D#217683

2/18/86 RH

UNITED STATES NAVY AND MARINE CORPS BASES, OVERSEAS

VA 67 .U554 1985

United States Navy and

UNITED STATES NAVY AND MARINE CORPS BASES, OVERSEAS

PAOLO E. COLETTA, *Editor*
K. Jack Bauer, *Associate Editor*

Greenwood Press
Westport, Connecticut • London, England

Library of Congress Cataloging in Publication Data
Main entry under title:

United States Navy and Marine Corps bases, overseas.

Companion vol.: United States Navy and Marine Corps bases, domestic. c1985.
Bibliography: p.
Includes index.
1. Navy-yards and naval stations, American—Foreign countries—Addresses, essays, lectures. 2. Military bases, American—Foreign countries—Addresses, essays, lectures. 3. United States. Navy—Facilities—Foreign countries—Addresses, essays, lectures. 4. United States. Marine Corps—Facilities—Foreign countries—Addresses, essays, lectures. I. Coletta, Paola Enrico, 1916-
II. Bauer, K. Jack (Karl Jack), 1926-
VA67.U554 1985 359.7′0973 84-4470
ISBN 0-313-24504-5 (lib. bdg.)

Library of Congress Catalog Card Number: 84-4470
ISBN 0-313-24504-5

First published in 1985

Greenwood Press
A division of Congressional Information Service, Inc.
88 Post Road West
Westport, Connecticut 06881

Printed in the United States of America

10 9 8 7 6 5 4 3 2 1

Contents

Preface

The need of the United States for naval bases both at home and abroad has changed in response to modifications in strategy that take into account the emergent global environment, advanced military technology, and the ever-growing importance of the world's oceans as sources of supply for edible and inedible resources. Given its global interests, the United States needs a worldwide network of bases, facilities, and overflight rights to sustain forward deployment and strategic mobility, to ship arms to friends, and to show the flag and influence foreign national policies. To some degree, the presence of U.S. bases in a foreign land assures the host country of American support, while the disestablishment of a base may be perceived as a loss of protection—and certainly of American dollars. Unfortunately, improved economic status, military strength, or political factors may cause a host country to raise the ante in negotiations with the United States over base rights. The Philippines are a case in point. And the loss of bases, as of the intelligence-gathering facilities in Pakistan, Turkey, and Iran, has put at least a temporary crimp in verifying Soviet missile tests.

After the U.S. Navy established its "distant stations" early in the nineteenth century, it had to depend for logistic support, and sometimes for ships themselves, upon friendly nations in the Caribbean, South Atlantic, Mediterranean, Pacific, and Far East. With the change from sail to steam, overseas bases became even more important, as they did in the Atlantic during the Spanish-American War and World War I. Worldwide bases were necessary during World War II, and bases in Japan, Okinawa, the Mariana Islands, and the Philippines were indispensable during the Korean and Vietnam wars. After Britain left its holdings "East of Suez" and the other Western European nations decolonized following World War II, the United States had to pick up the burden of policing the Persian Gulf and Indian Ocean as well as the Central and Western Pacific. Although nuclear-powered ships need return to base only infrequently for upkeep, they return fairly often in order to obtain fresh food and supplies and to give their crews rest, recreation, and refresher training. During the last thirty years, nevertheless, the number of important overseas naval and air bases has shrunk from about 150 to about 30, with most of the closures occurring after World War II, in the Western Pacific following the withdrawal from Vietnam, in the Mediterranean, and in the Near East. The Soviet invasion of Afghanistan and the creation of the U.S. Rapid Deployment Force may start a turnaround, at least in some geographical areas close to the Persian Gulf.

There is a vital distinction between "hard" bases, that is, those under American control, such as Roosevelt Roads, Puerto Rico, and "soft" bases, those in which sovereignty lies with the host country. Rota, Spain, is a good example of the latter.

The location of a base can be very important. With the closing of the New York (Brooklyn) Navy Yard and the decrease in activity of the New England yards—barring the submarine base at New London, Conn.—American naval operations in the North Atlantic are supported largely from Norfolk, Va., and Charleston, S.C., with help from the submarine base at Holy Loch, Scotland, and the U.S. Naval Air Facility in the Azores Islands. The Sixth Fleet Headquarters at Naples, Italy, the naval air station at Sigonella, Sicily, the naval base at Rota, Spain, and new arrangements being made with Greece provide support for the protection of the 2,500 ships that daily ply the Mediterranean. The new base at Diego Garcia Island supports the ships and aircraft that counter the Soviet naval presence in the Indian Ocean; the naval base at Guantánamo Bay, Cuba, and bases in Puerto Rico help police the Caribbean, in which the USSR enjoys a base (at Cienfuegos, Cuba); the bases in the Philippines provided vital support during the Vietnam War. Security in the Western Pacific is obtained by forces working particularly out of Yokosuka, Japan, and various naval air and Marine Corps air stations in Okinawa and Japan; and the security of the Central Pacific is assured by forces based in the Marianas. Were the U.S. Navy not to have such bases, it would have to rely upon an all-afloat posture that would severely impede its operations. Since the beginning of the Cold War, moreover, basing diplomacy has become an important component of "linkage politics" in which the United States and the USSR have competed for base rights in various parts of the world, especially in the Middle East and Africa.

This book provides entries, in alphabetical order, on overseas U.S. naval and Marine Corps bases and facilities. U.S. domestic bases are covered in a companion book, *U.S. Navy and Marine Corps Bases: Domestic*. By definition, domestic bases include those located in the fifty states of the United States, but exclude those located in Puerto Rico, the Virgin Islands, and Guam. The latter appear in this book. For the purposes of this book an overseas base is defined as a geographic area that permits overflight rights, port visits, and the use of offshore anchorages. "Strategic access," as to markets, raw materials, and media outlets, may or may not obtain.

As already indicated, a base may be "hard" or "soft." Robert E. Harkavy (*Great Power Competition for Overseas Bases: The Geopolitics of Access Diplomacy* [New York: Pergamon Press, 1982], p. 15), adds that "a rigid definition of the term 'base' concedes the existence of such only where the user has exclusive extraterritorial control, either via compulsion or by treaty." In addition, "where the power's use of an installation is controlled merely ad hoc, or where joint access and control [are] evident, it is now common to refer to a 'facility.' "

Generally, however, a base is considered a major installation and a facility the site of a smaller, more technical, and less obtrusive establishment. A *base*, then, can be defined as 1) a major installation from which operations are projected or supported; 2) an area or locality containing installations that provide logistic or other support; or 3) a home airfield. A *facility* is an activity that provides a specific kind of operating assistance to naval, ground, or air forces, thereby facilitating action or operations. Both bases and facilities are *establishments*, defined as installations, together with personnel and equipment, organized as operating entities. A *station* is a general term meaning any military or naval activity at a fixed land location, with each classified by the service in which it operates permanently or temporarily. A *section base* is a minor base under the administrative control of a larger base.

This book excludes very minor temporary support establishments but includes all important and historically significant bases and facilities, extant and extinct. Each entry discusses the form and function of the base or facility and gives something of its history and development. Bibliographies at the end of each entry provide sources for further research.

These bibliographies are divided into two sections: A, providing primary sources, and B, providing secondary sources. If, in some instances, there are no primary or secondary sources, one of the two sections may be omitted. Since Samuel Eliot Morison's fifteen-volume *History of United States Naval Operations in World War II* has been listed frequently throughout the work, the title of the entire history has not been repeated and only the title of the relevant volume is given.

In order to avoid having a plethora of entries alphabetized under "Navy," "naval," or "United States," entry headings generally begin with the base's location. The location is then followed by the base's name and the date it was created and disestablished, unless it is still operating. For historical reasons, however, some bases are discussed as part of a group rather than in separate entries. Some of these, such as the U.S. Northern Bombing Group Bases in World War I, were formed as a part of a particular military operation. Others, such as the World War II bases in Brazil, were significant as a group but not individually. Thus, when a group of bases forms a logical whole, the bases are discussed in a group entry rather than in separate entries.

The reader looking for these bases will be aided by entries providing cross-references from the specific base to the appropriate general entry. Thus, for instance, the reader looking for the World War II base at Arzew, Algeria, will find an entry reading "*See* North Africa; U.S. Naval Bases." Readers who know a base by its name only and are uncertain of its location will also be aided by entries providing cross-references as well as by Appendix B. When an entry mentions a base or facility discussed in a separate entry in this work, a cross-reference is indicated by (q.v.) or by a *see* reference.

Additional access is provided by the index and the three appendices. Appendix A lists bases according to type or major function, including, for instance, submarine bases and Marine Corps air facilities. Appendix B lists bases according to their geographical location, and Appendix C provides a time line or chronology. The time line readily illustrates the beginnings and the waxing and waning of bases, with sharp increases shown for war periods and quick demobilization following wars. It should aid those interested in the bases formed during a particular period in history.

Entries were written by a number of well-known scholars in naval history. While each contributor followed a basic outline, no attempt was made to restrict contributors to the outline or to deny them free use of their treatment and style. This is not an official history, and the opinions or assertions expressed herein are the personal ones of the authors and do not necessarily reflect the views of the Department of the Navy. I trust I speak for all contributors in believing that this volume will provide a valuable source of information for both scholars and students. The contributor's name is given at the end of each entry he or she wrote. I wrote those that are unsigned and assume responsibility for them.

My thanks are due to each author; to Dr. K. Jack Bauer for being a most cooperative associate editor and contributor as well; to Dr. Dean C. Allard and his staff at the Operational Archives Branch of the Naval Historical Center, and to Barbara Lynch and others at the Navy Department Library in the same center; to Brig. Gen. Edwin H. Simmons and his staff at the History and Museums Division of U.S. Marine Corps Headquarters; to Capt. Richard Knott, USN, and his staff at the Naval Aviation History Office; and to Cynthia Harris, Editor, Reference Books, Greenwood Press, for her excellent guidance.

PAOLO E. COLETTA
Editor-in-Chief

Introduction

The need to establish a navy yard in a particular place, and to maintain it there, is a matter of geography, general policy, and long-term domestic politics. But navies must be responsive to urgent short-term demands stemming from the needs of foreign policy or strategy. That requires ships to go from their domestic navy yards and operate, sometimes for long periods, in distant places. In war they must have a place as near as possible to the anticipated scene of battle where they can return for rest, repair, and replenishment. During the Quasi-War with France, 1798–1800, U.S. warships found British bases in the Caribbean open to them and were glad to have their use. During the Barbary Wars U.S. ships used Gibraltar (q.v.).

In the War of 1812 Britain and the United States were engaged in a military campaign on the U.S.–Canadian frontier, centering on Detroit. The British line of communications extended from the home country westward across the Atlantic, through the St. Lawrence, and through Lakes Ontario and Erie, transshipping to small craft or going overland briefly as geography dictated. The U.S. Navy made little effort to cut the line of communications across the Atlantic. The British Navy was so big and the American so small that nothing important could be expected from such an effort. But the British Navy had no warships on the lakes and could bring none up from the sea through the St. Lawrence. So even a small U.S. squadron in Lake Ontario could put a halt to the British supply traffic, thereby isolating the British Army's forces at Detroit. There was no such squadron. It had to be built. This was done at Sackett's Harbor, N.Y., near Lake Ontario's eastern end. A yard, or base, was built, and in it ships were built, but nothing came of the effort, for the British set up their own shipyard and base across the lake and built their own squadron. In this situation the opposing naval commanders, enterprising enough in the construction of their bases and ships, ran out of enterprise when it came to fighting. That was good enough for the British, who were able to keep their supplies flowing westward.

The Americans also built a shipyard at Erie, Pa., at the eastern end of Lake Erie. More interesting, the American commander on Lake Erie, Oliver Hazard Perry, built an advanced base at Put-In Bay in the Bass Islands, an archipelago only thirty miles from the British fort guarding the approaches to Detroit. From here, as close as he could get to the enemy, Perry's hastily built little ships hovered about Detroit and the nearby Canadian ports. To break the blockade, a small British squadron similar to Perry's offered battle. The offer was accepted, the battle was fought, and the British were defeated. This meant that their army, now with no hope of support, had to retreat eastward. The American western frontier was made safe, and an American army, ferried across the lake by Perry's vessels, pursued the retreating British.

When the war ended there was little need for the lake squadrons or their bases. Over the years both ships and bases vanished, albeit rather more slowly than one might think appropriate. Still, a visitor to Sackett's Harbor today will find there little but reeds and a sleepy village.

During the Mexican War the small navy yard established at Pensacola, Fla., in 1825 served as a base of supply and repair for the ships on blockade duty in the Gulf of Mexico. But, just as at Lake Erie in 1813, a location closer to the scene of action was needed. This was provided by Anton Lizardo, an anchorage only some ten miles from the main Mexican port of Veracruz. It was at Anton Lizardo that blockading ships coaled, repaired, and replenished themselves. And it was there that the invasion fleet gathered before landing Gen. Winfield Scott's conquering army on the beach just outside of gunshot of the forts guarding Veracruz.

The Spanish-American War was fought over Cuba. But the first important action of that war took place in the Philippines when Commo. George Dewey's small Asiatic squadron destroyed the Spanish squadron at Manila Bay in May 1898. By then American commercial ships had been sailing Pacific waters and visiting Pacific and Asian ports for more than a century. The U.S. Navy appeared in the Pacific in 1813 when the frigate *Essex* made her raiding cruise against British whalers in the southeastern part of that ocean. Shortly after the end of the War of 1812 the Navy established stations in both the Eastern Pacific and Asian waters. Neither had a base of its own and depended on the courtesy, or weakness, of other countries for the use of their harbors. But after the conquest of California during the Mexican War a navy yard was established at Mare Island, not far from San Francisco, and by 1898 another had been established at Bremerton, Puget Sound, Wash., not far from Seattle. The ships on the Pacific Station, though few in number, were adequately based.

Steam's conquest of sail in the U.S. Navy, which began with the *Fulton* in 1814, was complete by 1898. Only the first of the ships of the "New Navy," which began in 1883, carried any auxiliary sail, and in due course it was removed from them.

But steam required coal, and ships had to be refueled frequently. The need for a coaling station was among the reasons for American interest in acquiring the Hawaiian Islands. It was the main reason for American interest in acquiring Samoa.

Other countries were also interested in these remote islands, in the case of

Hawaii mainly the British and the Japanese; in the case of Samoa, mainly the British and the Germans. In 1889 the USS *Trenton*, the most powerful ship on the Pacific Station, was, with a couple of smaller consorts, at Samoa. British and German warships were there, too. A nasty controversy over who would control the native government developed between the Americans and the Germans, and some people even talked of war. What came was not war but a hurricane that destroyed the American and German squadrons. In due course the islands were split among the three countries. But the Germans lost their share of Samoa at the beginning of World War I. The British gave theirs up after the end of World War II. The United States still possesses its share, but the naval base has long since vanished. It never was much more than a coaling station, and its role in the events of World War II in the Pacific turned out to be very small.

Hawaii's story was different, of course. The islands were annexed during the Spanish-American War, on 7 July 1898, but it took a long time to establish a base there.

In the meantime, George Dewey, his country at war and he without a base, acquired one when he seized the Spanish navy yard at Cavite (q.v.), not far from Manila, after first having sunk the Spanish squadron there. The Spanish navy yard became a U.S. navy yard. Eventually, a floating dry dock was moored in Subic Bay (q.v.) to the north of the Bataan Peninsula, a seaplane base was established at Sangley Point (q.v.), not far from Cavite, and a few other places were put to other naval uses. All were lost quickly to the Japanese in 1941. The Philippines became independent in 1946 after the United States recaptured them from the Japanese. The U.S. flag was lowered for the last time from Cavite and Sangley Point long ago, but Subic Bay flourishes today as a U.S. naval base, with a major ship repair facility at Olongapo and, at nearby Cubi Point (q.v.), a huge air station.

As a byproduct of Dewey's campaign, the United States acquired the mid-Pacific island of Guam. Despite the recommendations of many, nothing was done to fortify the island before World War II. Thus, its fall to the Japanese, which was inevitable, was not a disaster on the scale of those at Bataan and Corregidor. When the island was recovered in mid-1944, it was turned into a huge naval and air base to support further attacks on Japan. Early in 1945 Adm. Chester W. Nimitz moved his headquarters there for the war's duration. In the years since the end of that war Guam has served mainly as a base for the Strategic Air Command's B–52s and the Pacific Fleet's ballistic missile submarines. With the recent entry into service of the very long-ranged Trident submarine-launched ballistic missile and the earlier easing of relations between China and the United States, the submarines no longer need to use the base at Guam (q.v.). During the Vietnamese War the island was important as a supply and repair base for the fleet in the South China Sea and for the B-52s bombing North Vietnam. It was also a refueling stop for the commercial airliners crossing the Pacific with troops bound for the war.

When the United States entered World War I the fleet scattered, mainly to European waters. The ships operated chiefly out of bases at Irish, Scottish, and French ports. Naval aircraft flew from bases in England, France, Italy, the Azores (q.v.), and elsewhere, escorting convoys, patrolling sea areas, and attacking enemy naval bases in Belgium and Austria-Hungary. Some of the aircraft were flying boats; others were on wheels. The wheeled aircraft did not need a base on the water, or even in sight of it, in order to be useful in the struggle for the sea. Special bases at Inverness and Invergordon, Scotland (*see* World War I U.S. Naval Bases in Europe) were used to prepare the mines dropped to form the North Sea Mine Barrage.

After the fall of France in 1940 the United States turned over fifty old destroyers to Britain in return for the opportunity to buy or lease land for bases—seven in British colonies in the Western Hemisphere and one in Newfoundland, then an independent member of the British Commonwealth of Nations. Some of these—Argentia (q.v.) in Newfoundland, Bermuda (q.v.), and Trinidad (*see* Caribbean, The, U.S. Naval Bases)—proved to be extremely useful in the war against the U-boats. Bermuda remains useful to this day, chiefly as a base from which A/S aircraft can patrol the waters off North America's eastern coast. That base in the Bahamas began to prove useful long after World War II was over when its deep, quiet, undisturbed Tongue of the Ocean began its long service as a testing ground for sonars and other submarine and A/S devices. The other bases acquired as a result of the destroyer deal, on Jamaica and some of the small islands of the Caribbean, never became important.

This country's preparation for, and entry into, World War II led to the establishment of bases successively across the Atlantic in Iceland, Ireland, England, and the Azores, in Brazil and Morocco, and then in the Mediterranean, first to provide for the ships and aircraft fighting the U-boats, and then to support the several Anglo-American invasions of Europe. Many of these bases were new. Others were added to existing British or French establishments, such as Portland-Weymouth, in England, and Mers-el-Kebir, Algeria (*see* North Africa, U.S. Naval Bases). When the need for these bases disappeared, ideally they disappeared, too, though in fact that did not always happen at once. What certainly did cause them to disappear rapidly was the quick departure from the Navy at the war's end of those officers and men who served, or at least, lived, at them.

The Japanese attack on Pearl Harbor, which destroyed so many airplanes and ships, did little harm to the base. To the west, Guam fell to invading Japanese, as did the Philippines. One of the first things the Pacific Fleet did was to escort convoys filled with troops and arms for the garrisoning of islands along the route from the United States to Australia, New Zealand, and lesser islands in the South and Southwest Pacific. There, more fighting ships, combat aircraft, and troop units were gathered, trained, supplied, and finally sent forth either to defend these holdings or to regain locations that the Japanese had taken. Many of the places fought for and retaken by the Allies took their turn as advanced bases from which new thrusts could be made. Sometimes, as at Manus (q.v.), in the

Admiralty Islands north of New Guinea, the Japanese were forced out. But because there were many big harbors in the Pacific which could be turned into good bases, it was not necessary to eject the foe from all of them. So the Japanese were allowed to stay in their great bases at Rabaul and Truk after the ships and airplanes they had served were destroyed or driven away. When those were gone, the bases had no more importance. To be sure, Kwajalein (q.v.) had to be taken and Guam retaken. But Ulithi (q.v.) in the northwestern Carolines was not garrisoned by the Japanese, and the United States took the atoll and its vast lagoon at no cost.

One of the interesting developments of World War II was the growth to maturity of the underway replenishment of warships at sea with fuel, ammunition, food, and other stores. These techniques reached their peak in the Pacific. Yet the need for bases—ever new bases as each one provided a springboard for the fighting forces to seize the next one on the way to Japan—did not end until the war also ended. At each new base tenders arrived to repair ships damaged in battle or worn by the high tempo of operations, while oilers and other replenishment ships were themselves replenished.

The war ended in September 1945 with American warships in Japanese harbors, American airplanes in Japanese air space, and American troops on Japanese soil. The bases built to support a war that now had ended were closed for the same reasons as elsewhere.

Everyone hoped that after the war the world would be different from the way it was beforehand. In that respect people got what they wanted, though, as it turned out, hardly anyone would say that the postwar arrangements were satisfactory. Postwar fears of Soviet aggression led, among other things, to the creation of the North Atlantic Treaty Organization and other alliances in which the United States was the principal partner. At war's end the fleets had withdrawn to home waters, leaving only a few ships here and there overseas. But trouble between the Yugoslavs and the Italians over possession of the Adriatic port of Trieste, Communist insurgency in Greece, Soviet pressure on Turkey, civil war in China, and other aspects of the world's unending upheaval quickly led to the dispatch of ships, undermanned though they were, to distant parts of the world. In most cases their successors, or their successors' successors, are in those parts today.

The Navy liked to boast that the force in the Mediterranean, soon to be called the Sixth Fleet, was based in Norfolk, with all support coming directly from that East Coast city. After a while the boast was no longer heard. An air facility appeared at Sigonella, Catania, Siciliy (q.v.), and a permanent berth of the Sixth Fleet's flagship was built at Gaeta, Italy, about sixty miles north of Naples, where the fleet's ships often anchored. Fuel dumps and ammunition dumps were built in various places.

In the Pacific the Navy took over the bases of the old Imperial Japanese Navy, notably the great yard at Yokosuka (q.v.) on Tokyo Bay. When war began in Korea in 1950 Yokosuka and other former Japanese naval bases supported the operations of the Seventh Fleet as the fleet in turn supported the U.S., United Nations, and South Korean armies ashore.

After three years the Korean War ended with the boundary between North and South Korea about where it had been before the war started. Crises came and went elsewhere in the Pacific before the next big war began, in Vietnam, far from Korea. Subic Bay and Guam, not especially useful in the Korean War, were very important when the United States entered the war in Vietnam. Day after day, year after year, the Seventh Fleet's carriers at Yankee Station in the Gulf of Tonkin launched their planes on raids against targets in North Vietnam. Ammunition ships, oilers, and store ships sailed heavy-laden out of Subic Bay to replenish the carriers and their escorts some 600 or 700 miles to the west. Empty, they returned to refill themselves and go out again. The carriers and their escorts also used Subic Bay for maintenance and repair. Replacement aircraft came aboard from the field at Cubi Point. From the same field patrol planes flew long surveillance flights over the South China Sea. Some kept track of the large foreign cargo ships and tankers which, even though headed for North Vietnamese ports and filled with arms, ammunition, food, and fuel, were allowed to pass unmolested. Others looked for small ships, "trawlers," which, filled with some of those arms, the North Vietnamese sent south clandestinely, intending them to reach the Viet Cong.

On the shallow coasts of South Vietnam and up the wide, muddy rivers, other naval bases were set up quickly at such places an An Thoi, (q.v.), Can Tho-Bin Thuy (q.v.), Nha Be (q.v.), Chu Lai (q.v.), and Danang (q.v.). There were based the multitude of small ships and boats that tried to keep the trawlers from reaching their destinations and to make the local waters safe for both South Vietnam's normal commerce and its military traffic. Sometimes the chief feature of such a base was an anchored repair ship or barracks ship converted from a World War II tank landing ship (LST). Sometimes it consisted mainly of a few piers and concrete barracks surrounded by wire and earthworks to provide protection from nearby hostile forces. In the course of time the United States tired of that war, the boats and their bases were turned over to the South Vietnamese, and the planes on the carriers stopped making their dangerous, unrewarded raids in the north. Now, years later, Subic Bay and Guam continue their activities, but at a much slower tempo. They support naval activities principally in the Indian Ocean rather than in the waters and on the coasts of the South China Sea. No longer the most advanced of our bases, they have passed that title on to Diego Garcia (q.v.), a barren atoll in the middle of the Indian Ocean where the World War I German raider *Emden* once anchored. At Diego Garcia supply and repair ships wait until their services are needed. Underway replenishment ships come in from time to time, as do combat ships in need of a tender's services. Patrol planes thunder off the runway to keep watch on whatever goes on below that might affect the oil traffic between the Persian Gulf and the ports of the United States and its allies.

In the meantime, the technologies of the rocket, the nuclear weapon, and the nuclear power plant have made it possible for submarines long at sea to carry and launch instruments of vast destruction at targets far inland. But since even nuclear-powered submarines cannot stay at sea indefinitely they, like other ships, must have bases to which they can return. Some of these are long established, such as the base at New London, Conn., from which submarines have sailed for generations. They may be existing bases converted from other uses, such as Guam, or they may be entirely new, such as those at Holy Loch, Scotland (q.v.), and Rota, Spain (q.v.). An excellent example of rapid change in the location of bases is the current use by ballistic missile submarines of new bases at Keyport, Wash., and Kings Bay, Ga., rather than of the older bases at Guam and Rota.

Clearly, then, U.S. overseas bases have been established for two main reasons: to provide support for forward forces engaged in war, and to support American foreign policy interests worldwide.

FRANK UHLIG, JR.

UNITED STATES NAVY AND MARINE CORPS BASES, OVERSEAS

A

ABEMAMA ATOLL.
See Apamama (Abemama) Atoll, U.S. Naval Air Base.

AGADIR, FRENCH MOROCCO.
See North Africa, U.S. Naval Bases.

AITAPE, NEW GUINEA, U.S. NAVAL ADVANCE BASE, 1944–1945 One prong in a series of three simultaneous landings on the northern New Guinea coast, Aitape (03°50′S., 143°E.) was part of the Southwest Pacific Area's great bypass operation to isolate and neutralize the Japanese forces at Wewak. This would open the rest of the New Guinea coast for conquest. Allied troops landed at Aitape on 22 April 1944 and quickly captured the enemy airfield there. Aitape became useful to the Seventh Fleet both as a PT operating base and as an amphibious staging point because of the large U.S. Army installations organized there. PT boats from Motor Torpedo Boat Squadrons 7 and 18 arrived at Aitape on 26 April and began patrols against barges in the bypassed Wewak area. They saw much action as the bottled-up Japanese tried to reopen their supply lines. Patrols from Aitape continued until September 1944, when the last PTs departed for Biak (q.v.).

As an amphibious supply and assembly point, Aitape staged the May 1944 landings at Toem-Wakde, further up the New Guinea coast. In August 1944 the Seventh Amphibious Force established an amphibious training center at Aitape to prepare Army troops there for landings on Morotai (September 1944) and at Lingayen on Luzon (January 1945). Thereafter Aitape was a small boat base until 30 March 1945, when naval facilities there were disestablished.

BIBLIOGRAPHY

A. U.S. Navy, "7th Amphibious Force Command History, 10 January 1943-23 December 1945" (Washington: Naval Historical Center, Operational Archives Branch); "U.S. Naval Activities Disestablished since July 1945," 27 Sept. 1954 (Washington: Naval Historical Center, Operational Archives Branch).

B. Samuel E. Morison, *New Guinea and the Marianas March 1944-August 1944* (Boston: Little, Brown, 1953); Capt. Robert J. Bulkley, *At Close Quarters: PT Boats in the United States Navy* (Washington: Navy Department, Naval History Division, 1962); Vice Adm. Daniel E. Barbey, *MacArthur's Amphibious Navy* (Annapolis, Md.: U.S. Naval Institute, 1969).

JOHN B. LUNDSTROM

AITUTAKI, SOUTH COOK ISLANDS, U.S. NAVAL AIR TRANSPORT SYSTEM BASE, 1943–1944 An atoll in the New Zealand-administered South Cook Islands, Aitutaki (18°52′S.,159°45′W.) was utilized beginning in 1943 as a fueling point for aircraft of the Naval Air Transport System on flights to and from the South Pacific. Aitutaki, located west of Bora Bora (q.v.) and east of Tongatabu (q.v.), served as a convenient stopping point for aircraft flying between those two points. Within the atoll on the small islands of Amuri and Tautu were four airfields encompassing an Army Air Forces base as well as the NATS base. Aitutaki also featured a seaplane landing. Naval installations were closed in September 1944.

BIBLIOGRAPHY

A. "U.S. Naval Activities Disestablished Since July 1949," 27 Sept. 1954 ("Monograph Histories of U.S. Naval Overseas Base, Vol. II. Pacific Area" (Washington: Naval Historical Center, Operational Archives).

B. U.S. Navy, "U.S. Naval Bases in the South and Southwest Pacific (and Central Pacific Forward) in World War II," 1 November 1954 (Washington: Naval Historical Center: Operational Archives Branch).

JOHN B. LUNDSTROM

ALBANY, AUSTRALIA, U.S. ADVANCE SUBMARINE BASE, 1942 Albany, West Australia (35°S, 117°E.), is a port on the southwest Australian coast about 300 miles south of Fremantle-Perth (q.v.). For four months (May-August 1942) it was the site of a U.S. naval submarine base. Fearing that Fremantle might be exposed to a surprise Japanese attack, Commander, Southwest Pacific Force ordered the submarine tender *Holland* and Submarine Squadron 2 to move south to Albany, which featured a good harbor and rail communications, although it was known as "Little Siberia" to sub crews. In June 1942 Rear Adm. Charles A. Lockwood, commanding the Fremantle-based submarines (Task Force 51), conducted important torpedo tests at Albany that showed that submarine torpedoes did not perform reliably. In August 1942, with the danger to Fremantle greatly lessened, Albany was abandoned as a submarine base.

BIBLIOGRAPHY

A. None.

B. Theodore Roscoe, *United States Submarine Operations in World War II* (Annapolis, Md.: U.S. Naval Institute, 1949); Clay Blair, *Silent Victory: The United States Submarine War against Japan* (Philadelphia: Lippincott, 1973).

JOHN B. LUNDSTROM

ALEXISHAFEN, DUTCH NEW GUINEA.
See Madang-Alexishafen, Dutch New Guinea, U.S. Naval Advance Base.

ALGIERS, ALGERIA.
See North Africa, U.S. Naval Bases.

ALMIRANTE, PANAMA, U.S. NAVAL AUXILIARY AIR STATION (SEAPLANE), 1942–1943 Almirante, on Panama's north shore at 8°N., 83°W, about half way between Panama's borders with Costa Rica and Colombia, was one of the numerous U.S. naval air stations established to counter U-boats operating in the Caribbean during World War II. It was commissioned as a seaplane facility on 16 July 1942 and decommissioned on 29 September 1943 after the worst of the U-boat campaign had subsided.

BIBLIOGRAPHY
A. "Almirante," in *Naval Air Stations*, 3 vols. (Washington, D.C., Navy Yard: Naval Aviation History Office, n.d.).

AMAPA, BRAZIL, U.S. NAVAL AIR BASE.
See Brazil, U.S. Naval Bases.

ANTARCTICA, U.S. NAVAL AND AIR BASES, 1929– Although others may have seen land in Antarctica before him, it was not until late 1839 when Lt. Charles Wilkes, USN, saw land at numerous points over a distance of 1,500 miles that the existence of a southern continent was accepted. However, interest in Antarctica did not revive until the early twentieth century, with numerous expeditions sent out by, among others, Britain, France, Germany, Russia, Japan, and Sweden. The British National Antarctic Expedition, 1901-1904, commanded by Capt. Robert Falcon Scott, used a base at Hut Point on McMurdo Sound. In 1907 British Lt. Ernest H. Shackleton's party located the South Magnetic Pole; in 1912 a Norwegian, Roald Amundsen, reached the geographic South Pole. (Like Arctic, the Antarctic has three poles: geographic, geomagnetic, and magnetic. The geographic pole is determined by the daily rotation of the earth. The geomagnetic pole is used by scientists to describe the earth's basic magnetic field. It is about 800 miles from the geographic pole. The magnetic pole is where you would arrive if you followed a compass needle southward.)

Until 1928, men or Mongolian ponies pulled the sleds used in exploring expeditions. Although air flights were pioneered on 26 November 1928 with an Australian, Sir Hubert Wilkins, and an American pilot, Carl B. Eielson, credit for using modern machines and communications methods goes to Rear Adm. Richard E. Byrd, USN. Beginning very late in 1928, Byrd flew out to each of the three successive bases built at Little America on the Bay of Whales. His Snow Cruiser, however, proved useless because of its weight and breakdowns.

A turning point came in 1929 when Congress authorized the establishment of the U.S. Antarctic Service Expedition under Byrd's command. Among its tasks was to determine the feasibility of establishing base sites and air bases.

Byrd used two bases in 1930: West Base, at Little America II on the Bay of Whales, and East Base, on Stonington Island in Marguerite Bay, on the west coast of the Antarctic Peninsula. These were to be manned permanently, with new men replacing those who wintered over and then returned home. World War II, however, forced the closing of the bases and the abandonment of a 1939 joint State, War, and Interior department plan to begin permanent occupation and scientific exporation of Antarctica.

Following World War II, the United States mounted Operation High Jump, with Byrd in command and Rear Adm. Richard H. Cruzen commanding Naval Task Force 68, comprised of thirteen ships, including a submarine, and more than 4,000 men. A great event was the flight of six twin-engine R4D *Skytrain* transports from the aircraft carrier *Philippine Sea* to the base of operations at Little America IV, on the Bay of Whales, and the first use of helicopters and of seaplanes from seaplane tenders. In 1948-1949 Comdr. Gerald L. Kitchum made even more extensive use of helicopters for taking aerial photographs.

Then came the worldwide all-out assault by sixty nations and 30,000 scientists in the International Geophysical Year (IGY), 1 July 1957-31 December 1958. Twelve nations engaged in the Antarctica part of the project. In anticipation of the IGY, the United States had sent the icebreaker *Atka* to the Antarctic in 1954 to locate sites for stations. The *Atka* found that icebergs had caused the Bay of Whales to disappear and had carried out to sea part of Little America IV. The American operation, Deep Freeze I (1955-1956), established two stations, Little America V at Kainana Bay, and Hut Peninsula, Ross Island, McMurdo Sound. The latter, named Naval Air Facility, McMurdo Sound, was renamed McMurdo Station in 1961. The first large aircraft—two standard *Skymaster* C-54s and two ski-equipped P3V *Neptunes*—landed there on 20 December 1955 after a 14.5 hour flight from New Zealand. These planes then explored almost 2 million square miles, about half of which had never been seen before. Their operations had been made possible because the *Edisto* had carried an advance party of thirteen officers and eighty men of the Mobile Construction Battalion (Special) and the detachment from Air Development Squadron Six (VX-6) to build an air operating facility at McMurdo Sound with a runway capable of accommodating Air Force *Globemaster* C-124 cargo planes. VX-6 also tested and developed air weapons for the Antarctic program at Patuxent River, Md., but operated first out of Quonset Point, R.I., and then out of Port Hueneme, Calif. In any event, the ninety-three men with the C-124s had to unload tons of equipment and materials from the cargo ships of Task Force 43, package it for air drops at the South Pole Station and at an auxiliary station to be built, and support the flight operations of VX-6. To house the personnel a "city" was built in six months, four of them totally dark, that included thirty-eight buildings, fourteen of them being steel Quonset huts, and twenty-four of prefabricated insulated panels. To supply aviation gasoline, fuel tanks that could hold 200,000 gallons were built; additional fuel came from two yard gasoline oilers (YOGs) that had been towed to Hut Point.

Deep Freeze II, 1956-1957, was the greatest invasion of Antarctica in history. The United States alone sent twelve ships and more than 3,000 men under Rear Adm. George J. Dufek, and eight Air Force C-124s in addition to naval planes. The large cargo planes dropped building supplies and materials at the South Pole as well as fuel for the tractor train carrying materials to the Byrd Station site. Meanwhile Dufek's Air Force-Army-Navy team built three coastal stations—at Cape Hallett on the Ross Sea, on the Knox Coast, and on the shore of the Weddell Sea, across the continent from McMurdo Station. When the ships and aircraft left Antarctica in February and March 1957, 317 Americans remained behind at the now seven U.S. stations. While McMurdo Station grew into the sea- and air-support base, Little America V was crushed by snow and Byrd Station and Amundsen-Scott (South Pole) Station were drifted over, two stations were transferred to other nations, and Hallett Station was used only during the summer. At the temporary interior stations, a burlap-and-board technique developed by Admiral Byrd served well. Deep Freeze III, 1957-1958, was largely a period of relief and resupply. Newcomers included two tracked vehicles, the Weasel and the Sno-Cat, which followed dog teams pulling a sled. The Sno-Cat, incidentally, is large enough for men to live in. Although the IGY had ended, the United States continued its effort with Deep Freeze IV, 1958-1959. Temporary structures now gave way to more permanent ones for an ongoing scientific program, with the International Antarctic Treaty of 1959 stating that the Antarctic "shall be used for peaceful purposes only."

The temporary buildings of Byrd's day were built on the surface and connected with enclosed passageways made of 2-by-4-inch boards covered with chicken wire and burlap. When the snow that covered them formed into ice, however, they were in a giant vise. Built in 1955-1956, Little America IV had to be closed down in 1959 before it actually collapsed. Other construction methods have been to use a geodesic dome, as at the South Pole Station, or to have a Sno-Miller cut trenches, span their tops with metal arches, and let the snow just blow over them. Insulated buildings in the tunnels left space for walkways, thus creating a veritable village under the snow. Only exhaust funnels, radio antennas, and scientific observatories are above the surface. Another method, much more expensive, is to place buildings on columns that can be jacked up. This method is fine where there is little snow accumulation but poor in such areas as the Bay of Whales, in which seventy feet of snow accumulated in thirty years. Prefabricated vans called wanigans are now in common use. These look like house trailers on skis and are pulled into place by tracked vehicles. They can be resited when snow piles up. In one instance, in 1963, to build Eights Station (named for the first American scientist in the Antarctic, James Eights) vans were fitted into a KC-130F *Hercules* cargo plane that flew forty trips over the 1,384 miles from McMurdo Station. There eight units, on skids, were pulled by a tractor into parallel rows of four each. With a floor between the rows and a common roof, a large building of eight rooms was constructed around a central hallway. Most of the research carried on was devoted to upper air physics. In 1965-1966 VX-6 duplicated its feat of 1963 by flying almost daily trips from McMurdo Sound to establish Plateau Station, located 11,900 feet above sea level on a stretch of ice 630 miles beyond the South Pole.

Given the austerity and monotony of the area, American designers have worked to improve both living and working conditions. At McMurdo, for example, there are a church, a store, movies, and a gymnasium for an average of 700 people in summer and 200 in winter. At the South Pole Station, some support personnel and only seventeen scientists wintered over in 1981.

To obtain water in Antarctica has been a serious problem. Some is obtained by melting snow with the exhaust pipes of electric-generator engines or oil-fired burners or, as at Hallett Station, which is on the site of a penguin rookery, by burning fuel for evaporators that desalt seawater. Fuel is the largest single item shipped to Antarctica. (During Deep Freeze 67, more than 2 million gallons of diesel and automotive fuels were delivered to U.S. stations and 4 million gallons were brought in for aviation use.) A great improvement came in 1962, when a nuclear reactor was installed at McMurdo to desalt seawater for drinking water and sewer flushing. Another problem is that of fire; in consequence, stations consist of several separate buildings, a number of them being well stocked with water and food for refugees from a fire.

While planes and helicopters carry men, ships bring the fuel and most of the dry cargo to McMurdo, following channels slowly opened by icebreakers. To improve upon tracked vehicle trains that formerly serviced interior stations, the Navy since 1964 has used ski-equipped KC-130s that land on flat areas called domes and pump fuel from their 3,500 gallon capacity fuselage tanks, into rubber storage bladders. Helicopters not only engage in ice reconnaissance but serve as ship-to-shore transports. To reach great heights, Army turbine-powered UH-1 *Iroquois* helicopters were delivered by KC-130s. For some experiments, such as seismic soundings, tracked vehicle trains are still important, and in mountainous areas dog teams were used until the early 1960s, when they were replaced by lightweight motor toboggans.

Supply involves the provision of adequate clothing, most of it devised by a group headed by Paul Siple. One can work in Antarctica in shirt sleeves on a calm day when the sun is shining. However, even a light wind will combine with low temperature into a wind-chill factor that quickly evaporates body heat. At 0°F and wind at 10 miles per hour, the effect on a man is the same as if the temperature were -20°F without wind. Outermost garments must therefore be windproof. Inside, various layers of garments trap body heat and serve as insulation. Special gloves, boots, caps, coats, and hooded parkas are needed, and sometimes a face mask to protect the nose and cheeks. The entire clothing package weighs thirty-five pounds. Emphasis is also placed on replacing men with data-recording machines powered by radioactive isotopes. If desired, such data can then be transferred to satellites in polar orbits. Satellites themselves have been found useful for work in meteorology, geophysics, and especially geodesy. Meanwhile submarines and special small submersibles are under development for use in Antarctic waters.

Except for the heavy military emphasis of Operation High Jump, the magnet that draws men to Antarctica is scientific study to unlock the secrets nature has stubbornly frozen in the polar environment. It is the function of others to transport, feed, clothe, and house the scientists. Even though both are funded by the National Science Foundation, there is a distinction between the scientists in the U.S. Antarctic Research Program and the military personnel, mostly Navy, who support them. The Navy gathers equipment, supplies, and personnel in the United States, sends the equipment and supplies forward by ship, and flies down the personnel. Annual costs for the United States since 1980 have been $9 million for research and $54 million to run the bases and provide logistic support. Since the principal American operating area lies south of New Zealand, transportation is staged through Christchurch, on New Zealand's South Island, where a U.S. Naval Communications Technical Group is also located. McMurdo Station, the primary U.S. supply base in Antarctica, lies 2,500 miles to the south. After the material and supplies are sorted out at McMurdo, they are forwarded from the coast to interior stations by aircraft. The number of inland permanent stations has varied since 1957 between four and seven. In 1967 five were manned: McMurdo, at 77°51′S., 166°37′E.; Amundsen-Scott South Pole Station, at the Geographic South Pole; Byrd Station, at 80°1′S., 119°32′W.; Plateau Station, at 79°15′S., 40°30′E.; and Palmer Station at 64°46′S., 64°5′W. The station at Hallett was occupied full time from 1957 to 1965, when damage occurred by a fire, and then was manned only during the summer. During the summer, too, various weather observation stations and temporary camps for scientists are maintained.

The amount of logistic support needed is great because the distances are great. From McMurdo to the South Pole is about 800 miles; to Byrd, 900; to the Plateau, now closed, 1,350. To provide this support is the duty of the U.S. Naval Support Force, Antarctica, established as part of the Atlantic Fleet on 1 February 1955, first commanded by a rear admiral but since about 1972 by a captain. At almost the same time Air Development Squadron Six was established; it has played an important part in the annual Deep Freeze operations and has revolutionized the art of Antarctic exploration. The last reciprocating engine aircraft in support of scientists in Antarctica occurred in 1972, when turbo-prop, ski-equipped KC-130s and twin-turbine UH-1Ns took over, with airlift to Antarctica from New Zealand provided for the most part by Air Force turbo-jet C-141 *Starlifters*. Extremely useful in building new stations is Naval Mobile Construction Battalion 71. Greatly easing the construction work is the transportation by KC-130s of crated, portable vans from McMurdo to the South Pole stations beginning in 1974; these are used as workshops by the scientists. During November and December 1974 VX-6, now renamed VXE-6, delivered fifty of the vans, whose total weight exceeded 1 million pounds.

When the Navy closed its facilities at Davisville, R.I., in 1974, the support force moved its winter headquarters to Port Hueneme, Calif., and former Task Force 68 became Task Force 199 based at Ford Island, Hawaii. Each year some ten Navy and Coast Guard ships manned by 1,500 officers and men deliver the food, fuel, doctors and medicines, fuel, lubricating oil, and spare parts to keep the operations going during the summer, when about 2,300 support personnel aid the 250-275 scientists. During the winter, however, only about thirty-five scientists stay over. During the last few years, four stations have been manned continuously: McMurdo, Amundsen-Scott South Pole, Palmer, and Siple, while three additional camps—Lake Bonney, Cape Crozier, and Byrd—have been activated each summer.

During the winter of 1974 about 350 men of VXE-6 spent four months in Antarctica. They hauled more than 3 million pounds of supplies, mostly to the South Pole Station, for the Navy Seabees who were building a massive geodesic dome there, somewhat like the Houston Astrodome, to house scientific workshops. The year 1975 marked the twentieth anniversary of VXE-6 in Antarctica. During that year it hauled materials and men to complete a new geodesic dome at the South Pole. The older station had been closed down because drifting snow weakened the supports of the original structure. Meanwhile Huey helicopters helped scientists explore one of the two active volcanoes and in addition moved 376 metric tons of supplies and transported more than 2,700 passengers. The year 1975 also marked the first time that 350 naval and Marine men in VXE-6 operated entirely from Point Mugu, Calif. The Coast Guard detachment, which began operating with Deep Freeze in 1967, is based at Mobile, Ala. Its staff of twenty-two officers and sixty enlisted men in 1980 operated ten Sikorsky HH-52As that deployed with an icebreaker.

VXE-6 Antarctic operations continued during the austral months beginning in late August 1980. Involved were some 400 officers and men operating two types of aircraft, seven ski-equipped KC-130F and R Hercules transports, and seven UH-1N twin Huey helicopters. Upon returning to Point Mugu in October and flying down again, VXE-6 began resupplying the permanent stations and remaining summer stations, preparing facilities for the operating season, and lifting scientific field parties to remote areas by helicopter, with ground time kept to a minimum and engines constantly turning over. By February 1981, with the end of the summer, the summer stations were closed, the permanent stations were restocked, and VXE-6 returned to Point Mugu by 1 March.

BIBLIOGRAPHY

A. Interview with Dr. Raymond R. Heer, Jr., former program director for Antarctic Atmospheric Research in the National Science Foundation, Annapolis, Md., 1 December 1981, Record Group 330, Center for Polar and Scientific Archives (Washington: National Archives).

B. Richard E. Byrd, *Little America* (New York: G. P. Putnam's Sons, 1930); George

J. Dufek, *Operation Deep Freeze* (New York: Harcourt, Brace, 1957); Paul Siple, *90° South: The Story of the American South Pole Conquest* (New York: G. P. Putnam, 1959); Ralph K. Andrist, *Heroes of Polar Exploration* (New York: American Heritage Publishing Co., 1962); Carl R. Eklund and Joan Beckman, *Antarctica; Polar Research and Discovery during the International Geophysical Year* (New York: Holt, Rinehart, and Winston, 1963); Ian Carmeron, *Antarctica: The Last Continent* (Boston: Little, Brown, 1974); JOC Willie Stephen, "Life Down Under," *Naval Aviation News*, May 1974, pp. 35-37; Comdr. W. S. Kosar, USN, "Hercules Unchained," U.S. Naval Institute *Proceedings* 102 (Oct. 1976): 151-53; National Science Foundation, *Flight to the South Pole: The New Age of Antarctic Exploration and Research* (Washington: 1979); JOC James M. O'Leary, "Aviation in Antarctica," *Naval Aviation News*, Feb. 1980, pp. 22-29; Lisle A. Rose, *Assault on Eternity* (Annapolis, Md.: Naval Institute Press, 1980); Margot Hornblower, "The Last Untouched Continent," *Washington Post*, 2 Feb. 1981.

AN THOI, REPUBLIC OF VIETNAM, U.S. NAVAL SUPPORT ACTIVITY, 1965–1971 Of all the Navy's bases in South Vietnam, An Thoi, on the southern tip of Phu Quoc Island in the Gulf of Siam, was the most isolated. Almost 1,000 miles from Subic Bay, it taxed the Seventh Fleet's mobile logistic support force during the Vietnam War. Still, naval leaders recognized early the strategic value of the site: from there naval forces could readily interdict sea infiltration of communist men and supplies from Cambodia. Another favorable consideration was the availability to American units of real estate near the Vietnamese Navy's existing compound.

Consequently, in the summer of 1965 An Thoi was selected as a Coastal Surveillance Force combat and logistic base. Due to the Navy's shortage of suitable vessels, the Coast Guard was called upon to initiate the patrol operation in that area. Coast Guard Division 11, with nine 82-foot cutters (WPBs), began Market Time coastal patrol operations from An Thoi that July. Subsequently, the unit was joined by U.S. naval forces employing fast patrol craft (PCF) and a gunboat of the Royal Thai Navy. In addition, a coastal surveillance command center was established to control operations in that sector.

While the Naval Support Activity, Saigon, Detachment An Thoi, worked to improve berthing, messing, supply, repair, transportation, security, and other support for the combat units, the fleet provided additional assistance. Repair ships *Krishna* (ARL-38) and *Tutuila* (ARG-4) and berthing and messing barges APL-55 and APL-21 were deployed to the site at various times from 1965 to 1969. Although new base facilities and a contractor-built 3,500-foot airstrip eased logistic problems, An Thoi continued to require much fleet support.

By May 1971, however, when the An Thoi Logistic Support Base was turned over to the Vietnamese Navy as part of the Vietnamization program, the installation furnished major overhaul services for river and coastal combat craft and supplied a number of smaller U.S. bases in the Gulf of Siam region.

BIBLIOGRAPHY

A. Commander Naval Forces, Vietnam, "The Naval War in Vietnam," May 1970 (Washington: Naval Historical Center, Operational Archives Branch); Service Force, U.S. Pacific Fleet, "Command Histories, 1967-1972" (Washington: Naval Historical Center,

Operational Archives Branch); Richard Tregaskis, *Southeast Asia: Building the Bases. The History of Construction in Southeast Asia* (Washington: GPO, 1975).

B. Herbert T. King, "Naval Logistic Support, Qui Nhon to Phu Quoc," U.S. Naval Institute *Naval Review* 95 (May 1969):84-111; Richard L. Schreadley, "The Naval War in Vietnam, 1950-1970," U.S. Naval Institute *Naval Review* 97 (May 1971):180-211; Edwin B. Hooper, *Mobilty, Support, Endurance: A Story of Naval Operational Logistics in the Vietnam War, 1965-1968* (Washington: GPO, 1972).

EDWARD J. MAROLDA

ANTIGUA, BRITISH WEST INDIES, U.S. NAVAL AIR FACILITY.
See Caribbean, The, U.S. Naval Bases.

ANTIGUES, FRANCE.
See World War I U.S. Northern Bombing Group Bases in England and France.

APAMAMA (ABEMAMA) ATOLL, U.S. NAVAL AIR BASE, 1943–1944 Apamama is an atoll seventy-five miles southwest of Tarawa in the Gilberts, an archipelago belonging to Great Britain that the Japanese occupied shortly after the attack on Pearl Harbor in December 1941. Measuring about fifteen miles long and six miles wide, the atoll embraces a protected lagoon with commodious anchorage. Abatiku Island occupies the southwest corner of the lagoon.

After aerial photography revealed in early 1943 that the Japanese had built a landing field on Betio Island (Tarawa) and a seaplane base on Butaritari Island (Makin), the Joint Chiefs of Staff ordered an attack on the Gilberts in an operation designated "Galvanic." Plans called for the capture of Apamama as well as Tarawa and Makin. The operation was to provide air bases from which to stage further aerial operations against the Marshalls and other neighboring Japanese-occupied islands, remove the threat from the Japanese in the Gilberts to Allied communications between Hawaii and Australia, and divert Japanese forces eastward from the Indian Ocean.

Since Apamama was held by only twenty-five Japanese, the atoll was actually captured by an advance company of Marine scouts landed from the submarine *Nautilus* on 19 November 1943. Elements for the air station reached the atoll about ten days later, and the Ninety-Fifth Construction Battalion completed a 4,500-foot fighter strip named O'Hare Field by 10 December 1943. The Seabees ultimately extended the main coral runway to 8,000 feet to handle heavy bombers, added a secondary 1,950-foot sand strip, and constructed nineteen miles of coral-surfaced roads, a 12,000-barrel tank farm, a 5,000-foot submarine pipeline, and a causeway that served as an unloading pier. Personnel on the atoll had increased to 5,000 by the peak month of February 1944, when O'Hare despatched 1,045 planes, more than 300 of them four-engined planes. Apamama was formally commissioned a Naval Air Base on 15 April 1944. As the war moved westward, however, activity at Apamama rapidly declined, and the base was decommissioned on 16 October 1944.

BIBLIOGRAPHY

A. Commander in Chief, U.S. Pacific Fleet, "Administrative History of the Marshalls-Gilberts Area," 6 vols., 1946 (Washington: Naval Historical Center, Operational Archives Branch); U.S. Navy, Bureau of Yards and Docks, *Building the Navy's Bases in World War II*, 2 vols. (Washington: GPO, 1947): ii:317-18.

B. Samuel E. Morison, *Aleutians, Gilberts and Marshalls, June 1942-April 1944* (Boston, Little Brown, 1951), pp. 179-82, 213.

WILLIAM R. BRAISTED

APPLEDORE, ENGLAND.
See United Kingdom, U.S. World War II Naval Bases.

ARCACHON, FRANCE.
See World War I U.S. Naval Air Stations in Europe.

ARGENTIA, NEWFOUNDLAND, U.S. NAVAL OPERATIONS BASE, 1941– Argentia is located in southeast Newfoundland on the Avalon Peninsula, on Placentia Bay, sixty-five miles west southwest of St. John's at 47°18′N., 53°59′W.

The U.S. National Defense Act passed on 28 June 1940 provided for the sale of naval and military equipment not essential for defense to foreign governments. Either the Chief of Naval Operations or the Chief of Staff of the Army had to approve all sales. It was this act that helped pave the way for the destroyers-for-bases agreement between the United States and United Kingdom. In this deal, signed on 2 September 1940, the United States turned over fifty old destroyers to be recommissioned in the Royal Navy. In return, the United States obtained ninety-nine-year leases for naval and air bases in eight British colonies from Newfoundland to British Guiana. Argentia was the first base built under this agreement.

Just two weeks after the agreement was signed, Adm. John Greenslade, on President F. D. Roosevelt's order, was touring possible base sites in Newfoundland. The location of the fishing village and old silver mine at Argentia was chosen partly because Placentia Bay is the only year-round ice-free harbor in Newfoundland. Moreover, Argentia harbor, 1.8 miles long, afforded excellent take-off and landing conditions for seaplanes and was connected to St. John's by road and rail.

The first survey crews arrived at Argentia in October 1940; construction began on 29 December. Civilian contractors came with 1,500 men from Quonset Point, R.I. Building aircraft runways and diverting a source of water to the base were priority items. Most of the land was covered with a layer of peat up to twenty feet deep that had to be removed. Crews took out 8.5 million cubic feet of peat, earth, and gravel before starting on the runways. The weather was another obstacle.

On 25 January 1941 the Third Provisional Company of the U.S. Marine Corps arrived at Argentia. These, with construction workers, lived aboard the USS *Richard Peck* in the harbor until barracks could be built. The Marines raised the American flag over the base on 13 February 1941. About 4,000 civilians from Newfoundland also worked at construction, with many of them living on schooners in the harbor.

On 3 May 1941 an Aerological Detail under Lt. F.B. Stephens arrived. Also in May, planning began for the arrival of Patrol Squadron 52, which would start American participation in Atlantic convoy escort activities. Reconnaissance flights began, and a destroyer division soon joined in the work. On 14 June 1941 the ninety-nine-year lease became official. Task Force 24 was to be based in Argentia, and its commander, Vice Adm. Arthur L. Bristol, took up residence in the destroyer tender *Prairie* (AD-15) in the harbor. On 15 July, Naval Operating Base Argentia was commissioned, Capt. G. Morgan commanding. Temporary asphalt runways had been built, and the Naval Air Station was commissioned on 28 August. South of the NOB, the Army built a coast artillery installation, Fort McAndrew (later McAndrew Air Force Base).

The historic Atlantic Conference between President Roosevelt and Prime Minister Winston Churchill held between 10 and 15 August 1941 took place aboard the HMS *Prince of Wales* and the USS *Augusta* (CA-31) in Argentia harbor, amid security so tight that convoys in the area at the time were assured of safe passage. It was this conference that produced the Atlantic Charter, the basic agreement of defense, war, and postwar cooperation between the United States and the United Kingdom.

The first U.S.-escorted convoy started on 17 September 1941 with five destroyers from Argentia. Argentia-based destroyers helped to pioneer the use of sonar for tracking submarines. The Placentia Project of November 1941 brought U.S. submarines to Placentia Bay for antisubmarine operations. As part of the Joint Army-Navy Newfoundland Defense Plan of 28 November 1941, PBYs were brought in for winter duty.

When the United States entered the war in December 1941, the German U-boat threat had to be met with full force to enable American troops to travel to Europe and North Africa. Argentia played a leading role in antisubmarine warfare. Patrol planes of Argentia's squadron VP-82 got the first two American U-boat kills in March 1942.

On 18 February 1942 the USS *Truxtun* (DD-229) and *Pollux* (AKS-2) ran aground in a snowstorm off the Burin Peninsula on their way to Argentia. Although 204 men died, local residents were instrumental in rescuing survivors and helping to provide care at the Argentia Naval Hospital. In appreciation, the U.S. government later built a hospital on the Burin Peninsula.

In 1942, the peak year for U-boat successes, the British also began to use Argentia for the maintenance of their escort destroyers. The U.S. Navy assembled the largest task force to sail under the American flag in the Atlantic: six escort carriers and fifty destroyers and destroyer escorts. Harbor Defense Plan 3 (Hypo Dog Prep-3) provided for patrol craft in the harbor around the clock. An anti-torpedo net with net tenders was used in Little Placentia Harbor. Aircraft sank U-boats at the approaches of the harbor.

American convoy escort duties declined after the Atlantic Convoy Conference of March 1943. Argentia was kept as a key base, however, and expansion of its facilities continued, including the addition of a large floating dry dock and a ship repair unit, and the establishment by the British of a naval air station. However, some projects were reduced starting in September 1943. Such battleships as the *Indiana* (BB-58), *South Dakota* (BB-59), *Alabama* (BB-60), and *Iowa* (BB-61) had their shakedown cruises out of Argentia. In early 1944 Argentia got Minesweeping Division 25 and a Harbor Approaches Patrol Unit.

In June 1944 the Royal Navy withdrew from Argentia, but that summer an American lighter-than-air squadron arrived for ASW reconnaissance and ferrying duties. Argentia was also an arrival point for German POWs. On 28 October 1944 the Air-Sea-Rescue Program was set up for the Newfoundland-Greenland-Iceland corridor. In April 1945, during Germany's final submarine offensive, ''Operation Wolfpack,'' the USS *Frederick C. Davis* (DE-136), a destroyer from Argentia, was torpedoed south of the Flemish Cap. Of the 192 crew members, 115 died. Units from Argentia sank *U-546* (the U-boat responsible) and captured thirty-three prisoners.

The naval forces at Argentia toward the end of the war were called by the new name of Placentia Bay Patrol. Argentia had already become the headquarters of the Greenland Patrol. Free French, Dutch, Canadian, and Polish forces, in addition, used NOB Argentia for repair and other support.

From a wartime high of more than 20,000 men, forces in Argentia declined rapidly after the end of the war. The Navy was still active, however, in air and sea rescue operations and in transporting forces from Europe to the Pacific theater and from Europe back to the United States.

In May 1949 the Coast Guard assumed the sea rescue and ice patrol missions in Argentia. On 30 June 1950 NOB Argentia and the NAS were disestablished and succeeded by Naval Station Argentia. In the 1950s the Navy assumed responsibility for the sea parts of the ''early warning'' system, the Atlantic and Pacific Barriers. In July 1955 Airborne Early Warning Wing, Atlantic, was commissioned. Seven aircraft from Airborne Early Warning Squadron 11 transferred from NAS Patuxent River, Md., to Argentia in April 1956. Th first flight of the Atlantic Barrier took off from Argentia on 1 May 1956. In December of that year the AEW Wing Atlantic and Commander Barrier Forces, U.S. Atlantic Fleet established Argentia as headquarters. The Barrier flights were made in EC-121 *Warning Stars*.

Meanwhile McAndrew Air Force Base was signed over to the Navy on 1 July 1955 and became known as ''Southside.'' Support facilities and housing were the main projects there. The ten-floor bachelor officers' quarters, Strain Memorial

Hall, known as the "Argentia Hilton," was Newfoundland's tallest building at the time; it was completed in 1957. In October 1959 Argentia got the top security Oceanographic Facility. In February 1956 Argentia had on board 2,163 military personnel.

WV-2s *Constellations* flew reconnaissance missions between Argentia and the Azores until late 1962, when they were replaced with P3-As *Orions*. In March 1960 the surface part of the Barrier systems was dropped, and only one of the sixteen destroyer escorts involved remained at Argentia. In 1962 the Navy Hydrographic Long Range Ice Reconnaissance and Ice Forecasting Facility began operations in Argentia. There were also meteorological and communications stations.

In 1964 Commander Barrier Forces Atlantic moved to Keflavik, Iceland (q.v.). The Airborne Early Warning Wing, Atlantic was decommissioned in August 1965.

Starting in early 1970, the "Phase Down" hit Argentia. Because of its increased speed and range, the P3 was no longer needed there; those from Patuxent and the Azores (q.v.) covered the North Atlantic. Most activities were either transferred or decommissioned. The overall base population, military and civilian, fell from a postwar high of 10,000 in the early 1960s to about 1,000 in late 1982.

Argentia did not die as a U.S. Navy installation, however. The Oceanographic Facility has become the basis for the current U.S. Naval Facility Argentia, a unit of the Oceanographic System, Atlantic, based at Norfolk, Va. Personnel strength at Argentia included 321 Navy (304 at the Naval Facility, 7 at the commissary, 6 at the Navy Exchange, and 4 in the Navy Broadcasting Service); 7 in the Air Force (Greenpine Activity); and 62 in the Canadian Forces—a total of 390.

BIBLIOGRAPHY

A. U.S. Navy, Bureau of Yards and Docks, *Building the Navy's Bases in World War II*, 2 vols. (Washington: GPO, 1947); U.S. Department of State, "Negotiations for Transfer of American Destroyers to the British Navy and for Establishment of American Naval and Air Bases in British Possessions in the Western Hemisphere," in *Papers Relating to the Foreign Relations of the United States, 1940* (Washington: GPO, 1961), III:49-77; U.S. Naval Facility, Argentia, Newfoundland, *Cruise Book, 1979* (Argentia: U.S. Naval Facility, 1979); U.S. Naval Facility, Argentia, Newfoundland, Public Affairs Office, *U.S. Naval Facility. FPO New York, 09597* (Argentia: NAVFAC PAO, [1982]); U.S. Naval Station Argentia, Newfoundland, *NS Argentia, NFLD* [report for 1956] (Washington: Naval Historical Center, Operational Archives Branch); U.S. Navy, Atlantic Fleet, Commander in Chief, *Commander Task Force Twenty-four*, Administrative History No. 139 (Washington: Navy Department, 1946).

B. William Bradford Huie, *Can Do! The Story of the Seabees* (New York: E. P. Dutton, 1944); George A. Weller, *Bases Overseas: An American Trusteeship in Power* (New York: Harcourt, Brace, 1944); R.A. Mackay, ed., *Newfoundland: Economic, Diplomatic, and Strategic Studies* (Toronto: Oxford University Press, 1946); Samuel E. Morison, *The Battle of the Atlantic September 1939-May 1943* (Boston: Little, Brown, 1947); William

L. Langer and S. Everett Gleason, *The Challenge to Isolation, 1937-1940* (New York: Harper and Brothers, 1952); William L. Langer and S. Everett Gleason, *The Undeclared War, 1940-1941* (New York: Harper and Brothers, 1953); Julius A. Furer, *Administration of the Navy Department in World War II* (Washington: GPO, 1959): Stetson Conn and Byron Fairchild, *The Framework of Hemisphere Defense. U.S. Army in World War II: Western Hemisphere* (Washington: Office of Chief of Military History, Department of the Army, 1960); Patrick Abbazia, *Mr. Roosevelt's Navy: The Private War of the U.S. Atlantic Fleet, 1939-1942* (Annapolis, Md.: Naval Institute Press, 1975); Edward W. Chester, *The United States and Six Atlantic Outposts: The Military and Economic Considerations* (Port Washington: Kennikat Press, 1980.

WILLIAM MCQUADE

ARUBA, NETHERLANDS WEST INDIES, U.S. NAVAL OPERATING BASE.
See Caribbean, The, U.S. Naval Bases.

ARZEW, ALGERIA.
See North Africa, U.S. Naval Bases.

ATSUGI, JAPAN, U.S. NAVAL AIR FACILITY, 1950– NAF Atsugi is located at 35°27′N., 139°27′E., near Tokyo and Yokohama. Its primary mission is to provide logistic support for aviation units of the Seventh Fleet. The base currently hosts the embarked air wing of the USS *Midway* and provides housing for families of crews whose ships participate in the Overseas Family Residency program.

Americans came to Atsugi in a dramatic way. On 30 August 1945, scarcely two weeks after Japan's surrender, Gen. Douglas MacArthur, newly designated Supreme Commander Allied Powers in Japan, arrived at Atsugi. His plane touched down at a facility that already had an exciting history. Begun in 1938 by the Imperial Japanese Navy, the base was originally intended to be a home for large experimental aircraft. Budget cuts prior to Pearl Harbor delayed its completion until 1943, when it was given the dual mission of training fighter pilots and providing air defense for Yokohama and Tokyo. By 1944 the base had its own air group, which consisted of seventy-two carrier fighters, twenty-four night fighters, and twelve reconnaissance aircraft. To protect Japan's waning air defense forces, local residents were mobilized to dig huge caves, which concealed aircraft from the American attackers' view. Early in 1945 some of those aircraft scrambled to strike back at U.S. Air Force and Navy bombers. When Emperor Hirohito announced Japan's surrender, some at Atsugi determined to defy his orders. For six days pilots, crewmen, and civilians clashed, forcing the base commander to call in troops from nearby Yokosuka (q.v.) to put an end to the internecine fighting. Then, in the two days remaining prior to MacArthur's scheduled arrival, some 8,000 people were brought in to remove the debris from Atsugi's runways.

When MacArthur arrived, all the world wanted to hear about Atsugi and its environs. The base was literally the window through which Americans got their first view of a people and nation most had known only as a savage and resourceful foe. But once it became clear that the occupation of Japan would be peaceful, Atsugi lost its notoriety. The U.S. Army's 188th Airborne Infantry Regiment used it for about a year, and thereafter only replacement trainees' boots trod over its scarred soil and pitted runways. In March 1949 the U.S. Army discontinued use of Atsugi.

The outbreak of war in Korea brought Atsugi back to life. When fighting began on the Korean peninsula, the U.S. Navy had but one carrier on station in the Western Pacific, with another scheduled to join it. Within six months, three carriers formed the nucleus of the Seventh Fleet. Their prospective presence, together with a demonstrated need for more shore-based patrol aircraft, prompted Washington in October 1950 to send a dozen Seabees to Atsugi to see what might be done with its rutted runways and charred hangars. The Seabees, together with Fleet Aircraft Squadron 11, which arrived in November, readied the base for its establishment as a Naval Air Station on 1 December 1950. Four officers and fifty enlisted men then launched Atsugi on a new career of service to the Seventh Fleet.

During the next decade, Atsugi grew into the preeminent American naval air station in the Western Pacific. Its complement skyrocketed, climbing to nearly 5,000 offices and men. When at the end of the Korean fighting Marine Air Group Eleven came to the base, Atsugi for a time had more Marines than Navy men on board. In 1954 the base became home for the newly created Commander Fleet Air, Western Pacific, its senior tenant command today. Atsugi's landscape was transformed over the next few years, as new photographic laboratories, a new control tower, and even a golf course were constructed. In 1957-1958 the base's runways were completely refurbished and extended to accommodate new high performance jets, such as the F3H *Demon*, F4D *Skyray*, FJ-4 *Fury*, and F11-F *Tiger* aircraft.

Growth brought new problems and unexpected pressures to Atsugi. As the base grew, so too did its neighboring cities. What had been countryside two decades earlier was now part of the Tokyo-Yokohama megalopolis. Residents grew increasingly unhappy about the noise created by the new jets, and they protested when occasional accidents damaged their property. In 1960 Atsugi achieved unwelcome political prominence when reporters disclosed that it provided a home for U-2 "black planes" similar to the surveillance aircraft shot down over the Soviet Union. Nine years later the base would again become a focal point for protests when North Korean fighters shot down an EC-121 reconnaissance plane that had taken off from Atsugi.

American naval leaders responded to these pressures as early as 1961, when they developed Kisarazu, an alternative field on the opposite and less densely populated side of Tokyo Bay. War in Vietnam further dispersed Atsugi's functions. Although the fighting there brought an unprecedented five carriers to the

Seventh Fleet, creating new needs for aviation support services, the focus of operations moved far to the south of the base. As task units moved south, tenant commands shifted away from Atsugi. In July 1965 MAG-11 returned to Iwakuni, Japan (q.v.), VC-5, which provided target, photographic, and other services for the fleet, followed in 1968, going to Okinawa (q.v.). By the end of the 1960s plans were also being made to move other major users of Atsugi's facilities—VQ-1, VRC-50, and HC-7, which provided reconnaissance, logistics, and helicopter support, respectively—to other bases.

During the 1970s a combination of naval resourcefulness and diplomatic ingenuity gave Atsugi a new lease on life and a fresh significance. A detachment was sent to Misawa (q.v.), 300 miles to the north, laying the groundwork for further dispersal of the base's functions. In 1975 Atsugi and Misawa alike were redesignated Naval Air Facilities. The homeporting of the USS *Midway* at Yokosuka in 1973 suggested better use for increasingly scarce space at Atusgi. It would remain an administrative center and become home for the dependents of crewmen whose ships were to remain far longer than the previous norm in Western Pacific waters. Finally, American and Japanese negotiators agreed that Atsugi would become a joint use facility. The base provided an alternative landing site for civilian aircraft in 1970, when a world's fair at Osaka and a major international exposition in Tokyo jammed all other available airports. On 1 July 1971 Japanese Maritime Self-Defense Forces established their first small operational unit on the base, assuming control of flight operations. A decade later, the JMSDF's Fifty-first Squadron would join American naval aircraft using Atsugi.

In this way, a facility built forty years earlier by Japanese to fight Americans became a base from which naval aviators of both nations could contribute to the maintenance of peace and stability in the Western Pacific.

BIBLIOGRAPHY

A. *Kanagawa no Beigun kichi*, (1982); "Atsugi, Japan, NAF," Naval Air Stations, 3 vols. (Washington, D.C. Navy Yard; Naval Aviation History Office, n.d.).

B. "Living Conditions in Atsugi, Japan," *All Hands*, June 1960, pp. 50-52; Russell Stone, "NAF Atsugi," *Naval Aviation News* 57 (Nov. 1975):28-33; "Living Overseas: In the Far East—Atsugi," *Navy Times*, 16 Aug. 1982, p. 26.

ROGER DINGMAN

AUCKLAND, NEW ZEALAND, U.S. NAVAL OPERATING BASE, 1942–1946 Auckland is a large city located near the northern tip of New Zealand's North Island at 38°46′S., 174°40′E. One of New Zealand's major ports, its harbor facilities are excellent. By March 1942 the U.S. Navy had earmarked Auckland as the site of a main fleet operating base for the South Pacific and as the principal terminus of the line of supply stretching from San Francisco. In April, with the organization of the Pacific Ocean Areas, it was designated the future location for the headquarters of the South Pacific Area under Vice Adm.

Robert L. Ghormley. Created there was the nucleus of the South Pacific Service Squadron, a major Service Force subordinate command. For the time being, its main activity was the procurement of such supplies and commodities as the New Zealand economy could offer to the Navy. In negotiations with the New Zealand government, it was decided to utilize the New Zealand Public Works Department as the principal construction agent for the U.S. Navy installations. Initial work involved erecting barracks and other buildings to help handle the greatly increasing number of personnel assigned to Auckland.

Admiral Ghormley, his temporary flagship the repair ship *Rigel*, reached Auckland late in May. Soon he was involved in preparations for what would become the offensive into the Solomon Islands. Consequently, on 26 July he strongly recommended to the Chief of Naval Operations that plans be expedited for transforming Auckland into the South Pacific's principal operating and supply base and requested that the necessary base forces be organized and sent as soon as possible. Meanwhile, planning and some work had begun on a large naval supply depot, two ammunition depots, two base hospitals, and a large fuel oil tank farm. However, events in August involving the Solomons drastically changed Auckland's role. Noumea, New Caledonia (q.v.), much closer than Auckland to the forward area, by necessity became one of the main South Pacific fleet and supply bases because of the need to supply the effort to hold onto Guadalcanal (q.v.) and Tulagi (q.v.). Even before the Guadalcanal landings (7 August 1942), Ghormley had moved his advance headquarters to Noumea, and on 21 October his successor, Vice Adm. William F. Halsey, formally recommended that Noumea, rather than Auckland, be developed as the main South Pacific base. By 8 November 1942 South Pacific Area headquarters had completed its move from Auckland to Noumea.

Thereafter, Auckland functioned at a greatly reduced level. Construction of the fuel oil tank farm was cancelled. Nevertheless, with its port facilities Auckland was still a useful rear area supply and staging point as well as a collection site for valuable New Zealand commodities. Its dockyards were enlarged to enable repairs to be made to small- and medium-sized ships. By February 1944, with the departure of most of the troops staging in New Zealand, roll-up at Auckland was begun, and by the end of 1944 naval activity was largely confined to a small receiving barracks. The naval operating base at Auckland was formally disestablished in March 1946.

BIBLIOGRAPHY

A. U.S. Naval Operating Base, Auckland, New Zealand, "War Diary, 1943-1944" (Washington: Naval Historical Center, Operational Archives Branch); Service Squadron, South Pacific, "History of Commander, Service Squadron, South Pacific, 7 December 1941-15 August 1945" (Washington: Naval Historical Center, Operational Archives Branch); U.S. Navy, Bureau of Yards and Docks, *Building the Navy's Bases in World War II*, 2 vols. (Washington: GPO, 1947); South Pacific Area and Forces, "History of New Zealand during World War II," Administrative History, Appendix 34 (16) (Washington: Naval Historical Center, Operational Archives Branch).

B. Samuel E. Morison, *Coral Sea, Midway and Submarine Actions May 1942-August 1942* (Boston: Little, Brown, 1949); Samuel E. Morison, *The Struggle for Guadalcanal August 1942-February 1943* (Boston: Little, Brown, 1949); Rear Adm. Worrall Reed Carter, *Beans, Bullets, and Black Oil* (Washington: GPO, 1953); Vice Adm. George C. Dyer, *The Amphibians Came to Conquer*. 2 vols. (Washington: GPO, 1971).

JOHN B. LUNDSTROM

AZORES ISLANDS, PORTUGAL, U.S. NAVAL BASE, 1943–1945 Although Lt. Albert B. Read, USN, flew the NC-4 into Horta and Ponta Delgada on 17 May 1919 on his trans-Atlantic flight, the last American whalers left the Azores in 1921, and American strategic interest in the islands disappeared until 1940, even though some trade continued. In March 1940 President Franklin D. Roosevelt spoke about possible future German actions against the Azores with the American Minister to Portugal, and in July the minister expressed Washington's concern for their future status to Libson. Finally, in September, British and American representatives in London agreed that in the event of war the United States would occupy the Azores (and the Cape Verde Islands as well). Should hostilities occur the Army's First Infantry Division and the First Marine Division were alerted for a possible invasion. In any event, the Portuguese Prime Minister, Antonio de Salazar, fearing a German occupation of the Iberian Peninsula, asked his country's ancient ally, Britain, with which it had been allied since the mid-fourteenth century, for help. Fortunately for his enemies, Hitler made no attempt to acquire the Azores, a site which would have given him an excellent air facility for operating in the Atlantic and attacking the United States with Focke-Wulf FW-200s based at Bordeaux.

Knowing that Portugal was suspicious of American expansionist proclivities, Washington several times during the spring of 1941 reassured its government that it had no intention of occupying the islands, and in the American-British-Canadian Staff Agreement of 27 March the islands were left as a British responsibility should the United States enter the war. But the War Plans Division of the Office of Chief of Naval Operations ranked the Azores very high as a strategic area, and on 22 May President Roosevelt directed the Chief of Naval Operations (CNO), Adm. Harold R. Stark, to be ready on thirty days' notice to occupy them. Finally, at the 11 August meeting with Winston Churchill off Argentia (q.v.) that produced the Atlantic Charter, it was agreed that American forces would occupy the Azores and the British the Cape Verdes, with a token Brazilian force to accompany the Americans for the sake of appearances. Other matters intervened until early 1943, when the Battle of the Atlantic raged at its height, yet the only step taken was to have Pan American Airways, whose clippers had begun to stop at Horta on the Long Island-to-Lisbon flights in 1939, arrange to improve the airfields on both Terceira—a volcanic island twenty miles long and twenty miles wide—and São Miguel. However, Portugal did grant fuel facilities at the Harbor of Praia Island to American warships as well as merchant vessels and on 17 August agreed that the British could use Lajes Field on Terceira, the port of Horta on the island of Fayal, and Santa Maria as a major military transportation field for troops destined for Western Europe. With the door opened by its British ally, Washington had its chargé in Lisbon, George Kennan, sound out Portugal while it reached an agreement with the British for the use of airfields in the Azores for transports and aircraft being ferried across the Atlantic, an agreement to which Salazar consented. On 6 June 1944 Adm. Ernest J. King set up U.S. Naval Forces Azores Command. Three days later men of the Ninety-sixth Construction Battalion (Seabees) arrived and, following belated approval from Salazar, began building a 6,000-foot-long by 150-foot-wide airstrip on Santa Maria at a time when the war in Europe had only six months to go. Army Engineers who followed did most of the expansion work that enabled Lajes Field to be used by both the Army Transport Command and the Naval Air Transport Service while the Ninety-sixth Seabees improved harbor facilities at Praia and erected Quonset huts, radio stations, hangars, ship buildings, dispensaries, mess halls, and office and recreational facilities for 600 officers and men at Santa Ritta Camp. In addition the Seabees constructed an 8-inch, 3,800-foot-long submarine pipeline that permitted tankers to unload fuel to gasoline farms on Santa Maria and Terceira. Before the Ninety-sixth Seabees left on 24 June 1944, 4 officers and 101 enlisted men were transferred to Mobile Construction Battalion Unit 613, which maintained the facilities. Much operational flying and rescue work was done by the PB4Y-1 squadron based at Terceira.

The war over, on 30 May 1946 the United States transferred the base at Santa Maria to Portugal and the British abandoned their control of Lajes. In 1951, after the United States and Portugal became allies in NATO, they signed a defense agreement that granted the United States base rights in the Azores in the event of war. The United States and Portugal jointly would construct facilities; when the latter were completed, Portugal would be responsible for their maintenance. On 15 November 1957 the agreement was extended to 31 December 1962. Meanwhile, in November 1958 the United States sent a number of Marines via Lajes to Lebanon; in 1961 the U.S. Air Force routed transports through Lajes on their way to Berlin and the Congo; and the United States built a secret storage area for missiles to be issued to Polaris submarines. When the Common Defense Pact expired in 1962, Portugal refused to extend it but invited the United States to remain on the islands on an ad hoc basis, whereupon the United States decreased the number of aircraft and personnel based at Lajes.

In 1968 the United States had only a dozen aircraft and 1,500 personnel at Lajes, about half the numbers of 1960. However, a new five-year Common Defense Agreement was signed in 1969, with the United States giving Portugal $436 million. In 1973, the still 1,500 Americans at Lajes spent most of their $13.8 million annual payroll locally. More importantly, they tended a vast underground antisubmarine network about the Azores and their antisubmarine planes could track any Soviet submarine within 1,000 miles either in the Atlantic or Mediterranean. During the last few years only about thirty American warships have called annually at Ponta Delgada. In any event, negotiations have been under way with respect to American aid needed to modernize Portugal's military forces. After speaking with Prime Minister Francisco Pinto Balsemao on 15 December 1982, President Ronald Reagan reaffirmed the commitment of the United States to provide military aid to Portugal in return for a new agreement on American military facilities and told Balsemao that he had asked for $90 million in military aid for Portugal in the fiscal year 1983 budget, a $25 million increase in such funding.

BIBLIOGRAPHY

A. Azores Naval Forces, "Establishing U.S. Naval Forces in the Azores, January to August 1944" (Washington: Naval Historical Center, Operational Archives Branch); U.S. Navy, Bureau of Yards and Docks, *Building the Navy's Bases in World War II*, 2 vols. (Washington: GPO, 1947).

B. Samuel E. Morison, *The Battle of the Atlantic September 1939-May 1945* (Boston: Little, Brown, 1947); Edward W. Chester, *The United States and Six Atlantic Outposts: The Military and Economic Considerations* (Port Washington, N.Y.: Kennikat Press, 1980), pp. 154-83.

B

BAHIA, BRAZIL, U.S. NAVAL AIR FACILITY AND NAVAL OPERATING FACILITY. *See* Brazil, U.S. Naval Bases.

BALBOA, PANAMA CANAL ZONE, U.S. NAVAL OPERATING BASE/NAVAL STATION, 1938– By General Order No. 108 dated 16 April 1938, naval property at and in the vicinity of Balboa was designated the U.S. Naval Operating Base, Balboa. It was comprised of the following administrative establishments: District Headquarters, Balboa; Naval Radio Station, Balboa; Naval Radio Station, Summit; Naval Ammunition Depot, Balboa; and all other naval activities on the west bank of the canal at the Pacific end. With the accretion of new facilities and the disestablishment of others, on 11 May 1943 Naval Operating Base, Balboa, became Naval Station, Balboa. It included Naval Radio Station, Farfan, which replaced the decommissioned Naval Radio Station, Balboa; Naval Ammunition Depot, Balboa, which included the naval magazine at Coco Solo (q.v.); and the naval reservation on the west bank of the Pacific end of the Panama Canal. Located therein in addition were the Naval Supply Depot, Balboa; Naval Fueling Activities, Fifteenth Naval District; Naval Supply Depot, Balboa; Naval Hospital, Balboa; Naval Radio Station, Summit; Naval Station, Taboga Island (q.v.); Naval Station, Balboa (q.v.); Submarine Operating Base, Balboa; Naval Net Depot, Balboa; Marine Barracks, Balboa; Advanced Base Depot; Defense Housing at Locona; and Section Base, mine and bomb disposal units, a salvage depot, and naval medical supply depot, Balboa. Harbor defense was provided by magnetic loops and radio sonobuoys controlled by a Joint Army and Navy Harbor Entrance Control Post, which had a signal station on Flamenco Island, Balboa.

See also Panama Canal Zone, Post-World War II Defense Arrangements.

BIBLIOGRAPHY

A. Defense Plans, in Office of Naval Records and Library, Subject File 1911-1927 (Washington: Record Group 45, National Archives); Records of the General Board of the Navy, 1903-1945 (Washington: Naval Historical Center, Operational Archives Branch);

U.S. Navy, Bureau of Yards and Docks, *Building the Navy's Bases in World War II, 2 vols*. (Washington: GPO, 1947), I: 4, 5, 27, 34, 40, II,5-21; *A Chronology of Events Relating to the Panama Canal*, prepared for the Committee on Foreign Relations, United States Senate, by Congressional Research Service, Library of Congress (Washington: GPO, December 1977); "Panama Canal Zone Files," Interdepartmental Committee on Regulations for Air Navigation in the Panama Canal Zone (Washington: Naval Historical Center, Operational Archives Branch); Record Group 80, Correspondence of the Secretary of the Navy (Washington: National Archives); Record Group 165, War College Division (Washington: National Archives); "U.S. Naval Administration in World War II. Commander 15th Naval District and Commander Panama Sea Frontier," 2 vols, microfilm (Washington: U.S. Navy Department Library).

BALBOA, PANAMA CANAL ZONE, U.S. NAVAL STATION 1917– With the Panama Canal approaching completion in 1914, the Navy decided to build two graving docks at Balboa, one large enough to take any ships that transited the canal, the other for small craft. Only Drydock No. 1 was completed, but plans for No. 2 were kept alive. Meanwhile tenders supported submarines. The naval station at Balboa, established in 1917, is located just east of Panama. Few improvements were made there during the disarmament doldrums of the 1920s and 1930s. Following congressional authorization of 1938 to increase the size of the Navy by 20 percent, however, Acting Secretary of the Navy Charles Edison appointed a board headed by Rear Adm. A. J. Hepburn to report on the nation's needs for "additional submarine, destroyer, mine, and naval air bases on the coasts of the United States, its territories, and possessions." The board stressed the importance of shore facilities to service the augmented fleet, a need also stressed on 9 May 1939 by the Chief of Naval Operations, Adm. William D. Leahy, to the House Naval Affairs Committee. As a consequence of the Hepburn Report, two construction contracts for the Canal Zone were signed, one on 17 June, one on 17 July 1940. Following the signing of the destroyer-for-bases deal with Great Britain on 2 September 1940, a board headed by Rear Adm. John W. Greenslade was appointed to survey the naval shore establishment with a view to determining the requirements of a two-ocean navy. The report became the blueprint for all subsequent base development in the Caribbean and contiguous areas in the Atlantic and Pacific.

On 6 June 1941, the Navy developed a small operating base at Balboa where a pier had been built in 1937 to afford access to an ammunition depot. The pier was extended, and two new finger piers were added, each 40 by 704 feet and built of reinforced concrete. Tunnels built into the piers provided space for fuel oil, water, and power lines. Several hundred feet from the shoreline a 50-by-834-foot head quay, or transverse wharf, was built to join the inboard ends of the three piers. Adjacent to the piers was built an industrial area. It contained shops for the repair and overhaul of torpedoes, batteries, communications equipment, and other facilities. Pacific-bound convoys were topped off with stores kept in a three-story,100-by-300 foot general storehouse. A steel-frame net and boom building and several temporary storehouses were also built for a new boom depot to the south of the industrial area. There was also a 12,000-square-foot paved area for the net weaving and a 74,000-square-foot area for storage. The Fifteenth Naval District headquarters area, covering 40 acres, was increased to 65 acres. Thereon a new office building, bombproof command center, and additional housing for service personnel were built. A four-story 80-by-220-foot converted storehouse adjacent to the Balboa piers, completed in November 1941, formed the nucleus of the Balboa supply depot. After Pearl Harbor, eight 50-by-300-foot temporary frame structures were erected half a mile north of the main warehouse. These were completed in March 1942, together with a sorting and handling shed and a 75,000-square-foot lumber storage yard. A refrigerator storehouse to replenish ships' food supplies was completed in May 1944.

Construction for Drydock No. 2, long deferred, began in January 1942 under a new design that permitted the accommodation of two destroyers or two submarines abreast. Alongside, with a common wall, Drydock No. 3 was built to service small craft.

The Fourth Supplemental National Defense Appropriation Act of 1941 finally funded the submarine base recommended by the Hepburn Board. In addition, two floating docks were transferred from Cristobal to Balboa so that ships on the Pacific side needing repairs need not transit the canal.

With a new pier, dry docks, pumping plant, electrical substation, and increased repair capacity, by the end of 1943 the repair facilities available in the Canal Zone were estimated to equal those at Pearl Harbor on 7 December 1941.

See also Panama Canal Zone, Post-World War II Defense Arrangements.

BIBLIOGRAPHY

A. U.S. Navy, Bureau of Yards and Docks, *Building the Navy's Bases in World War II*, 2 vols. (Washington: GPO, 1947), II:15, 18, 20, 22, 36, 39, 40, 41; "U.S. Naval Administration in World War II. Commander 15th Naval District and Commander Panama Sea Frontier," 2 vols., microfilm (Washington: U.S. Navy Department Library).

BALIKPAPAN, DUTCH BORNEO, U.S. NAVAL ADVANCE BASE, 1945 The Seventh Amphibious Force (Seventh Fleet, Southwest Pacific Area) conducted its last amphibious operation of World War II at Balikpapan (1°45′S., 117°E.), Dutch Borneo, in the Netherlands East Indies. Australian forces landed there on 1 July 1945. Supporting the operation were the tender *Mobjack* and PTs from Motor Torpedo Boat Squadrons 10 and 27. With the capture of Balikpapan, the Seventh Fleet organized an MTB advance base there. The PTs patrolled along the southeast coast of Borneo and across Makassar Strait toward the Celebes. After the Japanese surrender in September, naval forces at Balikpapan assisted freed Allied prisoners of war and refugees. The base remained open until December 1945.

BIBLIOGRAPHY

A. U.S. Navy, "7th Amphibious Force Command History, 10 January 1943-23 December 1945" (Washington: Naval Historical Center, Operational Archives Branch).

B. Samuel E. Morison, *Liberation of the Philippines October 1944-August 1945* (Boston: Little, Brown, 1959); Capt. Robert J. Bulkley, *At Close Quarters: PT Boats in the United States Navy* (Washington: Navy Department, Naval History Division, 1962); Vice Adm. Daniel E. Barbey, *MacArthur's Amphibious Navy* (Annapolis, Md.: U.S. Naval Institute, 1969).

JOHN B. LUNDSTROM

BANTRY BAY, IRELAND.
See World War I U.S. Naval Air Stations in Europe; World War I U.S. Naval Bases in Europe.

BARRANQUILLA, COLOMBIA, U.S. NAVAL AIR FACILITY.
See Hispanic South America, U.S. Naval Bases.

BASSENS, FRANCE.
See World War I U.S. Naval Bases in Europe.

BELEM, BRAZIL, U.S. NAVAL AIR FACILITY.
See Brazil, U.S. Naval Bases.

BENI-SAF, ALGERIA.
See North Africa, U.S. Naval Bases.

BEN KEO, REPUBLIC OF VIETNAM, U.S. NAVAL ADVANCED TACTICAL SUPPORT BASE, 1969–1971 This small village, on South Vietnam's Vam Co Dong River, was the location of a naval advanced tactical support base during the war in Southeast Asia. Naval leaders deployed river patrol boat (PBR) units there as part of the Giant Slingshot operation to interdict the movement of enemy troops and supplies across the Cambodian border.

Seabees brought in from the I Corps Tactical Zone in northern South Vietnam constructed the installation during 1969 and 1970. The naval constructionmen built a defensive perimeter, fuel and ammunition storage facilities, personnel accommodations, and a helicopter pad.

The completed facility was transferred to the Vietnamese Navy when U.S. naval forces were withdrawn from the forward area in April 1971.

BIBLIOGRAPHY

A. Commander Naval Forces, Vietnam, "The Naval War in Vietnam," May 1970 (Washington: Naval Historical Center, Operational Archives Branch).

EDWARD J. MAROLDA

BEN LUC, REPUBLIC OF VIETNAM, U.S. NAVAL SUPPORT BASE, 1968–1971 Located close to the junction of South Vietnam's Vam Co Tay and Vam Co Dong rivers, Ben Luc served as the main support base for the Navy's Giant Slingshot operation during the Southeast Asian Conflict. The main objective of this operation was to interdict communist infiltration from the nearby "Parrot's Beak" border area of Cambodia using river patrol, river assault, and helicopter units.

Beginning in December 1968, American naval forces deployed to forward staging positions along both rivers. At Ben Keo (q.v.), Go Dau Ha (q.v.), Hiep Hoa (q.v.), and Tra Cu (q.v.), on the Vam Co Dong, and at Moc Hoa (q.v.), Tan An (q.v.), and Thuyen Nhon (q.v.) on the Vam Co Tay, Seabees brought in from the Danang (q.v.) area set up advanced tactical support bases (ATSBs) that provided the combat units with base defenses, fuel and ammunition storage, a helicopter pad, sleeping and messing facilities, and other essentials.

Meanwhile, efforts were made to prepare facilities at Ben Luc, which would be responsible for the intermediate-level repair of the combat units' river patrol boats (PBRs) and for supply of the ATSBs. Because of its location in relation to the two key waterways of the area and on Route 4, the main road to Saigon, Ben Luc was geographically well suited for its role. However, the base site chosen, on the bank nearest to Saigon in case the bridge was dropped by the Viet Cong, was less than ideal. When the Navy's survey team arrived at Ben Luc, they found the site under water and river material inadequate for landfill use. In order to obtain funds for expensive truck-transported fill, naval leaders designated Ben Luc a combined U.S.-Vietnamese naval base, thereby enabling them to tap into available Vietnamization program allocations.

Other problems hindered the base development effort. Fears that the French had laid a minefield in the area prompted a thorough but time-consuming search by an explosive ordnance disposal team. The dredge *Western Eagle* was damaged by a Viet Cong 107mm rocket, and on another occasion a crane-bearing barge tipped over, dropping the machinery into the river. Finally, a tank landing ship (LST) from Danang transporting material required for construction of the installation was unable to offload its cargo; the facilities at Ben Luc were too rudimentary. The ship was diverted to Newport near Saigon and the resources were transferred to trucks for delivery to the site.

While base facilities were under construction, the Navy took interim measures to provide logistic support to the patrol forces upriver. YR-9, a floating workshop with spaces that were ideal for an operations and communications center, was grounded at the site. In addition, the *Harnett County* (LST-821) temporarily anchored in the river to provide berthing for the PBRs and crew accommodations.

The intermediate support base was commissioned in July 1969 as Naval Support Activity, Saigon, Detachment Ben Luc. By September of that year, 812 men worked at the installation and occasionally as many as seventy vessels tied up or anchored in the river.

As part of the Vietnamization of the war, the Vietnamese Navy relieved U.S. naval forces of control of the Giant Slingshot operation in May 1970. The following year, in April, the turnover process was completed when Ben Luc and the ATSBs on both rivers were turned over to the Republic of Vietnam.

BIBLIOGRAPHY
A. Commander Naval Forces, Vietnam, "The Naval War in Vietnam," May 1970 (Washington: Naval Historical Center, Operational Archives Branch).

BEREHAVEN, IRELAND.
See World War I U.S. Naval Air Stations in Europe.

BERMUDA, U.S. NAVAL BASES, 1918–1919, 1941– While the U.S. Navy has had bases on the islands of Bermuda, it has used several locations for these activities—establishing some, disestablishing others, and transferring authority here and there as needs changed. There has been no major base or station under the continuous authority of one military service since 1918. Hence general U.S. operations in Bermuda will be discussed by giving consideration to four primary sites.

The Bermuda Islands consist of some 360 small coral and limestone islands located in the Atlantic Ocean 568 miles due east of Cape Hatteras, N.C. There are no native Bermudians, for these islands were uninhabited when discovered in 1515 by Spanish navigator Juan de Bermudez. They were first colonized in 1609 by the same British organization that established Jamestown, Va. While noted as a perpetual garden spot and mecca for tourists, Bermuda has long had strategic military and naval significance. This is apparent from the remarkable variety of coastal fortifications representing many periods and the magnificent Royal Navy Dockyard at the western tip of the island, which today is both a historic site and home of the Bermuda Maritime Museum.

The seven largest islands have been connected by bridges and causeways to form what is termed "the mainland." Bermuda's total land area is approximately twenty-two square miles. Prior to achieving complete autonomy in 1968, it was the oldest self-governing colony in the British Empire. Its House of Assembly was the second oldest lawmaking body in that empire, preceded only by the national parliament in London.

Bermuda's strategic value first began to loom significantly to the United States during World War I, when the U.S. Navy opened Naval Base No. 24 on White's Island in Hamilton Harbor in March 1918. This facility was used for ASW and convoy escort duties. It was leased for a period of ten years, but the lease lapsed and the base closed in January 1919, following the war's end.

In 1940, during the early days of World War II, Anglo-American cooperation returned to Bermuda. In a historic action of 20 September 1940, the United States agreed to give Great Britain fifty old destroyers for a ninety-nine-year lease on various sites. Bermuda was one of these sites, and the United States moved rapidly to construct an Army airfield on the eastern end of Bermuda (on Long Bird and St. David's Islands) and a naval seaplane station in the central portion of the island (across the Great Sound from Hamilton, Bermuda's capital city).

In 1940 Bermuda had only three towns—Hamilton, St. George's, and Somerset—and a population of 32,000. Roads were primitive, automobiles were virtually unknown, and potable water was obtained only by unique rooftop collection methods. One can therefore easily imagine the impact the influx of foreigners building two major military bases had upon this small, fragile community. While the men of St. David's may as sailors have visited distant lands, most of the women rarely left the small island on which they had been born. In any event, with patriotic ardor the House of Assembly agreed to the "destroyer-bases deal" even though it well knew that grave economic, political, and social changes would result. Winston Churchill himself attested to these sacrifices, while President F. D. Roosevelt termed the base lease "the most important action in the reinforcement of our national defense that has been taken since the Louisiana Purchase."

Nonetheless, American bases ultimately brought not only previously forbidden automobiles, but tore at the very historic fiber of Bermuda itself. In one instance, the graves of descendents of one of the three men left on the island in 1610 had to be moved to make way for American construction work. Practicality and survival, however, reigned supreme, with the Colonial Secretary telling his people: "It could be real bombs knocking down your houses around your ears." The reality of the threat was also brought home when, during the summer of 1940, hardly a week went by without wounded and injured survivors from sunken ships being brought to Bermuda. Gradually, the shock of tearing up long-undisturbed land gave way to a sense of comradeship with the friendly Americans. Despite legal authorization in May 1941, even the dreaded automobile had to wait for its first paved road (from Fort Bell to Hamilton in 1945). In the interim, horse-drawn transport and a narrow-gauge railway (with tracks ending 1 1/2 miles from Fort Bell) moved most stores and equipment.

By 5 January 1941 the Chief of Naval Operations had established a three-pronged program to develop naval bases in Bermuda. Involved was the acquisition of both Morgan and Tucker Islands and their adjoining cays, an engineering survey for both short- and long-term construction needs, and establishment of a naval air station to support a squadron of seaplanes and two small seaplane tenders. An additional ramp and parking area for two more patrol squadrons, a cleared site for pesonnel and support structures, and emergency power also were desired. Finally, arrangements had to be made with the U.S. Army for a site able to house temporarily one carrier air group at the Army airfield being developed at Fort Bell. All these activities followed the recommendations of the Hepburn Board's report in 1938, which were echoed by the report of the Greenslade Board dated 6 January 1941.

Although the Greenslade Board had also urged establishment of additional shore facilities to support carrier, cruiser, destroyer, and submarine forces, the first Navy facility to be built was the naval seaplane base. In accordance with a Bureau of Yards and Docks fixed-fee contract, on 15 February 1941 a Civil Engineering Corps captain arrived in Bermuda as Officer in Charge of Construction (OIC) and conferred with architectural and engineering contractors. In addition to Morgan and Tucker Islands, the Navy leased a 113-acre mainland plot for the seaplane station.

In all, some thirty-nine related construction projects were begun by 28 March 1941. The Naval Operating Base, with headquarters for the Commandant in Hamilton, was commissioned on 7 April 1941. Navy contractors were established in the Elbow Beach Hotel, while a construction camp was erected for 2,000 workers at the leased site. American naval officers lived at the Inverurie Hotel. The seaplane station was commissioned on 1 July 1941.

Initially the narrow, funnel-shaped channel between Morgan and Tucker Islands was dredge-filled. This joined the two islands and increased their original area by at least one-third. The now-single island was then connected to the mainland at Kings Point by a causeway. Primary structures included a pier for a seaplane tender, three seaplane ramps, a seaplane parking area, a large seaplane hangar, barracks for 1,100 men, quarters for 140 officers, a bombproof power plant, and the usual industrial, administrative, and storage buildings needed at any air station. Underground storage was provided at Kings Point for fuel oil, diesel oil, and gasoline. In addition, there were barracks for men at the fueling depot and the air station, a fifty-bed dispensary, a large magazine area, and a radio station. Moreover, a 10-acre water catchment was developed along with storage for 5 million gallons of fresh water. All these installations were of a permanent nature and constructed of steel and concrete.

During this construction period, it became evident that air patrols were needed more quickly than facilities for them could be built. Therefore an airfield being used by commercial airlines on Darrell Island some two and a half miles east within Great Sound, was developed immediately as a temporary seaplane base. By March 1942, when the new naval seaplane station had been completed, naval operations ceased at Darrell Island.

No task of such magnitude could occur without many challenges. As early as June 1941, the bureau officer in charge reported unfavorably on the "attitude of Bermudians," saying that they resented not only the presence of American naval and military forces and especially the construction crews, but having to give up their land for the American bases. They also obstructed work by procrastination in handling requests for occupation of leased property, continued to charge customs duties and other taxes, and failed to issue licenses for official U.S. motor trucks. In great contrast, the British military and naval forces on the islands were "extremely friendly and helpful."

This report, however, paled in comparison to one made by a visiting naval officer and former residential American engineer and architect that attacked virtually every aspect of the construction effort, alleging misplaced priorities, faulty construction, lavish staff facilities, absent work force, and a lack of dredging. The former submarine commander concluded: "The Army contractors are estimated to have accomplished about seven times as much aviation work as the Navy contractors." Because this report was from a line officer without major construction experience, it appears to have been disregarded. The report of the OIC was accepted by both the Bureau of Yards and Docks and the Navy. Moreover, the seaplane station was ready for use in March 1942 as scheduled, and another naval Civil Engineer Corps (CEC) officer thought the work so well done that he recommended the builders be given an ''E'' award for efficiency.

The original contract also called for construction work outside the seaplane station. One such project began in June 1941 with the development of submarine support facilities on Ordnance Island, in St. George's Harbor, on the eastern end of the island close to Bermuda's sea lanes and the U.S. Army's Fort Bell. Use of this area was obtained under a short-term lease extending to December 1955. Involved were rehabilitating aged, dilapidated structures for use as housing and messing facilities for submarine crews while ashore, improving water and sewer systems, repairing waterfront buildings, and installing mooring facilities offshore.

The Riddle Bay area—which had been a golf course and resort area used by Bermudians themselves—was developed as a naval recreational area during the summer of 1942. Improvements were made to existing shower and dressing rooms and to water and electrical supply systems; new recreation buildings, athletic fields, and an outdoor movie theater were also built. The Hamilton Hotel became a United Service Organization (USO) club, with the Coral Island Cove and Elbow Beach pavilion as USO branches. For ''the duration,'' a 200-bed mobile hospital supplemented the small station dispensary.

Meanwhile the Army proceeded to construct Fort Bell and Kindley Field on Long Bird and St. David's Islands to handle all landbased Army and Navy planes. Fort Bell was named for Maj. Gen. George Bell, Jr., a graduate of West Point who commanded the Thirty-third Division of the American Expeditionary Force in France in 1918. He had worked closely with the British and was decorated by them.

The Kindley Field runway area (which in 1946 became Kindley Air Force Base) was named after Capt. Field E. Kindley, a young American officer who distinguished himself during World War I. He is credited by the United States with shooting down ten German aircraft—twelve in official British records. Kindley was killed in a crash at Kelly Field on 1 February 1920 during an air demonstration being prepared for Gen. John J. Pershing. An amphibious Army Air Corps field on Corregidor in the Philippine Islands that operated from about 1921 to 1929 had earlier been named for Kindley.

Commissioned 25 June 1941, Kindley Field included naval facilities for the temporary support of one carrier air group of ninety planes, barracks for 550 men and 125 officers, messing facilities, storage buildings, nose hangars, and radio aids. The high point of Army/Navy construction work came in June 1942, with 3,600 men working in Bermuda. British sources indicate total U.S. construction costs of $43 million through only 1943.

Southlands, located along the southern shoreline of Hamilton Island, was obtained under another short-term lease for development as an Anti-Aircraft Training Center (AATC) under the Commandant. Construction, begun on 1 July

1942, included a night vision training building, repair shops, magazine loading shops, magazines, instruction buildings, barracks, gun platforms, a control tower, and various roads, walkways, and service buildings.

The Navy's initial Bermuda construction contract terminated on 8 April 1943, and a new contract was issued which continued to 28 June 1944. Throughout the entire war, negotiations continued between U.S., British, and Bermuda authorities about such matters as the need for additional land by the American forces; the reorganization, paving, and maintenance of roads and bridges; immigration quotas for Bermudians into the United States (deemed necessary since the United States had taken some 10 percent of Bermuda's land); Bermudian tariffs on vegetables and customs collections on American imports; and the essential water supply issue. A unique wartime plan to camouflage the entire island and make the bases and air stations look like lovely Bermuda foothills complete with houses was also begun. Although this plan was never fully implemented, photographs of the scale model for this transmutation are in the Bermuda Maritime Museum.

American convoys began arriving at Bermuda in early 1943. These contained as many as ninety-seven ships and continued until May 1944. They helped the pre-D-Day build-up and included many landing craft. About the time the convoys ended, the NOB itself increased operations, thus bringing more U.S. naval ship traffic.

In addition to civilian contractor construction, there was considerable Seabee activity on Bermuda. The Thirty-first Construction Battalion, 27 officers and 1,027 men, arrived on 5 December 1942 to assist the contractor in building the operating base, seaplane station, and submarine base. On 27 February 1943 there arrived in addition the Forty-first CB, with 27 officers and 1,080 men. Primary activities included roads, utilities, grading, accessory buildings, and general cleanup. In addition these units began operation, maintenance, and repair work on the island's entire naval establishment under the direction of the Public Works Department. In October 1943 the Thirty-first CB returned home and was replaced by the 540th Maintenance Unit, and in December by the 551st Maintenance Unit. When the Forty-first CB departed, the two maintenance units combined to carry out the Navy's public works mission.

Throughout the entire period of construction there was only one fire and only forty-four civilian personnel were lost (a single ship sinking). While there was no combat on or near Bermuda during the entire war, food rationing for civilians had begun at the war's start in 1939. U-boat attacks brought a real threat of starvation in mid-1942. Then stocks were slowly built up, although rationing continued until the war's end. U.S. servicemen and women received a battle star on their American Campaign Medal for duty in Bermuda between 7 December 1941 and 2 September 1945. Civilian and contractor construction workers also were awarded a special pin for their contribution.

During all this time the Army was engaged in building Fort Bell and its Kindley Field runway on Long Bird and St. David's Islands under the direction of Army Engineers based at the St. George's Hotel, which later became a USO. Operations began in March 1941. On 16 April the first American troops arrived in the transport *American Legion* and were garrisoned at the elegant, luxurious Castle Harbor Hotel. Perhaps because of this luxury, Army enlisted personnel were prohibited from riding in the elevators and had to use the stairways. The first flag was raised over the airfield on 4 July 1941. A thirty-bed hospital opened the next month. The first runway pavement was laid and weathermen (the Twenty-fourth Signal Company) also arrived in August 1941.

Kindley Field opened for takeoffs and landings on 29 November 1941, and carrier aircraft landings began on 15 December. An F2A from the USS *Long Island* was the first carrier-based plane to land. An RAF B-24 *Liberator* was the first landbased plane to use the field, arriving on 20 December 1941. The first U.S. Army Air Corps planes landed 6 February 1942.

By 27 April 1942 the Army began ASW patrols, using B-17s and B-24s. Navy PBYs, operating from the Navy Seaplane Station, were also very active in this effort. These patrols continued until February 1944.

The Fort Bell Base Headquarters and the Kindley Field Air Base Squadron were organized in July 1942. Fort Bell also operated a cemetery until September 1967, when 128 bodies were removed by a Graves Registration Team. Of these, 125 were returned to the United States, one French sailor was returned to Paris, and two were reburied in Bermuda. These individuals had been military and civilian workers who died of natural causes, with the majority being shipwreck casualties.

Kindley Field's first aircraft of its own, a crated C-78 Cessna, arrived on 15 January 1943. It was put together and flown by 28 January. On 20 March a 150-bed hospital, which had cost more than $1 million to build, was opened. Army C-54s began a regular transportation schedule on 14 December 1943. A small Air Transport Command (ATC) unit arrived two weeks later, on 30 December. During 1944 and 1945, Kindley Field was a major refueling and rest stop for medical air evacuation flights, handling between 1,000 and 2,000 such patients a month. The base's first flight surgeon reported in February 1944. The ATC group grew gradually and formed the basis of the air base group that took over operation in January 1946 when the U.S. Army left, and Fort Bell became Kindley Air Force base under the U.S. Army Air Forces. In 1948 this became a U.S. Air Force Base because the U.S. Air Forces had become an independent service.

By the fall of 1944 naval activity in Bermuda began to decline as the war in Europe turned in favor of the Allies. U-boat activity in the Atlantic had all but halted. The Submarine Repair Facility at Ordnance Island was reduced to caretaker status in January 1945. That same month, the ATC was first transferred to Guantánamo Bay, Cuba (q.v.), then decommissioned on 1 April 1945. By that time the Navy had some 3,112 personnel stationed in Bermuda: 732 Seabees, 2,240 other sailors and airmen, and 140 Marines. In May of that year naval activities on the island included the Naval Operating Base, the Naval Air Station (seaplane), an Advanced Amphibious Training Center (AATC), a Naval Air Transport Service Unit, a Submarine Base, a Section Base, a Submarine Repair Facility (in reduced status), a Fuel Depot, a DE-DD Training Center (the former AATC), Repair Facilities, a YR Barge, a Degaussing Range, a Loop Station, a Port Director, Marine Barracks, and an ATC and Naval Detachment at the Army's Kindley Field.

On 23 July 1945 the Navy's portion of Kindley Field was turned over to the U.S. Army; on 31 July the Naval Air Station was reduced to a Naval Air Facility and the Naval Operating Base was reduced to a Repair Facility. Also during this same month, Ordnance Island was returned to its native owners; and on 15 August 1945 the Lend-Lease agreements ended. On 31 December 1950 total naval personnel on Bermuda numbered only 460 (131 Navy, 20 Marine Corps, 188 dependents, and 121 civilian employees). On 1 July 1950 both the NOB and the NAS were disestablished, and a Naval Station was established in their stead. It included an Air Department (Aerological Activity and Microseismic Activity), a Communications Department, a Seabee Detachment, a Marine Detachment, and two aviation squadrons—Patrol VP 49 and Service FASRon 795. The station's mission, as of 30 July 1950, was to:

> Provide facilities to support regular operations of fleet reconnaissance and anti-submarine aircraft. The organization and planning of the Naval Station to provide for the rapid transition of component departments to the status of separate activities upon mobilization. Marine Corps to provide base interior guard.

By 30 June 1951 total U.S. personnel in Bermuda had increased to 6,001 (3,225 Army, Navy, Air Force, and Marines, 876 civil servants; 300 contractor employees; and 1,600 dependents). Perhaps the USAF's most significant contribution to Bermuda was the Long Bird Bridge. Initially, St. George's could be reached only by boat or ferry. In 1871 a causeway had been built to connect the island and link up with St. George's via a swing bridge—which still permitted boats to pass between Long Bird and St. David's Islands. Construction of Fort Bell, however, closed this passage. To provide a waterway, a new channel was dredged through the old causeway. A temporary barge bridge, anchored on a pivot and powered by a small engine, now linked the causeway to itself. This barge could slowly swing open to allow boats to pass. While this barge bridge was slow, inconvenient to both cars and boats, and dangerous, funds for construction of the new swing bridge needed to replace the barge proved difficult to acquire. Finally, in February 1951, money was obtained by the Air Force. The new Long Bird swing bridge was dedicated on 4 December 1952 by Bermuda's governor as "a monument to the United States Air Force," which would "preserve a name steeped in the history of these islands and very dear to its people."

Culturally, the U.S. Air Force brought Bermuda another influence—television. The Army had operated a small radio station during World War II that provided music, a little news, and general diversion. This was disestablished in 1946 when Bermuda opened radio station ZBM. On 4 July 1955 Bermuda's first television station was installed by the Armed Forces Radio and Television Service. It was intended only for clubs, barracks, and on-station homes, since American films and TV programs were licensed only for viewing by military forces. By November 1956, however, arrangements were completed to permit the 1,500 American service families living off-base to receive TV broadcasts, which resulted in transmission to the entire island some sixty-two hours of programming weekly. On 18 January 1958 Bermuda's own ZBM-TV went on the air at 1740 hours, and the Kindley station was now limited, by mutual agreement, to telecasting only from noon until 1730. This joint plan continued until 25 February 1960, when ZBM-TV began full-time operation. ZFB-TV has begun since then.

Bermuda also serves as an interesting example of the contribution of women to military service. Christmas 1944 marked an unusual event as sixty members of the Women's Army Corp (WAC) reported for Bermuda duty. Another sixty arrived the following May, making considerable social changes in a base that lacked transportation and had only limited recreational opportunity. By May 1946 all but two female officers had departed. The Air Force assigned an occasional WAF (Women in the Air Force) officer to Bermuda, but enlisted women came only when accompanying a military husband. Since the Navy took over in 1970, nearly 500 naval women serve in a fully integrated air station.

Between 1954 and 1961 Kindley Air Force Base also served U.S. Navy airships. In April 1954 four blimps were moored at Castle Harbor for six weeks, leaving behind a mobile mooring mast. In December 1957 a NAS Lakehurst, N.J., blimp made a very challenging emergency landing during a major storm. Again, on 13 February 1958, a similar emergency came to a successful conclusion on the fifth landing attempt, when loss of an engine forced the blimp commander to release all helium from the bag, bringing about a sudden, dramatic descent. Two uneventful visits took place in 1960, athough on 12 and 13 December another weather-plagued blimp took four hours to fly ninety miles and had to wait another five-and-one-half hours for surface winds to calm sufficiently to permit a landing. The last two uneventful air ship missions took place in February and July 1961.

Upon request, the Chief of Naval Research obtained permission to establish a small research laboratory at Tudor Hill in Bermuda, the construction of which was completed late in 1960. Today this laboratory and its auxiliary site at High Point Cay are devoted to acoustic research programs as a detachment of the Naval Underwater Systems Center (headquartered in Newport, R.I., and with a major laboratory in New London, Conn., and major detachments in West Palm Beach, Fla. and the Bahamas—headquarters of the Navy's Atlantic Undersea Test and Evaluation Center). The Tudor Hill laboratory is outfitted with extensive digital and analog data acquisition, processing, and analysis equipment. It is also the terminal for a number of underwater acoustic installations varying in depth from 2,300 to more than 16,000 feet and covering a broad frequency range. The laboratory also includes a research ship for at-sea support of research efforts. The year 1960 also saw completion of a new Commissary Store at Kindley Air Field.

Navy control has resulted in consolidation of military beaches. From a high of eight beaches, NAS Bermuda now has only two—Clearwater Beach, established in 1952, and NASA Beach, which was formerly Long Bird Beach on Cooper's Island. A new Naval Exchange completed in 1980 is another important military landmark.

Continuing creative use of limited facilities is a mark of the U.S. military presence in Bermuda. A beer hall for construction workers from 1941 to 1943, for example, was converted to a chapel. It was used for that purpose until 1958, when a new chapel was completed. Another old Bermuda dwelling became a Red Cross "Hostess House" in January 1945, with as many as ten Red Cross hostesses providing recreational programs and assisting medical air evacuation patients during stopovers. In 1947 this building became a Service Club operated by Special Services. It provided dance classes, buffet suppers, game tournaments, dances, holiday parties, island tours, and a meeting place for hobby and club groups. In 1952 a new wing was added for $24,000. When the Navy took over the base in 1970, this building became, in turn, the Chief Petty Officer's Club, the Non-Alcoholic Center, and most recently the Community Center (again operated by Special Services and providing special interest classes, club meetings, unit or private parties, and evening classes in a variety of skills).

One of Bermuda's most historic structures is Long Bird House, which since 1959 has housed the base/station commanding officer and his family. Millionaire William Marcus Greve, who owned thirty-nine of the island's original sixty-two acres, had begun construction of this home, reported by *Life* magazine in 1941 as "a $200,000 pleasure dome." Later that year, the U.S. Army paid Greve $300,000 for his land, unfinished house, guest cottage, and outbuildings intended as a model dairy farm. By mid-1942 the house had been completed and converted into a headquarters and operations building. It provided offices for the Kindley Field commander and his staff, operations, traffic, weather, communications, message center, intelligence, and the sergeant major—as well as an officers' mess, kitchen, and bar. Atop the house was a control tower. The stables were converted to bachelor officers' quarters. Air operations moved to a new site in 1944, and Greve House became the residence of Fort Bell's commander and quarters for visiting VIPs. Named informally "Hotel DeGink," it housed up to twenty-two guests at one time, including such notables as Gen. Dwight D. Eisenhower, Andrei Gromyko, Herbert Hoover, Fiorello La Guardia, Lord Beaverbrook, Averill Harriman, Alexander Seversky, Clare Boothe Luce, Prince Abdil Ilah, and Generals Omar Bradley, Lucius Clay, H. H. Arnold, and Claire Chennault. In 1945 the stables were converted to WAC enlisted barracks, and the guest house to WAC officers' quarters. Distinguished visitors continued staying at Long Bird House until 1959, when the "Gulfstream" bachelor officers' quarters opened. Long Bird House's old control tower was removed only in early 1982 by a team of seven Seabees. This was a very challenging project because the tower was bordered on three sides by fragile Bermuda slate roofs and on the fourth by a fish pond. It also turned out to weigh some 23,000 pounds—an amount just below the critical weight limit of the only available crane.

Air station streets are named for two World War II battlefields (Corregidor and Bataan), flowers (Hibiscus, Holly, Oleander), functions (Wharf, Ferry, Hospital, and—enroute to the National Aeronautics and Space Administration's installation—Mercury), locations (Castle Harbor and Kindley Field), and for some fourteen American medal winners (thirteen officers, one enlisted; twelve Army Air Forces, and two Navy—including Capt. Colin P. Kelley, Jr., Lt. Gen. Frank M. Andrews, and Lt. Comdr. John C. Waldron, the last the leader of Torpedo Squadron Eight at the Battle of Midway). One civilian is so honored. Tommy Fox Road was named for Henry Mortiner "Tommy" Fox of St. David's, the "uncrowned king" of the community who died on 12 October 1942. This former whaling man was a Bible-quoting teetotaler and a colorful symbol of Anglo-American cooperation. It seems only fitting that there is at least this one tribute to a Bermudian who gave up so much so that the Free World might remain free.

As to the future, it would appear that as long as potential enemies operate submarines and long-legged aircraft, the U.S. Navy will consider Bermuda a viable advance base. Thus, while the U.S. Army, the U.S. Air Force, and even the Royal Navy of the United Kingdom have closed permanent military facilities and left this lovely island, the U.S. Navy will remain (at least until the year 2039, when the original ninety-nine-year lease will expire). Some things remain the same, and the U.S. Navy seems to have become as much a part of Bermuda as the Wednesday evening military tattoo in the town square of St. George's.

BIBLIOGRAPHY

A. "Information on Living Conditions in Bermuda" (U.S. Navy, mimeo., Nov. 1959); "History of Naval Air Facility, Bermuda, 1 July 1941 to 2 Sept. 1945" (Washington: Naval Historical Center, Operational Archives Branch); O.L. Carson, Acting Director, to Chief, Bureau of Yards and Docks, 20 Feb. 1946, "Subj.: Naval Facilities in Bermuda—Report on Establishment and Construction of" (Washington: Naval Historical Center: Operational Archives Branch); *NUSC Brief,* Technical Document 6060A for Fiscal Year 1981 (Newport, R.I.: Naval Underwater Systems Center); Bermuda File, Naval Facilities Engineering Command Historical Information Branch, Naval Construction Battalion Center, Port Hueneme, Calif.

B. "A Look into the History of the Air Station," series in NAS Bermuda, *Bermuda Tide-ings*, Sept. 1981-Apr. 1982; Lt. Comdr. Ian Stranach, RN (Ret.), *The Andrew and the Onions: The Story of the Royal Navy in Bermuda, 1795-1975* (Bermuda: The Island Press, n.d.).

DAVID L. WOODS

BIAK, DUTCH NEW GUINEA, U.S. NAVAL ADVANCE BASE, 1944–1946 Situated across the entrance of Geelvink Bay in northwestern Dutch New

Guinea, Biak and the other islands of the Schouten group commanded the Japan Strait and lay only 900 miles southeast of Mindanao in the Philippines. Southwest Pacific Area strategists intended to develop Biak (10°0′S., 131°0′E.) as a large air and advance naval base for the Fifth Air Force and the Seventh Fleet. It was to become a staging and repair point for light craft and aircraft. On 27 May 1944 Allied troops landed on Biak, but a skillful Japanese defense and prolonged resistance led to the decision by early June to occupy the small Paidado Islands a few miles south of Biak and build the bases there. On 2 June 1944 troops took over the islands of Owi and Mios Woendi. Owi became an airfield complex for Fifth Air Force heavy bombers and fighters, and Air Force headquarters remained there until November.

The small island of Mios Woendi became the focus of naval activity. On 6 June 1944 Motor Torpedo Boat Base 2 set up shop there to handle the boats of MTB Squadron 12, soon joined by Squadrons 21 and 9. Biak was threatened by the Imperial Japanese Navy, which tried to land reinforcements for its defenders, so there was much action for the PTs. On 26 June, Base 21 arrived from Dreger Harbor near Finchhafen (q.v.), and early in July two more MTB squadrons with three tenders arrived. Mios Woendi became the main PT base in the Southwest Pacific. Ashore, Seabees built a main overhaul and repair base and facilities to handle fifty boats. The base was operating on its own by early August. The PTs themselves saw much combat that summer, but contacts with the enemy gradually decreased until 16 November 1944, when the PTs ceased patrols and left New Guinea waters.

Meanwhile the naval base on Mios Woendi (formally commissioned on 11 June 1944) also developed facilities for handling landing craft, patrol planes, and submarines. Mobile Amphibious Repair Base 2 began arriving on 4 July and set up repair shops and floating dry docks to service landing craft as big as LSTs. Likewise in July, Naval Seaplane Base 2 was brought in to support operations and maintenance for Fleet Air Wing 17 flying boats. Mios Woendi was an important operating base for patrol planes searching north and west toward the Philippines and the Dutch East Indies. Finally, in September 1944, the submarine tender *Orion* set up at Mios Woendi an advance submarine base to fuel and supply submarines based at Fremantle-Perth (q.v.) hunting Japanese shipping in the Dutch East Indies and the southern Philippines. Stopping off at Mios Woendi for fuel and torpedoes greatly increased the amount of time they could patrol Japanese waters. On nearby Noesi Island was a fuel tank farm and on Oeriv Island a naval mine and ammunition depot.

Mios Woendi remained an important maintenance base for Seventh Fleet light craft operating in the Philippines and East Indies, although Owi was rolled up by the end of 1944. Mios Woendi functioned at full capacity until after VJ-Day and was disestablished on 19 January 1946.

BIBLIOGRAPHY

A. U.S. Navy, "7th Amphibious Force Command History, 10 January 1943-23 December 1945" (Washington: Naval Historical Center, Operational Archives Branch); U.S. Navy, Bureau of Yards and Docks, *Building the Navy's Bases in World War II*, 2 vols.

(Washington: GPO, 1947); "U.S. Naval Activities Disestablished since July 1949," 27 Sept. 1954 (Washington: Naval Historical Center, Operational Archives Branch); "Monograph Histories of U.S. Naval Overseas Bases. Vol. II. Pacific Area" (Washington: Naval Historical Center, Operational Archives Branch).

B. Rear Adm. Worrall Reed Carter, *Beans, Bullets, and Black Oil* (Washington: GPO, 1953); Samuel E. Morison, *New Guinea and the Marianas March 1944-August 1944* (Boston: Little, Brown, 1953); Capt. Robert J. Bulkley, *At Close Quarters: PT Boats in the United States Navy* (Washington: Navy Department, Naval History Division, 1962); Vice Adm. Daniel E. Barbey, *MacArthur's Amphibious Navy* (Annapolis, Md.: U.S. Naval Institute, 1969).

JOHN B. LUNDSTROM

BILIBID PRISON, MANILA, PHILIPPINE ISLANDS.
See Canacao, Bilibid Prison, Manila, Philippine Islands.

BINH THUY, REPUBLIC OF VIETNAM.
See Can Tho-Binh Thuy, Republic of Vietnam, U.S. Naval Support Activity.

BIZERTE, TUNISIA.
See North Africa, U.S. Naval Bases.

BORA BORA, SOCIETY ISLANDS, U.S. NAVAL STATION, 1942–1946 [BOBCAT] Bora Bora, or Borabora (16°25′S., 151°40′W.), is an island in the Leeward group of the Society Islands. It was the site of the first U.S. naval overseas base approved during the Pacific War. Dominated by towering volcanic peaks, the main island, some six by two-and-one-half miles in size, is surrounded by coral reefs but features a protected, deep harbor at Teavanui. Bora Bora was administered as a Free French colonial possession.

On 25 December 1941 Adm. Ernest J. King, prospective Commander in Chief, U.S. Fleet, advised the establishment in a remote, safe region of the South Pacific of a naval fueling base to service vessels traveling the routes between Panama and New Zealand-Australia—the vital lifeline to the Southwest Pacific. Five days later, the Chief of Naval Operations' War Plans Division recommended Bora Bora as the location of a tank farm holding 200,000 barrels of fuel oil and a seaplane base. An Army garrison would defend the island. Admiral King agreed, and on 8 January 1942 he secured a joint Army-Navy agreement for the establishment of the Bora Bora base.

Mounting a hastily organized expedition for Bora Bora proved chaotic, and only an ad hoc naval construction detachment could be assembled in time to sail from Charleston, S.C., on 27 January. The convoy arrived off Bora Bora on 17 February, and its commander, Rear Adm. John F. Shafroth, initiated negotiations with the Free French administrator for use of the island. In the formal agreement signed on 23 February, the French leased the necessary land and facilities to the United States. Great difficulty ensued in unloading the expedition's supplies and materiel, leading to delays in erecting base facilities. Bora Bora proved more rugged than expected, and water supplies were especially scanty. Not until 2 April was work begun on the fuel oil tank farm. The first eight storage tanks were functioning by 9 June, and thereafter ships began refueling at the rate of one or two per week. Naval construction troops prepared a seaplane base, Naval Air Station Bora Bora, capable of handling one patrol squadron of fifteen Consolidated PBY Catalina flying boats. Bora Bora eventually featured two airstrips as well. All naval construction was completed by March 1943.

Bora Bora in 1942-1943 fueled numerous vessels en route to or from the Southwest Pacific, but the base never became as logistically important as originally planned. In December 1942 numerous "fleets" of landing craft—LSTs, LSMs, and LCIs—headed out from the United States to join amphibious forces in the South and Southwest Pacific areas. They found Bora Bora a convenient, if not altogether comfortable (given the water scarcity), stopping point on their voyages. Bora Bora-based PBYs helped to run herd on some of the greener landing craft crews and guide them in. Likewise, numerous barge-towing convoys touched at Bora Bora en route to the southwest. To handle numerous small-boat repairs, Bora Bora had a small ship repair unit with one YR floating workshop and several small pontoon dry docks. A partial roll-up of facilities began in June 1943, but the base remained open to service small craft until well after VJ-Day. On 2 June 1946 Bora Bora Naval Station was disestablished, and the remaining facilities were turned over to the French colonial authorities.

BIBLIOGRAPHY

A. Bora Bora, Society Islands, Naval Station, "History of the United States Naval Station, Bora Bora, Society Islands of French Oceania," Shore Establishment, 9 July 1945 (Washington: Naval Historical Center, Operational Archives Branch); U.S. Navy, Bureau of Yards and Docks, *Building the Navy's Bases in World War II,* 2 vols. (Washington: GPO, 1947).

JOHN B. LUNDSTROM

BORDEAUX, FRANCE.
See World War I U.S. Naval Bases in Europe.

BRAZIL, U.S. NAVAL BASES, 1941–1945 With a long coastline jutting boldly out into the Atlantic, Brazil's geography gave it importance in America's plans for military preparedness during the late 1930s. Naval bases would be needed along its coast in order to challenge the German submarine menace. Furthermore, its relative closeness to West Africa made it an important site if planes and war materials had to be shuttled to combat zones that might develop in Europe and the Mediterranean. As early as March 1941, Adm. Ernest J. King, Chief of Naval Operations, and Rear Adm. Jonas Ingram, then commanding a cruiser patrol division in the Caribbean and South Atlantic, agreed that the seaports the cruisers were already using at San Juan, Puerto Rico (q.v.), and Guantánamo Bay, Cuba (q.v.), would be inadequate if major A/S activity developed in the Atlantic. Both admirals felt that the use of ports like Recife and Bahia would greatly ease the Navy's patrol problems. Accordingly, contact was made with the government of Brazil, which granted the United States permission to use a number of locations for naval bases.

Recife, U.S. Naval Advance Base, 1942-1945

Located on the hump of Brazil where it pushes brazenly into the South Atlantic, Recife during the war was Brazil's third largest city, with 400,000 people. While its location was ideal for the Navy's needs, its harbor was small and narrow and could handle only ships with a draft of less than twenty-five feet. Throughout 1941 the U.S. Navy merely used the modest facilities already at the port. In 1942, after it entered the war, the United States undertook a dramatic expansion program both in the dock area and at Ibura Airfield, the latter just beyond the edge of the city. It erected housing and storage facilities and a 150-bed hospital. Six kilometers beyond the city an ammunition dump was established. In December construction began on a destroyer repair unit. At the same time, Admiral Ingram moved his headquarters ashore and into a rented ten-story building. Nevertheless, the facility that contributed most to the war effort was the fuel tank farm. At the start of the war, when the tanks were full—which was not often—they contained only enough oil for two weeks of normal operations, and its pumps, owned by the Caloric Oil Corp., could pump only 125 tons per hour into the bunkers of a waiting ship. To solve the delay problem, the Navy in July 1942 sent Lt. Comdr. Charles C. Dunn to Recife as a Convoy Routing Officer. Loading activity was speeded up, and new fuel tanks for added storage were built. Attention to such improvements soon paid off. One of the most important convoys of World War II, AS-4, including ten cargo ships carrying the new Sherman tanks to Gen. Bernard L. Montgomery's Eighth Army in North Africa, made a special fueling stop at Recife in midsummer 1942 before proceeding to its destination at Port Suez by way of the Cape of Africa. By outflanking German U-boats, the move made possible the timely delivery of tank units that, as Winston Churchill later remarked, guaranteed the Allied victory at El Alamein.

Expansion at Recife continued in 1942. Camp Ingram, named for the admiral, comprised twelve barracks for housing upwards of 1,000 men. A destroyer repair unit contained 745 men; by 1944 it was able to undertake major repairs on destroyer-sized vessels. Finally, a rest and rehabilitation center and an experimental farm for growing crops for the use of American servicemen were established. By late 1944, after the Battle of the Atlantic had been won and the naval emphasis shifted toward the Pacific, Recife and her sister ports became less important to the war effort. In November 1945, after Japan's surrender, naval facilities at the port were decommissioned and the ship repair installation was handed over to the Brazilian government. In the 1960s and 1970s, when the Caribbean was taking on new importance because of the need for space tracking stations and because of the threat of Communist Cuba, Brazil was too distant geographically to play a role in America's current naval basing needs. Her role for that purpose had ended in 1945.

Bahia, U.S. Naval Air Facility and Naval Operating Facility, 1943-1945

The second most important port in Brazil was the city of Bahia, located 400 miles south of Recife along the Atlantic coast. Because it lay beyond the hump of Brazil, it initially enjoyed a lesser role in the war against Axis submarines. Nevertheless, it had an excellent natural harbor compared to the meager one at Recife. Furthermore, from the American sailor's point of view, it was considered a good liberty port.

Three military installations were built at Bahia. The first was the Aratu seaplane base located twelve miles to the north of Bahia, one of five such bases the United States built in Brazil. It had half a squadron of patrol bombers, these being twelve *Martin PBM*, to which two PBY *Catalinas* were soon added, and eventually an LTA mast, radio station, and the Naval Air Transport (NATS) Unit. Built by the U.S. Army for Navy use, the Aratu base was operational by April 1943 and on 26 November 1943 was commissioned as a Naval Air Facility. New construction by the Navy added a cost of $700,000 to the site. Included were an Assembly and Repair Facility Class D, ships, a nose hangar, a ramp, 100,000-gallon underground gasoline storage, and berthing and messing facilities for the 70 officers and 540 men of the facility and for the 50 officers and men of the seaplanes based there—with all facilities enjoying paint camouflage. Because potable water was unavailable in the area, water was brought in by tank truck and a water barge. Although used extensively for convoy protection and ASW until the end of the war, Aratu was too far from the "Slot," the route U-boats took between 22° and 25°W., and by October 1942 it had only three of its original planes left and had been transferred to Galeao for administrative purposes. Although Aratu was restored as an independent command on 23 January 1944, it was later transferred to Natal, on 10 June 1944. It was disestablished on 30 June 1945 and transferred to the U.S. Army.

The second military installation at Bahia was a new electric power plant and a 3,000-ton floating dry dock that served as a destroyer repair facility to the end of the war. Gradually added to the Naval Operating Facility were a NATS unit, Harbor Detection Station, Sonobuoy Radio Station, Escort Vessel Station, Degaussing Range, and Radio and Radio D/F stations. The third facility, already mentioned, was the fuel oil storage depot that eventually included two 10,000-barrel tanks and two 80,000-barrel tanks.

Bahia did not figure as dramatically in the war effort as her neighbor Recife did, but two events served as stark reminders that the hot war was not too far away. The first was the arrival in November 1942 of a British convoy of troopships carrying 15,000 British soldiers for the invasion of North Africa. Although Bahia was not geographically the ideal Atlantic Ocean port for this rendezvous point, it had to do, for no other port along the South Atlantic was large enough to accommodate such a huge convoy. This pattern was repeated, and on a number of occasions as much as 250,000 tons of shipping was in the port at one time.

Finally, the port was also used in 1944 for the convoying of the Brazilian Expeditionary Force, an army contingent of Brazilian soldiers who served with the Allies in the Italian campaign.

In late 1945 the U.S. naval facilities at Bahia were decommissioned and the government of Brazil regained control of the installations, as had been provided under the Lend-Lease agreement.

Natal, U.S. Naval Air Facility, 1943-1945

The third major port of interest to the U.S. Navy was Natal. Although this city was less significant than Bahia and Recife, the Navy's interest in Brazilian sites commenced with Natal. That interest began in November 1940, when the U.S. Secretary of War entered into a contract with Pan American Airways (PAA) (which had landing facilities there for its trans-Atlantic flights) for the purpose of creating certain landplane and seaplane bases in Brazil and for improving existing ones. It was agreed that the actual development would be done by the Airport Development Program (ADP), a construction subsidiary of PAA, and that the facility would accommodate twelve seaplanes and a small number of landplane patrol bombers that would be used for convoy protection and ASW in the South Atlantic. By October 1941 a Navy patrol plane squadron was aboard and operating from the Rio Potengy on the northern edge of the city of Natal. They obtained their gasoline at the PAA station. Including some earlier work at the site by the U.S. Army, total construction costs amounted to more than $935,000. By December a Marine contingent had arrived, followed by seaplane tenders to serve the air squadron.

The beginning of America's war with Germany on 8 December 1941 created a problem. While the United States was now at war, Brazil was not, and armed Marines were needed to guard the newly established air facilities. Technically, as a neutral, Brazil could not permit the carrying of arms by citizens of a nation at war. The solution found was practical and diplomatic. Brazil would allow American Marines to arrive in Brazil, but their weapons would be boxed and would arrive separately. This procedure applied to all American base facilities in Brazil. All Marine guard patrols would be undertaken with truncheons as arms. When Brazil entered the war in August 1942, this procedure was changed and well-armed Marines resumed their patrols.

The facilities at Natal included installations for six Navy patrol bombers; a landplane base eight miles beyond the city with two runways at a site called Parnamarin Field; and naval housing, shops, and operating facilities. An extended mission called for the basing of three patrol bomber squadrons and for the commissioning of the naval facilities as a Naval Air Facility on 25 September 1943. Navy construction costs at the seaplane base were $300,000; at the land field, $635,000. As of 1 December 1944 there were on board eleven large patrol bombers, thirteen medium patrol bombers, one observation plane, and eight multi-engine seaplanes. Personnel at the time included 232 officers and 1,431 men. Grim reminders to both Americans and Brazilians of the horrors of war came in 1943 when many survivors from torpedoed ships in the South Atlantic were processed through the port. With the war in Europe over, on 30 June 1945 the NAF was disestablished and turned over to the U.S. Army

The remaining naval facilities established in Brazil during the war operated either aircraft or blimps. The impetus for their establishment came in September 1942 when President Getulio Vargas responded to his nation's declaration of war and ordered his Navy to operate under the command of U.S. naval forces. This placed the Brazilian Navy under the command of Rear Adm. Jonas H. Ingram, Commander, South Atlantic Force. With the war moving into high gear, Capt. Robert Trexel, USN, was directed to make a two-week tour of Brazil and recommend to the Secretary of the Navy where air facilities should be established. The result was the utilization of a half dozen or more sites well located for ASW and surface raider patrols along the Brazilian coast.

Amapa, U.S. Naval Air Base, 1943-1945

The most northerly air base was at Amapa, located near the Amapa Grande River, about 140 miles inland from the border of French Guiana, on flat prairie land. There the U.S. Army had built an airfield, begun in 1941 and completed in the spring of 1942. The field was turned over to the Navy on 22 June 1943, with six months of construction work to follow at a cost of $632,000, for a total cost of $2 million. Two runways, each extended to 5,000 feet in length, originally served three land patrol bombers in providing convoy protection, ASW patrol, and an emergency landing site in the vast jungle north of the Amazon River. An expanded mission was to base two blimps, which were considered better search vehicles than land patrol bombers for coastal patrol, and another half squadron of land patrol planes, with the planes of VP-83 covering convoys between Trinidad and Bahia. For the blimps, two mooring circles were built. There was an Assembly and Repair Class D facility for both HTA and LTA as well as storage for 40,000 gallons of gasoline. Amapa was principally operated by the Army engineers but served as an NATS stop and was also used by the U.S. Army Air Forces. Quarters and messing facilities were also provided. With personnel down to 27 officers and 126 men on 1 November 1944, preparations were made to return the base to the Brazilian government at the end of the war. It was decommissioned on 30 June 1945.

Camocim, U.S. Naval Seaplane Base, 1941

Construction by the United States of a naval seaplane base at Camocim, an isolated spot 400 miles north of Natal, began in October 1941. But the Navy soon found that other sites closer to the mouth of the Amazon on the one hand and nearer to the bight of the hump of Brazil on the other were more suitable. In consequence the base was never completed.

Caravellas, U.S. Naval Air Facility, 1943-1945

Caravellas is a modest-sized port some 300 miles down the coast about half way between Bahia and Rio de Janeiro. Before the war began, Air France had operated a field there. In late 1943 the United States took the establishment over and added facilities for two blimps that would engage in convoy protection and ASW patrol. A landplane base was then added for six patrol planes that operated from a 5,000-foot runway. Lack of good paving material and very wet weather delayed the completion of the base. However, it had Navy housing for eighteen officers and sixty men, fuel storage, and a single mast blimp refueling base operated by ten officers and forty men. Even when the landplane field became operational, on 1 August 1944, it was used only for the emergency landing of patrol planes. Yet it had value, for the Naval Air Transport Service used the field almost daily for fuel topping off and for freight and passenger offloadings. The total cost of construction at Caravellas was slightly more than $2 million. It was decommissioned soon after the end of the war in Europe, on 1 August 1945.

Belem, U.S. Naval Air Facility, 1943-1945

Another facility was established at Belem, located on the south bank of the Amazon River near its wide junction with the Atlantic. Because of its key location it was the first of the five seaplane bases the United States built in Brazil to obtain new air facilities. Runways were already in place because Pan American and Brazilian Airlines and Air Force had facilities there, and the U.S. Navy on 18 March began flying some amphibian aircraft from the original Army field, named Val de Caens. The U.S. Army Engineers did some of the early construction, then turned the work over to the Navy on 23 September 1943. A seaplane base for six patrol craft was added, and a hangar, barracks, and fuel storage tanks were soon built. Now the seaplane tenders *Humboldt* and *Thrush*, which had supported the seaplanes, departed. An expanded mission increased to twenty-four the patrol bombers at Belem. It was commissioned on 26 November 1943, when construction costs amounting to $837,000 had provided an Assembly and Repair facility Class D; two 6,000-by-250-foot asphalt Army runways that were connected by taxiways to the seaplane ramps on the Para River; a portable hangar; a shop; radio and radio D/F stations; an NATS unit; and personnel facilities for 40 officers and 160 men, the number increasing to 72 officers and 186 men by 1 November 1944. The landplanes and patrol seaplanes were operated by an additional 81 officers and 422 men. Between early April and 1 December 1943 a Tactical Center was built, but recommendations for adding blimps and their supporting facilities were vetoed by Washington, which pointed out that LTA craft operated out of Igarape Assu.

Belem was used not only by the U.S. Army and U.S. Navy, but by Pan Am, the Brazilian Air Force, and Panair do Brazil, with the U.S. Navy accounting for only 14 percent of its use. The facility was decommissioned on 15 June 1945.

Fortaleza, U.S. Naval Air Facility, 1943-1945

The first use of blimps in Brazil came at the air base at Fortaleza, a port city 300 miles northwest of the easternmost tip of Brazil. In April 1943 construction began on facilities to accommodate a unit of two blimps and a half squadron, or six patrol bombers, that made use of a paved 5,000-foot runway. Living quarters, fuel storage, a radio station, an LTA mast base, and a helium storage building were eventually added at what was called Pici Field. The U.S. Army and the Brazilian Air Force also used the facility, and an NATS unit operated from the nearby Adjacento Field. In 1943 four-engine bombers were ferried via Fortaleza to North Africa. The air facilities at Fortaleza were heavily used until late 1944. Decommissioning came six months later, in June 1945.

Galeao, U.S. Naval Air Facility, 1943-1945

While most of the U.S. naval air bases were at some distance from major cities in Brazil, such was not the case with Galeao. Located near Rio de Janeiro, it operated only seaplanes and took on increased importance as the U-boats were pushed southward in 1943. It was not closed until 1945.

Igarape Assu, U.S. Naval Air Facility, 1943-1945

Construction work at Igarape Assu was begun by the U.S. Army on 2 August 1943 at a site along the banks of the Amazon River near the major river port of Belem. Since Belem already had a U.S. naval patrol plane facility, Igarape was developed solely as a blimp base, with buildings added for quarters, storage, shop space, maintenance, and fuel storage. Building costs to 30 October 1943 approximated $414,000, and the facility was declared to be in full operating status on 23 December 1943. The blimps that flew from two mooring circles and a take-off mat engaged in convoy protection and ASW patrol in the Southwest Atlantic. The closest place to Belem where an LTA station could be established—it was only seventy-five miles away—Igarape Assu was fully utilized at the height of the war, yet it was closed earlier than most other U.S. naval installations, with the Navy departing in April 1945.

Maceio, U.S. Naval Air Facility, 1943-1945

The naval air facility at Maceio, 200 miles south of the major port of Recife, was established to fill in the patrol gap along Brazil's hump that extended above Bahia. Plans in mid-1941 called for establishing facilities for six patrol bombers, but these were scrapped for about two years, when a new plan called for supporting installations for two blimps and six landbased patrol bombers. It was ready for operations on 18 March 1943 and was commissioned on 14 December 1943, with costs at that time amounting to $720,000 for the LTA facilities and $310,000 for the seaplane facilities. Available were a 4,500-by-150-foot asphalt runway at Army Field, two mooring circles for the blimps, an Assembly and Repair Class D facility, and personnel facilities for the 56 officers and 230 men who operated the planes and blimps. Maceio was one of five seaplane bases the United States built in Brazil. Although original plans did not call for it to be in active commission, on 3 April it was deemed necessary to triple the requirement for the facilities there, in large part because it was to become a two-mast blimp base. The seaplanes used Lagoa de Norte (North Lake), which was three by five miles in extent; facilities were built there costing $600,000. The base remained in full operation until it was transferred to Brazil in November 1945 under a Lend-Lease agreement.

Florianopolis, U.S. Naval Operating Facility, 1943-1945

Florianopolis was not only a U.S. Naval Operating Facility but served the Brazilian Air Force as well. It was a minor installation, as were the America-built facilities discussed below under "Minor U.S. Naval Facilities in Brazil, 1943-1945."

Minor U.S. Naval Facilities in Brazil, 1943-1945

A number of U.S. naval air facilities and naval bases were built along the hump of Brazil; in addition a naval air facility was constructed on the island of Fernando de Naronha. The first facilities were built by the U.S. Army through a cooperative contract with the Pan American Airport Development Corporation. Later ones were built by lump sum or cost-plus-fixed-fee contracts issued by the Navy's Bureau of Yards and Docks. They served in the antisubmarine campaign in the South Atlantic and provided stepping stones on the air route from the United States to Africa. They are listed from north to south with the major utilities they contained.

Fernando de Noronha is a rocky, volcanic island located 210 miles off the eastern hump of Brazil. Construction of an Army base began in 1943 included two runways, one 6,000-by-150 feet, the other 2,950-by-130. When it became apparent that the Army could make only limited use of the facility, it was transferred to the U.S. Navy, which added a blimp take-off mat and mooring circle and operated a Naval Air Transport Service unit. As the tactical situation required, patrol bombers and LTA craft were based there, and the Army Transport Command occasionally used it for refueling on flights from the United States to Africa. It was decommissioned in June 1945.

Ipitanga. As in the case of Fernando de Noronha, the facilities at Ipitanga were originally built to serve landplanes of the U.S. Army. Construction which began in January 1942 included a paved runway 1,968-by 131 feet. When it became apparent that the Army could make little use of Ipitanga, it was transferred to the U.S. Navy, which used it for half a patrol squadron and two blimps. In addition by 1944 the Navy erected housing, storage, and administration buildings, two 5,000-foot paved runways, a parking area, two prefabricated nose hangars, and a blimp take-off mat with two mooring circles. The base was disestablished in July 1945.

Santa Cruz. At this location the U.S. Navy assisted the Brazilian government to speed the construction of a 5,000-by-168-foot runway, taxiways, and parking areas to serve six patrol bombers and also a Naval Air Transport Service unit, and also built LTA facilities, a radio station, and repair shops. The base, shared with the Brazilian Air Force, was decommissioned in September 1945 and then under Lend Lease arrangements transferred to Brazilian control.

Victoria. At Victoria Airport, seven miles north of the city of Victoria, the Brazilian government had built a 5,000-by-168 foot runway, small hangar, and radio station. In April 1944 the U.S. Navy added a take-off area and mooring circles for LTA. All U.S. Navy had left the site by Oct. 1945.

Rio de Janeiro was shared by the U.S. Navy with the Brazilian government. There the United States had a naval attaché, an administrative operating base, a port director, an air facility (at Galeao), and a small radio station. Available to the U.S. Navy were a fairly large Brazilian dry dock and adequate repair facilities. A major port, Rio de Janeiro was used for convoy assembly, and substantial use was made of it by Brazilian landplanes and seaplanes. All U.S. Navy forces had left the site by November 1945.

BIBLIOGRAPHY

A. "Records of the U.S. Tenth Fleet, Convoy and Routing Files for 1942, Box 2, Convoy AS-4" (Washington: Naval Historical Center, Operational Archives Branch); "Shore Establishment/Advanced Bases," Directory, December 1944 (Washington: Naval Center, Operational Archives Branch); U.S. Navy, Bureau of Yards and Docks, *Building the Navy's Bases in World War II*, 2 vols. (Washington: GPO, 1947); "Administrative History of the Caribbean Sea Frontier till VE-Day," and "Commander in Chief, U.S. Atlantic Fleet," and "Commander South Atlantic Force, Brazil," in "Naval Administration in World War II" (Washington: Naval Historical Center, Operational Archives Branch).

B. Waldo G. Bowman and others, *Bulldozers Came First* (New York: McGraw-Hill, 1944); Samuel E. Morison, *The Atlantic Battle Won, May 1943-May 1945* (Boston: Little, Brown, 1956); Douglass R. Burnett, "Mission Improbable," U.S. Naval Institute *Proceedings* 107 (Jan. 1981):52-57.

WILLIAM L. CALDERHEAD

BREMERHAVEN, GERMANY, U.S. NAVAL ADVANCE BASE, 1945– Germany surrendered unconditionally on 7 May 1945. On 1 June, Drew 4 and Drew 6 (Drews were units ready to establish overseas harbor facilities) were decommissioned and then recommissioned as Naval Advanced Base Bremerhaven and NAB Bremen, respectively. The activity at Bremerhaven consisted of an advance base, a salvage group, a Construction Battalion Unit, and a fifty-bed dispensary. On 1 July 1945 the following change in the organization of U.S. Forces Europe became effective: Commander Naval Forces Germany assumed operational command of all U.S. naval forces in the European Theater of Operations (ETO), and reported and became responsible to the Supreme Commander Allied Expeditionary Force; and on 11 November NAB Bremerhaven and NAB Bremen were redesignated as NAB Weser River, TF 124.2. Naval personnel on board approximated 256 officers and 1,495 men, and headquarters was moved to Bremerhaven. On 1 November 1946 the USN Port Director, Bremerhaven, was disestablished and port control was transferred to the Office of the Military Government (OMG).

As of 1 January 1948, the mission of the naval forces command, through the OMG for Germany, was to care for former enemy naval vessels until they were disposed of; to dispose of certain former German merchant vessels assigned to the United States; to dispose of enemy captured war materials; to support and assist U.S. shipping; and to furnish logistic support to Commander Naval Forces Germany (COMNAVFORGER), Commander in Chief, Naval Forces Eastern Atlantic and Mediterranean (CINCNELM) in London and, as required, to fleet units visiting the Enclave (foreign unit on German soil) and European waters. In 1950 Headquarters COMNAVFORGER was moved to Heidelberg. On 11 November of that year the Chief of Naval Operations directed the disestablishment of NAB Bremerhaven and the establishment of Naval Activities Bremen Enclave, effective 1 July 1951, with military control vested in COMNAVFORGER and management control under the CNO. A new mission issued at this time directed that the activity be prepared, organized, trained, and equipped for combat operations incident to the establishment and conduct of port operations in any port on the continent of Europe. In addition it would train officers and men to perform military demolition, radiological safety, and artificer duties. Last, it would provide logistic support to other naval activities in Europe. Among the last were the staff of COMNAVFORGER in Heidelberg; a Naval Technical Unit in Berlin; CINCNELM in London; fleet units visiting the Enclave about Germany and European waters; and Communications Unit 8, which would serve U.S. naval activities in Germany, naval forces in the Eastern Atlantic, and the MSTS at Bremerhaven. Authorized personnel complement was 20 officers, 199 men, and 186 German civilians, the last paid for out of the costs of occupation.

On 24 March 1950 there was also established a Rhine River Patrol Unit. A separate command with its own commanding officer, the 12 officers, 193 men, and 57 German civilians would conduct training in boat handling, river navigation, and demolition, and patrol between Bergen and Karlsruhe.

As of March 1952 the Bremerhaven Enclave had on board the U.S. Naval Advance Base; Communication Unit 8 and Communication Unit 32 (half team); Minesweeping Readiness Unit; Weser River Patrol and Security Unit; Ship Maintenance and Repair Facility; Special Projects (the USS *Northwind* and USS *Westwind*); and a combined MSTS/NCSO.

BIBLIOGRAPHY

A. "Monograph Histories of U.S. Naval Overseas Bases. Vol. I. Atlantic Area, 22 December 1953" (Washington: Naval Historical Center, Operational Archives Branch).

BREST, FRANCE.

See World War I U.S. Naval Air Stations in Europe; World War I U.S. Naval Bases in Europe.

BRISBANE, AUSTRALIA, U.S. ADVANCE SUBMARINE BASE, NAVAL AIR STATION, NAVAL OPERATING BASE, 1942-1946 The capital of Queensland in northeastern Australia, Brisbane is a large port city (27°29′S., 153°8′E.) located on the Brisbane River about fourteen miles in from the coast. In 1942 it was placed within the Southwest Pacific Area. During World War II it became the largest U.S. Navy base in Australia. It was the best base from which to support operations in the New Guinea-Coral Sea area.

The first U.S. naval activity at Brisbane was the creation of an advance submarine base. On 15 April 1942 the submarine tender *Griffin* and six old S-boats from Submarine Division 53 arrived at Brisbane after a long trans-Pacific voyage from Panama. At New Farm Wharf on the Brisbane River, they set up an operating base and within a few days conducted their first war patrols into the Coral Sea. Joined shortly thereafter by five S-boats from Fremantle-Perth (q.v.) in southwestern Australia, the Brisbane-based boats formed the Eastern Australia Submarine Group (Task Force 42) under the Commander, Southwest Pacific Force (in March 1943 redesignated Seventh Fleet).

Especially after July 1942, with the transfer of headquarters, Southwest Pacific Force to Brisbane, naval facilities there were developed to support increased fleet operations. Base personnel, with the help of Australian labor, built a naval supply depot as well as a seaplane base on the Brisbane River, the nucleus of Naval Air Station Brisbane. Plans envisioned using Brisbane as an expanded submarine base, an amphibious base (supply, assembly, and repair of landing craft), an advance supply depot, and a ship repair unit (which had already begun, as at Hamilton, with three ferries rigged as floating workshops). Located at the terminus of the long supply route from the United States (and with the highly active South Pacific Area in between), Brisbane's development was slow in the fall and winter of 1942.

On 15 January 1943 headquarters of the Amphibious Force, Southwest Pacific Area (Rear Adm. Daniel E. Barbey) was organized at Brisbane, and two days later the naval base was formally commissioned. Early in 1943 naval construction troops arrived to expedite completion of a number of vital projects. That spring they set up an advance base construction depot and associated "Camp Seabee," which became the primary staging point for naval construction battalions in the Southwest Pacific Area. To service the fleet, they erected a mine depot and a naval ammunition depot as well as greatly expanding the facilities of the ship repair unit. Port facilities for Liberty ships were increased so that Brisbane wharfs were able to unload up to 40,000 tons a day. NAS Brisbane was expanded until it encompassed two airfields as well as the seaplane base. In May 1943 Rear Admiral Barbey's redesignated Seventh Amphibious Force took over a landing craft depot at Toorbul Bay at the mouth of the Brisbane River and turned it into an amphibious training command center.

Thus by the summer 1943 Brisbane was fast becoming the chief supply point for the Seventh Fleet's assault on eastern New Guinea. Materiel from the United States was unloaded there and transshipped to forward bases. The vast numbers of small landing craft required by the Seventh Amphibious Force assembled there, where crews were trained and the vessels were repaired before heading north into combat. Brisbane's submarines (redesignated Task Force 72 after the creation of the Seventh Fleet) continued to be very active in 1943, with war patrols against Japanese shipping in the Upper Solomons, Rabaul, and points north.

In December 1943 advance headquarters of the Seventh Amphibious Force advanced to Milne Bay (q.v.) in eastern New Guinea, and thereafter some roll-up of installations occurred at Brisbane as bases such as Milne Bay became more important. In January 1944 the mine assembly depot was dismantled and sent forward, and in May Brisbane's submarines were reduced in number in favor of bases at Manus (q.v.) in the Admiralty Islands and at Fremantle. Concentrations of enemy shipping had simply moved too far north for Brisbane to remain an effective base. Roll-up at Brisbane increased greatly in the summer of 1944 after organization of the naval base at Hollandia, Dutch New Guinea (q.v.). With headquarters of the Seventh Fleet moved to Lake Sentani at Hollandia in July, so much traffic was diverted north from Brisbane that in January 1945 the last supply representative for the Seventh Amphibious Force left for Hollandia. In February and March 1945 the submarine base at Brisbane was closed as the submarine tender *Fulton* and the few remaining submarines advanced to Subic Bay, Luzon (q.v.). Facilities at Brisbane remained open until 14 January 1946, when the base was disestablished.

BIBLIOGRAPHY

A. U.S. Navy, "7th Amphibious Force Command History 10 January 1943-23 December 1945" (Washington: Naval Historical Center, Operational Archives Branch); U.S. Navy, Bureau of Yards and Docks, *Building the Navy's Bases in World War II*, 2 vols. (Washington: GPO, 1947); U.S. Navy, "U.S. Naval Bases in the South and Southwest Pacific (and Central Pacific Forward) in World War II," 1 November 1954 (Washington: Naval Historical Center, Operational Archives Branch).

B. Theodore Roscoe, *United States Submarine Operations in World War II* (Annapolis, Md.: U.S. Naval Institute, 1949); Rear Adm. Worrall Reed Carter, *Beans, Bullets, and Black Oil* (Washington: GPO, 1953); Vice Adm. Daniel E. Barbey, *MacArthur's Amphibious Navy* (Annapolis, Md.: U.S. Naval Institute, 1969); Clay Blair, *Silent Victory: The United States Submarine War against Japan*, 2 vols. (Philadelphia: Lippincott, 1973).

JOHN B. LUNDSTROM

BRUNEI BAY, BRITISH NORTH BORNEO, U.S. NAVAL ADVANCE BASE, 1945–1946 On 10 June 1945 Australian Army forces transported by the Seventh Amphibious Force (Seventh Fleet, Southwest Pacific Area) invaded Brunei Bay (5°N., 115°E.), British North Borneo, on the large island's northwest coast. Supporting the operation were Motor Torpedo Boat Squadrons 13 and 16 with the tender *Willoughby*. PTs operating from Brunei Bay patrolled the western coast of Borneo and, after VJ-Day, assisted with the evacuation of Allied prisoners of war and refugees. The Seventh Fleet at Brunei Bay operated a port director's office until 27 January 1946.

BIBLIOGRAPHY

A. U.S. Navy, "7th Amphibious Force Command History, 10 January 1943-23 December 1945" (Washington: Naval Historical Center, Operational Archives Branch); "7th Fleet Administrative History, Motor Torpedo Boats" (Washington: Naval Historical Center, Operational Archives Branch).

B. Samuel E. Morison, *Liberation of the Philippines October 1944-August 1945* (Boston: Houghton Mifflin, 1959); Capt. Robert J. Bulkley, *At Close Quarters: PT Boats in the United States Navy* (Washington: Navy Department, Naval History Division, 1962); Vice Adm. Daniel E. Barbey, *MacArthur's Amphibious Navy* (Annapolis, Md.: U.S. Naval Institute, 1969).

JOHN B. LUNDSTROM

BUNA, NEW GUINEA, U.S. NAVAL ADVANCE BASE, 1943–1944 The site of extremely savage fighting in the first stage of the reconquest of New Guinea, Buna (8°40′S., 148°23′E.) is located on the north coast of the Territory of Papua in eastern New Guinea. In January 1943, after the fighting there ended, forces of the Southwest Pacific Area organized Buna as a troop staging and supply point. It became an important base for U.S. and Australian Army troops and consequently an amphibious center. The Seventh Amphibious Force used it as a staging point for the invasions of Lae (September 1943), Finchhafen (September 1943), Cape Gloucester, New Britain (December 1943), and the Admiralty Islands (February 1944). From August to November 1943 Buna was also the site of a temporary motor torpedo boat support base. The PT tender *Hilo*, joined in October by the new repair ship *Portunus,* conducted PT overhaul and repairs. In November they advanced to Morobe, (q.v.), further up the New Guinea coast. The Seventh Fleet continued using the troop facilities at Buna until July 1944.

BIBLIOGRAPHY

A. U.S. Navy, "7th Amphibious Force Command History, 10 January 1943-23 December 1945" (Washington: Naval Historical Center, Operational Archives Branch); U.S. Navy, "U.S. Naval Bases in the South and Southwest Pacific (and Central Pacific Forward) in World War II," 1 November 1954 (Washington: Naval Historical Center, Operational Archives Branch).

B. Capt. Robert J. Bulkley, *At Close Quarters; PT Boats in the United States Navy* (Washington: Navy Department Naval History Division, 1962; Vice Adm. Daniel E. Barbey, *MacArthur's Amphibious Navy* (Annapolis, Md.: U.S. Naval Institute, 1969).

JOHN B. LUNDSTROM

C

CAIRNS, AUSTRALIA, U.S. NAVAL ADVANCE BASE, 1942–1945 Cairns, Queensland (17°0′S., 145°47′E.), is a small port on Trinity Bay in extreme northeastern Australia. In December 1942, personnel from Motor Torpedo Boat Base 4 arrived there to establish a support base for Southwest Pacific Force PTs beginning to operate in eastern New Guinea. Cairns served as their main engine overhaul base. Conditions were primitive, as Cairns lies on a flat, swampy coastal plain.

In the late spring of 1943, Seventh Fleet decided to use Cairns as a minor logistical support and repair base for escort vessels and landing craft. June 1943 saw the establishment there of a Seventh Amphibious Force training center. In early October elements of the Fifty-fifth Naval Construction Battalion arrived from Brisbane (q.v.) to work on base facilities, while on 18 October MTB Base 4 left for Kana Kopa at Milne Bay, New Guinea (q.v.). Cairns itself was established formally as a naval base on 20 November 1943. Seabees by 1 January 1944 had completed Escort Base One, set up as a destroyer and small-craft repair, mine maintenance, and naval supply base. In 1944 this was further expanded with floating dry docks (ARD-7, AFD-10) for destroyer work, making the facility equivalent to one fully equipped destroyer tender. Other base installations included water storage tanks and a naval ammunition depot.

Cairns was utilized extensively by escort vessels and landing craft operating between northern Australia and New Guinea. It also served as an important hospital and medical supply complex. Roll-up and transfer of facilities to forward areas began in late 1944 and was largely completed by January 1945. The Cairns base was disestablished on 21 March 1945.

BIBLIOGRAPHY

A. U.S. Navy, "7th Amphibious Force Command History, 10 January 1943-23 December 1945" (Washington: Naval Historical Center, Operational Archives Branch); U.S. Navy, Bureau of Yards and Docks, *Building the Navy's Bases in World War II*, 2 vols. (Washington: GPO, 1947); U.S. Navy, "U.S. Naval Bases in the South and Southwest Pacific (and Central Pacific Forward) in World War II," 1 November 1954 (Washington:

Naval Historical Center, Operational Archives Branch); ''7th Fleet Administrative History: Motor Torpedo Boats'' (Washington: Naval Historical Center, Operational Archives Branch).

B. Capt. Robert J. Bulkley, *At Close Quarters: PT Boats in the United States Navy* (Washington: Navy Department Naval History Division, 1962).

JOHN B. LUNDSTROM

CALAIS (OYE), FRANCE.
See World War I U.S. Northern Bombing Group Bases in England and France.

CALLAO, PERU.
See Hispanic South America, U.S. Naval Bases.

CAMOCIM, BRAZIL, U.S. NAVAL SEAPLANE BASE.
See Brazil, U.S. Naval Bases.

CAMPAGNE, FRANCE.
See World War I U.S. Northern Bombing Group Bases in England and France.

CAMP GARCIA, VIEQUES ISLAND, PUERTO RICO.
See Vieques Island, Puerto Rico, U.S. Marine Corps Camp Garcia.

CAMP SMEDLEY D. BUTLER.
See Okinawa, Japan, U.S. Marine Corps Camp Smedley D. Butler.

CAM RANH BAY, REPUBLIC of VIETNAM, U.S. NAVAL BASE, 1965–1972 The naval base at Cam Ranh Bay, in the Republic of Vietnam, served as the nerve center of the Navy's Market Time anti-infiltration operation during the Southeast Asian Conflict. With one of the largest natural harbors in the Far East and centrally placed on the 1,500-mile coast of South Vietnam, Cam Ranh Bay was long seen as a strategic site. Russian Admiral Rozhdestvenski's fleet anchored there in 1905 before steaming on to its fateful meeting with the Japanese fleet in the Strait of Tsushima. The Japanese had used it during World War II until 1944, when U.S. Naval Task Force 38 blasted it.

Almost sixty years later American naval leaders evaluated the bay as a possible fleet anchorage and seaplane base from which to support the foundering South Vietnamese nation. During 1964 Seventh Fleet reconnaissance aircraft, seaplane tender *Currituck* (AV-7), and Mine Flotilla 1 units carried out hydrographic and beach surveys and explored sites for facilities ashore.

This preparatory work proved fortuitous when a North Vietnamese trawler was discovered landing munitions and supplies at nearby Vung Ro Bay in February 1965; the incident led U.S. naval leaders to develop Cam Ranh as a major base to support the Coastal Surveillance Force. During the following years, the

Navy deployed there fast patrol craft (PCF), Coast Guard cutter (WPB), destroyer escort (DER), and patrol gunboat (PG) units. The site became the center of coastal air patrol operations with the establishment in April 1967 of the U.S. Naval Air Facility, Cam Ranh Bay, and the basing there of P-2 *Neptune* and P-3 *Orion* patrol aircraft. That summer, Commander Coastal Surveillance Force and his staff moved their headquarters from Saigon (q.v.) to Cam Ranh Bay and set up an operational command post to control the Market Time effort. Country-wide coordination also was enhanced with the establishment of the Naval Communications Station.

In the beginning, shore facilities at Cam Ranh Bay were extremely limited, requiring interim measures to support assigned naval forces. Army depots provided common supplies, while Seventh Fleet light cargo ships *Mark* (AKL-12) and *Brule* (AKL-28) delivered Navy-peculiar items from Subic Bay (q.v.) in the Philippines. Until mid-1966, when shore installations were prepared to take over the tasks, messing and quartering of personnel were handled by APL-55, anchored in the harbor. Also, a pontoon dock was installed to permit the repair of the coastal patrol vessels. Gradually, the Naval Support Activity, Saigon, Detachment Cam Ranh Bay, improved the provision of maintenance and repair, supply, finance, communications, transportation, postal service, recreation, and security support.

With the concentration at Cam Ranh Bay of Market Time headquarters and forces during the summer of 1967, the demand for base support became extraordinary. Accordingly, the Naval Support Activity, Saigon, Detachment Cam Ranh Bay, was redesignated the Naval Support Facility, Cam Ranh Bay, a more autonomous and self-sufficient status. A greater allocation of resources and support forces to the shore installation resulted in an improved ability to cope with the buildup of combat units. In time, the Cam Ranh Bay facility accomplished major vessel repair and dispensed a great variety of supply items to the anti-infiltration task force. In addition, the naval contingent at the Joint Service Ammunition Depot issued ammunition to the coastal surveillance, river patrol, and mobile riverine forces as well as to the Seventh Fleet's gunfire support destroyers and landing ships. Seabee Maintenance Unit 302 provided public works assistance to the many dispersed Naval Support Activity, Saigon, detachments.

As a vital logistic complex, Cam Ranh Bay continued to function long after the Navy's combat forces withdrew from South Vietnam as part of the Vietnamization of the war. However, between January and April 1972 the Naval Air Facility, the Naval Support Facility, and the Naval Communications Station turned over their installations to the Vietnamese Navy and were duly disestablished. The headquarters and naval operations center of Commander Coastal Surveillance Force redeployed to Saigon, thus ending the Navy's seven-year operation at Cam Ranh Bay.

BIBLIOGRAPHY
A. Commander Naval Forces, Vietnam, "The Naval War in Vietnam," May 1970 (Washington: Naval Historical Center, Operational Archives Branch), and Commander Naval Forces, Vietnam, "Monthly Historical Reports, 1965-1971" (Washington: Naval Historical Center, Operational Archives Branch).

B. Herbert T. King, "Naval Logistic Support, Qui Nhon to Phu Quoc," U.S. Naval Institute *Naval Review* 95 (May 1969):84-111; Frank C. Collins, Jr., "Maritime Support of the Campaign in I Corps," U.S. Naval Institute *Naval Review* 97 (May 1971):156-79; Richard L. Schreadley, "The Naval War in Vietnam, 1950-1970," U.S. Naval Institute *Naval Review* 97 (May 1971):180-211; Edwin B. Hooper, *Mobility, Support, Endurance: A Story of Naval Operational Logistics in the Vietnam War, 1965-1968* (Washington: GPO, 1972).

EDWARD J. MAROLDA

CANACAO, OR BILIBID PRISON, MANILA, PHILIPPINE ISLANDS, U.S. NAVAL HOSPITAL Through the foresight of Robert W. Kentner, PhM1C, USN, a record remains of how Americans captured at Canacao Naval Hospital were treated during the Japanese occupation. On 8 December 1941 there were at the hospital 19 officers, 5 pharmacists, 12 nurses, about 75 hospital corpsmen, and 255 patients. The personnel planned to evacuate to the Sternberg General Hospital, Manila, taking along the supplies in the Medical Supply Depot, Canacao. On the ninth, 147 patients were transferred to Sternberg, with others going elsewhere, and Canacao was now ready, under Capt. R. G. Davis, MC, USN, to treat war casualties. Two days later they had 500 patients as a result of the Japanese aerial bombing of the navy yard at Cavite (q.v.), which destroyed the dispensary there. With the survivors from Cavite on board, a field hospital was established at Canacao in the Sangley Point (q.v.) area. From there patients were moved to new quarters in Philippine Union College, Balintawak. Counting casualties from an air raid on Sangley Point, by 21 December there were 126 patients on board, with the census increasing to 163 on the thirty-first.

On 1 January 1942 Captain Davis restricted all personnel to another site, Santa Scholasta's College, Manila, a former U.S. Army Hospital Annex, to await the occupation of Manila by the Japanese Expeditionary Forces. These arrived on the second, conferred with Captain Davis, and acquired a muster list of the personnel on board. Immediately the daily ration was cut to two meals a day, with coffee to be served only in the morning. All radios and automobiles were sequestered, and Japanese sentries guarded the grounds. After taking all the quinine, the Japanese also removed 160 iron beds and their mattresses, pillows, and linen, and moved some patients and staff to a prison camp. By 11 March the Japanese had taken all X-ray machines and other supplies while transferring still other Americans to a prison camp at Pasay. Finally, on 27 May, they took over the entire hospital; by 29 January 1945 those who survived were allowed a mere 840 calories a day.

On 25 January 1945 all at the hospital could hear bombs falling in the Manila area throughout the day. More bombers came on the twenty-sixth, and on the twenty-eighth P-38s were over Manila and B-24s were sighted over Manila Bay. One can only imagine the feeling of Kentner as he noted that day, "Many U.S. planes sighted over Manila today." But he also noted that there were many deaths attributable to malnutrition. On 31 January Kentner recorded, "Two USN Grumman fighters over camp at 1930 today, flying at high speed and very low altitude. A grand sight." On that day there were 101 patients on board with dysentery and 236 with vitamin deficiency. By 2 February Army bombers were over Manila, and on the third Kentner heard machine gun fire and tanks. On the fourth, the Japanese said they were leaving immediately. They released all POWs and left at 1245 hours. At 1900 hours "Yanks" broke through the north-south wall of Bilibid Prison, and its inmates could see Manila ablaze. "This day will be the most unforgettable day of all our lives," wrote Kentner, adding on the fifth, "This morning the American troops moved into Bilibid. LIBERATED. Japs being brought in as prisoners."

BIBLIOGRAPHY

A. "Kentner's Journal. Bilibid Prison, Manila, PI, From 12-8-41 to 2-5-45. A Daily Journal of Events Connected with the Personnel of the U.S. Naval Hospital, Canacao, PI" (Washington: Naval Historical Center, Operational Archives Branch).

CANADA.
See World War I U.S. Naval Air Stations in Canada.

CAN THO-BINH THUY, REPUBLIC OF VIETNAM, U.S. NAVAL SUPPORT ACTIVITY, 1966–1972 Can Tho, situated in the center of South Vietnam's economically and militarily vital Mekong Delta, was the hub of U.S. naval operations in that region. The site was chosen because its location on the Bassac River made Can Tho ideal as a base from which naval forces could operate against Viet Cong supply traffic on surrounding waterways. Another attractive feature was the city's accessibility to logistic vessels deployed in the South China Sea. In addition, an existing Vietnamese Navy installation could partially accommodate the first increment of the U.S. River Patrol Force scheduled to deploy there. And in Can Tho, the largest city west of Saigon, were concentrated the headquarters of key Vietnamese naval and military commands.

As a result, in May 1966 a ten-boat section of River Division 51 deployed to Can Tho to inaugurate the Game Warden river interdiction operation in that area. Although the Vietnamese River Assault Group base possessed a marine railway and a number of storage buildings, at first logistic support for the Americans was austere. Quartering was a special problem, necessitating the acquisition of facilities in the city. However, when the Naval Support Activity, Saigon, Detachment Can Tho, was established that August, conditions soon improved. Seabees installed portable fuel storage bladders and connected a number of pontoons to form a small pier for the river patrol boat (PBR) unit. In October, YRBM-9, a repair, berthing, and messing barge, arrived at Can Tho, easing support problems enough to allow the deployment from Saigon (q.v.) of Commander River Patrol Force and his staff.

At the same time, the naval support activity detachment oversaw the development of a major base complex at nearby Binh Thuy, and by mid-summer 1967 this facility was prepared to receive tenants.

In July 1967 the headquarters of the River Patrol Force was moved to Binh Thuy, and shortly afterward the Naval Support Activity, Saigon, Detachment Can Tho, was redesignated Detachment Binh Thuy. Another headquarters took shape in the area when the Deputy Commander Naval Forces, Vietnam, was charged in late 1968 with implementing the Sea Lords strategy, which sought to interdict the infiltration of communist troops and supplies from Cambodia.

To enhance support from Binh Thuy of naval combat units throughout the delta, a great effort was made during 1968 to improve the airstrip at Can Tho and to complete a 1,500-foot airstrip, hangars, aircraft repair shops, and berthing and messing facilities at Binh Thuy. As a result, in 1969 major components of Helicopter Attack (Light) Squadron 3, the "Seawolves," and Light Attack Squadron 4, the "Black Ponies," the Navy's only combat air support units based in South Vietnam, were established there.

Even as the Sea Lords operations got under way, steps were taken, under the Vietnamization program, to diminish the Navy's role in the delta and to enhance that of the Vietnamese Navy. Between 1969 and 1972 American naval personnel trained their Vietnamese counterparts, turned over to them river craft, equipment, and installations, and conducted the U.S. withdrawal. The turnover of the Binh Thuy Logistic Support Base and the disestablishment of the naval air squadrons and the Naval Support Activity, Saigon, Detachment Binh Thuy, in April 1972, concluded the major U.S. naval presence in the Can Tho-Binh Thuy area.

BIBLIOGRAPHY

A. Commander Naval Forces, Vietnam, "The Naval War in Vietnam," May 1970 (Washington: Naval Historical Center, Operational Archives Branch); Commander Naval Forces, Vietnam, "Monthly Historical Reports, 1965-1971" (Washington: Naval Historical Center, Operational Archives Branch); Service Force, U.S. Pacific Fleet, "Command Histories, 1967-1972" (Washington: Naval Historical Center, Operational Archives Branch).

B. Herbert T. King, "Naval Logistic Support, Qui Nhon to Phu Quoc," U.S. Naval Institute *Naval Review* 95 (May 1969):84-111; S.A. Swarztrauber, "River Patrol Relearned," U.S. Naval Institute *Naval Review* 96 (May 1970):120-57; Richard L. Schreadley, "The Naval War in Vietnam, 1950-1970," U.S. Naval Institute *Naval Review* 97 (May 1971):180-211; Edwin B. Hooper, *Mobility, Support, Endurance: A Story of Naval Operational Logistics in the Vietnam War, 1965-1968* (Washington: GPO, 1972).

EDWARD J. MAROLDA

CANTON ISLAND, U.S. NAVAL AIR FACILITY, 1941–1946 Canton Island is a coral atoll in the Phoenix Group about 800 miles south of Palymra and 1,600 miles southwest of Hawaii on the air route between Hawaii and the

Southwest Pacific commonwealths of Australia and New Zealand. In the mid-1930s, when the United States was searching for unclaimed Pacific islands to serve as fueling stations for the Navy's patrol planes and commercial aircraft, the American and British governments both claimed Canton and neighboring Enderbury Island. President Franklin D. Roosevelt held, however, that the British claim was invalid because the islands had not yet been settled. After the Hepburn Board on the needs of the shore establishment recommended in December 1938 that the lagoon be dredged for use by naval patrol planes and tenders, Britain formally asserted its interest in Canton, and the two nations finally agreed in April 1939 to place both Canton and Enderbury under their joint control for fifty years. Taking advantage of a proviso allowing American companies to construct facilities at Canton, Pan American Airways, with American naval encouragement, proceeded in 1939 to develop the lagoon for use by its planes flying between Hawaii and the Southwest Pacific. The Navy simultaneously undertook to store at the facility a cache of 100,000 gallons of aviation gasoline and corresponding quantities of lubricating oils.

By 1941 the Navy and the Marines were so occupied with building and defending other island air stations that the Army and Army Engineers were assigned the task of constructing a landing field and defenses at Canton. While the Army remained in command of Canton Island after the outbreak of World War II, the Navy took over the Pan American Airways installation and developed a naval air facility able to handle up to a dozen patrol planes, harbor works capable of unloading 400 tons a day, and minor ship repair shops. All naval facilities in Canton Island were disestablished on 14 October 1946.

BIBLIOGRAPHY

A. Record Group 80, General Records of the Navy Department, 1927-1940, A21-5 File (Washington: National Archives); U.S. Navy, Bureau of Yards and Docks, *Building the Navy's Bases in World War II*, 2 vols. (Washington: GPO, 1947), II:160-61; "Monograph Histories of U.S. Naval Overseas Bases. Vol. II. Pacific Area" (Washington: Naval Historical Center, Operational Archives Branch).

B. Francis X. Holbrook, "United States National Defense and Trans-Pacific Air Routes, 1933-1941," Ph.D diss., Fordham University, 1969.

WILLIAM R. BRAISTED

CAPE CROZIER STATION, ANTARCTICA, U.S. NAVAL BASE.
See Antarctica, U.S. Naval and Air Bases.

CAPE HALLETT COASTAL STATION, ROSS SEA, ANTARCTICA, U.S. NAVAL BASE.
See Antarctica, U.S. Naval and Air Bases.

CARAVELLAS, BRAZIL, U.S. NAVAL AIR FACILITY.
See Brazil, U.S. Naval Base.

CARDIFF, WALES.
See World War I, U.S. Naval Bases in Europe.

CARIBBEAN, THE, U.S. NAVAL BASES, 1940– During the first forty years of the twentieth century, American interests in the Caribbean were largely political, with the exception of our military posture in areas like Cuba and Puerto Rico. As World War II approached, however, American military and political interests extended to other Caribbean lands as well.

Trinidad, British West Indies, U.S. Naval Operating Base, 1942-1967

Undoubtedly the most important of the Caribbean Islands is the British island of Trinidad. On the southeastern edge of the Caribbean 800 miles southeast of Puerto Rico, it is fairly large in size (thirty-five miles wide, fifty-five miles long) and stands as a sentry guarding the shipping lanes along the coast of South America and those leading to the Venezuelan oil fields and the Panama Canal.

America's first military interest in Trinidad occurred in September 1940 when President F. D. Roosevelt announced his "destroyers for bases" deal whereby the United States would acquire eight base sites along the rim of the Atlantic Ocean from Great Britain for fifty overage destroyers. Trinidad was one of these bases. In October of the same year, Rear Adm. John Greenslade surveyed possible sites for a naval base at Trinidad, and a 12-square-mile segment on the northwest tip of the island was chosen as the best location. In early 1941 the British government signed an agreement to lease the site to the United States, and steps were begun to move out the natives living there. It was then decided that rather than build an air station, as originally planned, the Navy would establish a large naval operating base. Capt. Arthur W. Radford, USN, who would become a famous figure in the Navy of the 1940s and 1950s, was in overall command of the activity, while the actual building operations were placed in the hands of the James Stewart Construction Co. of New York. The U-boat sinkings of two Allied ships in early 1942 near the island's chief harbor, Port of Spain, was a grim reminder of the need for haste. Seaplane facilities were quickly completed, and in February 1942 four PBY *Catalinas* began regular patrols. A year later a squadron of six blimps began operations, and in October 1943 a naval squadron of Vega PV-1 *Ventura* planes replaced the Army patrol planes that had operated there from early 1942. Finally, in the fall of 1944 a naval fleet anchorage was estalished in the waters off the naval operating base, protection being afforded by an A/S net and Coast Guard patrols.

In addition to air operation facilities, the naval base also included a self-contained shore establishment at Teteron Bay. This involved the operation and maintenance of minesweepers, net vessels, harbor entrance control units, and living accommodations for over 900 men. At nearby Chaguaramos Bay an escort (ship) repair base was built including three floating dry docks. It was capable of repairing merchant ships and operating damage to destroyers and of making minor engineering repairs for cruisers and carriers. The base grew during the war years, the peak in personnel coming in 1944, when 8,700 enlisted men and 769 officers were stationed there. A receiving station also housed 3,000 transients a month. Ancillary support was provided by a public works section, supply depot, warehouse, and base hospital. In January 1945 the escort repair base was decommissioned and the lighter-than-air operation was dropped. Finally, in July, the remaining two air squadrons were transferred and in 1950 the base was placed in a partial maintenance status. A new Lend-Lease agreement was signed in 1952 extending American rights to the property held, but in 1962 Trinidad became an independent nation. Four years later the Navy began to phase out its control and turned over all of its base facilities to the new government in 1967.

Jamaica, British West Indies, U.S. Naval Air Base, 1942-1944

The second large British-owned island that played a role in the war years was Jamaica. Located just south of Cuba and Hispaniola and the Windward Passage (the broad strait of water between those two islands), it was an ideal spot for an American air base. The base itself was placed on Little Goat Island, just south of Jamaica and about fifty miles from the capital, Kingston. The island was small (150 acres) but it had a land-locked harbor that was perfect for seaplane operations. Two piers, a seaplane ramp, two administration buildings, a power plant, and a shop were built on the base. In addition, housing facilities and a medical dispensary providing for the needs of seventy-five men and twenty-five officers who handled the two squadrons of seaplanes stationed there were also constructed. After private contractors had performed the major building operations, the station Public Works Department took over until the base was decommissioned in September 1944. Through the 1950s the United States still maintained physical possession of Little Goat Island.

Antigua, British West Indies, U.S. Naval Air Facility, 1942-1945

A much smaller but extremely important site because of its location was the British island of Antigua in the Leeward Islands chain. Antigua was leased to the United States in the destroyers-for-bases deal made with Great Britain in 1940. Just 200 miles east of Puerto Rico, it lies on the extreme eastern edge of the arc of islands in the Lesser Antilles chain. This made it an important spot for A/S patrols. These were carried out during the war by one squadron of seaplanes supported by a seaplane tender. The base was completed in June 1942, but the rising threat of enemy submarines necessitated an increase in the operating force. Once that threat subsided, the base became an auxiliary one in 1944; it was remanded to caretaker status in 1945.

St. Lucia, British West Indies, U.S. Naval Air Station, 1942-1943

A similar pattern developed at the island of St. Lucia. Lying 250 miles south of Antigua in the same chain that guards the southeastern edge of the Caribbean, St. Lucia was acquired in the destroyers-for-bases deal with Britain in 1940. Its value lay in its potential as an air base. In 1941 a tract of 245 acres was set aside on the island at Gros Inlet for a seaplane station. This was not the first time that this inlet had played a role in war, for Adm. George Rodney had used it as a base for his fleet in the waning years of the American Revolution. The twentieth-century facility included a seaplane ramp, a parking apron, and a 350-foot pier. Accommodations were also built to house 200 men and 25 officers. The base was active until its decommissioning in September 1943, when it was to be maintained in caretaker status by a small Coast Guard detail. The United States still retains possession of the site.

Curacao and Aruba, Netherlands West Indies, U.S. Naval Operating Base, 1942-1945

The last foreign-owned locations in the West Indies to become an American naval base were the Netherlands-owned islands of Aruba and Curacao. Lying just fifty miles north of the coast of Venezuela, the islands are sizable (each is over 100 square miles) and are located strategically close to Lake Maracaibo, a major source of America's petroleum during World War II. The Navy's interest in these islands, though, goes back to the days of the Spanish-American War. Once the Spanish fleet had steamed across the Atlantic in its effort to succor Cuba, it was nearly out of fuel and hence was vulnerable to American attack. Denied access to Cuba by the American blockade, the Spaniards, in a sly move, refueled at Curacao. Nevertheless, the respite was temporary, for the fleet was soon trapped and destroyed. But it pointed up to the U.S. Navy the fact that any territory in the West Indies in unfriendly hands could cause disproportionate harm to American interests in those waters.

The early events of World War I seemed to foreshadow a repetition of this danger. When the Netherlands fell to Nazi Germany in May 1940, there was the possibility that Hitler's forces would seize the islands, thus creating a vital base for their operations in the West Indies and threatening the nearby oil fields and refineries. To prevent both threats, the British Navy moved swiftly and occupied both Dutch islands. Eighteen months later, just after Pearl Harbor, the United States made arrangements with the Dutch and British governments to take them over. In February 1942 U.S. Army troops landed from two transports and occupied the areas. An interallied command was then created which lasted throughout the war. The American contribution comprised three squadrons of both sea and land patrol planes, a naval maintenance and repair office, a naval observer office to gather intelligence, and housekeeping facilities, which were established at a site that was named U.S. Naval Camp Parera. Three important missions accomplished by this naval operating base were harbor security against fire and sabotage; convoy routing to insure quick turnaround for the 150 vessels per month that were staged through the area; and protection of the lake fleet tankers carrying oil north to the United States. After the war in the Pacific had been concluded, both bases were disestablished and were returned to the Dutch government in October 1945.

See also Guantanamo Bay, Cuba, U.S. Naval Base; La Fe, Cuba, U.S. Naval Air Facility; St. Thomas, Virgin Islands, U.S. Naval Bases; Santa Fe, Isle of Pines, Cuba, U.S. Naval Air Facility; Vieques Island, Puerto Rico, U.S. Marine Corps Camp Garcia.

BIBLIOGRAPHY

A. *U.S. Navy, Building the Navy's Bases in World War II,* 2 vols. (Washington: GPO, 1947); "Administrative History of the U.S. Operating Base, Trinidad, BWI, and Trinidad Sector," in "U.S. Naval Administration in World War II" (Washington: Naval Historical Center, Operational Archives Branch); "Administrative History of the Aruba, Curacao Command," in "U.S. Naval Administration in World War II" (Washington: Naval Historical Center, Operational Archives Branch); "Administrative History of the Caribbean Sea Frontier till VE Day," in "U.S. Naval Administration in World War II" (Washington: Naval Historical Center, Operational Archives Branch).

B. Samuel E. Morison, *The Battle of the Atlantic, September 1939-May 1943* (Boston: Little, Brown, 1947); Samuel E. Morison, *The Atlantic Battle Won, May 1943-May 1945* (Boston: Little, Brown, 1956).

WILLIAM L. CALDERHEAD

CASABLANCA, FRENCH MOROCCO, U.S. NAVAL OPERATING BASE.
See North Africa, U.S. Naval Bases.

CASTLETOWNBERE, IRELAND.
See World War I U.S. Naval Air Stations in Europe.

CAT LAI, REPUBLIC OF VIETNAM, U.S. NAVAL INTERMEDIATE SUPPORT BASE, 1965–1971 This South Vietnamese town, on the Dong Nai River east of Saigon, was developed into a naval logistic installation during the war in Southeast Asia. Designated an intermediate support base, Cat Lai supplied American and Vietnamese river force operating bases in the capital region with maintenance, financial, repair, material, and administrative support. After training Vietnamese Navy personnel to carry out these logistic responsibilities, the U.S. Navy withdrew its advisors and disestablished the base in September 1971.

BIBLIOGRAPHY

A. Commander Naval Forces, Vietnam, "Monthly Historical Reports, 1965-1971" (Washington: Naval Historical Center, Operational Archives Branch).

EDWARD J. MAROLDA

CAT LO, REPUBLIC OF VIETNAM, U.S. NAVAL COMBAT AND LOGISTICS BASE, 1965–1971 Cat Lo, on the northern shore of South Vietnam's

Cape Vung Tau, served as a naval combat and logistics base during the Vietnam War. U.S. naval leaders chose the site for several reasons: with ready access to the South China Sea, the river approaches to Saigon, and the Mekong Delta, Cat Lo was strategically placed; and facilities at the Vietnamese Navy base were immediately available to U.S. units.

Three distinct operational forces were based at Cat Lo: components of the Coastal Surveillance Force; the Saigon area minesweeping force; and the River Patrol Force. Beginning in late 1965, naval units began scouring the coast for communist seaborne infiltrators, and soon afterward minesweeping craft initiated their escort and patrol mission on the narrow waterways leading to Saigon, the country's main port. Cat Lo also acted as a staging and logistic base for the move deep into the Mekong Delta of the Navy's river force. From March to June 1966, the *Belle Grove* (LSD-2) and the *Tortuga* (LSD-26) brought the first river patrol boats (PBRs) into Vietnam with the deployment to Cat Lo of River Division 53 and River Division 54 elements. Once the more ideally placed base at Nha Be (q.v.) became operational in mid-year, the PBR units relocated there, but other river forces remained, such as Patrol Air Cushion Vehicle (PACV) Division 107. Until redeployment to the Danang area in June 1968, the experimental PACVs were tested in the swamp, river, and coastal environment around Cat Lo.

To maintain the various combat forces, Naval Support Activity, Saigon (q.v.), established a detachment at Cat Lo that provided berthing, messing, supply, repair, transportation, communication, and other logistic support. Although Amphibious Construction Battalion 1 installed a pontoon pier and built a ramp for the PACVs, additional measures were required to support the American units before shore facilities were established. First YD-220 and then YD-174, both floating cranes, were stationed at Cat Lo to prepare newly arrived PBRs for in-country operations and to overhaul the coastal patrol's ''Swift'' boats (PCFs).

The naval facility at Cat Lo gradually diminished in importance as minesweeping activities were concentrated at Nha Be south of Saigon, and as bases deeper into the delta were used by the river patrol units. As part of the process of Vietnamization, Cat Lo's resources were turned over to the Vietnamese Navy in April 1971.

BIBLIOGRAPHY

A. Commander Naval Forces, Vietnam, ''The Naval War in Vietnam,'' May 1970 (Washington: Naval Historical Center, Operational Archives Branch); Service Force, U.S. Pacific Fleet, ''Command Histories, 1967-1972'' (Washington: Naval Historical Center, Operational Archives Branch).

B. Herbert T. King, ''Naval Logistic Support, Qui Nhon to Phu Quoc,'' U.S. Naval Institute *Naval Review* 95 (May 1969):84-111; S.A. Swarztrauber, ''River Patrol Relearned,'' U.S. Naval Institute *Naval Review* 96 (May 1970):120-57; Richard L. Schreadley, ''The Naval War in Vietnam, 1950-1970,'' U.S. Naval Institute *Naval Review* 97 (May 1971):180-211; Edwin B. Hooper, *Mobility, Support, Endurance: A Story of Naval Operational Logistics in the Vietnam War, 1965-1968* (Washington: GPO, 1972).

EDWARD J. MAROLDA

CAVITE, LUZON, PHILIPPINE ISLANDS, U.S. NAVAL BASE, 1898–1948 Cavite lies south of the city of Manila on the east side of Manila Bay. It had been used by the Spaniards as an arsenal beginning in 1799 and had been so developed that by 1834 a frigate was built there. It was the only arsenal and the principal naval station in the Philippines; although covering only 71.619 acres, it was the command center for all Spanish naval operations in the Philippine Islands. Following the destruction on 1 May 1898 of the collection of marine antiquities Adm. Patricio Montojo had anchored off Cavite rather than fight off Manila and endanger the city, Adm. George Dewey ordered Lt. Comdr. Edward P. Wood, commanding the gunboat *Petrel*, to enter the shallow waters about Cavite, destroy any ships that had taken refuge there, and burn the smaller Spanish ships located beyond Cavite Point. From the *Petrel*'s small boat her executive officer and navigator, Lt. Bradley A. Fiske, commandeered two large tugs, three steam launches, and several smaller boats that proved quite useful in providing services to the larger American ships. On the morning of 2 May, the *Petrel* in the lead, Dewey took his squadron to Cavite, obtained the surrender of the arsenal, and placed a force of Marines in charge of it. It was thereafter used for docking and repairing American ships. From it ships enforced the blockade Dewey established in Manila Bay, small boats provided transportation to the beach as American troops arrived, and Dewey sailed to support the demand for the capitulation of Manila on 13 August Philippine time. As yet, repair facilities were so poor that Dewey's larger ships had to go to Hong Kong (*see* Far Eastern Naval Bases to 1898) for docking, but small craft obtained repairs there that enabled them to fight the Filipino insurgents that rebelled against American control starting 4 Februrary 1899 and ending with the capture of Emilio Aguinaldo in 1901, and thereafter patrolled Philippine waters.

In 1905 a floating dry dock built in Baltimore, Md., was towed to Cavite, and during the world cruise of the Great White Fleet from 1907 to 1909, 8 percent of the 434,906 tons of coal it consumed was acquired at coaling stations at Cavite and Honolulu. However, the Joint Board of the Army and Navy advised against any extensive outlays for insular fortifications in the Philippines. Because of this advice, congressional penuriousness, disagreement between the Army and Navy on what base sites to develop in the Philippines, and the restrictions upon adding to American fortifications west of Hawaii in the Five Power Naval Treaty written by the Washington Conference of 1921-1922, nothing was done to improve the defenses of the Philippines even after 1936, when the treaty was a dead letter. This meant that in the event of war in the Western Pacific both the Philippines and Guam (q.v.) would fall at once to the Japanese and that bases for the support of American forces would have to be rewon against enemy opposition.

On 7 December 1941 Cavite was the headquarters of the Sixteenth Naval District, of Adm. Thomas Hart's tiny Asiatic Fleet (he had at Cavite one cruiser, four old World War I destroyers, two submarine tenders, and twenty-nine submarines), and of the Asiatic Communication Officer. At the navy yard there were a submarine base in decommissioned status, fuel depot, naval air station at Sangley Point (q.v.), shore signal station, naval prison, receiving ship, port director of the naval transportation service, fleet radio school, naval ammunition depot, and naval hospital and medical supply depot Canacao (q.v.).

On the night of 9-10 December 1941, Japanese planes bombed the Army's Fort McKinley and Nichols Field, and on 10 December, a clear day with unlimited visibility, twenty-seven Japanese twin-engined bombers flying at between 20,000 and 25,000 feet approached from the northwest, while others came from the south. The only defenses at Cavite were ships' batteries and nine 3-inch AA guns whose range was too short to be effective. The first bombs dropped started fires on the submarine tender *Canopus* (AS-9). With Cavite's water mains disrupted, fires were fought with bucket brigades of sand. While fires on the submarine *Seadragon* (SS-194) were brought under control, a lighter with forty-eight torpedoes was destroyed, as were all the cargo and torpedoes and spare parts ready to go aboard the submarine tender *Otus* (AS-20). Damaged also were the destroyer *Peary* (DD-226) and the minesweeper *Bittern* (AM-36). With no fighter aircraft to oppose them, Japanese bombers took deliberate aim and directly destroyed or started fires that wiped out all the important installations at the yard: the power plant, torpedo repair shop, signal office, warehouses, radio stations, and service facilities, and several small ships as well. The aircraft shop and ammunition depot were not hit, but fear that the latter would explode caused the yard to be evacuated. About 500 persons were killed or wounded. Thus the only U.S. naval repair base in the Far East had been virtually destroyed, and without adequate air protection Admiral Hart's surface units were placed in grave danger. On 19 December Hart therefore sent the tenders *Otus* and *Holland* (AS-3), the destroyer *Pope* (DD-225), and a converted yacht southward, leaving the *Canopus* and *Pigeon* (ASR-6) in Manila Bay to service the submarines for as long as possible. On 25 December, with most other Allied commanders in retreat, he left for Java on the *Shark* (SS-174).

On 4 February 1945 U.S. troops entered Manila; on the fourteenth they captured the Cavite naval base and Nichols Airfield. However, as of 30 June 1946 there were only 5 officers and 157 men in ship's company and a total of 41 officers and 568 men on board. There were no general supplies or ammunition storage, only a small pontoon dry dock, some lighters, light cranes, and a picket boat, and the personnel lived in Quonset huts. Cavite's function was to repair small boats in the Manila Bay area. With the buildup of naval installations in Subic Bay (q.v.), it was really no longer needed, and it was disestablished on 15 January 1948.

BIBLIOGRAPHY

A. Dewey to Secretary of the Navy, 13, 14, January 1899, in "The Philippines," ZE File (Washington: Naval Historical Center, Operational Archives Branch); Charles H. Stockton to the Secretary of the Navy, enclosing Lt. A. P. Niblack, "What the Acquisition of the Philippines Will Require of the U.S. Navy" ("The Philippines," ZE File (Washington: Naval Historical Center, Operational Archives Branch).

B. French Ensor Chadwick, *The Relations of the United States and Spain: The Spanish-American War,* 2 vols. (New York: Charles Scribner's Sons, 1911); William R. Braisted, *The United States Navy in the Pacific, 1897-1909* (Austin: University of Texas Press, 1958); William R. Braisted, *The United States Navy in the Pacific, 1899-1922* (Austin: University of Texas, 1971); Paolo E. Coletta, *Admiral Bradley Allen Fiske and the American Navy* (Lawrence: Regents Press of Kansas, 1979); James W. Leutze, *A Different Kind of Victory: A Biography of Admiral Thomas C. Hart* (Annapolis, Md.: Naval Institute Press, 1981); David F. Trask. *The War with Spain in 1898* (New York: Macmillan, 1981); Walter G. Winslow, Captain, U.S. Navy (Ret.), *The Fleet the Gods Forgot: The U.S. Asiatic Fleet in World War II* (Annapolis, Md.: Naval Institute Press, 1982).

CENTRAL AMERICA, U.S. NAVAL BASES, 1907–1946 In contrast to the limited interest that the U.S. Navy had in naval base facilities in South America, the situation in Central America was quite different. The region was much closer to the U.S. mainland, it was contiguous to vital shipping lines in the Caribbean, and its close proximity to the Panama Canal constantly presented the potential of a serious threat. The story of American naval interests in this area has been a reflection of that concern.

Fonseca, Nicaragua, U.S. Naval Air Facility, 1942-1943

Once the construction of the Panama Canal had commenced, it became clear that while the canal would have adequate protection on the Atlantic side through the U.S. bases at Guantanamo Bay, Cuba (q.v.), and at San Juan, Puerto Rico, the Pacific Ocean approaches to the canal were void of any protective screen. Two possibilities presented themselves: Cocos Island and Fonseca Bay. Cocos Island was a small and isolated spot 100 miles south of the canal. Although several opportunities came along by 1914 to purchase it, the United States decided not to do so due to the bleakness of the island. The second site was at Fonseca Bay on the Pacific coast of Nicaragua, 1,100 miles northwest of Panama. Happily, the United States had a treaty with Nicaragua giving it the right to lease land at Fonseca for a base or a coaling station. In 1907 and again in 1913 the Navy, through its General Board, considered the feasibility of a base but took no action. After World War I began in Europe, the board in 1915 considered the matter again, and again rejected the idea of acquisition. Two points were stressed in the decision. First, the direct distance from Panama to San Francisco (the United States' chief West Coast naval base) was only 100 miles greater than the route from Fonseca Bay to San Francisco. Consequently this minor difference in mileage lessened the value of Fonseca as a coaling station. Second, it was noted that due to the unexpected success of using colliers for refueling during the Navy's world cruise of 1907-1909, the need for land based coaling stations was less pressing, and excessive numbers of coaling stations would only dissipate the Navy's strength. Nevertheless, it was emphasized that while Fonseca would not be of much benefit to the United States, if it were in the hands of an unfriendly nation in time of war it would pose a grave threat. Accordingly the General Board urged that the wording of the treaty with Nicaragua be changed to give the United States the exclusive right of using Fonseca Bay. In 1916 an agreement was made with Nicaragua that did not provide this guarantee but that did grant the right to establish a base at Little Corn and Great Corn Islands for ninety-nine years. This right was never exercised.

One year later, with America now at war, the General Board noted that since Fonseca was one of only two feasible base sites on the Pacific coast below California (Magdalena Bay, Mexico, was the other) the United States should take steps to establish a base there by dispatching a naval vessel to examine the bay for its use as a fueling station. The cruiser *Cincinnati* was dispatched and found the bay to be suitable, but it was felt that more sheltered water further north in Honduras or El Salvador might be preferable. The war ended before the United States considered the matter again, but in 1920 the General Board observed that while there was no need for a base in the near future, the United States should be given exclusive rights to establish one.

Here the matter stood until World War II. In the spring of 1942 an advanced naval seaplane base was established at Money Penny Anchorage at Fonseca Bay. The site was to be the northwestern apex of the great air search triangle that guarded the western approaches to the canal. The lack of a sheltered bay, noted twenty-five years earlier, made seaplane landings hazardous, so this seaplane unit was moved southward to Corinto. Two other problems plagued the Fonseca base—the lack of a deep-water anchorage, which necessitated bringing cargo ashore in lighters, and the lack of road and rail connections. This forced the Navy to use a forty-mile shuttle service by boat with Managua, the capital. These conditions were endured till late 1943, when the base was decommissioned and all activities were moved to Corinto.

Corinto, Nicaragua, U.S. Naval Auxiliary Air Facility, 1942-1946

Corinto is located 100 miles southeast of Fonseca Bay along the Nicaraguan coast. In the early part of the century it had been disregarded as a possible base for ships, but in the air age the picture was changing. After World War II began, Corinto served as a naval auxiliary air facility beginning in September 1942. When the Fonseca planes were moved over, it operated at full capacity till the late spring of 1944. Original plans called for two squadrons of patrol seaplanes and two squadrons of PT boats. In addition, base facilities were to be built to accommodate 1,000 men. Fortunately, Corinto had what Fonseca lacked: a deep-water anchorage, dock, railroad sidings, and ample building materials such as stone and lumber. All the standard units that an advanced air base needed were eventually in place, including a twenty-two bed hospital dispensary. Plans for a torpedo maintenance facility were dropped when it was finally decided not to station PT boats there. Active patrol plane operations continued until the spring of 1944, when the squadron base was shifted to the Galapagos. Limited daily reconnaissance continued, though, and the base proceeded to provide ships of the fleet operating in that area with supplies of fuel, water, and provisions. After the war, in mid-1946, the station was decommissioned and the facilities were returned to Nicaragua.

Puerto Castillo, Honduras, U.S. Naval Base, 1942-1946

Two hundred miles due north of Fonseca Bay but on the Atlantic side of the isthmus and in Honduras lay the site of another American base, Puerto Castillo. Rights to use this site were obtained in July 1942, and the base was commissioned that November. Because the United Fruit Company had built modern facilities in the nearby town of Trujillo for shipments of bananas, the Navy was able to use these facilities as it built up its operations. The United States acquired the base site without limitation or cost with the proviso that at the end of the war the permanent installations would be handed over to Honduras. Seabees, supplemented by local workers, constructed a seaplane ramp, a floating pier, and oil tanks and water tanks, as well as two pump houses. A large dock that could handle the Navy's biggest ships was already available and had good rail facilities alongside. Furthermore, most of the personnel stationed there considered the living quarters to be excellent. The base served as a facility for fueling and provisioning ships and for making minor repairs. In addition it served as a naval auxiliary air facility, but its aircraft saw only minor service in a backwater area of the war. Still, the Navy continued to use its supply facilities and did not return the base to Honduras until February 1946.

See also Panama Canal Zone, Post-World War II Defense Arrangements; Panama Canal Zone, U.S. Naval Radio Stations.

BIBLIOGRAPHY

A. U.S. Navy, Bureau of Yards and Docks, *Building the Navy's Bases in World War II*, 2 vols. (Washington: GPO, 1947); U.S. Navy General Board Reports, Letterbook File, 1900-1947 (Washington: Naval Historical Center, Operational Archives Branch); "Records of the Field Liaison and Records Section, Base Maintenance Section, Monographs and Histories of Overseas Bases, Canal Zone, 1904-1942" (Washington: Naval Historical Center, Operational Archives Branch); "U.S. Naval Overseas Bases: A Current Survey" (Prepared by Direction of Chief of Naval Operations), 1957 (Washington: Naval Historical Center, Operational Archives Branch); "Administrative History of the Caribbean Sea Frontier Till VE Day," in "U.S. Naval Administration in World War II" (Washington: Naval Historical Center, Operational Archives Branch); "Fifteenth Naval District, Panama, the Canal Zone, and Honduras" (Washington: Naval Historical Center, Operational Archives Branch).

B. Daniel Wicks, "The Lake Nicaragua Naval Base Scheme," U.S. Naval Institute *Proceedings* 106 (Aug. 1980):56-60.

WILLIAM A. CALDERHEAD

CHARLOTTE AMALIE, VIRGIN ISLANDS, U.S. MARINE CORPS AIR FACILITY.

See St. Thomas, Virgin Islands, U.S. Naval Bases.

CHAU DOC, REPUBLIC of VIETNAM, U.S. NAVAL COMBAT BASE, 1969–1970 Chau Doc, on the Bassac River in the Republic of Vietnam, was the site of a naval combat base during the Southeast Asian Conflict. American and Vietnamese river forces staged from the base while patrolling the rivers and canals along the Cambodian border as part of the Sea Lords anti-infiltration strategy of 1969-1970.

BIBLIOGRAPHY
A. Commander Naval Forces, Vietnam, "Monthly Historical Reports, 1965-1971" (Washington: Naval Historical Center, Operational Archives Branch).

EDWARD J. MAROLDA

CHEFOO, KOREA.
See Far Eastern U.S. Naval Bases to 1898.

CHERBOURG, FRANCE, U.S. NAVAL ADVANCE BASE, 1944–1945 Following the capture of Cherbourg at the conclusion of the Battle of Normandy, on 26 July 1944 the U.S. Navy began to build a series of facilities for an advance base in the major harbor at the center of the northern shore of the Cotentin Peninsula. Included were a salvage base, radio material office, mine and bomb disposal unit, harbor entrance control post, port director, radio station, fuel office, and net depot. The airfields in the area were under U.S. Army control, but the British established a minesweeper base at Cherbourg.

BIBLIOGRAPHY
A. Shore Establishment/Advanced Bases, "Directory, December 1944" (Washington, D.C., Navy Yard: Naval Aviation History Office).

CHERCHEL, ALGERIA.
See North Africa, U.S. Naval Bases.

CHO MOI, REPUBLIC OF VIETNAM, U.S. NAVAL LOGISTICS INSTALLATION, 1969–1971 Cho Moi, a small population center on South Vietnam's Mekong River, was the site of a naval logistic installation during the Vietnam Conflict.

Cho Moi was chosen for this role by U.S. naval leaders during 1969, when they developed a new strategy, called Sea Lords, to interdict Viet Cong and North Vietnamese infiltration into the Mekong Delta from Cambodia. The Cho Moi intermediate support base provided U.S. and Vietnamese river forces patrolling the waterways in the area with supplies and boat repairs.

Once the Vietnamese Navy was prepared to unilaterally handle this task, in September 1971, U.S. naval forces withdrew and the base was disestablished.

BIBLIOGRAPHY
A. Commander Naval Forces, Vietnam, "Monthly Historical Reports, 1965-1971" (Washington: Naval Historical Center, Operational Archives Branch).

EDWARD J. MAROLDA

CHORRERA, REPUBLIC OF PANAMA, U.S. NAVAL ADVANCE BASE, 1943–1944 Chorrera is located about thirteen miles west of Balboa, seven miles inland from the Pacific Ocean, and forty miles north of Taboga Island. To the emergency fighter base built by the U.S. Army in 1943 was added a blimp facility. After the Army withdrew in 1943, the Navy used the base for about a year, for it was put in caretaker status in November 1944.

BIBLIOGRAPHY
A. "Fifteenth Naval District and Commander Panama Sea Frontier," in "U.S. Naval Administration in World War II," 1945 (Washington Navy Yard: Navy Department Library); U.S. Navy, Bureau of Yards and Docks, *Building the Navy's Bases in World War II,* 2 vols. (Washington: GPO, 1947). Vol. II.

WILLIAM L. CALDERHEAD

CHRISTCHURCH, NEW ZEALAND, ANTARCTIC SUPPLY BASE AND U.S. NAVAL TECHNICAL COMMUNICATIONS GROUP.
See Antarctica, U.S. Naval and Air Bases.

CHU LAI, REPUBLIC OF VIETNAM, U.S. NAVAL SUPPORT ACTIVITY, 1964–1971 Almost overnight, this site fifty-six miles southeast of Danang in the Republic of Vietnam became a major naval logistic base. In the latter months of 1964, U.S. naval leaders concluded that an additional air facility was required in the I Corps Tactical Zone to ease the current and projected overcrowding of units and aircraft at the Danang (q.v.) airfield. Soon after construction of the proposed 8,000-foot jet-capable airfield was ordered, Pacific Fleet units moved ashore. In May 1965 Amphibious Construction Battalion 1, protected by Marine forces, installed two pontoon causeway piers and an amphibious fuel line along the sea bottom, and Naval Mobile Construction Battalion 10 laid down aluminum matting for the runway and taxiway. By the end of the month, half of the airfield was completed, enabling the immediate operation from Chu Lai of Marine Air Group 12 elements.

Assuring adequate logistic support by sea to the air group, the growing Marine ground force, and some of the Navy's Coastal Surveillance Force units was an absolutely essential but difficult task for the Naval Support Activity, Danang, Detachment Chu Lai. The Viet Cong interdicted the roads and rail line in the vicinity of the coastal site, and air transport resources were limited. Although relatively secure from enemy action, the sea line of communication was threatened by natural conditions. There was no harbor at Chu Lai, at the mouth of the Truong River, and the unprotected coastal site was subject to heavy seas, especially during the northeast or winter monsoon period; both the causeway and the fuel line were damaged in 1965. Initially, there were few facilities ashore, and the deep, powdery beach sand hindered both over-the-shore movement and construction.

While the establishment of permanent base facilities was under way, interim steps were taken to maintain support. Landing craft transferred supplies from Danang, and tank landing ships (LSTs) delivered cargo, especially ammunition, from the naval depots at Subic Bay (q.v.) in the Philippines and from Sasebo, Japan (q.v.). By the fall of 1965, smaller LSTs were crossing the Truong River bar at high tide to offload at the temporary Cus Ho ramp. The river was finally opened to larger ships, including LSTs, fuel barges, and coastal freighters, when dredges cleared a 16-foot channel in the spring of 1966. The weather continued to hamper operations at Chu Lai, witnessed by the loss of the *Mahnomen County* (LST-912) in January 1967. The ship broached off Chu Lai beach after being torn from her anchor by 18-foot waves and subsequently broke apart on the rocks.

However, the construction of permanent facilities continued to improve the logistic situation. By 1967 portable fuel storage bladders were replaced by a rigid-wall tank farm that was connected to additional fuel lines laid along the sea bottom. A hard-topped road and ramp complex enabled sailors to offload as many as six LSTs simultaneously. Chu Lai soon became the second busiest port in I Corps, after Danang. By September 1969 the Naval Support Activity, Danang, Detachment Chu Lai, handled over 86,000 measurement tons of cargo each month in support of First Marine Division and First Marine Aircraft Wing elements. The naval presence in Chu Lai diminished after June 1970, when logistic facilities were turned over to the Army, whose units were playing a greater operational role in the southern I Corps region. The coastal patrol operating base there was turned over to the Vietnamese Navy in May 1971 as part of the Vietnamization of the war.

BIBLIOGRAPHY

A. Service Force, U.S. Pacific Fleet, "Command Histories, 1967-1972" (Washington: Naval Historical Center, Operational Archives Branch).

B. Frank C. Collins, Jr., "Maritime Support of the Campaign in I Corps," U.S. Naval Institute *Naval Review* 97 (May 1971):156-79; Edwin B. Hooper, *Mobility, Support, Endurance: A Story of Naval Operational Logistics in the Vietnam War, 1965-1968* (Washington: GPO, 1972); K.P. Huff, "Building the Advanced Base at DaNang," U.S. Naval Institute *Naval Review* 94 (May 1968):88-113; Jack Shulimson and Charles M. Johnson, *U.S. Marines in Vietnam: The Landing and the Buildup, 1965* (Washington: USMC Headquarters, History and Museums Division, 1978); Richard Tregaskis, *Southeast Asia: Building the Bases: The History of Construction in Southeast Asia* (Washington: GPO, 1975).

EDWARD J. MAROLDA

COCO SOLO, PANAMA CANAL ZONE, U.S. NAVAL AIR STATION AND SUBMARINE BASE, 1917–1950 While the U.S. Navy kept station ships off both coasts of Panama during the second half of the nineteenth century, the land defense of the isthmus was vested in small detachments of Marines based primarily at Coco Solo, on the Atlantic side of the canal two miles east of Colon, and at Balboa (q.v.) and Panama City on the Pacific side. In 1914, with the canal about to open, the Marines gave way to the Army. Soon thereafter the Navy Department directed that a main submarine base be established at Coco Solo and an auxiliary base at Balboa.

Capt. A.W. Grant, USN, head of the Submarine Service, started construction work at Coco Solo for a temporary submarine base in 1917, and in July of that year there arrived the submarine tender *Tallahassee* and the submarines C-1, C-2, and C-3. The submarines returned to the United States in December 1918. Meanwhile, on 6 May 1918, Lt. R.G. Pennoyer placed Naval Air Station Coco Solo in commission as a seaplane base. It was built on 131 acres, of which 42 acres were water and marsh. With dredging work started in May 1917 and completed in February 1918, construction began on two storehouses, mess hall, machine shop, hospital, ordnance shed, and quarters for fifty-two submarine officers and six naval aviators. Many of the facilities of the submarine base and the NAS were used in common, although the former reported to the Bureau of Yards and Docks and the latter to the Commandant, Fifteenth Naval District and the Bureau of Aeronautics. The missions of NAS Coco Solo were to provide services and operating facilities; to aid in maintaining assigned aircraft squadrons to protect the eastward approaches of the Panama Canal; to repair and overhaul naval aircraft assigned; and to maintain utility aircraft (the latter provided transportation, photographic, aerological, and target-towing services). Soon a radio station was built so that the base could communicate with its pilots and also report weekly to Washington on weather conditions encountered by the pilots. To extend aerial observation over the Caribbean entrance to the canal, in 1918 an auxiliary seaplane base was established at Porvornier Island in the San Blas country. In addition to searching for enemy submarines and mines, seaplanes from Coco Solo provided cover for convoys entering and leaving port. So important was this work that in 1923 the Navy made the submarine base at Coco Solo a permanent facility and also authorized the construction of a naval station at Balboa.

Following the end of World War I, the 1,183 men at the Coco Solo installations were greatly reduced in number and the submarine base was abandoned. The naval air station was left with one operating R-type aircraft, seventeen HS-21s (landplanes), two R-9 seaplanes, and seven HS-1L planes. On 2 December 1919 Lt. Comdr. Victor D. Herbster, USN, relieved Pennoyer as commanding officer, but the Navy placed the station in reserve in 1922, leaving only skeleton personnel aboard. These men, and those who followed, suffered the lethargy imposed by the climate, the dampness, corrosion, and rot, the malaria, and the dysentery. The antidote provided by the station commander was athletic programs and a rotation policy back to the United States after eighteen months of duty.

In addition to the enervating climate, airmen suffered from restrictive regulations. According to rules issued by the Interdepartmental Air Navigation Committee in the Panama Canal Zone, aircraft could not carry arms, munitions, or explosives and could carry cameras and radios only after obtaining special permission. While air navigation regulations should not interfere with the operation of Panamanian aircraft, which must conform to American regulations, all American hands were warned to guard against the disclosure of information about the fortifications defending the approaches to the Canal and to ward off danger to its locks by malicious or demented persons.

Although opinion in Washington in the 1920s and early 1930s was divided over whether Pearl Harbor or Panama should have precedence as a naval base site that would be immune from attack, it finally was decided that Pearl Harbor would be the main base and that while the stationing of the fleet at Panama was improbable it should serve as a supply base for ships transiting the canal. According to the Army, no additional defenses were needed for the Canal Zone, yet the Navy continually worried about possible sabotage to ships from Panamanians or from an increasing number of Japanese near the Zone, and the leaders of the various fleet exercises held off Panama in the twenties and thirties called for the utmost number of aircraft possible to be based there. Among new types of aircraft in the late 1920s were T3M-2s, OLs, and VOSs, torpedo, patrol, and observation aircraft.

The Panama Canal Zone was excluded from the freeze on the building of additional fortifications dictated in the Washington Naval Disarmament Conference of 1922. In consequence, upon deeming the defenses of the Panama Canal Zone inadequate, the Joint Army-Navy Committee on 27 April 1927 recommended the expenditure of $38 million for new Army and Navy projects in addition to the $22,342,618 spent to that date. Given the limits placed upon the building of capital ships in the Washington Treaty, the committee demanded that ships in the Zone be properly protected and stated that only naval forces could provide the adequate protection necessary for them and for the canal as well. Although the canal was neutralized in time of peace, no enemy ship must be allowed to transit it in time of war, and any suggestion that defensive forces be limited or reduced must be taken as revealing a hostile attitude. While an enemy landing in the Zone could be discounted, a speedy fleet could approach it and it would take only one bomb to disable a canal lock. Because ships from the United States could not reach the zone in time if an attack were made, the Navy concluded that the defenses of the Zone should be made second only to those of Hawaii. Most important would be the provision of seaplanes able to scout 300 miles out to sea. Moreover, submarines and aircraft had made even 16-inch guns sited on land obsolete as defensive arms.

Few changes were made in the naval installations in the Panama Canal Zone during the disarmament doldrums of the 1920s. In 1930, in accordance with the Navy's Shore Station Development Board, a 1,200-by-120-foot landing field was built for use by landplanes attached to the station and visiting aircraft from the fleet. In consequence, NAS Coco Solo was designated a Fleet Air Base in 1931 and for a decade executed routine gunnery, bombing, navigation, and radio flights in addition to providing search and rescue. On board in the 1930s were three fleet squadrons supported by about 1,000 men and two fleet tenders. The first twelve PBY *Catalina* aircraft arrived in 1937, when the installation of lights at the station made night operations possible. Meanwhile, in 1932 the Shore Station Board was authorized by the Secretary of the Navy to use some land opposite Balboa for the establishment of a Naval Operating Base. The latter was built in 1936 and 1937 on 704 acres of land, expanded to 1,345 acres in 1939.

Following congressional authorization in 1938 to increase the Navy by 20 percent and to establish a naval air strength of 3,000 planes, Acting Secretary of the Navy Charles Edison appointed a board headed by Rear Adm. A.J. Hepburn to report on the nation's needs for "additional submarine, destroyer, mine, and naval air bases on the coasts of the United States, its territories, and possessions." The board stressed the importance particularly of shore facilities to service the increased number of aircraft, a need also stressed on 9 May 1939 by the Chief of Naval Operations, Adm. William D. Leahy, to the House Naval Affairs Committee. Among the sites to be further developed in accordance with the Hepburn Report, dated 1 December 1938, was Coco Solo, where the facilities since 1918 had been called Submarine Base and NAS, Coco Solo. The latter, however, was designated as a Naval Air Station in 1938. The Secretary of the Navy, Claude A. Swanson, submitted the report to the Speaker of the House soon after Christmas, and an administration-sponsored bill was prepared. Because of the limit of $65 million in the bill, Coco Solo was one of three sites deleted. Nor was it included in the regular naval appropriations bill for fiscal years 1940 and 1941. However, following the destroyer-bases deal with Great Britain of September 1940, funds to build base sites and develop others, including $8 million for the submarine base at Coco Solo to service six submarines, were authorized in the Fourth Supplemental National Defense Appropriation Act of early 1941.

At the time of the Japanese attack on Pearl Harbor, NAS Coco Solo had on board Patrol Wing 3, comprised of VP-31, VP-32, and VP-33, each with twelve PBYs and various spares. VP-34 was soon added, and also some PBY-3s. From 67 officers and fewer than 1,000 men, the personnel complement expanded to 316 officers and 3,900 men by September 1945. In 1939 NAS Coco Solo was headquarters for the three squadrons of Patrol Wing 3. Although the headquarters were to be shifted to the Albrook Army Air Field nearby on 10 August 1942, the operating squadrons remained at Coco Solo. On 8 September 1939, meanwhile, the headquarters for the staff of the Fifteenth Naval District was located at Balboa. Nearby, on Amador Road just north of the entrance to Fort Amador, was property designated for a naval radio station. With space at headquarters becoming insufficient, and with its work being seriously disturbed by movement of trains and locomotives, the Bureau of Yards and Docks built a new administration building on this property; it was occupied on 5 July 1941.

As a consequence of the Hepburn Report, two construction contracts for the Canal Zone had been signed on 17 June and 17 July 1940. Following the signing of the destroyer-bases deal on 2 September, a board headed by Rear Adm. John W. Greenslade was appointed to survey the naval shore establishment with a view to the requirements of a two-ocean navy. The report became the blueprint for all subsequent base development in the Caribbean and contiguous areas in the Atlantic and Pacific.

Although the naval defense of the Panama Canal rested on the Atlantic side, mainly with forces based at Guantánamo Bay (q.v.), Puerto Rico, and Trinidad (*see* Caribbean, The, U.S. Naval Bases), the planes and submarines at Coco Solo played their part. By the end of 1940, a third contract provided for erecting 1,100 housing units, and in the summer of 1941 work began on building a new hospital about three miles from the air station. During the spring of 1942, in addition, the ammunition depot built in 1937 was enlarged from 700 to 1,500 acres, increasing its potential fourfold.

In 1939 NAS Coco Solo occupied 185 acres of the sand-flea infested land on the east side of Manzanillo Bay. Facilities included a small landing field, three plane hangars, one blimp hangar, barracks, officers' quarters, three seaplane ramps, gasoline storage, and a few miscellaneous buildings. Plans approved on 1 August 1940 called for expanding the site rather than building an additional air base elsewhere. The shore facilities could not support the seven patrol squadrons now assigned to Coco Solo. Moreover, a wide stretch of open water between the eastern breakwater and Margarita Point permitted heavy ocean swells to enter Manzanillo Bay and often made seaplane operations hazardous. To overcome the hazard, the 3,800-foot gap in the breakwater was closed by dumping stones and concrete blocks onto a 15-foot coral mat. On 30 acres of land reclaimed by dredging in the area of Coco facing the sea, there were added three large steel hangars, four seaplane ramps, 700,000 square feet of concrete parking area, engine test stands, and a large aircraft assembly and repair shop. Other construction encompassed barracks and a mess hall for 1,400 men, a bombproof command center, an operations building, a large administration building to house the administrative offices of both the air station and adjoining submarine base, and several large warehouses. Dredging operations at the air station also provided coral fill for new runways at the Army's adjacent France Field. When that field was complete, a 1,700-by-66-foot concrete taxiway was built to connect the two stations. After May 1943 the Navy could use the Army field to operate its landplanes.

Following the attack on Pearl Harbor urgent need was seen for increasing the defenses of the Panama Canal Zone proper and for establishing strategically located bases to guard the approaches to the Atlantic and Pacific entrances to the canal. Although responsibility for the defense of the Canal Zone was vested in the Commanding General, Caribbean Defense Area, this general created an Air Task Force that authorized Army planes to operate over land and naval planes to operate over water. As a consequence of plans already made by the Army and Navy Joint Planning Board, Advanced Base Depot at Balboa was built on the West Bank of the Canal for the storage of material, a wise move because Panama was to become the major link in future logistic operations in the South Pacific. Because the Navy was to "furnish the United States with timely information of any enemy approach to the canal,'' the selection of sites for advanced bases for air and sea scouting units was of primary concern to the Commandant of the Fifteenth Naval District. While the assignment of said commandant to serve also as Commander Panama Sea Frontier made little difference in administrative matters and danger was expected more from sabotage than from enemy suicide or nuisance raids, perhaps from carriers, he assigned his forces the task of patrolling his area of responsibility by ships and aircraft, searching and destroying enemy submarines by Hunter-Killer groups of ships and aircraft, escort ships and convoys by surface ships and aircraft, patrolling and defending harbors and their approaches (a task taken over from local naval defense forces of the Fifteenth Naval District), and routing and convoying of shipping.

To expand sea surveillance, advance bases were established at the Galapagos Islands; Puerto Castillo, Honduras; Barranquilla, Colombia; Fonseca and Corinto, Nicaragua; Salinas, Ecuador (*see* Central America, U.S. Naval Bases; Hispanic South America, U.S. Naval Bases); and Grand Cayman Island, British West Indies. On a four-day schedule, planes left Coco Solo to fly to these bases and return, thus investigating the sea for 800 miles from the main base. By January 1942 Patrol Wing 3 had been increased to thirty-two planes, all dependents had been evacuated, blackout regulations had been disseminated, and special air defense drills had commenced. Radar was installed at the station and also in the patrol planes (rather than at Norfolk), and Patrol Squadron 3 was directed to use whatever planes were available. It soon acquired VF, VOS, VJ, and VJR types. The station gave support to both American and British aircraft and to LSTs, PT boats, and other craft heading for operational areas in the Pacific and in addition provided biweekly transportation on a Naval Air Transport Service (NATS) schedule that flew from Miami via Portland Bight, Jamaica.

By letter of 11 May 1943 the Secretary of the Navy disestablished Submarine Base, Coco Solo, redesignated the facility thereat as U.S. Naval Station, Coco Solo, and also established a Naval Operating Base. The latter was comprised of a naval station, a section base at Cristobal, and a Naval Tank Farm, but on 24 October 1944 the base lost control of NAS Coco Solo.

Among the training activities at NAS Coco Solo were a joint school for the instruction of enlisted men in free aerial machine gunnery (32 men every four weeks), a refresher course offered to 644 men between 24 April and 30 November 1944, a pilots' navigation refresher course, a pilots' flight refresher course, an enlisted air combat crewmen refresher course, and Link instrument training.

The first enemy action reported was the firing of a torpedo at an American ship 225 miles northeast of the Galapagos Islands, the last on 7 May 1944 when two torpedoes hit the U.S. tanker *Kittaning* while she was forty miles northeast of Cristobal. No success was achieved by planes flying intelligence runs along the north coast of Colombia to learn where and how U-boats were refueled and reprovisioned.

Operating under the influence of demobilization following the war, NAS Coco Solo disestablished its Recreation Camp at Trinidad Island and the advance seaplane stations in Honduras and Ecuador, and merged many of its services with those of the naval station. The 1,299 men aboard in September 1945 were reduced to 630 by 30 June 1946, a large number of the latter being eligible for demobilization within the next two months.

With demobilization complete on 15 August 1946, NAS Coco Solo transferred its surplus property and obtained a new mission: to provide full-time support for the VP(ML), two VP(MS) squadrons, and Class "A" overhaul facilities, scheduled NATS operations, and part-time support for one Carrier Air Group (CVG). Moreover, it was to use civilian rather than military personnel as much as possible. With its complement reduced to 70 percent of its wartime high, NAS Coco Solo had to train new men assigned to it and suffered while personnel dropped as low as 70 to 80 percent of that allowed. Not until 30 September 1947 did it have 650 enlisted men on board, and not until 30 September 1948 did its complement reach 95 percent of allowance. Word came during the third quarter of 1949 that it would be placed in maintenance status and that it should combine its civilian personnel with that of the Naval Operating Base and reduce its personnel from 1,102 to 675. By 1 February 1950 even the overhaul and repair department had been deactivated.

Submarine Base, Coco Solo

Established in 1917 and later modernized, the submarine base occupied a 130-acre peninsula bounded on the north by Margarita Bay and on the west and south by Manzanillo Bay. With no extension of land, important additions to all facilities were begun in 1940. Included to the north were a 300-foot-wide mole pier equipped with water, oil, and air lines, a railway spur, a large transit shed, several storehouses, and shop buildings. To the south, similarly, the existing quay was extended by 500 feet and equipped with water, oil, and electric services, A 16,000-square-foot paved area for net weaving and a large storage building comprised a net depot. On 20 acres of new land created by dredging were built the main housing areas for the station and the chapel, library, and recreation buildings.

To protect the above-ground fuel oil, diesel oil, and gasoline tank farms and pumping stations on both ends of the canal, these were replaced with underground storage in 1942, with the Gatun farm, about two miles southwest of Coco Solo, servicing both the naval and military facilities nearby. To provide the speedy delivery of fuel oils particularly while U-boats were ravaging tankers in the Caribbean, pipelines were built to connect the Gatun farm with a new Arrajan farm near Balboa. These were duplicated in 1944. Meanwhile, however, Secretary of the Navy Frank Knox ordered that a Naval Operating Base be established in the Panama Canal Zone that would include the naval air station, naval station, naval hospital, net depot, and naval defense housing at Coco Solo, with the submarine base there to be disestablished and its facilities redesignated United States Naval Station, Coco Solo.

See also Panama Canal Zone, Post-World War II Defense Arrangements.

BIBLIOGRAPHY
A. "Records of the General Board of the Navy, 1903-1945," (Washington: Naval Historical Center, Operational Archives Branch); "Coco Solo" (ZE File Washington: Naval Historical Center, Operational Archives Branch); "History of Coco Solo Naval Air Station, 1937 to 2 September 1945" (Washington: Naval Historical Center, Operational Archives Branch); U.S. Navy, Bureau of Yards and Docks, *Building the Navy's Bases in World War II*, 2 vols. (Washington: GPO, 1947), I:4,5,26, 34, 36, 40, II:15-21; *A Chronology of Events Relating to the Panama Canal*, prepared for the Committee on Foreign Relations, United States Senate, by Congressional Research Service, Library of Congress (Washington: GPO, December 1977); "Commander 15th Naval District and Commander Panama Sea Frontier," In "U.S. Naval Administration in World War II" (Washington: U.S. Navy Department Library); "Panama Canal Zone," files in "Interdepartmental Committee on Regulations for Air Navigation in Panama Canal Zone" (Washington: Naval Historical Center, Operational Archives Branch); Record Group 45 Defense Plans, in Office of Naval Records and Library, Subject File 1911-1927 (Washington: National Archives); Record Group 80, Correspondence of the Secretary of the Navy (Washington: National Archives); Record Group 165, War College Division (Washington: National Archives).

COLON, PANAMA CANAL ZONE, RADIO STATION.
See Balboa, Panama Canal Zone, U.S. Naval Operating Base/Naval Station.

CONSTANTINOPLE, TURKEY, U.S. NAVAL BASE, 1919–1923 In World War I the United States took no part in the defeat and occupation of Turkey, which was largely a British show. After the armistice, the Allies used High Commissioners to enforce the armistice terms; the United States followed suit by having the former Secretary of the American Embassy at Constantinople serve as Commissioner, while the Swedish Legation handled American diplomatic affairs.

To represent his government and look after American interests in Turkey, at the request of the State Department the Chief of Naval Operations, Adm. William S. Benson, detailed Rear Adm. Mark Lambert Bristol to Constantinople on 8 January 1919. His area of responsibility extended over the waters east of longitude 21°, which included all of Greece except Corfu and the region to the east. Bristol raised his flag on the converted yacht USS *Scorpion*, the station ship, on 28 January. Finding accommodations on board inadequate for business and entertainment purposes, he moved into the American Embassy, which also provided him with radio communications. Other naval activities, however, were based elsewhere. A leased building on the waterfront served as a naval supply base, with dental, dispensary, engineering, machine shop, and port offices nearby. Fuel oil storage was rented from the Standard Oil Company. Private shipyards were available for repair and overhauling the ships in the detachment. In 1919 this included three converted yachts, four submarine chasers, and four destroyers. One of the twelve destroyers on duty in 1920 was commanded by Capt. William D. Leahy.

Bristol performed diplomatic as well as naval duties. He supported the Near East Relief Program by detailing port officers at Smyrna, Constantinople, and Derindje, as well as Constanza, Romania, and provided ship travel for the relief agents as well as taking care of their mail and radio communications. One of his officers sat on the Associated Governments' Advisory Trade Committee and helped American business concerns, especially the Standard Oil Company of New York, operating in the Near East.

To improve his relations with other Allied representatives, Bristol on 12 August 1920 was made a High Commissioner, hence ranking over all American diplomatic and consular representatives. He received his orders from the State Department via the Navy Department and headed both a diplomatic and a naval staff. Capt. Lyman A. Cotten served him as naval chief of staff for about a year after 15 April 1921; from that time until the post was discontinued in the spring of 1924, the billet was filled by Capt. Arthur J. Hepburn.

Bristol's largest problem was handling the evacuation of Armenian and Greek refugees from Asia Minor to Greece during the Greek-Turkish War of 1920-1922, one of the greatest folk movements in world history. The admiral attended the first session of the Lausanne conference, from 26 November 1922 to 4 February 1923. With peace about to be restored, twelve of his destroyers were detached, leaving eight with him. Once the new Ataturk government assumed power, on 4 August 1923, foreigners began to evacuate Constantinople, with the last American ship leaving the city on 4 October. However, the State and Navy departments agreed that a detachment of six destroyers, a subchaser, and the *Scorpion* would remain in the Eastern Mediterranean for at least six months. With political conditions quieting, in the spring of 1924 the detachment was transferred to the Commander, Naval Forces, Europe, with surplus stores at Constantinople returned home.

BIBLIOGRAPHY

A. Record Group 45, Subject File WT-Turkey, 1918-1927 (Washington: National Archives); Henry P. Beers, *U.S. Naval Detachment in Turkish Waters, 1919-1942* (Washington: Navy Department, 1943).

B. Walter Hiatt, "Admiral Bristol: American Naval Diplomat," *Current History* 27 (Feb. 1928):676-80; Peter M. Buzanski, "Admiral Mark L. Bristol and Turkish-American Relations, 1919-1922," Ph.D. diss., University of California, Berkeley, 1960; Thomas S. Bryson, *American Diplomatic Relations with the Middle East, 1784-1975: A Survey* (Metuchen, N.J.: Scarecrow Press, 1977); Thomas S. Bryson, *Tars, Turks, and Tankers: The Role of the United States Navy in the Middle East, 1800-1979*, (Metuchen, N.J.: Scarecrow Press, 1980).

CORFU, GREECE.
See World War I U.S. Naval Bases in Europe.

CORINTO, NICARAGUA, U.S. NAVAL AUXILIARY AIR FACILITY.
See Central America, U.S. Naval Bases.

CROIX D'HINS, FRANCE, LAFAYETTE RADIO STATION, 1917–1920 Because of the possibility that the Germans might cut the trans-Atlantic cables during World War I, the U.S. Navy planned to provide secure means of radio communications with France. It was not until 29 October 1917, however, that André Tardieu, the French High Commissioner in the United States, cabled Paris that the Navy had asked about building a new and very powerful radio station in France and that if necessary it would supply the material. On 31 October Secretary of the Navy Josephus Daniels asked the U.S. naval attaché in Paris what material would be needed. Then, on 29 November, Gen. John J. Pershing, commanding the American Expeditionary Force, cabled the Navy Department to speed up its efforts. Because of wartime conditions, the poor quality of commercial radio equipment, and Pershing's having only field communications, the material and equipment had to be provided by the Navy. At meetings of the Inter-Allied Radio Commission held at New London, Conn., on 4 and 12 December, it was decided to build a station in France, a proposal approved by the Inter-Allied Communications Committee, which sat in Paris. To coordinate matters, Lt. Comdr. E. H. Loftin, USN, was sent to Paris. The design, fabrication, installation, and erection of the radio apparatus, antenna supporting towers, and connected public works were assigned to the Bureau of Engineering and the Bureau of Yards and Docks, with the French to provide the site and construct the buildings and the foundations for the towers. The Bureau of Yards and Docks had never built towers more than 600 feet in height, and the eight 820-foot towers to be built at the little country village of Croix D'Hins, fourteen miles southwest of Bordeaux, would be the second highest structures in the world after the Eiffel Tower. Ordered to construct the towers, the Philadelphia Navy Yard began work on them in January 1918 and sent them across by October.

Instead of the manhandled gin poles used in erecting some of the hangars at American naval air stations in France, workers at Croix D'Hins were provided steam-driven, and later motor-driven, hoists. While 600 skilled steel erectors worked on the towers, electrical engineers and a force of experienced linemen strung an 11-mile high-tension power transmission line to bring in the electrical power for a 1,000-kilowatt arc transmitter, the most powerful radio station in the world after the one at Annapolis, Md., which served Washington, D.C.

The construction of the camp itself began in April 1918; when completed it contained buildings with a total of 97,757 square feet of space. Construction on the towers, begun on 4 October 1918, was incomplete as late as mid-December. Indeed, the radio station was not satisfactorily tested until 20 September 1920. Meanwhile it had been decided to complete only four of the towers because the high power greatly exceeded French needs, to send the work crews home, and to keep only a caretaker crew on board. The French, however, wished to continue the work as a postwar project and requested the Navy to push on. France paid for the subsequent costs of all labor, material, and equipment. On 4 May 1919 work began again, and all work except painting was finished on 14 January

1920. On 15 November the station was turned over to French radio operators, and on 18 December it was formally turned over to the French government. Its total cost was $3.5 million.

Rebuffed by Secretary Daniels when he suggested serving during the war in naval uniform and again when he wished to visit Europe during the early part of the war, Assistant Secretary of the Navy Franklin D. Roosevelt finally obtained permission to visit the Allied countries in order to tend to expenditures, leases of buildings and land, and other contracts. With a small staff he left from New York on a destroyer on 9 July 1918 and arrived at Portsmouth, England, on the twenty-first. Of his visit to Croix d'Hins he wrote:

> On our way back to Bordeaux we ran south about 15 miles to the wonderful new radio station which our Navy is putting up for the French Government at Croix d'Hins. Lieut. Commander George C. Sweet, my old friend of the Pacific Coast trip, is in charge. None of the steel for the 8 great towers is up, but the material is rapidly arriving.

Roosevelt returned home in October, only to be sent across again early in 1919 to supervise the demobilization of American naval personnel and equipment. He was authorized to determine the status of all major contracts and financial obligations of the U.S. Navy and in addition to approve and enact settlements of any obligations or claims resulting from U.S. naval operations undertaken in the fifty-four naval bases, twenty-five port offices, and several radio stations in Europe. As he put it, his "biggest deal" concerned the Lafayette Radio Station. When the French attempted to delay a settlement, he informed the Prime Minister, Tardieu, that all uninstalled equipment and material would be returned to the United States unless he agreed immediately to take the station over. Tardieu perforce replied that France wanted the station finished and would pay for it on the basis of its cost to the United States, to which Roosevelt agreed.

BIBLIOGRAPHY

A. U.S. Navy, Bureau of Yards and Docks, *Activities of the Bureau of Yards and Docks, Navy Department, World War, 1917-1918* (Washington: GPO, 1921); U.S. Navy Department, Bureau of Engineering, *History of the Bureau of Engineering, Navy Department, During the World War* (Washington: GPO, 1922).

B. D. Graham Copeland, "Steel Tower Construction at the World's Greatest Radio Station," U.S. Naval Institute *Proceedings* 46 (Dec. 1920):1903-19; Elliott Roosevelt, ed., *F.D.R.: His Personal Letters, 1905-1928* (New York: Duell, Sloan, and Pearce, 1948), p. 437; Capt. L.S. Howeth, USN (Ret.), *History of Communications-Electronics in the U.S. Navy* (Washington: GPO, 1963), pp. 208-9, 238-39.

CUA VIET, REPUBLIC OF VIETNAM, U.S. NAVAL SUPPORT ACTIVITY, 1967–1970 The most northerly of the Navy's bases in the Republic of Vietnam, Cua Viet was for much of the war there under mortar, rocket, artillery, or ground attack by the North Vietnamese Army. But because of its location at the mouth of the Cua Viet River, which skirted the southern boundary of the Demilitarized Zone (DMZ), the base was well situated to provide fuel, ammunition, supplies, and construction material to forward Marine and Army combat forces. In addition, the headquarters and sizable river patrol units of Task Force Clearwater used Cua Viet as a base to secure the vital river line of communication. Although the Army dredge *Hyde*, the *Coconino County* (LST-603), and YFU-59 were damaged and YFU-62 and a mechanized landing craft (LCM-8) were sunk between 1967 and 1969, the task force and attached minesweeeping units kept the waterway open. This was especially critical during the trying days of the Tet Offensive of 1968.

In March 1967 the Naval Support Activity, Danang, Detachment Cua Viet, was established to augment the efforts of the nearby base at Dong Ha (q.v.) in the provision of logistic support to American and allied forces in the DMZ area. Cua Viet served as a transshipment point for supplies intended for Dong Ha. The detachment's tasks were made difficult not only by enemy action, but also by the physical environment. The wind and rain of the northeast monsoon were particularly harsh there. Outside the river entrance, shoals posed a great hazard to naval vessels making the 90-nautical-mile passage to and from Danang. Crossing the bar proved equally dangerous until the *Helbar*, a Canadian dredge, cleared a channel, a task other craft repeated in following years. The river itself was difficult to traverse because of shifting sand bars and enemy direct fire weapons. In March 1967 the *Caroline County* (LST-1126) became the first ship of that size to enter the river and tie up at Cua Viet.

The sixty-one-man naval logistic detachment gradually improved the facilities at the base. Initially, the LST ramp consisted of connected metal matting, but by the end of 1967 a more permanent soil and cement hardpan was in place. The naval unit also increased the efficiency of the existing ship-to-shore fuel line and storage tank facility. Tankers discharged fuel at Cua Viet, and it was then transferred to LCM-8s and towed bladders for the run to Dong Ha. In addition, the detachment operated a small-boat repair facility and cargo staging area.

As the South Vietnamese began to assume a greater combat role in the war, U.S. forces were withdrawn from forward areas such as the DMZ. Task Force Clearwater headquarters and a number of river patrol units deployed to Tan My in February 1970. At the same time, Naval Support Activity, Danang, Detachment Cua Viet, was disestablished, and the site was redesignated an advanced tactical support base for limited support of forward naval units. Soon afterward, all U.S. naval forces at Cua Viet were withdrawn to the Danang area.

BIBLIOGRAPHY

A. Commander Naval Forces, Vietnam, "The Naval War in Vietnam," May 1970 (Washington: Naval Historical Center, Operational Archives Branch).

B. K. P. Huff, "Building the Advanced Base at Danang," U.S. Naval Institute *Naval Review* 94 (May 1968):88-113; S. A. Swarztrauber, "River Patrol Relearned," U.S. Naval Institute *Naval Review* 96 (May 1970):120-57; Frank C. Collins, Jr., "Maritime Support of the Campaign in I Corps," U.S. Naval Institute *Naval Review* 97 (May 1971):156-79; Richard L. Schreadley, "The Naval War in Vietnam, 1950-1970," U.S.

Naval Institute *Naval Review* 97 (May 1971):180-211; Edwin B. Hooper, *Mobility, Support, Endurance: A Story of Naval Operational Logistics in the Vietnam War, 1965-1968* (Washington: GPO, 1972); Richard Tregaskis, *Southeast Asia: Building the Bases: The History of Construction in Southeast Asia* (Washington: GPO, 1975).

EDWARD J. MAROLDA

CUBI POINT, LUZON, REPUBLIC OF THE PHILIPPINES, U.S. NAVAL AIR STATION, 1951– NAS Cubi Point is located on Subic Bay, on the island of Luzon, Bataan Peninsula, Republic of the Philippines, sixty air miles northwest of Manila. It is on land owned by the Republic of the Philippines and used in accordance with the 1947 bases agreement made by the United States with the Philippines. It is leased to the United States for a period of ninety years on a rent-free basis.

Because of the vision of Admiral Arthur W. Radford, then Commander in Chief, U.S. Pacific Fleet, plans for Cubi Point were formulated in early 1951; construction started in December of that year. It was built entirely by Seabees, who undertook the greatest earthmoving project ever attempted. Some ninety-foot cuts were made, and eighty-five foot fills, by moving about 18 million cubic yards of earth and 15 million yards of coral. The station was commissioned on 25 July 1956, Capt. Page Knight, USN, commanding.

The mission of Cubi Point was to "maintain and operate facilities and provide services and material to support operations of aviation activities and units of the operating forces of the Navy and other activities and units, as designated by the Chief of Naval Operations." Among its tasks were: to provide dockside services to fleet aviation ships; to serve as a secondary stock point; to maintain air terminal facilities for logistic aircraft and authorized commercial air lines; to operate and maintain limited seaplane facilities; to provide support for personnel assigned to the Naval Magazine, Subic Bay (q.v.); to provide support for personnel assigned to communication units present; to support operations of transient aircraft; and to provide administrative, aerological, aircraft maintenance facilities, ammunition storage, berthing, chaplain, clothing and small stores, communications, dental, educational, flight operations, fuel issue, industrial relations, legal, medical, messing, ordnance, photographic, postal, recreational, security, service information, small boat, station maintenance, supply, telephone, transportation, and utilities support for station operation and tenant activities as required. The original activities and units for which support was to be provided were Headquarters, Commander Naval Air Base, Fleet Air, Philippines; one fleet aircraft service squadron; one utility squadron detachment; and Naval Magazine, Subic Bay.

Cubi had just shaken down when it was called upon to deal with various crises. In mid-December 1957, because of the Indonesian crisis, Marine Air Group 11 began phasing into the station for training exercises. Various other air units came aboard, then divisional troops, and finally a Marine Expeditionary Force consisting of attack aircraft, helicopters, and ground troops. The Force embarked in an antisubmarine carrier and, upon completing its mission, returned to the station. Although MAG 11 was replaced by MAG 12, MAG 16, and other groups, a Marine Air Group remained at Cubi through June 1958.

Because of the Formosan crisis, in August 1958 various transport, reconnaissance, attack, and fighter squadrons deployed to Cubi Point, and air groups from various carriers in the area used its field for training and exercises. Involved were seven air group detachments, an antisubmarine helicopter detachment, and two MAGs. At various times the following carriers called: *Ticonderoga* (CVA-14), *Bon Homme Richard* (CVA-31), *Princeton* (CVS-37), *Hornet* (CVA-12), *Philippine Sea* (CVS-47), *Shangri La* (CVA-38), *Hancock* (CVA-19), and *Kearsarge* (CVA-33). All the requirements of these carriers and their air groups were met by station personnel totaling 45 officers, 459 men, and 593 civilians.

All construction at Cubi Point was of a permanent nature. Because wood was subject to quick deterioration and termite damage, structures were built of reinforced concrete. There were six berthing spaces for ships; six 180-man barracks; one 260-man bachelor officers' quarters; a 8,000-by-200-foot runway; twenty-six married officers' quarters, twenty-four married enlisted men's quarters; and ammunition at NAVMAG, Subic Bay, located adjacent to the air station. In addition there were a Marine Barracks and the usual utilities and recreational areas.

With the departure of Mobile Construction Battalion Unit 5 on 14 March 1959, all construction and repairs devolved upon the Public Works Department and local contractors. Although Commander Fleet Air Philippines was redesignated Commander Fleet Air Southwest Pacific and relocated as NAS Agana, Guam (q.v.), Cubi remained the headquarters of Commander Naval Air Base Philippines. In addition to many VIPs, eight carriers were serviced by Cubi in 1959.

With the Vietnam War warming up, Cubi became ever more important. In June 1960, E-15 arresting gear became operational, and on 17 July, E-28, the latter being the first operational installation in the Navy. On 20 August station personnel began working a six-day week, and on 12 December Cubi became the primary stock point for all aircraft engines in the Southwest Pacific. In addition to its own departments, in 1966 Cubi had the following tenant commands: Fleet Intelligence Center Pacific Facility; VRC-50 Fleet Tactical Support Squadron; VAP-61, Heavy Photographic Squadron; VQ-1, Fleet Air Reconnaissance Squadron; VAW-1, Carrier Airborne Early Warning; and VC-5A, Fleet Composite Squadron, the last of which could carry nuclear weapons, a stockpile of which was kept at Cubi.

In addition to Philippine Air Lines, which provided commercial service on a revocable permit basis, on 6 June 1966 there was established at Cubi a Naval Air Terminal Cargo Office/Naval Overseas Cargo Office, with most of the personnel and cargo going to Vietnam. Also, on 14 October, a Special Landing Force Camp that used fifty-five buildings, came under the command of the air station commander. The increased pace at Cubi, due largely to the Vietnam war, can be measured by the doubling of engine repair work in 1966; an average of

9,434 air flights per month; and an increase in cargo and ordnance handling from 200,000 pounds a month in 1965 to over 1 million pounds a month in 1966. Soon forty-five C-118, C-121, C-124, C-130, C-135, C-141, DC-7, CD-8, CL-44, and 707-type transport aircraft were serving as a direct channel for transportation from Cubi Point to Danang, Republic of Vietnam (q.v.).

In addition to increasing its terminal operations 78 percent in 1966, Cubi furnished 3 million gallons of aviation gasoline and JP-5 fuel per month; requisitions for supplies increased from 6,202 in December 1965 to 11,000 a year later; and 8,000 units of equipment and components from aircraft carriers in the South China Sea were either repaired or shipped to the United States for overhaul. To be able to perform all this work, the personnel level at Cubi was increased more than 40 percent during the year—from 708 in January to 1,000 on 31 December 1966. So pressing was the load of work, however, that the station commander asked for another increase, to 1,362 men. The increased pace was also shown in construction projects, with fifty-one projects authorized at a cost of $13.3 million; fifteen under way at a cost of $13.1 million; and five others costing $1 million. Medical monthly outpatient examinations alone increased 25 percent. There was also one serious tragedy, as reported in the station newspaper, the *Afterburner*: a disastrous fire in the *Oriskany* (CVA-34) on 26 October 1966 resulted in the return of forty-three bodies to Cubi.

The year 1967 brought still further pressure on Cubi Point. While there was no change in tenants, aircraft maintenance had to be expanded and geared to repair such aircraft as the A-4 *Skyhawk*, F-8 *Crusader*, and F-4 *Phantom*. In consequence, what in July 1965 had been one of the smallest aircraft maintenance departments had grown to be the largest of its kind in the Pacific Fleet, with between 30 and 60 percent of the work involving support to aviation units based elsewhere, including 4,500 transient aircraft alone in 1967. At the end of that year the capital investment at Cubi Point approached $21 million, and its annual budget was about $2.61 million. The year set many new records: 171,733 landings and takeoffs, for a monthly average of 14,311; lifting 60 million pounds of cargo; augmentation of the station's Paramedic Rescue Training Activity; expansion of the jet fuel storage facility by adding another 50,000-barrel tank—and VIPs calling without end.

Cubi enjoyed no letup in 1968 and 1969 except for a forty-five-day period during which its runway was closed so that it could be lengthened to 9,000 feet—at a cost of $1.2 million. (The extra load was placed on NAS Sangley Point [q.v.].) But some respite came in 1970, when three squadrons departed and flight operations were about 20,000 less than in 1969, cargo lifted being about half that of 1969. Yet carriers were in port on forty-one occasions for a total of 141 days, twenty-six aircraft carriers, landing and personnel helicopters (LPHs) were in port for 149 days, and thirty-nine additional ships visited, as did 367 VIPs.

By 1971 the Navy-wide reduction in manpower hit Cubi as it did many other installations. Sangley transferred two squadrons, which meant an increase of 50 percent in workload with an 11 percent decrease in personnel. During the year thirty-five carriers called for 189 days, as did ten LPHs for 116 days, and an amazing 461 VIPs arrived. A newcomer was the P-3 antisubmarine *Orion* aircraft. Another first came in 1973 in the form of the first two women line officers. On 17 August Admiral Radford, who had suggested building Cubi, died of cancer; appropriate memorial serivces were held. With the Vietnam pullout in progress, flight operations at Cubi reached their greatest total ever—176,459—and crash programs were instituted on fuel conservation, race relations education, and drug education, with seminars for 1,400 personnel being held on race relations alone in 1973. Ample attention was also devoted to Project Handclasp, through which hospital beds, food, medical supplies, toys, and so on were given to sufferers of natural disasters or to the poor; native youths were employed for summer work programs; and tours were given, not only to VIPs, but to schoolchildren and other groups, by members of the Public Affairs Office. Flight operations diminished somewhat, to 190,165; almost as many passengers were taken out (19,936) as were taken in (17,586); and more than twice as much cargo and mail were flown out as were shipped in. Medivac flights numbered 123, and construction worth $5.5 million was under way.

The year 1975 saw many volunteers from Cubi work to prepare their major recreation center, at Grande Island, to receive Vietnamese refugees. For three months, berthing, food, medical care, and recreational facilities were provided for 82,190 persons. In addition, 12,271 tons of cargo were handled. It took 282 Air Force C-141 and C-130 aircraft to receive and load that number around the clock; in addition, the Cubi air terminal processed over 40,000 persons and received 1 million pounds of cargo.

Flight operations at Cubi numbered 149,813 in 1978, with these undertaken by the latest models of transport aircraft and HH-46A and CH-46D helicopters. There were fewer flight operations in the next two years. In 1980 the last Southeast Asian refugees departed from the 500-man camp on Grande Island.

In 1983 Cubi Point had five permanent aviation units and twenty-seven tenant commands. Its great period of growth was from 1957 to 1975, coinciding with the rise and fall of the U.S. effort in Vietnam. It still handles between 100 and 150 flights daily and its key location remains valuable, for it serves as the primary support base in the logistics pipeline for both the Pacific and the Indian Ocean.

BIBLIOGRAPHY

A. "Command History, Naval Air Station, Cubi Point, Luzon, Republic of the Philippines," 1951- (Washington: Naval Historical Center, Operational Archives Branch); "Cubi Point Naval Air Station," Summary Cards (Washington Navy Yard: Naval Aviation History Office).

CURACAO/ARUBA, NETHERLANDS WEST INDIES, U.S. NAVAL OPERATING BASE.

See Caribbean, The, U.S. Naval Bases.

D

DAKAR, FRENCH MOROCCO.
See North Africa, U.S. Naval Bases.

DANANG, REPUBLIC OF VIETNAM, U.S. NAVAL SUPPORT ACTIVITY, 1964–1973 At the height of the Vietnam War, the support establishment at Danang in the Republic of Vietnam was the Navy's largest overseas shore command. From that port city, over 200,000 U.S., South Vietnamese, and allied forces fighting in the I Corps Tactical Zone were supplied with all the necessities of war.

Long before that conflict, in 1845, the U.S. Navy first made contact with Danang (then called Tourane by Westerners) when Capt. John "Mad Jack" Percival sailed the USS *Constitution* into the harbor to free a French missionary purportedly imprisoned there. Whether he succeeded or not is unclear, but the zealous officer's use of an armed landing party to take hostages was an afront to the Vietnamese that subsequent American apologies did not completely assuage.

Apparently the passage of 119 years settled the issue, for when U.S. naval forces established facilities for an advisory detachment at Danang in 1964, the South Vietnamese government was anxious for military assistance in the desperate struggle against its communist foe. At that point, both American and Vietnamese leaders recognized the port city's strategic importance. Danang was South Vietnam's second largest city after Saigon, the capital, and boasted the only natural harbor capable of accommodating deep-water vessels in the northern region of the country. The city lay astride the only road and rail routes that paralleled the long coast of South Vietnam, and commanded the approaches from North Vietnam through the Demilitarized Zone (DMZ) that separated the two antagonists. In addition, aircraft flying from Danang's airfield would be able in a short time to reach targets in northern South Vietnam, in the Laotian and North Vietnamese panhandles, and in the Gulf of Tonkin.

The possession of Danang by friendly forces was considered vital. Concluding at the end of 1964 that the conflict in Southeast Asia was about to enter a period of open hostilities, Pacific commanders initiated defensive measures and made preparations for the construction of additional airfield runways and for base and port facilities, to include piers, warehouses, ammunition magazines, and fuel storage tanks. Marine helicopter and ground security units were stationed at the airfield.

When major Marine ground and air forces deployed to Danang in March 1965, the action symbolized the beginning of large-scale conventional warfare in Southeast Asia. For the next four years, the two-division III Marine Amphibious Force and various Army divisions joined the Army of Vietnam in a campaign to defeat the enemy in the I Corps region. The Navy also provided combat formations, such as the Coastal Surveillance Force, which patrolled the northern littoral in search of infiltrating trawlers and junks, and Task Force Clearwater, whose river patrol boats (PBRs) fought to keep the rivers of I Corps open to allied logistic traffic. Based at Danang were the headquarters of the Thirtieth Naval Construction Regiment and, later in the war, those of the Third Naval Construction Brigade and the Thirty-second Naval Construction Regiment.

When the Marines moved ashore in the spring of 1965, naval commanders found the port at Danang inadequate for sustained logistic support of large forces. Most oceangoing vessels were unable to approach offloading sites, which were located along either bank of the Han River. Only coastal vessels, junks, sampans, and other small craft could make the passage up the narrow, 15-foot channel to the piers and the quay. Lightering operations also proved difficult when ships anchored in the roadstead were subjected to the heavy seas and high winds of the winter monsoon. Winds of 35 knots and 14-foot swells were not uncommon.

Port facilities were limited to three small piers, three tank landing ship (LST) ramps, and a stone quay. Warehouses were small and few in number, and cargo staging areas were constricted by residential and commercial buildings. The main road exiting the waterfront made a narrow passage through the congested downtown area. Only one limited-capacity bridge connected both sides of the river. What cargo handling equipment existed was unsuitable.

Because U.S. leaders were not sure how long the Marine Expeditionary Force would be deployed ashore in the Danang area, they hesitated in establishing a permanent, landbased naval logistic command during the first half of 1965. As a result, the Seventh Fleet's Amphibious Force managed the initial support effort in I Corps. Elements of the Pacific Fleet's Service Force and Mine Force, Naval Beach Group 1, Cargo Handling Battalions 1 and 2, and nucleus port crew, amphibious, underwater demolition team, and explosive ordnance disposal units moved in to develop and protect the supply line into the port. The III Marine Amphibious Force was charged with staging cargo and distributing it to forward units.

In mid-July, however, naval units in Danang assumed responsibility for receiving, offloading, stowing, and delivering supplies, fuel, and ammunition to allied forces in I Corps. This included the transshipment of material from Danang to outlying ports and beaches and the operation of those terminals. Harbor defense and other security duties also were assigned tasks. Finally, the Navy was directed to construct and manage a station hospital.

On 15 October 1965 the Naval Support Activity (NSA), Danang, was formally established and took on the logistic support mission, once it was clear that the deployment of Marine forces to the northern reaches of South Vietnam would not be temporary. To accomplish his tasks, the NSA commander controlled a wide variety of craft, including mechanized landing craft (LCM-3, LCM-6, and LCM-8), utility landing craft (LCU), harbor utility craft (YFU), small harbor tugs (YTLs), open lighters (YCs), refrigerated barges (YFRN), Army LARCs, and a refrigerator ship. In addition the fleet provided several LSTs, a dock landing ship (LSD), and an attack transport (APA), the latter to quarter and mess the men of NSA while base construction was underway. Most of the men moved ashore in March 1967. The harbor security force operated 50-foot picket boats, 16-foot Boston Whalers, and landing craft.

The Navy's Seabees began the construction project in Danang, which eventually became one of the largest port and base complexes in the world, using material assembled in Advanced Base Functional Component packages. Based on World War II experience, naval leaders had recognized that certain building materials and equipment were essential for the rapid establishment of forward logistics facilities. Thus within one year of its establishment NSA Danang boasted three deep-draft piers, which jutted from a landfill behind Observation Point, for deep-draft ships; two 300-foot wooden piers; and a facility designated the Bridge Cargo Complex that consisted of 1,600 feet of wharf for lighters, 500,000 square feet of covered storage space, and 300,000 cubic feet of refrigerated storage space. Although the combat forces in I Corps would require even more support, by October 1966 NSA Danang was able to handle over 200,000 measurement tons of cargo each month.

Naval logisticians also worked to improve the provision of fuel. Existing facilities and tanker trucks owned by the Shell and Esso oil companies were augmented by Marine vehicles, portable storage bladders, and an amphibious fuel line laid along the sea bottom between Red Beach and an offshore point; another line extended to the Marine air station at nearby Marble Mountain.

During this same period, the Seabees constructed the Naval Support Activity, Danang, Station Hospital, which cared for the increasingly heavy battle casualties. Although the Viet Cong destroyed a 100-bed unit with rockets and mortars in October 1965, by the following June the eighteen-building medical facility had 330 beds operational. And by then the wards and operating rooms were air conditioned. In August 1966 over 400 beds were available for the wounded and sick.

During the first year of operation, the NSA's problems were legion. A number of landing craft and harbor craft types were found to be inadequate; cargo handling equipment was scarce; improper cargo loading, packaging, and palletizing caused delays; and port personnel were inadequate. The effort to acquire additional real estate for port construction was delayed by the need to respect

Vietnamese religious and cultural customs and by the South Vietnamese government, U.S. Marine, and Military Assistance Command Vietnam (MACV) bureaucratic processes. The winter monsoon brought with it rough weather that often stopped cargo operations at Danang and increased the danger and difficulty of transshipping supplies to outlying ports in I Corps. These problems, combined with a surge of ship arrivals at the end of 1965, created a temporary logistic bottleneck.

However, moderating weather, incoming equipment and personnel, and refined operating procedures soon eased the situation. By February 1966 there was a thirty-six-hour period in which no cargo remained to be offloaded from waiting ships. NSA Danang handled 135,500 short tons of supplies, on the average, each month during the year.

The next two years witnessed additional efforts to improve the port's logistic capability. Over 130 rough terrain and warehouse forklifts and 20 cranes were dispatched to Danang to lessen waterfront congestion. NSA established a small craft repair facility to maintain its growing fleet of harbor and coastal vessels. This work was aided by a small floating dry dock (AFDL) stationed in the harbor. A ten-section causeway was installed so that LSTs could better unload bulky construction material. New facilities at Danang enabled the SS *Bienville* to inaugurate containerized cargo operations in South Vietnam during August 1967. Three months later, the SS *Transglobe*, a newly designed "roll-on roll-off" ship, began transporting vehicles between Okinawa and the Republic of Vietnam. At the same time, Danang became the largest military-commercial fuel complex in-country with a storage capacity of over 500,000 barrels. And the Danang Station Hospital treated over 21,500 combat casualties, 44,000 non-battle patients, and 1 million outpatients during the first four years of the facility's operation.

Even as Danang burgeoned, NSA detachments at outlying ports in I Corps enhanced the flow of logistic support to the combat units. The naval units established at Cua Viet (q.v.) and Dong Ha (q.v.) on the Cua Viet River during 1967 provided the Third Marine Division fighting south of the DMZ with fuel, ammunition, food, and other supplies transported from Danang. That same year, the NSA detachments at Hue and Tan My (*see* Hue-Tan My-Phu Bai, Republic of Vietnam, U.S. Naval Support Activity) secured the logistic lifeline to allied troops in the vicinity of the old Vietnamese imperial capital. This effort was helped by the mooring at Tan My in December of Mobile Base I, which consisted of a number of connected pontoons that carried supply, repair, maintenance, and other shops. The unit had been assembled in Danang and then towed to the mouth of the Hue River. NSA continued to back up the detachment established earlier in the war at Chu Lai (q.v.) to the south, while a naval contingent was deployed to Sa Huynh (q.v.) in 1968 to support Army combat forces in the Duc Pho region. With this logistic network in place, the Navy was able to maintain vital support to allied troops fighting desperately to defeat the enemy's Tet Offensive.

NSA Danang reached its peak of performance in 1969 as the war entered a new phase. The command controlled almost 250 ships, landing craft, lighters, tugs, barges, and floating cranes, making it the greatest concentration of such vessels in Southeast Asia. The command was manned by 450 officers and 10,000 sailors and controlled a civilian work force of over 11,000 Vietnamese and civilian contractor personnel. Deep-draft vessels were able to discharge their cargo at three piers, while LSTs and smaller craft used the Tien Sha, Bridge, Museum, and Ferry cargo facilities. The port controlled 900,000 square feet of supply depot space, 2.7 million square feet of open storage space, and 500,000 cubic feet of refrigerated storage space. On the average, NSA handled over 320,000 short tons of cargo each month. The two major fuel tank farms at Danang reached a capacity of 50 million gallons that year.

As U.S. forces began withdrawing from I Corps in 1969, the logistic mission at Danang was redirected to support the Vietnamization of the war. In May NSA Danang was charged with assisting the Vietnamese armed forces to establish a functioning logistic system for the I Corps area prior to the turnover of resources by American naval units. Part of this entailed a comprehensive training program, the purpose of which was to replace skilled and semi-skilled Korean and other workers with Vietnamese. December 1969 witnessed the move to Okinawa (q.v.) of the Thirtieth Naval Construction Regiment headquarters and the transfer to the Vietnamese Navy of various landing craft, barges, and lighters. In May 1970 the Station Hospital at Danang was turned over to Army control. The following month, the support activity was redesignated Naval Support Facility, Danang. Thereafter, the naval command concentrated on training Vietnamese replacements as the Army asssumed responsibility for support of allied forces in I Corps. The naval presence in Danang was reduced further in November 1971 when the Third Naval Construction Brigade hauled down its colors. The support facility was disestablished in April 1972. Finally, by 29 March 1973, several fleet air detachments and the Naval Communications Station, Philippines, Detachment Danang, the last naval units in the Danang area, had been redeployed or disestablished in place. Thus ended the Navy's momentous nine-year sojourn in Danang.

BIBLIOGRAPHY

A. Commander, Naval Forces, Vietnam, "The Naval War in Vietnam," May 1970 (Washington: Naval Historical Center, Operational Archives Branch); Commander Naval Forces Vietnam, "Monthly Historical Reports, 1965-1971" (Washington: Naval Historical Center, Operational Archives Branch); Service Force, U.S. Pacific Fleet, "Command Histories, 1967-1972" (Washington: Naval Historical Center, Operational Archives Branch).

B. K. P. Huff, "Building the Advanced Base at DaNang," U.S. Naval Institute *Naval Review* 94 (May 1968):88-113; Charles J. Merdinger, "Civil Engineers, Seabees, and Bases in Vietnam," U.S. Naval Institute *Naval Review* 96 (May 1970):254-75; Richard L. Schreadley, "The Naval War in Vietnam, 1950-1970," U.S. Naval Institute *Naval Review* 97 (May 1971):180-211; Edwin B. Hooper, *Mobility, Support, Endurance: A*

Story of Naval Operational Logistics in the Vietnam War, 1965-1968 (Washington: GPO, 1972); Edwin B. Hooper, Dean C. Allard, and Oscar P. Fitzgerald, *The Setting of the Stage to 1959*, Vol. 1 of *The United States Navy and the Vietnam Conflict* (Washington: GPO, 1976).

EDWARD J. MAROLDA

DARIEN, PANAMA CANAL ZONE.
See Panama Canal Zone, U.S. Naval Radio Stations.

DARTMOUTH, ENGLAND.
See United Kingdom, U.S. World War II Naval Bases.

DARWIN, AUSTRALIA, U.S. NAVAL ADVANCE BASE, 1942–1945 A deep-water port in northeastern Australia, Darwin (12°28′S., 130°50′E.), in the Northern Territory became an advance naval base for U.S. naval forces in the Southwest Pacific. It was the most northerly port in Australia and faced the Netherlands East Indies. Before the outbreak of the Pacific War it featured Royal Australian naval and air force stations, but it came into prominence in December 1941 when the Chief of Naval Operations selected it as the prospective main logistics base for the Asiatic Fleet. By January 1942 several auxiliaries and tenders had gathered there to support the main Asiatic Fleet operating base at Surabaya, Java (q.v.), 1,200 miles northwest of Darwin. Late in January it was decided to shift the main fleet supply base to safer waters at Fremantle-Perth (q.v.) in southwestern Australia. A surprise Japanese air raid on 19 February 1942 sank eight ships at Darwin and led to its abandonment as a U.S. naval base. However, it remained an important air base where Australian and U.S. Army Air Forces air units fought for air supremacy with Japanese aviation forces based on Timor.

American naval activity at Darwin resumed in the spring of 1943 when Motor Torpedo Boat Base 10 was sent there to support PTs operating in Torres Strait between Australia and New Guinea. Darwin was prepared should the PTs have to withdraw from NAS Thursday Island (q.v.), but that did not occur, and PTs never operated from Darwin. However, MTB Base 10 personnel helped service patrol planes and became the nucleus of a light craft base at Darwin. That summer the U.S. Navy agreed to supply the Royal Australian Air Force with aerial mines for use against Japanese shipping in the Dutch East Indies, and Seabees in August 1943 arrived to construct a mine depot. Concurrently, personnel from the submarine base at Fremantle set up at Darwin an advance submarine base where boats could stop for fuel and obtain additional torpedoes. Darwin was a convenient site for mid-patrol refurbishing by submarines headed north and back south toward Fremantle.

The Darwin advance naval base was formally established on 21 November 1943, and in January 1944 Seabees, after improving base and harbor facilities, finally started work on the mine depot at the RAAF station on Frances Bay. They completed it in April 1944. Darwin continued supporting submarine operations until the spring of 1945, when the Fremantle base was moved to the Philippines. U.S. naval activities ceased at Darwin after 31 July 1945.

BIBLIOGRAPHY

A. U.S. Navy, Bureau of Yards and Docks, *Building the Navy's Bases in World War II*, 2 vols. (Washington: GPO, 1947); U.S. Navy, "U.S. Naval Bases in the South and Southwest Pacific (and Central Pacific Forward) in World War II," 1 November 1954 (Washington: Naval Historical Center, Operational Archives Branch); "U.S. Naval Administration in World War II: Submarine Commands," 2 vols. (Washington: Naval Historical Center, Operational Archives Branch).

B. Samuel E. Morison, *The Rising Sun in the Pacific 1931-April 1942* (Boston: Little Brown, 1948); Theodore Roscoe, *United States Submarine Operations in World War II* (Annapolis, Md.: U.S. Naval Institute, 1949); Capt. Robert J. Bulkley, *At Close Quarters: PT Boats in the United States Navy* (Washington: Navy Department, Naval History Division, 1962).

JOHN B. LUNDSTROM

DELLYS, ALGERIA.

See North Africa, U.S. Naval Bases.

DEPTFORD, ENGLAND.

See United Kingdom, U.S. World War II Naval Bases.

DIEGO GARCIA ISLAND, INDIAN OCEAN, U.S. NAVAL BASE, 1973–

Situated near the center of the Indian Ocean, at 7°21′S., 72°28′E. is the tiny atoll of Diego Garcia, British Indian Ocean Territory (BIOT). Its eleven square miles of low-lying sand and coral make it the largest of the five coral islands comprising the Chagos Archipelago. Although the origin of its name is clouded, many believe that it is derived from the name of the Portuguese mariner who is reputed to have discovered the atoll in the late fifteenth century. The territory has been British ever since the Royal Navy wrested control of the Indian Ocean from the French during the Napoleonic Wars.

The Indian Ocean is the third largest in the world. Its waters link sixteen countries bordering the Indian Ocean basin and an additional five island nations, such as the Seychelles and Sri Lanka. Its vast expanse covers 28 million square miles. Oil tankers sail in and out of the area via the Cape of Good Hope, the Suez Canal, the Indonesian Straits, and the waters off Australia. The distances from Diego Garcia to mainland points are formidable: 3,500 miles to Simonstown, South Africa; 3,550 miles to the U.S. naval base in Subic Bay (q.v.), the Philippines; and 2,850 miles to Cockburn Sound, Australia (site of a U.S. communications station).

The island boasts a myriad of exotic birds, land crabs, and, unfortunately, flies, which are a major nuisance. Rainfall may be as low as four inches a month, or as high as fourteen. Sunny days prevail with occasional rain and light winds, with monthly temperatures ranging from 85°F to 76°F. October to March is the season of the northwest monsoon.

When World War II ended, the United States, as the leader of the so-called free world, assumed the status of global policeman. At the same time Washington officials became aware that if the United States were to preserve peace in the postwar world, its armed forces would need island bases to support its naval and air operations. Among those individuals who foresaw this need were Paul H. Nitze, then an official in the Foreign Economic Administration, and Capt. Arleigh A. Burke, USN, at the Navy Department.

By 1960, when Nitze had become Assistant Secretary of Defense for International Security Affairs and Admiral Burke was Chief of Naval Operations, the move to acquire base rights at Diego Garcia received attention from the high command. Among the senior officers on Admiral Burke's staff who were prime movers on the project were Rear Adms. Roy Johnson, Thomas H. Moorer, Horacio Rivero, and George H. Miller. Capt. (later Rear Adm.) John M. Lee, Stuart M. Barker, a senior civilian staff member, and Rear Adm. E. P. Aurand also pressed hard for the base.

From this point on, the concept of a shared British-American base went smoothly. Prime Minister Harold Wilson was persuaded that Britain could continue to maintain a presence only with the help of the United States. The U.S. State Department expressed its satisfaction inasmuch as the idea of a joint command would demonstrate to an uneasy Congress that the U.S. Navy was not "going it alone" in the Indian Ocean.

As a naval and air base, Diego Garcia offered the Navy a potential communications station to keep contact with nuclear submarines as well as with ships and aircraft operating in the Indian Ocean. Additionally, planes of the Navy and Air Force would have a convenient refueling and repair base to support their aerial surveillance of shipping. Diego Garcia is in a key position in a line from Australia to the horn of Africa and the Persian Gulf. Last, a U.S. base at Diego Garcia would demonstrate to uneasy neutralist nations that the U.S. presence in the area was fixed and firm.

Concurrently, the Soviet Navy began to increase its activity in the Indian Ocean area as the shrinking British Navy recalled its ships to home waters. By 1968 the Soviet Indian Ocean squadron rivalled the U.S. Navy's small Middle East Force, which had symbolized American sea power in the Persian Gulf since 1949. On land, the Soviets had established fleet facilities at Aden, Hodeida, and Socotra, and on the Dahlak Archipelago in Eritrea.

Problems in acquiring the island arose in 1965. At the time, Diego Garcia was attached administratively to Mauritius, a British colony that was scheduled to become independent in 1968. However, Britain arranged for Diego Garcia to be detached from Mauritius, compensating the latter for the loss of the atoll by payment of £3 million. Thereupon, on 10 November 1965, Britain declared the island to be British Indian Ocean Territory, thus paving the way for a U.S.-U.K. treaty for a joint naval base.

The new pact (an executive agreement) became official on 30 December 1966 when both nations agreed to make use of the atoll for defense purposes for fifty years. Administration of the island would be a joint affair. It now remained for the Navy to persuade Congress as well as Pentagon civilian officials to approve the appropriation of funds to convert the atoll into a military base and communications station. As matters turned out, the funds eventually were provided, but only after much delay and persuasion of skeptical members of Congress who believed that if the United States built up Diego Garcia, then the Russians would react by enlarging their bases in the region.

By 1971 the British government had moved out about 1,200 copra plantation contract workers and their families from Diego Garcia to Mauritius or the Seychelles. Meanwhile, thanks to $5.4 million authorized by Congress, the Navy Seabees in 1970 and 1971 began construction of a communications facility and lengthened the airfield to accommodate giant C-130 *Hercules* cargo aircraft. On 20 March 1973 the U.S. Naval Communications Station was activated, while at the same time the Royal Navy established its small administrative command.

Between 1971 and 1974 Congress authorized $48 million, enabling the Seabees to dredge the lagoon, enlarge the airfield, and build shops, quarters, and warehouses. These latest improvements ensured that the Air Force and Navy could count on a base for their long-range aircraft, including B-52 bombers. Likewise, the Indian Ocean battle group now had a replenishment port, thus removing a large burden borne by the logistics ships that had regularly replenished the battle groups under way. By late 1973 the Navy could boast of a base that could communicate globally via satellite with distant ships and stations. Large carriers could anchor in the lagoon. Finally, combat ships and aircraft could be furnished with fuel, provisions, and repair assistance.

Predictably, the buildup of this defense base met with opposition abroad from neutralist groups. In the British Parliament, Labor Party spokesmen asserted that the base would destroy the "equilibrium" of the region. India, fearful of China and anxious to form ties with Russia, condemned the U.S. presence at Diego Garcia. In the United States, William Colby, head of the Central Intelligence Agency, predicted in 1974 that if the government established a base "of some size" on Diego Garcia, the Soviets would take similar steps to expand their bases on the Indian Ocean shores. He did not mention that the Russians had already built an air and naval base at Berbera, Somalia.

Spurred on by their respective national interests, supporters of Diego Garcia included the Shah of Iran; Pakistan, an apprehensive neighbor of Russia; and China, still an implacable enemy of the Soviet Union. This small minority was opposed in the United Nations when, on 16 December 1971, the General Assembly voted to adopt a "Declaration of the Indian Ocean as a Zone of Peace." In Washington, Sen. Mike Mansfield of Montana called on the Senate to disallow appropriations for Diego Garcia on the grounds that the nation was generating an arms buildup in the Indian Ocean. The Senate voted the funds after Defense Secretary James Schlesinger pointed out that Diego Garcia would serve as a balance to the Soviet base at Berbera.

The growing importance of the island became clear on 25 February 1976 when Washington and London signed an executive agreement providing for expansion of the anchorage, the airfield, and the base. This pact was followed by an announcement in October 1977 officially naming the base as a U.S. Naval Support Facility. Its stated mission was to provide air terminal operations, search and rescue, aerology services, aviation shops, and fuel and supply support for planes and ships.

The fall of the Shah of Iran in 1979, followed eventually by Washington's break in diplomatic relations with the revolutionary government, underlined the stark fact that the West's supply of Middle East oil could no longer be taken for granted. The Soviet invasion of Afghanistan during Christmas week in 1979 brought into sharp relief the strategic value of Diego Garcia. President Jimmy Carter announced the possibility that the invasion might be a stepping-stone to Soviet control of the world's oil supply. He responded by immediately ordering two battle groups to the Indian Ocean. He then sought agreement from Britain to again enlarge the base at Diego Garcia. State Department officials were flown to the Middle East to obtain the use of aviation and port facilities at Oman, Kenya, and Somalia. By January 1980 twenty-five U.S. warships were cruising the Arabian Sea, while an equal number of Soviet naval vessels steamed in the area. The strategic value of Diego Garcia had now been demonstrated. However, the security of free world shipping depended on the ability of the U.S. Navy to control the waters of the Indian Ocean.

BIBLIOGRAPHY

A. *Command History, U.S. Naval Communications Station, Diego Garcia, 1973* (Washington: Naval Historical Center, Operational Archives Branch); U.S. Congress, Congressional Research Service, Library of Congress, Report: *Means of Measuring Naval Power with Special Reference to U.S. and Soviet Activities in the Indian Ocean*, 12 May 1974 (Washington: 1974); U.S. Pacific Fleet Instruction 5451.30 of 8 December 1977, Chief of Naval Operations, OPNAV Notice 5450 of 3 November 1977; U.S. Defense Mapping Agency, Hydrographic Topographic Center, *Sailing Directions (enroute) for East Africa and the South Indian Ocean*, Pub. No. 171 (Washington: GPO, 1978).

B. Michael Getler, "U.S. Navy Extends Operation of Warships in Indian Ocean," *The Washington Post*, 7 Jan. 1972; Monoranjan Bezboruah, *U.S. Strategy in the Indian Ocean* (New York: Praeger Publishers, 1977); Alvin J. Cottrell and Walter F. Hahn, *Naval Race or Arms Control in the Indian Ocean* (New York: National Strategy Information Center, Inc., 1978); James H. Noyes, *The Clouded Lens: Persian Gulf Security and U.S. Policy* (Stanford, Calif.: Hoover Institution Press, 1979); Paul B. Ryan, *First Line of Defense: The U.S. Navy since 1945* (Stanford: Hoover Institution Press, 1981).

PAUL B. RYAN

DONG HA, REPUBLIC OF VIETNAM, U.S. NAVAL SUPPORT ACTIVITY, 1967–1970 The base at Dong Ha, located only a few miles south of the

Demilitarized Zone (DMZ) separating North and South Vietnam, was exposed to more enemy action during the war than any other naval facility. The site, on the south bank of the Cua Viet River, was within range of North Vietnamese artillery, rockets, and mortars, and sappers often tested the perimeter defenses. During August and September 1967 alone, the communists destroyed thirteen 10,000-gallon fuel storage bladders and an ammunition dump. In addition, enemy swimmers and water mines inflicted great damage on allied craft tied up at the pier or transiting the river. Still, because of Dong Ha's strategic position astride a river to the sea and the Republic of Vietnam's major north-south highway, Route 1, the risks were warranted. Responsive logistic support for American and allied forces fighting near the DMZ was vital.

Beginning in mid-1966, landing craft transported fuel, ammunition, supplies, and construction material ninety miles from Danang (q.v.) to the mouth of the Cua Viet River and then eight miles upriver to a rudimentary landing at Dong Ha. But these vessels, primarily utility landing craft (LCU) and harbor utility craft (YFU), were ill-suited to this task, especially during the northeast monsoon period, when heavy seas and high winds drove craft into the numerous coastal shoals. Crossing the bar into the Cua Viet was also a dangerous operation. And on the last leg of the journey the vessels were subject to enemy mines and direct fire from the banks.

In March 1967, to improve the efficiency of logistic support operations in the northern I Corps Tactical Zone, naval leaders split the Naval Support Activity, Danang, Detachment Dong Ha, into two sections, with nearby Cua Viet (q.v.) becoming a separate facility. Thereafter, seagoing vessels put in at Cua Viet, where their cargo was transferred to smaller mechanized landing craft (LCM-8) for the short but dangerous trip to Dong Ha.

For the remainder of 1967, the one officer and thirty-four sailors of the detachment at Dong Ha and the attached Marine cargo handling unit worked to push forward such things as 175-mm guns, construction material for a proposed defensive line south of the DMZ, and materials for a major airfield at Quang Tri. In addition, the small airstrip at Dong Ha required continuous repair support due to enemy shelling. By November 1967 the detachment was handling 72,453 measurement tons of supplies a month. Seabees built two offloading sites that could accommodate LCUs and barges, and this additional capacity proved a boon during 1968, for during that year Army and Marine units fought major battles with the North Vietnamese in the DMZ area. That the American combat forces prevailed over the enemy was partly due to the responsive support of the Navy's Dong Ha detachment. In February 1970, after another productive year, the naval unit at Dong Ha was disestablished and its facilities turned over to the Vietnamese as part of the Vietnamization program.

BIBLIOGRAPHY

A. Commander Naval Forces, Vietnam, "The Naval War in Vietnam," May 1970 (Washington: Naval Historical Center, Operational Archives Branch); Service Force, U.S. Pacific Fleet, "Command Histories, 1967-1972" (Washington: Naval Historical Center, Operational Archives Branch).

B. K. P. Huff, ''Building the Advanced Base at DaNang,'' U.S. Naval Institute *Naval Review* 94 (May 1968):88-113; Frank C. Collins, Jr., ''Maritime Support of the Campaign in I Corps,'' U.S. Naval Institute *Naval Review* 97 (May 1971):156-79; Edwin B. Hooper, *Mobility, Support, Endurance: A Story of Naval Operational Logistics in the Vietnam War, 1965-1968* (Washington: GPO, 1972).

EDWARD J. MAROLDA

DONG TAM, REPUBLIC OF VIETNAM, U.S. NAVAL SUPPORT ACTIVITY, 1966–1971 Dong Tam, in South Vietnam's Mekong Delta, was the home ashore during the Southeast Asian Conflict for a unique joint service formation, the Mobile Riverine Force. Composed of a brigade of the Army's Ninth Infantry Division and the Navy's Riverine Assault Force, the 5,000-man unit was created to launch swift, wide-ranging offensive operations against the Viet Cong by using the many waterways in the region. To retain flexibility, logistic support resources initially were concentrated on river-based ships, smaller craft, and pontoon barges that deployed with the combat units.

However, recognition that supplemental shore facilities also were needed prompted the search for a suitable site. Anticipating operations against the Viet Cong in the southern and western approaches to Saigon, Army and Navy leaders sought a base site that was centrally located and on a major river in the region. The My Tho area possessed some assets, but there was a scarcity of unoccupied land on which to locate a base. However, about five miles west of the city, at Dong Tam, there were several hundred acres of abandoned rice paddy that could be developed to support a base.

Accordingly, in August 1966, dredges began filling a 1-square-mile area with river sand and at the same time excavating a boat-turning basin. This work was dangerous; three of the five dredges used at Dong Tam from 1966 to 1969 were damaged or sunk by Viet Cong swimmers. Another vessel was sunk when it dredged up live ordnance that exploded.

Regardless of the risk, by January 1967 the site was ready to receive construction forces. Seabees moved ashore and began work on berthing, messing, administrative, and recreational facilities with prestocked materials transported from Saigon by the *Brule* (AKL-28), *Mark* (AKL-12), and YFR-889. In addition, the naval constructionmen installed a pier using six pontoons.

In January 1967 the Naval Support Activity, Saigon, Detachment Dong Tam, was established to provide the naval component of the Mobile Riverine Force with fuel, ammunition, and supplies. Maintenance and repair of river craft also was a responsibility. As the detachment strove to build up the logistic establishment, interim measures were taken to support the assault force. A 12,000-gallon fuel barge, eight mechanized landing craft (LCM-3), repair, berthing, and messing barges YFNB-24 and YRBM-17, barracks craft APL-26, and floating crane YD-220 were dispatched to the site in the first half of 1967.

With the base prepared to receive them, River Assault Squadron 9 elements of the Navy's assault force deployed to Dong Tam in March and April 1967.

Each squadron consisted of various converted landing craft, including two command craft (CCB), five monitors, twenty-six armored troop carriers (ATC), sixteen assault support patrol boats (ASPB), and one refueler. Mobile support for the entire Mobile Riverine Force was provided by two self-propelled barracks ships (APBs), two tank landing ships (LSTs), two tugs (YTBs), a non-self-propelled barracks barge (ARL), and a repair barge (YFNB).

By the end of 1967 the base at Dong Tam was able to provide boat berthing, dry-dock, maintenance and repair, supply, communications, sleeping, and messing facilities for one river assault squadron. The Army compound accommodated an infantry battalion and an artillery battalion. These units periodically rotated with their counterparts afloat. In addition, a detachment of the Navy's Helicopter Attack (Light) Squadron 3 was based at Dong Tam for support of the force.

During 1968 the responsive logistic support provided by the detachment at Dong Tam, as well as the support contingent afloat, enabled the Mobile Riverine Force to surprise and destroy widely separated enemy units. During the Tet Offensive the force was credited with saving My Tho, Can Tho, and Vin Long from complete enemy destruction.

Although the Mobile Riverine Force was disbanded in August 1969, Dong Tam continued to serve the Navy in Vietnam. As a Logistic Support Base, it provided river craft with major overhauls and stocked large amounts of supply items for smaller installations in the area. In September 1971, once the Vietnamese Navy was prepared to take on the responsibility for support of river operations in the region, the U.S. Navy turned over its facilities at Dong Tam.

BIBLIOGRAPHY

A. Service Force, U.S. Pacific Fleet, "Command Histories, 1967-1972" (Washington: Naval Historical Center, Operational Archives Branch).

B. Herbert T. King, "Naval Logistic Support, Qui Nhon to Phu Quoc," U.S. Naval Institute *Naval Review* 95 (May 1969):84-111; W. C. Wells, "The Riverine Force in Action, 1966-1967," U.S. Naval Institute *Naval Review* 95 (May 1969):46-83; S. A. Swarztrauber, "River Patrol Relearned," U.S. Naval Institute *Naval Review* 96 (May 1970):120-57; Edwin B. Hooper, *Mobility, Support, Endurance: A Story of Naval Operational Logistics in the Vietnam War, 1965-1968* (Washington: GPO, 1972).

EDWARD J. MAROLDA

DUNKESWELL, DEVONSHIRE, ENGLAND, U.S. NAVAL AIR FACILITY.

See United Kingdom, U.S. World War II Naval Bases.

DUNKIRK, FRANCE.

See World War I Northern Bombing Group Bases in England and France.

E

EASTLEIGH, ENGLAND, U.S. NAVY ASSEMBLY AND REPAIR BASE. *See* World War I U.S. Naval Air Stations in Europe; World War I U.S. Northern Bombing Group Bases in England and France.

EDZELL, SCOTLAND, U.S. NAVAL SECURITY GROUP, 1959– This facility is located in northeastern Scotland midway between Aberdeen and Dundee at about 56°30′N., 3°W. Its mission is to support U.S. Fleet units operating in the area, provide navigational service relating to air-sea rescue, and conduct technical research in support of Navy electronic projects.

On 1 December 1959 a memorandum of understanding governing the occupancy of the Royal Air Force Base at Edzell by the United States was signed by United States and United Kingdom representatives. On 11 February 1960 occurred the "Marching On" ceremony, after which the station was officially occupied by one American officer and eight enlisted personnel. Operations began on 15 August 1960 while construction for operations buildings and permanent housing areas began. To the original site were added the Royal Air Force Base Kinnaber, on 11 October 1962, and family quarters at Inverbervie, on 29 January 1963. A Marine Detachment began its security functions on 20 April 1963. Construction of a Courier Transfer Station at Prestwick, Scotland, began on 1 January 1963. Operations began there under the command of the commanding officer at Edzell on 1 July 1963, with the aircraft furnished by the 6321st Air Base Group. U.S. Air Force, Prestwick.

Temporary housing for servicemen with dependents, originally eight mobile homes, has been replaced with permanent structures known as "USAHOMES." Several hotels are available about three miles from the base, which contains quarters for 24 officers and 120 enlisted families. At Inverbervie, twenty miles away, there are 17 enlisted units, and at Brechin, six miles away, 102 enlisted units.

Given its location close to the North Sea and the Grampian Mountains, the climate of Edzell is characterized by fog, wind, cold temperatures, and between

30 and 35 inches of rain a year. The personnel allowance for Edzell is 24 Navy and 2 Marine Corps officers and 388 Navy and 52 Marine Corps enlisted personnel.

Educational facilities for children K-8 are available on the base or in Scottish schools, but the nearest American high school is in London, 500 miles away. University of Maryland courses for higher education are offered at the base. Indoor sport facilities abound, while the outdoorsman can take advantage of the rod and gun club, trap range, and on-base trout fishing. Medical, dental, chapel, and banking facilities are located on the base.

Personnel arriving at Edzell are met by a "buddy" who acts as a sponsor in helping one get located and indoctrinated in the classified work of the Naval Security Group.

In 1966 the commanding officer of Naval Security Group, Edzell, went to London to receive the U.S. Ambassador's Award for Community Relations Programs for stations with less than one thousand personnel. The award was presented by Hon. David E. E. Bruce.

BIBLIOGRAPHY

A. "Command History, 9 February 1967, U.S. Naval Security Group Activity, Edzell, Scotland" (Washington: Naval Historical Center, Operational Archives Branch).

B. "Living Overseas: Edzell, Scotland," *Navy Times*, 20 September 1982, p. 30.

EFATE, NEW HEBRIDES ISLANDS, U.S. NAVAL OPERATING BASE, 1942–1946 [ROSES] Efate, approximately 17°42′S., 168°23′E., is a strategically sited outpost both for New Caledonia (300 miles southwest) and Fiji (600 miles southeast). In 1942 a principal island of the New Hebrides Co-Dominium administered jointly by Britain and France, it is heavily forested, with rugged mountain crests in the north of its twenty-five-mile length. There were two main anchorages: Vila on the southwest coast, and Port Havannah in the northwest.

On 18 February 1942 Efate was proposed by Adm. Ernest J. King, Commander in Chief, U.S. Fleet, as a site for an advance naval base. King envisioned it as the vital "first rung" in his emerging step-by-step strategic advance into the British Solomon Islands toward the Japanese naval bastion at Rabaul on New Britain. Approval by the Joint Chiefs of Staff followed on 20 March, outlining plans for an advanced naval base, a seaplane base, and airfields. Five days later a small Army detachment from Noumea (q.v.) occupied Efate. Meanwhile, Admiral King diverted Task Force 13 (the Fourth Marine Defense Battalion and ground elements of Marine Air Group 24), en route to the Tongatabu Islands (q.v.), to Efate instead. This force arrived at Vila on 8 April. Another convoy with naval construction forces reached the island a month later. First priority was given to the construction of an airfield near Vila, and on 27 May Marine fighters began operating there. By 1 June the seaplane base (nucleus of Naval Air Station Efate) was ready for a patrol plane squadron.

In July and August 1942 Efate served as a valuable staging point for the offensive into the Solomons (Operation Watchtower), beginning with the invasions of Guadalcanal and Tulagi. Army heavy bombers staged through Efate's fields for reconnaissance and raids in the lower Solomons, while Marine fighting squadrons backed up the squadrons operating from 20 August out of Henderson Field on Guadalcanal (q.v.). A second fighter strip, this one at Port Havannah, was ready that fall, and a bomber field was completed in January 1943. Likewise, in the summer and fall of 1942 construction battalions initiated a number of base facilities to help support fleet operations including fuel oil depots at Vila and Port Havannah, a small ammunition depot, a naval camp at Malapoa Point, and an important base hospital to help deal with the flow of casualties from the Solomons.

Although far overshadowed by the emerging giant fleet base at Espiritu Santo (q.v.) about 120 miles to the northwest, Efate in the role of a minor fleet operating base did service and fuel considerable numbers of ships. At Port Havannah the repair ship *Medusa* conducted routine and limited emergency repairs. The Marine Corps integrated Efate's airfields into its complex network of rear area staging and training bases supporting its air offensive in the Solomons. Squadrons bound for combat were able to shake down and train there or rest after coming out of battle. In October 1943 Efate served as rehearsal point for the I Marine Amphibious Corps' invasion of Bougainville scheduled for November. Again, a month later, it similarly played host to the Second Marine Division practicing for landings on Tarawa Atoll (q.v.) in the Gilbert Islands. Efate's depots issued supplies and ammunition for some of the forces headed into the Gilberts.

By early 1944 naval construction on Efate had ceased, and a gradual roll-up of base facilities was begun. That June, Marine aviation activities on Efate ended with the transfer of headquarters Marine Air Wing 2 to Espiritu Santo. The naval operating base on Efate was disestablished on 17 February 1946, ending the history of another installation which, because of changing strategical situations, never did fulfill as important a role as originally envisioned.

BIBLIOGRAPHY

A. Service Squadron, South Pacific, "History of Commander Service Squadron South Pacific, 7 December 1941-15 August 1945," Type Commands, 1946 (Washington: Naval Historical Center, Operational Archives Branch); U.S. Navy, "U.S. Naval Bases in the South and Southwest Pacific (and Central Pacific Forward) in World War II," 1 November 1954 (Washington: Naval Historical Center, Operational Archives Branch); U.S. Navy, Bureau of Yards and Docks, *Building the Navy's Bases in World War II*, 2 vols. (Washington: GPO, 1947).

B. Robert Sherrod, *History of Marine Corps Aviation in World War II* (Washington: Combat Forces Press, 1952); Rear Adm. Worrall Reed Carter, *Beans, Bullets, and Black Oil* (Washington: GPO, 1953).

JOHN B. LUNDSTROM

EMIRAU, NEW IRELAND, NEW GUINEA, U.S. NAVAL ADVANCE BASE, 1944–1945 Emirau Island (1°40′S., 150°0′E.) in the St. Matthias Group (Australian-administered Mandated Territory of New Guinea) is located about 100 miles northwest of Kavieng on New Ireland. It is admirably suited to command the approaches to Kavieng, and as such recommended itself to the Allies as an air and naval base. Roughly eight by two miles in size and with generally level terrain, it featured two anchorages, Hamburg Bay in the northwest coast, and Eulolou harbor on the opposite side of the island.

Early in 1944 the Allies decided to capture Emirau both to contain the Japanese base at Kavieng and as an outpost for the huge naval base in the Admiralty Islands to the northwest. On 22 March 1944 the Fourth Marines (reinforced) under the jurisdiction of the Third Fleet (South Pacific Area) invaded Emirau and captured it after little resistance. Three days later elements of the Eighteenth Naval Construction Regiment arrived there to begin building the air and naval base. The same day (25 March) Motor Torpedo Boat Squadron 11 with the tender *Mobjack* advanced to Emirau to begin PT patrols off New Hanover and New Ireland. They were soon joined by PTs from Squadron 5.

Construction of the Emirau base (formally commissioned on 28 April 1944) continued through the spring and summer of 1944. Two airfields, North Cape and Inland, were made operational for fighters and heavy bombers to pound New Britain and New Ireland. The Seabees also built a seaplane base for patrol planes. Regarding naval base facilities, headquarters for the Emirau base were erected on the southwest tip of the island. Across a small channel from headquarters, PT personnel set up MTB Base 16 on little Eanusau Island. The base offered quarters, an overhaul base, and a small boat pool, as well as supplies and material for the PTs operating from Emirau. Emirau's main harbor facilities were at Hamburg Bay, which offered a good anchorage and a capability for unloading 750 tons a day. Situated there were a naval supply depot and a small-boat repair unit with a Landing Craft Infantry (LCI) floating dry dock to service landing craft.

On 15 June 1944 Emirau shifted from the South Pacific Area to control by the Southwest Pacific Area and became part of the Allied Naval Forces, Northern Solomons (Task Group 70.8), headquartered at Torokina, Bougainville (q.v.). By the fall of 1944 the threat constituted by Japanese forces at Rabaul and Kavieng had lessened so greatly that containment bases such as Emirau became much less vital to the war effort. On 24 November 1944 Emirau's PTs discontinued combat patrols, and the roll-up of MTB Base 16 was ordered two weeks later. PTs and base soon departed for other duty with the Seventh Fleet. Likewise, the remaining naval facilities at Emirau were dismantled, and the base was disestablished in March 1945. Seabee maintenance units finally pulled out in May 1945.

BIBLIOGRAPHY

A. Service Squadron, South Pacific, "History of Commander Service Squadron South Pacific, 7 December 1941-15 August 1945," Type Commands, 1946 (Washington: Naval Historical Center, Operational Archives Branch); U.S. Navy, Bureau of Yards and Docks, *Building the Navy's Bases in World War II*, 2 vols. (Washington: GPO, 1947); U.S. Navy, "U.S. Navy Bases in the South and Southwest Pacific (and Central Pacific Forward) in World War II,'' 1 November 1945 (Washington: Naval Historical Center, Operational Archives Branch).

B. Robert Sherrod, *History of Marine Corps Aviation in World War II* (Washington: Combat Forces Press, 1952); Rear Adm. Worrall Reed Carter, *Beans, Bullets, and Black Oil* (Washington: GPO, 1953).

JOHN B. LUNDSTROM

ENIWETOK ATOLL, U.S. ADVANCED FLEET ANCHORAGE, NAVAL AIR BASE, AND NAVAL OPERATING BASE, 1944-1947

Eniwetok is a circular atoll in the Western Marshalls endowed with a 388-square-mile lagoon that can provide commodious anchorages for perhaps 2,000 vessels. Located 326 miles northwest of Kwajalein, about 1,000 miles east of the Marianas, and 669 miles northeast of Truk, Eniwetok was superbly located for staging both American fleet and air operations in the Western Pacific. Three of the small islands dotting the atoll's rim were suited for naval development: the triangular Engebi at the north of the atoll; the two-mile-long, club-shaped Eniwetok at the south; and the tear-shaped Parry on the southeastern rim. After Japan acquired the Marshalls as mandate from the League of Nations at the close of World War I, American naval men became interested in Eniwetok's strategic possibilities. The cruiser *Milwaukee* made a surprise call at Eniwetok in 1923, but the atoll thereafter remained closed, mysterious, and undefended. Only in November 1942 did the Japanese build an airfield on Engebi, their most important facility on the atoll. In January 1944 the Japanese Army finally despatched an amphibious brigade to provide Eniwetok with at least light defense.

When he turned during World War II to plan Operation Flintlock for the occupation of the Marshalls, Adm. Chester W. Nimitz concluded that Eniwetok could be occupied along with Kwajalein and Majuro if the reserves for the operation were not exhausted in capturing the two eastern atolls. The reserves having remained intact, the Twenty-second Marine Regiment and elements from the Army's Twenty-seventh Division, supported by fleet units under the overall command of Rear Adm. Henry W. Hill, between 17 and 23 February secured Eniwetok against determined Japanese resistance. Thereafter, Eniwetok was developed as a Navy and Marine air base and as a fleet anchorage supported exclusively by floating forces, except for a recreational area.

Army engineers and the 126th Construction Battalion moved first to restore the Japanese field at Engebi to support four Marine fighter squadrons until the main air base on Eniwetok had been completed. Commissioned Wrigley Airfield, the facility eventually included a 3,950-foot fighter strip and a 146,000-gallon aviation gasoline tank farm.

On the southern part of the island, the 110th Seabees built a wholly new base for bombers at Stickell Field, which was equipped with a 6,800-foot runway, engine overhaul shops, and a tank farm of twelve 1,000-barrel tanks. Eniwetok Island was also provided with two coral piers, small-boat repair shops, and a floating dock for small ships. Parry Island was developed as a seaplane base using an existing Japanese ramp and adding parking areas and repair shops. Medical facilities were provided on Engebi, Eniwetok, and Parry by dispensaries with a total capacity of 200 beds. Named overall atoll commander was Capt. E. A. Cruise, USN.

Eniwetok became a major staging base for attacks on the Marianas, the Palaus, the Philippines, Iwo Jima, and Okinawa. Its harbor was a key center for marshalling forces and routing ships to and from the Western Pacific. The Shipping Control Office Forward Area (SCOFA) and Service Squadron 10 were located at Eniwetok from May 1944 until they were moved to the Marianas in the autumn of 1944. In July 1945 alone 1,000 ships sailed from Eniwetok. It was assigned to serve as a main base for Task Force 38 in the prospective invasion of Japan and became the base for twenty units of the British Fleet Train. Indeed, Eniwetok provided more services to the British Pacific Fleet than to the American fleet at the close of World War II. The Naval Air Base and the Naval Station at Eniwetok were disestablished on 23 May 1947.

BIBLIOGRAPHY

A. Commander in Chief, U.S. Pacific Fleet, "Administrative History of the Marshalls-Gilberts Area," 6 vols., 1946 (Washington: Naval Historical Center, Operational Archives Branch); U.S. Navy, Bureau of Yards and Docks, *Building the Navy's Bases in World War II*, 2 vols. (Washington: GPO, 1947), II:324-26; "World War II Command File and Base Maintenance Division Records" (Washington: Naval Historical Center, Operational Archives Branch).

B. Samuel E. Morison, *Aleutians, Gilberts and Marshalls June 1942-April 1944* (Boston: Little, Brown, 1951), pp. 282-304.

WILLIAM R. BRAISTED

ESPIRITU SANTO, NEW HEBRIDES ISLANDS, U.S. NAVAL OPERATING BASE, 1942–1946 [BUTTON] The largest island of the New Hebrides Co-Dominium of Britain and France, Espiritu Santo (15°15′S., 166°51′E.), became one of the two most important bases in the South Pacific. About seventy miles long and forty miles wide, it is mountainous and densely forested, particularly in the west. Its plantations and main anchorages are located on the southeast coast on Segond Channel. Its importance as a naval base grew as the Allies contemplated a counteroffensive into the Solomons northwest of the New Hebrides. Espiritu Santo is strategically located about 400 miles north of Noumea (q.v.) and 500 miles southeast of Guadalcanal (q.v.) (about 200 miles closer to Guadalcanal than Efate (q.v.), the other naval base in the New Hebrides). On 28 June 1942 a small reconnaissance party arrived on the island, and on 3 July Rear Adm. John S. McCain (Commander, Air, South Pacific) recommended that an airfield be built there.

In response to McCain's suggestion, work began on 8 July on an airfield at Turtle Bay on the southeast coast. From there, Army heavy bombers would be able to strike the Japanese airfield under construction at Guadalcanal. McCain had the seaplane tender *Curtiss* advanced to Espiritu Santo to direct the landbased air forces in the impending invasion of the Solomons. On 28 July the first fighters began operating from Espiritu Santo, and two days later Boeing B-17 heavy bombers conducted their first raid on Guadalcanal. With the 7 August landings on Guadalcanal and Tulagi, airfield construction was the first priority on Espiritu Santo, with the object of building the island into a major air support base for the Solomons. On 11 August Construction Unit Battalion-1 (CUB-1), with aviation specialists and naval construction troops, reached the island and began construction of a second fighter field and two full-fledged bomber bases. Late that fall, in addition to staging squadrons to Guadalcanal's Henderson Field, aviation shops at Espiritu Santo acted as an overhaul point for aviation engines. Airfield construction continued well into 1943, as Espiritu Santo became one of the largest air complexes in the South Pacific.

With increasing fleet commitments in the rapidly expanding Solomons naval campaign, Espiritu Santo became important as the site of an advance naval base. Recoiling from the 9 August 1942 defeat at Savo Island, transports from Guadalcanal and Tulagi (q.v.) withdrew to Espiritu Santo and dropped off troops and supplies. These became part of a new First Marine Base Depot, part of which served as the nucleus of a similar installation set up at Noumea. This was the beginning of Espiritu Santo's role as a major South Pacific supply base at the expense of Auckland, New Zealand (q.v.). The primary orders developing Espiritu Santo as a naval base were issued by the Chief of Naval Operations on 25 August 1942. Gathering and transporting the men and material to transform Espiritu Santo into a major naval base took time. During the fall of 1942, Seabees began constructing basic naval base facilities and a seaplane base. Meanwhile, Espiritu Santo became a forward fleet base for warships challenging the Japanese in Ironbottom Sound off Guadalcanal. For service and emergency repairs, these cruisers and destroyers were handled by the repair ship *Rigel* and the personnel of CUB-13. CUB-1 erected a naval ammunition depot whose size increased steadily. Espiritu Santo's increasing value in assisting fleet operations led Vice Adm. William F. Halsey to recommend that the island's development into a major operating base be expedited.

Naval activities on Espiritu Santo really took off after February 1943 with the arrival of the first elements of LION ONE, an integral base force with the task of creating the fleet operating base, a naval supply depot supporting vast offensive operations, repair facilities capable of dealing with all types of ships, a fuel depot, and an air center handling all types of aircraft including at least two carrier air groups. By June 1943 all of the installments of LION ONE had arrived, and the major projects were well underway with the formal commissioning of the naval base on 1 July. At Aore Island just off the southeast coast, Seabees erected a huge fuel depot that eventually stored 500,000 barrels of fuel oil, 20,000 barrels of diesel, 17,000 barrels of gasoline, and 23,000 barrels of aviation gasoline. From November 1943 this fuel depot was one of the busiest in the Pacific, fueling ships directly, transshipping oil from chartered tankers to fleet oilers, and maintaining a continuous reserve of five tanker loads of fuel. A huge naval supply depot on Segond Channel constituted the actual supply base; it handled tremendous amounts of materiel, both for the fleet and for advance bases in the Solomons and points north. Espiritu Santo's ammunition depot eventually grew to 175 separate magazines, which at its peak (September 1944) rearmed 120 warships.

In addition to fuel and supply, Espiritu Santo boasted an impressive ship repair unit and numerous specialist shops, including torpedo overhaul, aviation engine overhaul, pontoon assembly, and a mine depot. Housed on little Aesi Island in Pallikulo Bay on the southeast coast, the ship repair unit, operating by the summer of 1943, became the most impressive in the South Pacific. It offered extensive routine and battle damage repairs to hundreds of ships. Joining the unit in December 1943 was the massive ABSD-1 (Advance Base Sectional Dock 1), a floating dry dock 844 feet long with a lift potential of 81,000 tons. It was just one of many floating docks of different sizes. For the smallest warships, PT-Base 2 arrived in early 1943 and became a major engine overhaul installation for the South Pacific's PT squadrons. By November 1943 it was turning out an average of fifty-four restored engines a month. In connection with all of the vessels being serviced, supplied, and repaired there, Espiritu Santo developed an extensive fleet welfare and recreation center.

The Marine Corps eventually turned Espiritu Santo into one of its main aviation bases, initially as a main air support base for the Solomons, then as a great training, staging, and rest center. The island's complex of airfields was useful for indoctrinating new squadrons before they departed for combat. First under headquarters Marine Air Wing 1 and later under Marine Air Wing 2, Espiritu Santo functioned as one of the Corps' primary aviation areas until early 1945.

Throughout 1943 and 1944 Espiritu Santo helped to supply and stage an impressive portion of all of the South Pacific Area's campaigns and fleet operations as well as the Central Pacific's invasions of the Gilbert and Marshall islands. The last big operation involving the base was in February-March 1945 with the mounting of Operation Iceberg, the invasion of Okinawa. Espiritu Santo supplied and fueled many vessels, including the floating reserve (Second Marine Division). The decision to begin a major roll-up was made in December 1944, and dismantling started in force early in spring 1945. Key installations were disassembled, crated, and sent forward to such bases as Manus (q.v.) in the Admiralty Islands and the Philippines. Espiritu Santo remained important as a fuel and supply base until well into 1946, as the Navy pulled out of the South Pacific. On 12 June 1946 the base was formally disestablished; it was abandoned on 18 November 1946.

BIBLIOGRAPHY

A. Service Squadron, South Pacific, "History of Commander, Service Squadron, South Pacific 7 December1941-15 August 1945" (Washington: Naval Historical Center, Operational Archives Branch); Lt. D. W. Kralovec, "A Naval History of Espiritu Santo, New Hebrides," 2 vols. Shore Establishment, 1945 (Washington: Naval Historical Center, Operational Archives Branch); U.S. Navy, Bureau of Yards and Docks, *Building the*

Navy's Bases in World War II, 2 vols. (Washington: GPO, 1947); Espiritu Santo, New Hebrides, Naval Air Base, "A History of Naval Aviation at Espiritu Santo," Administrative Histories, Appendix, South Pacific Administrative History 6" (Washington: Naval Historical Center, Operational Archives Branch).

B. Samuel E. Morison, *Coral Sea, Midway, and Submarine Actions May 1942-August 1942* (Boston: Little, Brown, 1949); Samuel E. Morison, *The Struggle for Guadalcanal August 1942-February 1943* (Boston: Little, Brown 1949); Samuel E. Morison, *Breaking the Bismarcks Barrier 22 July 1942-1 May 1944* (Boston: Little, Brown, 1950); Robert Sherrod, *History of Marine Corps Aviation in World War II* (Washington: Combat Forces Press, 1952); Rear Adm. Worrall Reed Carter, *Beans, Bullets, and Black Oil* (Washington: GPO, 1953); Vice Adm. George C. Dyer, *The Amphibians Came to Conquer*, 2 vols. (Washington: GPO, 1972).

JOHN B. LUNDSTROM

ESSEQUIBO, BRITISH GUIANA, U.S. NAVAL AIR FACILITY.
See Hispanic South America, U.S. Naval Bases.

EXETER, ENGLAND.
See United Kingdom, U.S. World War II Naval Bases.

EXMOUTH GULF, AUSTRALIA, U.S. NAVAL SECTION BASE, 1943–1945 Exmouth Gulf, on the west coast of Australia at 22°6′S., 114°30′E., operated as a U.S. naval fueling station from 1943 to 1945. It first became prominent, despite its lack of facilities, in March 1942 as an emergency fueling point for warships withdrawing from the inferno at Java. In June 1942 Rear Adm. Charles A. Lockwood, commanding the Task Force 51 submarines based at Fremantle-Perth (q.v.), envisioned Exmouth Gulf as a site for an advance submarine base. Basing there would save the submarines two days of fuel. A small force was sent in late 1942 to Exmouth Gulf, and in early May 1943 the submarine tender *Pelias* sailed for there to operate at the base, formally commissioned on 10 April 1943. Exmouth Gulf lasted only one month as the site of a complete advance submarine base. Poor weather, primitive facilities, and the threat of enemy air attack from Timor forced a closing of the facilities. However, the Exmouth Gulf base remained as a fuel stopping point for Fremantle-based submarines as well as major fleet units. In May 1944 the British Eastern Fleet operated from there for a short time. The fueling station remained open until 19 July 1945.

BIBLIOGRAPHY

A. U.S. Navy, "U.S. Naval Bases in the South and Southwest Pacific (and Central Pacific Forward), in World War II," 1 November 1954 (Washington: Naval Historical Center, Operational Archives Branch); "United States Naval Administration in World War II: Submarine Commands," 2 vols. (Washington: Naval Historical Center, Navy Library); Exmouth Gulf, Australia, Advance Base, "Notes on Exmouth Gulf Advance Base: World War II Operation POTSHOT," Shore Establishment (Washington: Naval Historical Center, Operational Archives Branch).

B. Theodore Roscoe, *United States Submarine Operations in World War II* (Annapolis, Md.: U.S. Naval Institute, 1949); Clay Blair, *Silent Victory: The U.S. Submarine War against Japan*, 2 vols. (Philadelphia: Lippincott, 1975).

JOHN B. LUNDSTROM

F

FALMOUTH, ENGLAND.
See United Kingdom, U.S. World War II Naval Bases.

FAR EASTERN U.S. NAVAL BASES TO 1898 Commo. Edmund P. Kennedy, the first commander in chief of the "U.S. Naval Forces in the East India and China Seas," otherwise known as the East India Squadron, was also the first to advise the Navy Department with regard to possible base sites. In 1835, on his way home from the station, which was notorious for its unhealthful conditions—a reputation enhanced by his squadron's losses to dysentery and cholera—Kennedy wrote that only Macao, the Portuguese city on the western side of China's Canton River estuary, was "favorable in point of view of health, for vessels of war to replenish at." He considered Singapore, off the tip of the Malay Peninsula, reasonably salubrious and very convenient for commerce, while Manila in the Philippine Islands he thought as suitable as any of the remaining ports, although it was subject to periodic outbreaks of cholera.

Whatever its advantages, however, Singapore was too far from the Chinese coast to provide satisfactory logistic support for the East India Squadron, so the Board of Navy Commissioners had stores shipped to Macao and Manila, where they were landed in care of the U.S. consuls. Officers of the squadron surveyed these stores periodically, often finding extensive deterioration caused by the climate and rats, particularly at Manila, which U.S. warships visited infrequently.

When the British established a settlement at Hong Kong, across the Canton River estuary from Macao, during the Opium War (1839-1842), it superceded Macao as the site of the American naval depot, presumably because of its fine harbor and the political stability expected of a British colony. But Hong Kong had its disadvantages: it was very humid and unhealthful during the summer (southwest) monsoon; rents were much higher than those in Macao; and its waters teemed with Chinese pirates, some of whom attacked the squadron's storehouse in 1844. Commo. Foxhall A. Parker, who amassed this list of deficiencies, added another—American stores at Hong Kong would be lost at once in the event of hostilities between the United States and the United Kingdom, as would any of the squadron's warships caught in that confined harbor. Parker would have preferred that the squadron's supplies be kept in a storeship moored in a secure harbor on the coast of China; in the absence of such a vessel, he obtained from the governor of Macao the privilege of landing the provisions and stores duty-free and rented a godown in which to house them. Thus, Macao became the squadron's base once more in 1844, and its lack of ship repair facilities was soon alleviated by the construction of a dry dock at Whampoa, the merchant ship anchorage below Canton and distant some sixty-five miles from Macao.

Seven years later, the Navy Department proposed to Commo. John H. Aulick that rapidly growing Hong Kong be considered as a base site. The commodore conferred with the U.S. consuls at Macao and Hong Kong before responding that the latter's fine harbor was its only advantage and that so long as Portugal maintained a sufficient military force in Macao, it was the best location for the East India Squadron's stores.

But none of Macao's advocates had mentioned its harbor. In fact, its shallow waters forced oceangoing vessels to anchor in an open roadstead three miles from the city. Thus, all supplies had to be lightered from the cargo ships to the godown and from the godown to the warships at considerable expense. Moreover, this transshipping was interrupted whenever the wind sprang up, for the lighters could not lie alongside the vessels if even a good topgallant breeze were blowing. To compound the problem, steamships were appearing in the Far East—Aulick's flagship, the paddle-frigate *Susquehanna*, was the first steamer assigned to the East India Squadron—and the difficulty of transporting the hundreds of tons of coal that they would require to and from the shore under these conditions was immediately apparent to Aulick's successor, Commo. Matthew Calbraith Perry.

After his first visit to the Canton River estuary, in 1853, Perry enumerated Hong Kong's advantages: the largest ships could anchor within a thousand yards of the shore and discharge or embark supplies in almost any weather; virtually all articles of provisions and stores could be purchased there; and ship and engine repair facilities were being developed. Anglo-American relations had been harmonious since the settlement of the Oregon boundary question in 1846, and Perry thought that the squadron's stores would be safer in the British colony than in Macao, "a small badly defended Town, surrounded by a numerous population of Chinese." The commodore conceded that Macao was healthier, but he believed that the dangers of Hong Kong had been exaggerated.

Having located a suitable building in Hong Kong at an annual rental much lower than that paid for the Macao godown, Perry had a small pier constructed nearby and obtained the British governor's permission to have the squadron's stores landed there henceforth. Perry's successors found no reason to question his decision; with the exception of the American Civil War years, when British unfriendliness caused the few U.S. warships in Asian waters to turn to Macao,

Hong Kong served as the East India Squadron's principal South China port of call for the remainder of the nineteenth century.

From the Canton River estuary, Perry sailed to Shanghai, which he thought another potential base site—until he became acquainted with its hydrographic features. Located on the narrow, winding Hwangpoo River, which flows into the Yangtze-Kiang estuary some twenty miles from the sea, Shanghai was difficult of access especially because of the hazardous entrance to the estuary. The outer bar had but a twenty-foot depth at low water and an entrance channel only one and a half miles wide with dangerous shoals on either hand. The coast could not be seen from the bar; no beacons, buoys, or lighthouses existed; and the tidal currents were notoriously swift and irregular. Three of Perry's vessels touched on the south shoal while crossing the outer bar, while the fourth, entering without a pilot, grounded on the north side, from which she was refloated with difficulty. Not surprisingly, Perry decided not to establish a depot at Shanghai.

Perry's opinion notwithstanding, Shanghai would obviously figure prominently in the East India Squadron's future. The city's position as the natural entrepot for the vast and heavily populated Yangtze basin and the friendliness of its inhabitants to foreigners would soon enable it to surpass Canton as the focal point for trade with China. The international settlement, which had arisen beside Shanghai on a spacious tract made available for that purpose by the imperial government, contained consulates and the buildings of the major commercial companies as well as luxurious dwellings, clubs, a race course, and even Christian churches. A dry dock and ship and engine repair facilities added to the city's importance, and in 1855 Chinese authorities were persuaded to engage a boat's crew under Lt. George H. Preble, USN, to survey and buoy the estuary. Preble also prepared sailing directions, and a lightship was moored off the outer bar. The largest warships, however, could not ascend the Hwangpoo and so had to anchor at Woosung, where the river enters the estuary; there they were coaled and supplied by smaller vessels from Shanghai. The anchorage offered little beyond good holding ground; its strong tidal currents occasionally swept ships ashore or caused damage to their hawsepipes.

Perry, of course, was mainly interested in his mission to open Japan to American commerce. To this end, he visited Naha, Okinawa, in the Ryukyu Islands, and Port Lloyd, Chichi Jima, in the Bonin Islands, with an eye to utilizing them as bases. The former served as the anchorage at which his steam-propelled warships were coaled from chartered vessels and storeships en route to and from Japan in 1853 and 1854, but the treaty that Perry negotiated with the Okinawa regent contained no mention of Naha's use as a naval base, nor did the East India Squadron frequent its waters thereafter.

Perry's interest in the Bonin Islands was due in part to his belief that the United States had a valid claim based on their reputed discovery by an American warship in 1823. He thought Port Lloyd admirably sited to serve as a coaling station for trans-Pacific steamers and purchased a tract of land on which to build the coal depot. Following his visit, Perry ordered the commanding officer of the sloop of war *Plymouth* to take formal possession of the southernmost group of the islands in the name of the United States, subject to confirmation by the government. His superiors in Washington, however, showed no interest in the Bonins, and few American warships visited Port Lloyd.

The major vessels of the East India Squadron were ordered home in 1861, and when the squadron was reestablished at the end of the Civil War (it became the Asiatic Squadron in 1866), Rear Adm. Henry H. Bell described Hong Kong as "the center of commerce and mails in the China Seas." As such, he thought that it must remain the squadron's headquarters. Since it was so far from the northern Chinese ports and Japan, an additional base was needed. He ruled out Shanghai, "the sickliest port in China and not safe to approach without expensive pilotage," and Yokohama, where the Japanese government had assigned each of the foreign navies a depot site, because it was to windward of all other ports on the Asiatic Station during the summer monsoon. Nagasaki, on the other hand, was centrally located on the station and had a good harbor free of navigational difficulties. Healthful and moderately cool during most of the year, this principal seaport on the western side of Kyushu could provide good water, fresh provisions, and coal of fair quality from the nearby Takashima mines, all at reasonable prices. Nagasaki's lack of docks and machine shops was alleviated somewhat by the availability of both at Shanghai, 460 miles across the East China Sea. Admiral Bell recommended that an old frigate be moored at Nagasaki to serve as storeship and hospital; vessels bringing supplies from the United States could divide their cargoes between the frigate and the Hong Kong depot.

Rumors of the loss of an American merchant schooner in Korean waters led Bell to send the screw-sloop *Wachusett* to investigate in 1867. Considering it likely that a punitive expedition would have to be sent, Bell ordered Comdr. Robert W. Shufeldt to reconnoiter Port Hamilton in the Kŏmun Do, "situate among the islands to the southward of Corea," as a possible base site. The commander reported enthusiastically on the harbor's potential, and the admiral held that "the possession of so small a place does not indicate the least ambition for territorial aggrandizement." As usual, the U.S. government showed no interest in acquiring any possession in Asian waters.

Bell's relief, Rear Adm. Stephen C. Rowan, recognized Nagasaki's advantages, but he observed that "Yokohama must be the commercial head centre for Japan and the headquarters of all the European naval powers" because of its proximity to Edo, soon to be Tokyo, the political capital of the Japanese Empire. He condemned Nagasaki as "the worst place in the East" for a seamen's hospital because of the prevalence of venereal diseases there and urged that a small hospital be built on the heights overlooking Yokohama. Rowan also ordered the sailing storeship *Idaho* from Nagasaki to Yokohama. Reduced to a hulk after suffering severe damage in an 1869 typhoon, the *Idaho* remained in Tokyo Bay as a receiving ship and storeship until her sale in 1874.

Rear Adm. John Rodgers, Rowan's successor, agreed that Yokohama should be his squadron's Japanese base and arranged the purchase of coal sheds that the Pacific Mail Steamship Company had erected on the U.S. Navy's lot there. In 1871 the imperial government completed a dry dock at nearby Yokosuka (q.v.), the first installation in what was destined to be the Japanese Navy's principal dockyard, and that autumn Rodgers's flagship, the screw-frigate *Colorado*, was repaired there after grounding in the Strait of Shimonoseki. Meanwhile, the admiral supervised the construction of a two-story hospital at Yokohama.

Rodgers's tenure of command of the Asiatic Squadron was notable mainly for the punitive expedition against Korea in June 1871. Following this operation, the squadron withdrew to Chefoo, a port on the northern side of China's Shantung Peninsula. The admiral chose Chefoo because it had regular steamship service to Shanghai and because telegraphic communication between the latter and Washington, D.C., had recently been established. Almost equally important, Chefoo's moderate temperatures provided a welcome respite from Korea's scorching summer heat. Although Chefoo could offer little beyond fresh provisions and a sheltered anchorage, it soon became a favorite summer rendezvous for vessels of the Asiatic Squadron. Officers and men debilitated by weeks in the oppressive heat of the Canton estuary and the Yangtze Valley looked forward eagerly to an opportunity to recuperate at Chefoo.

Rowan and Rodgers may have believed that they had settled the location of their command's Japanese base, but Rear Adm. Thornton A. Jenkins, who hoisted his flag in the *Colorado* at Yokohama in 1872, had other ideas. Citing Admiral Bell's arguments in favor of Nagasaki, he added that the Japanese government was building a dockyard there and that it was the best harbor on the station during the typhoon season, while the Yokohama anchorage was exposed to those violent winds. News that the dockyard project had been abandoned did not deter Jenkins; he informed the Secretary of the Navy that he would utilize Nagasaki and Shanghai as his squadron's principal bases. The admiral leased premises at Nagasaki late in 1873 and ordered that the stores at Yokohama and Hong Kong be sent there. Recognizing that coal might be purchased more cheaply at Hong Kong than anywhere else on the station, Jenkins kept a coal depot at the British colony, and he retained the hospital at Yokohama.

Subsequent commanders in chief had mixed feelings about Nagasaki's desirability as a base. Indeed, several manifested a growing feeling that it would be more economical for their vessels to purchase provisions, coal, and supplies at Hong Kong, Shanghai, and Yokohama than to have these materials shipped to Nagasaki from the United States.

The Navy Department directed that the owners of the Nagasaki depot site be given notice that the lease would be terminated on 1 January 1884, but the question of another depot had not been settled by that date. Almost a year later, Rear Adm. John Lee Davis and several of his commanding officers strongly opposed a suggestion that the depot be relocated at Yokohama. All preferred that everything be purchased on the open market and considered Hong Kong and Shanghai preferable to Yokohama in the event that a depot were to be continued.

Thereafter, the Asiatic Station really had no depot or base as such until after the Spanish-American War. Its commanders in chief and paymasters made such arrangements as they could, always intent upon spending as little money as possible. When the expense of using the Yokosuka dry dock was held to be exorbitant, recourse was had exclusively to commercial docks elsewhere, although this sometimes resulted in lengthy delays because merchant ship operators often scheduled docking well in advance. Thus, Yokosuka continued to be used on occasion, although foreign warships were not permitted to enter the dockyard during the Sino-Japanese War of 1894-1895.

Germany's seizure of Kiaochow Bay on the Shantung Peninsula in 1897 inspired proposals that the United States lease a base site, with Chefoo and one or another of the harbors in the Chusan Archipelago mentioned as the most likely locations. Nothing had come of these proposals by 1898, however, so Commo. George Dewey found himself commanding a squadron thousands of miles from the nearest base to which it could depend on access should the United States become involved in hostilities.

In the event, this lack of a base did not prove a serious handicap. Dewey's vessels had almost completed their preparations for war at Hong Kong when Britain's declaration of neutrality in the Spanish-American War made their departure mandatory, and then the warships merely steamed to Mirs Bay, thirty miles to the eastward in Chinese territorial waters. Here they continued to utilize Hong Kong's repair and communication facilities until they weighed anchor to seek out and engage the Spanish naval forces in Philippine waters. None of the American men-of-war suffered serious damage in the Battle of Manila Bay, and the war itself ended before any required docking or major repair. An assured supply of coal, Dewey's greatest need, was provided by British-owned colliers at anchor in Manila Bay when the Asiatic Squadron arrived. The American flag officer commandeered their cargoes on the rather dubious ground that they were contraband of war. His offer to pay for the coal was refused by the British consul, who protested the entire proceeding. The commander in chief of Britain's China Fleet concurred in the consul's action—and, of course, did nothing more.

Throughout the nineteenth century, U.S. naval forces in Asian waters were kept at a minimal size, and the arrangements for their supply and repair, haphazard though they sometimes were, proved to be adequate for their needs. Commanders in chief might have welcomed a base of their own, at which they would not have been dependent upon another nation's good will. They probably would have agreed, on the other hand, that the burden of defending such a base would have more than offset its usefulness.

BIBLIOGRAPHY

A. Record Group 45, "Letters from Officers Commanding Squadrons, 1841-1845, East India and Asiatic Squadrons" (Washington National Archives); Record Group 45, "Letters Received by the Secretary of the Navy from Officers Commanding Ships of War; Logs, Journals, and Diaries of Officers of the United States Navy at Sea, March 1778-July 1908" (Washington: National Archives); U.S. Navy, Hydrographic Office,

Asiatic Pilot, Vol. II: *The Japan Islands*, 2nd ed. (Washington: GPO, 1920); U.S. Navy, Hydrographic Office, *Sailing Directions for the Western Shores of the China Sea: From Singapore Strait to and Including Hong Kong*, 3rd ed. (Washington: GPO, 1937); U.S. Navy Department, Hydrographic Office, *Sailing Directions for the Coast of China: From the Yalu River to the Approach to Hong Kong*, 4th ed. (Washington: GPO, 1943); British Admiralty Station Records, China Correspondence. Adm. 125 (London: Public Record Office).

B. Samuel E. Morison, *"Old Bruin": The Life of Commodore Matthew Calbraith Perry, 1794-1858* (Boston: Little, Brown, 1967); Maurice Collis, *Foreign Mud: The Opium Imbroglio at Canton in the 1830's and the Anglo-Chinese War* (1946; repr. New York: W. W. Norton, 1968); Charles O. Paullin, *American Voyages to the Orient, 1690-1865* (Annapolis, Md.: U.S. Naval Institute, 1971); Robert E. Johnson, *Far China Station: The U.S. Navy in Asian Waters, 1800-1898* (Annapolis, Md.: Naval Institute Press, 1979).

ROBERT E. JOHNSON

FARFAN, PANAMA CANAL ZONE, RADIO STATION.
See Balboa, Panama Canal Zone, U.S. Naval Operating Base/Naval Station.

FEDALA, FRENCH MOROCCO.
See North Africa, U.S. Naval Bases.

FERNANDO DE NORONHA, BRAZIL, U.S. NAVAL AIR FACILITY.
See Brazil, U.S. Naval Bases.

FERRYVILLE, TUNISIA.
See North Africa, U.S. Naval Bases.

FINCHHAFEN, NEW GUINEA, U.S. NAVAL ADVANCE BASE, 1943–1945 Finchhafen (6°34′S., 147°0′E.) is a small but excellent harbor located north of Huon Gulf and in close proximity to Cape Cretin, Langemak Bay, and Dreger Harbor. In 1943 it was officially a part of the Mandated Territory of New Guinea. Allied troops from the Southwest Pacific Area landed near Finchhafen on 22 September 1943 and captured the harbor on 2 October. The Seventh Fleet decided to utilize the Finchhafen area as an amphibious staging and supply point, a naval supply depot, and a light craft repair and maintenance base. Such facilities would greatly expedite basic Southwest Pacific Area strategy for further amphibious operations west along the north New Guinea coast to neutralize Japanese strength in the region.

On 5 November 1943 the first Seabee unit, the Sixtieth Naval Construction Battalion, arrived but it constructed an Army Air Forces airfield before starting on the intended naval base. Meanwhile, headquarters Motor Torpedo Boat Squadrons, Southwest Pacific Area, selected Dreger Harbor on Huon Gulf southwest of Finchhafen as the site of a PT operating and repair base. Dreger Harbor became the most important PT base in New Guinea. On 25 November 1943 PTs from Squadron 21 moved to Dreger Harbor from Morobe (q.v.). A few days later they began patrolling up the New Guinea coast and across Vitiaz Strait toward New Britain in order to cut the Japanese supply line to Madang.

In December 1943 base construction was begun at Finchhafen, and by the time the base was formally commissioned on 1 February 1944, most important projects were well under way. Seabees improved harbor facilities, piers, wharfs, and moorings, so that Finchhafen could accommodate up to fourteen Liberty ships at one time. To handle the supplies and materiel, a large naval supply depot was set up, as was a fuel oil tank farm. At Langemak Bay, a fueling station served submarines. Finchhafen also featured a ship repair unit, including a floating dry dock, to handle small craft up to the size of LSTs. The Seventh Amphibious Force established an amphibious training center to help prepare troops stationed at several important Army camps in the area. Facilities at Dreger Harbor were greatly improved into a major PT supply and repair installation known as PT Base 21.

Finchhafen's main importance to the Allies was as an amphibious staging and supply base. Troops assembling there conducted invasions in April 1944 at Aitape and Humbolt Bay on New Guinea, while the base's last major effort was helping to mount the invasion of Leyte, October 1944. Finchhafen also served as an important naval supply and small craft maintenance point within Seventh Fleet's network of rear area bases. In November 1944 all major projects were cancelled, and roll-up of facilities began. The PT facilities at Dreger Harbor functioned until January 1945, then departed for Mindanao. Likewise, dismantling of the supply depot and ship repair unit proceeded. On 1 April 1945 the Seventh Fleet turned over remaining installations to the U.S. Army.

BIBLIOGRAPHY

A. U.S. Navy, "7th Amphibious Force Command History, 10 January 1943-23 December 1945" (Washington: Naval Historical Center, Operational Archives Branch); U.S. Navy, Bureau of Yards and Docks, *Building the Navy's Bases in World War II*, 2 vols. (Washington: GPO, 1947); U.S. Navy, "U.S. Naval Bases in the South and Southwest Pacific (and Central Pacific Forward) in World War II," 1 November 1954 (Washington: Naval Historical Center, Operational Archives Branch); Motor Torpedo Boat Squadrons, Philippine Sea Frontier, "Command History of MTB Squadrons, Philippine Sea Frontier, formerly MTB Squadrons, 7th Fleet," 5 vols. (Washington: Naval Historical Center, Operational Archives Branch).

B. Samuel E. Morison, *Breaking the Bismarcks Barrier 22 July 1942-1 May 1944* (Boston: Little, Brown, 1950); Rear Adm. Worrall Reed Carter, *Beans, Bullets, and Black Oil* (Washington: GPO, 1953); Capt. Robert J. Bulkley, *At Close Quarters: PT Boats in the United States Navy* (Washington: Naval History Division, 1962); Vice Adm. Daniel E. Barbey, *MacArthur's Amphibious Navy* (Annapolis, Md.: U.S. Naval Institute, 1969).

JOHN B. LUNDSTROM

FLORIANOPOLIS, BRAZIL, U.S. NAVAL OPERATING FACILITY. *See* Brazil, U.S. Naval Bases.

FONSECA, NICARAGUA, U.S. NAVAL AIR FACILITY.
See Central America, U.S. Naval Bases.

FORTALEZA, BRAZIL, U.S. NAVAL AIR FACILITY.
See Brazil, U.S. Naval Bases.

FOWEY, ENGLAND.
See United Kingdom, U.S. World War II Naval Bases.

FREETOWN, SIERRA LEONE, U.S. NAVAL ADVANCE BASE, 1942–1943 Located as it is on the Atlantic Ocean near the southern extremity of the western African ''bulge''—9°N., 13°W.—Freetown provided a site from which the Allies in World War II could defend against a possible German drive toward South Africa, send supplies to those engaged in the invasion of North Africa, and harbor ships that operated in the South Atlantic. To this end, the British government early in 1942 began to develop Freetown's harbor facilities as well as those of British West Africa (independent after 1961). To serve ships up to cruiser size, they also planned to install one large and one small floating dry dock at Freetown, to erect a hospital, and to build an ammunition dump, refrigerated warehouse space, fuel depots, and housing for personnel. In February 1942 the British asked the United States for material assistance. In consequence, the United States had a timber floating dry dock, the *Triumph*, towed by an American and a British tug from New York to Freetown.

Because of the absence of skilled labor in Sierra Leone and because the food supply consisted of little other than rice and coffee, in June 1942 the United States organized two Civil Engineering Corps officers, a doctor, a dentist, and forty enlisted men into an advance base unit and ordered them to Freetown. In July they were joined by 10 additional officers and 250 men, and in December by Construction Battalion Detachments 1001 and 1002, each consisting of 250 officers and men. On 3 March 1943, CBD 1001, CBD 1002, and the advance base unit were combined to form the Sixty-fifth Construction Battalion.

After the Axis forces were driven out of North Africa in mid-May 1943, the need for Freetown as an advance base ceased to exist, and the United States withdrew its forces there in June 1943.

BIBLIOGRAPHY

A. U.S. Navy, Bureau of Yards and Docks, *Building the Navy's Bases in World War II*, 2 vols. (Washington: GPO, 1947), II:93-94.

FREMANTLE-PERTH, AUSTRALIA, U.S. NAVAL ADVANCE BASE, 1942–1946 Fremantle is a port in West Australia closely associated with the city of Perth which is only twelve miles inland from there on the Swan River. It was an important Royal Navy Australian base in the early days of 1942, when it was selected as a refuge for ships from Naval Forces, Southwest Pacific, escaping from the Netherlands East Indies. On 3 March 1942 the submarine tender *Holland* arrived from Java with the submarines of the Submarine Force. Naval headquarters, Southwest Pacific, leased wheat-unloading sheds at Fremantle for use as an advance submarine base—at location at 31°40′S., 115°50′E. The submarines began operating as Task Force 51 for war patrols past the Malay Barrier into the South China Sea. The submarines and submarine base (changed to Task Force 72 in March 1943 with the activation of the Seventh Fleet) performed vital duties throughout 1943 and 1944. By May 1944 upwards of thirty fleet submarines based out of Fremantle. Base personnel with the help of Australian labor constantly improved facilities, erecting a naval supply depot and other installations to support the submarines. In late 1943 the floating dry dock ARD-10 arrived to assist with submarine overhaul and repair. Fremantle-based submarines saw much action in 1944 and early 1945, but on 20 March 1945 submarine headquarters and base personnel were shifted to Subic Bay, Luzon (q.v.).

Fremantle also became very important as a fuel oil staging point for the Seventh Fleet and the British Pacific Fleet. Much of the oil was shipped in directly from refineries in the Persian Gulf. By June 1945 Fremantle had tank farms storing some 700,000 barrels of fuel oil and 206,000 barrels of diesel oil. The U.S. Navy base at Fremantle was disestablished on 15 January 1946.

BIBLIOGRAPHY

A. U.S. Navy, "7th Amphibious Force Command History, 10 January 1943-23 December 1945" (Washington: Naval Historical Center, Operational Archives Branch); U.S. Navy, Bureau of Yards and Docks, *Building the Navy's Bases in World War II*, 2 vols. (Washington: GPO, 1947); U.S. Navy, "U.S. Naval Bases in the South and Southwest Pacific (and Central Pacific Forward) in World War II," 1 November 1954 (Washington: Naval Historical Center, Operational Archives Branch); Motor Torpedo Boat Squadrons, Philippine Sea Frontier, "Command History of MTB Squadrons, Philippine Sea Frontier, formerly MTB Squadrons, 7th Fleet," 5 vols. (Washington: Naval Historical Center, Operational Archives Branch).

B. Samuel E. Morison, *Breaking the Bismarcks Barrier 22 July 1942-1 May 1944* (Boston: Little, Brown, 1950); Rear Adm. Worrall Reed Carter, *Beans, Bullets, and Black Oil* (Washington: GPO, 1953); Capt. Robert J. Bulkley, *At Close Quarters: PT Boats in the United States Navy* (Washington: Naval History Division, 1962); Vice Adm. Daniel E. Barbey, *MacArthur's Amphibious Navy* (Annapolis, Md.: U.S. Naval Institute, 1969).

JOHN B. LUNDSTROM

FRENCH FRIGATE SHOALS, U.S. NAVAL AIR FACILITY, 1943–1946 Although the reputed discoverer of French Frigate Shoals was the French explorer Jean François de Gelup, Comte de la Perouse, Lt. John M. Brooke, USN, commander of the schooner *Fenimore Cooper*, made the first recorded landing on the shoals in 1858 and claimed them for the United States the following year. About eighteen miles in diameter, the shoals include six islets and a high rock, La Perouse Pinnacle, which has the appearance of two frigates under full sail. The shoals lie 530 miles northwest of Hawaii on the direct air route between Pearl Harbor and Midway (q.v.).

To protect them against bird poachers, President Theodore Roosevelt by executive order in 1909 included the shoals in a wildlife preserve, along with other islands to the northwest of Hawaii except Midway. The U.S.S. *Rainbow*, Lt. Comdr. F. T. Horne commanding, completed a hydrographic survey of the shoals in 1914, and Lt. John Rodgers, then commandant of the Pearl Harbor Naval Air Station, determined in 1924 that the waters of the shoals were suitable for seaplanes. The Navy used the shoals as a site for amphibious landings and fleet problems as well as an advanced base during the 1930s. In the early days, PBYs were staged through the shoals, some personnel living on East Island.

After the outbreak of World War II, French Frigate Shoals were viewed by American naval officers as a possible staging point for enemy air attacks on Oahu and as a convenient site for an aviation fuel and emergency repair station. After two Japanese aircraft in March 1942 used the shoals to stage an attack on Pearl Harbor, the United States established an observation post protected by mines and a small Marine detachment (twelve enlisted men). This small occupation force apparently sufficed to deter the Japanese from using the shoals as a rendezvous prior to the Battle of Midway.

After the Japanese attack on Midway convinced the Americans that the island needed additional protection, the Navy decided to establish a naval air facility at French Frigate Shoals as a refueling station for fighters, as a staging and emergency landing point for either sea- or landplanes, and as an observation outpost for the defense of Pearl Harbor. In July 1942 the Fifth Construction Battalion began improvements at the shoals that within a year provided a channel 200 feet wide and 20 feet deep leading into the lagoon, a 3,100-foot runway on Tern Island at the northern extremity of the shoals, and an 8,000-foot seaplane runway. Around Tern Island the Seabees sank 5,000 steel pilings, into which they poured crushed coral, thereby forming a stationary airplane carrier that mounted defenses of barbed wire and light guns of various calibers. Other facilities included an administration building, quarters for officers and enlisted men, a radar tower, fresh-water evaporators and towers, and storage for 100,000 gallons of gasoline and 6,000 gallons of diesel oil. The total cost of the air facility was estimated at $2 million.

When the Seabees returned to Pearl Harbor in March 1943, the French Frigate Shoals Naval Air Facility was formally commissioned as a sub-department of the Pearl Harbor Naval Air Station, Lt. W. S. Tenhagen in charge. Naval personnel at the facility gradually increased to 4 officers and 123 enlisted men in 1944. In addition to providing emergency landing and staging facilities for planes moving between Pearl Harbor and Midway, the air facility daily despatched reconnaisance flights covering a 100-mile radius and beamed radar for 40 miles.

Maintenance was a serious problem at French Frigate Shoals, since salt in the air and water caused metals to rust rapidly and eroded the seawall. Boredom also plagued the personnel, whose only diversions were fishing and movies seven nights a week. The tedium was briefly broken, however, when the *Queen Mary* and her consorts called at the shoals for fueling in March 1943.

Having lost its usefulness to the Navy with the end of World War II, the air facility was closed effective 9 June 1946, and the property was turned over to the Hawaiian government for use as a fishing station. A Coast Guard Loran Transmitting Station, which had originally been constructed on the shoal's East Island, was reconstructed and commissioned on Tern Island in 1948.

BIBLIOGRAPHY

A. U.S. Navy, Bureau of Yards and Docks, *Building the Navy's Bases in World War II*, 2 vols. (Washington: GPO, 1947), II:161-62; Amerson A. Binion, "French Frigate Shoals, a History: 1786-1969" (Washington: Naval Historical Center, Operational Archives Branch); "Monograph Histories of U.S. Naval Overseas Bases. Vol. II. Pacific Area" (Washington: Naval Historical Center, Operational Archives Branch).

WILLIAM R. BRAISTED
PAOLO E. COLETTA

FROMENTINE, FRANCE.
See World War I U.S. Naval Air Stations in Europe.

FUNAFUTI, ELLICE ISLANDS, U.S. NAVAL ADVANCE BASE, 1942–1946 Funafuti, a coral atoll of the Ellice Islands, was in 1942 part of the British Crown Colony of the Gilbert and Ellice Islands. Located at 8°31′S., 179°8′E., the atoll is ten by eight miles in size and comprises thirty small islands, with Funafuti being the largest. Featuring a ship channel into its somewhat shallow lagoon, it was the only port of entry for the Ellice Islands. Situated about 700 miles southeast of Japanese holdings in the Gilberts and about 500 miles north of Fiji, it received consideration as early as 5 February 1942 as the site of an advance base. However, the idea was not adopted until late summer 1942 when concern mounted for Samoa after the Japanese began reinforcing their bases in the Gilberts.

On 2 October 1942 the Fifth Marine Defense Battalion and elements of the Second Naval Construction Battalion occupied Funafuti atoll. First priority was the construction of an airfield from which long-range reconnaissance flights could keep an eye on the southern Gilberts and Nauru. Open in November and improved to all-weather capability by the spring of 1943, Funafuti airfield was used beginning in April by heavy bombers to attack Tarawa in the Gilberts. In the meantime, Seabees likewise set up a small seaplane base for flying boats as well as a PT boat base from which several PTs from Squadron 3 operated until mid-1943.

Aside from its role as an outpost, Funafuti in the fall of 1943 became important in connection with preparations for Operation Galvanic, the invasion of the

Gilberts. The nearest naval base to the objectives of Tarawa and Makin, Funafuti acted as a staging and support point. On 1 November the fleet activated Service Squadron 4 (composed of twenty-four repair and supply vessels) at Funafuti. SERVRON 4 handled fuel, supplies, and minor repairs for many ships participating in Operation Galvanic. These services involved only SERVRON 4 vessels, as there were few facilities ashore. The naval base, such as it was, was commissioned on 15 November 1943. Funafuti also became a focal point for the landbased air forces supporting the invasions. Rear Adm. John H. Hoover, the air commander, was there from November 1943 until January 1944.

After the November-December 1943 conquest of the Gilberts, Funafuti also helped to support the subsequent invasion of the Marshall Islands (Operation Flintlock) commencing in January 1944. Again the atoll's submarine-proof anchorage served as a convenient supply and staging point, although part of SERVRON 4 had already advanced to newly captured Tarawa (q.v.). At Funafuti, chartered tankers transferred oil to the fleet oilers to take out to the combat ships. With the capture in February 1944 of the fine fleet anchorage at Majuro (q.v.), Funafuti's usefulness as a naval base was largely over. SERVRON 4 quickly moved north into the Marshalls. Thereafter, Funafuti's main value was its airfield, a necessary stopping point for Naval Air Transport Service flights to and from the South Pacific. Roll-up of facilities began in May 1944, but Funafuti's airfield was used until the base's disestablishment on 12 June 1946.

BIBLIOGRAPHY

A. U.S. Navy, Bureau of Yards and Docks, *Building the Navy's Bases in World War II*, 2 vols. (Washington: GPO, 1947); U.S. Navy, "U.S. Naval Bases in the South and Southwest Pacific (and Central Pacific Forward) in World War II," 1 November 1954 (Washington: Naval Historical Center, Operational Archives Branch).

B. Rear Adm. Worrall Reed Carter, *Beans, Bullets, and Black Oil* (Washington: GPO, 1953); Samuel E. Morison, *Aleutians, Gilberts, and Marshalls June 1942-April 1944* (Boston: Little, Brown, 1953); John B. Lundstrom, *The First South Pacific Campaign: Pacific Fleet Strategy, December 1941-June 1942* (Annapolis, Md.: Naval Institute Press, 1976).

JOHN B. LUNDSTROM

G

GALEAO, BRAZIL, U.S. NAVAL AIR FACILITY.
See Brazil, U.S. Naval Bases.

GATUN, PANAMA CANAL ZONE, RADIO STATION.
See Panama Canal Zone, U.S. Naval Radio Stations.

GEORGETOWN, BRITISH GUIANA, U.S. NAVAL AIR STATION AND NAVAL AIR FACILITY.
See Hispanic South America, U.S. Naval Bases.

GIBRALTAR, U.S. NAVY TENANT NAVAL BASE, 1801–1807, 1917–1919, 1941– The declaration of war on the United States by Tripoli on 14 May 1801 caused the United States in June 1801 to send Commo. Richard Dale from Norfolk with three frigates and a war schooner to the Mediterranean. Lacking a base, Dale by permission of the British governor used the naval facilities at Gibraltar. These were located west of ''The Rock'' on a sandy peninsula that joins The Rock to the Spanish mainland between 36°7′ and 36°9′N and 5°22′ and 5°21′W. Because American supply ships would not venture east of Gibraltar, he established a naval supply base at Syracuse, Sicily. His ships, which operated in the Straits and off the coast of North Africa, obtained water occasionally at Malta (*see* Mediterranean, The, U.S. Naval Bases, 1800-1917) and supplies through the firm of DeButts and Purviance, of Leghorn, Italy, but these were paid for through the London House of J. Mackenzie and A. Glennie. When supplies were either short or not forwarded in time from home, Dale exercised the prerogative of squadron commanders to borrow, lease, or even buy supplies overseas, including small warships.

In 1802 Dale was relieved by Commo. Richard Morris, who performed so perfunctorily that he was ordered home and cashiered from the service. The much more vigorous Commo. Edward Preble arrived at Gibraltar in September 1803 with two frigates, two brigs, and three schooners and was soon able to obtain a pledge from the Emperor of Morocco to abide by the 1787 treaty of peace and friendship. Preble then shifted his base to Syracuse, from where he could both police the Mediterranean and maintain his blockade of Tripoli. While there, in early 1804 he approved Lt. Stephen Decatur's plan to destroy the frigate *Philadelphia*, which had grounded and had been captured off Tripoli. Decatur's heroic exploit need not be retold. With peace with the Barbary nations concluded—temporarily—President Thomas Jefferson directed the Mediterranean squadron—usually two frigates and various brigs, schooners, and gunboats—to stay on station. Based on Syracuse and Malta, it did so until 1807, when economy measures forced the abandonment of Syracuse and a return to Gibraltar while Navy agents remained at Syracuse, Leghorn, Naples (q.v.), and Malta to handle details of repairing and provisioning American ships. Meanwhile, in 1806 Secretary of the Navy Samuel Smith centered naval administration in the Mediterranean at Port Mahon, Minorca.

During World War I, while Queenstown, Ireland, and Brest, France (*see* World War I U.S. Naval Air Stations in Europe; World War I U.S. Naval Bases in Europe), were the major American naval bases "over there," Gibraltar was important because it guarded the Atlantic-Mediterranean gateway. Vice Adm. William S. Sims, USN, Commander, U.S. Naval Forces Operating in European Waters, established a base there, and on 18 August 1917 there arrived the flagship of the patrol force of the U.S. Atlantic Fleet, the scout cruiser *Birmingham*. On the twentieth, Sims detached Rear Adm. Henry Wilson from Gibraltar and directed him to command the American naval base at Brest. Wilson had already obtained the complete cooperation of the British admiral in command as well as of French and Italian representatives at Gibraltar. Made available to Wilson had been supplies of all kinds, food, fuel oil, coal, and repair facilities. The same cooperation was extended to Wilson's relief, Rear Adm. Albert P. Niblack. The American ships at Gibraltar—cruisers, destroyers, and Coast Guard cutters—escorted convoys between The Rock and England and those that traversed the Mediterranean or made passage to the Azores Islands (q.v.). Though not quite as good as the record established at Queenstown, American ships at Gibraltar were at sea for 57 percent of the time—about six days at sea, four in port. The gateway for more traffic than any other port in the world, the 18,256 ships that passed by were escorted during World War I. At the time of the Armistice, the U.S. Navy had there two cruisers, four gunboats, five Coast Guard cutters, nine yachts, one tender, six destroyers, and eight submarine chasers.

During World War II the naval dockyard was constantly used to repair Allied ships; since then it has served many ships of the NATO nations.

BIBLIOGRAPHY

A. "American Naval Vessels Actually Present in European Waters upon the Cessation of Hostilities, Grouped by Bases: Statistics" (Washington: Naval Historical Center, Operational Archives Branch).

B. Gardner W. Allen, *Our Navy and the Barbary Corsairs* (Boston: Houghton Mifflin,

1905); James A. Field, *America and the Mediterranean World, 1776-1882* (Princeton, N.J.: Princeton University Press, 1969); Christopher McKee, *Edward Preble: A Naval Biography, 1761-1807* (Annapolis, Md.: Naval Institute Press, 1972).

GO DAU HA, REPUBLIC OF VIETNAM, U.S. NAVAL ADVANCE BASE, 1969–1971 This site, located close to the Cambodian border on South Vietnam's Vam Co Dong River, provided U.S. naval forces with an advanced base of operations during the Southeast Asian War. River patrol boat (PBR) units staged there in the effort to hinder communist infiltration that threatened nearby Tay Ninh and Saigon, further southeast.

Initially, acquiring sufficient land at Go Dau Ha proved a problem, but during 1969 the Army's engineers created a land-filled and metal-reinforced base area on the river bank. Soon afterward, Seabee units built sleeping and messing facilities, fuel and ammunition storage, defensive works, and a helicopter pad.

Go Dau Ha was turned over to the Vietnamese Navy in April 1971, as U.S. naval forces were withdrawn from the war.

BIBLIOGRAPHY

A. Commander Naval Forces, Vietnam, "The Naval War in Vietnam," May 1970 (Washington: Naval Historical Center, Operational Archives Branch).

EDWARD J. MAROLDA

GREEN ISLAND, SOLOMON ISLANDS, U.S. NAVAL ADVANCE BASE, 1944–1945 Green Island (also known as Nissan) is a coral atoll (4°38′S., 154°15′E.) situated roughly halfway between Buka and New Ireland. The most northerly of the Solomon Islands, in 1942 it was administered by Australia as part of the Mandated Territory of New Guinea. It is about seven by five miles in size, with a ship channel permitting anchorage by small vessels in the lagoon.

On 15 February 1944 troops of the Third New Zealand Division landed on Green Island to utilize it as part of the campaign to contain and neutralize powerful Japanese bases on New Britain and New Ireland northwest of there. Bombers operating from Green Island would be able to strike Rabaul and Kavieng as well as Truk in the Carolines to the north. An airfield on Green Island was operating by mid-March 1944 and eventually was expanded into an air complex capable of supporting a large number of aircraft.

The same day as the first landings on Green Island, the personnel and facilities of Motor Torpedo Boat Base 7 were put ashore, and on 16 February PT boats from MTB Squadron 10 began operating from the new base. The PTs executed patrols along the coast of New Ireland and raided the approaches to Rabaul. Seabees built a small naval supply depot on Green Island as well as a small fuel tank farm. To support the small craft using the atoll's facilities, a small-boat repair unit was established. On 15 June 1944 overall control of Green Island was transferred from the South Pacific Area to the Southwest Pacific Area, specifically the Seventh Fleet. Green Island became part of Allied Naval Forces, Northern Solomons Area (Task Group 70.8).

Combined air and sea assaults on the supply lines and installations surrounding Rabaul and Kavieng tamed those two previously feared Japanese bastions. The quieting down of Japanese naval activity permitted the roll-up of many installations in the Northern Solomons Area. At Green Island, MTB Base 7 was dismantled beginning 8 December 1944. The base itself was disestablished in March 1945, although Seabee maintenance forces remained there until August 1945.

BIBLIOGRAPHY

A. U.S. Navy, Bureau of Yards and Docks, *Building the Navy's Bases in World War II*, 2 vols. (Washington: GPO, 1947); U.S. Navy, "U.S. Naval Bases in the South and Southwest Pacific (and Central Pacific Forward) in World War II," 1 November 1954 (Washington: Naval Historical Center, Operational Archives Branch).

B. Robert Sherrod, *History of Marine Corps Aviation in World War II* (Washington: Combat Forces Press, 1952); Rear Adm. Worrall Reed Carter, *Beans, Bullets, and Black Oil* (Washington: GPO, 1953); Samuel E. Morison, *Aleutians, Gilberts, and Marshalls June 1942-April 1944* (Boston: Little, Brown, 1953).

JOHN B. LUNDSTROM

GREENLAND, U.S. NAVAL BASES, 1941– The coming of air travel made Greenland a strategic location, one particularly vital for meteorological stations. Knowing Greenland's weather today enables military strategists and forecasters to have a good idea about Europe's weather tomorrow. One consideration that went into planning the D-Day Normandy invasion was the weather report from Greenland.

Since Greenland belonged to Denmark, the German occupation of Denmark on 9 April 1940 greatly alarmed Greenlanders. The United States started negotiations to have a consulate set up in Greenland, and on 3 May Greenland requested American protection. The American consulate at Godthaab opened on 25 May, with James K. Penfield in charge.

As early as 18 May 1940 the Navy had plans to defend the cryolite mine at Ivigtut in south Greenland because cryolite was vital in the production of aluminum. In July 1940 the USCG *Campbell* (CG-65) arrived at Ivigtut with guns and ammunition. Some Coastguardsmen took off their uniforms and served as guards at the mine.

The United States was also sending survey teams, such as the South Greenland Survey Expedition, which arrived on 31 March 1941. Although the United States did not want to occupy Greenland, it did not want it to be occupied by a belligerent like Great Britain or Canada either. U.S. officials were slowly assuming the view that Greenland came under the Monroe Doctrine and welcomed Danish Minister Henrik de Kauffmann's negotiations in Washington.

On 25 March 1941 Germany extended the war zone to the east coast of Greenland. In the meantime, negotiations at Washington were progressing. On 5 April President F. D. Roosevelt allocated $5 million for construction of air bases in Greenland. Then, on the ninth, the first anniversary of the German occupation of Denmark, he and de Kauffmann signed the Agreement Relating to the Defense of Greenland. In the agreement the United States recognized Danish sovereignty in Greenland and assumed responsibility for its defense because of the inability of Denmark to provide it at the time. The U.S.-built bases in Greenland were to be made available to all nations of the Western Hemisphere. The legality of the agreement was doubtful because the Nazi-dominated Danish government denied it and Kauffmann wisely remained in Washington after he was recalled as minister. The Danish people and the Greenlanders apparently were considerably happier with the agreement.

In May 1941 President Roosevelt placed the seagoing vessels and personnel of the Coast Guard under the Navy because the former had the vessels to deal with ice, an outgrowth of its work with the International Ice Patrol created in 1912. The Northeast Greenland Patrol was established on 1 June 1941 under the leadership of Comdr. (later Rear Adm.) Edward H. "Iceberg" Smith, USCG, an explorer and oceanographer. The South Greenland Patrol started shortly afterward. In October of the same year the two would merge.

Meanwhile, on 7 June 1941 the Basic Joint Army-Navy Plan for the Defense of Greenland (the NOAH Plan) was issued. The Navy had three main tasks: 1) to defend sea communications between Greenland and North America; 2) to defend shipping in Greenland's coastal waters; and 3) to aid the Army in keeping away any hostile elements from the continent and its territorial waters. U.S. Army troops occupied Greenland on 13 June 1941.

Commander Smith had already learned from natives about a place called Narssarssuaq, or "large, level place." It proved to be the best place for the main air base to be built in Greenland. In addition to providing convoy escort with the Northeast Greenland Patrol, Smith started the Northeast Greenland Sledge Patrol. This consisted primarily of Danes with dogsleds on watch for any Nazi activity. Acting on a tip from this patrol, the Coast Guard cutter *North Star* (WPG-59), Lt. Comdr. Frank Meals, captured the SS *Buskoe*, a Norwegian sealer carrying a German meteorological and communications expedition, on 12 September 1941. Later some men and gear were rounded up on shore on the east coast of Greenland. This was the first American prize of World War II.

Also before Pearl Harbor the Navy authorized base construction in Greenland, on 28 November 1941. The four objectives for the Navy's initial phase were the naval facilities at Narssarssuaq and Gronnedal, a radio station at Gamatron, and a Loran navigation station at Frederiksdal.

By 25 October 1941 there was only one combined Greenland Patrol. About Christmastime, Commander Smith set up his three-man Greenland Patrol Headquarters in the Boston Navy Yard. The headquarters was later moved to Argentia, Newfoundland (q.v.). There was also a Senior Officer Present Ashore (SOPA) in Greenland, at Narssarssuaq. Duties of the Patrol included: 1) keeping up Greenland communications on the Allied side (some Norwegians had been broadcasting pro-Nazi propaganda); 2) preventing all Axis operations in Greenland; 3) escorting shipping in the area; 4) maintaining icebreakers to keep waters as ice-free as possible for shipping; 5) providing reconnaissance and plane-guarding operations; and 6) supplying the Army.

Greenland Patrol also had to have the cutters and PBY patrol craft available to support the Army's Operation Bolero for ferrying a million men and many aircraft to the British Isles. This operation began on 26 June 1942 and continued through the warm weather months of that year and 1943. The Greenland Patrol was working with old converted trawlers to supplement its cutters.

During World War II thirteen U.S. bases were known as "bluies" in Army code, a term the Navy adopted. These bases were built by private contractors working under the Army. The Navy's Bureau of Yards and Docks supplied many of the materials, especially for the bases that most concerned the Navy. The bases were as follows.

Bluie West 1—Narssarssuaq, located in southwest Greenland, forty miles inland at the head of Tunugdliarfik Fjord at 61°9′N., 49°25′W. It also carried the code name "Onoto." This was the main air base and the location of the SOPA as well as the command post for the Greenland Patrol's air operations. Narssarssuaq proved very valuable to the aircraft-ferrying phase of Operation Bolero, which operated between Presque Isle, Me., and Prestwick, Scotland. Narssarssuaq is located approximately 775 miles from Goose Bay, Labrador, and Reykjavik, Iceland. The base was commissioned on 1 January 1943 and turned over to Denmark on 15 July 1946. The Naval Air Facility, however, operated until 5 February 1951.

Bluie West 2—Kipisaka, on a narrow channel in the Cape Farewell Archipelago on the southern tip of Greenland at about 59°47′N., 43°55′W.

Bluie West 3—Simiutak Island (also known as Cruncher Island), at the mouth of Skovfjord, in the south at 60°42′N., 46°33′W. A high-frequency direction finder station was built there.

Bluie West 4—Faeringhavn, at 63°42′N., 51°33′W.

Bluie West 5—Godhavn, at the southern tip of Disko Island on Davis Strait at the mouth of Disko Bay, at 69°15′N., 53°32′W.

Bluie West 6—Thule, in northwest Greenland on the south shore of Wolstenholme Fjord, an inlet of North Baffin Bay, at 76°33′N., 68°47′W. Thule became the major air base after the war.

Bluie West 7—Gronnedal, a Naval Operating Facility on the east side of Arsuk Fjord at 61°14′N., 48°6′W., near the cryolite mine at Ivigtut. It carried the code name "Biped." It started in May 1942, and the fuel depot and base were commissioned on 1 April 1943. It was turned over to Denmark on 10 August 1951.

Bluie West 8—Sondre Stromfjord, 100 miles inland, 10 miles from the ice cap, and just north of the Arctic Circle at 67°1′N., 50°43′W. It was an airfield commanded by Col. Bernt Balchen, a famous aviator and polar explorer. Balchen became well known for organizing and carrying out rescues of downed flyers on the Greenland Ice Cap. This base was also known as "Bodkin." It is still in American hands and is known as Sondrestrom Airfield.

Bluie East 1—Torgilsbu, near Cape Farewell on the southern tip of Greenland at 59°47′N., 43°55′W.

Bluie East 2—Ikateq, on Angmagssalik Island at 65°36′N., 37°36′W. It was built in 1942 as an airfield and was connected with the Canadian Arctic Task Unit's Crimson Project. It was abandoned in 1946.

Bluie East 3—Gurreholm, on the east side of Northeast Bay at Scoresby Sound, 71°17′N., 25°5′W. The radio station was started 12 October 1941.

Bluie East 4—Ella Island, on the west side of the King Oscar's Fjord on Davy Sound at 72°10′N., 23°40′W.

Bluie East 5—Eskimonaes, at the southernmost point of Clavering Island at 74°5′N., 21°16′W. This was a radio station and headquarters of the Northeast Greenland Sledge Patrol. On 24 March 1943 Germans from the Sabine Island meteorological station attacked and burned Eskimonaes. One Sledge Patrol member was killed and another captured, but the latter overpowered his captor and escorted him on the long journey to Gurreholm, arriving in May.

By 14 May 1943 Colonel Balchen's planes were bombing Eskimonaes, which the Germans had already abandoned. On 25 May the combination of Balchen's forces on land and in the air and those of Capt. Carl C. von Paulsen on the sea captured the German post at Sabine Island. A new U.S. station was set up at Myggbukta, also called McKenzie Bay or Mosquito Bay, at 73°29′N., 21°35′W.

Two important Navy posts were not in the Bluie chain. The naval radio station at *Gamatron Island* was on the eastern side of Skovfjord in southern Greenland at about 60°40′N., 46°32′W. The secret Loran navigation station was at *Frederiksdal*, the southernmost Danish settlement in Greenland, at 60°0′N., 44°40′W. It was also known as Navy 226.

The Greenland Patrol also had escort duties at the "Crystal" bases in the Canadian Arctic: Crystal 1 at Fort Chimo, Quebec; Crystal 2 at Upper Frobisher Bay, Baffin Island; and Crystal 3 at Padloping Island, near Baffin Island.

In order to spot German activity around eastern Greenland as early as possible, Admiral Smith in 1943 decided to establish a high-frequency direction finder station on Jan Mayen Island, 250 miles east of Scoresby Sound, Greenland. Norway controlled Jan Mayen, and "free" Norwegians operated a radio station there. Capt. Charles W. Thomas in the cutter *Northland* (WPG-49) arrived in November 1943, and the crew built a station in one month, overcoming many problems with the weather and rough surf. The base, called "New Chicago," later became part of the Iceland Base Command.

There were other encounters with the Germans around Greenland. The *Northland* chased and captured the trawler *Kehdingen* near Great Koldewey Island on 1 September 1944. On 4 October the Americans captured the German weather station on Little Koldewey Island, along with 500 land mines. On 14 October 1944 the *Eastwind* (WAG-279) and *Southwind* (WAG-280) captured the Nazi trawler *Externstein* with its communication system and crew of twenty. The Americans then used this ship under the name *East Breeze*.

Naval operations in Greenland were scaled down toward the end of the war, even though the airfields continued to be important. After the war, while the Army and Air Force rebuilt airfields and conducted experiments on the Greenland Ice Cap, the Navy continued its gradual withdrawal. But there was little doubt that the United States would stay in Greenland. The 1947 Inter-American Treaty of Reciprocal Assistance (Rio Treaty) included Greenland in the sphere of American security.

On 27 April 1951 a new Danish-American agreement under NATO was signed. One provision was the transfer of the Naval Station Gronnedal to Denmark. NOB Greenland was disestablished on 10 August 1951. As of 1952, U.S. Navy personnel were no longer stationed in Greenland.

All Navy connection with Greenland did not end, however. Operation Blue Jay in 1951 was a secret operation to build the modern air base at Thule, original site of Bluie West 6. The Military Sea Transportation Service, consisting of Navy ships and time-chartered commercial vessels, transported many of the men and materials to Greenland. Elements of the Atlantic Fleet were involved too. On 1 June 1951 the USS *Edisto* (AGB-2), with the Coast Guard's *Eastwind*, began to break the ice in Baffin Bay. Victory and Liberty ships followed with construction materials. The Navy used LSTs and LSDs as well as Underwater Demolition Teams to blast underwater obstacles. The project continued in 1952 under the name Operation SUNAC (Support of North Atlantic Construction). A total of 148 vessels fought fog and icebergs to bring materials to Thule, which has a shipping season of only forty-five to sixty days a year because of the ice. Ships also originally had to serve as barracks for the construction crews.

The U.S. Navy still flies aircraft into Greenland. Its Antarctic Development Squadron Six (VXE-6) has used its LC-130 *Hercules* with skis during northern summers to support the National Science Foundation's Greenland Ice Sheet Project. The Navy has also participated in joint service polar exercises such as East Arctic '81, with Greenland as a jumping-off point. With an apparent revival recently of U.S. interest in Greenland, perhaps the Navy will become involved again.

BIBLIOGRAPHY

A. U.S. Navy, Atlantic Fleet, Commander in Chief, *Commander Greenland Patrol*, Administrative History No. 140 (Washington: Navy Department, 1946); U.S. Navy, Bureau of Yards and Docks, *Building the Navy's Bases in World War II*, 2 vols. (Washington: GPO, 1947); U.S. Department of State, *Agreement between the Government of the United States of America and the Government of the Kingdom of Denmark, Pursuant to the North Atlantic Treaty, Concerning the Defense of Greenland, 27 April 1951* (Washington: GPO, 1952); U.S. Defense Mapping Agency, Hydrographic Topographic Center, *Sailing Directions for East Greenland and Iceland*, H. O. Pub. No. 17 (Washington: GPO, 1976); U.S. Defense Mapping Agency, Hydrographic Topographic Center, *Sailing Directions for West Coast of Greenland (Kap Farvel to Kap Morris Jesup)*, 3rd ed., H. O. Pub. No. 16 (Washington: GPO, 1976); U.S. Department of State, *Agreement Relating to the Defense of Greenland, 9 April 1941* (Washington: GPO, 1971).

B. Philip E. Mosely, ''Iceland and Greenland: An American Problem,'' *Foreign Affairs*

18 (July 1940):742-46; Vilhjalmur Stefansson, *Greenland* (Garden City, N.Y.: Doubleday, Doran, 1942); Bernt Balchen, Corey Ford, and Oliver La Farge, *War below Zero: The Battle for Greenland* (Boston: Houghton Mifflin, 1944); Richard Van Alstyne, *American Diplomacy in Action: A Series of Case Studies* (Stanford, Calif.: Stanford University Press, 1944); Hans W. Weigert, "Iceland, Greenland and the United States," *Foreign Affairs* 23 (Oct. 1944):112-22; Samuel E. Morison, *The Battle of the Atlantic September 1939-May 1943* (Boston: Little, Brown, 1947); Arthur Pocock, *Red Flannel and Green Ice* (London: Herbert Jenkins, 1950); Charles W. Thomas, *Ice Is Where You Find It* (Indianapolis: Bobbs-Merrill, 1951); William L. Langer and S. Everett Gleason, *The Challenge to Isolation, 1937-1940* (New York: Harper and Brothers, 1952); William L. Langer and Everett Gleason, *The Undeclared War, 1940-1941* (New York: Harper and Brothers, 1953); Harvey Mitchell, "Where Sailors Did NOT Want Liberty," *All Hands* 432 (Feb. 1953):10-12; Geoffrey Williamson, *Changing Greenland* (New York: Library Publishers, 1954); David Howarth, *The Sledge Patrol* (New York: Macmillan, 1957); Stetson Conn and Byron Fairchild, *The Framework of Hemisphere Defense. U.S. Army in World War II: The Western Hemisphere* (Washington: Office of Chief of Military History, 1960); John A. Logan, *No Transfer: An American Security Principle* (New Haven: Yale University Press, 1961); William S. Carlson, *Lifelines through the Arctic* (New York: Duell, Sloan and Pearce, 1962); Borge Fristrup, *The Greenland Ice Cap* (Seattle: University of Washington Press, 1967); Jefferson H. Weaver, "Greenland As Part of the U.S.," *New York Times*, 13 Aug. 1970; Patrick Abbazia, *Mr. Roosevelt's Navy: The Private War of the U.S. Atlantic Fleet, 1939-1942* (Annapolis, Md.: Naval Institute Press, 1975); "Antarctic Airplanes Aid Greenland Program," *Antarctic Journal of the United States* 12 (Sept. 1977):13; Orlen L. Brownfield, "An Arctic Odyssey," *MAC Flyer* 24 (Sept. 1977):12-14; John H. Cloe, "Skibirds on the Ice Cap," *American Aviation Historical Society Journal* 22 (Summer 1977):42-53; Finn B. Sorenson, "Greenland Its Relevance to North American Security," *Naval War College Review* 32 (Nov.-Dec. 1979):88-102; Edward W. Chester, *The United States and Six Atlantic Outposts: The Military and Economic Considerations* (Port Washington, N.Y.: Kennikat Press, 1980); Geir Lundestad, *America, Scandinavia, and the Cold War, 1945-1949* (New York: Columbia University Press, 1980); A. V. Stephenson, "Up North on East Arctic," *Airman* 25 (Dec. 1981):44-48; "Secret U.S.-Greenland Policy?" *Christian Science Monitor*, 14 Jan. 1983, p. 2.

WILLIAM MCQUADE

GUADALCANAL, SOLOMON ISLANDS, U.S. NAVAL ADVANCE BASE, 1942-1946 [CACTUS, LATER MAINYARD] The prime objective of the first U.S. counteroffensive of the Pacific War, Guadalcanal was the largest island in the British Solomon Islands Protectorate in the South Pacific. Approximately eighty miles long and twenty-five miles wide, it features a mountainous spine and a northern coastal plain. In 1942 activity on the island centered around Lunga Point (9°25′S., 160°5′E.) on the north-central coast, where the Japanese in June began constructing an airfield a month after they first occupied the island. In July 1942 the Joint Chiefs of Staff approved Guadalcanal as the major objective in Operation Watchtower, the reconquest of the lower Solomons as the first step of an island-by-island campaign toward the main Japanese base at Rabaul, on New Britain in the Bismarck Archipelago. On 7 August 1942 the First Marine Division (reinforced) executed landings on Guadalcanal and also on Tulagi and Florida Islands eighteen miles to the north across Sealark Channel. It was the beginning of a bitter seven-month land, sea, and air struggle to hold onto and expand beachheads in the face of determined enemy counterattacks. Guadalcanal was finally secured on 9 February 1943 after a Japanese evacuation.

During the actual fighting on the island, NAB Guadalcanal's main contribution, other than destroying enemy troops there, was as a vital air base contesting for air superiority over the southern Solomons. In plans for Watchtower, provisions were made for rapidly capturing and activating the Japanese airfield on Guadalcanal. During the landings on 7-8 August, Vice Adm. Robert L. Ghormley (Commander, South Pacific Area) put his amphibious commander, Rear Adm. Richmond Kelly Turner, in charge of developing the air base. On 20 August two squadrons (one fighter—VMF-223, one dive bomber—VMSB-232) from Marine Air Group 24 arrived at Guadalcanal's newly christened Henderson Field. They were the first of many Marine, Navy, and Army air units to operate from Guadalcanal as the "Cactus Air Force." On 29 August the headquarters and elements of CUB-1 arrived from Espiritu Santo (q.v.) to help run the airfield. Turner wanted advance naval base facilities set up on Guadalcanal because it possessed virtually no port or unloading areas other than beaches, despite urgent supply requirements for ground and aviation forces. However, CUB-1 and Seabees, who followed in September, had to concentrate on airfield development; this was hindered by almost daily Japanese air and artillery attacks along with occasional naval bombardments. Elements of the Sixth Naval Construction Battalion set about building three auxiliary airfields around Henderson Field to aid dispersal. One of the fields was named Carney (for Capt. James V. Carney, USMC), another Sailer (for Maj. Joseph Sailer, USMC). In addition Seabees constructed fighter strips at Kukum and Lunga and two bomber fields at Koli Point. An involved project, with airfields, aviation gasoline tank farms, and base facilities, it transformed north-central Guadalcanal into a massive air base complex.

By the very end of the Guadalcanal campaign in early 1943, Seabees had gradually improved port facilities at Lunga, Kukum, Point Cruz, and Tetere on the island's north coast. Guadalcanal became a valuable staging and supply point to help support the northwestward advance through the Solomons. Construction troops set up camps, depots, and hospitals all along the north coast, serviced by a complex network of roads. No fewer than seventeen naval construction battalions served on Guadalcanal, remaking much of the island's real estate. Unloading capacity was raised to about 2000 tons a day to handle the flow of men and materiel to and from the island. A ship repair unit serviced the profusion of small boats and landing craft using Guadalcanal. In October 1943, headquarters South Pacific Area moved to Koli Point.

At Guadalcanal, troops staged for such operations as Bougainville (November 1943) and Guam (July 1944). Likewise the island was a staging point for landbased aviation, particularly Marine Corps, a link between Espiritu Santo and the forward bases. Guadalcanal's last big effort came in February-March 1945, when troops from there helped mount Operation ICEBERG, the invasion of Okinawa. Island depots issued supplies and ships to a total of 207 were loaded with men and materiel or otherwise serviced by floating repair units. With their departure by 15 March 1945, Guadalcanal faced a drastic roll-up of installations. The naval air station was the last to go, and on 12 June 1946, Guadalcanal's advance naval base was disestablished.

BIBLIOGRAPHY

A. Lt. (jg) Eugene E. McLeary, "History of U.S. Naval Advance Base Guadalcanal, 1942-1945," 2 vols. Shore Establishment, 1945 (Washington: Naval Historical Center, Operational Archives Branch); Service Squadron, South Pacific, "History of Commander, Service Squadron, South Pacific 7 December 1941-15 August 1945" (Washington: Naval Historical Center, Operational Archives Branch); U.S. Navy, Bureau of Yards and Docks, *Building the Navy's Bases in World War II*, 2 vols. (Washington: GPO, 1947).

B. Samuel E. Morison, *Coral Sea, Midway, and Submarine Actions May 1942-August 1942* (Boston: Little, Brown, 1949); Samuel E. Morison, *The Struggle for Guadalcanal August 1942-February 1943* (Boston: Little, Brown, 1949); Samuel E. Morison, *Breaking the Bismarcks Barrier 22 July 1942-1 May 1944* (Boston: Little, Brown, 1950); Robert Sherrod, *History of Marine Corps Aviation in World War II* (Washington: Combat Forces Press, 1952); Rear Adm. Worrall Reed Carter, *Beans, Bullets, and Black Oil* (Washington: GPO, 1953); Vice Adm. George C. Dyer, *The Amphibians Came to Conquer*, 2 vols. (Washington: GPO, 1972).

JOHN B. LUNDSTROM

GUAM, MARIANA ISLANDS, U.S. NAVAL STATION AND NAVAL OPERATING BASE, 1898– Guam is the largest and most southern of the Mariana Islands, an archipelago that is part of a semi-submerged mountain chain extending southward from Japan. Located in the middle of the Western Pacific, it is 1,555 miles east of Manila, 1,550 miles south of Tokyo, and 3,644 miles west of Honolulu. It is roughly the shape of a footprint enclosing 225 square miles, and is thirty miles long and twelve miles wide. It possesses one harbor on the west coast, San Luis d'Apra, which has been developed as a protected anchorage capable of berthing a large number of ships. The island has been devastated twice by typhoons since World War II.

The native inhabitants of Guam are Chamoros, a Micronesian people who intermarried extensively with the Spanish. The first European to discover Guam was Ferdinand Magellan, sailing for Spain in 1529. Spain ruled the Marianas from their bloody conquest in the seventeenth century until the Spanish-American War of 1898. When President McKinley decided to send reinforcements to Adm. George Dewey following the Battle of Manila Bay, Capt. Henry Glass, with the cruiser *Charleston* escorting three transports of the first Philippine expeditionary force, stopped briefly at the defenseless island to secure its surrender to the United States and to convey the Spanish governor and his staff as prisoners to the Philippines. In August 1898 the Navy Department's Strategy Board recommended that the United States acquire a coaling and cable station in the Marianas along with stations at Pearl Harbor, the Philippines, and China. Guam was to be one of a chain of stations along a naval route extending from the Atlantic via an isthmian canal and across the Pacific to the Far East. The board cautioned, however, that the United States should only acquire the overseas positions that it was prepared to defend, and the United States thus secured only Guam and the Philippines, in the Pacific, from Spain by the Treaty of Paris in 1898, leaving the remaining Marianas and other Spanish mid-Pacific islands to be acquired by Germany by purchase from Spain the following year. Guam was assigned by the President to the Navy in 1899, and the naval governor of Guam from 1899 to 1949 was also commandant of the Guam naval station.

Guam seemed all but forgotten during the decade after the Spanish-American War. A Guam Survey Board under Capt. John F. Merry in 1901 recommended building a fortified base on the island, and the 1905 Joint Army and Navy Board on Coast Defense chaired by Secretary of War William Howard Taft included Guam among the strategic positions in the Pacific that should be fortified. Its funds for overseas bases being limited, however, the Navy Department concentrated initially on building a fleet base at Subic Bay (q.v.) in the Philippines and, after 1908, at Pearl Harbor. The Pacific Cable Company established a landing for its trans-Pacific cable at Guam in 1903, and in 1905 the Bureau of Equipment had a modest coal pile of 5,000 tons at Guam.

Only gradually did Guam begin to loom more important in American naval thinking as Japan, after about 1905, moved from the position of sure friend to that of possible enemy. With the main units of their battle fleet habitually concentrated in the Atlantic as protection against Germany, naval strategists sought means by which the battle fleet during a war with Japan (known as the Orange Plan) could be moved to and maintained in the Western Pacific preparatory to the expected climactic battle with the Japanese fleet. Army experts insisted that the Army could not hold the Navy's proposed base at Subic Bay against Japanese attack until the arrival of the American fleet from the Atlantic, and the Joint Army and Navy Board in 1908 decided that the Navy should concentrate on building Pearl Harbor as its principal overseas base in the Pacific. As the American fleet could not operate effectively in the Western Pacific 5,000 miles from a base at Pearl Harbor, Guam assumed significance as a point from which the Navy might organize support for the fleet on its transit from Hawaii to the Far East.

The Navy's prestigious General Board finally affirmed in 1909 that Guam should be defended "as a naval base of the first order" because the fleet would require the island as an "intermediate point of support" during its transit across the Pacific. That year the board also persuaded the Navy Department to land six old 6-inch guns from the gunboat *Concord* at Guam to serve in an improvised defense. The Naval War College in its 1911 Orange Plan concluded that the central route across the Pacific by way of Hawaii and Guam was the best course for the fleet to follow in its passage to the Far East. Both the Army and the Navy War College declared the following year that, since Pearl Harbor and Guam were the two foci from which the battle fleet could operate effectively in the Pacific, Guam should be provided with defenses sufficient to prevent its capture by any force that might be brought against it. These recommendations were finally adopted by the Joint Army and Navy Board and approved by President Woodrow Wilson during an immigration crisis with Japan in May 1913. The Navy also gave at least tentative support to the concept of a base at Guam in 1913 by moving the Marines and sixty guns of an advanced base outfit from Subic Bay to Guam.

This mild upsurge on behalf of Guam was followed by years of indecision, drift, and debate. In April 1914 a subordinate Joint Army and Navy Board at Guam drew up a scheme for the defense of the entire island with fixed defenses mounting guns ranging up to 14-inch-rifles and a mobile garrison of 8,500 men, but this report lay unattended for the next five years in the files of the Joint Army and Navy Board in Washington. The proposals by successive island governors similarly failed to generate response from higher authority. This inaction in Washington reflected, in part, uncertainty as to the Navy's role in the Western Pacific should the Philippines gain the independence promised them in the 1916 Jones Bill, and, in part, from a tendency to delay decisions affecting the Pacific until World War I was safely won in the Atlantic.

With the destruction of German naval power in World War I and the opening of the Panama Canal, the U.S. Navy was finally able to station a battleship fleet in the Pacific, the better to protect Guam and other American insular possessions. Japan, however, had extended its power eastward in the Pacific by seizing German island possessions that paralleled the Navy's natural trans-Pacific route and practically surrounded Guam: the Marianas, the Marshalls, and the Carolines. Anxious to keep the islands out of neutral hands and reduce the threat they posed to the Navy's trans-Pacific line of communications, American naval officers agreed to leave the islands to Japan as mandates from the League of Nations with the proviso that the island empire would neither fortify nor build naval bases in its new possessions. Perhaps inadvertently, Japan thus acquired the positions that would prove invaluable to the United States in its island-hopping movement across the Pacific during World War II. By insisting that Japan refrain from fortifying its Pacific islands, however, the Americans provided Japan with an opportunity to demand a *quid pro quo*: that the United States refrain from building additional naval and military installations in Guam and the Philippines.

Nevertheless, American naval officers after 1919 pressed for the construction of a base at Guam. In 1919 the Parks-McKean Board on navy yard development declared itself "convinced of the necessity" for building a first-class base at Guam and a second-class base in the Philippines, and the reorganized Joint Army and Navy Board affirmed in its 1919 paper, "Strategy in the Pacific," that the fleet required fortified bases at Hawaii, Guam, and the Philippines so that the fleet could move to establish a blockade of Japan. The following year, the Joint

Board, the Navy's General Board, and war planners in the CNO's office all resolved that building a base at Guam was second only to construction of a naval operating base at Pearl Harbor. The enthusiasm of naval professionals for Guam, however, was not shared by their civilian chiefs or by Congress, and Guam remained without significant naval facilities or permanent fortifications when representatives of the five leading naval powers in 1921 met at the Washington Conference on arms limitation.

American naval professionals hoped to exclude naval bases from the discussions at the Washington Conference. The Japanese, however, were unwilling to accept a fleet inferior to that of the United States if the Americans retained the right to build bases at Guam and in the Philippines from which their fleet could menace the Japanese homeland. In consequence, in Article XIX of the Five Power Naval Treaty of 1922 the United States agreed to refrain from building new naval or military installations in its island possessions west of Hawaii, while Japan accepted a battle fleet having 60 percent of the tonnage of the American fleet. Japan also undertook not to build military or naval facilities outside its home islands. American naval officers deeply resented the prohibition placed on Guam even as they ignored in their public statements the advantage gained by the United States from Japan's promise to leave its Pacific islands unfortified.

Article XIX effectively eliminated Guam as a significant factor in American naval strategy for at least fifteen years. As the Joint Army and Navy Orange Plans still contemplated a movement by the American fleet to the Philippines, American planners looked increasingly to the unfortified Japanese mandates, rather than to Guam, as way stations available to the fleet during its westward progress. The Hoover administration practically demilitarized Guam in 1930-1932 by withdrawing all naval aircraft from the island, removing its principal ordnance, and reducing the Marine garrison to 10 officers and 121 enlisted men.

Only with the expiration of the Five Power Naval Disarmament Treaty of 1922 on 31 December 1936 was the United States again free to build a base at Guam, and thereafter strong sentiment emerged within the Navy, especially among naval airmen, for the construction of a base on the island. In 1935 the Navy granted to Pan American Airways the right to develop facilities at Guam as well as Midway and Wake for its famed China Clipper, facilities that would be available to the Navy during an emergency. As in the past, however, the naval agitation in favor of the base tended to collide with political, diplomatic, and even naval considerations that ultimately weighed heavily in favor of inaction. The United States rejected a proposal from Britain that they agree with Japan to continue the nonfortification arrangement even after the expiration of the Washington treaty, but the Chief of Naval Operations, Adm. William D. Leahy, cautioned in the spring of 1938 that it was then inappropriate to ask Congress for legislation for a Guam base. Finally, in response to a request from Congress to the Navy Department for its recommendations on air, submarine, and destroyer bases, the Hepburn Board (chaired by Rear Adm. A. J. Hepburn) exceeded the Board's original precept, to recommend "major and minor base sites,'' to urge the development of Guam as a ''Major Advanced Fleet Base'' because such a base would assure the Philippines ''practical immunity'' against attack, ''reduce to its simplest terms'' the defense of Hawaii and the continental United States, and provide the fleet with greater freedom to meet emergencies in the Atlantic. The Hepburn Board also recommended construction of a major air and submarine base at Guam with defenses sufficient to render its capture a serious undertaking for any probable enemy. A modest provision of $5 million largely for harbor improvement at Apra was disapproved by Congress in 1939, as was a somewhat smaller appropriation in 1940. Finally in 1941, after the Rear Adm. John Greenslade Board had recommended the building of an ''Outlying Subsidiary Base'' at Guam capable of supporting minor task forces, Congress approved modest expenditures for breakwater and harbor improvement, fuel storage, and additional seaplane facilities.

As naval war planners in 1941 were increasingly diverted from the Pacific by the gathering crisis in the Atlantic, their plans for the Pacific became more defensive. Guam in 1941 was placed in ''Category F'' in defense planning, under which local forces under attack would attempt no more than to destroy those items that should not fall into enemy hands, and the Navy Department decided against establishing a Marine Defense Battalion on the island because the unit could not be expected to provide any effective defense. Asked by the Secretary of the Navy whether Guam should be provided with permanent defenses, the General Board recommended in November 1941 that the island not be fortified under current circumstances because any move to increase its defenses might provoke the crisis with Japan that the Navy then desired to avoid. Work on the limited improvements authorized by Congress, undertaken under contract by a private firm, was hardly under way when Guam fell to the Japanese on 10 December 1941. During their brief occupation, the Japanese constructed a 4,500-foot airstrip on Orote Peninsula and nearly completed a similar strip close to the capital, Agana.

The Americans recaptured Guam in July and August 1944 as part of Operation Forager, whose purpose was to secure naval and air base sites in the three principal Mariana Islands: Guam, Saipan, and Tinian. The first landing on Guam was a two-pronged thrust by the Marines and Army north and south of Apra harbor to encircle and seize the harbor and Orote Peninsula airfield. The field was operational by 30 July, and Seabees moved rapidly to construct a 17,000-foot barrier enclosing the outer harbor, extensive quay walls and pontoon piers, and a dredged inner harbor for small craft. The core of the naval base was LION 6, whose components as assembled in California prior to shipment to Guam had the capacity of Pearl Harbor at the outbreak of World War II. Naval Operating Base Guam eventually acquired floating dry docks with lifting capacity up to 80,000 tons and shops capable of repairing all classes of ships. Apra claimed second place after Antwerp as the busiest foreign port under American control. The base's ammunition dumps covered 6,910 acres; its huge supply depot distributed supplies valued at $1 billion during the war.

Also of prime importance on Guam were the five reconstructed or newly built airfields. Orote Airfield, its runways rebuilt and extended to 5,000 feet, initially supported fighter operations and later serviced 1,800 planes for the fleet and the Marines. The extended Agana Airfield handled passenger and freight traffic. North of the Agana field was the large Harmon Field, which first launched B-29 bombers for Japan in November 1944. And finally there were completed two entirely new fields, each with 8,500-foot airstrips, North and Northwest Fields, for B-29 traffic. Guam also became a major fuel station in the Western Pacific, boasting a tank capacity of 328,000 barrels of aviation gasoline, 130,000 barrels of diesel oil, 40,000 barrels of gasoline, and 448,000 barrels of fuel oil. The facilities, in short, provided for all branches of the armed forces. In addition to the Naval Operating Base, the Naval Air Base, and the Army airfields, Guam was also the advanced headquarters of Commander in Chief Pacific Fleet-Pacific Ocean Area (CINCPAC-CINCPOA) (Adm. Chester W. Nimitz), the Commander Forward Area Central Pacific, and the Marine island commander.

Although Guam experienced considerable retrenchment after World War II, it remained one of the Navy's key positions in the Western Pacific. Being American soil, it is the only American base west of Pearl Harbor where the Navy's tenure is not subject to dispute by a foreign landlord, as have been Subic Bay in the Philippines, Cam Ranh Bay (q.v.) in Vietnam, or Yokosuka (q.v.) in Japan. Atop Nimitz Hill to the west of Agana is the headquarters of the Commander, U.S. Naval Forces Marianas, who serves as coordinator for a variety of naval activities in Guam, the Northern Marianas, and the Trust Territories of the Pacific Islands. The Navy's senior officer on Guam has not been involved in administering civil government since 1949. His job, however, has drawn him into diplomatic and civil projects, such as his coordination of the evacuation of some 119,919 refugees from Southwest Asia in 1975.

There being no question that Guam would continue as a site for important naval activities, the Navy immediately after 1945 was tasked with reconstructing in more permanent form the temporary facilities that had been hastily contrived during the war. Guam was the immediate beneficiary of roll-ups of other Western Pacific bases that brought to the island a large amount of useful material. Deactivation of the famous Seabees forced the Navy to turn to civilian contractors for such important work as dredging and equipping Apra Harbor. A consortium of firms, the Brown-Pacific-Maxon Construction Company, was awarded construction contracts amounting to $261,839,291 over a period of more than nine years, an average of well over $2 million a month. The Korean and Vietnam wars also stimulated new construction, as did devastating typhoons, notably Karen in 1962 and supertyphoon Pamela in 1976.

Oldest of the island's naval utilities is the Naval Station, which included the entire island at the time of its founding in 1899. After Guam's recapture from Japan in 1944, the station emerged around Apra Harbor as the Guam Naval Operating Base, was redesignated a Naval Base in 1952, and then returned to the status of a Naval Station in 1956. The station is home port of Commander

Submarine Squadron Fifteen (Comsubron Fifteen) including the tender *Proteus* and eight fleet ballistic missile submarines based on "Polaris Point." SUBRON Fifteen also provides logistic support to Seventh Fleet nuclear attack submarines. Spread over more than 1,000 acres around Apra Harbor is the U.S. Naval Supply Depot, Guam, which provides supplies and services to the fleet as well as numerous shore activities on Guam.

The former Industrial Department of the Guam Naval Operating Base was separated from the base in 1951 and redesignated the U.S. Naval Ship Repair Facility, Guam. The facility's mission is "to provide logistic support, including drydocking, repair, alteration, and conversion of naval ships and service craft and ships of other departments." In addition, the facility has repaired ships of such friendly states as the Philippines, the Republic of China, and South Vietnam. Greatly reduced from its World War II capacity, the facility's usefulness has been restricted by the want of a large graving dock. The large number of Filipinos in the facility's labor force has been replaced since the late 1960s by American citizens.

The Guam Naval Air Station is centered on the two runways of the Guam Naval Air Base built after the recapture of Guam in 1944. The air station was a support base for photographic reconnaissance and early warning squadrons during the Vietnam War. Operating from the station is the Fleet Reconnaissance Squadron, VQ-1, whose 700 personnel operate some sixteen aircraft. Also at the station is the Anti-Submarine Warfare Center, which houses some of the most sophisticated computers and electronic equipment possessed by the Navy. The center's primary missions are to conduct ASW and to provide intelligence to the Seventh Fleet.

Isolated on 8,800 acres of a wildlife refuge in the south-central region of the island are 231 earth-covered magazines of the U.S. Naval Magazine. Much reduced from its flourishing World War II days, the magazine was active during the Korean and Vietnam wars. Today it is a major ammunition storage area to support contingency plans in the Western Pacific. A tenant on the magazine's acreage is MOMAG UNIT EIGHT, the largest Mobile Mine Assembly Group Unit in the world.

The largest naval command on Guam is the Naval Communications Area Master Station, Western Pacific (NAVCAMS WEST PAC), employing some 1,400 military personnel and serving the entire Western Pacific and Indian Ocean areas. Other significant facilities on Guam are the Naval Oceanographic Command Center, which specializes in typhoon warning; the Naval Calibration Laboratory, which serves numerous other units on Guam; the U.S. Naval Facility, Guam, which is engaged in oceanographic research; and the 800-bed Naval Regional Medical Center.

BIBLIOGRAPHY

A. Record Group 80, General Records of the Navy Department, 1897-1922, File No. 1351 (Washington: National Archives); U.S. Navy, Bureau of Yards and Docks, *Building the Navy's Bases in World War II*, 2 vols. (Washington: GPO, 1947), II:343-58; "Monograph Histories of U.S. Naval Overseas Bases. Vol. II. Pacific Area, Guam'' (Washington: Naval Historical Center, Operational Archives Branch); Records of the General Board of the Navy, 422 File (Washington: Naval Historical Center, Operational Archives Branch); ''Selected Papers, World War II Command Histories'' (Washington: Naval Historical Center, Operational Archives Branch).

B. Henry P. Beers, ''American Naval Occupation and Government of Guam, 1898-1902,'' *Administrative Reference Service Report No. 6* (Washington: National Archives); Samuel E. Morison, *New Guinea and the Marianas, March 1944-August 1944* (Boston: Little, Brown, 1944); William R. Braisted, *The United States Navy in the Pacific, 1909-1922* (Austin: University of Texas Press, 1958); Samuel E. Morison, *The Rising Sun in the Pacific, 1931-April 1942* (Boston: Little, Brown, 1958); Francis C. Holbrook, ''United States National Defense and Trans-Pacific Commercial Air Routes, 1933-1941'' (Ph.D. diss., Fordham University 1969).

WILLIAM R. BRAISTED

GUANTANAMO BAY, CUBA, U.S. NAVAL BASE, 1898- The U.S. naval base at Guantanamo Bay, Cuba, is situated at the southeastern tip of the island at 19°15′N., 75°9′W. The bay's proximity to the Windward Passage, the shortest sea route from the east coast of North America and Europe to the Caribbean, and the bay's large and commodious harbor have attracted the attention of Americans and Europeans for centuries, but its possible use as a naval station was not seriously mentioned until the American Civil War, when Secretary of the Navy Gideon Welles listed it among various locations in the Caribbean useful as coaling and repair facilities in order to maintain a naval blockade of the Confederacy. Arrangements were made to send coal there, but no concerted effort was made to establish a station. However, the desirability of a coaling and repair station near the Windward Passage increased during the postwar decades as the Navy continued to convert from sail to steam; as trade increased across the Caribbean and the fear of a European presence in the hemisphere grew; as the Navy assumed an ever greater role as protector of American life and property abroad; and as the prospect of an isthmian canal emerged. Capt. Alfred T. Mahan, USN, who repeatedly stressed the need for naval bases in the Caribbean, influenced the development of a Navy station and of coaling stations there. While domestic stations along the Gulf Coast and the southwestern Atlantic coast could help maintain a fleet when it entered the Caribbean, it was apparent that it was far better, and even essential, to have facilities in the West Indies. Still, Guantanamo Bay might not ever have been taken over by the United States had not war erupted with Spain in 1898.

Upon learning that Spanish Adm. Pascual Cervera had slipped into Santiago de Cuba, the value of Guantanamo Bay as a logistics support base was realized both by the U.S. naval commander in the Caribbean, Rear Adm. William T. Sampson, and the Navy Department, the latter of which directed Comdr. Bowman H. McCalla and some Marines from Key West to seize it. The war proved the military usefulness of the bay to both civilian and military leaders in Washington while the American press made sure that the general public took notice of it. Even so, its retention after the war was not a foregone conclusion. However, on 16 August 1898 a special board established by the Navy Department in June to examine future naval coaling needs recommended its acquisition and retention. Just before it was disestablished, the Naval Strategy (or War) Board seconded the recommendation not only because Guantanamo Bay could serve as a logistic support base but also because it could be useful to defend a proposed isthmian canal. Another endorsement came on 27 September from Comdr. Royal B. Bradford, Chief of the Bureau of Equipment.

Having obtained the right to remain in Cuba, Secretary of the Navy John D. Long, for one, told his diary that reconstructing and protecting Cuba would require naval stations there and found support from Bradford and Rear Adm. Henry C. Taylor, Chief of the Bureau of Navigation, who reflected the opinions of most officers in the Atlantic Fleet. Secretary of War Elihu Root and Army leaders in Cuba agreed. The problem facing the McKinley administration was how to acquire a naval station without negating the promise of Cuban independence. Pressure to reach a decision came from the General Board of the Navy, which on 16 April 1899 recommended the acquisition of Guantanamo Bay. Additional pressure came from the military governor of Cuba, Gen. Leonard Wood, who investigated ownership of the proposed naval reservation and on 18 July 1900 spoke about the matter with Root and McKinley. In November, the Cuban Constitutional Convention assembled in Havana while Wood sought to prepare various influential Cubans to accept the terms the United States would offer them. By the end of January 1901 the Senate Committee on Relations with Cuba had drafted eight demands as conditions for a U.S. withdrawal from Cuba. Second on the list was a demand for naval stations. Now to be overcome were objections from not only radical Cubans but even from moderate ones that selling or leasing land to the United States violated Cuban independence. On 21 February, when the Platt Amendment was offered the Cubans, anti-American demonstrations were held in Cuba. There was also some opposition to the Platt Amendment in the U.S. Senate on the ground that the maintenance of naval stations in Cuba was imperialism and would lead to continued involvement in the island and to problems of empire. However, the amendment passed easily, and President William McKinley signed the bill into law on 2 March 1901.

Opposition to the Platt Amendment came from many Cubans inside and outside the Constitutional Convention, and on 12 April the Cubans voted it down. With the amendment changed to read that the granting of sites for naval stations did not give the United States the right to intervene in domestic Cuban affairs, the Cubans were satisfied. Their official agreement came on 12 June 1901.

Although the way was not clear to start building needed facilities at Guantanamo Bay, neither McKinley nor his successor, Theodore Roosevelt, felt he could move until the new Cuban government was placed in operation in the spring of 1902. That government, under President Tomas Estrada Palma, proposed that the United States lease rather than own naval stations and that it accept only two bases. Upon the recommendation of the General Board, Washington asked only for Guantanamo Bay and a defense area of ten miles' radius from Toro Cay, and in November sent Bradford to try to secure approximately 280 square miles as the site of a station. The Cubans offered about a fifth of what Bradford requested. The issue of how many bases the Cubans would allow was not finally resolved until 16 February 1903, when the United States agreed to accept two sites, Bahia Honda, on the north side of Cuba near Havana, and Guantanamo Bay. These would be leased rather than purchased. While a joint Cuban-American survey was completed on 8 July, the formal transfer of the land took another five months due to the difficulty of purchasing the private land on the proposed naval reservation. On 10 December 1903 Rear Adm. Albert S. Barker formally accepted the U.S. auspices over Guantanamo Bay. Because both U.S. and Cuban officials were unsure of the reaction in Cuba to the transfer of the bay, no high-ranking Cuban dignitary attended the ceremony.

The possibility of controversy surrounding the bay did not deter the Navy from requesting an appropriation of $1,015,000 for Guantanamo in fiscal year 1904-1905. However, members of the House Naval Affairs Committee soon fell into dispute, not so much over the importance or functions of the base as over how much construction and expenditure were needed to make it functional. In the end, the amount appropriated was much less than that granted either Subic Bay (q.v.) or Cavite (q.v.), in the Philippines. A radio station was established in 1904.

Over the following years, the funding situation for Guantanamo Bay remained basically the same. The General Board inevitably asked the House Naval Affairs Committee for more than Congress was willing to authorize, yet each year Guantanamo came out relatively well compared to all foreign stations. One way or the other, and often through the secretary's discretionary budget, naval base proponents and Guantanamo Bay supporters obtained funding for the Cuban base. Moreover, appropriations for Guantanamo during some of those turbulent years actually surpassed those for several Gulf stations.

Nevertheless, Guantanamo Naval Station never achieved the size and development sought by the Navy General Board. In addition to those problems already mentioned, the base suffered after 1904 from a growing debate over the bay's defensibility. In the opinion of Guantanamo's opponents, hills surrounding the bay and new higher-powered ordnance made Guantanamo vulnerable to attack. As a result, the Navy tried to expand the boundary of Guantanamo during the American occupation of Cuba, 1906-1909, to include the nearby hills. The Roosevelt administration, however, refused to take action, for obvious political reasons, while the United States controlled the island's government. After the occupation, the Navy succeeded in getting the State Department to sign an agreement with the Cuban secretary of state to expand the boundary of Guantanamo Naval Station, but the Cuban Senate refused to ratify it.

The paucity of fresh water on the naval reservation also caused growing concern during the years after the United States took control of Guantanamo. The Navy had known about the fresh water shortage before assuming control of the area, but it had always thought that deep wells would alleviate the problem. When digging proved fruitless, it became obvious that the only continuous source of fresh water would have to come from rivers several miles beyond the station boundary. This caused concern since the water pipes would have to pass through Cuban territory and the water would constantly face the possibility of disruption from radical elements within the island.

Finally, in 1910, after years of controversy within both Congress and the Navy, which had included everything from suggestions that the Navy abandon Guantanamo to recommendations that it make its Cuban base the largest non-contiguous station, the Taft administration decided to definitely retain the bay but to designate it as an Emergency Repair Facility. The decision was primarily that of Navy Secretary George von L. Meyer, whom Admiral Dewey had lobbied extensively on the values of Guantanamo. The fact that the bay was still designated a limited facility reflected all the positions taken against the bay's retention during its first decade in American hands, but especially the questions of cost and defense. Contrary to much opposition, Guantanamo Bay was retained because it appeared to fulfill its basic roles as a training facility and as a first line of defense despite its limited development and the small expenditure there.

By 1911 the main station at Guantanamo had moved from Toro Cay to its present site just inside the southeastern portion of the bay. Only a few permanent structures were in place, and much of the land remained uncleared. Yet the bay had no trouble acting as a winter home for the fleet that carried out maneuvers and training exercises in the area. It additionally provided an important location for the Marines not only to practice their amphibious advanced base training but to be closer to potential Caribbean hot spots should unrest develop. Nor did the bay's limited state of development prevent it from being used for aviation instruction, preemptive positioning, advanced base positioning along the most important sealane in the Caribbean, and as a demonstration of America's presence in the Caribbean.

Over the next half decade the Navy created some new buildings, expanded some older structures, and ordered the handful of naval aviators in the fledgling Aviation Camp at Greenbury Point, Annapolis to operate out of an Aviation Camp established at Fisherman's Point, Guantanamo Bay, in 1913. Their operations showed that aircraft could spot mines and submarines in shallow waters and work with the fleet in other ways. The General Board and the Joint Board of the Army and Navy also continued to fight for the development of Guantanamo's defenses, including the expansion of the station boundary. Nevertheless, the bay's development remained sparse through the eve of World War I and the initial years of that conflict. Its uses did not change except in the intensity of training and the introduction of more aircraft and submarine practice. In fact, the station's most important function during those years, in terms of carrying out U.S. policy, may have been its training and sending of Marines to pacify Haiti in 1915 and the Dominican Republic the following year. The base also served as a door through which Marines entered Cuba in 1917 to protect U.S. life and property, just as they had five years earlier; in addition, Guantanamo acted as a base for the Ninth Marines, who waited in readiness for dispatch to the Panama Canal in case of trouble.

Still, it was not until 1917 that Guantanamo Naval Station got an appropriation from Congress to increase fleet facilities, and those were not complete until just prior to the war's end, in the fall of 1918. Guantanamo, in other words, contributed little to the war effort, although there was little action in or near the Caribbean to warrant a massive buildup at the station during the war years.

Over the next two decades Guantanamo barely changed in its size or function. This reflected many developments, including the limitations placed on arms at the Washington Conference of 1922; the demobilization of the Navy following World War I; a preoccupation with domestic affairs; the continuing problems of fresh water and defense at Guantanamo (among other objections to developing the base); and a growing concern with Pacific rather than Caribbean affairs. However, the Atlantic Fleet and the Marine Corps continued their winter training at the bay, and ships regularly stopped there for provisions, water, and fuel, or to use some of the training facilities, such as the rifle range. Early dirigibles and seaplanes also conducted test flights from the new McCalla Field during those years, and planes that patrolled the Panama Canal used Guantanamo as a base during the rainy months from October to December. As a result of these activities, the late 1920s and early 1930s witnessed the construction of several new piers and buildings at Guantanamo, as well as a water distilling plant.

In August 1933 the Gerardo Machado regime fell. A growing anti-Yankeeism, due in part to America's relationship with Machado and in part to the economic depression of the preceding few years, for which America was blamed, led to the U.S. abrogration of the Platt Amendment except for the portion related to Guantanamo Bay. On 29 May 1934 a treaty was signed between the United States and Cuba granting Guantanamo to America in perpetuity unless the United States abandoned the bay or both parties mutually agreed to terminate the lease. The only restrictions placed upon America were that the reservation could only be used as a naval station, that Cuban vessels could travel freely through the bay if they were engaged in trade, that private enterprise was forbidden on the reservation, and that the United States agreed to help prevent the smuggling of goods in and out of Cuba through the bay. While many Cubans had desired the United States out of their country completely, the treaty reflected the preference of others that the United States retain its naval station at Guantanamo to protect the island from foreign invasion.

In 1938 the naval station at Guantanamo Bay had a complement of 17 naval officers, 153 bluejackets, 5 Marine officers, and 129 leathernecks. Its shops, storehouses, training facilities, and small airfield were still only basically sufficient to satisfy the fleet's maneuvers from January through April. But as the possibility of war in Europe grew, the Navy conducted several studies on Guantanamo to determine the adequacy of its defense and its potential usefulness in a war situation. One such report by the influential Hepburn Board, which visited Guantanamo in 1938 under Rear Adm. A. J. Hepburn, recommended considerable expansion of the station's facilities, especially its airfield. A water system was also started by July 1939 that carried water to the station from the Yateras River, a few miles north.

On 7 January 1939 the Secretary of the Navy declared Guantanamo and sixteen other bases a Naval Defense Area (NDA). This designation, recommended by the General Board the previous December, restricted visitors to Guantanamo as well as the aircraft that could fly near the station. The name NDA was changed in November 1939 to Defensive Sea Area and Airspace Reservation.

The following year, Adm. Harold R. Stark, Chief of Naval Operations, wrote Rear Adm. John W. Greenslade, senior member of the Board of Survey and Report on the Adequacy and Future Development of Naval Shore Establishments, that the Caribbean was among the world's most strategic areas which America had to control and that the Navy therefore needed to develop Guantanamo Bay since it was America's most important base in the West Indies. Despite the station's earlier problems, which had inhibited its development, the government obviously considered Guantanamo vital. As a 1940 article in *Time* observed, Guantanamo was like a boxer's extra 6-inch reach that would act as a buffer to a growing German submarine presence in the Caribbean.

President Franklin D. Roosevelt and Congress saw to it that Guantanamo and other American bases were developed by appropriating millions of dollars to such facilities in June 1940. The importance the President placed on Guantanamo was demonstrated as well by his visit there in December 1940. Over the next few years, some $34 million was spent on expanding the Cuban station, which led to some 9,000 civilian and 4,000 government workers being employed there by fall 1943. Part of the sum went toward building a self-contained Marine Corps base at Deer Point for approximately 2,000 men, while another sizable portion went into construction of aviation facilities for the Marines. In 1940 the First Marine Aviation Group, commanded by Lt. Col. Field Harris and attached to the First Brigade of Brig. Gen. Holland M. Smith, USMC, was sent to Guantanamo. It soon underwent extensive training at McCalla Field, including support for ground forces, fixed and experimental gunnery, bombing exercises, and landing exercises on aircraft carriers.

As for General Smith, who designed the Marine amphibious assault in the Pacific during World War II, he spent February 1941 leading Force Landing Exercise 7 (FLEX 7), a joint operation between the Marines and the First Army Division. Smith's men and the Fourth Defense Battalion had also been assigned the job of protecting the Panama Canal. In September 1942 the Thirteenth Defense Battalion, under Cols. Bernard Dubal and Richard Cutts, moved into Guantanamo, where they remained until 1944, to take up the canal's defense. During the war years as many as 1,200 Marines held regular duty at Guantanamo Bay, while another 6,000 Marines underwent training there.

In keeping with the bay's expanded role during the war, it began functioning as a Naval Operating Base on 1 April 1941. This grouped together the Naval Station, Naval Air Station, Marine Corps Base, and Naval Net Depot under the command of Capt. George L. Weyler, USN. In July 1942 the Anti-Aircraft Training Center was added. That year, too, the commandant of the Naval Operating Base was designated as commander of Guantanamo Sector, Caribbean Sea Frontier. This put him in charge of the Coast Guard, naval personnel, air-sea rescue, communications, harbor patrols, and other operations in his area. By 1942 Guantanamo was also acting as an important base for reconnaissance and ASW aircraft in the Caribbean. Due to the presence of German submarines, especially in the southeastern Caribbean Sea, Guantanamo became the focal point for convoys where ships heading in the same direction would meet and regroup. In keeping with this effort, an Escort Vessel Administration was established at Guantanamo Bay in 1942.

By 1944 Germany was contained, and the general expansion of the base began to subside. By the summer of the following year families returned to Guantanamo Bay, and the station was converted into a training school for foreign personnel whose countries had purchased American military hardware. In 1946, for example, 79 officers and 1,088 men of the Chinese Navy visited Guantanamo for maneuvers aboard American ships. The station additionally resumed its earlier functions as a winter training facility for the fleet and as a site for amphibious operations of the Marine Corps. By the late 1940s the population of the base hovered around 5,000 people, approximately 3,000 of whom were civilian employees, 1,500 military personnel, and the rest their dependents. This was down from the nearly 5,500 military and 5,000 civilians who populated the station in January 1944.

The Korean War affected Guantanamo to the extent that ships activated for duty in the Orient often conducted their shakedown training in the Caribbean. The war also led to a greater naval appropriation, which permitted new buildings at the Cuban base. This caused the number of persons there to grow to about 8,000 residents and 3,000 commuters, most of them Cuban workers. In addition, ship crews at Guantanamo Bay numbered as many as 15,000 men during the winter months.

On 18 June 1952 the name U.S. Naval Operating Base, Guantanamo Bay, Cuba, was changed by the Secretary of the Navy to U.S. Naval Base. The components making up the base included the Naval Station, Naval Air Station, Marine Barracks, Naval Supply Depot, Naval Hospital, Naval Dental Clinic, and Fleet Training Center.

The following year a struggle began in Cuba to overthrow the government of Fulgencio Batista. The revolt's leader, Fidel Castro, was captured and later exiled to Mexico. He returned to his homeland in 1956, however, to continue his revolutionary struggle. Because he and his men operated in the Sierra Maestra near Guantanamo Bay, they caused concern to the commander of the naval base there. Finally, in March 1958, the station commandant, Adm. R. B. Ellis, wrote the American ambassador to Cuba, Earl Smith, about his concerns for the safety of the Yateras River water plant located several miles outside of the north boundary of the naval station. The guerrillas had been seen in the area and rumors persisted that they planned to blow up the plant.

On 27 June 1958 a group of rebels led by Raul Castro, Fidel Castro's brother, captured a busload of thirteen U.S. civilians and thirty military personnel in north Oriente Province. This was to protest the United States' allowing Batista to refuel his bombers at Guantanamo Bay. In response, Admiral Ellis ordered U.S. aircraft to fly over the revolutionaries to scare them, while Ambassador Smith wanted to send Marines from the base into Cuba to free the captives. The U.S. State Department, however, opposed direct American intervention, and the dilemma was resolved when Castro released the prisoners in mid-July.

Shortly thereafter, fighting erupted between rebels and Cuban government forces near the Yateras River. Once more fearful of having the station's fresh water supply disrupted, Admiral Ellis dispatched Marines to the water plant as a precaution. The Batista government requested that the Marines remain in the area, but protests from a cross-section of the Cuban public and the promise of Fidel Castro not to damage the water supply prompted the American government to pressure Batista to keep his own men at the river as the Marines withdrew.

On 1 January 1959 Fidel Castro came to power in Cuba. Four months later he told the American Society of Newspaper Editors in Washington, D.C., that he would respect Cuba's international obligations and would keep his hands off Guantanamo Bay. But over the next year and a half, Cuba's relationship with the United States steadily deteriorated as Castro's regime moved to the left and the United States withdrew what little support it had shown for the revolution.

Amid these tensions, in July 1960, a *Washington Post* article warned of possible sabotage at Guantanamo by pro-Castro Cubans working on the base. It also expressed concern over the vulnerability of the bay's fresh water supply, which traveled by pipe through Cuban territory. A few months later, after the USS *Boxer* arrived at Guantanamo with a contingent of Marines, the Cuban government accused the United States of building up its forces in Cuba to invade the island. The United States responded that such troop visits to Guantanamo were regular occurrences, and President Dwight D. Eisenhower reaffirmed the U.S. right to Guantanamo Bay. The Cuban government subsequently announced that it would never attack the American base, but it would do everything in its power to legally regain "its sovereign territory."

The American position on Guantanamo was partly predicated upon the need to appear tough before a leftist regime, but it also emanated from the sincere belief that Guantanamo remained a useful base. As Adm. Arleigh Burke, Chief of Naval Operations, stated in November 1960, Guantanamo Bay remained an important site for watching the Windward Passage, all the Caribbean islands, and the Panama Canal. It also served as an excellent training area. "The weather is ideal," he said, "and we are not interfering with a lot of airplanes. We can do gunnery exercises, bombing exercises, missile training. . . a lot of things we can't do anywhere else."

For the above reasons, President Eisenhower made it clear to the Cubans that the status of the American base was unchanged when he severed diplomatic relations with the island nation in January 1961. Subsequently, no attempt was made by the Castro regime to move against the American base, although the two nations remained the worst of enemies over the following years due to such incidents as the Bay of Pigs fiasco and the missile crisis of 1962. On the latter occasion, the United States deployed at Guantanamo Bay two Marine battalions, with a strength of over 5,000 men, and 400 Marine Corps aircraft as tensions mounted with the Soviet Union. The incident undoubtedly reinforced Castro's belief that a move against the U.S. base would prove militarily disastrous for him. Yet the Cuban government never stopped claiming that the bay should be under its control, and Castro reacted to the U.S. buildup at Guantanamo by fortifying the area around the base with large guns and tanks. He also began harassing the Cubans who still worked on the base and traveled to the station each day. It was in February 1964, however, that Castro took his most direct action against the base, when he seized the water pipeline from the station to the Yateras River.

Fidel Castro claimed that Cuba's 1903 treaty with the United States said nothing about the U.S. naval base at Guantanamo receiving water from outside the reservation. The United States countered that the shut-off violated a 1938 contract with the Cubans that was reaffirmed in 1947. The U.S. government also noted that on numerous occasions Castro had promised not to seize the fresh water supply to Guantanamo Bay.

After a month of tension, the Cuban government reopened the pipeline, but the Navy installed a desalination plant at the base to prevent future water problems. President Lyndon Johnson also retaliated by firing about 2,000 of the 3,000 Cuban workers at the base. Most of them were replaced with Jamaicans.

Since the mid-1960s tensions have continued between the United States and Cuba over control of Guantanamo Bay. As a result, the debate over retaining "Gitmo," as naval personnel call the base, has also persisted. Perhaps the strongest argument for relinquishing control is that the bay is more of a convenience than a necessity and its return to the Cubans would go a long way in restoring better relations with America's one-time friend. Supporters of this position usually contend that Roosevelt Roads, Puerto Rico can fulfill Guantanamo's functions. Furthermore, they argue that holding Guantanamo for preemptive reasons does not prevent the Soviets from acquiring naval stations elsewhere in Cuba, and there is no certainty that a U.S. withdrawal from Guantanamo would lead to a Soviet buildup at the bay. In fact, Fidel Castro might find it difficult to explain his giving the Russians Guantanamo Bay after so many years of trying to remove the Americans and criticizing a foreign naval presence in Cuba. On the other hand, the argument can be made that if the Soviets, or even the Cubans, retain Guantanamo as a major naval installation, U.S. forces could still reach the bay in fifteen minutes by jet in an emergency, while the U.S. Navy could dispatch ships there from Roosevelt Roads. These latter points support one last argument against the retention of Guantanamo Bay, namely, that the base is obsolete in a modern age of missiles and at a time when America's policy in the Caribbean is not likely to include the sending of Marines from Guantanamo into neighboring countries.

The proponents of Guantanamo claim, first, that America has every legal right to remain at the bay since the 1934 treaty with Cuba specifies that the American presence there can only be terminated by mutual consent. They also argue that no other location in the Caribbean has the military advantages of Guantanamo Bay, not even Roosevelt Roads, and even if that location did possess the physical and geographic features of Guantanamo, it would cost millions of dollars to develop the Puerto Rican base, and the United States would have to abandon millions of dollars in unmovable equipment and structures at Guantanamo Bay. Proponents also contend that even if there were another base that could replace Guantanamo, or even if there existed legal and moral reasons for relinquishing control over it, the importance of Gitmo to America's foreign policy and national security would outweigh them. According to this reasoning, Guantanamo is, at the very least, an important bargaining chip in the Cold War whose time to be cashed in has not yet arrived. Others contend that America should keep the base if for no other reason than because it irritates the communists in Cuba. Former Sen. Margaret Chase Smith has additionally remarked that America should keep Guantanamo Bay because withdrawal would be a sign of weakness and make it appear that we were giving in to the demands of the communists.

A more substantial argument for the retention of the bay is that it continues to serve as an important site for the fleet. Each year well over a hundred ships, scores of aircraft, and some 20,000 men train at Guantanamo. Moreover, Guantanamo continues to fulfill its function as a guardian of the Windward Passage and as a convenient location for the deployment of U.S. forces in the Caribbean or South America should the need arise, as it did in the Dominican Crisis of 1965.

Having Guantanamo also provides the United States with a nearby location to demonstrate displeasure with the Soviet presence in Latin America and the Soviet military buildup in Cuba without having to find a potentially more dangerous form of protest. This became evident when President Jimmy Carter dispatched Marines to Guantanamo in 1979 after learning about a Soviet brigade in Cuba. Naval bases, in short, are still important in limited confrontations, and they broaden a president's options. While naval strategy and the means by which wars are fought have changed considerably since Guantanamo was founded and Captain Mahan postulated the numerous advantages of naval bases, nothing has detracted from the fact that naval stations are still useful and that "despite the enormous technical advances of the last fifty years. . . the transport of armies [still] requires the essential support of ships."

The future of Guantanamo as a major U.S. naval base depends considerably upon what type of relationship the U.S. government wants to have with Cuba. It is clear that Guantanamo remains important from a strategic-military standpoint but that it is not vital for national security. As a result, the Carter administration, as part of an attempt to better relations with Latin America generally during the fall of 1977, gave "serious consideration," in the words of a senior naval official at the Pentagon, to moving fleet training from Guantanamo Bay to Roosevelt Roads as a first step toward abandoning Guantanamo. Subsequent events, however, such as Cuba's support of the Soviet invasion of Afghanistan and Cuba's military forays around the world in favor of pro-communist regimes, ended the possibility of returning Guantanamo to Cuban control. Since then, the election to the presidency of Ronald Reagan, a vehement anti-communist who would go to almost any length to harass Fidel Castro, has made it less likely than ever that America's policy on Guantanamo Bay will change in the near future.

Meanwhile, Castro continues to use every major public forum to criticize the U.S. presence at Guantanamo Bay. The base has given him an opportunity to repeatedly claim that America retains Guantanamo for an invasion of the island and that America is two-faced for criticizing Cuban "imperialism" abroad while maintaining an unwelcome military installation in Cuba. While Castro is not likely to take any military action to get the base back, for obvious reasons, neither are the Cubans likely to lose their determination to regain control of the bay. Whether the United States will let that happen depends considerably on how future policy makers weigh the strategic and tactical advantages of Guantanamo Bay against the potential complications in foreign policy that retention of the bay might cause.

BIBLIOGRAPHY

A. Record Group 59, General Records of the Department of State, Miscellaneous Letters File, 1898-1909, Numerical File, 1906-1910; and Record Group 84, Records of Foreign Service Posts of the Department of State, General Dispatches to 1906 (Washington: National Archives); Records of the General Board of the Navy (Washington: Naval Historical Center, Operational Archives Branch); Department of the Navy, *Annual Reports of the Secretary of the Navy* (Washington: GPO, 1880-1910); U.S. Department of the Navy, Bureau of Supplies and Accounts, *Statement Showing the Total Amount of Money Expended on the Naval Station Guantanamo, Cuba, from Time of Its Occupation by the United States to End of the Fiscal Year 1912—And Also the Annual Expenditures for Maintenance During That Time* (Washington: Bureau of Supplies and Accounts, March 29, 1913).

B. Marion Murphy, *The History of Guantanamo Bay, Cuba* (Guantanamo Bay, Cuba: District Publications and Printing Office, Tenth Naval District, 1964); Richard Wellington Turk, "U.S. Naval Policy in the Caribbean, 1865-1915," Ph.D. diss., Fletcher School of Law and Diplomacy, Tufts University, 1968; Richard D. Challener, *Admirals, Generals, and American Foreign Policy, 1898-1914* (Princeton, N.J.: Princeton University Press, 1973); Martin J. Scheina, "The U.S. Presence in Guantanamo," *Strategic Review* 4 (Spring 1976):81-88; David F. Trask, *The War with Spain in 1898* (New York: Macmillan, 1981); Bradley M. Reynolds, "Guantanamo Bay, Cuba: The History of an American Naval Base and the Relationship to the Formulation of United States Foreign Policy and Military Strategy toward the Caribbean, 1895-1910,'' Ph.D. diss., University of Southern California, 1982.

BRADLEY REYNOLDS

GUINES, FRANCE.
See World War I U.S. Northern Bombing Group Bases in England and France.

GUIPAVAS, FRANCE.
See World War I U.S. Naval Air Stations in Europe.

GUJAN, FRANCE.
See World War I U.S. Naval Air Stations in Europe.

H

HALIFAX, NOVA SCOTIA.
See World War I U.S. Naval Air Stations in Canada.

HA TIEN, REPUBLIC OF VIETNAM, U.S. RIVER PATROL BOAT STAGING AREA, 1968–1970 The American naval base at Ha Tien, on the South Vietnamese-Cambodian border in the Mekong Delta region, served as a forward staging area for river patrol boat (PBR) units engaged in anti-infiltration operations along the Vinh Te Canal. In keeping with the Vietnamization of the war, the Ha Tien facility was turned over to the Vietnamese Navy in December 1970 after two years of operation.

BIBLIOGRAPHY

A. Commander Naval Forces, Vietnam, "Monthly Historical Reports, 1965-1971" (Washington: Naval Historical Center, Operational Archives Branch).

EDWARD J. MAROLDA

HIEP HOA, REPUBLIC OF VIETNAM, U.S. NAVAL ADVANCED TACTICAL SUPPORT BASE, 1969 Located on the Vam Co Dong River northwest of Saigon in the Republic of Vietnam, Hiep Hoa served as an advanced tactical support base for U.S. naval forces in the Vietnam War. River patrol boat (PBR) units patrolled the sector of river around the site as part of the Giant Slingshot anti-infiltration operation. The river forces attempted to disrupt the constant flow of communist men and munitions into the capital region.

During 1969 Seabees and construction materials were transported from Danang (q.v.) to Hiep Hoa for development of the shore facility. While the river sailors used a partially destroyed, abandoned sugar mill for sleeping quarters, the Seabees began construction of better quarters, base defenses, fuel and ammunition storage, and a helicopter pad. However, the lack of troops for protection from ground attack forced the evacuation of the naval force to nearby Tra Cu (q.v.) later in the year.

BIBLIOGRAPHY
A. Commander Naval Forces, Vietnam, "The Naval War in Vietnam," May 1970 (Washington: Naval Historical Center, Operational Archives Branch).

EDWARD J. MAROLDA

HISPANIC SOUTH AMERICA, U.S. NAVAL BASES, 1907–1947 The position the U.S. Navy took toward the matter of naval bases beyond its borders was naturally related to the role it would have to play in defending America's interests. In the twentieth century and in the Western Hemisphere that role was delineated by three specific objectives: 1) enforcing the Monroe Doctrine; 2) protecting the Panama Canal; and 3) minimizing the threat major outside powers, such as Germany in World Wars I and II, might pose.

One region of Latin America that held minimal interest in terms of naval bases, at least until World War II, was the mainland of South America. Too far from the United States to be a serious threat before the days of air power and situated geographically in such a way as to pose, at the utmost, a manageable challenge to the Panama Canal, mainland South America was largely neglected by American geopolitical interests through the first forty years of the twentieth century.

Georgetown, British Guiana, U.S. Naval Air Station and Naval Air Facility, 1942-1944

Four different South American countries came to figure in American naval planning. In 1907 authorities of the government of British Guiana offered to sell the U.S. government a tract of land on St. Bartholomew's Island to be used as a coaling station. Not needing a station in that area and not wanting to become overextended with vulnerable and far-flung bases, the General Board of the Navy rejected the proposal. A third of a century passed before the area would again become of interest to the Navy. In January 1941 the Rear Adm. John Greenslade Board on the Shore Establishment stressed the importance of naval bases in the Guianas as a means of thwarting German U-boat activity and keeping open Atlantic trade routes with South America in the event of war. In response to this report, legal rights to land were obtained from Great Britain in the destroyer-for-bases deal of September 1940, and a naval air station was established at Georgetown in February 1942 on the right bank of the Essequibo River forty miles upstream from the Atlantic Ocean. Seaplanes operating from the station, which cost $1.45 million to build, guarded the Trinidad-Recife convoys as they made passage along the shoulder of northeast South America. At the same time, Navy blimps operated from Atkinson Field, a U.S. Army base, on the Demerara River. There was a Port Director there, and the station was a flag stop for the Naval Air Transport Service. The station was placed in caretaker status on 22 July 1944 and decommissioned two days later.

Nearby, ten miles downriver, a Naval Air Facility had been established under the name Essequibo, British Guiana. At this site, selected in February, 1941 by

Rear Adm. Raymond A. Spruance, then Commander Caribbean Sea Frontier, clearing began on 8 March in an environment completely free from malaria-bearing mosquitoes. It remained in operating status until 25 November 1946, when it was inactivated. It was decommissioned in March 1947.

Paramaribo, Surinam, Dutch Guiana, U.S. Naval Base, 1943-1944

The neighboring country of Dutch Guiana also became the site of U.S. naval operations with the coming of World War II. A squadron of blimps was established at the seaport city of Paramaribo in August 1943. Later a squadron of seaplanes arrived; these were serviced by seaplane tenders using the harbor of the port city. Twenty-five miles inland, at an Army base at Zandry Field, several squadrons of Navy planes operated through late 1943 and most of 1944. The base was inactivated and then disestablished in August 1944.

Barranquilla, Colombia, U.S. Naval Air Facility, 1943-1945

In contrast to the Guianas, those countries that lay closer to the Panama Canal were of much greater concern to American naval interests. The Republic of Colombia was a case in point. As early as 1902 the General Board of the Navy noted that if an isthmian canal were built the Navy would need a base along the coast of Colombia as a security measure. Over the next ten years, though, no effort was made to acquire one. Then in 1912 an opportunity for a base presented itself when Colombia expressed its willingness to lease three Caribbean islands near the isthmus to the United States. However, the need for such "strategic" areas was no longer felt, and the U.S. government dropped the matter. The coming of World War II, of course, changed that. In the spring of 1943 a U.S. naval refueling unit was established at the port of Barranquilla, a city some 300 miles east of the Panama Canal. Both landplanes and blimps used the airport facilities there, which had been operated by Pan American Airways. Included were Soledad Airport, six miles south of the city, which had two paved 3,500-foot runways; two hangars; a main repair shop belonging to Airanca, the Colombian national airline; storage for 45,000 gallons of gasoline, all of which Airanca shared with the Colombian Army and Pan American; a seaplane base at which the planes used the Magdalena River; tent quarters for American men and a screened-in porch for officers; and a PT refueling base. The Navy originally used five Grumman A/S aircraft for daily patrol and convoy cover. They were replaced early in 1944 by Douglas SBD scout bombers. Although there were no blimp facilities there, by 15 May 1944 an LTA mast was ready to receive balloons.

Air operations out of Barranquilla were important because they guarded the shipping lanes of the oil ports of Colombia and the approaches to the Panama Canal. In November 1944, with the maritime threat from Germany rapidly fading, operations were sharply curtailed. The facilities were disestablished in March 1945.

Salinas, Ecuador, and South Seymour, Galapagos Islands, U.S. Naval Air Facilities, 1942-1946

Guarding the Panama Canal from the Pacific side was also a concern of the United States. The South American country of Ecuador was substantially involved with us in this long-standing concern. From the start of its independence in the early nineteenth century, Ecuador held sovereignty over the Galapagos Islands, a small chain of barren islets several hundred miles off the Ecuadorian coast. For much of the nineteenth century they had little importance and were known chiefly for their rich guano deposits. In 1899 the picture changed dramatically. Anticipating the coming of an isthmian canal and realizing the importance of the Galapagos' location, 800 miles south of Panama, the U.S. State Department exchanged notes with Ecuador concerning the lease of a possible base site. By 1903 the U.S. decided that such a base was not needed, observing that although the islands would have little value in American hands, they would be a grave threat if they fell under the control of a major foreign power that was unfriendly toward the United States. Considerations were again made in 1909, 1913, and 1917 for a facility there as well as one in Ecuador proper (1910), but no final action was taken.

With the approach of World War II, the report of the Greenslade Board on the naval shore establishment emphasized the significance of the islands to the security of the canal on the Pacific side. As a result, Ecuador leased to the United States the island of South Seymour in the Galapagos, which in 1942 was used as a seaplane base for two squadrons of patrol bombers. Facilities were built by the Army and the Seabees to accommodate 125 officers and 1,050 men, a fuel depot, and a radio station. There was also an auxiliary air field. There was absolutely no fresh water on the island, so water was shipped in "for the duration." A second base was located at Salinas, a small city on the northwestern edge of Ecuador at Santa Elena Bay. At first this location was to serve as a boat base; then plans were changed to make it a seaplane refueling base, then a complete patrol plane base, and finally just an emergency refueling depot with a naval radio station. Despite its chameleonlike existence, it served the Navy well. It was the eastern anchor of a large air-search triangle with the Galapagos Islands and Fonseca, Nicaragua (*see* Central America, U.S. Naval Bases), the two other points of the triangle. The Navy returned control of the base to Ecuador after the war, in February 1946.

Talara, Peru, incidentally, was used as a joint U.S. Army and Navy air base, and Callao as a naval supply base.

BIBLIOGRAPHY

A. U.S. Navy, Bureau of Yards and Docks, *Building the Navy's Bases in World War II*, 2 vols. (Washington: GPO, 1947); "U.S. Naval Overseas Bases: A Current Survey," Prepared by direction of Chief of Naval Operations, 1957 (Washington: Naval Historical Center, Operational Archives Branch); "Administrative History of the U.S. Operating Base, Trinidad, BWI, and Trinidad Sector" (Washington: Naval Historical Center, Operational Archives Branch); Records of the General Board of the Navy, Letterbook File, 1900-1947 (Washington: Naval Historical Center, Operational Archives Branch); "Shore Establishment: Summary Cards" (Washington, D.C., Navy Yard, Naval Aviation History Office); "U.S. Naval Administration in World War II: Administrative History of the Caribbean Sea Frontier till VE Day" (Washington: Naval Historical Center, Operational Archives Branch).

B. Waldo G. Bowman and others, *Bulldozers Came First* (New York: McGraw-Hill, 1947); Samuel E. Morison, *The Battle of the Atlantic September 1939-May 1943* (Boston: Little, Brown, 1947); Samuel E. Morison, *The Battle of the Atlantic Won May 1942-May 1945* (Boston: Little, Brown, 1956).

WILLIAM L. CALDERHEAD

HOI AN, REPUBLIC OF VIETNAM, U.S. PATROL BOAT BASE, 1969–1971 This South Vietnamese coastal city was the site of a U.S. patrol boat base during the Southeast Asian Conflict. Located at the mouth of the meandering Cua Dai River south of Danang, Hoi An was well placed to support patrols inland by the river patrol boat (PBR) units based there. In keeping with the thrust of the Vietnamization program, the base was turned over to the Vietnamese Navy in 1971.

BIBLIOGRAPHY

A. Commander Naval Forces, Vietnam, "The Naval War in Vietnam," May 1970 (Washington: Naval Historical Center, Operational Archives Branch).

EDWARD J. MAROLDA

HOLLANDIA, DUTCH NEW GUINEA, U.S. NAVAL ADVANCE BASE, 1944–1945 Located on Humboldt Bay on the north-central coast of New Guinea, Hollandia (2°30′S., 141°50′E.) was a settlement and fine anchorage in Dutch New Guinea. As the best site for a potential naval base between Wewak and Geelvink Bay, it became the focus of Gen. Douglas MacArthur's strategic bypass of the Japanese Eighteenth Army at Wewak, both to isolate a Japanese strongpoint and to create a major supply installation for supporting the return to the Philippines. On 22 April 1944 Allied troops landed at Hollandia and at Tanahmerah Bay twenty-five miles to the west, capturing both areas against only light resistance. PT operations from Hollandia began on 2 May, when the tender *Oyster Bay* and a Motor Torpedo Boat Squadron conducted patrols toward Geelvink Bay until 5 June 1944, when they moved to Mios Woendi near Biak (q.v.).

Despite the PT crews' disappointment in not fighting the Japanese from Hollandia, the Seventh Fleet preferred the absence of the enemy in constructing its advance base in Humboldt Bay. Beginning in May 1944 Seabees greatly improved port facilities at Hollandia, completing the first Liberty ship pier by July and a second by November. Eventually there were five ship docks and anchorages for an additional fifteen Liberty ships. Unloading capacity rose to 1,200 tons per day. Also at Hollandia, the Seabees built a big naval supply depot, a base for convoy escorts, a destroyer repair unit with five small floating dry docks, a naval ammunition depot, and a pontoon assembly area. At Tanahmerah Bay there was established a fuel oil depot, completed by October 1944, which stored 110,000 barrels of fuel oil and 10,000 of diesel oil. At Lake Sentani, inland eight miles west of Hollandia, Seventh Fleet headquarters relocated, beginning in July, from Brisbane (q.v.).

The importance of the Hollandia naval advance base was its close association with extensive Army camps to create a vital staging and supply point for amphibious operations in New Guinea and the Dutch East Indies, and ultimately for the invasion of the Philippines. It became the transshipment point for most of the supplies forwarded to Southwest Pacific Area combat units. Troops from there participated in the Leyte landings in October 1944. The base was particularly valuable for logistic support in 1945 for the conquest of the southern Philippines. By August 1945 only a few facilities there had been rolled up, but the close of hostilities brought a rapid dismantling. The base was disestablished on 1 November 1945 and the remaining facilities were turned over to the Dutch government.

BIBLIOGRAPHY

A. U.S. Navy, "7th Amphibious Force Command History, 10 January 1943-23 December 1945" (Washington: Naval Historical Center, Operational Archives Branch); U.S. Navy, Bureau of Yards and Docks, *Building the Navy's Bases in World War II*, 2 vols. (Washington: GPO, 1947); U.S. Navy, "U.S. Naval Bases in the South and Southwest Pacific (and Central Pacific Forward), in World War II," 1 November 1954 (Washington: Naval Historical Center, Operational Archives Branch).

B. Rear Adm. Worrall Reed Carter, *Beans, Bullets, and Black Oil* (Washington: GPO, 1953); Samuel E. Morison, *New Guinea and the Marianas March 1944-August 1944* (Boston: Little, Brown, 1953); Capt. Robert J. Bulkley, *At Close Quarters: PT Boats in the United States Navy* (Washington: Navy Department, Naval History Division, 1962); Vice Adm. Daniel E. Barbey, *MacArthur's Amphibious Navy* (Annapolis, Md.: U.S. Naval Institute, 1969).

JOHN B. LUNDSTROM

HOLY LOCH, SCOTLAND, U.S. FLEET BALLISTIC SUBMARINE BASE, 1961– Holy Loch, Grennock, Scotland, located at 55°59′N., 4°54′W., is a Clyde dockyard port that serves both British and American ballistic missile submarines in a restricted area, the Americans being north and west of Carraig Mhaol, the British at nearby Faslane. Holy Loch has good holding ground and is sheltered from all but northwesterly winds that suddenly sweep down the valley between the precipitous mountains fringing the head of the loch.

Four previously built advance base section docks in ordinary at the Atlantic Reserve Fleet at Green Cove Springs, Fla., were towed across the Atlantic to Holy Loch, where they were joined to form the auxiliary floating dry dock *Los Alamos* (AFDB-7), which would serve at the fleet ballistic submarine base the U.S. Navy established there on 3 March 1961 under Commander, U.S. Naval Activities, United Kingdom, with Headquarters in London. The *Los Alamos* served not only the Fleet Ballistic Missile (FBM) boats of Submarine Squadron 14 but also the two submarine tenders assigned to the base. By perfecting an "off center" dock plan, she was able to dock two FBMs at a time. Original personnel numbered more than 1,100 military and 450 civilians. This number increased to 390 officers and 2,384 enlisted personnel in 1970, who brought with them 3,586 dependents. These figures remained quite steady for the next decade.

The functions of the Naval Activity Support Facility at Holy Loch are to provide material and personal support for naval units associated with the *Polaris/ Poseidon* program.

Fresh, potable water is supplied to Holy Loch by a five-mile overland and three and a third mile submarine waterline built in 1966. Security is provided by a small Marine Corps detachment; educational facilities by branches of a number of American universities and colleges. Housing and medical/dental facilities increased apace with the growth of personnel, and air flights to most other U.S. naval facilities in England and Scotland, and also to McGuire Air Force Base, Trenton, N.J., are scheduled biweekly. Incoming air cargo approximates 1 million short tons annually, while surface cargo brings in only 113 tons. The reverse is true for outgoing cargo; in the sample year 1970, 430 tons went by air but 1,630 tons went by sea. The annual payroll for both military and civilian personnel is about $15 million.

The USS *Hunley* (AS-31), built by the Newport News Shipbuilding and Dry Dock Co. in 1961-1962, had the distinction of being the first ship designed and built up from the keel to service and maintain the U.S. Navy's nuclear-powered Ballistic Missile Submarine Fleet. After shakedown, repairs, and visits to several northern American ports, she stood out of the Norfolk Operating Base on 29 December 1962 for Holy Loch. She was relieved by the *Proteus*, which had served Submarine Squadron 14 at Rota, Spain (q.v.). On 12 April 1964 she returned to the United States for conversion that enabled her to handle the new A-3 Polaris missile. She resumed her duties at Holy Loch on 14 June 1964. In December 1965, when the *Thomas A. Edison* came alongside to begin the 100th refit of a Nuclear Powered Ballistic Submarine (SSBN), this meant that none of the 100 SSBN submarines had been late in leaving her or returning to her from patrol. When she returned to the United States late in 1966 and began operating out of Charleston, S.C., she was succeeded in turn by the *Canopus* (AS-34) and the *Holland* (AS-32).

BIBLIOGRAPHY

A. "Command History, Commander U.S. Naval Activities United Kingdom, 1962-1980" (Washington: Naval Historical Center, Operational Archives Branch).

B. Robert E. Wood, JOC, "Air Support for Polaris Submarines," *Naval Aviation News*, July 1962, pp. 13-14; "*Canopus*," "*Holland*," "*Hunley*," "*Los Alamos*," and "*Proteus*," in *Dictionary of American Naval Fighting Ships*, 8 vols. (Washington: Naval History Division, 1959-1981), II:27, III:348-49, IV:143, V:394-95.

HONG KONG, CHINA.
See Far Eastern U.S. Naval Bases to 1898.

HUE-TAN MY-PHU BAI, REPUBLIC OF VIETNAM, U.S. NAVAL SUPPORT ACTIVITY, 1965–1970 From a modest beginning, the Navy's facilities in the area of Hue, Vietnam's old imperial city and the third largest population center in the Republic of Vietnam, developed into a major combat and logistic complex. This followed the deployment there, especially after 1967, of large Marine, Army, and South Vietnamese forces.

Even though the Marine presence near Hue, primarily at Phu Bai, was limited in the early stages of deployment, the Navy worked to provide responsive logistic support. Naval leaders recognized that the most direct line of communication to the South China Sea, by way of the Hue River and a six-mile-long road, had the best potential. Alternate road, rail, and air approaches from Danang were subject to frequent enemy interdiction or were unable to accommodate the many tons of supplies needed. In addition, Tan My, at the mouth of the Hue River and terminus of the short road, was well placed to support the growth of allied forces north and west of Hue.

From 1965 to 1967 steps were taken to improve logistic facilities at Hue and Tan My and the line of communication between. An old boat ramp at the Hue city park was refurbished and an adjoining cargo staging area enlarged. The ramp was manned by a detachment of Naval Support Activity, Danang (q.v.). Utility landing craft (LCU) carrying supplies and later fuel regularly plied the twelve miles of river between the city and the Col Co (Colonial Company) ramp at Tan My. On occasion, fleet amphibious cargo ships (AKA) anchored off the coast and shuttled their landing craft directly upriver to Hue.

The road between the city and Tan My was unimproved and wound its way through rice paddies and insecure villages before crossing a causeway to the Col Co ramp. The roadway frequently was inundated during the monsoonal deluge. During this period, however, Seabee units resurfaced and widened the road in key spots. It soon became the preferred approach to Phu Bai, where another detachment of the Danang support activity was established.

The Col Co ramp at Tan My, previously operated by a private concern to service Vietnamese sampans and junks, was gradually improved to accommodate the simultaneous berthing and offloading of four tank landing ships (LSTs). And before the construction of a pipeline to Hue, the facility was used to transfer fuel from suitably equipped landing craft to tanker trucks. The vessels shuttled between Col Co and nearby Thuan An (q.v.), where a fuel storage tank farm and floating offshore discharge line were installed in April 1966. Subsequently, a more permanent bottom-laid line connected tankers with the storage tanks. This facility was operated by a thirty-eight-man detachment of Naval Support Activity, Danang. Other naval units stationed in Tan My lagoon included a contingent of the Coastal Surveillance Force and a refrigerated covered lighter that maintained cold provisions for the forces in the region.

The Navy's units in the Hue area were especially taxed to maintain logistic support for allied combat forces during the enemy's Tet Offensive of 1968. The ramp and cargo staging facilities in the city were under constant attack by rockets, mortars, and ground forces from 31 January 1968 to 3 February 1969 and periodically thereafter. The fuel storage tank there was set ablaze. For a time, the unit at the ramp was forced to seek protection at the Military Assistance Command, Vietnam, compound. At the same time, the vessels at Tan My had to put out to sea to avoid Viet Cong fire. Later, they transported civilian refugees to Danang. River cargo operations were halted for ten days, but despite the loss of eighteen men and two LCUs and damage to forty-four other craft, naval units continued to deliver vital supplies and ammunition to the American combat troops fighting to recapture Hue.

The severity of the enemy's Tet campaign demanded a great reinforcement of allied commands in the I Corps Tactical Zone and a commensurate increase in naval combat and support forces. Early in 1968, units of the Navy's River Patrol Force were deployed there from stations further south in the Mekong Delta region. These river patrol boat (PBR), minesweeping, and patrol air cushion vehicle (PACV) units comprised Task Force Clearwater, which was charged with securing the two major waterways of the I Corps Tactical Zone, the Cua Viet and Hue Rivers. The PBR element of the Hue River Security Group, and at various times the task force headquarters, were located in Tan My lagoon on board Mobile Base I, a floating base consisting of large connected pontoons that served berthing, messing, repair, and command-control functions. The other units and the Naval Support Activity, Danang, detachment usually were stationed ashore.

As security on the river was improved during 1969 and 1970, the American naval force was gradually relieved by Vietnamese Navy units as part of the Vietnamization process. At the same time, logistic responsibilities in the Hue area were relinquished. Consequently, in the spring of 1970 Naval Support Activity, Danang, withdrew Mobile Base I and disestablished the detachments at Phu Bai and Tan My.

BIBLIOGRAPHY

A. Commander Naval Forces, Vietnam, "The Naval War in Vietnam," May 1970 (Washington: Naval Historical Center, Operational Archives Branch); Service Force, U.S. Pacific Fleet, "Command Histories, 1967-1972" (Washington: Naval Historical Center, Operational Archives Branch).

B. K. P. Huff, "Building the Advanced Base at DaNang," U.S. Naval Institute *Naval Review* 94 (May 1968):88-113; S. A. Swarztrauber, "River Patrol Relearned," U.S. Naval Institute *Naval Review* 96 (May 1970):120-57; Frank C. Collins, Jr., "Maritime Support of the Campaign in I Corps," U.S. Naval Institute *Naval Review* 97 (May 1971):156-79; Richard L. Schreadley, "The Naval War in Vietnam, 1950-1970," U.S. Naval Institute *Naval Review* 97 (May 1971):180-211; Edwin B. Hooper, *Mobility, Support, Endurance: A Story of Naval Operational Logistics in the Vietnam War, 1965-*

1968 (Washington: GPO, 1972); Richard Tregaskis, *Southeast Asia: Building the Bases: The History of Construction in Southeast Asia* (Washington: GPO, 1975).

EDWARD J. MAROLDA

I

IE SHIMA, RYUKYU ISLANDS, U.S. NAVAL ACTIVITIES, 1945 Ie Shima is a small, elliptical island located at 26°43′30″N., 127°47′30″E., three and a half miles west of Bise Sake, the northwestern end of the Motobu Peninsula on Okinawa. It is only about five and a half miles long in an east-west direction and two and three quarters miles wide in a north-south direction, but it is flat and has four good beaches from 9 to 35 yards wide and from 125 to 900 yards long on the southern and eastern shores. The mission of its invaders was "to provide a close-in major air base for use against the Japanese home islands."

While the island was commanded by Brig. Gen. C. E. Thomas, USA, harbor installations, the communications center, and the Seabees were under naval control. The military heart of the island was its four airfields, each with a strip between 6,000 and 7,000 feet long, although there were no hangars. To support American operations was the function of the Navy, which used two small pontoon piers and five ship mooring buoys, and had sixty-four berths 1,000 yards wide, sufficient for all vessels of any size. While there were no ship repair facilities and all personnel slept in tents, U.S. military personnel at the end of the war, when all facilities were rolled up, included 18,105 Army, 1,145 Navy, and 2,489 Marine Corps. It was on this island that the famous correspondent Ernie Pyle was killed.

BIBLIOGRAPHY

A. "Base Facilities Summary: Advance Bases Central Pacific Area, June 30, 1945 (U.S. Pacific Fleet and Pacific Ocean Area)," (Washington: Naval Historical Center, Operational Archives Branch).

IGARAPE ASSU, BRAZIL, U.S. NAVAL AIR FACILITY.
See Brazil, U.S. Naval Bases.

ILE TUDY, FRANCE.
See World War I U.S. Naval Air Stations in Europe.

INCHON, KOREA, U.S. NAVAL FLEET ACTIVITIES, 1950–1951 Inchon is the site of Korea's largest shipyards. It also has machine tool factories, textile mills, a motor vehicle plant, copper refining and fabrication plants, and a sizable construction materials industry. A secondary military base there contained a barracks and storage compound built by U.S. occupation forces. The Korean Navy, however, depends upon commercial facilities for repairs and fueling. U.S. Naval Fleet Activities Inchon was established 1 October 1950 by Commander Naval Forces Far East; it was disestablished on 22 January 1951. On 20 June 1951 Fleet Activity Group 1 (ex-Chinnampo) was redesignated and reestablished as U.S. Naval Fleet Activities Inchon by the Chief of Naval Operations, and consolidated with the Military Sea Transportation Service and Naval Control of Shipping Office. On 19 January 1951 Commander, Naval Forces, Far East, had recommended disestablishing the facilities at Inchon because almost all U.S. personnel wounded in Korea had been shipped out. In fact, on 1 December 1950 he had ordered that everything there be backloaded and that the personnel there prepare to evacuate 6,000 stretcher cases. The statistics are startling: 1 December 1950—7,000 U.S. Army litter patients were transported to the USS *Repose* from Chinnampo with destination Inchon; 3 December, with the temperature at 17°F—three APAs and two AKAs arrived and took on ROK Army and Marine wounded and also some POWs; 4 December, a relatively warm 28°F—word was received that the Eighth Army's defense line near Pyongyan was broken and that Chinnampo had only about four hours to clear the port before the arrival of a Chinese regiment there. Evacuation to the SS *Seaborne* began at 2300 hours and was completed early on 5 December, when Fleet Activities Chinnampo was disestablished.

BIBLIOGRAPHY

A. "Monograph Histories of U.S. Naval Overseas Bases. Vol. II. Pacific Area," (Washington: Naval Historical Center, Operational Archives Branch); Commander Fleet Activities, Japan-Korea, "War Diary, January 1-31, 1951" (Washington: Naval Historical Center, Operational Archives Branch).

INVERGORDON, SCOTLAND.
See World War I U.S. Naval Bases in Europe.

INVERNESS, SCOTLAND.
See World War I U.S. Naval Bases in Europe.

IPITANGA, BRAZIL, U.S. NAVAL AIR FACILITY.
See Brazil, U.S. Naval Bases.

IWAKUNI, JAPAN, U.S. MARINE CORPS AIR STATION, 1958– On the island of Honshu, Japan, near Hiroshima, is the Iwakuni Marine Corps Air Station. Since 1969 it has served as the Headquarters (Rear) of the First Marine

Aircraft Wing. It is also the home for five tactical air squadrons. Operating around the clock from the station's 8,000-foot runway, they perform between 8,000 and 10,000 flights per month.

The land where the base is located is very young, having only arisen from the sea about 350 years ago. Prior to that the area was part of Japan's Inland Sea. After the emergence of the land literally from the depths, it remained the site of a small fishing village until the eve of World War II, when the Japanese Navy built an air station there. As a result, by 1940 the population of the area had soared to 51,000. Throughout the war the station was a flight training facility for students from the Eta Jima Naval Cadet School, with ninety-six training aircraft at the base performing that function. One-hundred-fifty Zero fighters were also there. Some of their small hangars still exist at the base. The station emerged relatively unscathed from the war, suffering only a single strafing attack from a carrier-based strike force in July 1945, just a month before the end of the conflict.

U.S. Marines were the first occupying forces on the scene at Iwakuni following the Japanese surrender. The Army shortly followed, as did forces from Great Britain, India, New Zealand, and Australia. From 1948 to 1952 the Royal Air Force controlled the base. Then the U.S. Air Force took over. Throughout the Korean War, front-line tactical air support missions were flown out of Iwakuni along with strategic bombing runs against North Korea. The station was also a troop processing center, earning it the nickname "Gateway to Korea."

On 1 October 1954 the Air Force turned Iwakuni over to the Navy. In July 1956 the First Marine Aircraft Wing moved to it from Korea and on 1 January 1958 assumed command of the base as a Marine Corps Air Facility. Finally, in July 1962 Iwakuni officially became a U.S. Marine Corps Air Station.

From being the "Gateway to Korea" Iwakuni became in the 1960s the "Airways to Vietnam." It was from there that Marine Aircraft Group 12 sent its Air Base Squadron ashore in April 1965 at Chu Lai (q.v.) to construct a Marine Expeditionary airfield in South Vietnam. The group's tactical aircraft and First Marine Aircraft Wing followed shortly. The Indochina War had a debilitating impact on the manning level at Iwakuni as its strength shrank from over 6,000 personnel to 2,700. Meanwhile, Marine Corps Headquarters in Washington authorized accompanied tours of duty for those assigned to the base, resulting in a concurrent increase in dependents at the station from zero to nearly 1,200.

With the winding down of the Vietnam War, Marine aviation units began to return to Iwakuni. In April 1971, after six years of combat duty, the headquarters of the First Marine Aircraft relocated back. Today Iwakuni Marine Corps Air Station's main task is to serve as the Headquarters (Rear) of the First Marine Aircraft Wing in support of the Wing's Headquarters (Forward) at Futema Marine Corps Air Station on Okinawa (q.v.).

BIBLIOGRAPHY
B. MSgt Paul Sarokin, "Japan: Iwakuni," *Leatherneck*, March 1958, pp. 16-20, 91; Tom Bartlett, "MCAS Iwakuni Japan," *Leatherneck*, Jan. 1982, pp. 38-43.

ROGER T. ZEIMET

IWO JIMA, U.S. ADVANCE AIR BASE, 1945–1946 Iwo Jima is a pear-shaped island in the Volcano group 625 miles north of Saipan in the Marianas and 660 miles south of Tokyo. On the southern tip, the stem of the pear, the slumbering volcano Mount Suribachi rises about 350 feet above sea level. The central and northern section of the island is a plateau covered for the most part by volcanic ash. The coasts, rocky and inhospitable, lack any natural harbor. Beaches extending northward and eastward from Mount Suribachi were used by the Americans for on-beach unloadings. Commo. Matthew Calbraith Perry in 1853 purchased land for a coaling station from American settlers at Port Lloyd (*see* Far Eastern U.S. Naval Bases to 1898) in Chichi Jima, in the neighboring Bonin group, but the United States failed to contest Japan's claims to sovereignty over the islands. In 1944 Iwo Jima was inhabited by about 400 Japanese engaged in raising sugar and pineapples, and in sulphur extraction. All were evacuated after Japan decided to convert the island into a bastion of imperial defense.

By 1944 both the Japanese and the Americans recognized the strategic value of Iwo Jima as a potential air base. The Japanese finished two air fields (South and Central Fields) and were constructing a third, North Field, by 1945. These fields provided the Japanese with bases from which to harass B-29 bombers flying between the Marianas and Tokyo. For the Americans, they could serve as advanced air bases for P-51 fighter escorts and for emergency landings by B-29 superforts unable to complete the long flight from Japan to the Marianas. American war planners in October 1944 decided to seize Iwo Jima for an air base. After an ineffective bombardment, the Third, Fourth, and Fifth Marine Divisions of the Fifth Amphibious Corps landed on Iwo Jima's beaches on 19 February 1945. Confronted with a masterful, in-depth defense by the Japanese, the Marines only secured the island on 16 March after one of the bloodiest campaigns in Leatherneck history.

Even before fighting was concluded, Seabees began reconstructing and extending the Japanese fields. In April 1945 the first landbased fighter escort took off from South Field to accompany B-29s in a strike against Japan, and by July 1945 the main runway at South Field had been extended to 6,000 feet and paved with emulsified asphalt. An 8,500-foot strip for B-29s was completed at Central Field on 7 July 1945 to receive 102 B-29s returning from a raid on Tokyo that day. Eventually Central Field included two 9,800-foot airstrips and a 6,000-foot fueling strip. North Field was constructed entirely anew by Seabees and Army Engineers in extremely difficult terrain. By VJ-Day, North Field was furnished with a 6,000-foot strip paved to 5,500 feet, 10,000 feet of taxiways, and 129 hardstands.

Two main tank farms, East and West, supported lesser distributing farms at the three airfields. East Tank Farm attained a capacity of 85,000 barrels of aviation gasoline; West Tank Farm, of 160,000 barrels of aviation gasoline, 50,000 barrels of motor gasoline, and 20,000 barrels of diesel oil. Unloading was entirely across the beaches. After an improvised breakwater of blockships was broken up by storm, the Americans never again attempted seaward protection for their ships at Iwo Jima. Since Iwo Jima was endowed with no constantly flowing streams, the Americans further developed the system of wells, water catchments, and reservoirs inherited from the Japanese. The island was also furnished with considerable storage facilities, housing for 37,000 officers and men, hospitals with a capacity of 1,250 beds, radar equipment atop Mount Suribachi, and sixty miles of primary and secondary roads. American naval air facilities were rolled up at Iwo Jima on 14 August 1946.

BIBLIOGRAPHY
A. U.S. Navy, Bureau of Yards and Docks, *Building the Navy's Bases in World War II*, 2 vols. (Washington: GPO, 1947), II:337-74.
B. Samuel E. Morison, *Victory in the Pacific, 1945* (Boston: Little, Brown, 1961).

WILLIAM R. BRAISTED

J

JAMAICA, BRITISH WEST INDIES, U.S. NAVAL AIR BASE.
See Caribbean, The, U.S. Naval Bases.

JOHNSTON ISLAND, U.S. NAVAL AIR FACILITY, 1941–1948 Johnston Island, a coral atoll situated 720 miles southwest of Oahu, includes a lagoon and two small islands—the 60-acre Johnston Island and the still smaller Sand Island. In the mid-1930s, when the United States was involved in a scramble for Pacific island air bases, the Navy recognized the significance of Johnston Island as a strategic position from which air patrols could be operated to detect hostile forces penetrating the Eastern Pacific. By executive order, in December 1934 President Franklin D. Roosevelt placed Johnston under naval control, and the U.S. Fleet undertook minor improvements to prepare the lagoon for tender-based operations by patrol planes: blasting coral heads, clearing a 3,600-foot runway and ship-channel into the lagoon, and building a boat landing. Air units of the fleet used the lagoon during Fleet Problem XVIII in 1937. In line with recommendations on naval bases made by the Hepburn Board, the Navy engaged a civilian contractor to construct permanent facilities for tender-based planes. Two years later the Greenslade Board on naval air facilities confirmed that Johnston Island should serve as a secondary air base to provide strategic security against enemy operations approaching Hawaii, the Panama Canal, and the west coast of South America. The Navy placed a small Marine detail on Johnston Island in March 1941, and the Johnston Air Station was formally commissioned in August 1941.

By the time war broke out with Japan in December 1941, the civilian contractors had dredged three runways for amphibians, had begun a landing field on Johnston Island, and had erected living quarters, a fifty-bed hospital, and storage for 25,000 gallons of aviation gasoline and 16,000 barrels of fuel oil. Although the island was shelled by a Japanese submarine on 15 December 1941, the civilians continued work on runway extensions until they were relieved by elements of the Fifth and Tenth Seabee Battalions. As the war moved into the

Marshalls and farther west, Johnston became a fueling station for submarines and a major stop on the air transport route westward across the Pacific. When improvements were completed by the summer of 1944, the area of Johnston had been increased fourfold to 160 acres. It then included accommodations for 70 officers and 1,118 enlisted men and capacity for thirteen amphibians and seventy-six land planes. The Naval Air Facility was inactivated on 1 July 1948 and transferred to the Air Force.

BIBLIOGRAPHY

A. Record Group 80, General Records of the Navy Department, 1927-1940, A21-5 File (Washington: National Archives); ''Monograph Histories of U.S. Naval Bases. Vol. II. Pacific Area'' (Washington: Naval Historical Center, Operational Archives Branch).

B. Francis X. Holbrook, ''United States National Defense and Trans-Pacific Commercial Air Routes, 1933-1941,'' Ph.D. diss., Fordham University, 1969.

WILLIAM R. BRAISTED

K

KEFLAVIK, ICELAND, U.S. NAVAL STATION, 1941- Keflavik, the site of the naval station that forms part of the NATO Base, is located in southwest Iceland on the northwest shore of the Reykjanes Peninsula, Faxa Bay, at 64°N., 22°35′W., and twenty-two miles west-south-west of Reykjavik.

With the outbreak of World War II in Europe in 1939, the days of Iceland's historic isolation were numbered. The Germans had courted Iceland before the war and were planning to establish a base there. On 10 May 1940, about a month after the German occupation of Denmark, Great Britain occupied Iceland and began building two air bases there. The United States had established diplomatic relations with the Danish government in exile a month earlier and in October 1940 sent Lincoln McVeagh as its first minister to Iceland. However, a request by Iceland in December 1940 for military aid was rejected by the United States.

In March 1941, when Germany extended the war zone to Iceland, the United States, Britain, and Canada reached agreement on war strategy in the ABC-1 Staff Paper and on providing aid to Iceland. In April 1941 the U.S. destroyer *Niblack* fired on a U-boat after picking up survivors from a Dutch ship off the coast of Iceland. On 18 April Adm. Ernest J. King, USN, the Commander of the Atlantic Fleet, issued an order defining the Western Hemisphere to include western Iceland. British troops were urgently needed elsewhere, but President F. D. Roosevelt was reluctant to have Americans relieve British troops in Iceland without a request from the Icelandic government. Even so, preparations for a landing were secretly under way in the United States.

By 22 June 1941 the First Marine Brigade (Provisional), Brig. Gen. John Marston, commanding, had sailed from Charleston, S.C., with orders to aid the British in defending Iceland. The brigade was delayed in Placentia Bay, Newfoundland, while an invitation was extracted from Prime Minister Herman Jonasson of Iceland. The invitation, offered on 1 July, was accepted that very day, and the Marines arrived at Reykjavik on the seventh. President Roosevelt then told Congress that three German threats had prompted the occupation: the threat to Greenland and to North America itself, the threat to Atlantic shipping, and the threat to the already considerable flow of American munitions to Britain.

While the first Marine base camp was near Alafoss, twelve miles from Reykjavik, the Marines were spread over 300 square miles, building bases of Nissen huts and patrolling the coast. With the arrival of U.S. Army troops in August, the Marines were unwillingly attached to the command of Maj. Gen. C. H. Bonesteel. After the Marines were firmly established and the United States had entered the war, they were needed elsewhere, and by March 1942 they had left Iceland.

Meanwhile a Navy contract had been signed on 25 September for civilian personnel to go to Iceland from Newfoundland and Quonset Point, R.I., to build a fleet air base near Reykjavik and also a fuel storage tank farm at Hvalfjordhur. On 8 November 1941 Naval Operating Base Iceland was established under the control of the Commander in Chief, Atlantic Fleet, with Rear Adm. J. L. Kauffman named as the commandant. Kauffman did not set up headquarters on the beach until 23 December, in the meantime using as headquarters the USS *Williamsburg* (ex-yacht *Aras*), anchored at Hvalfjordhur with seventy-five officers and men on board. Despite severe damage to the base by a 130 mph hurricane, it was commissioned on 21 January 1942.

On 22 April 1942 the U.S. Army officially took over control of Iceland Base Command from the British, most of whose troops had been withdrawn. At the same time the United States, despite General Bonesteel's counterproposal of a U.S. military government in the event of an attack, assured Iceland that all facilities would revert to Icelandic control after the war, with landing rights to be decided upon later. Because Icelanders had had no military forces or wars for centuries and were not accustomed to having foreigners occupy their country, the presence of the British and American troops caused much resentment among the populace. For their part, the troops were thrown into a tedious and often boring tour of duty in a harsh and isolated setting. They behaved as soldiers often do in similar situations and created some ugly incidents, especially in 1941 and 1942. As early as 4 October 1941 the Icelandic government sent Secretary of the Navy Frank Knox a list of twenty grievances against U.S. policies and American misbehavior toward Icelanders; most of these were attributable to the Army, however, rather than to the Marines or the Navy.

On 16 May 1942 Naval Operating Base Iceland (NOBI) moved ashore when Camp Knox, near Reykjavik, was commissioned. The base had already become an important link in the convoy system set up in 1941 between the United States and the Newfoundland-Greenland-Iceland passage to Britain. Ships, and later aircraft, served the convoys as escorts and for search and rescue purposes. NOBI also maintained a Port Director's Office.

In August 1942 Seabee (Construction Battalion) units of the Navy began to arrive in Iceland to take over from contractor personnel the duty of building the facilities. Their duties included building the Naval Operating Base, including a 100-bed hospital, two airfields, a tank farm, and an ammunition depot at Hvalfjordhur and recreational facilities at Falcon Camp, in the same area. They unloaded many of the supply ships themselves and worked under extreme weather conditions and severe logistical problems. Despite their numerous difficulties, the first American aircraft landed at Meeks Field, the Army's air base, on 26 March 1943. Meeks became one of the most important fields of the European War and later the Keflavik International Airport, around which the current NATO base has grown. Meeks and the Navy's Patterson Field were usably complete by August 1943, and by October the Seabees began to leave Iceland.

Escort of convoys from Iceland continued to be important not only for the passage to Britain but also for the Murmansk run, which furnished supplies to the Soviet Union under Lend-Lease after Hitler invaded Russia. While periodic small-scale German strafing and bombing raids occurred on or near Iceland, a major attack was never launched. In the spring of 1943 British and Canadian ships took over the escort of convoy function, and U.S. naval strength began to dwindle; in April 1943 it was down to 4,428 men, while the Army still had 38,000 troops there.

In the Hvalfjordhur area, British salvage and fuel depots dwarfed similar American installations, and with American naval functions being whittled down Rear Adm. A. C. Bennett, commander, NOBI, recommended to Adm. Royal E. Ingersoll, Commander in Chief of the Atlantic Fleet, that most of the U.S. facilities be closed, maintained in caretaker status, or turned over to the British. He reckoned without the British, who particularly did not want to lose the service of the American long-range PBY *Catalina* flying boat squadron based there.

On 13 June 1943 Admiral King directed Admiral Ingersoll to proceed with the reduction of NOBI but to maintain the Fleet Air Base until at least October and in addition to keep Falcon Camp ammunition storage facility ready for use if needed. Two days later, however, a new base commander, Commo. R. S. Wentworth, was ordered to turn the salvage and fuel depots over to the British, to withdraw the two American tankers there, to place Falcon Camp in caretaker status, and to proceed to turn over the Fleet Air Base to the British. The Joint Chiefs of Staff approved this process despite an increase of U-boat activity in the Iceland area, and on 20 December 1943 Admiral King decided to close the Naval Air Facility.

NOBI did not change much until May 1944, when a new reduction was ordered. Falcon Camp was dismantled, while Camp Knox was consolidated and maintained as a supply depot. Some personnel from "Project 719," supporting the High-Frequency Radio Direction Finding Station on Jan Mayen Island, about 300 miles to the northeast, were held over at NOBI.

By November 1944 NOBI had become Naval Operating Facility Iceland, the token American presence commanded by a commander in grade. Camp Knox still had several Quonset huts, a few barges, and the Port Director's Office, but American personnel numbered merely 40 officers and 330 enlisted men. For the rest of the war the Navy's responsibility would be to supply the Army. Yet the air-sea rescue provided for the Iceland-Greenland-Newfoundland route kept morale high on the ships and aircraft carrying troops from Europe both before and after VE-Day. On VJ-Day, 2 September 1945, only 17 U.S. naval officers and 190 enlisted men, many of them Seabees, remained in Iceland.

Fortunately, relations between the American military forces and Icelanders improved despite disputes between them over the American censorship of mail and the prices charged by the Navy when selling American oil to them. The Icelandic government, still under the Danish king in 1940, had declared itself independent when Germany occupied Denmark in 1940, and it was determined to remain independent when the Act of Union expired in 1944. On 17 June 1944, when Iceland officially became a republic, the United States was the first country to extend recognition to it.

Although many Icelanders realized that they could not return to the isolation and "cultural purity" of prewar days, most of them expected the United States to honor the 1941 Defense Agreement and withdraw from the island after the war. The U.S. Navy was still involved there, however, because in November 1945 the British turned their naval air station, fuel depot, and naval ammunition depot back to the United States, and in October 1945 the U.S. State Department had petitioned Iceland for the lease of some bases. When the Icelandic government stalled, a political struggle ensued. Finally, on 7 October 1946, the Keflavik Agreement gave U.S. military aircraft the right to use the Keflavik airfield to help maintain American occupation forces in Germany. In return, the 1941 Defense Agreement was allowed to expire, which meant that the American occupation had to end within six months. The last American troops left Iceland in April 1947.

During the tensions of the Cold War, Iceland was persuaded to join the North Atlantic Treaty Organization, in 1949, but was required neither to establish native military forces nor to harbor foreign troops during peacetime. Within the NATO framework a new defense agreement between Iceland and the United States was signed on 5 May 1951. On 6 July the Iceland Defense Force became a NATO command under the control of the U.S. Air Force, with Naval Station Keflavik established as part of that command.

After the Korean War ended in 1953, antimilitary feeling and economic disputes with the United States caused Iceland to start reevaluating the NATO base. On 28 March 1956 the Icelandic Althing passed a resolution calling for the withdrawal of American forces, but the Middle East War and the Soviet Union's reaction to the Hungarian Revolution of that year prevented the carrying out of the resolution. The North Atlantic Council also recommended that Iceland not deprive itself of NATO and U.S. protection. However, this time Iceland and the United States bypassed NATO and reached a new agreement on 6 December 1956. In 1959 a series of incidents involving American military men and Icelanders led to more anti-American sentiment and more diplomatic disputes. In 1960 the U.S. Army withdrew from Iceland. On 1 July 1961 the U.S. Navy took over the host role of the Iceland Defense Force from the U.S. Air Force and shifted a number of early warning aircraft from Argentia, Newfoundland (q.v.), to Keflavik.

Periodic cultural and political disputes have prompted movements in Iceland for the removal of the Americans. Between 1971 and 1973 a review of the defense agreement was fueled by a protest in 1972 against U.S. involvement in Vietnam. Under the terms of the 1951 agreement, after either government requests NATO review, failure to reach a new accord can lead to termination of the 1951 agreement a year later. Such a termination could have occurred in January 1974, but a petition signed by half of the eligible voters in Iceland requested the government not to terminate it.

A memorandum of understanding signed on 22 October 1974 provided for a lower American military profile in Iceland and more attention to Iceland's domestic interests. In consequence, the number of U.S. personnel was reduced, the Marine guards at Keflavik Airport were detached, and since then all U.S. military personnel have had to live on base. Moreover, all enlisted men of E-5 rank or below have to obey a curfew beginning at 2300 hours in Reykjavik. The United States has installed a cable television system to stop the old Icelandic complaint of the corrupting influence of American TV. It has also taken steps to upgrade the facilities of Keflavik Airport and to separate them from the NATO Base. On the other hand, in 1974 Iceland agreed to sell geothermal heat to the United States—the process being completed in 1982—and cooperation between the Iceland Defense Force and the Icelandic Coast Guard, civil defense, and civil aviation personnel has greatly improved.

The U.S. Navy's role in Iceland now includes coordination of the Iceland Defense Force activities, which are headed by a flag officer, support services, and ASW. The commanding office of Naval Station Keflavik is also Commander, Naval Forces Iceland. A major feature is the patrol squadron of nine P-3C *Orion* aircraft for ASW operations, one of the twenty-four such squadrons in the U.S. Navy. The squadron has 58 officers and 280 enlisted men under Fleet Air Keflavik. Other naval units are the Naval Oceanography Command Detachment, Naval Communications Station, Marine Barracks, Naval Security Group Activity, Naval Investigative Service Resident Agency, Navy Broadcasting Service Detachment Eight, and Resident Officer in Charge of Construction. The NATO Base includes 920 family housing units and 15 buildings for unaccompanied military personnel. The total base population is about 5,000, of which 2,000 are dependents. As of 31 March 1982 the actual count, by military service, of those on active duty in Iceland was: Navy, 1,712; Marine Corps, 122; Air Force, 1,119; and Army, 2—for a total of 2,955.

BIBLIOGRAPHY

A. Eric Linklater, *The Northern Garrisons* (London: HMSO, 1941); U.S. Office of the Deputy Chief of Naval Operations (Air), *Air Task Organization in the Atlantic Ocean Area* (Washington: Navy Department, 1946); U.S. Navy, Atlantic Fleet, Commander in Chief, *Naval Operating Base Iceland* (Washington: Navy Department, 1946); U.S. Navy, Bureau of Yards and Docks, *Building the Navy's Bases in World War II*, 2 vols. (Washington: GPO, 1947); U.S. Department of State, *Defense Agreement Pursuant to the North Atlantic Treaty between the United States of America and the Republic of Iceland* (Washington: GPO, 1951); U.S. Department of State, *Defense of Iceland Pursuant to the North Atlantic Treaty: Agreement Effected by an Exchange of Notes Signed at Reykjavik December 6, 1956* (Washington: GPO, 1957); U.S. Department of State, *Aviation: Joint Financing of Certain Air Navigation Services in Iceland and in Greenland and the Faroe Islands* (Washington: GPO, 1979); U.S. Navy, Atlantic Fleet, Commander in Chief, Iceland Defense Force, *Newcomers Guide, NATO Base, Keflavik, Iceland, 1980-81* (Keflavik: Commander Iceland Defense Force, 1980); *White Falcon, Special Edition, 1981* (Keflavik: Iceland Defense Force Public Affairs Office, 1981).

B. Philip E. Mosely, "Iceland and Greenland: An American Problem," *Foreign Affairs* 18 (July 1940):742-46; Hugh B. Cave, *We Build, We Fight: The Story of the Seabees* (New York: Harper, 1944); Clyde H. Metcalf, ed., *The Marine Corps Reader* (New York: G. P. Putnam's Sons, 1944); Hans W. Weigert, "Iceland, Greenland and the United States," *Foreign Affairs* 23 (Oct. 1944):112-22; Samuel E. Morison, *The Battle of the Atlantic September 1939-May 1943* (Boston: Little, Brown, 1947); Richard W. Johnston, *Follow Me: The Story of the Second Marine Division in World War II* (New York: Random House, 1948); Agnes Rothery, *Iceland: New World Outpost* (New York: Viking Press, 1948); John L. Zimmerman, "Force in Readiness," U.S. Naval Institute *Proceedings* 83 (Feb. 1957):164-71; Donald E. Neuechterlin, *Iceland: Reluctant Ally* (Ithaca, N.Y.: Cornell University Press, 1961); John Joseph Hunt, "The United States Occupation of Iceland, 1941-1946," Ph.D. diss., Georgetown University, 1966; Patrick Abbazia, *Mr. Roosevelt's Navy: The Private War of the U.S. Atlantic Fleet, 1939-1942* (Annapolis, Md.: Naval Institute Press, 1975); Johannes Nordal and Valdimar Kristinsson, *Iceland, 874-1974. A Handbook Published by the Central Bank of Iceland on the Occasion of the Eleventh Centenary of the Settlement of Iceland.* (Reykjavik: Central Bank of Iceland, 1975); Katharine Scherman, *Daughter of Fire: A Portrait of Iceland* (Boston: Little, Brown, 1976); Edward W. Chester, *The United States and Six Atlantic Outposts: The Military and Economic Considerations* (Port Washington, N.Y.: Kennikat Press, 1980); Robert A. Fliegel, "Iceland: Unique in NATO," U.S. Naval Institute *Proceedings* 106 (Aug. 1980):32-37; Richard F. Tomasson, *Iceland: The First New Society* (Minneapolis: University of Minnesota Press, 1980); Frank Fisher, "Outpost in the North Atlantic," *All Hands* 789 (Oct. 1982):16-21; "Where They Serve," *Defense 82*, Almanac Issue, Sept. 1982, p. 26.

WILLIAM MCQUADE

KIEN AN, REPUBLIC OF VIETNAM, U.S. AND REPUBLIC OF VIETNAM RIVER FORCES OPERATING BASE, 1969-1970 Situated on the Cai Lon River in South Vietnam's Mekong Delta, Kien An served as an operating base for U.S. and Vietnamese river forces during the Southeast Asian Conflict. Developed during 1969, the base was turned over to the Vietnamese Navy in December 1970 when American forces began withdrawing from the war.

BIBLIOGRAPHY
A. Commander Naval Forces, Vietnam, "Monthly Historical Reports, 1965-1971" (Washington: Naval Historical Center, Operational Archives Branch).

EDWARD J. MAROLDA

KILLINGHOLME, ENGLAND.
See World War I U.S. Naval Air Stations in Europe.

KIRIWINA ISLAND, NEW GUINEA, U.S. NAVAL ADVANCE BASE, 1943-1944 Kiriwina is one of the Trobriand Islands located to the northeast of Milne Bay in extreme eastern New Guinea. Occupied on 30 June 1943 by troops of the Southwest Pacific Area, Kiriwina (8°30′S., 151°3′E.) was utilized beginning 2 October 1943 as an advance base for PT boats. Boats from Motor Torpedo Boat Squadron 7 patrolled from Kiriwina against Japanese barge traffic off the New Britain coast. They found few targets, and on 27 February 1944 closed their base there.

BIBLIOGRAPHY
A. U.S. Navy, "7th Amphibious Force Command History, 10 January 1943-23 December 1945" (Washington: Naval Historical Center, Operational Archives Branch); U.S. Navy, Bureau of Yards and Docks, *Building the Navy's Bases in World War II*, 2 vols. (Washington: GPO, 1947); U.S. Navy, "U.S. Naval Bases in the South and Southwest Pacific (and Central Pacific Forward) in World War II," 1 November 1954 (Washington: Naval Historical Center, Operational Archives Branch).
B. Rear Adm. Worrall Reed Carter, *Beans, Bullets, and Black Oil* (Washington: GPO, 1953); Samuel E. Morison, *New Guinea and the Marianas March 1944-August 1944* (Boston: Little, Brown, 1953); Capt. Robert J. Bulkley, *At Close Quarters: PT Boats in the United States Navy* (Washington: Navy Department, Naval History Division, 1962); Vice Adm. Daniel E. Barbey, *MacArthur's Amphibious Navy* (Annapolis, Md.: U.S. Naval Institute, 1969).

JOHN B. LUNDSTROM

KNOX COASTAL STATION, ANTARCTICA, U.S. NAVAL BASE.
See Antarctica, U.S. Naval and Air Bases.

KWAJALEIN, MARSHALL ISLANDS, U.S. NAVAL AIR BASES, NAVAL OPERATING BASE, AND HEADQUARTERS COMMANDER MARSHALLS-GILBERT AREA 1944- Kwajalein Atoll in the Marshall Islands is the second largest coral atoll in the world, embracing a 655-square-mile lagoon that extends 66 miles in length and up to 20 miles in width. Shaped like an old-fashioned pistol pointing westward, the atoll is dotted by more than ninety islets whose total land area amounts to only a little over six square miles. Only three points possess sufficient land for military or naval installations: Ebadon Island to the west, at the pistol's mouth; the linked islands of Roi-Namur to the north; and Kwajalein Island with neighboring Ebeye, at the southern or butt end of the pistol. Channels in the north and south afford ready access from the ocean to the lagoon's protected waters. Prior to World War II, the Japanese had constructed an important air base at Roi-Namur, a naval installation on Kwajalein, and a seaplane base and repair facilities on Ebeye.

When Adm. Chester W. Nimitz and his Commander in Chief Pacific Ocean Area (CINCPOA) staff projected their westward island-hopping strategy in Operation Flintlock, they planned to secure effective control of the Marshalls by capturing Kwajalein Atoll in the middle of the group, Majuro to the east, and Eniwetok to the northwest. The anchorage at Kwajalein could be readily developed to support the fleet in its operations farther west, and American aircraft could use fields on Kwajalein either as staging points on trans-Pacific flights or as bases from which to neutralize Japanese positions east and west. Kwajalein, therefore, was to serve as a fleet anchorage with minor repair facilities and a major air center.

The American attack on Kwajalein was two-pronged. A Northern Attack Force including the Fourth Marine Division captured the Roi-Namur area by 2 February 1944; and a Southern Attack Force, the Army's Seventh Infantry Division, completed the conquest of Kwajalein and neighboring islets by 4 February. Accompanying the attacking forces were the Seabees, the base components, and the occupation forces essential to begin work on facilities contemplated in Kwajalein's mission. Kwajalein also became the headquarters of the Commander Marshalls-Gilbert Area, Rear Adm. Alva D. Bernard, whose command was designated Task Force 96. Kwajalein Island was under Army command until it was transferred to the Navy in July 1945.

Roi-Namur looks like two buck teeth jutting from a jaw-shaped formation at the northeast extremity of the atoll. Roi measures about 1,250 by 1,170 yards; Namur, about two-thirds that size. The two islands are linked by a narrow coral strip that the Americans widened with fill drawn from the lagoon. Accompanying the invasion force were elements for an advanced naval air base (ACORN 21), naval base components of Gropac 3, Communications Unit 6, Carrier Air Service Unit (CASU) 20, the 109th Construction Battalion, the 15th Marine Defense Battalion, and Marine Air Group (MAG) 31.

Beginning on 5 February 1944, the 109th Seabees undertook to clear Roi of the debris of battle and to restore the main Roi runway, which was 4,300 feet long. They thus enabled the first fighter squadrons to begin operations from the base on 13 February notwithstanding a devastating Japanese bombing attack. Later two additional runways were restored so that by the formal commissioning of the base in May 1944 it supported 100 planes (fighters, light bombers, and patrol planes) that operated daily against the Japanese on Wotje, Jaluit, and Truk. The largest single sortie from Roi included 240 planes launched against Maleolop on 14 December 1944. Thereafter, the sorties declined as fighting moved westward.

In March 1944 the Ninety-fifth Seabees landed on Namur to build an aviation supply depot that provided large quantities of aviation material during the Marianas campaign. Other facilities fabricated on Namur included a 4,000-barrel tank farm, three dispensaries, a housing compound of floored tents and Quonsets, and repair shops for small boat repairs. The limited water front facilities boasted a 4-by-30-foot pontoon pier and a restored 450-by-30-foot Japanese pier. Personnel on Roi-Namur reached 6,500 by 1 April 1944.

About forty miles south of Roi-Namur at the southeast tip of the atoll are the three-mile-long, boomerang-shaped Kwajalein Island and attendant islets extending northward: Ebeye, Berlin (Gugegwe), and Bennett (Bigej). The nucleus of the naval base at Kwajalein was the components of Gropac 2, the first elements of which moved ashore on the island's sea side the day before the island was declared secure. Among the minor naval facilities constructed by the Seabees on Kwajalein were a restored and extended Japanese pier, a 100-foot seawall, and some light repair shops. The most important single utility on Kwajalein, however, was the reconstructed 6,300-foot coral runway to which the Seabees added two 80-foot taxiways and 100 hard stands for heavy bombers. When the Army turned command of Kwajalein Island over to the Navy on 1 July 1945, the field became the principal element of a new Kwajalein Naval Air Base (officially designated U.S. Naval Air Base #824). The base also served the Naval Air Transport Service and the Army Transport Command.

Because of the crowded conditions on Kwajalein Island, naval utilities spilled northward to small Berlin Island. There the Japanese had already established a supply depot, repair shops for small craft, a marine railway, a small pier, and a foundry capable of pouring steel. After the Seabees had bulldozed and leveled the island, men of the E-6 repair unit went to work building carpentry, electrical, machine, and engine overhaul shops until Berlin Island became practically a separate naval repair station with the best repair facilities located between Pearl Harbor and Guam (q.v.). Two important units transferred from Kwajalein to Berlin Island were a floating dry dock, the USS AFDL-7, which had lifting capacity of 1,900 tons, and the Repair Barge (YR-25). Although specifically assigned to repair light craft of Task Force 96, Berlin Island soon responded to calls from small craft of many commands.

Three miles north of Kwajalein Island lies Ebeye, measuring about 5,300 by 700 feet, where two Japanese seaplane ramps had escaped destruction during the island's capture. The 107th Seabees and men from ACORN 23 pushed to complete a seaplane base, Naval Air Base #807, by clearing a parking area and building repair shops, housing, a dispensary, covered storage, and a 4,000-barrel aviation gasoline farm. The base's mission in December 1944 was to support medium and heavy bomber squadrons. Perhaps to escape dominance by the Army on Kwajalein, the naval atoll commander also established his headquarters on Ebeye. Other major facilities established in the vicinity of Kwajalein Island were a 60,000-barrel fuel oil tank farm on Bennett Island, a Joint (Army, Navy, Marine) Communications Center on Carlson Island, and an underwater detection unit on Bascombe Island.

Kwajalein remained active even as the war moved westward. Between April

1944 and March 1945 its harbor handled 157,925 tons of cargo and afforded anchorage to unnumbered ships awaiting routing to various points in the Pacific. Kwajalein Air Field served as a major staging point for aircraft flying the Pacific. Its fuel tanks made a crucial contribution to the fleet's fuel requirements in the major battles farther west. And from Kwajalein American aircraft continued the air surveillance of the bypassed bases in the Marshalls and Carolines.

After World War II the naval presence at Kwajalein continued, but in reduced form. By 1949 the base was seriously run down as the result of corrosive weather conditions, shortage of personnel, and inadequate financing. Kwajalein's chief responsibility was to provide a staging point for trans-Pacific flights, to support the civil administration, and to conduct search and rescue operations. In 1947 the combined utilities were defined as a naval station; three years later they were placed under the Commandant, Fourteenth Naval District; and in 1951 the station was reorganized and placed under the Bureau of Aeronautics. There was considerable naval construction on Kwajalein in the mid-1950s, mostly of housing and recreational facilities. By 1959 the Navy had decided to assign its remaining responsibilities to a civilian contractor, to deactivate the naval station, and to gradually phase out naval personnel as civilians arrived to take over. In 1982 the Air Force retained a Missile Range at Kwajalein for the observation of intercontinental ballistic missiles fired from Vandenberg Air Force Base, Calif. Also in 1982, protesting islanders demanded indemnification for dislocations suffered through the years.

BIBLIOGRAPHY

A. Commander in Chief, U.S. Pacific Fleet, ''Administrative History of the Marshalls-Gilberts Area,'' 6 vols. (Washington: Naval Historical Center, Operational Archives Branch); U.S. Navy, Bureau of Yards and Docks, *Building the Navy's Bases in World War II*, 2 vols. (Washington: GPO, 1947), II:320-24; Selected Papers from World War II Command Files and Base Maintenance Records (Washington: Naval Historical Center, Operational Archives Branch).

B. Samuel E. Morison, *Aleutians, Gilberts and Marshalls June 1942-April 1944* (Boston: Little, Brown, 1951), pp. 207-81, 305-7.

WILLIAM R. BRAISTED

L

L'ABER VRACH, FRANCE.
See World War I U.S. Naval Air Stations in Europe.

LA FE, CUBA, U.S. NAVAL AIR FACILITY, 1943–1944 In 1940 agreement was reached between the Navy Department and the government of Cuba for the use of various Cuban sites for defense purposes. One of these was at La Fe, 22°2′N., 84°16′W., on the northern side of the western tip of Cuba and 210 miles southwest of NAS Key West. It was thus well located for air and surface craft to patrol the Yucatan Channel, the narrow waters that divide Cuba from the Yucatan Province of Mexico and join the waters of the Gulf of Mexico and the Caribbean Sea.

At a cost of $247,000, during 1941 and 1942 the Frederick Snare Corp. built a facility capable of storing 275,000 gallons of gasoline, quarters for sixteen officers and seventy-five men, diesel oil storage, and facilities for six seaplanes and three PT boats. Although no planes were sent there, the facilities were frequently used by PBM *Mariners* that flew search and block patrols out of Key West. With the U-boat threat largely evaporated by late 1943, Commander Gulf Sea Frontier recommended turning over to the Cuban Navy all structures except those necessary to support activities emanating from NAF San Julian (q.v.), ten miles to the east. The Chief of Naval Operations agreed, and all fixed installations and construction were turned over to the Cuban government at no cost. The facility was disestablished on 12 September 1944.

BIBLIOGRAPHY
A. "Naval Air Facility, La Fe, Cuba," Summary Cards (Washington, D.C., Navy Yard: Naval Aviation History Office).

LA FRENE, FRANCE.
See World War I U.S. Northern Bombing Group Bases in England and France.

LA GOULETTE, TUNISIA.
See North Africa, U.S. Naval Bases.

LAJES, AZORES ISLANDS, PORTUGAL, U.S. NAVAL AIR FACILITY, 1957– Located on Portuguese Air Base Four, Terceira Island, Azores, the Naval Air Facility is a tenant organization of the U.S. Air Force 1605th Air Base Wing, Military Airlift Command, with both commands being guests of the Portuguese government. Construction of the NAF on the southwest side of Lajes Field started in August 1954 and was completed in December 1957, with authorization for its establishment directed by the Secretary of the Navy on 18 January 1957. Comdr. G. C. Gilmore, USN, was the acting commander until relieved by Capt. C. L. Lipham, USN, in July 1957 as the first commanding officer.

The primary mission of NAF Lajes was to maintain and operate facilities and provide services and materials in support of aviation operations for units of operating forces of the Navy and other activities as designated by the Chief of Naval Operations. The facilities included a hangar, attached shops and offices, taxiways, and aircraft parking spaces. During the early days most of the support provided was for Atlantic barrier aircraft in Airborne Early Warning Squadrons until the barrier was disestablished in 1965. Attached to the facility, but located about a mile from it, is the Advanced Underseas Weapons Complex, which was completed in February 1972.

On 1 January 1962 the Commander in Chief Atlantic Fleet (CINCLANTFLT) directed the establishment of Commander Fleet Air Azores (COMFAIR-AZORES) and assigned the additional duties to the commanding officer of NAF, Lajes, who on 26 September assumed ever greater responsibility when he was designated as the Commander Azores Sector ASW group. Given the increased emphasis on ASW operations in the Atlantic, the introduction of the P-3A *Orion*, and the strategic location of Lajes in mid-Atlantic, NAF Lajes became intimately involved in Atlantic ASW operations and in coordinating its efforts with adjoining U.S./NATO commands. It provided maintenance and logistics and communications support to five different patrol squadrons that conducted aerial surveillance in the mid-Atlantic and Mediterranean during the Cuban missile crisis of 1962. In addition to servicing and providing logistic support for naval aircraft, NAF Lajes routinely services transient Marine Corps as well as naval aircraft.

By May 1974 NAF Lajes had moved to a new site on the northeast side of Lajes Field. The renovated facilities there included a hangar with maintenance shop spaces, administration buildings, and a Tactical Support Center. Since that time NAF Lajes has increased its maritime air activity. It has five P-3 aircraft and crews which, including ground support personnel, add up to more than 100 officers and men. At various times, Naval Air Reserve Squadrons from the United States take their active duty for training periods at Lajes. Helping both Regulars and Reservists is an Antisubmarine Classification and Analysis Center in the Operations Control Center. Established in October 1968, it provides a post-flight analysis capability. With the establishment of a new Antisubmarine Warfare Operations Center in July 1974, Lajes could still better provide operational and logistical support for the P-3C *Orion*.

Currently under the command of Capt. William H. Ketchum, NAF Lajes has a personnel complement of 18 officers and 164 enlisted men.

BIBLIOGRAPHY

A. Ens. James T. Ross, USNR, U.S. Naval Air Facility, Lajes, Azores Islands, to the writer, 14 Oct. 1982, with enclosed "History of U.S. Naval Air Facility, Lajes, Azores," n.d.

LAKE BOLSENA, ITALY, NAVAL AIR STATION.
See World War I U.S. Naval Air Stations in Europe.

LAKE BONNEY, ANTARCTICA, U.S. NAVAL BASE.
See Antarctica, U.S. Naval and Air Bases.

LA MADDALENA, SARDINIA, U.S. NAVAL SUPPORT OFFICE, 1944, 1973– With the capitulation of Italy in September 1943, the islands of Corsica and Sardinia fell into American hands. Because of their convenient location, sites there were used for PT boat bases, with the boats engaged in warfare against German E-boats and other enemy vessels operating out of southern French and northern Italian ports. Because of the short range of the PT, many bases were established, the most important being the one at Maddalena. There, on 13 April 1944, a detail of one officer and twenty-seven men from the 1005th Detachment, at Bizerte (*See* North Africa, U.S. Naval Bases), arrived and erected pontoon dry docks, finger piers, and Quonset huts. With their work completed by 3 July 1944, the detail returned to Bizerte.

Current U.S. Naval facilities near the Emerald Coast at La Maddalena (41°12′N., 9°25′E.) cover parts of three of the seven main islands in the Archipelago of Maddalena off the extreme northeast part of Sardinia: the Island of Santo Stefano, the Island of La Maddalena, and the city of Palau on northern Sardinia. At Santo Stefano a submarine tender is homeported alongside a NATO missile depot. In addition there are port services, commissary and exchange, and various recreational facilities. Palau has a Fleet Landing Pier and hotels that provide temporary housing for those awaiting permanent quarters. Barren and rocky, yet thickly populated, La Maddalena is the site for the U.S. Naval Support Office (NSO), which includes administration services, supply and disbursing, personal property office, housing referral, legal services, public works offices, transportation, recreation center, library, chaplain's services, and a grade school, a high school, and an extension of the University of Maryland. To the 12 military housing units there in 1973, 122 more were added by August 1981.

Formerly a detachment of Naval Support Activity, Naples (q.v.), NSO was commissioned independently on 1 January 1973. The submarine tender *Howard W. Gilmore* (AS-16) arrived on 6 April 1973, swelling the number of personnel at La Maddalena from 3 officers, 2 chief petty officers, and 7 enlisted men by more than 900 men and ten dependent families. By 1 January 1980 NSO had grown to thirteen officers, eleven CPOs, and thirty-six enlisted men.

One great public relations problem has been to convince communist and socialist Sardinians that American nuclear submarines do not harm the ecology of the Mediterranean Sea. A second has been to stand fast to the authority granted in the Status of Forces Agreement that commissary and exchange stores may operate without a sales license and local sanitation and safety inspections. A third has been to counter terrorist destruction of American property. Some local hostility has evaporated in consequence of such civil works as refurbishing a local Catholic orphanage and summer camp, the hiring of local inhabitants in the public works program, and sports contests with resident Italian naval personnel.

In addition to the 40,000 mostly Italian and French visitors to La Maddalena each summer, the island has been visited by such American officials as the Chief of Information; Commander in Chief, U. S. Navy, Europe; various assistant secretaries of the Navy; Commander Submarines, Atlantic; Commander of Sixth Fleet; American Ambassador to Italy; the Chief of Naval Operations; and many units of the Sixth Fleet.

In July 1980, the *Howard W. Gilmore* was relieved by the USS *Orion* (AS-18), which services American nuclear submarines and other fleet units with the support of NSO, Maddalena.

BIBLIOGRAPHY

A. U.S. Navy Department, Hydrographic Office, *Sailing Directions*, H. O. Pub. No. 130 (Change 1) (Washington: GPO, 1972), pp. 257-58; "Narrative" and "Command History" of La Maddalena provided the writer by the Human Resources Management Officer, NSO, La Maddalena.

LA PALLICE, FRANCE.
See World War I U.S. Naval Air Stations in Europe.

LA TRINITE, FRANCE.
See World War I U.S. Naval Air Stations in Europe.

LAUNCETON, ENGLAND.
See United Kingdom, U.S. World War II Naval Bases.

LE CROISIC, FRANCE.
See World War I U.S. Naval Air Stations in Europe.

LEYTE, REPUBLIC OF THE PHILIPPINES, U.S. NAVAL SHORE FACILITIES, 1944–1947 The island of Leyte lies south of Luzon and south and west of Samar, with its capital, Tacloban, at about 12°N., 124°E. To the east is the Pacific Ocean; to the south, via Surigao Strait, lies the Mindanao Sea, which leads westward to the Sulu Sea and then to the South China Sea. Following the capture in October 1944 of Leyte Gulf by the Seventh Fleet supported by the Fifth Fleet and Army forces, the Navy established around the gulf an anchorage section, Naval Shore Facility Tacloban, a naval operating base, receiving station, and a boat repair unit at San Antonio, as well as a naval air base at Jinamoc. In addition there were a degaussing unit, fleet recreation centers at Macarat and Osmena, a fleet service center at Lipata (on Samar [q.v.]), and a ship watering point at Balusao. Construction was undertaken by the Second and Seventh Seabee brigades consolidated into Construction Forces, Samar. Following the war the anchorage section was turned over to the U.S. Army, the naval air base at Jinamoc was transferred to Puerto Princessa, Palawan (q.v.), and between 15 November 1945 and 12 August 1947 all the other facilities were disestablished.

BIBLIOGRAPHY

A. U.S. Navy Bureau of Yards and Docks, *Building the Navy's Bases in World War II*, 2 vols. (Washington: GPO, 1947), Vol. I; "Monograph Histories of U.S. Naval Overseas Bases. Vol II. Pacific Area" (Washington: Naval Historical Center, Operational Archives Branch); "Report of Board Appointed to Inquire into and Submit Recommendations on Postwar Development Philippine Islands" (Washington: Naval Historical Center, Operational Archives Branch).

LINDBERGH BAY, VIRGIN ISLANDS, U.S. MARINE CORPS AIR FACILITY.

See St. Thomas, Virgin Islands, U.S. Naval Bases.

LINGAYEN, LUZON, REPUBLIC OF THE PHILIPPINES, U.S. NAVAL FACILITIES, 1945–1946 About six weeks after U.S. forces invaded Luzon via the Gulf of Lingayen in January 1945, the U.S. Navy established there a section base, PT base, Port Director, and Mobile Amphibious Repair Base. All these installations were disestablished on 3 February 1946.

BIBLIOGRAPHY

A. "Monograph Histories of U.S. Naval Overseas Bases. Vol. II. Pacific Area" (Washington: Naval Historical Center, Operational Archives Branch).

LISBON, PORTUGAL, U.S. NAVAL BASE.

See Mediterranean, The, U.S. Naval Bases, 1800-1917.

LITTLE AMERICA I–IV, ANTARCTICA, U.S. NAVAL BASES.

See Antarctica, U.S. Naval and Air Bases.

LOCH ERNE, IRELAND.

See United Kingdom, U.S. World War II Naval Bases.

LOCH RYAN, SCOTLAND.

See United Kingdom, U.S. World War II Naval Bases.

LONDONDERRY, IRELAND, U.S. NAVAL OPERATING BASE. *See* United Kingdom, U.S. World War II Naval Bases.

LONG BINH, REPUBLIC OF VIETNAM, U.S. RIVER FORCES OPERATING BASE, 1969–1970 This vast Army command and logistic complex northeast of Saigon in the Republic of Vietnam also served as a naval operating base during 1969-1970. River patrol units carried out their anti-infiltration duties on the waterways of the area from this facility on the Dong Nai River. As part of the Vietnamization of the conflict, Vietnamese Navy units relieved their American counterparts there in November 1970.

BIBLIOGRAPHY
A. Commander Naval Forces, Vietnam, "Monthly Historical Reports, 1965-1971" (Washington: Naval Historical Center, Operational Archives Branch).

EDWARD J. MAROLDA

LONG PHU, REPUBLIC OF VIETNAM, U.S. INTERMEDIATE SUPPORT BASE, 1969–1971 Long Phu, located at the mouth of the Bassac River in the Republic of Vietnam, served as a logistic facility for American and Vietnamese river and coastal units during the Southeast Asian Conflict. As an intermediate support base, Long Phu provided smaller operating bases in the region with fuel, maintenance, administration, and supplies. As part of the Vietnamization program, the installation was turned over to the Vietnamese Navy in September 1971, and American naval forces withdrew from the area.

BIBLIOGRAPHY
A. Commander Naval Forces, Vietnam, "Monthly Historical Reports, 1965-1971" (Washington: Naval Historical Center, Operational Archives Branch).

EDWARD J. MAROLDA

LONG XUYEN, REPUBLIC OF VIETNAM, U.S. ADVANCED SUPPORT BASE, 1966–1971 The austere facility at Long Xuyen, in the Republic of Vietnam, served as an advanced staging and support base for U.S. naval forces during the Vietnam War. From August 1966 to April 1967, the twenty river patrol boats (PBRs) of River Division 52 patrolled a segment of the Hau Giang River as part of Operation Game Warden, which was designed to deny the Viet Cong free waterborne movement in the strategic Mekong Delta. The combat unit was provided with boat repair, supply, and other logistic support by a detachment of Naval Support Activity, Saigon (q.v.).

U.S. naval leaders chose the Long Xuyen site because it was accessible by water and air (with a 3,000-foot airstrip) and because a South Vietnamese Navy River Assault Group base already existed there. It was hoped that co-location of American and Vietnamese forces would foster allied cooperation and lessen the need for the construction of new facilities. However, steps were taken in 1967 to improve this forward base, including the installation of a pontoon pier and a fuel storage bladder, extension of an existing boat ramp, and deployment there of a fuel oil barge. U.S. naval forces were shifted to Tan Chau (q.v.) on the Cambodian border in 1969 and the Long Xuyen facility was disestablished when the enemy presence in this area diminished.

Later in the war, the Navy developed at Long Xuyen an intermediate support base that provided supplies and repairs to the river units operating along the Cambodian border. This facility was turned over to the Vietnamese Navy as part of the Vietnamization program in September 1971.

BIBLIOGRAPHY

A. Commander Naval Forces, Vietnam, "The Naval War in Vietnam," May 1970 (Washington: Naval Historical Center, Operational Archives Branch).

B. Herbert T. King, "Naval Logistic Support, Qui Nhon to Phu Quoc," U.S. Naval Institute *Naval Review* 95 (May 1969):84-111; S. A. Swarztrauber, "River Patrol Relearned," U.S. Naval Institute *Naval Review* 96 (May 1970):120-57; Edwin B. Hooper, *Mobility, Support, Endurance: A Story of Naval Operational Logistics in the Vietnam War, 1965-1968* (Washington: GPO, 1972).

EDWARD J. MAROLDA

LORIENT, FRANCE.
See World War I U.S. Naval Bases in Europe.

LOUGH FOYLE, IRELAND, U.S. NAVAL AIR STATION.
See World War I U.S. Naval Air Stations in Europe.

LOUGH SWILLY, IRELAND, U.S. NAVAL KITE BALLOON STATION.
See World War I U.S. Naval Air Stations in Europe.

M

MACAO, CHINA.
See Far Eastern U.S. Naval Bases to 1898.

MACEIO, BRAZIL, U.S. NAVAL AIR FACILITY.
See Brazil, U.S. Naval Bases.

MACKAY, AUSTRALIA, ADVANCE NAVAL BASE, , 1943–44 Mackay, Queensland, a small port located on Australia's northeastern coast between Brisbane and Townsville, became a small landing craft depot (Lat. 21°10′S., Long. 149°10′E.). The depot was activated in March 1943 for the 7th Amphibious Force, Seventh Fleet, in the Southwest Pacific Area. It participated in the amphibious training command and helped staged operations in eastern New Guinea until February 1944, when facilities were shipped to forward bases and Mackay disestablished.

BIBLIOGRAPHY
A. U.S. Navy. "7th Amphibious Force Command History, 10 January 1943-23 December 1945." (Washington: Naval Historical Center Operational Archives Branch).
B. Barbey, VADM Daniel E. *MacArthur's Amphibious Navy*. (Annapolis, 1969).

MCMURDO SOUND, ANTARTICA, U.S. NAVAL AIR FACILITY, MCMURDO STATION.
See Antarctica, U.S. Naval and Air Bases.

MACTAN ISLAND, CEBU ISLAND, REPUBLIC OF THE PHILIPPINES, U.S. NAVAL AIR BASE, 1945–1947 On Mactan Island, which administratively is part of Cebu Island, the U.S. Navy on 5 May 1945 established a naval air base capable of supporting both landplanes and seaplanes. Four airstrips were begun but were incomplete when the war ended on 2 September 1945. The facility was inactivated on 1 December 1946 and disestablished on 17 March 1947.

BIBLIOGRAPHY
A. Summary Cards (Washington Navy Yard: Naval Aviation History Office).

MADANG-ALEXISHAFEN, DUTCH NEW GUINEA, U.S. NAVAL ADVANCE BASE, 1944–1945 Faced with a long run up the New Guinea coast between main bases at Finchhafen (q.v.) and newly established Hollandia (q.v.) the Seventh Amphibious Force (Seventh Fleet, Southwest Pacific Area) requested establishment of a landing craft staging and repair base at Alexishafen in the Madang District of the Mandated Territory of New Guinea. Located on Bostrem Bay, Alexishafen (5°10′S., 145°45′E.) offered an excellent sheltered anchorage for small craft. On 13 June 1944 a detachment of the Ninety-first Naval Construction Battalion, utilizing materiel from Finchhafen and Milne Bay (q.v.), began work at Alexishafen, first on a section base, then on the landing craft maintenance base. The base was commissioned on 17 August and operated by Service Force, Seventh Fleet. That fall, Floating Repair Unit 1, with extensive workshop and small dry-dock facilities, was established there. Madang-Alexishafen played a vital role in maintaining the flow of landing craft for the invasions of the Carolines, Morotai, and Leyte. By late November 1944 it was evident that the base was too far in the rear to continue performing that function. Roll-up began in December, and by the end of January 1945 Madang-Alexishafen Naval Advance Base had been closed.

BIBLIOGRAPHY
A. U.S. Navy, "7th Amphibious Force Command History, 10 January 1943-25 December 1945" (Washington: Naval Historical Center, Operational Archives Branch); U.S. Navy, Bureau of Yards and Docks, *Building the Navy's Bases in World War II*, 2 vols. (Washington: GPO, 1947); U.S. Navy, "U.S. Naval Bases in the South and Southwest Pacific (and Central Pacific Forward) in World War II," 1 November 1954 (Washington: Naval Historical Center Operational Archives Branch).
B. Rear Adm. Worrall Reed Carter, *Beans, Bullets, and Black Oil* (Washington: GPO, 1953); Vice Adm. Daniel E. Barbey, *MacArthur's Amphibious Navy* (Annapolis, Md.: U.S. Naval Institute, 1969).

JOHN B. LUNDSTROM

MADISONVILLE, MASSACHUSETTS BAY, MARQUESAS ISLANDS, U.S. NAVAL BASE, 1813 To repair his frigate *Essex* after its historic voyage around the Horn in 1813, Commo. David Porter built the first overseas American naval base in the Pacific Ocean at Madisonville, Massachusetts Bay, in the Marquesas Islands, about 800 miles northeast of Bora Bora. As he put it:

> Agreeably to the request of the chiefs, I laid down the plan of the village about to be built. The line on which the houses were to be placed was already traced by our barrier of water casks. They were to take the form of a crescent, to be built on the outside of

the enclosure, and to be connected with each other by a wall twelve feet in length and four feet in height. The houses were to be fifty feet in length, built in the usual fashion of the country, and of a proportioned width and height.

On the 3d November, upwards of four thousand natives, from the different tribes, assembled at the camp with material for building, and before night they had completed a dwelling-house for myself, and another for the officers, a sail loft, a cooper's shop, and a place for our sick, a bake-house, a guard-house, and a shed for the sentinel to walk under. The whole were connected by the walls as above described. We removed our barrier of water casks, and took possession of our delightful village, which had been built as if by enchantment.

The base, begun in October, served Porter until he left in mid-December to "seek glory" off the west coast of South America.

BIBLIOGRAPHY

A. David Porter, *Journal of a Cruise Made to the Pacific Ocean, by Captain David Porter, in the United States Frigate Essex, in the Years 1812, 1813, and 1814*, 2 vols.(1815; repr. Upper Saddle River, N.J.: The Gregg Press, 1970), II:62-63.

B. Archibald D. Turnbull, *Commodore David Porter, 1780-1843* (New York: The Century Co., 1929); Frank Donovan, *The Odyssey of the "Essex"* (New York: David McKay, 1969); David F. Long, *Nothing Too Daring: A Biography of Commodore David Porter, 1780-1843* (Annapolis, Md.: U.S. Naval Institute, 1970).

MAJURO, MARSHALL ISLANDS, FLEET ANCHORAGE, NAVAL BASE, AND NAVAL AIR FACILITY, 1944–1947 Majuro is a roughly rectangular atoll in the eastern Marshalls at the center of a triangle formed by Jaluit, Maloelap, and Mille atolls. Majuro is composed of fifty-six islands that enclose a commodious lagoon about twenty-one miles long by six to seven miles wide. The largest of the islands, Majuro, forms the southwestern edge of the lagoon, but the most important islands from a naval point of view are Darrit, Uliga, and Dalap, on the lagoon's eastern extremity. Germany established a minor supply base on Darrit prior to World War I, and the Japanese briefly placed a small garrison on the island early in World War II. American naval planners during the late 1930s conceived that the atoll might provide accommodation for the fleet should it undertake a westward movement against Japan. When Adm. Chester W. Nimitz and his staff drew up plans in 1943 to capture Kwajalein and Eniwetok atolls in Operation Flintlock, they also provided for the occupation of Majuro, whose lagoon they expected to use for mobile service units. Nimitz appreciated that American planes operating from Majuro and from new bases in the Gilberts could effectively neutralize the Japanese airstrips in the eastern Marshalls. As approved by Commander in Chief Pacific Ocean Area (CINCPOA) in March 1944, Majuro was to include an advanced fleet anchorage without shore facilities, a submarine base with floating repair support, and air facilities for one fighter squadron, two scout bomber squadrons, and one amphibious patrol squadron.

Army assault forces from the 106th Regiment, 27th Division were scheduled to occupy the atoll on 31 January 1944, but an advance intelligence unit of Marines actually was the first to discover that the Japanese had deserted Dalap, Uliga, and Darrit and to overrun them. The 100th Construction Battalion, together with the occupying troops, was landed the next day, and by 3 February some thirty ships were anchored in the lagoon, with fifty more expected shortly. Arriving components included those for a naval air station (Acorn 20), a naval station (Gropac 4), a radar air defense unit (Argus 18), a carrier air service unit (CASU 20), and Communications Unit 6. The Argus, Acorn, and Gropac components were eventually merged to form U.S. Naval Base Majuro.

The Japanese left intact on Darrit Island a 400-foot pier, a seaplane ramp, and numerous structures that the Seabees converted into administrative offices, barracks, warehouses, transient quarters, and a hospital. To the south on Dalap Island they completed a 5,800-by-445-foot coral-surfaced runway, equipped with parking aprons, housing, and repair shops. Twelve 1,000-gallon gasoline tanks on neighboring Biggariat Island were connected to the Dalap airstrip with 4-inch pipes. After it was decided to establish a carrier replacement pool at Majuro, a second strip, measuring 4,000 feet by 175 feet, was built on Uliga Island with a two-lane causeway connecting to Dalap. Submarines and Coast Guard units were also established on their separate islands, the submarines at Mysore and the Coast Guard at Lorraine.

Military government was responsible for surveillance of some 4,000 Marshallese inhabitants on Majuro and neighboring islets. The atoll commander, Capt. V. F. Grant, was notably successful in dealing with the natives. A program was developed by which submarines secretly evacuated hundreds of friendly natives from the Japanese-controlled atolls neighboring Majuro: Jaluit, Wotje, Maloelap, and Mille. The many Protestant Christian natives employed by the base were provided with hospital facilities and ministered to by the Navy's Protestant chaplain. The Navy also encouraged native handicrafts that were sold to servicemen at a public market.

Majuro harbor was used to service and supply carrier and other fleet units throughout the remainder of the war. Marine aircraft operating from Majuro's fields effectively neutralized the neighboring enemy bases, assisted with A/S operations, conducted inshore patrol and rescues at sea, and engaged in searches and reconnaissance. The naval facilities were rolled up on 23 June 1947.

BIBLIOGRAPHY

A. Commander in Chief, Pacific Fleet, "Administrative History of the Marshalls-Gilberts Area," 6 vols. (Washington: Naval Historical Center, Operational Archives Branch, 1946); U.S. Navy, Bureau of Yards and Docks, *Building the Navy's Bases in World War II*, 2 vols. (Washington: GPO, 1947), II:318-20.

B. Samuel E. Morison, *Aleutians, Gilberts and Marshalls June 1942-April 1944* (Boston: Little, Brown, 1951), pp. 225-29, 305-6.

WILLIAM R. BRAISTED

MALTA, U.S. NAVAL BASE.

See Mediterranean, The, U.S. Naval Bases, 1800-1917.

MANDINGA, REPUBLIC OF PANAMA, U.S. LIGHTER-THAN-AIR STATION, 1944–1945 Mandinga, located on the Caribbean side of Panama about seventy-five miles from the canal entrance, like Chorrera (q.v.) had its first construction undertaken by the U.S. Army on land acquired in a lease from the government of Panama. In early 1944 the Navy took over and established a lighter-than-air-base as a feature of the defense screen for the canal. In early 1945, however, the blimps were transferred to Barranquilla, Colombia (*See* Hispanic South America, U.S. Naval Bases), and the site was returned to Panama.

BIBLIOGRAPHY

A. "U.S. Naval Administration in World War II. Administrative History, Fifteenth Naval District and Commander Panama Sea Frontier," 2 vols., 1945 (Washington: U.S. Navy Department Library); U.S. Navy, Bureau of Yards and Docks, *Building the Navy's Bases in World War II*, 2 vols. (Washington: GPO, 1947), Vol. II.

WILLIAM L. CALDERHEAD

MANILA, LUZON, PHILIPPINE ISLANDS.
See Far Eastern U.S. Naval Bases to 1898.

MANUS, ADMIRALTY ISLANDS, U.S. NAVAL OPERATING BASE, 1944–1947 Manus, the largest of the Admiralty Islands, is located in the Bismarck Sea north of New Guinea and northwest of New Britain in the Bismarck Archipelago. About fifty by seventeen miles in size, its most important feature is the harbor its northeastern end forms along with small, crescent-shaped Los Negros Island. Known as Seeadler Harbor (2°1′S., 147°25′E.), it is a superb protected anchorage fifteen miles long and four miles wide.

With the final decision in 1943 to bypass the Japanese main base of Rabaul on New Britain, the Admiralties loomed important as a substitute main fleet base about 350 miles northwest of Rabaul. Such a base was vital to support offensives to the west and north, beginning in the spring of 1944 with the Southwest Pacific Area's grand strategy of leaping far ahead on the New Guinea coast to Hollandia (q.v.). The invasion of the Admiralties was conducted by the Seventh Amphibious Force of the Southwest Pacific Area, beginning on 29 February 1944 with landings on Los Negros. Resistance was unexpectedly heavy. Elements of the Fourth Naval Construction Brigade arrived to work on Momote Airfield and came under fire, but by 5 March the situation was more favorable. The first fighters began operating out of Momote on 10 March. That day the tender *Oyster Bay* with fifteen PTs from Motor Torpedo Boat Squadrons 18 and 21 arrived to begin patrols to help protect the Admiralties and support combat operations on Manus, where the remnants of the Japanese garrison had withdrawn. The PTs continued patrols until mid-April 1944, then left for other duty.

The development of Manus into a main fleet operating base, a source for supplies, fuels, and repairs, was undertaken by the Third Fleet (South Pacific Area). Earmarked for Manus were the personnel and equipment of LION FOUR, a huge, prepackaged base force sent from the United States. Beginning in mid-April 1944, a massive transformation of northeastern Manus and Los Negros was undertaken. Construction there seemed ubiquitous, and in terms of eventual outlay of expense Manus was the third largest advance base in the Pacific (after Guam [q.v.] and Leyte [q.v.]). The base was commissioned on 18 May 1944. It is best to describe it by sketching the categories of installations that comprised the complex base.

For handling ship repair and service, one of Manus's prime functions, a main ship repair base was set up inside Seeadler Harbor at Lombrum Point on Los Negros. The facility offered docking, repair, workshops, and maintenance equal to the best-equipped tenders. By fall, installed there was a wide variety of floating dry docks, including the Advance Base Sectional Dock 2 (100,000 tons lift) and ABSD-4 (70,000 tons). Manus offered major repairs for all classes of ships. Lombrum Point was also the site of a landing craft repair base for LCTs, LSM, and smaller boats. Manus featured a submarine overhaul base after May 1944 with the arrival of the submarine tender *Euryale*, joined later by another tender. The base that summer serviced submarines relocating from Brisbane (q.v.). Operating out of Manus greatly shortened their trips into the combat area. At Papitalai Point on Los Negros was a main PT overhaul and repair base. Hyane Harbor on the east coast of Los Negros featured highly developed port facilities, piers, warehouses, cranes, a repair pier for Liberty ships, and an 800-foot fuel pier. Seabees at Hyane also operated a small-boat repair unit.

With regard to supply, materiel, and fuel, Manus comprised a number of huge installations. On Manus itself was a massive Naval supply depot opened on 2 July 1944 but constantly expanding until it consisted of 180 buildings serviced by two long piers and an LST beach. It provided necessary supplies for the whole base and for forces afloat. At Hyane Harbor on Los Negros was an aviation supply depot that became the main sorting and transshipping agency for aviation in the whole Southwest Pacific Area. It included an aviation overhaul and repair unit. Also at Hyane Harbor was Pontoon Assembly Depot 1, which assembled some 900 pontoon cells a month for the forward areas. An installation at Lorengau on Manus (which was also main base headquarters) offered fresh water for ships and the base. At Papitalai Point on Los Negros a huge fuel oil tank farm was begun on 23 June 1944. It was one of the main Seabee projects and eventually comprised storage for 630,000 barrels of fuel oil. Also at Papitalai was a dry dock storage facility.

Manus also contained a number of important aviation bases. At Momote and Mokerang on Los Negros were Army Air Forces fields, while Lombrum Point featured a main seaplane overhaul and repair base, shops, ramps, hangars, a tank farm, and facilities for operating one patrol plane squadron. Ponam Island, off the north coast of Manus, in the summer of 1944 became a fighter base. It offered facilities for two carrier air groups and one landbased patrol squadron, as well as aviation overhaul and repair shops. At Pityilu Island, just northwest of Seeadler Harbor, was another big naval air station with a capacity similar to

Ponam Island, but it also had repair and storage for 350 aircraft. Both Ponam and Pityilu were vital for continued operations of fast carrier task forces in the forward areas. Of the two, Pityilu was more fun to visit, because it also had a fleet recreation center handling up to 10,000 bluejackets at a time.

Manus contributed mightily to fleet operations well before construction there was complete. In April 1944 it was a major fuel source for the fast carrier task forces supporting the invasion of Hollandia, a supply point where the fleet oilers could get oil from chartered tankers. In May and June, during preparations for the invasion of the Marianas, fleet units and transport convoys stopped at Manus for supplies and fuel. In August-September 1944 came the biggest buildup yet at Manus, as its installations neared completion. Along with Eniwetok Atoll (q.v.), it became the Third Fleet's principal base for executing STALEMATE II, the invasion of the Western Carolines. Tremendous amounts of supplies and materiel were collected at Manus. Service Squadron 10 of the Pacific Fleet assembled there, greatly augmenting its ship repair capabilities. The big floating dry docks arrived at that time to be based at Lombrum Point. In September 24 fleet oilers operated from Manus to serve the fleet, and that month over 4 million barrels of fuel oil were delivered to Manus. In addition to Third Fleet's operations, Manus in September also helped support the Seventh Fleet's invasion of Morotai in the Dutch East Indies.

In October, with Third Fleet opening another main base at Ulithi Atoll (q.v.) in the Carolines, Seventh Fleet utilized Manus to service ships preparing for the invasion of Leyte in the Philippines. Throughout operations to the northwest and west, Manus functioned as a vital part of fleet supply and repair. By early 1945 some of its services were gradually assumed by fleet bases at Guam, Ulithi, and Leyte, but Manus was still going strong until well past VJ-Day. It assisted in the roll-up of many other bases in the Southwest Pacific and finally was disestablished on 1 September 1947.

BIBLIOGRAPHY

A. Motor Torpedo Boat Squadrons, Philippine Sea Frontier, "Command History of MTB Squadrons, Philippine Sea Frontier, Formerly MTB Squadrons, 7th Fleet," 5 vols., Type Commands, 1945 (Washington: Naval Historical Center, Operational Archives Branch); U.S. Navy, "7th Amphibious Force Command History 10 January 1943-23 December 1945" (Washington: Naval Historical Center, Operational Archives Branch); U.S. Navy, Bureau of Yards and Docks, *Building the Navy's Bases in World War II*, 2 vols. (Washington: GPO, 1947); U.S. Navy, "U.S. Naval Bases in the South and Southwest Pacific (and Central Pacific Forward) in World War II," 1 November 1954 (Washington: Naval Historical Center, Operational Archives Branch).

B. Theodore Roscoe, *United States Submarine Operations in World War II* (Annapolis, Md.: U.S. Naval Institute, 1949); Samuel E. Morison, *Breaking the Bismarcks Barrier 22 July 1942-1 May 1944* (Boston: Little, Brown, 1950); Rear Adm. Worrall Reed Carter, *Beans, Bullets, and Black Oil* (Washington: GPO, 1953): Samuel E. Morison, *New Guinea and the Marianas March 1944-August 1945* (Boston: Little, Brown, 1953); Samuel E. Morison, *Leyte June 1944-January 1945* (Boston: Little, Brown, 1958); Capt. Robert J. Bulkley, *At Close Quarters: PT Boats in the United States Navy* (Washington: Navy

Department, Naval History Division, 1962); Vice Adm. Daniel E. Barbey, *MacArthur's Amphibious Navy* (Annapolis, Md.: U.S. Naval Institute, 1969); Clay Blair, *Silent Victory: The United States Submarine War against Japan* (Philadelphia: Lippincott, 1975).

JOHN B. LUNDSTROM

MEDITERRANEAN, THE, U.S. NAVAL BASES, 1800–1917 In his monumental work, *The Mediterranean and the Mediterranean World in the Age of Philip II* Fernand Braudel wrote, "The Mediterranean is not. . .a *single* sea, it is a complex of seas; and these seas are broken up by islands, interrupted by peninsulas, ringed by intricate coastlines." This inland sea, some 2,330 miles long, is enclosed by Southern Europe on the west, the Near East on the east, and North Africa on the south. Historically, the Mediterranean was the maritime crossroads for the development of the civilizations of Europe, Asia, and Africa. It became and has remained one of the world's busiest highways.

American commercial interests from the colonial period to the present have been attracted to the Mediterranean world. American merchant vessels under the British and later the U.S. flag plied the inland seas as far to the east as the Levant. The Mediterranean world has also been of interest to other Americans, particularly government officials, missionaries, educators, tourists, and in times of war, servicemen.

Even in peacetime the Navy maintained an almost continuous presence in the Mediterranean. The Mediterranean Squadron was the first of several squadrons established in various parts of the world, as the U.S. Navy adopted a peacetime policy of dispersing its warships on distant cruising stations. The Mediterranean station was founded in 1801 because of depredation on American commerce by the Barbary corsairs. Even after the Barbary Wars ended in 1805, the flag continued to be shown in the Mediterranean. Two years later, however, the station was discontinued and the vessels called home because of the developing crisis with Great Britain. No American warships patrolled the Mediterranean until the war with Great Britain ended. In 1815 the station was reestablished because the Barbary States had taken advantage of the war to renew their attacks on U.S. shipping. Because of instability in the Mediterranean world, an American naval squadron would be maintained in the inland sea from 1815 until the outbreak of the Civil War in 1861.

Port Mahon and Gibraltar, Spain; Malta; Pisa, Italy

The more than 3,000 miles' distance from the United States posed logistical problems. A base was needed to house stores and provisions and to provide repair facilities. British base facilities were utilized at Malta and Gibraltar (q.v.) during the conflict with the Barbary States. In 1815 the Mediterranean Squadron commander approached the Spanish government concerning the establishment of a base at Cartagena, Port Mahon, or Algeciras. After a lengthy period of negotiation lasting several years, he was successful in gaining permission to use Port Mahon in the Balearic Islands as a temporary base. However, efforts to persuade the Spanish government to agree to a more permanent arrangement were unsuccessful. The unstable diplomatic relationship between the United States and Spain arising out of differences over the Louisiana boundary, Florida, and the Latin American revolutions all contributed to this situation.

From 1816 to 1821 the principal stores depot and repair facility had remained at Gibraltar and the naval hospital at Pisa, while the vessels rendezvoused at various Mediterranean ports during the winter season. In 1821 the Spanish government's permission to use Port Mahon resulted in the squadron's moving its stores depot and fleet rendezvous to that island. The bases's existence was brief, however. In 1822 the Spanish government refused to extend permission when the United States decided to recognize the new Latin American states. In 1825 permission was received again, this time on a more permanent basis. Port Mahon provided the Navy with its first overseas base. Its deep and sheltered anchorage, along with excellent liberty for officers and men, gave the Mediterranean Squadron an ideal port for more than twenty years.

In 1846 the Spanish government informed the United States that the base privilege on Port Mahon was to be terminated. Although American diplomatic officials were able to delay the closing for two years, in 1848 the base was liquidated.

Spezia, Italy

During this two-year period the Mediterranean Squadron commander, Commo. George C. Read, searched for a suitable site to replace Port Mahon. Three locations were considered: Porto Ferraio on the island of Elba; Syracuse on the island of Sicily; and Spezia on the Italian mainland. Syracuse was preferred, but the political instability on the island persuaded the squadron commander to recommend Spezia.

Throughout the 1850s and 1860s the squadron was based at Spezia on the Gulf of Genoa. Nevertheless, the site was considered temporary. The Piedmontese government planned to establish a naval base at Spezia and when this occurred the United States would be required to find another location for its squadron. The outbreak of the American Civil War and the withdrawal of the Mediterranean Squadron temporarily postponed the problem.

Lisbon, Portugal

In 1865 American naval vessels entered the Mediterranean for the first time since the outbreak of the Civil War. The Navy Department decided to reestablish a station in European waters in the spring of that year in order to be able to counter a threat similar to that the Confederate States had posed to Union commerce. The naval force, however, would no longer be known as the Mediterranean Squadron, but as the European Squadron. A naval force would be based almost continuously in European waters until early in the twentieth century.

In 1865 the Navy Department selected Lisbon, Portugal, as the site for the European Squadron's base and winter rendezvous. A number of sites in the

Mediterranean were considered, including two former bases, Port Mahon and Spezia, but the expansion of the squadron's cruising area to include Northern Europe as well as the Mediterranean was the major factor in deciding on Lisbon.

No shore facilities of any kind were established at Lisbon. The Navy's logistical policy at that time was to utilize floating storeships anchored at the designated rendezvous. Dry stores and machinery parts were easily brought from the United States. Perishable articles, such as bread and fresh provisions, could be purchased locally. Coal was contracted for with local merchants. As in the past, the squadron had to depend upon European yards for repairs. Throughout the period until the early twentieth century, Gibraltar was the major repair center for the American warships in European waters.

To those who were most conscious of its potential value—the American diplomatic representatives—an American naval base remained an attractive goal. Periodically, proposals were put forward recommending particular localities. In the spring of 1866 the American consul at Spezia urged the reestablishment of at least a coal depot there. Also in that year the United States diplomatic representative on the island of Crete recommended the acquisition of that island as the site of a naval base. A French company sought to obtain permission from the Greek government to purchase a site in that country and lease it to the United States for ninety years. In the mid-1870s Michel Vidal, the American consul at Tripoli, investigated and made lengthy reports concerning the suitability of Cyrenaica for a naval base. Even the Cape Verde Islands were recommended.

Villefranche, France

During these years the Navy Department expressed little interest in establishing a permanent base in the Mediterranean. Nevertheless, in 1869, for reasons of economy, squadron commanders were ordered to shift from floating storeships to store facilities ashore. In February 1870, Rear Adm. William Radford, the European Squadron commander, recommended Villefranche, France, to the department as the site for a supply depot. The recommendation was approved and the admiral proceeded to lease a warehouse. The agreement was informal, however, and "rest[ed] solely upon the good feeling and 'politesse' of the French government." For thirteen years, the logistic support base of the European Squadron remained limited, to all intents and purposes, to a rented warehouse on the French Riviera.

Outside of sporadic visits to Villefranche to replenish, the squadron's only stay there occurred during the winter months. This had become standard practice during the early years of the Mediterranean Squadron's existence when the fierce winter gales made routine port-to-port cruises hazardous, and it continued in the post-Civil War years.

In November 1882 Secretary of the Navy William Chandler ordered the logistical facility at Villefranche abandoned. This was primarily an economy move, as the European Squadron had declined in importance and size throughout the 1870s. The squadron continued to use Villefranche as a winter rendezvous until 1889, when the European station was deactivated.

The European Station, 1894-1917

Although the European station was reestablished in 1894, no effort was made to acquire a base. Instead, the squadron returned to a logistical policy of local purchase and repair along with replenishment by occasional supply ships. No change in this policy occurred even during the Near Eastern crisis in the mid-1890s, which required the continuous presence of an American naval force in the Eastern Mediterranean. The growing trouble with Spain over Cuba resulted in the station's again being abandoned in 1898.

The Navy seriously considered establishing a base in the Canary Islands or along the Moroccan coast during the Spanish-American War, and the Balearic Islands were again considered. The idea was dropped with the armistice. There is no evidence that the American negotiators at Paris approached the Spanish government about obtaining a site for a naval station in the Mediterranean or Eastern Atlantic.

Shortly after its creation in 1900, the Navy's General Board, an advisory body of professional officers, began to study the idea of acquiring naval bases outside the United States. Although the European station was activated once again in 1901, the General Board showed no interest in establishing an overseas support base for it.

In January 1905 the Navy Department announced that the European station was to be abandoned. This was a result of a reorganization of the Navy that culminated with the designation of the Asiatic Squadron, the creation of a Pacific Fleet, and the concentration of all the battleships in the Atlantic Fleet. This reorganization marked the end of the peacetime policy, established early in the nineteenth century, of permanent distant stations. The European station would not be revived until the United States entered World War I.

One final episode occurred a few years before the war began. In 1909 the government of the tiny Balkan kingdom of Montenegro apparently offered a bay and adjacent land to the United States for a naval base. The offer was not seriously considered. We no longer had a European Squadron, and warships visiting the Mediterranean could be coaled and reprovisioned from commercial depots, supply ships, and colliers.

BIBLIOGRAPHY

A. None

B. Howard R. Marraro, "Spezia: An American Naval Base, 1848-68," *Military Affairs* 7 (Winter 1943):202-8; Richard D. Challener, "Montenegro and the United States: A Balkan Fantasy," *Journal of Central European Affairs* 17 (Oct. 1957):236-42; James A. Field, Jr. "A Scheme in Regard to Cyrenaica," *Mississippi Valley Historical Review* 44 (Dec. 1957):445-68; James A. Field, Jr., *America and the Mediterranean World 1776-1882* (Princeton, N.J.: Princeton University Press, 1969); Fernand Braudel, *The Mediterranean and the Mediterranean World in the Age of Philip II*, 2 vols. (New York: Harper & Row, 1972); Thomas A. Bryson, *Tars, Turks, and Tankers: The Role of the United States Navy in the Middle East, 1800-1979* (Metuchen, N.J.: Scarecrow Press,

1980); William N. Still, Jr., *American Sea Power in the Old World: The United States Navy in European and Near Eastern Waters, 1865-1917* (Westport, Conn.: Greenwood Press, 1980).

WILLIAM N. STILL

MERAUKE, DUTCH NEW GUINEA, U.S. NAVAL ADVANCE BASE, 1943 In 1943 Merauke was a small harbor and naval base on the south coast of Dutch New Guinea across the Torres Straits from Australia. Located two miles from the mouth of the Merauke River on a swamply, tropical coastal plain (8°30′S., 140°22′E.) it was selected in the spring of 1943 as the site of an airfield and small-boat operating base to prevent Japanese penetration southward into that region of New Guinea. The base operated in connection with bases at Thursday Island (q.v.) and Cairns (q.v.) in northeastern Australia.

On 8 May 1943 elements of the Fifty-fifth Naval Construction Battalion arrived to construct a motor torpedo boat operating base at Merauke, which was defended by Australian troops and Royal Netherlands Navy light forces. The Seabees also constructed an airstrip. All facilities were completed in September 1943. Meanwhile, Seventh Fleet PT boats had assembled at Thursday Island in late spring 1943 with the intention of basing at Merauke should the Japanese threaten that base. Conditions around Merauke were difficult for the PTs because of shallow water. The PTs never did base permanently at Merauke and left the area in August 1943. All U.S. naval activities at Merauke ceased in December 1943, but the base was used extensively by Australian and Dutch forces.

BIBLIOGRAPHY

A. Motor Torpedo Boat Squadrons, Philippine Sea Frontier, "Command History of MTB Squadrons, Philippine Sea Frontier, Formerly MTB Squadrons, 7th Fleet," 5 vols., Type Commands, 1945 (Washington: Naval Historical Center, Operational Archives Branch); U.S. Navy, Bureau of Yards and Docks, *Building the Navy's Bases in World War II*, 2 vols. (Washington: GPO, 1947); U.S. Navy, "U.S. Naval Bases in the South and Southwest Pacific (and Central Pacific Forward) in World War II," 1 November 1954 (Washington: Naval Historical Center, Operational Archives Branch).

B. Capt. Robert J. Bulkley, *At Close Quarters: PT Boats in the United States Navy* (Washington: Navy Department Naval History Division, 1962).

JOHN B. LUNDSTROM

MERS-EL-KEBIR, ALGERIA.
See North Africa, U.S. Naval Bases.

MIDWAY ISLANDS, U.S. NAVAL AIR STATION AND SUBMARINE BASE, 1941– Midway is a coral atoll almost exactly in the middle of the North Pacific about 900 miles northwest of Honolulu. The atoll embraces a lagoon surrounded by coral reefs of twenty-eight square miles and two islands, Sand and Eastern. The former island measures about one and one-half square miles, while the latter is somewhat smaller. With the advent of airpower, Midway assumed considerable strategic significance as a station for planes patrolling the approaches to Hawaii and for refueling trans-Pacific flights.

Midway was first claimed for the United States in 1859 by Capt. N. C. Brooks of the Hawaiian bark *Gambia*, and the islands were formally annexed for the United States by Capt. William Reynolds of the USS *Lackawanna* in 1867. The atoll constituted the first island group acquired by the United States beyond its continental limits. Acting in response to complaints against Japanese bird poachers, President Theodore Roosevelt in 1903 placed Midway under the jurisdiction of the Navy Department. The same year, the Commercial Cable Company established a cable landing for its trans-Pacific cable, and Lt. Comdr. Hugh Rodman, commanding the USS *Iroquois*, designated the company's local manager the naval custodian with instructions to prevent wanton destruction of birds that bred on the islands. A Marine contingent occupied the islands from 1904 to 1908. Naval development of Midway was prohibited by Article XIX of the 1922 Washington naval limitations treaty.

Midway assumed increasing significance as a potential air base following Japan's denunciation of the naval limitation treaties in 1934. In 1935 the Navy gave to Pan American Airways the right to develop support facilities for the air boats of its trans-Pacific China Clipper service. These facilities would be open to the Navy during an emergency. The Army Engineers also dredged the lagoon, ostensibly for commercial use, and the Hepburn Board on naval stations declared in late 1938 that building an air base at Midway was second only in importance to developing Pearl Harbor. Specifically, the board wanted facilities at Midway for two squadrons of patrol planes including expanded harbor works, increased fuel storage, and modest repair facilities. The later (1941) Greenslade Board confirmed that submarines and air patrols should be stationed at Midway to survey the route between Hawaii and the Philippines.

In March 1940 contract labor began the construction envisioned by the Hepburn Board. The more important new improvements included three asphalt-paved runways on Eastern Island, minor industrial repair facilities, additional ramps and hangars for seaplanes, underground gasoline storage, a hospital in buildings provided by the cable company, and barracks for Marine and naval personnel. A Marine defense battalion returned to garrison Midway in June 1940, and the Midway Naval Air Station was formally commissioned in August 1941.

Work at Midway was seriously curtailed after the withdrawal of civilian construction workers following the Japanese attack on Pearl Harbor on 7 December 1941. Marine and naval aircraft based on Midway joined with American carrier air craft to repulse the Japanese in the famed Battle of Midway in early June 1942, but the attackers managed to damage seriously or destroy the hospital, fuel tanks, a torpedo shop, the seaplane hangar, and other works.

As the war in the Pacific moved westward, Midway's status changed from defensive outpost to offensive operating base. In July 1942 the Secretary of the Navy formally established the Naval Operating Base, Midway Islands, embracing the Naval Air Station, a new Submarine Base, and all other naval facilities on the island. The Naval Air Station on August 1942 was named Henderson Field in honor of Maj. Loften R. Henderson, USMC, one of the heroes of the Battle of Midway. The Fiftieth and Tenth Construction Battalions lengthened two airstrips on Sand Island to 7,500 and 8,600 feet, respectively, to accommodate heavy bombers, and the anchorage was expanded to provide moorings for six cruisers, five destroyers or submarines, and a repair ship. Other new facilities included additional underground fuel storage tanks, an underground hospital, shop buildings, and a power plant. Work on the base by the Seabees was officially completed in December 1944.

After Japan's surrender, Midway steadily declined as a naval facility until the base was ordered inactivated effective 1950. Also, Pan American Airways shifted its mid-Pacific activities from Midway to Wake in 1952, and the Commercial Cable Company two years later closed the office that it had maintained on Midway since 1903.

The outbreak of the Korean War, however, brought a marked turn in Midway's fortunes. The Secretary of the Navy ordered the Naval Air Station reopened in August 1950, and Midway was declared ready for air traffic in September. Thereafter, Midway expanded as an air traffic center and as a port of call for ships. In 1968, a hight point in the Vietnam War, some 313 ships called at Midway for fuel or other services; 11,077 aircraft, 4,261 of them from the Military Air Command, were logged at Midway air terminal. With the winding down of the Vietnam War by 1972 flights were down to 2,279, passengers to 5,018, and ships to 170.

BIBLIOGRAPHY

A. Record Group 80, General Records of the Navy Department, 1927-1940, A21-5 File (Washington: National Archives); U.S. Navy, Bureau of Yards and Docks, *Building the Navy's Bases in World War II*, 2 vols. (Washington: GPO, 1947), II:154-57; Selected Papers, World War II Command File and Base Maintenance Division Records (Washington: Naval Historical Center, Operational Archives Branch).

B. Samuel E. Morison, *Coral Sea, Midway, and Submarine Actions May 1942* (Boston: Little, Brown, 1958), pp. 69-160; Francis X. Holbrook, ''United States National Defense and Trans-Pacific Commercial Routes, 1933-1941,'' Ph.D. diss., Fordham University, 1969.

WILLIAM R. BRAISTED

MILDENHALL, SUFFOLK, ENGLAND, U.S. NAVAL AIR FACILITY, 1964– NAF Mildenhall is situated aboard the Royal Air Force Station, Mildenhall, about sixty-five miles northeast of London and only eighteen miles northeast of Cambridge, as a tenant activity of the U.S. Air Force 513 Tactical Airlift Wing. It was commissioned on 1 July 1964. As a tenant, it occupies office space in parts of two hangars, the latter of which may upon request be used for aircraft maintenance. It also has a Bachelor Enlisted Quarter (BEQ) for assigned and transient personnel.

The mission of NAF Mildenhall is to provide air logistic services and aircraft maintenance to support aviation units and activities of the operating forces of the U.S. Navy in the United Kingdom, military units in the Northern European area, and other commands as directed. To accomplish this mission it operates three C-131F *Convairs* and, when needed, a C-2 from Logistic Support Squadron 24 (VR-24).

During fiscal year 1980 Mildenhall aircraft lifted 854,400 pounds of cargo and 2,464 passengers, with the cargo including mail, baggage, and courier packages for twenty-nine ships and fifty-four airfields in fourteen countries. Most destinations, in order of priority, were in England, West Germany, and France, but flights were made as far north as Norway and as far south as Morocco. Cargo delivered to the USS *Nimitz* alone weighed almost ten tons. To accomplish this mission, Mildenhall aircraft made an average of 57.5 sorties a month, with flight time approximating 1,165 hours. Its service to personnel may be gauged by the fact that in fiscal year 1980 it offered assistance to transient Navy, Marine Corps, and Coast Guard personnel arriving on 150 commercial flights, the crews of sixty naval aircraft, 500 men engaged in fleet exercises, and a number of hospital patients from United Kingdom Commands. It did this with a crew of eight officers, forty enlisted men, and seven civilian employees at a cost of $648,362.

Government quarters at Mildenhall are so scarce that newcomers are advised that they must live off base on the economy for from six to eight months before they are available. Both American and British schools for children K-8 are available. Large American automobiles are discouraged because of the left-hand drive, limited availability of parts and high gasoline prices.

BIBLIOGRAPHY

A. "Command History 1980 (OPNAV Report 5750-1, Mildenhall Naval Air Facility," dated 20 Jan. 1981, (courtesy Jini E. Hesse, SK2, Public Affairs Officer, Naval Air Facility Mildenhall).

B. "Living Overseas: England—Mildenhall," *Navy Times*, 27 Sept. 1982, p. 37.

MILFORD HAVEN, ENGLAND.
See United Kingdom, U.S. World War II Naval Bases.

MILNE BAY, NEW GUINEA, U.S. NAVAL ADVANCE BASE, 1942–1946 Situated in a cleft between two peninsulas comprising the extreme eastern tip of New Guinea, Milne Bay is a body of water about twenty miles long and seven miles wide making a deep, well-protected anchorage. Before 1942 the only organized settlement in the area was the small port on Samarai Island (10°45′S., 151°30′E.) located just south of the entrance to Milne Bay proper. Samarai fronted China Strait, the close passage through the Louisiade Archipelago jutting into the Coral Sea beyond eastern New Guinea. In the spring of 1942 Allied forces occupied Milne Bay to deny it to the Japanese and built airfields from which to strike at enemy bases on the north Papuan coast and on New Britain. In August and September 1942 troops at Milne Bay successfully repulsed a Japanese offensive to capture the airfields there. Under the control of the Royal Australian Navy, the Allies utilized Milne Bay as a collecting point for small craft to run supplies from there northwestward to Allied ground troops fighting at Buna.

The first real U.S. naval activity at Milne Bay began in December 1942 with the arrival of the tender *Hilo* and four PT boats from Motor Topedo Boat Squadron 6. They organized an operating base at Kana Kopa on the bay's southeast shore, under the control of Task Group 50.1, MTB Squadrons, Southwest Pacific Force. In February 1943 MTB Base 6 arrived at Kana Kopa to function as a support base for New Guinea-based PTs, which operated by early 1943 from an advance base at Tufi (q.v.) on the northern Papuan coast. The personnel at Kana Kopa had to cope with highly adverse climatic and terrain conditions.

In the spring of 1943 headquarters of the Seventh Fleet (redesignated on 15 March 1943 from Southwest Pacific Force) decided to develop Milne Bay as a naval advance base to supplant the distant Australian ports in supporting amphibious operations on New Guinea. Under these plans, it was to become a major supply, transshipment, and staging area for Allied forces operating in New Guinea, a major overhaul base for PTs, and a destroyer-light craft repair base.

Beginning in mid-1943, naval construction battalions arrived at Milne Bay to erect several different installations at sites around its shore and the islands just south of it. At Kana Kopa MTB facilities were expanded to include barracks, a gasoline tank farm, wharfs, and two pontoon dry docks. After June 1943 Kana Kopa functioned as a main overhaul and repair base, taking over so much work from MTB Base 4 at Cairns (q.v.) in northeastern Australia that on 18 October that installation was moved to Milne Bay and absorbed into Base 6. Not until June 1944 were the PT facilities at Milne Bay closed down and forwarded to the base at Dreger Harbor in Huon Gulf. (*See* Finchhafen, New Guinea, U.S. Naval Advance Base).

Gamadodo, on Milne Bay's south shore, became the site of a huge naval supply complex. By late 1943 Seabees had greatly improved berthing facilities there and began work first on an advance base construction depot and then on an ammunition depot, a naval supply depot, and a pontoon assembly depot. Gamadodo also served as an Army staging camp for 10,000 troops. Related installations included the Seabee Base headquarters at Ladava and hospitals and recuperation centers at Hilimoi.

Milne Bay also featured facilities servicing ships and aircraft. At Gohora Bay, on the western shore, there was an important destroyer repair unit with shops, piers, and four floating dry docks capable of handling destroyer-sized and smaller vessels. After October 1943 the submarine tender *Fulton* operated in Milne Bay, conducting refits for submarines formerly operating out of Brisbane (q.v.). The Seventh Amphibious Force in late 1943 relocated facilities of the old Toorbul Bay (Brisbane) amphibious training center in new quarters at Stringer Bay on the northwestern shore of Milne Bay. The base offered training and repair for landing craft units. Headquarters, Seventh Amphibious Force moved there in December 1943. Finally, at Samarai Island and in Jenkins Bay on nearby Sariba

Island two seaplane bases with ramps, hangars, and aviation gasoline tank farms were erected in late summer 1943.

Formally commissioned on 1 March 1944, the Milne Bay naval advance base offered vital logistic support for all subsequent operations in the New Guinea area. It took over most of the functions formerly performed for Seventh Fleet in the Australian ports now much farther from the combat area than Milne Bay. The base performed at peak capacity until the fall of 1944, until a similar base at Hollandia (q.v.) began supplanting Milne Bay's role. Thereafter a roll-up of facilities at Milne Bay took place. In March 1945 the amphibious training center at Stringer Bay advanced to Subic Bay (q.v.), and the supply depots followed later. The base at Milne Bay was disestablished on 21 June 1946.

BIBLIOGRAPHY

A. Motor Torpedo Boat Squadrons, Philippine Sea Frontier, ''Command History of MTB Squadrons, Philippine Sea Frontier, Formerly MTB Squadrons, 7th Fleet,'' 5 vols., Type Commands, 1945 (Washington: Naval Historical Center, Operational Archives Branch); U.S. Navy, ''7th Amphibious Force Command History, 10 January 1943-23 December 1945'' (Washington: Naval Historical Center, Operational Archives Branch); U.S. Navy, Bureau of Yards and Docks, *Building the Navy's Bases in World War II*, 2 vols. (Washington: GPO, 1947); U.S. Navy, ''U.S. Naval Bases in the South and Southwest Pacific (and Central Pacific Forward) in World War II,'' 1 November 1954 (Washington: Naval Historical Center, Operational Archives Branch).

B. Samuel E. Morison, *Breaking the Bismarcks Barrier 22 July 1922-1 May 1944* (Boston: Little, Brown, 1950); Rear Adm. Worrall Reed Carter, *Beans, Bullets and Black Oil* (Washington: GPO, 1953); Capt. Robert J. Bulkley, *At Close Quarters: PT Boats in the United States Navy* (Washington: Navy Department, Naval History Division, 1962); Vice Adm. Daniel E. Barbey, *MacArthur's Amphibious Navy* (Annapolis, Md.: U.S. Naval Institute, 1969).

JOHN B. LUNDSTROM

MINDORO ISLAND, PHILIPPINE ISLANDS, U.S. NAVAL FACILITIES, 1945–1946 Following the Leyte campaign, which began in October 1944, American plans for the capture of Manila included the seizure of an island to the west of Luzon that had clear weather and on which airfields could be built. While the Third Fleet stood to the east of Luzon and for three days struck its airfields, a Seventh Fleet amphibious force moved from Leyte Gulf via Surigao Strait toward Mindoro. The Japanese reacted vigorously by sending out their Second Striking Force from Indochina ports and by attacking with more than 150 kamikazes. Planes from the escort and fleet carriers successfully covered the Mindoro landings, however, and the invaders went ashore on 15 December without opposition and rapidly began to construct two airstrips. A resupply echelon reached them in late December. Constructed also near San Jose were a section base and advanced PT base No. 4. In addition there was ACORN 19 (advanced air base construction unit) and facilities for planes of the Naval Air

Transport Service. While records do not show the exact date of the disestablishment of the facilities, they most likely were closed either late in 1945 or early in 1946.

BIBLIOGRAPHY

A. "Monograph Histories of U.S. Naval Overseas Bases. Vol. II. Pacific Area" (Washington: Naval Historical Center, Operational Archives Branch).

MISAWA, JAPAN, U.S. NAVAL AIR FACILITY, 1975– Naval Air Facility, Misawa, is located at 40°3′N., 141°4′E., not far from the northern extremity of the island of Honshu. Its primary mission is to provide support, facilities, and materiel for the aviation activities of the Seventh Fleet. The base also carries out other activities as designated by higher authority. It comes under the command of Commander in Chief, Pacific Fleet, through Commander Naval Air Forces, U.S. Pacific Fleet, and Commander Fleet Air, Western Pacific.

Misawa was designated a naval air facility on 1 October 1975, when Capt. William S. Myers assumed command. However, a detachment from Naval Air Station Atsugi (q.v.) had been stationed at Misawa since 1970, when the Navy took over responsibility for the base from the Air Force. The latter had controlled the base since its occupation in September 1945 by U.S. Army troops. When the first Americans arrived there, they found the base almost destroyed by the attacks of U.S. fighters and B-29 bombers. It had served the Imperial Japanese Navy as a research and training facility since 1942, providing a site for the instruction of kamikaze pilots and for improvement of Japan's Zero and Jack aircraft. The Imperial Japanese Army had built its airstrip, beginning in 1938.

The base presently supports fleet operations in a variety of ways. Its six departments provide administrative, medical, operational, maintenance, and supply services to patrol aircraft from the fleet, to visiting tactical aircraft from Marine Corps Air Station, Iwakuni (q.v.), and to Japanese civilian and Air Self-Defense Force aircraft. Misawa hosts a patrol squadron on a rotational basis. Detachments from the Naval Oceanographic Command, the Naval Security Group, and the Naval Mobile Construction Batallions are located on the base. It has facilities for arrested landings, as well as the Ripsaw Bombing Range, which is used to train tactical aviators. In recent years, Misawa has provided support for the COPE NORTH exercises of the Japanese Self-Defense Forces.

BIBLIOGRAPHY

A. "Command Histories, 1975-1982" (U.S. Naval Air Facility, Misawa, Japan).

B. P. T. Mullikin, "Outpost Misawa," *Naval Aviation News* 61 (June 1979):36-37; "Living in the Far East: Misawa," *Navy Times*, 16 August 1982, p. 48.

ROGER DINGMAN

MOC HOA, REPUBLIC OF VIETNAM, U.S. NAVAL ADVANCED TACTICAL SUPPORT BASE, 1968–1971 This site, on the Vam Co Tay River north of the Republic of Vietnam's Plain of Reeds, served as a naval advanced tactical support base during the war in Southeast Asia. Moc Hoa sat astride an infiltration route from Cambodia that had long been used by the Viet Cong. The U.S. Navy established the staging base there for river patrol boat (PBR) units that patrolled this sector of the Vam Co Tay in Operation Giant Slingshot.

In 1969 the Navy's Seabees deployed to the site from the Danang area and soon provided the river force with a suitable base. The naval constructionmen installed sleeping and messing facilities, fuel and ammunition storage, a helicopter pad, defensive bunkers, and an operations center.

When U.S. naval forces withdrew from South Vietnam, U.S. installations were turned over to the Vietnamese Navy; the base at Moc Hoa was transferred in April 1971.

BIBLIOGRAPHY

A. Commander Naval Forces, Vietnam, "The Naval War in Vietnam," May 1970 (Washington: Naval Historical Center, Operational Archives Branch).

EDWARD J. MAROLDA

MONROVIA, LIBERIA, U.S. NAVAL TENANT PORT, 1944–1945 After finding several sites inhospitable, a small colony of free Negro slaves from America in 1822 chose Monrovia for the capital of Liberia, the only "Land of Freedom" in Africa, then controlled by foreign powers. Located on the Atlantic Ocean at 5°3′N., 10°2′W., about 200 miles south of Freetown, Sierra Leone, and 300 miles north of Cape Palmas, the southern extremity of the "bulge" of Western Africa, it enjoys quite a balanced economy, with agriculture, fishing, mining, and some manufacturing. Most important for the Allies in World War II, its harbor was suitable for development as a commercial port. To this end, on 13 December 1943 the American and Liberian governments agreed that the United States would supervise the construction of such a port. On 27 April 1944 the Navy's Bureau of Yards and Docks let a cost-plus-fixed-fee contract for the construction of a commercial port, port works, and access roads in Liberia, at an estimated cost of $20 million. In this case the Navy acted as the agent of the Department of State, and officers of the Civil Engineer Corps supervised the construction. All facilities were turned over to the government of Liberia following the end of World War II in the Atlantic on 8 May 1945.

BIBLIOGRAPHY

A. U.S. Navy Bureau of Yards and Docks, *Building the Navy's Bases in World War II*, 2 vols. (Washington: GPO, 1947), II:94.

MOROBE, NEW GUINEA, U.S. NAVAL ADVANCE BASE, 1943–1944 Morobe was a district headquarters of the Australian-administered Mandated Territory of New Guinea. A well-situated, protected anchorage (7°45′S., 147°39′E.) at the mouth of the Morobe River on New Guinea's northern coast, Morobe was chosen on 20 April 1943 as the site of an advanced operating base for PT boats. Boats making patrols from Morobe could cover Huon Gulf and beyond. Motor Torpedo Boat Squadron 8 of Task Group 70.1 (Seventh Fleet, Southwest Pacific Area) was the unit to advance to Morobe from the base at Tufi (q.v.). PT patrols continued into early fall 1943, and the base was used by them until December 1943. Meanwhile, Morobe also became a staging point for coastal traffic and an important U.S. Army base for engineer special troops. Seventh Fleet naval forces utilized the Morobe base until May 1944.

BIBLIOGRAPHY

A. U.S. Navy, "7th Amphibious Force Command History 10 January 1943-23 December 1945" (Washington: Naval Historical Center, Operational Archives Branch); U.S. Navy, "U.S. Naval Bases in South and Southwest Pacific (and Central Pacific Forward) in World War II," 1 November 1954 (Washington: Naval Historical Center, Operational Archives Branch).

B. Capt. Robert J. Bulkley, *At Close Quarters: PT Boats in the United States Navy* (Washington: Navy Department, Naval History Division, 1962); Vice Adm. Daniel E. Barbey, *MacArthur's Amphibious Navy* (Annapolis, Md.: U.S. Naval Institute, 1969).

JOHN B. LUNDSTROM

MOROTAI, NETHERLANDS EAST INDIES, U.S. NAVAL ADVANCE BASE, 1944–1946 Morotai, an island in the Molucca group, Netherlands East Indies, is located west of New Guinea and about fifty miles north of the much larger island of Halmahera, in 1944 strongly held by the Japanese. It lies almost on a direct line from the western tip of New Guinea to Mindanao in the Philippines. In Allied hands, it would serve as a valuable air and staging base to facilitate the return to the Philippines. Naval forces on Morotai could contain Japanese forces at Halmahera. Morotai itself (about forty-eight miles by twenty-eight miles in size) was mountainous and densely wooded. The most useful area appeared to be the Gila Peninsula (1°55′N., 128°7′E.) on the south coast, where the terrain was more level.

Troops from the Southwest Pacific Area invaded Morotai on 15 September 1944, the same day as landings in the Western Carolines to the east. The first objective was to seize the area around Gila Peninsula and establish an air and naval base. On 16 September a force of forty-one PT boats and two tenders from the Seventh Fleet began operating from Gila Harbor with patrols to isolate Morotai and harass Japanese forces on Halmahera. It was the beginning of nearly a year-long effort by the PTs, which in 1,300 patrols destroyed 50 barges and nearly 150 smaller craft and prevented the enemy on Halmahera from interfering with operations on Morotai.

On 27 September 1944 the Eighty-fourth Naval Construction Battalion reached Morotai to begin construction of the advance base. Port facilities at Gila were greatly improved to permit docking by Liberty ships to supply the base, the airfields, and important Army camps on the island. On little Soemsoem Island in the harbor, Motor Torpedo Boat Advance Base 4 was operating by early October 1944 to service the PTs based at Morotai. Also at Morotai was a small-boat repair unit to handle landing craft. The Morotai base facilitated supply for

Army forces staging there for the reinforcement of the invasion of Luzon, as well as landings on Borneo in the spring and summer of 1945. Aircraft based there helped assure air superiority in the region. Morotai functioned well after the end of hostilities during the withdrawal of forces from the area. The naval base was disestablished on 21 January 1946, and part of it was turned over to the Royal Australian Navy.

BIBLIOGRAPHY

A. Motor Torpedo Boat Squadrons, Philippine Sea Frontier, Formerly MTB Squadrons, 7th Fleet,'' 5 vols., Type Commands, 1945 (Washington: Naval Historical Center, Operational Archives Branch); U.S. Navy, ''7th Amphibious Force Command History 10 January 1943-23 December 1945'' (Washington: Naval Historical Center, Operational Archives Branch); U.S. Navy, Bureau of Yards and Docks, *Building the Navy's Bases in World War II*, 2 vols. (Washington: GPO, 1947); U.S. Navy, ''U.S. Naval Bases in the South and Southwest Pacific (and Central Pacific Forward) in World War II,'' 1 November 1954 (Washington: Naval Historical Center, Operational Archives Branch).

B. Samuel E. Morison, *Leyte June 1944-January 1945* (Boston: Little, Brown, 1958); Capt. Robert J. Bulkley, *At Close Quarters: PT Boats in the United States Navy* (Washington: Navy Department, Naval History Division, 1962); Rear Adm. Daniel E. Barbey, *MacArthur's Amphibious Navy* (Annapolis, Md.: U.S. Naval Institute, 1969).

JOHN B. LUNDSTROM

MOSTAGANEM, ALGERIA.

See North Africa, U.S. Naval Bases.

MOUTCHIC-LACANAU, FRANCE.

See World War I U.S. Naval Air Stations in Europe.

MY THO, REPUBLIC OF VIETNAM, U.S. NAVAL SUPPORT ACTIVITY, 1966–1969 This strategically placed city in the Republic of Vietnam's Mekong Delta region was the home for several river patrol boat (PBR) units from the U.S. Navy's River Patrol Force during the Vietnam War. Naval leaders chose to develop a base there because My Tho lay at the junction of Route 4—the only relatively good road traversing the delta—and the My Tho River. This river was important for the Navy's conduct of the Game Warden waterway interdiction operation, and it provided easy access for logistic ships deployed in the South China Sea. Another factor in its selection was its proximity to Kien Hoa Province, purportedly the birthplace of the Viet Cong National Liberation Front and long a communist stronghold. The subsequent enemy mortar and rocket attacks on the U.S. naval installation certainly attested to the validity of this assessment. Finally, location of American naval units at the Vietnamese Navy River Assault Group base, it was hoped would foster allied cooperation and make use of existing facilities.

In June 1966 a ten-boat section of River Division 53 began patrol operations from the My Tho base, which then hardly warranted that description. Repair parts, supplies, and ammunition were stored in tents or rudimentary shelters. Personnel were quartered away from the waterfront in leased buildings, including the less than sumptuous two-story Victory Hotel. To alleviate these problems, construction began in November on new structures at a nearby site. Although this base was fully operational by March 1967, with the establishment of the Naval Support Activity, Saigon, Detachment My Tho, additional construction provided helicopter facilities at the existing 1,600-foot airstrip, a 1,000-barrel fuel tank farm, and a mine defense net upriver. As part of the Vietnamization process, the My Tho base was turned over to the Vietnamese Navy in November 1969.

BIBLIOGRAPHY

A. Service Force, U.S. Pacific Fleet, "Command Histories, 1967-1972" (Washington: Naval Historical Center, Operational Archives Branch).

B. Herbert T. King, "Naval Logistic Support, Qui Nhon to Phu Qoc," U.S. Naval Institute *Naval Review* 95 (May 1969):84-111; S. A. Swarztrauber, "River Patrol Relearned," U.S. Naval Institute *Naval Review* 96 (May 1970):120-57; Edwin B. Hooper, *Mobility, Support, Endurance: A Story of Naval Operational Logistics in the Vietnam War, 1965-1968* (Washington: GPO, 1972).

N

NAGASAKI, JAPAN.
See Far Eastern U.S. Naval Bases to 1898.

NAM CAN, REPUBLIC OF VIETNAM, U.S. NAVAL MOBILE FACILITY, 1969–1971 One of the most remote of all the Navy's bases in the Republic of Vietnam was Nam Can, situated on the north bank of the Cua Lon River in the Ca Mau Peninsula. Establishment of a shore facility at Nam Can resulted from a strategic decision to penetrate recognized Viet Cong strongholds in order to disrupt enemy supply lines and hinder waterborne movement. Reasserting the sovereignty of the South Vietnamese government over this area was another prime consideration. Consequently, in June 1969 naval harbor craft towed the first of thirteen pontoons that were to comprise a floating base complex to a mooring point off the deserted Vietnamese town of Nam Can.

Operations from this mobile facility, named Sea Float, soon improved security in the surrounding area, prompting plans to develop an installation ashore on the site of the destroyed town. Designated Solid Anchor, the base was designed to protect and support U.S. and South Vietnamese naval forces engaged in river and coastal operations.

Construction problems were legion. Building materials had to be shipped in from distant areas, especially Saigon (q.v.), which was 150 miles from the site. Because local dredged fill was unsuitable, even sand was barged in. In addition, the heavy equipment of Seabee Battalion 1 repeatedly became mired in the extremely porous ground. Equally difficult was the task of clearing the surrounding scrub and brush away from the perimeter. Nonetheless, during 1970 the Nam Can intermediate support base became functional and provided the allied combat units in the Ca Mau Peninsula with vital logistic assistance.

In keeping with the direction of the Vietnamization program, the Vietnamese Navy assumed the Solid Anchor mission in April 1971, thus ending the last major U.S. combat operation in Vietnam. In September of that year, U.S. naval personnel turned over control of the shore facility to their Vietnamese counterparts.

BIBLIOGRAPHY
A. Commander Naval Forces, Vietnam, "The Naval War in Vietnam," May 1970 (Washington: Naval Historical Center, Operational Archives Branch).
B. Richard L. Schreadley, "The Naval War in Vietnam, 1950-1970," U.S. Naval Institute *Naval Review* 97 (May 1971):180-211.

EDWARD J. MAROLDA

NANDI-SUVA, FIJI ISLANDS, U.S. NAVAL ADVANCE BASE, 1942–1945 [FANTAN] A large and populous island group of the South Pacific, Fiji in 1942 was a British Crown colony with its capital at Suva (18°8′S., 178°25′E.) on the main island of Vitu Levu. Located strategically to cover the vital line of communication from the United States to New Zealand and Australia, Fiji was at first defended by a garrison of New Zealand ground and air forces. With the establishment of the Australia-New Zealand (ANZAC) Area in February 1942, the ANZAC Squadron (later Task Force 44) of Allied cruisers and destroyers was based at Suva. On 13 May the United States took over responsibility for Fiji's security, and the first American ground troops arrived in June. That summer naval construction battalions were earmarked for Vitu Levu. The U.S. Navy chose to develop facilities on Vitu Levu's western shore, especially on the coastal plain around Nandi (17°45′S., 177°25′E.), a large anchorage that already featured a Royal New Zealand Air Force base. Initial plans involved a minor naval operating base at Nandi and a naval air station with seaplane bases at Saweni and Latuoka Bay just to the north.

In July 1942, with base construction just under way, Fiji served as a staging point and rehearsal site for the impending offensive that August into the Solomon Islands. During the Guadalcanal-Tulagi campaign (August 1942-February 1943), Fiji acted as a minor support base. Naval construction troops that fall started erecting a small fuel oil tank farm at Latuoka and completed it in April 1943. Fiji was host in late 1942 to a small task force built around the old battleships *Maryland* and *Colorado*. In November, Motor Torpedo Boat Base 3, a PT boat main engine overhaul installation, arrived at Nandi, but early in 1943 it shifted northwest to the massive naval base at Espiritu Santo (q.v.) in the New Hebrides closer to the forward area. In May 1943 additional naval construction and base troops of CUB-3 reached Fiji to complete development of fuel and supply facilities. They also opened a third port at Vunda Point, north of Nandi.

The additional work accomplished by CUB-3 became useful in the fall of 1943 when Fiji served as an important staging, supply, and fueling base for Operation Galvanic, the invasion of the Gilbert Islands. Fiji proved especially valuable as a convenient base for chartered tankers to transship fuel oil to fleet oilers heading back to the combat area. Thereafter naval activities on Vitu Levu gradually wound down. By August 1944 Seabee maintenance units had withdrawn, leaving the Naval Air Transport Service Base at Lauthala Bay near Suva as a functioning element of naval forces on Fiji. On 1 July 1945 the Navy turned over the remaining installations to the Army.

BIBLIOGRAPHY
A. Lt. Alfred B. Potts, "Historical Narrative, Fiji Islands," South Pacific Command Administrative History, 34, 6 November 1945, Appendix (Washington: Naval Historical Center, Operational Archives Branch); Service Squadron, South Pacific, "History of Commander, Service Squadron, South Pacific 7 December 1941-15 August 1945," Type Commands, 1946 (Washington: Naval Historical Center, Operational Archives Branch); U.S. Navy, Bureau of Yards and Docks, *Building the Navy's Bases in World War II*, 2 vols. (Washington: GPO, 1947):II, 195, 218-20; U.S. Navy, "U.S. Naval Bases in the South and Southwest Pacific (and Central Pacific Forward) in World War II," 1 November 1954 (Washington: Naval Historical Center, Operational Archives Branch).

B. Rear Adm. Worrall Reed Carter, *Beans, Bullets, and Black Oil* (Washington: GPO, 1953); Vice Adm. George C. Dyer, *The Amphibians Came to Conquer*, 2 vols. (Washington: GPO, 1972).

JOHN B. LUNDSTROM

NANOMEA, ELLICE ISLANDS, U.S. NAVAL ADVANCE BASE, 1943–1944 Nanomea, the northernmost island in the Ellice Islands, is located about 375 miles northwest of Funafuti. That placed the island much closer to the Japanese-held Gilbert Islands than other air bases in the Ellice Islands. Nanomea (also spelled Nanumea) is a small island (at 5°39′S., 176°8′E.), surrounded by a coral reef. Beginning on 5 September 1943, when American forces reached the island, Seabees from the Sixteenth Naval Construction Battalion labored furiously to ready an airfield on its low, level coral terrain. By 17 September the field was serviceable, and eleven days later Marine Fighter Squadron 441 began operating from it. In November two Army Air Forces heavy bomber squadrons staged into Nanomea to begin strikes on the Gilberts and other Japanese bases in the Marshall Islands. By December 1943 the Army Air Forces had taken over Nanomea's air effort, but the field and its associated facilities also served as an alternate air base for Naval Air Transport System aircraft flying to and from the South Pacific. Roll-up of naval facilities was begun as early as May 1944, and the base itself was dissolved in December 1944.

BIBLIOGRAPHY
A. U.S. Navy, Bureau of Yards and Docks, *Building the Navy's Bases in World War II*, 2 vols. (Washington: GPO, 1947); U.S. Navy, "U.S. Naval Bases in the South and Southwest Pacific (and Central Pacific Forward) in World War II," 1 November 1954 (Washington: Naval Historical Center, Operational Archives Branch).

B. Robert Sherrod, *History of Marine Corps Aviation in World War II* (Washington: Combat Forces Press, 1952); Samuel E. Morison, *Aleutians, Gilberts, and Marshalls June 1942-April 1944* (Boston: Little, Brown, 1953).

JOHN B. LUNDSTROM

NAPLES, ITALY, HEADQUARTERS, COMMANDER NAVAL FORCES NORTHWEST AFRICAN WATERS, 1944-1947, AND HEADQUARTERS, ALLIED FORCES SOUTH (NATO), 1951- Naples first assumed importance to the American Navy during the Barbary Wars. Commo. Edward Preble made use of it for needed stores; more important, he convinced its ruler to lend him the small gunboats and bomb ketches he needed to carry out his offensive operations against Tripoli. Throughout the 1800s Naples continued to be a visiting port for the Navy, but World War II and the Cold War made it vitally important.

At the Trident Conference at Washington in May 1943, a decision was made to expand the Sicilian operation into an invasion of mainland Italy in order to knock it out of the war, tie up as many German divisions as possible, and thus weaken Germany on the projected French invasion front. Following the speedy taking of Sicily and the fall of Mussolini on 25 July, the Salerno Bay area was selected as the landing site for the Fifth Army. It was essential that Naples be taken and opened as soon as possible. Since it was expected that the Germans would carry out extensive demolition at Naples, Salerno was to be taken on D-Day and used as the entry port until Naples was ready. Naples was scheduled to be taken by D-plus-12 and to be in operation within ten to fourteen days.

Naples was not taken until D-plus-22, 1 October 1943. The British Port Party landed on 3 October. Special salvage teams had been set up to expedite clearing Salerno and Naples. Commo. William A. Sullivan, USN, principal salvage officer on the staff of Allied Naval Commander, Mediterranean, had collected a team of bluejackets and Army engineers to work with a similar British team and with a firefighter unit under Comdr. W. L. Worten, USNR.

Naples was a nightmare of destruction. For three weeks the Germans, aided by constant Allied bombings, had systematically wrecked it. Hundreds of craft had been used to block the harbor and her satellite ports. Bulkheads had been blown to prevent the refloating of the wrecks. Cranes and locomotives had been piled crazily on top of wrecks to make clearance even more difficult. Machinery and buildings had been demolished and fires set along the waterfront. The city's electricity and water had been cut off. Much of the destruction seemed aimed more at punishing the Italians for their failures as allies than at insuring the closing of the port.

The salvage teams got to work. Piers were cleared and wrecks that could not be moved were bridged over and made into new piers, while access roads were bulldozed through ruined buildings near the waterfront. Two graving docks were put back into operation within ten days and opened for loading. Approach channels were swept and, within two days of their being taken, berths were available for five Liberty ships and six coasters along with eight holding berths. Within one month the port was restored sufficiently for deep-draft vessels that supported the Allied effort through this one port. By the end of the year, Allied tonnage exceeded the maximum official capacity of the port before the war.

Initially, the Navy's role had been to help the British open Naples to supply the Allied invasion, but the Navy rejected the idea of setting up a naval establishment there. However, in January 1944 it was decided to establish a headquarters at Naples for the Commander Naval Forces Northwest African Waters. A minimum of personnel was assigned at first, but as traffic continued heavy through Naples more and more functions and personnel were added until its final shutdown in April 1947.

With the creation of the North Atlantic Treaty Organization, Naples again assumed importance as the headquarters of the southern defense area, Allied Forces South, in June 1951. In this role, it serves as the support base for the U.S. Sixth Fleet in the Mediterranean. Included are a Naval Air Facility, Naval Communications Center, Naval Regional Medical Center, and the Support Activity.

BIBLIOGRAPHY

A. U.S. Office of Naval Records and Library, *Naval Documents Related to the United States Wars with the Barbary Powers*, 6 vols. (Washington: GPO, 1939-1944); United States Naval Administrative Histories of World War II, Commander U.S. Naval Forces, Northwest African Waters, "Naval Forces, Northwest African Waters and the Eighth Fleet," 5 vols. (Washington: Naval Historical Center, Operational Archives Branch, 1945).

B. Samuel E. Morison, *Sicily, Salerno, and Anzio* (Boston: Little, Brown, 1954); "Naples and Its Aviation Activities," *Naval Aviation News*, Dec. 1964, pp. 22-23.

FRANCIS X. HOLBROOK

NATAL, BRAZIL, U.S. NAVAL AIR FACILITY.
See Brazil, U.S. Naval Bases.

NEMOURS, ALGERIA.
See North Africa, U.S. Naval Bases.

NEW GEORGIA, SOLOMON ISLANDS, U.S. NAVAL ADVANCE BASE, 1943–1945 New Georgia and its associated islands, such as Rendova and Vangunu, supported during the Solomons campaign a number of small naval and air bases wrested from the Japanese. Located 100 to 150 miles northwest of Guadalcanal (and like it a part of the British Solomon Islands Protectorate), New Georgia in the spring of 1943 became the central objective of an Allied offensive into the Central Solomons. The Japanese in late 1942 had begun construction of an airfield at Munda Point on its north coast. For the Allies to gain a foothold in that area, they had to capture the airfield and turn it against its builders, as they had done in August 1942 on Guadalcanal. Only now, with Munda's defenses intact. the Allies could not take it by a coup de main, but rather would have to occupy a number of places in New Georgia and build up for the assault on Munda.

The first Allied landing in the New Georgia area took place on 21 June 1943, when a small reconnaissance party occupied Segi Point (8°35′S., 157°53′E.) on Vangunu Island. Seabees quickly hacked out and leveled land for an airstrip that was ready in late July for operation by light planes coordinating close air combat support in the ground attack on Munda. Despite enemy air attacks, the airfield at Segi Point was continuously improved and in time expanded to three runways. Eventually Navy fighters operated from there until more forward bases rendered it useful mainly as an emergency field. The installation was finally abandoned in July 1944.

The best natural harbor in the New Georgia group was to be found on the north coast of Rendova (8°50′S., 157°3′E.), an island about sixteen miles long situated just southwest of New Georgia. On 30 June 1943 Army troops landed there against limited resistance, and the same day PT boats from Motor Torpedo Boat Squadron 9 set up a base on little Lumbari Island in Rendova Harbor. The PTs patrolled north of New Georgia to help isolate the Japanese defenders from supplies and reinforcements filtering in by barge runs and escorted convoys. The PTs at Rendova were themselves steadily reinforced, until in September, after the capture of New Georgia proper, their patrols extended north and northeast to threaten all of Vella Lavella and the west coast of Choiseul.

Because of increased operations from Rendova Harbor, it was decided in October 1943 to shift the main base facilities across the harbor to Bau Island. Roomier and better situated, Bau Island permitted expansion of the PT overhaul and repair facilities. That same month the naval base at Rendova was formally established. Even after operations in the New Georgia area wound down, Rendova remained important as a base offering repair and overhaul service to MTB squadrons in the northern Solomons. In January 1944 the facilities at Rendova were organized as PT Base 11, and eventually headquarters, MTB Squadrons, South Pacific Force, moved there from Tulagi (q.v.).

On the northeast coast of New Georgia, another PT base was set up at Lever Harbor. PTs began operating from there beginning 24 July 1943 to patrol the east coast of New Georgia past Kolombangara toward Vella Lavella and Choiseul. By October contacts with Japanese barge traffic had dwindled, and the temporary PT base at Lever Harbor was abandoned on 1 November 1943.

The landings on New Georgia itself took place on 2 July 1943 with Munda (8°0′S., 157°15′E.) as the main objective. The drive on the airfield took much longer than expected because of the skilled Japanese defense, difficult terrain, and inexperience. Not until 5 August was the enemy airfield captured. By 15 October Seabees had restored it to full operating condition and had also constructed a fighter strip on Ondonga Island, six miles north of Munda. Aircraft flying from the two bases were vital in securing air superiority over Vella Lavella and southern Bougainville. At Munda itself and on Ondonga Island, naval construction troops established small-boat repair units that serviced the craft so vital in supplying small island bases lacking adequate port facilities. Both repair units were operating by February 1944.

The New Georgia air and naval bases played an important role in the continued campaigns northward up the Solomons chain: Vella Lavella, the Treasury Islands, and Cape Torokina on Bougainville. Thereafter the bases at Rendova (Bau Island) and Munda-Ondonga supported containment operations against bypassed strong Japanese garrisons on Choiseul and Bougainville. On 15 June 1944, along with a number of other bases in the area, New Georgia passed to the overall control of the Southwest Pacific Area, specifically the Seventh Fleet. New Georgia became part of Allied Naval Forces, Northern Solomons Area. Headquarters MTB Squadrons, South Pacific Area Force, moved from Bau Island to Torokina (q.v.). MTB Base 11 on Bau Island remained open until January 1945, and the remaining installations on New Georgia were rolled up and closed in March 1945.

BIBLIOGRAPHY

A. Motor Torpedo Boat Squadrons, Philippine Sea Frontier, "Command History of MTB Squadrons Philippine Sea Frontier, Formerly MTB Squadrons, 7th Fleet," 5 vols., Type Commands 1945 (Washington: Naval Historical Center, Operational Archives Branch); Service Squadron, South Pacific, "History of Commander, Service Squadron, South Pacific 7 December 1941-5 August 1945" (Washington: Naval Historical Center, Operational Archives Branch); U.S. Navy, Bureau of Yards and Docks, *Building the Navy's Bases in World War II*, 2 vols. (Washington: GPO: 1947); U.S. Navy, "U.S. Naval Bases in the South and Southwest Pacific (and Central Pacific Forward) in World War II," 1 November 1954 (Washington: Naval Historical Center, Operational Archives Branch).

B. Samuel E. Morison, *Breaking the Bismarcks Barrier 22 July 1942-1 May 1944* (Boston: Little, Brown, 1950); Robert Sherrod, *History of Marine Corps Aviation in World War II* (Washington: Combat Forces Press, 1952); Capt. Robert J. Bulkley, *At Close Quarters: PT Boats in the United States Navy* (Washington: Navy Department, Naval History Division, 1962).

JOHN B. LUNDSTROM

NHA BE, REPUBLIC OF VIETNAM, U.S. NAVAL SUPPORT ACTIVITY, 1966–1972 The U.S. naval establishment at Nha Be, seven miles south of Saigon, capital of the Republic of Vietnam, was a major combat and logistic base during the Southeast Asian Conflict. As naval leaders concluded early, the site was strategically placed at the junction of the Long Tau and Soirap, the main rivers between the port of Saigon and the South China Sea. In addition, Nha Be lay astride waterways traversing the Viet Cong-infiltrated Rung Sat swamp and the eastern Mekong Delta region. To support river patrol and minesweeping operations, Nha Ba was ideally located. In addition, the Vietnamese Navy's River Assault Group compound there initially was suitable for a small American force.

In March 1966 a detachment of Mine Squadron 11, employing 57-foot minesweeping boats (MSBs) and converted landing craft, became the first U.S. naval unit to deploy to Nha Be. During the next five years the U.S. minesweeping force patrolled the water approaches to Saigon, escorted commercial and military vessels, and worked to keep the ship channels free of enemy mines. While a number of vessels were damaged or sunk, the absolutely vital water line of communication never was severed by Viet Cong action.

Also in March 1966, the first units of the Navy's River Patrol Force tied up at Nha Be and soon afterward began operations against Viet Cong waterborne logistic traffic in the Rung Sat and in the Mekong Delta. Eventually, the base was able to support forty river patrol boats (PBRs) engaged in this operation, designated Game Warden. Other components of the force were Helicopter Combat Support Squadron 1 and Helicopter Attack (Light) Squadron 3, detachments of which flew from helicopter pads at nearby Cruickshank Airfield. Both the surface and air units of the River Patrol Force based at Nha Be took part in Operation Giant Slingshot, which sought to interdict communist men and supplies infiltrating from Cambodia on the Vam Co Dong and Vam Co Tay Rivers during 1969-1971.

The support base at Nha Be developed into a major logistic complex. Initially, the river sailors had to rely on Army depots in Saigon for supply items common to both services and were quartered in tents at the Vietnamese installation. However, once the Naval Support Activity, Saigon, Detachment Nha Be, was established, conditions improved. A pier for the PBRs was fashioned with Army pontoons, and YFNB-16, a large covered lighter, was stationed at the site, making berthing, repair, spare parts, and supplies available. An Army crane was used for hull repair of the MSBs. These and other measures were taken to provide interim support.

Meanwhile, 20 acres of nearby swampland were filled with dredged soil, and by December 1966 work was begun on permanent base facilities, which included depot-level repair, administrative, communications, storage, maintenance, quartering, and messing buildings, four 1,000-barrel fuel storage tanks, and a boat pier. Although securing potable water and shoring up the landfill presented problems, Nha Be became a key naval support complex in the Saigon area. By late 1968 eighty-four craft and the recently deployed headquarters of Naval Support Activity, Saigon (q.v.), were based there. The facility continued to serve the Navy's needs until its turnover to the Vietnamese Navy and the disestablishment of Naval Support Activity, Saigon, Detachment Nha Be, in April 1972.

BIBLIOGRAPHY

A. Commander Naval Forces Vietnam, "The Naval War in Vietnam," May 1970 (Washington: Naval Historical Center, Operational Archives Branch); Commander Naval Forces, Vietnam, "Monthly Historical Reports, 1965-1971" (Washington: Naval Historical Center, Operational Archives Branch).

B. Herbert T. King, "Naval Logistic Support, Qui Nhon to Phu Quoc," U.S. Naval Institute *Naval Review* 95 (May 1969):84-111; S. A. Swarztrauber, "River Patrol Relearned," U.S. Naval Institute *Naval Review* 96 (May 1970):120-57; Richard L. Schreadley, "The Naval War in Vietnam, 1950-1970," U.S. Naval Institute *Naval Review* 97 (May 1971):180-211; Edwin B. Hooper, *Mobility, Support, Endurance: A Story of Naval Operational Logistics in the Vietnam War, 1965-1968* (Washington: GPO, 1972); Richard Tregaskis, *Southeast Asia: Building the Bases: The History of Construction in Southeast Asia* (Washington: GPO, 1975).

EDWARD J. MAROLDA

NHA TRANG, REPUBLIC OF VIETNAM, U.S. NAVAL OPERATING STATION, 1965–1971 Located thirty miles north of Cam Ranh Bay in the

Republic of Vietnam, Nha Trang served as an operating station for naval units during the Southeast Asian Conflict. Between 1965 and 1967 the Navy established there a 20-man coastal surveillance center to coordinate anti-infiltration patrol operations by American and Vietnamese units and a 120-man harbor security unit to protect vessels delivering supplies to the Army's port complex. The Navy's base facilities were turned over to the Vietnamese when U.S. forces withdrew from the war in 1970 and 1971.

BIBLIOGRAPHY
A. Commander Naval Forces, Vietnam, "Monthly Historical Reports, 1965-1971" (Washington: Naval Historical Center, Operational Archives Branch).

EDWARD J. MAROLDA

NORTH AFRICA, U.S. NAVAL BASES, 1942–1978 Given the great distance from the United States, limited shipping space, U-boat peril, lack of information concerning its responsibilities in North Africa, and uncertainty as to how long any bases would be kept and the extent of their development, the U.S. Navy found planning advance bases in North Africa especially frustrating.

The supplies for establishing beachheads or bases were to be provided by the Chief of Naval Operations, but when these had been established responsibility for their future supply shifted to the Navy's Service Force, except for food, which was the job of the U.S. Army.

In Operation Torch, in early November 1942, American and British forces struck at the Axis in North Africa in the greatest amphibious invasion in history up to that time, with 850 ships divided to strike at Casablanca, Oran, and Algiers simultaneously. The functions of the U.S. Navy until the attacks were launched were to safely transport the Army and its supplies, to provide adequate offshore protection of supply lines afloat and forces ashore, to refuel warships during the crossing of the Atlantic from Norfolk, Va., and to prevent the enemy from interfering with these efforts. Following the initial assaults it became necessary to establish bases from which naval ships could obtain fuel, ammunition, and supplies, have their operational and battle damage repaired, and support additional assaults as the front moved eastward and then toward the ultimate objective—Europe.

Casablanca, French Morocco, U.S. Naval Operating Base, 1942-1945

Among the most important northwest African ports was Casablanca, located on the Atlantic coast of French Morocco at 33°39′N., 7°35′W., about 200 miles southwest of Tangier. Given the amount of supplies that would be needed by the 35,000 men in the American Western Task Force, TF34, Vice Adm. H. Kent Hewitt, USN, commanding, it made sense to acquire a harbor that could handle the 600 to 700 tons of supplies needed each day from adequate berthing, unloading, and stowage facilities. Casablanca was a modern man-made port protected by an adequate breakwater and possessing piers and other facilities. Included in TF34 were members of the second section of the 17th Construction Battalion (Seabees), later augmented by the second section of the 53rd Seabees and reformed to constitute the 120th Seabees. They built the naval operating base, as noted below, that served U.S. military forces outside of the Mediterranean.

On 7 November 1942 Admiral Hewitt sent a Southern Attack Group 125 miles south of Casablanca to the small phosphate port of Safi to land troops and tanks that would attack Casablanca from the south; a Center Attack Group to the small port of Fedala, 14 miles northwest of Casablanca, with troops to attack the city from the north; and a Northern Attack Group to the coastal village of Mehedia, 65 miles north of Casablanca, to capture the airfield at nearby Port Lyautey. The landings, made early on the eighth, resulted in securing Fedala by noon, with numerous French ships sunk and clogging the harbor; the port of Lyautey and its airport, the only one in Morocco having all-weather concrete runways, were also secured. Supported by naval gunfire, American troops broke through to the airfield on 10 June and Army planes flown from carriers soon began operating from it. While the salvage of French and Dutch ships and various American boats proceeded in the Wadi Sebou River, the merchant vessel *Contesa* delivered a cargo of bombs and aviation gasoline in drums and the escort carrier *Chenango* launched forty-five P-40s, which flew to Lyautey. The task of establishing a naval air station there was entrusted to the seaplane tender *Barnegat*. At 0800 hours on 13 November, Patrol Squadron 73 arrived from Lyneham, England, and began operations.

Members of the Seventeenth Seabees were sent to both Fedala and Safi, meanwhile, where they cooperated with the Army, which was responsible for most of the construction work undertaken there. A monumental salvage task was faced at Fedala, where high waves had wrecked 169 of the 330 landing boats. However, the naval advance bases at Fedala and Safi had only a third of the facilities of those at Casablanca and served for only a short time as section bases. They were decommissioned early in October 1943. Incidentally, Seabees not only built up the naval air station at Port Lyautey but also built a similar station at Agadir, several hundred miles to the south, and still another at Dakar, still further south.

On 12 November 1942 the first contingent of the Casablanca Base Unit, 33 officers and 188 men trained in engineering, arrived at Casablanca. They established a harbor entrance control post and radio station, began salvage work to clear the harbor, and used lighters and barges for unloading ships. On 19 November Rear Adm. John L. Hall was designated Commander Moroccan Sea Frontier Forces, with headquarters at 10 Place de France, Casablanca, and Capt. H. G. Sickel became the commandant of Naval Operating Base, Casablanca. Hall had the double tasks of protecting the coast and operating ports against U-boats and keeping supplies flowing to the Army, with speed at Casablanca imperative because a convoy was due there five days after the assault. Hall divided his sea frontier forces into three parts. The Casablanca naval operating base supervised salvage and construction in Casablanca, Fedala, and Safi, with work hindered by the lack of tugs. Yet by mid-January 1943 the nine ships sunk at Casablanca and the merchant ships damaged during the assault on Safi and Fedala were cleared away and incoming convoys were emptied quite rapidly. Meanwhile, a minecraft squadron escorted convoys and laid protective minefields at Casablanca and Fedala, and submarine chasers, patrol craft, minesweepers, repair ships, and a net tender arrived to flush out the ships needed to operate a naval operating base. Winning the friendship of the defeated French, Hall was pleased when the latter removed some damaged merchant ships and loaned him tugs and pilots for American convoys. In turn, they kept control of their ships and coastal and antiaircraft batteries. Knowing of the emotional attachment the French had to their now disabled battleship *Jean Bart*, Hall let her remain in port and take up valuable space rather than taking her out to sea and sinking her.

Hall and his Army counterpart, Gen. George Patton, made the arrangements for the conference held in Casablanca by President F. D. Roosevelt, Winston Churchill, and their staffs even though they did not attend it. By the time Hall left Casablanca to report to Gen. Dwight D. Eisenhower as commander of Amphibious Forces, Northwest African Waters, and prepare for the invasion of Sicily, he left behind in Casablanca about 5,600 officers and men and a hustling, secure port for the entry of men and supplies. Among the facilities were officer's quarters, barracks, galley and mess hall, warehouses, hospital, ammunition depot, radio station, ship repair shop and assembly point for pontoon barges and cranes, harbor entrance control posts and signal towers, a water supply, oil line and tanks, and facilities maintenance, the last undertaken by Seabee crews on a reduced basis following the invasion of southern France but not ending until the base was decommissioned on 1 August 1945.

Following the submission of recommendations by the Naval Inspector General, the U.S. Army took over Agadir; repair materials at Casablanca were turned over to the French; the sonobuoys and loops were removed; the base hospital was closed and replaced with a dispensary; and a naval air facility was retained. Remaining materials were turned over to the U.S. Army for future disposition, while the Seabees were sent to Port Lyautey.

BIBLIOGRAPHY

A. United States Naval Administration Histories of World War II. Commander, U.S. Naval Forces, Northwest African Waters, ''Naval Forces, Northwest African Waters and the Eighth Fleet,'' 5 vols. (Washington: Naval Historical Center, Operational Archives Branch, 1945); U.S. Navy, Bureau of Yards and Docks, *Building the Navy's Bases in World War II*, 2 vols. (Washington: GPO, 1947), II;75-85; ''Command File, World War II'' (Washington: Naval Historical Center, Operational Archives Branch).

B. Harley Cope, ''Play Ball Navy,'' U.S. Naval Institute *Proceedings* 69 (Oct. 1943):1311-18; Waldo G. Bowman and others, *Bulldozers Came First: The Story of United States War Construction in Foreign Lands* (New York: McGraw-Hill, 1944); William B. Huie, *Can Do: The Story of the Seabees* (New York: Dutton, 1945); Samuel

E. Morison, *The Battle of the Atlantic September 1939-May 1943* (Boston: Little, Brown, 1947); Worrall Reed Carter and Elmer Ellsworth Duvall, *Ships, Salvage, and Sinews of War* (Washington: GPO, 1954); Samuel E. Morison, *The Atlantic Battle Won May 1943-May 1945* (Boston: Little, Brown, 1956); John H. Clagett, "Admiral H. Kent Hewitt, U.S. Navy. Part II: High Command," *Naval War College Review* 28 (Fall 1975):60-86; S.W.C. Pack, *The Battle for North Africa, 1942* (New York: Mason/Charter, 1976); Susan H. Godson, *Viking of Assault: Admiral John Lesslie Hall, Jr., and Amphibious Warfare* (Washington: University Press of America, 1982).

Oran, Algeria, U.S. Naval Operating Base, 1942-1945

Among the most important northwest African ports was Oran, Algeria, which the U.S. Navy selected as the site of a large supply department to serve all American forces inside the Mediterranean. It lies almost on the Greenwich meridian at 35°45′N. and sits on a shelf about 450 feet above the level of the middle sea. Its 20,000 inhabitants in 1942 could look down upon a protected harbor suitable for deep-draft ships, one well developed by the French as one of their major naval bases. Five miles to the west lies Mers-el-Kebir, similarly large and well-protected.

The task of building an advance naval base at Oran was given to Rear Adm. A. C. Bennett, who proceeded there from Rosneath, Scotland (*see* United Kingdom, U.S. World War II Naval Bases), with 94 officers and 759 naval men, 3 Marine Corps officers and 3 men, and 9 U.S. Army officers and 209 men, They brought with them salvage officers and repair materials and ten qualified divers. They arrived in October and November 1942 and found that an advance party under Capt. Walter C. Ansel, USN, along with British personnel had landed on 8 November and seized all shipping in the harbor, thus preventing sabotage to it. On 10 November the American and British party left Arzew for Oran and Mers-el-Kebir to engage in salvage work and found scuttled twenty-three ships, three dry docks, and two British warships. However, the outer port, or Avant port, was clear and usable. American and British naval port parties, soon aided by the French, raised the dry docks, cleared the harbor, and installed antisubmarine nets to protect it. Of the dry docks, Number One (722 feet by 111.5 feet) had a 25,000-ton capacity; Number Two (394 feet by 64.4 feet), 3,000 tons; Number Three (394 feet by 44.8 feet), 1,500 tons. Number One had two five-ton cranes; Number Two, two four-ton cranes; and Number Three, none. There were also three slips that could handle up to 500 tons or vessels up to 120 feet long. Various stationary and mobile cranes could lift up to thirty tons. The original commandant in charge of the U.S. Naval Operating Base Oran Area, including Mers-el-Kebir, was Admiral Bennett. He was succeeded by Commo. C. M. Yates. Commanding the naval station at Oran was Comdr. C. L. Andrews; at Mers-el-Kebir, Lieut. Comdr. G. H. Burnham.

Because the deep-water wells at Oran provided hard and contaminated water, American authorities took over the system and placed it under medical supervision. Sites for Navy housing, storage, and supplies were limited, and scattered throughout the city. The 120th Construction Battalion (Seabees) therefore built a supply depot. Using fifty-six standard 40-by-100 foot utility buildings and putting them end to end, they provided twenty-eight 200-foot warehouses. In addition they erected three 20-by-48-foot huts for general storage and fifty-six 40-by-200-foot Quonsets for the recipt of shipping. They also installed electric lights and heating systems and graded outside storage areas and built concrete access roads to them. While some good storage areas were available in fourteen buildings in the city, a refrigerator storehouse was badly needed. The only permanent Navy structures in Oran were two storehouses built of cinder-block with concrete flooring and tile roof that covered about 96,000 cubic feet of space. Upon completing their construction assignment, Construction Mobile Battalion Unit 513 was ordered to the base to provide for its maintenance, repair, and transportation.

Once developed as a major ship repair, hospital and storage area, and receiving station, Oran served as a jumping-off place for the amphibious operations launched against Sicily, Italy, and Southern France. Joining were men trained in advanced amphibious bases at Bizerte, Tunis, and Ferryville, Tunisia, and at Mers-el-Kebir, Beni-Saf, and Tenes, Algeria. Rehearsals for the important operations were held at assembly areas at Cherchel, Bone, Nemours, and Mostaganem, Algeria, with detachments from the 54th, 70th, and 120th Seabees providing what little these towns lacked in the way of installations.

To the south of Oran, the Seabees' largest construction effort involved building a naval supply depot. For the purpose they erected eighty-one Quonset huts with electrical and sewage systems. With some tents, space was made available for 1,500 men. Nearby the 120th Seabees built a 500-bed hospital (U.S. Navy Base Hospital 9) out of 110 Quonset huts, all with electricity, water, and sewage systems and with covered concrete walks connecting them. Nearby, too, were seventy-five Quonset huts with complete utilities that served as the receiving station. For their own use the 120th Seabees built seventeen Quonset huts useful for such general purposes as mess halls and ship's stores; and at St. Remy, a small town about ten miles to the southwest of Oran, they built an ammunition depot consisting of twenty-nine magazines. At Oran, in addition, there were a Radio Material Division, Communcications Division, Net Detail, and Joint Army/Navy Intelligence Collecting Agency.

As the fighting moved eastward and then into Europe, the Naval Inspector General recommended making substantial reductions in all personnel and facilities except at the supply depot, reducing the Seabees, turning the naval base hospital over to the French, ending the use of Oran as a transfer point for naval personnel, and turning over all port and base functions except supply to the French. The Commander in Chief U.S. Fleet (COMINCH) decided to offer the hospital to the U.S. Army or to the French military forces; it also directed the Commander of the Naval Operating Base to turn Oran and Mers-el-Kebir over to the French as expeditiously as possible, to close the harbor defense facilities as of 14 May 1945, to cease training for Atlantic convoy escorts as of 1 June, and to turn over convoy routing duties to the Freench on or about 8 June. Following the departure of the last landing craft for the United States, the NOB would be reduced to a Naval Detachment that would serve until the supply depot was removed and the naval hospital was disposed of.

After VE-Day, 9 May 1945, the United States turned the port of Oran back to the French. The receiving station was decommissioned on 26 June 1945, the naval station on 26 July, the naval operating base on 29 July, the naval magazine on 7 September, and the naval supply depot, Base Hospital 9, and the medical storehouse by 30 September, leaving a naval detachment to assume custody of all supplies and materials. Vehicles were transferred to the U.S. Army, all surplus was sold to the French Provisional Government on 6 October, and the Army handled the real estate problem via reverse Lend-Lease.

BIBLIOGRAPHY

A. United States Naval Administrative Histories of World War II Commander, U.S. Naval Forces, Northwest African Waters, ''Naval Forces, Northwest African Waters and the Eighth Fleet,'' 5 vols. (Washington: Naval Historical Center, Operational Archives Branch, 1945); U.S. Navy, Bureau of Yards and Docks, *Building the Navy's Bases in World War II*, 2 vols. (Washington: GPO, 1947), II:75-85; ''Command File, World War II'' (Washington: Naval Historical Center, Operational Archives Branch).

B. Waldo G. Bowman and others, *Bulldozers Came First: The Story of United States War Construction in Foreign Lands* (New York: McGraw-Hill, 1944); William B. Huie, *Can Do: The Story of the Seabees* (New York: Dutton, 1945); Samuel E. Morison, *The Battle of the Atlantic September 1939-May 1943* (Boston: Little, Brown, 1947); Worrall Reed Carter and Elmer Ellsworth Duvall, *Ships, Salvage, and Sinews of War* (Washington: GPO, 1954); Samuel E. Morison, *The Atlantic Battle Won, May 1943-May 1945* (Boston: Little, Brown, 1956); S.W.C. Pack, *The Battle for North Africa 1942* (New York: Mason/Charter, 1976).

U.S. Naval Advance Section and Advance Amphibious Training Bases, 1942-1945

After Gen. Dwight D. Eisenhower and his staff in London developed plans for the attack by combined British and American forces on the Axis troops in North Africa, the plans were sent to the U.S. amphibious forces assembled in American waters. These would mount, transport, and maintain U.S. assault troops; defend the localities chosen as advance bases; and control selected harbors in French Morocco, Algeria, and Tunisia. After seizing ports in French Morocco and Algeria, on 11 November 1942 Adm. H. Kent Hewitt, USN, Commander Naval Forces North Africa Waters, had naval operating bases established at Casablanca, French Morocco, and Oran, Algeria. Meanwhile Rear Adm. Richard L. Conolly, Commander Landing Craft North African Waters, began to establish Advance Amphibious Training Bases (AATBs). In just 113 days Hewitt had organized his forces and assembled 1,700 ships and 250 craft to carry 136,000 troops, 30,000 vehicles, and 20,000 tons of ammunition.

South of Casablanca, Hewitt had three section bases established, as one proceeds southward, at Fedala, Safi, and Dakar. *Fedala*, located at 33°43′N., 7°25′W., was captured on 8 November 1942. The small section base established there only fifteen and a half miles east-north-east of Casablanca was valuable for only a short time as a debarkation port for men and supplies. American personnel included only 25 officers and 155 men, and it was disestablished on 11 September 1943.

Safi, located at 32°18′N., 9°13′W., was also occupied on 8 November 1942 and served for a year as a naval section base. It had a Harbor Entrance Control Post and radio station and depended upon the U.S. Army for defense. In June 1943 American naval personnel included 28 officers and 227 men, but these were reduced to 11 officers and 73 men in September 1943, and the facilities were disestablished in November 1943.

Dakar, located at 14°14′N., 14°5′W., at the westernmost tip of the western African bulge, was already in use as a French naval air base. In June 1943 the Naval Air Transport Service (NATS) began using it as a staging point, and in September a Naval Air Facility was established there. A year later, a radio station was added, while the French used Dakar as a naval base and in addition had an airfield and seaplane base at Geree Bay. Operations remained unchanged until September 1945, when the American facilities were placed in caretaker status; on 8 June 1946 they were disestablished.

While Oran was the major supply point for Army operations in Tunisia, two small naval stations were established nearby, one at Mers-El-Kebir, four miles to the west, and one at Arzew, thirty-five miles to the east at 35°51′N., 0°13′W. The workload at these places increased sharply when word came in December 1942 to establish amphibious forces in the Mediterranean for use in invading Sicily. Arzew, where a Landing Craft Group was established on 15 January 1943, became a landing craft maintenance and operating base, had a Material Recovery Unit and U.S. Army Base Defense Force, and was a French air base. In February 1943 there were 103 American naval officers and 1,204 men there. After October 1944, however, Arzew was placed in reduced status when much of its equipment was sent to Salerno, Italy (q.v.). The 20 officers and 202 men there at the time remained until June 1945, when all facilities were disestablished.

Advance Amphibious Training Bases, 1942-1945

On 25 December 1942 officers of the Base Maintenance Division of the Office of the Chief of Naval Operations had made a 175-page report on a nineteen-day observation trip of base sites in North Africa. On the basis of this report, AATBs were established, from west to east, at Nemours, Beni-Saf, Mers-El-Kebir, Arzew, Mostaganem, Tenes, Cherchel, Dellys, Ferryville, Bizerte, and La Goulette (Tunis).

Established on 23 March 1943, *Nemours*, Algeria, at 3[illegible]1′N., 1°48′W., was at its peak in June, but it was comprised of only 20 officers and 214 men. It was disestablished on 15 August 1943.

Beni-Saf, Algeria, located at 35°21′N., 1°21′W., was established on 23 March

1943. Even with a naval diesel oil tank farm on the site, at the peak of its operations there were only 33 officers and 300 men there. With the number reduced to 23 officers and 216 men in September 1943, it was disestablished on 1 October 1943.

Americans occupied *Mers-El-Kebir*, Algeria, located at 35°44′N., 0°42′E., on 26 April 1943; it originally served as the assembly point for the battleship striking forces in the Mediterranean Fleet. In June it began to serve as a naval air station, AATB, and diesel oil farm. In September it became a British naval base. By February 1944 the U.S. Navy had established a radio station there and the French a net depot. A bit over a year later, in March 1945, only 13 American naval officers and 181 men remained, and the American facilities were disestablished on 11 June 1945.

Bizerte, Tunisia, located at 37°15′N., 9°49′E., was established on 12 May 1943. In June a mobile repair unit came on board, and in September an AATB was created, along with such other facilities as a Spare Parts Distribution Center, Material Recovery Unit, and British naval base. American personnel originally numbered 173 officers and 2,973 men. The AATB lasted until February 1944, when the staff headquarters of Commander Landing Craft North African Waters came aboard, as did an ammunition dump, MTB Squadron 15, PT Base No. 12, radio material office, and NATS, with personnel increasing to 278 officers and 2,674 men. The AATB was replaced by an Advance Training Base in October 1944, when American personnel had been reduced somewhat, to 157 officers and 2,620 men. Decommissioning occurred on 15 May 1945 even though there were still 80 officers and 847 men on board.

Tunis, Tunisia, is located at 36°51′N., 10°15′E. An AATB was established in the La Goulette area of the harbor on 22 May 1943, as were a naval auxiliary air facility and NATS seaplane base. Meanwhile it had served as headquarters for Commander Landing Craft North West Africa (ComLandCrabNAW), an Army Air Facility, and Military Air Transport Service (MATS) stopped at the naval auxiliary air facility. Personnel numbering 48 officers and 313 men were reduced in September 1943 to 26 officers and 169 men in February 1944, and the facilities were disestablished on 20 March 1944 following the end of the Sicilian and Italian campaigns.

Among the numerous facilities of the U.S. Navy at *Oran*, Algeria, was an AATB established in June 1943. Although it was disestablished soon after the invasion of Sicily, the American facilities there were not decommissioned until 22 December 1945.

An AATB and Naval Air Facility were established at *Arzew*, Algeria, on 24 March 1943 and served until October 1944, when the naval facilities there were reduced to a naval station and placed under the command of the NOB at Oran.

On 23 March 1943 American naval personnel entered *Mostaganem*, Algeria, which lies at 35°56′N., 0°5′E., and used it in part as an AATB until September 1943, in part as a diesel oil tank farm. At its peak its personnel numbered only

27 officers and 248 men. These were reduced to 19 officers and 204 men in September, and the facilities were disestablished on 19 December 1943.

Algiers, Algeria, (36°41′N., 3°4′E.) was captured by the Eastern Naval Task Force, Rear Adm. Harold M. Burrough, RN, commanding. The mission of this force was to occupy the port of Algiers and adjacent airfields, establish necessary communications, build up a striking force, and occupy Tunisia at the earliest possible date. Algiers was not only a British naval base but headquarters Allied Forces. Naval planning for the invasion of Sicily prior to that of Italy and then of Southern France began at Algiers, where Admiral Hewitt established the headquarters of his Northwest Africa Naval Forces. On 23 March 1943, meanwhile, an AATB had been established with 65 officers and 500 men. By September, after the Husky (Sicily) operation, the number of personnel was reduced to 39 officers and 354 men, and the base was disestablished on 1 October 1943, with Admiral Hewitt and the remainder of Supreme Headquarters moving on 8 July 1944 to Naples (q.v.). American naval personnel numbered 200 officers and men in September 1943. After an Allied Fuel Depot and a Salvage Force were added in February 1944, their numbers increased to 233 officers and 598 men. However, the movement of the fighting front elsewhere reduced the number of men to 68 officers and 264 men in October 1944, and to a mere 7 officers and 28 men in March 1945. The base was disestablished on 27 July 1946.

Dellys, Algeria, located at 36°55′N., 3°55′E., was established as a naval section base in February 1944 with TF84, later TG89.6, on board. There were never more than 63 American officers and 492 men there, and the facility was disestablished in January 1945.

At *Tenes*, Algeria, located at 36°31′N., 0°19′E., an Amphibious Training Base was established on 3 March 1943, as was a diesel oil tank farm with 65 officers and 568 men on board. Personnel were reduced to 38 officers and 384 men in September 1943, and the facilities were disestablished on 1 October 1943.

The AATB at *Cherchel*, Algeria, located at 36°37′N., 2°11′E., was established in June 1943. There soon followed MTB Base 12 and engine and overhaul facilities to support eighteen PT boats. Involved were 27 officers and 246 men. The facilities served until they were disestablished on 15 August 1943.

Ferryville, Tunisia, is located at 37°9′N., 9°48′E. In addition to having an AATB established there in February 1944, it was also a loading and repair center for LCT (5) flotillas 9, 10, and 11 and in addition was a British naval base and a French naval base and naval dockyard. The U.S. Navy turned over its holdings there to the French in May 1944.

The mission assigned the AATBs was that they would be used "for the assignment of personnel, landing craft, equipment and supplies, and the establishment of training and maintenance facilities." Those hurriedly created between March and May 1943 west of Algiers to prepare for Husky were never considered to be anything but temporary, and as soon as Tunis fell and the large base at Bizerte was developed they were progressively abandoned.

The southernmost of the five naval installations the United States built in French Morocco was at *Agadir* (30°30′N., 9°34′W.). An advanced aircraft base, it was used by Fleet Air Wing Fifteen, which engaged in ASW patrol off lower French Morocco and the Canary Islands. Construction there, begun in April 1943, included the efforts of both U.S. Seabees and the French Public Works Department at a cost of $600,000, which was paid through reciprocal aid. Operations and billeting facilities were in tents until June 1943. In September there were 71 American officers and 187 men on board. With the completion of the 5,200-foot runway and the belief that the installation would become permanent, native stone and wood were used to build permanent barracks and messing facilities, storerooms, administration offices, classrooms, and a control tower. Naval control of the installation was maintained until May 1945, when U.S. personnel were relieved by French personnel. There were 91 American officers and 348 men there in October 1943, and 164 officers and 620 men in February 1944. In July 1945 the base was turned over to the U.S. Army Transport Command.

Meanwhile, by the time Admiral Conolly appeared in Bizerte, varying numbers of LSTs, LCIs, LCTs, minelayers and minesweepers, patrol craft, submarine chasers, and tugs had arrived in areas recently cleared of Axis forces but utterly devastated by Allied bombing and Axis sabotage. With various vessels altered to serve as headquarters ships for task force commanders and commanders of regimental combat teams embarked in LCI(Ls), much use was made in the advance bases of floating pontoon dry docks to repair landing craft damaged during training operations. Meanwhile a continuous flow of supplies came from the supply depot at Oran, and seventy-two old torpedoes were overhauled, repaired, tested, and issued to PT boats. Although the ammunition ship *Mount Baker* was the principal floating source of naval ammunition, reserves of certain types of charges, projectiles, fuses, and component parts for depth charges and antisubmarine projectors were stocked at Bizerte as well as at Oran. French provisions obtained from the U.S. Army and clothing and small stores were stocked at Oran, Bizerte, and La Goulette. While the smaller landing craft were used to transport wounded men from beaches, LSTs served as hospital evacuation ships that transferred their cases to one of the fifteen hospital ships in the Mediterranean.

By early October 1943, following the invasion of Sicily, the major bases on the Atlantic coast of French Morocco were either placed in maintenance status or decommissioned, except for the U.S. Naval Air Station at Port Lyautey. The naval base at Oran remained in full operation, and Arzew, formerly headquarters for the AATBs, shifted to handling cargo ships, repairing boats, and shipping amphibious materials to the amphibious training bases in forward areas. Mostaganem similarly ceased engaging in amphibious operations and training and was used mostly for the handling of cargo ships by the Army. AATBs at Tenes and Cherchel were closed, but Bizerte assumed new importance. Despite the severe pounding it had received from both friend and foe, it loaded and reloaded amphibious craft of all types, operated the French submarine base and seaplane base and a receiving ship for amphibious men, contained extensive ship repair shops and facilities, and was the staging point for survivors of active fronts. Much use was made there of advanced base type equipment, such as two 250-ton pontoon dry docks, one 350-ton pontoon dry dock, and one 100-ton pontoon dry dock. Found invaluable were several pontoon-type floating cranes and pontoon barges. Fully operational was the pontoon assembly plant that assembled all kinds of structures but particularly pontoon causeways. Some of the work was undertaken by the Fifty-fourth Seabees, part of the Seventieth Seabees, and Special Seabee Detachments Nos. 1005, and 1106.

The AATB at Tunis specialized in the maintenance and repair of small craft but also repaired commercial ships and small boat engines. Much use was made of its small graving dock, approximately 182 feet in length, with a floating-type caisson, which had been repaired.

Following the fall of Sicily, which can be dated from the capture of Messina on 3 August 1943, only three weeks remained for training in amphibious warfare and for the repair of ships and craft that would take part in the projected landings on Italy itself, one by British forces from Messina onto the toe of the Italian boot, the other by American and British troops at Salerno, just south of Naples. Logistic support for these operations came in part from bases in Sicily and Malta, in greater part from Algiers, Bone, Bizerte, Tripoli, Tunis, Sousse, and Sfax. Water was carried from Bizerte to Salerno by thirteen U.S. LSTs and by a British ship. While food was provided by the U.S. Army, clothing stocks were available at Bizerte and Oran. At various North African ports a number of 250-ton and 350-ton pontoon dry docks were available for small craft, and repair ships were stationed at Bizerte, Algiers, and Ferryville, with repair facilities for small craft at Arzew, Bizerte, and Tunis. Harbor salvage work would be undertaken in cooperation with the Army. Ammunition stocks were located at Bizerte and Oran, with minor reserves in Arzew, Tenes, and Tunis. All landing craft stocked up with food, fuel, ammunition, water, and medical supplies prior to leaving port.

Although two convoys sailed to Italy from Sicily, the bulk of the more than 600 American and British warships destined to attack Salerno on 9 September 1943 came from Oran, Algiers, Bizerte, and Tripoli. As the result of German action (Italy had surrendered conditionally on 8 September), ten Allied warships, three merchant ships, about fifteen amphibious craft, and one hospital ship were damaged or sunk and thirty-six Allied warships, eight merchantmen, two hospital ships, and about twenty-five landing craft were damaged. By 1 October, however, Naples was in Allied hands and ship repairs were undertaken there rather than at African ports. The total number of personnel involved in the Salerno operation approximated 100,000. These were fed in part from U.S. Army dry stores and some fresh provisions but also from provision storeships despatched from the United States.

In sum, with the Allies ensconced at Palermo (q.v.) and Naples and the military front destined to move northward in Italy, the AATBs in North Africa were relegated to maintenance status or closed between 15 August and 1 October 1943.

BIBLIOGRAPHY

A. United States Naval Administrative Histories of World War II. ''Commander U.S. Naval Forces Northwest African Waters and the Eighth Fleet,'' 5 vols. (Washington: Naval Historical Center, Operational Archives Branch, 1945); U.S. Navy, Bureau of Yards and Docks, *Building the Navy's Bases in World War II*, 2 vols. (Washington: GPO, 1947), II:75-89; ''Monograph Histories of U.S. Naval Overseas Bases. Vol. 1. Atlantic Area,'' 1953 (Washington: Naval Historical Center, Operational Archives Branch); ''U.S. Naval Activities Disestablished since July 1949,'' 27 Sept. 1954 (Washington: Naval Historical Center, Operational Archives Branch).

B. Worrall Reed Carter and Elmer Ellsworth Duvall, USN (Ret.), *Ships, Salvage, and Sinews of War* (Washington GPO, 1954), pp. 157-323; Susan H. Godson, *Viking of Assault: Admiral John Lesslie Hall, Jr., and Amphibious Warfare* (Washington: University Press of America, 1982), pp. 57-106.

Port Lyautey, French Morocco, U.S. Naval Air Station, 1942-1978

In their strategic concept of a North African operation named ''Torch,'' the Combined Chiefs of Staff demanded

establishment of firm and mutually supported lodgments (a) between Oran and Tunisia on the Mediterranean and (b) in French Morocco on the Atlantic, in order to secure bases for continued and intensified air, ground, and sea operations, and (2) vigorous and rapid exploitation of these lodgments in order to acquire complete control of French Morocco, Algeria, and Tunisia, and extend offensive operations against the rear of Axis forces to the eastward.

The U.S. Navy found planning advance bases in Africa especially frustrating because of the great distance involved, limited shipping space, uncertainty as to how long any bases would be kept and the extent of their development, and the U-boat peril. Moreover, unless political arrangements were made with Vichy France, both the American Army and Navy were given only a 50 percent chance of success.

The Chief of Naval Operations was responsible for providing the supplies for establishing beachheads or bases. However, except for food, which would be provided by the Army, once beachheads and bases had been established, responsibility passed to the Navy's Service Force.

On D-Day, 8 November, American and British forces launched the greatest amphibious invasion in history up to that time. Simultaneously, 850 ships divided to strike at Casablanca, Oran, and Algiers. Prior to the assaults, the Navy was responsible for safely transporting the Army and its supplies and fueling and defending the ships involved. Following the assaults, it had to establish bases from which naval ships could obtain ammunition, fuel, and supplies, repair operational and ship damage, and support future operations that sought the ultimate objective—Europe. Among the most important northwest African ports was that at Mehedia, French Morocco, sixty-five miles north of Casablanca, because it led along the sinuous Wadi Sebou River to the airfield at Port Lyautey, formerly Kenitra, nine miles up the river, the only airfield in Morocco having all-weather concrete runways. A fortunate characteristic of the river is that it has two very straight stretches of water well suited for seaplane operations. In addition, the French had established a seaplane landing site in Morocco, in 1919. In 1932 they also prepared a grass landing field adjacent to it which was turned over to their navy in 1936. Port Lyautey was also a key position on the roads and railroads from Casablanca through Fez to Algeria. It was chosen over the capital, Rabat, which had only political importance. Moreover, Rabat was a holy city, and an attack upon it might trigger a native uprising.

While other American and British forces assaulted Casablanca, Oran, and Algiers, early on 8 November 1942 about 9,000 men of the Ninth Division under Brig. Gen. L. K. Truscott, Jr., supported by naval gunfire, were landed; they broke through to the airfield by 10 November. Army planes catapulted from carriers soon began operating from it. By capturing Port Lyautey they also secured control of the railroad that connected with the areas in which the Northern and Southern attack forces would land. Meanwhile various French and Dutch ships and American landing craft were repaired in the Sebou River, a merchant ship offloaded bombs and aviation gasoline, and an escort carrier flew off forty-five P-40s to Lyautey. Comdr. J.A. Briggs, USN, was made responsible for establishing a naval air station there. At 0800 on 13 November, Patrol Squadron 73 (PBY-A) arrived from Lyneham, England, and began operations. With the occupation of the Port Lyautey airfield and its use by American planes, and the establishment of a naval air station on 28 December, the principal purpose of the landings at Mehedia had been fulfilled.

By October 1943 new construction at Port Lyautey undertaken first by the Army and then by the Navy had been completed with the exception of additional barracks for aviation personnel. American personnel and some local labor had extended and widened the runways, built extra housing, improved the water system, and facilitated the use of seaplanes by means of pontoon units. Among the activities provided were a Naval Communications Facility, Marine Barracks, Fleet Weather Central, Fleet Intelligence Center, Fleet Tactical Support Squadron 24, Naval Mobile Construction Battalion, Air Navigation Office, and Overseas Air Cargo Terminal. By June 1944 there were also an Advanced Amphibious Training Base (established 23 March 1943), Refueling Depot, Naval Air Transportation Service Unit, Headquarters Fairwing-15 (to which two Army B-24 squadrons were attached on 9 March 1943 and which merged with the NAS on 8 June 1943), and Hedron Unit. The U.S. Army had its own air base and defense forces, while the French operated an ammunition depot. At their peak, American naval personnel reached 4,191. The increase in fuel storage by that time may be measured by the fact that there was now available storage for 2,787,000 gallons of aviation gasoline, 1,201,000 gallons of mogas, and 95,000 gallons of diesel fuel, and warehousing had been extended to 188,000 square feet. On 12 January 1944, after the Army's B-24 squadron departed, by order of the CNO FAW-15 became NAS Port Lyautey.

With the war in Europe almost over, in April 1945 American naval personnel at Port Lyautey were reduced to 195 officers and 876 men. Between May and November the Army Air Transport Command used the station as a staging point to return troops to the United States. Finally on 1 January 1948, the station was returned to the French government with reservations as to use, only to be re-designated Naval Air Activities, Port Lyautey, with VRU-4 Detachment, Aerological Activity, Naval Communication Station, 100-bed dispensary, completed fuel pier, and Marine Corps security detachment. On 1 July the Naval Air Activities was disestablished, whereupon it became a Naval Air Facility. Located on the same field as the Army's Craw Field, two miles from the city, the facility included a Naval Communications Facility, Naval Ordnance Facility, and Marine Detachment. Personnel on board as of the end of February 1951 numbered 2,269. With base housing in short supply, personnel sought quarters either in the city of Lyautey or at Mehedia, five miles away at the mouth of the Sebou River. The primary mission of the facility was to conduct ASW patrol and search, with Patrol Squadron 73 operating out of Port Lyautey and Patrol Squadron 92 out of Casablanca.

The greatest limiting factor at the port of Lyautey was the size of the ships that could be accommodated. However, there were a 2,800-foot quay with an 18-foot water depth, six 3-ton locomotive cranes, and five 2.5-ton locomotive cranes. As for the airfields, these had been extended from 3,200 feet of concrete to at least 5,000 feet in a NNE-SSE and approximately E-W direction. For support there were tank storage for about 30,000 barrels of oil, ten warehouses, three sheds each 135 feet square, and adequate water and electrical power. Good road and railroad communications were available to reach all parts of northwest Africa.

Soon after the dropping of atomic bombs on Japan, the Navy began to wonder if the almost five-ton bomb could be fitted to an aircraft capable of operating from a carrier. Among these who believed that it could were the aviator, Comdr. John T. Hayward, and Rear Adm. Daniel V. Gallery, in charge of the Navy's guided missiles. In 1948 and 1949 two modified long-range P2V *Neptunes* were flown off carriers. On 1 September 1949 the even heavier AJ-1 *Savage* was received, and on the ninth the Navy formally commissioned Hayward's experimental development group as Composite Squadron Five (VC-5) at NAS Moffett Field, Calif., with VC-6 joining on 6 January 1950. On 9 December 1950, six *Savages* and three *Neptunes* proceeded to Port Lyautey, whence they periodically went aboard the carriers *Midway*, *Franklin D. Roosevelt*, and *Coral Sea* in the Mediterranean for exercises and cruises. In the event of war, the planes could either be loaded aboard the carriers by dockside cranes or fly missions from Port Lyautey or other Mediterranean land bases. Additional *Savages* and *Neptunes* reached Port Lyautey on 14 October 1951.

After 1 July 1951 NAS Port Lyautey served the Commander in Chief of NATO forces in the Mediterranean with a carrier-based (rotational) squadron, transport squadron, Military Air Transport Service Detachment, Fleet Air Service Squadron, aircraft pool, and an LP Patrol Squadron on a rotational basis. Personnel involved at that date included 2,169 Navy, 75 Marine Corps, 554 civilians, and 440 contract workers, with 657 dependents on board.

In January 1952 a NAS Communication Center began transmitting general fleet broadcasts, and the major runway was extended to 500 feet in width and 8,000 feet in length. In 1953 a diesel-powered plant of six 550 kw generators and a hangar were completed. For the personnel, in 1954 there were elementary and high schools for dependents and a permanent thirty-five-bed dispensary. Although high temperatures were the norm, low humidity made them bearable, and recreation facilities abounded after the station acquired a "new look."

With 3,500 acres, Port Lyautey was the largest shore installation the U.S. Navy had in the European and Mediterranean area. As its importance in the Western European defense picture increased, so its physical character was changed. In 1947 personnel quarters consisted of twenty-man temporary Quonsets and tents, with few Quonsets for families. Flight operations were controlled from an elongated Quonset at the end of the one usable airstrip, and only one hangar was under construction. Primary recreation areas were the officers' club and enlisted men's clubs in leased quarters in the city of Lyautey. The mostly unpaved streets were dusty in summer and muddy during the winter rains, and sidewalks were almost unknown. Things began to change in 1951, when a vigorous building program was undertaken. Two-, three, and four-family units edged with gardens and separated by lawns replaced the Quonset huts. Nine new cubicle-type barracks were provided for single personnel and a new junior officers' quarters could serve 300 officers. As many as a thousand men could eat in the new mess hall and galley. Since French Morocco was considered an isolated area, the station was made as nearly self-sufficient as possible. A shopping center built near the new housing units could serve 10,000 people, among them Air Force personnel in the area and State Department people from Rabat and Sidi Smaine. In addition to the new hospital and school, there was a new chapel. To bolster morale, which suffered from many offbase restrictions, a new recreation building, enlisted men's club, 50-meter swimming pool, and skating rink with night lighting were provided. The golf course was open to all, and plants and shrubs were planted along the now paved streets and sidewalks.

As directed by higher authority, the mission of Port Lyautey was to provide facilities to support regular operations of fleet reconnaissance and ASW attack aircraft and transport aircraft and their supporting FASRONS; support temporary occasional basing of carrier air groups; serve as a secondary aeronautical supply point and support all shorebased naval and Marine Corps aircraft in the Commander in Chief North Atlantic and Eastern Mediterranean (CINCNELM) area, and provide emergency support for the Sixth Fleet; operate a class "Special" photographic laboratory and camera repair facility in support of the naval forces in the CINCNELM area; and provide facilities to support the Naval Communications Facility (Supply) and the Naval Ordnance Facility. Given its base loading and construction, NAS Port Lyautey reached its apogee in 1957. In 1958, however, naval activity was greatly reduced because of the movement of several units to Rota, Spain (q.v.). Nevertheless, the station played its part during the Lebanon crisis of 1958.

Some of the construction and maintenance work at Port Lyautey, under Seabee supervision until 1958, was undertaken by Arab (mostly Moslem) laborers, and relations with them as well as with the French remained cordial after the landings in 1942. Morocco gained its independence from France in 1955; to counter communist and Third World criticism, command at Port Lyautey, was shifted to Morocco in 1965. In 1976, however, Washington decided to disestablish the base, which cost $7 million a year to operate, and to replace it with satellite facilities. In December 1976 the radio receiver station at Sidi Yahi was turned over to Moroccans, whereupon the unguarded facility was promptly looted. On 30 September 1978 naval Capt. William Parris handed over to Morocco all that remained of the multi-million dollar installations.

BIBLIOGRAPHY

A. ''Command History of Port Lyautey, 1942-1945'' (Washington: Naval Historical Center, Operational Archives Branch); United States Naval Administrative Histories of World War II. Commander U.S. Naval Forces, Northwest African Waters, ''Naval Forces, Northwest African Waters and the Eighth Fleet,'' 5 vols. (Washington: Naval Historical Center Operational Archives Branch, 1945); ''Brief History of Port Lyautey'' (Washington: Naval Historical Center, Operational Archives Branch); ''NAS Lyautey, Kenitra, Morocco'' (Washington: Naval Historical Center, Operational Archives Branch).

B. ''What Gives at NAVACTS Port Lyautey,'' *Naval Aviation News*, July 1953, p. 29; ''Port Lyautey Has New Look,'' *Naval Aviation News*, Jan. 1956, pp. 16-19; Commander, U.S. Naval Activities, Port Lyautey, Kenitra, Morocco, *Welcome to Morocco: The Sun-drenched Land of Mosques and Veils*, 27 March 1963 and *People to People Report* (Washington: Naval Historical Center, Operational Archives Branch); ''Moroccans Have Kenitra,'' *Naval Aviation News*, Feb. 1964, p. 2; ''U.S. Turns Over Last Base in Africa,'' *Washington Post*, 1 Oct. 1978; Chuck Hansen, ''Nuclear Neptunes: Early Days of Composite Squadrons 5 and 6,'' *American Aviation History Society Journal* 24 (Winter 1979):262-68; Paolo E. Coletta, *The U.S. Navy and Defense Unification, 1947-1953* (Newark, Del.: University of Delaware Press, 1981).

NOUMEA, NEW CALEDONIA, U.S. NAVAL OPERATING BASE, 1942–1947 [WHITE POPPY] Capital of the French colony of New Caledonia, Noumea in 1942 grew haphazardly into one of the most important naval bases in the South Pacific. Confronting the eastern waters of the Coral Sea, New Caledonia is a large island almost 250 miles long situated roughly 900 miles east of Australia and 1,000 miles north of New Zealand, admirably located to protect (or menace) vital lines of communication to either place. Noumea (at 22°16′S., 166°27′E.), on the southwest coast, was the only serviceable port.

With a population of 11,000 (in 1936), Noumea offered an excellent spacious anchorage but relatively few port facilities.

In prewar discussions between Britain and the United States, New Caledonia fell into the British sphere of defense. Its role was envisioned as a stopping point on the Army Air Corps' air ferry route to Australia, but no construction had begun before December 1941. With the outbreak of war, Free French authorities at Noumea greatly feared a Japanese invasion and eagerly requested Allied troops to defend New Caledonia. In January 1942, during the ARCADIA conference in Washington, D.C., the United States recognized the value of New Caledonia as an air base and as a source of nickel. Despatched to garrison the island was Task Force 6814, Army troops under Maj. Gen. Alexander M. Patch. On 7 March Patch opened negotiations at Noumea with French Admiral Georges d'Argenlieu, New Caledonia high commissioner, for use of New Caledonia. Patch's troops arrived on 12 March, covered by Australia-New Zealand (ANZAC) naval forces including carrier Task Force 11 with the *Lexington*. The Army discovered one airfield already built at Tontouta (thirty miles north of Noumea) and another under construction at Plaine des Gaics, 150 miles northwest of Noumea.

In March and April 1942, Rear Adm. Frank Jack Fletcher's Task Force 17 including the carrier *Yorktown* operated in the Coral Sea west of Noumea. Fletcher hoped to base at Noumea, but Adm. Ernest J. King, Commander in Chief, U.S. Fleet, felt that the port was too exposed to Japanese attack. That spring, Noumea was not considered, despite its favorable potential for development, as an advanced naval base. Plans for even a small fuel oil depot to be located there were cancelled. The Navy preferred Auckland, New Zealand (q.v.), as the site of its main naval base in the South Pacific. For now, Noumea's main role was as a seaplane base for the tender *Tangier*, whose patrol planes would search the Coral Sea and the lower Solomon Islands. In May Marine Fighting Squadron 212 operated briefly from Tontouta field before shifting north to Efate (q.v.) in the New Hebrides. In an inspection tour the next month by Rear Adm. Richard E. Byrd's South Pacific bases committee, there were no recommendations for the development of Noumea other than as a port to supply Army troops based on New Caledonia.

With the inception in July 1942 of Operation Watchtower (invasions of Guadalcanal and Tulagi in the Solomons), Noumea drew limited interest by becoming the advance headquarters of Vice Adm. Robert L. Ghormley, Commander of the South Pacific Area. On 1 August he arrived there from Auckland. The rapidly changing situation in the Solomons brought Noumea into prominence. On 7-8 August the First Marine Division (reinforced) landed at Guadalcanal and Tulagi, but the disaster of the Battle of Savo Island (9 August) compelled the transports to withdraw before they had completed unloading supplies. Rear Adm. Richmond Kelly Turner, Commander, Amphibious Forces, South Pacific, quickly resolved upon Noumea as the best place from which to supply the beleaguered Marines in the Solomons. On 20 August he established at Noumea a Marine advanced supply depot and rerouted many vessels there. However, Noumea, despite its large harbor, was largely unprepared for its new vital role. Lacking were sophisticated port facilities, unloading gear, storage warehouses, and trained men. Nevertheless, it would have to do.

In September 1942 Ghormley requested more support personnel to reduce the chaos at Noumea and on 17 October recommended the establishment there of a 20,000-man naval base. That was twice the size of a LION, the Navy's largest prepackaged advance base force. Four days later, the new Commander of the South Pacific Area, Vice Adm. William F. Halsey, seconded his predecessor's proposal, formally advising what was already becoming an accomplished fact—substitution of Noumea for Auckland as the South Pacific's main fleet base. On 8 November his headquarters completed its transfer to Noumea. Port congestion was intense as supply ships rushed materiel for transshipment to the forces in the Solomons. From late 1942 into early 1943, up to 100 ships at a time waited to unload their cargoes. The first naval construction battalion to arrive, the Twentieth, was pressed into service that fall as stevedores. In November 1942 another Seabee battalion began building an advance base construction depot, and a third improved pier and wharf facilities. By February 1943 the worst was over with respect to berthing capacity.

In early 1943 Seabees began constructing massive facilities for the naval operating base and naval supply depot. On nearby Ducos Peninsula they erected a 370,000-barrel fuel oil tank farm. Ile Nou in Noumea was an excellent location for a number of specialist installations, including a large ship repair unit (including several floating dry docks), aircraft engine overhaul base, aviation gasoline tank farm, amphibious boat pool, seaplane ramp, and many other logistic and repair facilities. East of Noumea, a naval air station was set up at Magenta Bay. In conjunction with Espiritu Santo (q.v.) in the New Hebrides, Noumea became the main focus of supplies bound for the South Pacific. At Noumea's huge naval supply depot cargoes were stored, then repacked for shipment to forward areas. Thus Noumea supplied most of the materiel for the South Pacific's amphibious campaigns, while Espiritu Santo was primarily a fleet base. Noumea base facilities also serviced, fueled, and repaired the ships that handled this massive supply effort. New Caledonia also became important for the Marine Corps both as a supply depot and as a staging area. In March 1943 headquarters I Marine Amphibious Corps moved to Noumea, and that year Marine Air Group 25 units operated Tontouta field.

Roll-up of installations at Noumea was very gradual, so as not to disrupt the important work under way there. At first only those facilities that could not function properly in a remote rear area—the pontoon assembly detachment, aircraft engine overhaul base, and part of the advance base construction depot—were dismantled and moved forward. Marine aviation also shifted north in 1944. Thus Noumea operated at nearly full capacity throughout 1944. In November of that year, more dismantling began. Noumea played its last important part in helping to stage the forces invading Okinawa in April 1945. Thereafter the roll-up proceeded in force. By June 1945, when the Seabee maintenance units left, dismantling neared completion, but the base functioned until after the final roll-ups of other bases in the South Pacific. Noumea Naval Operating Base was disestablished on 27 May 1947.

BIBLIOGRAPHY

A. Service Squadron, South Pacific, "History of Commander, Service Squadron, South Pacific 7 December 1941-15 August 1945" (Washington: Naval Historical Center, Operational Archives Branch); U.S. Navy, Bureau of Yards and Docks, *Building the Navy's Bases in World War II*, 2 vols. (Washington: GPO, 1947); South Pacific Area and Forces, "New Caledonia," Administrative Histories, Appendix 34 (10) (Washington: Naval Historical Center, Operational Archives Branch).

B. Samuel E. Morison, *Coral Sea, Midway, and Submarine Actions May 1942-August 1942* (Boston, Little, Brown, 1949); Samuel E. Morison, *The Struggle for Guadalcanal August 1942-February 1943* (Boston: Little, Brown, 1949); Rear Adm. Worrall Reed Carter, *Beans, Bullets, and Black Oil* (Washington: GPO, 1953); Vice Adm. George C. Dyer, *The Amphibians Came to Conquer*, 2 vols. (Washington: GPO, 1972).

JOHN B. LUNDSTROM

NUKUFETAU, ELLICE ISLANDS, U.S. NAVAL ADVANCE AIR BASE, 1943–1944 Located about sixty miles northeast of Funafuti, also a part of the British Ellice Islands, Nukufetau became useful in the summer and fall of 1943 as an airfield for attacks on the southern Gilbert Islands. Nukufetau is a small coral atoll at 8°0′S., 178°30′E., with a shallow lagoon accessible through a ship channel. U.S. Marines occupied the atoll on 25 August 1943; five days later elements of the Sixteenth Naval Construction Battalion arrived to build the airfields. First completed was a fighter strip on 9 October, and fighters from Marine Fighter Squadron 111 operated from there by the end of the month. The bomber field was finished by early November and became host for two squadrons of heavy bombers and one of Marine dive bombers. The long-range bombers begain air strikes on the Gilberts to help soften them up for the invasions planned later in November. After the capture of the Gilberts, Nukufetau-based bombers patrolled and raided bypassed Japanese bases in the Marshalls. By early 1944 the air units had shifted from Nukufetau to bases further north, leaving the airfield as an alternate air staging point and emergency field. Roll-up of facilities on Nukufetau began in May, and the base was disestablished in December 1944.

BIBLIOGRAPHY

A. U.S. Navy, Bureau of Yards and Docks, *Building the Navy's Bases in World War II*, 2 vols. (Washington: GPO, 1947); U.S. Navy, "U.S. Naval Bases in the South and Southwest Pacific (and Central Pacific Forward) in World War II," 1 November 1954 (Washington: Naval Historical Center, Operational Archives Branch).

B. Samuel E. Morison, *Aleutians, Gilberts, and Marshalls June 1942-April 1944* (Boston: Little, Brown, 1952); Robert Sherrod, *History of Marine Corps Aviation in World War II* (Washington: Combat Forces Press, 1952).

JOHN B. LUNDSTROM

O

OKINAWA, RYUKYU ISLANDS, JAPAN, U.S. MARINE CORPS CAMP SMEDLEY D. BUTLER, 1957– Camp Smedley D. Butler on the island of Okinawa is unique among military bases in that instead of being a *place* it is a *thing*. It actually is an administrative unit that serves the needs of the operational Marine Corps units, primarily the III Marine Amphibious Force, that are stationed in the Western Pacific. Thus its name is an organizational designation, not a geographical location.

The Marine Corps named this novel facility in honor of Maj. Gen. Smedley D.Butler, one of the most colorful and dynamic leaders in the Corps' history. He won two Congressional Medals of Honor, the only person so far to do so. He earned the first in 1914 during the Marines' landing at Vera Cruz, Mexico, the second the following year in Haiti. In both instances he was cited for courage and conspicuous leadership in battle.

The Marines formally created Camp Butler on 1 April 1957 by changing the designation of their base support company in Okinawa to Headquarters and Service Company, Camp Smedley D. Butler, U.S. Marine Corps, Tengan, Okinawa. That same year the final units of the Third Marine Division transferred to Okinawa from mainland Japan. That process had been under way since 1955 as the result of an agreement with the Japanese government to remove all American ground troops from that nation.

Initially, the Third Marine Division exercised direct control over its camps in Okinawa. Then, on 1 November 1956 responsibility for their upkeep devolved upon the Base Camp Company. The creation of Camp Butler finalized this new arrangement. It resembled an existing relationship between the Second Division and Camp Lejeune in the United States. Its purpose was to free the division to concentrate on readiness training while leaving base housekeeping to Camp Butler. For example, the tenant units on Okinawa are deployable; the Marine Corps Base Command is not. Thus, if the troops do depart in a hurry, they need not detail people to remain behind to take care of the camps and other facilities on the island.

One of the principal functions of Camp Butler has been to serve as the Marines' landlord on Okinawa. From its headquarters at Camp Foster in the center of the island it has been responsible for that facility and the six other Marine bases on Okinawa—Camps Courtney, Hansen, Kinser, McTureous, and Schwab, and Futenma Air Station. The Marines also have two large training areas in the northern and central parts of the island as well as the Camp Fuji/Nunazu training site in Japan. All told, Camp Butler oversees 73,000 acres. In that capacity it fulfills its mission of supporting the III Marine Amphibious Force as America's "Force-in-Readiness" in the Western Pacific.

BIBLIOGRAPHY

A. U.S. Congress, Senate, Committee on Veterans Affairs, *Medal of Honor Recipients, 1863-1978*, 96th Cong., 1st sess., 1979; Public Affairs Officer, Camp S. D. Butler, to the Department of History, U.S. Naval Academy, 26 Feb. 1982; Camp Butler, Posts and Station Files, (Washington: U.S. Marine Corps Historical Center).

B. MSgt Paul Sarokin, "Okinawa," *Leatherneck*, Apr. 1958, pp. 22-27, 82; LtCol Thomas M. Burton, "Okinawa in Review," *Marine Corps Gazette*, Sept. 1958, pp. 28-30; MSgt Clay Barrow, "Okinawa," *Leatherneck*, June 1961, pp. 16-23; SSgt Paul A. Berger, "Camp Butler," *Leatherneck*, June 1965, pp. 36-41; Herb Richardson, "Okinawa," *Leatherneck*, March 1978, pp. 18-29; Tom Bartlett, "Camp Butler," *Leatherneck*, Apr. 1982, pp. 22-27.

ROGER T. ZEIMET

OKINAWA, RYUKYU ISLANDS, JAPAN, U.S. NAVAL AIR BASES AND NAVAL OPERATING BASE, 1945- The U.S. Naval Operating Base, Okinawa, is located at 26°26′20″N., 127°41′E., on the main island of the Ryukyu group, which is also known as the Nansei Shoto, Southwestern Islands, and Loochoo (Liu Chiu) Islands. Okinawa forms a natural barrier to the East China Sea and the approaches to Korea as well as to Japan's southernmost main island of Kyushu. It is about sixty miles long and from three to sixteen miles wide at its broadest part. Its population in 1980 numbered about 850,000, concentrated mostly in the southern third of the island. Its most important towns in 1940 were Naha, a harbor on the east coast, and Shuri, about five miles from Naha.

American naval interest in Okinawa dates from the mid-nineteenth century. In 1852 Commo. Matthew Calbraith Perry used the island as a base during prolonged negotiations with the Japanese government. He was successful, and Japan accordingly opened some of her ports to western traders. Soon thereafter Okinawa fell under Japanese rule together with the entire Ryukyu chain. As a consequence, American interest in Okinawa dwindled until by the 1930s it had almost reached the vanishing point.

In 1944, as World War II neared its climax, American interest in Okinawa abruptly revived. Okinawa would be needed again for the same reasons as in 1852, as an advance base for operations against Japan. This mission of those who seized Okinawa would be

> to establish bases from which to attack the mainland of Japan and its sea approaches. To support future operations in the regions bordering on the East China Sea. To sever Japanese sea and air communications between the Empire and the mainland of Asia, Formosa, Malaya, and the Netherlands East Indies. To establish secure sea and air communications through the East China Sea to the coast of China and the Yangtze Valley. To maintain unremitting pressure against Japan.

To those ends preliminary training began in California to create the U.S. Naval Operating Base, Okinawa. If all went well, combat troops would invade Okinawa in the spring of 1945. Thousands of construction troops would follow to develop the base. They would also rebuild or create from scratch numerous airfields and a seaplane station. By October 1945, everyone hoped, Okinawa would be ready to become the England of the Pacific, America's advance outpost for the forthcoming invasion of Japan.

Okinawa was well suited for this role. In climate it was subtropical, being hot and wet in the summer but reasonably cool and pleasant during the fall, winter, and early spring. Its only major drawback was the frequency with which typhoons struck the island; during them the Okinawans would join their ancestors in the lyre-shaped tombs that dot the islands. Visiting ships would have to take shelter, preferably at anchorages on the western or lee-side, for typhoons always come from the southwest. Aircraft—if they could—would have to take off for a haven outside the reach of the whirling storms' hundred-knot or better winds.

Typhoons aside, however, Okinawa was a pleasant locale. Its beaches, particularly in the mountainous northern two-thirds of the island, were well situated for recreation and water sports. Several anchorages protected by fringing islands were adaptable for naval use, especially on the island's eastern shore. Major Japanese airfields already existed at Yomitan and Kadena. Others could be readily built to take runways up to 10,000 feet in length.

The invasion of Okinawa by U.S. forces began on 1 April 1945. Operation Iceberg, as the landing was called, was the largest amphibious assault of the Pacific War and featured four divisions touching down abreast, two Army and two Marine.

The attack went easily at first against minor opposition but within a week the campaign had bogged down. Lt. Gen. Mitsuru Ushijima, the Japanese commander, had created a defense zone that included the port and capital city of Naha and most of the important installations at the south end of the island. Days extended into weeks as a ferocious battle, supported by naval forces, raged by air and land. The site of the projected American naval base on Buckner Bay on the east side of the island could not be used until both Naha and Ushijima's defense zone had fallen.

To defend Okinawa from the air, the Japanese employed their kamikazes against naval and merchant shipping. Hundreds of naval personnel died from the impact of direct hits by suicide planes. The outlying Kerama Retto islands, offshore of Okinawa to the west and south, became a haven for scores of battered ships of all sizes, especially destroyers. The land campaign could not end until most of the Japanese had died after fighting with the utmost bravery. Dead, too, was Lt. Gen. Simon Bolivar Buckner, the American commander. A stone fragment flung out by one of the very last shells fired by an artillery piece of the Japanese Thirty-second Army had taken his life.

By 24 June 1945, the day the campaign was declared over except for mopping up, total American casualties on land and sea had run to 12,620 killed and approximately 37,000 wounded, the heaviest loss for a single campaign of the Pacific War. Japanese losses, including those of Okinawan levies, though not known exactly, stood at well over 100,000 killed in action. In summary, though fought superbly well by the Japanese and far too unimaginatively by the Americans, the final outcome could have only one ending.

Command at Okinawa devolved upon the U.S. Army. As the campaign neared its end, Okinawa already resembled a gigantic construction site. Maj. Gen. Fred C. Wallace had on the island when the fighting ended some 87,000 construction troops of all the services. Included was a large Navy contingent commanded by Commo. (later Rear Adm.) Fred D. Kirtland, with Rear Adm. John D. Price commanding the Naval Operating Base and Commo. W. M. Dillon in command of the naval air bases. Stationed at first in a landing craft, Kirtland ultimately moved to Baten Ko at the south end of Buckner Bay. Named for the deceased American commander, Buckner Bay was to be both a naval anchorage and a port of embarkation for amphibious units.

By August, the planners had decreed, Okinawa would boast no fewer than twenty-two airfields, with airstrips from 5,000 to 8,500 feet long, enough to accommodate the entire Eighth Air Force from England as redeployed and reequipped. Navy and Marine aircraft would share some of these airfields and occupy a seaplane station located at Chimu Wan on the eastern shore. In addition to flying from Yomitan and Kadena airfields, Marine F4U *Corsair* fighters already had begun moving onto fighter strips at Awase and Chimu and onto a major base called Plumb Field on Ie Shima Island (q.v.), nearby to the west. There the famed war correspondent Ernie Pyle had earlier lost his life. Six 10,000-foot bomber strips were nearly ready to land their first B-29 *Superfortress* and B-32 *Dominator* bombers.

The harbor facilities at Naha, Chimu Wan, Buckner Bay, and Nago Wan were under naval control, At Katchin Hanto, on the eastern coast directly across from Kadena airfield, facilities including several permanent piers were progressing rapidly. There were no fuel or water supplies as yet, and no ship repair facilities, salvage gear, or shops, but there were 20,000 feet of beaches that could support LSTs and LCTs. By late October it seemed all but certain that Okinawa would be ready to embark GIs and Marines bound for Kyushu. Operation Olympic, the seizure of the southernmost Japanese home island, was set to go on 1 November 1945. Tokyo would be taken in Operation Coronet the following spring. For both invasions Okinawa would serve as the main advance staging and air base. Ready for future operations were 179,000 Army, 42,390 Navy, and 64,134 Marine personnel, and storage had been provided for 1,344,000 gallons of aviation gasoline and 126,000 gallons of motor gasoline.

Perhaps fortunately, neither Olympic nor Coronet was fated to occur. On 6 August 1945 the B-29 named *Enola Gay* dropped the first atomic bomb on Japan. The Soviet Union entered the war two days later, a second A-bomb fell on Nagasaki on 9 August, and by 15 August Emperor Hirohito had ordered Japan's armed forces to surrender. As abruptly as it had begun, World War II was over. All of the elaborate installations being rushed to support Olympic and Coronet could be drastically cut back or cancelled outright.

It was well, however, that construction of the naval station at Baten Ko could begin at once to taper off. On 16-17 September and 9-10 October typhoons hit the island. The first was small as these storms go, with winds reaching seventy-five knots, but the second was a major blow. Nevertheless, both caused major damage, enough to demonstrate that many installations would have to be strengthened or relocated.

Many piers made of heavy timbers fell apart under the impact of pounding seas. A decision followed to shift some of the main base facilities from Baten Ko to White Beach, farther north. The antennas of the busy naval communication station also suffered. These had been transmitting 975,000 encoded letter groups weekly, making the radio station then, as now, one of the most vital installations on the island. It too was restored and strengthened. Tents had proved useless as personnnel shelters, blowing flat immediately. Only steel Quonset huts stood up, though many lost all or part of their roofs. A decision was subsequently made to strengthen all buildings to withstand wind velocities of up to 200 mph. The worst loss of all was in the form of eighty-nine officers and bluejackets lost aboard four motor minesweepers and a subchaser that had foundered.

What necessitated a continued American presence on Okinawa was North Korea. Construction plans had all but vanished in 1945 and 1946 in the rush to "send the boys home." But when North Korea invaded South Korea in 1950, the island suddenly assumed a new importance. It once more became a vital stepping-stone to East Asia as well as a secure communications center. B-29s again found Okinawa useful as an air base, flying numerous strikes at North Korea from Kadena airfield, now the vital air installation on the island.

Once more Okinawa became a beehive of construction activity, with focus on the "Commo Center," now located at the former airfield site at Awase, while White Beach became the main naval station. Naha continued as the chief civilian port. In 1951 Comdr. J. T. Workman took over as the first of more than twenty successors (to the present) as Commander, Fleet Activities, Okinawa, and of U.S. Naval Air Facility, Okinawa, headquartered at Kadena.

After the Korean War's end in 1953, the chief mission of Fleet Activities, Okinawa, became the support of the amphibious forces of the U.S. Seventh Fleet. If war came again, whether in Korea, in the Taiwan Straits, or in Southeast Asia, then Marines based in Okinawa could be expected to be called. Japan was too congested to make a good maneuvering area. White Beach would thus become an important staging point. It had already become necessary to regularize the American presence on the island.

In 1951, with the Korean War stalemated, the State Department had accordingly decided to sign a peace treaty with Japan. Article 3 of the treaty would replace what amounted to an American military occupation of Okinawa with an agreed legal status. Continued unrest both in Japan and on Okinawa, however, made impossible the acceptance of Okinawa as a permanent American-owned base. Leftist leaders, such as Kamejro Senaga of the Okinawa People's Party, continued to agitate for the eventual return of Okinawa. Secretary of State John Foster Dulles seemed to agree, also, for by American admission Japan retained "residual sovereignty" over the islands. Nevertheless, the Eisenhower and subsequent U.S. administrations rejected Okinawa's reversion to Japan while the communist threat continued in the Far East.

In the latter 1950s and in the 1960s the movement to have Okinawa revert to Japanese rule became irresistible on Okinawa, in Japan, and in the United States. The Defense Department continued to term retention of Okinawa and unrestricted use of U.S. bases vital to American national security. Its position was bolstered by the support being given for the Vietnam War from the island's Marine units and its B-52 bombers. For its part, the State Department bent toward reversion, as Japan's politics in steadily rising crescendo insisted on the island's return. In part this was in response to communist pressure in Japan. On Okinawa, led by students from Okinawa University—located on grounds formerly occupied by the old castle at Shuri—youthful agitators and left-wing politicians demanded Okinawa's immediate unrestricted reversion. They paid no heed to the economic importance for their own livelihood of the American military, which furnished some 70 percent of the island's national income.

In 1969, coincidental with the climax of the Vietnam War, the agitation peaked. Yielding to Japanese pressure, the United States sought to devise the reversion of Okinawa while protecting American base rights. The Japanese government now sought unconditional reversion. It was his "firm determination," said Japanese Premier Eisako Sato in a speech to the Japanese Diet, to reunite Okinawa with Japan. Left-wing Okinawans and the radical Zengakuren students in Japan proper rushed to the gates of U.S. bases in Japan and Okinawa to reinforce demands for their immediate return with barrages of rocks and Molotov cocktails. Under joint socialist and communist sponsorship, they proclaimed 28 April 1969 to be "Okinawa Day." One observer termed Okinawa a "general's dream and a politician's nightmare."

Patient diplomacy finally paid off. In November 1969, as he had promised, Premier Sato traveled to the United States to meet the new president, Richard M. Nixon, who had begun a policy of gradual withdrawal of U.S. troops from Vietnam. Both chiefs of state agreed that negotiations should begin "with a view" to the transfer of Okinawa from U.S. to Japanese rule in 1972. The U.S. would retain only such bases as were needed for "national security." These would include Kadena airfield and the White Beach naval station. Sato's visit hardly satisfied the left in either Japan or Okinawa, but it forwarded an irreversible negotiating process.

Details proved to be extraordinarily complex. Complicating them further were additional demands by the Japanese to have the United States withdraw all atomic weapons and stocks of poison gas from Okinawa. To these demands the United States agreed. Also, both parties had to decide which bases the United States would continue to occupy and which the Japanese should take over. Finally, in 1971, a draft agreement was completed; it was to be signed and ratified the following year. On 15 May 1972 twenty-seven years of U.S. rule on Okinawa came to an end.

The day was not greeted with joy among most people in Naha nor among the Okinawa civilians working on U.S. bases, including White Beach. Many of the strongest opponents of the military had come to realize how much their living depended on the American presence. The leftist leaders, however, were not daunted. Their new goal, much muted and watered down, came to be to get *all* U.S. troops and bases off the island; at the same time they insisted that the Americans were responsible for Okinawa's economic plight. Faced with this criticism, Tokyo now had to subsidize the Okinawan economy. In the course of the next ten years Japan had to agree to furnish Okinawa, now a regular Japanese perfecture, with $5.5 billion worth of development assistance. This was to combat unemployment, which soon ranged up to three times the level of the homeland. Nevertheless, the left continued to protest the presence of U.S. bases, and on the tenth anniversary of Okinawa's reversion to Japan managed to stage a demonstration by 4,000 protestors.

Between 1969 and 1982 U.S. forces on Okinawa declined from about 40,000 until the figure finally stabilized at about 29,000. These included the Third Marine Division, permanently stationed on the island, with White Beach its designated debarkation area. White Beach is also the homeport of Commander, Amphibious Group VCTF 76. The main naval airfield was Kadena, where a patrol squadron was stationed, while Japanese F-104 fighters and a pair of missile battalions took over Okinawa's air defense. In 1973 the U.S. Navy had agreed to move all naval air units from Naha airfield as part of its force reduction. The island's protection was now a shared U.S.-Japanese responsibility. At White Beach the United States keeps an aviation patrol squadron and at least one squadron of the First Marine Air Wing.

How long will Okinawa remain a U.S. base—albeit one shared with the Japanese—and White Beach a U.S. naval station? This, of course, depends on events. So long as the Third Marine Division stays on Okinawa a substantial U.S. presence will probably continue. But if Washington should decide to withdraw the Marines, then the United States may pull out most of its combat units and White Beach will become a purely Japanese installation and Kadena a Japanese airfield—as the latter had been at the beginning of 1945.

In addition to Commander, Fleet Activities Okinawa and U.S. Naval Air Facility Kadena, American installations in Okinawa include four organizations whose functions are self-explanatory: Naval Regional Medical Center, Camp Kuwae, Okinawa; Naval Security Group Activity Hanza; Naval Regional Dental Center Yokosuka Branch; and Mobile Construction Battalion Shields.

Americans assigned to Okinawa must enter either through Kadena Air Base or the commercial airport at Naha. In either case they will be met by a ''buddy'' who will furnish information on transportation and temporary lodging. Additional information will include the wisdom of using a small Japanese rather than an American-made automobile because of stringent emission control standards; the location of nine schools from kindergarten through high school; that the Air Force is responsible for all government quarters on the island; and that living costs are very high.

BIBLIOGRAPHY

A. U.S. Department of the Army, ''Tentative Operation Plan ICEBERG 1-45, 6 Jan. 1945, Annex 3'' (Washington: World War II Records Center, National Archives); U.S. Department of the Navy. ''CINCPAC/CINCPOA Information Bulletin, 161-44. 1945'' (Washington: World War II Records Center, National Archives); ''Base Facilities Summary: Advance Bases Central Pacific (U.S. Pacific Fleet and Pacific Ocean Area), 31 Mar. 1945'' (Washington: Naval Historical Center, Operational Archives Branch); U.S. Department of State, ''Multilateral Treaty of Peace with Japan, 28 April 1952,'' *U.S. Treaties and Other International Agreements*, Vol. III, Part 3, 1952, pp. 3169-3425; U.S. Senate, Sub-committee on Security Agreements and Commitments Abroad. *Hearings*. 26-29 January 1970, (91st Cong., 2nd Sess.); U.S. Department of State, ''U.S. and Japan Sign Agreement on Reversion of Okinawa.'' Statements by President Nixon and Secretary Rogers. Text of agreement and related memoranda. *Department of State Bulletin* 65 (12 July 1971):33-41; U.S. Senate, ''President's Message to the Senate Transmitting the Agreement Between the United States and Japan on the Ryukyu Islands, 21 September 1971.'' Compilation of Presidential Documents 1305-07, 27 Sept. 1971); U.S. Sentate. Committee on Foreign Relations. *Hearing on Ex J.*, 82-1, 27-29 Oct. 1971, (92nd Cong., 1st Sess.)

B. Francis L. Hawks, *Narrative of the Expedition of. . .Commodore M.C. Perry*, 3 vols. (Washington: GPO, 1856); Roy E. Appleman and others, *Okinawa: The Last Battle* (U.S. Department of the Army. Historical Division). *The United States Army in World War II* (Washington: GPO, 1948); Charles Nichols and Henry I. Shaw, Jr., *Okinawa: Victory in the Pacific* (Washington: Historical Division, Headquarters, U.S. Marine Corps, 1955); Samuel E. Morison, *Victory in the Pacific* (Boston: Little, Brown, 1960); A. R. Campbell, ''Why We're Returning Okinawa to Japan,'' *New Republic* 160 (14 June 1969):11-13; M. D. Morris, *Okinawa: A Tiger by the Tail* (New York: Hawthorne, 1969); Robert Epp, ''The U.S.-Japan Treaty Crisis,'' *Current History* 58 (Apr. 1970):202-10; James H. Belote and William M. Belote, *Typhoon of Steel: The Battle for Okinawa* (New York: Harper and Row, 1970); Akio Watanabe, *The Okinawan Problem: A Chapter in Japan-U.S. Relations* (Melbourne, Australia: Melbourne University Press, 1970); Herbert A. Kampf, ''The Resolution of the Triangular Dilemma: The Case of Okinawan Reversion,'' *Asian Forum* 4 (Apr.-June 1972):37-48; Philip Dion, ''Return to Okinawa: This

Week the Ryukyan (sic) Is. Were Formally Returned to Japan; But the Economic Battle Has Only Just Begun,'' *Far Eastern Economic Review* 76 (20 May 1972):19-21.

JAMES H. BELOTE

ORAN, ALGERIA, U.S. NAVAL OPERATING BASE.
See North Africa, U.S. Naval Bases.

OYE (CALAIS), FRANCE.
See World War I U.S. Northern Bombing Group Bases in England and France.

P

PAIMBOEUF, FRANCE, U.S. NAVAL AIR STATION.
See World War I U.S. Naval Air Stations in Europe.

PALERMO, SICILY, U.S. NAVAL OPERATING BASE, 1943–1946 The decision to invade Sicily reached at the Casablanca Conference in January 1943 made it imperative to create an advanced naval base to support the beachhead buildup and the follow-up campaign to clear Sicily of Axis forces. Palermo was pinpointed due to its known facilities supporting the Italian Navy and its position near the beachheads, which gave hopes of an early capture. An advanced base unit was set up in the United States, first under Capt. H. G. Sickel, USN, and then under Capt. Leonard Doughty, Jr., USN. The unit's objectives were to set up minor bases at Gela, Porto Empedocle, and Licata, which were to serve as supply and unloading sites until the major base, Palermo, could be put into operation. In May, the base unit shipped out to the North African staging area, minus the ship repair section assigned to service Base Palermo. The speedy capture of Palermo (22 July) and its quick reopening (27 July) rendered the minor bases of little value after the first few weeks.

Axis forces had carried out considerable demolition at Palermo, already battered by frequent Allied bombing attacks since the spring. Machinery had been smashed, belts slashed, parts removed. The German command predicted that both the harbor and the city would prove useless to the Allies. The harbor was cluttered with the hulks of scuttled vessels both large and small; moles had been demolished and quayside buildings had been shattered. The city had neither power nor water.

But Palermo did have one great advantage that was to make it superior to other bases in the Mediterranean. Its shipyard, Cantieri Navali Reuniti, had been developed far beyond Allied intelligence estimates and was relatively undamaged. The underground oil tanks on Monte Pelligrino, with a capacity of about 1 million barrels, and the pipeline to the harbor were intact. Available at Palermo after the first few weeks was an immense reservoir of local labor, both skilled and unskilled. Commo. William A. Sullivan, USN, a salvage expert, went to work supported by the Seabees and the Army Engineers. The harbor was cleared; the dry dock repaired; the city's services restored; and a staging area for 15,000 troops constructed. The port reopened for shipping on 27 July 1943, and on the following day Naval Operating Base Palermo was established under the command of Captain Doughty with responsibility to serve the forces afloat, provide adequate harbor defense, and assist the Army in operating the port. The Army base units at Palermo had served with naval base units in Morocco, so that relations between the two services were excellent. The port facilities were shared with the Army until July 1944, when the latter withdrew from Sicily.

By 30 July, half the shipping berths had been cleared and it was possible to unload twelve ships simultaneously. This allowed the rapid landing of the Ninth Infantry Division on 1 August. During August, 44,878 personnel and 116,369 long tons of supplies were landed.

The Luftwaffe provided an early problem with a series of raids starting in early August on the city and the harbor, but after 23 August the enemy was unable to launch further major raids, and operations at the port were never seriously hampered. Palermo did have one unusual moment when one dawn it found a portion of the Italian fleet at the harbor's mouth. Fortunately, the Italians were on their way to Malta to surrender and had only stopped for medical supplies and food after having had a brush with their former allies.

The city was found to provide excellent billet accommodations although the base did suffer for some time from a shortage of storage facilities due to the Army's appropriation of most of the available warehouse storage facilities. Most of the work of restoring buildings to usefulness was carried out by the Seabees of the 120th Battalion. The shipyard was quickly put back into operation, as were the port facilities, including the fuel installations. Some 400,000 tons of heavy shipbuilding materials were found in the shipyard to help operations. The 750-ton floating dry dock was soon back in operation, but the 538-foot graving dock, which had been damaged by Allied bombing and had had a destroyer scuttled in it, took much longer to repair. A Naval Ammunition Depot with a capacity of 35,000 tons was established near Palermo at Mondello. The small breakwater harbor there permitted ammunition to be brought directly to Mondello instead of passing through Palermo.

The major repair facilities had suffered slight damage and were soon restored. Because ship repair personnel were never shipped for Palermo, Doughty called in the ship repair detachments from the three minor bases. These men, together with returning Italian workers, made it possible to conduct repair operations on a much larger scale. Palermo developed into a repair yard of some magnitude, especially during the Anzio operation, handling vessels ranging from LSTs and LCIs through merchant ships, destroyers, and even cruisers. From 77 officers and 491 men in September 1943, the number of naval personnel increased to 202 officers and 1,695 men in February 1944. In October 1944, in addition to 179 naval officers and 1,615 men, there were 19 Seabee officers and 612 men.

At its peak the base also employed 3,200 civilians, which made it the economic mainstay of Palermo. Base Palermo gained a reputation as a "can do" organization. In a one-year period 960 ships were drydocked for repairs and 750 were overhauled. This fine performance was due to the leadership of Comdr. Edward M. Ragsdale, USN, the Ship Repair Officer.

Palermo served as a repair base for the Anzio invasion and again as a support base for the invasion of southern France. In addition to its repair and support facilities, it had a Harbor Entrance Control Post, Port Director and Port Office, degaussing facility, bomb disposal unit, material recovery unit, merchant marine detail, radio station, and fleet post office. After the invasion of southern France, activity at the base decreased until January 1945, when the decision was made to concentrate the amphibious forces in the Palermo area. For a short period, base activity reached new heights until the withdrawal of the forces in the summer of 1945. At that time, a decision was reached to keep Base Palermo in commission as long as necessary to support the war in the Far East, but to reduce personnel and facilities as rapidly as possible. With the surrender of Japan, the workload at the base declined rapidly. On 1 January 1946 NOB Palermo was reduced to the status of Naval Detachment Palermo, and a time schedule was established to withdraw completely as of 31 March 1946, which was done.

BIBLIOGRAPHY

A. Commander Naval Operating Base, Palermo, "Organization Book" (NOB Palermo, 1 Nov. 1943); United States Naval Administrative Histories of World War II. Commander U.S. Naval Forces, Northwest African Waters, "Naval Forces, Northwest African Waters and the Eighth Fleet," 5 vols. (Washington: Naval Historical Center, Operational Archives Branch, 1945); U.S. Navy, Bureau of Yards and Docks, *Building the Navy's Bases in World War II*, 2 vols. (Washington: GPO, 1947).

B. Samuel E. Morison, *Sicily, Salerno, and Anzio* (Boston: Little, Brown, 1954).

FRANCIS X. HOLBROOK

PALMER STATION, ANTARCTICA, U.S. NAVAL BASE.
See Antarctica, U.S. Naval and Air Bases.

PALM ISLAND, AUSTRALIA, U.S. NAVAL ADVANCE AIR BASE 1943–1944 Located twenty miles north of Townsville in Queensland on Australia's northeastern coast, Palm Island in late 1942 served as a minor operating base for cruiser-destroyer forces patrolling off northeastern Australia. However, its main function for the Seventh Fleet, Southwest Pacific Area, was as a major patrol plane repair base. On 6 July 1943 a detachment of the Fifty-fifth Naval Construction Battalion arrived to construct a camp for 1,000 men, as well as ramps, hangars, and shops for twelve flying boats ashore and eighteen moored in the bay. On 25 October the fleet air facility (18°45′S., 146°35′E.) was ready for operations. From then until 1 May 1944 Palm Island averaged overhaul and repair of four seaplanes a day. Roll-up began on 1 June 1944, and facilities were dismantled for shipment to forward bases. Palm Island was disestablished in July 1944.

BIBLIOGRAPHY

A. U.S. Navy, Bureau of Yards and Docks, *Building the Navy's Bases in World War II*, 2 vols. (Washington: GPO, 1947); U.S. Navy, "U.S. Naval Bases in the South and Southwest Pacific (and Central Pacific Forward) in World War II," 1 November 1954 (Washington: Naval Historical Center, Operational Archives Branch).

JOHN B. LUNDSTROM

PALMYRA ISLAND, U.S. NAVAL AIR STATION, 1941–1947 Palmyra Island is an atoll in the Hawaiian group 960 miles south of Honolulu. The atoll was formerly composed of fifty-two islets, the largest only 46 acres, enclosing three lagoons. Ownership of most of the islands was claimed by the Fullard Leo family, and the Interior Department in the late 1930s aspired to convert the lagoon into a national monument and nature reserve.

With the emergence of air power as an increasingly significant factor in the mid-1930s, American naval officers conceived of Palmyra, along with other outlying islands, as strategically suited for tender-based patrol planes. The Hepburn Board in December 1938 recommended that a channel be dredged and coral heads removed to provide accommodations for small craft and tender-based planes, and in January 1940 the Navy let contracts for this minor development. By 1941 the Navy's plans were expanded to provide for a 5,000-foot airstrip constructed partly from coral fill dredged from the lagoons and deposited between Menge and Cooper Islands. In 1940 the Chief of Naval Operations also ordered a small Marine detachment to Palmyra for protection against hostile raids. Although still far from completed, the Palmyra Naval Air Station was formally established on 15 August 1941.

With the outbreak of war in December 1941 the civilian laborers turned to the construction of defenses, perhaps the most notable feature of which was a twelve-mile roadway of crushed coral, dredgings from the lagoons, that linked the islands in a horseshoe extending from northeast to southwest. Palmyra suffered only one brief and ineffectual Japanese bombardment, on 24 December 1941. Under pressure of war its facilities were immensely expanded; eventually they included a 100-room hotel, storage capacity for 400,000 gallons of aviation gasoline and 18,500 barrels of oil, an additional landplane runway, and facilities for small boats. Palmyra's usefulness, however, passed with the end of the war and the lengthening range of planes. The Naval Station was deactivated on 15 February 1947, and the facilities were shifted to the Civil Aeronautics Authority.

BIBLIOGRAPHY

A. Record Group 80, General Records of the Navy Department, 1927-1940, A21-5 File (Washington: National Archives); U.S. Navy, Bureau of Yards and Docks, *Building the Navy's Bases in World War II*, 2 vols. (Washington: GPO, 1947), II:121-22, 154-55.

B. Francis X. Holbrook, "United States National Defense and Trans-Pacific Commercial Air Routes, 1933-1941" Ph.D. diss., Fordham University, 1969.

WILLIAM R. BRAISTED

PANAMA CANAL ZONE, POST-WORLD WAR II DEFENSE ARRANGEMENTS With the signing on 18 May 1942 of a Defense Sites Agreement, the United States planned to build 134 bases on land leased from the Republic of Panama "for the duration," for which Panama received $20 million in addition to the annual rental charge paid for land occupied by U.S. forces. The sites were to be retroceded within a year following the end of the war. In addition the United States would pay up to a third of the costs of repairs made to roads used by its forces, build a new concrete highway (Rio Hato), and permit Panama to construct an oil pipeline connecting Panama and the port of Balboa.

By 1 September 1946, 51 of the 134 new bases had been abandoned, but 83 still remained. Panama said that the remaining bases violated her sovereignty and should be vacated. Much emotional talk, especially from communists, was heard about an "imperialist outrage" on Panamanian soil. On 11 September President Harry S. Truman said that the remaining bases would be evacuated, yet various bases remained manned under the contention of Washington that since no peace treaty had been signed the emergency under which the act of 18 May 1942 had been signed still existed. Nevertheless, in October 1947 fourteen months of negotiations began by which the United States obtained a twenty-year lease on an air base and five-year leases on twelve radar station sites—but not without communist-inspired student riots and demonstrations. For an annual rent of $28,015 for thirteen bases covering 28,838 acres and $137,500 for road repairs, the United States awaited Panama's decision.

With 10,000 students outside the Assembly building, on 22 December 1947 the delegates rejected the pact, whereupon Washington directed that the bases be evacuated—a step taken with military precision on the twenty-fourth.

Early in his administration, President Dwight D. Eisenhower made certain concessions in extant treaties that decreased American control in the Zone and thus increased that of Panama. Among these were a single pay scale for American and Panamanian workers; the flying of the Panamanian flag jointly with the Stars and Stripes in the Zone and on ships transiting the Canal; the addition of Spanish to English as an official language therein; and much higher payments to Panama from toll collections. In return the United States was given, among other concessions, the use of 19,000 acres in the Rio Hato region for military training and maneuvering. But student demonstrations occurred again, with 10 killed and nearly 100 wounded in May 1958. In 1956 and again in 1958 Panama rejected American requests for two sites for Nike bases. On 3 November 1959 former foreign minister Aquilino Boyd headed a presidential campaign "sovereignty" march into the Zone, after which he retired. Communist-led students used the incident to demonstrate; unable to quell the mob, the Zone police were aided by U.S. Army troops, who succeeded in doing so without killing anyone and inflicting only minor injuries, but only after a group had entered the American embassy, lowered the U.S. flag, and desecrated it. Eisenhower had agreed to let the Panamanian flag fly along the American one as "visual evidence that Panama does have titular sovereignty over the region." The "dual flag" policy remained a constant sore to Americans in the Zone, while Panamanian tempers flared over the Bay of Pigs and Cuban missile crises and heated up demands for a revision of the basic 1903 treaty and the abolition of the perpetuity clause, among other things. Renewed demonstrations against the United States occurred in 1964.

The Future of American Defenses in Panama

Half a century after the completion of the Panama Canal, the Republic of Panama became increasingly inbued with the nationalistic spirit that swept the rest of the Third World, viewing American operation of the canal and of the Canal Zone as a vestige of colonialism and a national indignity. After the serious anti-American riots of 1955, 1958, and 1964 President Lyndon B. Johnson agreed to renegotiate the Hay-Bunau-Varilla treaty of 1903. By 1974 Washington had agreed in principle to return the Canal Zone to Panama. The decision was based in part on the fact that only 10 percent of American waterborne commerce used the canal, which was too small to serve supertankers and U.S. aircraft carriers.

Following his inauguration, President Jimmy Carter put Panama high on his list of priorities and soon named veteran diplomats Ellsworth Bunker and Sol Linowitz to represent the United States in negotiating a treaty that would enable both parties to cooperate in protecting an efficient, secure, and neutral canal. As it transpired, two treaties were negotiated. The first called for Panama to take legal jurisdiction of the Canal Zone within three years and to assume a gradually larger role in the operation and defense of the canal until it would be turned over completely by the United States on 31 December 1999. The second, which other nations could also sign, pledged open and nondiscriminatory access to the canal even after Panama assumed control. Still to be settled was the issue of payments the United States would make to Panama and the right of the United States to intervene in case open access to the canal was denied.

American public opinion opposed the return of the canal, while the Navy supported its retention and the Army its retrocession. In Panama and in most other Latin American countries, objection was voiced to the right granted the United States to intervene indefinitely to defend the canal against a third country even after the canal had passed into Panamanian hands. The first of the two treaties—the Panama Canal Treaty—abolishes the Canal Zone, transfers its territorial jurisdiction to Panama, and grants Washington authority to operate and defend the canal until 31 December 1999. The second treaty restates the authority of the United States to defend the canal until the year 2000 and after that to have the permanent right to defend its neutrality even if the number of American troops and bases is reduced. The treaties were signed on 7 September 1977 with proper pomp and ceremony in Washington in the presence of high officials from twenty-three other Western Hemispheric nations. The treaties were submitted to the U.S. Senate on 16 September. A plebiscite on them held in Panama approved them by a vote of two to one. Among other matters that held up the vote in the U.S. Senate was the testimony given the Armed Services Committee by the Chief of Naval Operations, Adm. James Holloway, with respect to a top-secret U.S. communications intelligence facility on Galeta Island, at the Atlantic end of the canal. Called a "naval group security facility," it was manned by fifty men who engaged in high-frequency direction finding as part of SOSUS, the acronym for a network that tracks Soviet submarines, obtains bearings on surface ships and planes, and collects communications intelligence. The southernmost station in SOSUS, it participated in about two-thirds of all Atlantic Ocean fixes and was also important in detecting Soviet submarines operating in U.S. West Coast waters. Holloway concluded that the removal of the station would greatly reduce the capability of SOSUS and that it would be "enormously expensive" to relocate it on other foreign soil, where geography in addition would not allow the correct angles for a geometric fix. Whether the station would remain in U.S. hands after the year 2000, when the Zone would revert to Panama, remained to be seen. In any event, on a roll call taken on 16 March 1978 the first treaty passed with one vote to spare, 68 to 32. On 18 April, by exactly the same vote, the second treaty passed also. In sum, Panama was granted sovereignty over the Canal Zone and would gradually assume a larger role in the operation and defense of the canal until it would be turned over completely by the United States on 31 December 1999. Thereafter the United States could intervene only in case open access to the canal was denied.

BIBLIOGRAPHY

A. *A Chronology of Events Relating to the Panama Canal*, prepared for the Committee on Foreign Relations, United States Senate, by Congressional Research Service, Library of Congress (Washington: GPO, December 1977).

B. Ralph Minger, "Panama, the Canal Zone, and Titular Sovereignty," *Western Political Quarterly* 14 (June 1961):144-54; Jules Dubois, *Danger over Panama* (Indianapolis, Ind.: Bobbs-Merrill, 1964); Lawrence O. Ealy, *Yanqui Politics and the Isthmian Canal* (University Park: Pennsylvania State University Press, 1971); Jon P. Speller, *The Panama Canal: Heart of America's Security* (New York: Roger Speller and Sons, 1972); Paul B. Ryan, *The Panama Canal Controversy: U.S. Diplomacy and Defense Interests* (Stanford, Calif.: Hoover Institution Press, 1977); Walter LeFeber, *The Panama Canal: The Crisis in Historical Perspective* (New York: Oxford University Press, 1978); files of the *U.S. Department of State Bulletin*, 1977-1982.

PANAMA CANAL ZONE, U.S. NAVAL RADIO STATIONS, 1905– The Republic of Panama granted the United States permission to erect a wireless radio station twenty-five miles south of Colon along the Panama Railroad at Darien on the Atlantic side of the proposed canal, on a reservation containing 87.5 acres. Using a narrow-gauge railroad, locomotives, and cars left behind by French workers, American workmen by the end of 1905 had erected quarters, office, and radio buildings and three towers 600 feet high and about 800 feet apart; the radio equipment itself was provided by the American De Forest Wireless Telegraph Co. at a cost of $58,666. With electric power obtained from the Panama Canal transmission line, Darien was able to maintain contact with U.S. Naval Radio Station Key West and occasionally reach the station at Manhattan Beach, Coney Island, N.Y., a distance of 2,150 miles, as well as that at Arlington, Va. In 1908 U.S. Naval Radio Station Colon was commissioned and handled the traffic of the Navy, the Army, and all other government agencies in the area, as well as commercial traffic. In 1911 in accordance with recommendations of the Joint Army and Navy Board, an intricate system of radio communications linked the principal ports and bases of the Isthmus and naval headquarters in Washington, while a vast system of land and submarine cable telephone and telegraph circuits connected the various American facilities in the Canal Zone. In 1912 the Zone was tied into a radio system connecting Arlington, Va., with stations on the California coast, Hawaii, American Samoa, Guam (q.v.), and the Philippines. Tests conducted in 1915 paved the way for long-distance radio telephone systems as well.

In 1913 Radio Balboa was established at what was then known as Camp Elliott, where La Boca is now located, to handle traffic on the Pacific side of the canal. Its radius of operations being 3,000 miles, it could maintain direct communications with Washington. Moreover, it took over the transmitting end of the radio work from Balboa Radio Station. The Cape Mala Naval Radio Station, established on 1 March 1920 on the Pacific side of the Republic of Panama, served as a direction finder station, as did a similar station on Toro Point on the Atlantic side of the canal.

Under a 1926 treaty between the United States and Panama, the United States was permitted the use of areas lying outside of the Panama Canal Zone.Taking advantage of this treaty, the U.S. Navy built the Gatun Radio Station in 1932. During that year, however, the president of Panama signed a decree abrogating American radio communications in his republic. In consequence, naval radio underwent great changes during the middle and late 1930s. The work at Darien was moved to Summit by the fall of 1934, and Darien itself was decommissioned in 1937. In 1940 the Bureau of Yards and Docks authorized the establishment of Radio Farfan, which would receive traffic for Balboa and operate the transmission equipment at Summit by remote control. Construction was completed by May 1942. A World War II reorganization placed the Panama Canal Zone and its radio stations at Balboa, the District Center, and Colon, in the Fifteenth Naval District.

See also Panama Canal Zone, Post-World War II Defense Arrangements.

BIBLIOGRAPHY

A. U.S. Navy, Bureau of Yards and Docks, *Building the Navy's Bases in World War II*, 2 vols. (Washington: GPO, 1947), II:15, 20-21; "U.S. Naval Administration in World War II. Commander 5th Naval District and Commander Panama Sea Frontier," 2 vols., microfilm (Washington: U.S. Navy Department Library).

B. Lt. R.S. Crenshaw, USN, "The Naval Radio Stations of the Panama Canal Zone," U.S. Naval Institute *Proceedings* 42 (July-Aug. 1916):21-18; Capt. L. S. Howeth, USN (Ret.), *History of Communications-Electronics in the United States Navy* (Washington: GPO, 1963), pp. 215, 221.

PARAMARIBO, SURINAM, DUTCH GUIANA.
See Hispanic South America, U.S. Naval Bases.

PAUILLAC, FRANCE, U.S. NAVAL AVIATION BASE.
See World War I U.S. Naval Air Stations in Europe.

PELELIU, PALAU ISLANDS, U.S. NAVAL BASE 1944–1947 Peleliu, in the Palaus (Western Carolines), is an island five and one-half miles long and two and one-half miles wide. The Japanese had developed the Palaus as a major base for fuel, ammunition, and other supplies; they retired there after their base at Truk was rendered untenable by American air attacks. Japanese shore facilities included repair shops for small craft, and three airfields: the largest on Peleliu, a smaller strip on Ngesebus just to the north of Peleliu, and a partially constructed field at Airai still farther north on Babelthuap Island. The Americans moved in the late summer of 1944 to capture Peleliu and Angaur, the southernmost of the Palaus, thereby interrupting Japanese supply lines to the Southwest Pacific and securing for themselves anchorages and air stations for the pending invasion of the Philippines.

The First Marine Division landed on Peleliu on 15 September 1944 and managed to capture the principal airfield by the following evening. Since the Japanese retreated to previously prepared cave positions in a ridge to the north, however, the Americans only finally secured the island after suffering heavy losses. Even as the fighting progressed, the naval base components (Gropac 9) were landed, and three Seabee groups began constructing minimal shore facilities. By D-Day plus seven, fighter squadrons were operating from the former Japanese airfield, and the field in succeeding months was expanded to include a 6,000-foot bomber runway, 4,000-foot fighter strip, and extensive taxiways and parking areas. Early work was conducted under enemy mortar fire.

The Peleliu tank farm included twenty 1,000-barrel tanks for aviation gasoline, one 10,000-barrel tank for motor gas, and three 1,000-barrel tanks for diesel oil. Also built were supply depots for the Army, aviation, and spare parts. The Army Evacuation Hospital, the Naval Base Hospital, and several dispensaries eventually acquired a 1,500-bed capacity. The dredged inner harbor was equipped with a marine railway and shops for small boat repair.

A dozen miles south of Peleliu at the tip of the Palaus, the Eighty-first Army Division captured the five-square-mile Angaur Island on 23 October 1944. There the Army Engineers, assisted by Seabee units, constructed an Army air base with a 7,000-foot runway, taxiways and parking areas, and a tank farm. Angaur also boasted a naval ammunition dump and a Coast Guard Loran Station. Kossol

Passage between Peleliu and Angaur was used extensively for replenishment from service vessels during the Leyte campaign.

The Palaus lost their significance as the war moved northward after the conquest of the Philippines. The Army abandoned its Angaur base in June 1946, and the Navy disestablished its operations on Angaur and Peleliu in 1946 and 1947, respectively.

BIBLIOGRAPHY

A. "History of U.S. Naval Base Peleliu, 8 October 1945" (Washington: Naval Historical Center, Operational Archives Branch, World War II Command File); U.S. Navy, Bureau of Yards and Docks, *Building the Navy's Bases in World War II*, 2 vols. (Washington: GPO, 1947), II:326-32.

B. Samuel E. Morison, *Leyte Gulf, June 1944-January 1945* (Boston: Little, Brown, 1958).

WILLIAM R. BRAISTED

PENARTH, WALES.
See United Kingdom, U.S. World War II Naval Bases.

PERTH, AUSTRALIA.
See Fremantle-Perth, Australia, U.S. Naval Advance Base.

PESCARA, ITALY.
See World War I U.S. Naval Air Stations in Europe.

PHU BAI, REPUBLIC OF VIETNAM.
See Hue-Tan My-Phu Bai, Republic of Vietnam, U.S. Naval Support Activity.

PHU CUONG, REPUBLIC OF VIETNAM, U.S. NAVAL ADVANCED TACTICAL SUPPORT BASE, 1969–1970 Situated at the foot of a major bridge crossing South Vietnam's Saigon River, the naval combat base at Phu Cuong provided a relatively secure staging area for river patrol boat (PBR) units operating against communist infiltrators to the northwest of the capital city.

Initially, the Army provided the naval contingent with logistic support, but once Phu Cuong was designated an advanced tactical support base, supplies emanated from the Naval Support Activity, Saigon (q.v.) depot at nearby Newport.

As American forces withdrew from the war in Southeast Asia, South Vietnamese units took on greater combat tasks. In this regard, the Phu Cuong facility was turned over to the Vietnamese Navy in November 1970.

BIBLIOGRAPHY
A. Commander Naval Forces, Vietnam, "The Naval War in Vietnam," May 1970 (Washington: Naval Historical Center, Operational Archives Branch).

EDWARD J. MAROLDA

PHUOC XUYEN, REPUBLIC OF VIETNAM, U.S. NAVAL ADVANCED TACTICAL SUPPORT BASE, 1969–1971 This town, in the Republic of Vietnam's Mekong Delta region, was the site of one of the Navy's advanced tactical support bases during the conflict in Southeast Asia. River patrol boat (PBR) units taking part in the Sea Lords strategy of interdicting communist infiltration from Cambodia received basic supplies, such as fuel, food, and ammunition, from the facility. The base was turned over to the Vietnamese Navy in April 1971, after more than two years of American operation, when U.S. forces withdrew from the combat area.

BIBLIOGRAPHY
A. Commander Naval Forces, Vietnam, "Monthly Historical Reports, 1965-1971" (Washington: Naval Historical Center, Operational Archives Branch).

EDWARD J. MAROLDA

PISA, ITALY.
See Mediterranean, The, U.S. Naval Bases, 1800-1917.

PLATEAU STATION, ANTARCTICA, U.S. NAVAL BASE.
See Antarctica, U.S. Naval and Air Bases.

PLYMOUTH, ENGLAND.
See United Kingdom, U.S. World War II Naval Bases. *See also* Vicarage Barracks, Plymouth, Devon, United Kingdom, U.S. World War II Naval Bases.

POOLE, ENGLAND.
See United Kingdom, U.S. World War II Naval Bases.

PORT HAMILTON, KOREA.
See Far Eastern U.S. Naval Bases to 1898.

PORTLAND-WEYMOUTH, ENGLAND.
See United Kingdom, U.S. World War II Naval Bases.

PORT LLOYD, BONIN ISLANDS.
See Far Eastern U.S. Naval Bases to 1898.

PORT LYAUTEY, FRENCH MOROCCO.
See North Africa, U.S. Naval Bases.

PORT MAHON, SPAIN.
See Mediterranean, The, U.S. Naval Bases, 1800-1917.

PORT MORESBY, NEW GUINEA, U.S. NAVAL ADVANCE BASE 1943–1944 The capital of the Territory of Papua, Port Moresby (9°20′S., 147°9′E.) was a vital Allied base highly sought by the Japanese to complete their conquest of eastern New Guinea. Located on the southeastern coast of New Guinea, Port Moresby in 1942-1943 was the principal Allied air base in the area. Naval activities in general were handled by the Royal Australian Navy, which used it as a small-craft base and harbor. The U.S. Navy in June 1943 sent to Port Moresby a detachment of the Fifty-fifty Naval Construction Battalion to build for the Seventh Fleet a large radio communications center. In connection with the installation, which opened on 15 July 1943, Seventh Fleet provided port director facilities for Port Moresby. Roll-up of the facilities began in October 1944 and was completed by 1 November.

BIBLIOGRAPHY
A. U.S. Navy, Bureau of Yards and Docks, *Building the Navy's Bases in World War II*, 2 vols. (Washington: GPO, 1947); U.S. Navy, "U.S. Naval Bases in the South and Southwest Pacific (and Central Pacific Forward) in World War II," 1 November 1954 (Washington: Naval Historical Center, Operational Branch).

JOHN B. LUNDSTROM

PORTO CORSINI, ITALY.
See World War I U.S. Naval Air Stations in Europe.

PORT STEPHENS, NEW SOUTH WALES, AUSTRALIA, U.S. NAVAL ADVANCE BASE, 1943–1944 With the establishment of the Amphibious Force, Southwest Pacific Force (later Seventh Amphibious Force), the U.S. Navy took control of an Australian joint operations training school at Port Stephens, New South Wales. Located at Nelson's Bay 100 miles north of Sydney, Port Stephens (32°43′S., 152°6′E.) on 1 March 1943 became headquarters of the Amphibious Training Command. Ill-equipped and located far from troop concentrations, it nevertheless offered fine beaches and anchorages for amphibious training. Divisions were brought there in the spring of 1943 to be trained in amphibious techniques in landing craft serviced by a newly created equipment depot at Port Stephens. In June 1943 training facilities were shifted northward to Port Toorbul at Brisbane (q.v.), which was much closer to where the infantry divisions were quartered. The amphibious equipment depot at Port Stephens remained open until September 1944.

BIBLIOGRAPHY
A. U.S. Navy, "7th Amphibious Force Command History 10 January 1943-23 December 1945" (Washington: Naval Historical Center, Operational Archives Branch).

B. Vice Adm. Daniel E. Barbey, *MacArthur's Amphibious Navy* (Annapolis, Md.: U.S. Naval Institute, 1969).

JOHN B. LUNDSTROM

PUERTO CASTILLO, HONDURAS, U.S. NAVAL BASE.
See Central America, U.S. Naval Bases.

PUERTO PRINCESSA, PALAWAN, PHILIPPINE ISLANDS, U.S. NAVAL AIR BASE, 1945–1947 Puerto Princessa is located on the eastern shore of the island of Palawan at about 9°30′N., 118°E. There the U.S. Navy established a naval air base that could care for a fleet air wing, three carrier air service units, three patrol bomber squadrons, and two patrol squadrons. Commissioned on 5 May 1945, it had an administration building; two nose hangars; Class C shops; barracks for 1,000 men and 52 Marines; a BOQ for 80 men; underground fuel storage for aviation gasoline, motor gasoline, and diesel fuel; storage for aircraft spare parts and general service items; a commissary store; cold storage; thirty-bed dispensary; power plant; small arms magazine; small craft pier; radio station; and section base. The base served until inactivated in December 1946, when both the section base and landplane operating facilities were turned over to the Army. All other facilities were disestablished on 8 February 1947.

BIBLIOGRAPHY

A. Summary Cards (Washington Navy Yard: Naval Aviation History Office); "Monograph Histories of U.S. Naval Overseas Bases" 2 vols. Vol. 1. Pacific Area, 1 May 1957 (Washington Navy Yard: Naval Historical Center, Operational Archives Branch).

PUSAN, KOREA, U.S. NAVAL FLEET ACTIVITIES, 1950– The naval base at Pusan, in extreme southeastern Korea, is located twenty miles to the west at Chinae. The base is built around three contiguous basins, which open on a large, nearly land-locked anchorage that can accommodate a fleet of any size. The city is the southern terminus of the double-track, standard-gauge Kyongson-Mukden railroad line, which has branches leading to all major cities in Korea. Many highways also lead from Pusan to all parts of the peninsula.

U.S. Naval Fleet Activities Pusan was established on 11 December 1950 and consolidated the Military Sea Transportation Service and Naval Control of Shipping Office established there on 1 October 1950. As of 31 December 1952, the commander, Comdr. J. B. Williams, Jr., had on board four officers, sixteen men, and thirteen natives, the last used as interpreters and drivers. If monthly arrivals and departures of naval ships were few—with twenty-three arriving in February 1953 and twenty-two departing—merchant ship sailings were numerous. In February 1953, for example, 281 arrived and 263 departed.

The mission of the activity is to receive, store, and transship general stores and small craft parts to meet the requirements of the activity, and to support local naval units and other naval and Marine units in Korea. Illness is almost epidemic, for in January 1950 there were 250 patients in sick bay and, despite frequent lectures on venereal disease, there were 12 VD cases.

The men billeted there engage in disbursing, maintain and operate a fleet cargo center, and provide a general mess for activity personnel and personnel of the Naval Advisory Group, Republic of Korea Navy, Military Sea Transport Service/ Navy Control of Shipping Office (MSTS/NCSO) personnel, and even Republic of Korea merchant marine personnel. Overhaul and repairs of the headquarters ship and five small craft of the LCM and LCVP type are accomplished in Sasebo, Japan (q.v.).

BIBLIOGRAPHY

A. Commander, Fleet Activities, Pusan, Korea, ''Command History,'' 1952 and supplements (Washington: Naval Historical Center, Operational Archives Branch).

Q

QUEENSTOWN, IRELAND, SEAPLANE BASE.
See World War I U.S. Naval Air Stations in Europe.

QUEENSTOWN, IRELAND, U.S. NAVAL BASE.
See World War I U.S. Naval Bases in Europe.

QUI NHON, REPUBLIC OF VIETNAM, U.S. NAVAL SUPPORT ACTIVITY, 1965–1971 Located on the central coast of South Vietnam, Qui Nhon provided an operating base and logistic center for the Navy's Coastal Surveillance Force during the Southeast Asian Conflict. With easy access to coastal waters and the shipping lanes of the South China Sea, the port was well placed to support the Market Time anti-infiltration operation.

Beginning in the second half of 1965, fast patrol craft (PCF) units deployed to Qui Nhon to initiate the patrol. Subsequently, naval leaders established there a coastal surveillance command center to coordinate the efforts of U.S. and South Vietnamese elements and American patrol aircraft. On several occasions, other naval units sortied from the base, such as the inland foray by river patrol boats (PBR) in April 1968.

At first, resources to provide the PCF force with supplies and other assistance were limited. The naval unit drew upon Army stores for materials common to both services and looked to periodic resupply by the light cargo ships *Mark* (AKL-12) and *Brule* (AKL-28) for Navy-peculiar items, especially spare parts. These ships carried cargo from Subic Bay (q.v.) to various bases along the South Vietnamese littoral before stopping at Qui Nhon.

In April 1966 naval leaders established the Naval Support Activity, Saigon, Detachment Qui Nhon, to better administer logistic support of the coastal surveillance units. This task included the provision of berthing space, supplies, and repairs to the boats and transportation, messing, laundry, recreation, and base security.

Initially, the detachment relied on field expedients, such as using the tide to beach vessels for maintenance and repair of the hulls. Eventually, however, the Qui Nhon facility provided sophisticated support from a complex consisting of Seabee-built barracks, mess halls, repair, supply, and administrative buildings, an ammunition magazine, and a floating fuel system. When the Qui Nhon facility, by then designated an intermediate support base, was turned over to the Vietnamese Navy in September 1971, it functioned with an efficiency acquired from years of experience.

BIBLIOGRAPHY

A. Commander Naval Forces, Vietnam, ''Monthly Historical Reports, 1965-1971'' (Washington: Naval Historical Center, Operational Archives Branch).

B. Herbert T. King, ''Naval Logistic Support, Qui Nhon to Phu Quoc,'' U.S. Naval Institute *Naval Review* 95 (May 1969):84-111; S. A. Swarztrauber, ''River Patrol Relearned,'' U.S. Naval Institute *Naval Review* 96 (May 1970):120-57; Richard L. Schreadley, ''The Naval War in Vietnam, 1950-1970,'' U.S. Naval Institute *Naval Review* 97 (May 1971):180-211; Edwin B. Hooper, *Mobility, Support, Endurance: A Story of Naval Operational Logistics in the Vietnam War, 1965-1968* (Washington: GPO, 1972); Richard Tregaskis, *Southeast Asia: Building the Bases: The History of Construction in Southeast Asia* (Washington: GPO, 1975).

EDWARD J. MAROLDA

R

RACH SOI, REPUBLIC OF VIETNAM, U.S. NAVAL INTERMEDIATE SUPPORT BASE, 1969–1971 This town, on the western coast of South Vietnam's Mekong Delta region, was the site of a naval logistic base during the conflict in Southeast Asia. U.S. naval leaders selected Rach Soi during 1969 as a base from which to support a new strategy, called Sea Lords, to interdict the flow of communist supplies and troops from Cambodia. Located at the western end of two major canals, which American and Vietnamese river forces patrolled as a key part of the overall plan, Rach Soi was well placed to provide the area's river patrol boat (PBR) operating bases with supplies and boat repairs.

After U.S. forces withdrew from the region, in keeping with the Vietnamization of the war, the base continued to support the Vietnamese Navy. In June 1971, once it was clear that the Vietnamese were ready to assume this logistic task, the intermediate support base at Rach Soi was disestablished.

BIBLIOGRAPHY

A. Commander Naval Forces, Vietnam, "Monthly Historical Reports, 1965-1971" (Washington: Naval Historical Center, Operational Archives Branch).

EDWARD J. MAROLDA

RECIFE, BRAZIL, U.S. NAVAL ADVANCE BASE.
See Brazil, U.S. Naval Bases.

RIO DE JANEIRO, BRAZIL, U.S. NAVAL OPERATING BASE.
See Brazil, U.S. Naval Bases.

ROCHEFORT, FRANCE.
See World War I U.S. Naval Air Stations in Europe.

ROOSEVELT ROADS, PUERTO RICO, U.S. NAVAL BASE, 1941– Roosevelt Roads Naval Station lies in Ensenada Honda, eleven miles south of Cape San Juan, on the east coast of Puerto Rico. Including the 29,000 acres on Vieques Island (q.v.), "Roosey Roads" is the largest naval station in the world.

Before World War II the Navy operated a radio station on fifty-four acres at Cayey (18°7′10″N., 66°9′50″W.), located on Henry Barracks Military Reservation. In eastern Puerto Rico the Navy's only facility was a small reservation on Culebra Island, which had served as a rendezvous for the fleet and as a landing site for a Marine battalion during the maneuvers commanded by Adm. George Dewey in 1902-1903. In 1919 Lt. Robert L. Pettigrew, USN, surveying eastern Puerto Rico, recommended Vieques Sound as a potential location for a naval installation.

Lying on Vieques Passage, named for the small island off Puerto Rico that became such a source of controversy in the late 1970s, Roosevelt Roads was planned as the most important operating base in the Caribbean. As planners envisioned in World War II, it would ultimately provide anchorage, docking, and repair facilities, as well as fuel and supply sources for 60 percent of the Atlantic Fleet. The five-year project for completing the base, it was estimated in 1941, would cost more than $100 million.

The east coast of Puerto Rico was the only place on the island that could accommodate a naval base of this size—6,680 acres on Puerto Rico itself and most of Vieques Island, seven miles across the passage. The plan was to excavate rock from Vieques and create a breakwater between the two islands. In May 1941 work began; when the Japanese attacked Pearl Harbor, the number of workers had increased from a paltry 200 to 3,000, dredging operations commenced, and a pier was constructed for bringing in supplies.

But after the United States entered the war, pressing needs elsewhere—especially the commitment of a large number of ships in the Pacific—and shortages of supplies forced naval planners to alter the work schedule on Roosevelt Roads. Through 1942 the contractors worked almost exclusively on completing the drydock, machine shops, and airstrip. The supply depot, radio station, hospital, and seaplane base, as provided for in the 1941 plan, remained on the drawing board. But the 1,100-by-155 foot drydock was finished, initially used in July 1943, and dedicated in February 1944 as Bolles Drydock, after Capt. Harry A. Bolles, USN, killed in Alaska during the war. As imposing as the drydock was a power plant containing two 5,000-kilowatt generators protected by 4-foot thick concrete walls. The air station had three concrete runways, each 6,000 feet long. On Vieques the Navy constructed an ammunition depot of more than 100 buildings. From the Vieques quarry came the rock for the breakwater, and between October 1942 and August 1943, when work was suspended, 7,000 feet of the breakwater were constructed. On 15 July 1943 the Navy formally commissioned Roosevelt Roads as an operations base; on 1 November 1944 it became a naval station and was put into caretaker status.

The basic design of Roosevelt Roads had taken form in three years, but in 1943 the base was far from being the major installation planned in 1940. Though there was considerable German submarine activity in the Caribbean in 1942, when there occurred a spectacular attack on the oil installations of Dutch Aruba, the war seemed far away from Puerto Rico. Almost impulsively the naval planners who had envisioned the Caribbean as the cockpit of the war in 1940 had concluded by 1943 that a major naval operations base in Puerto Rico was unnecessary. In the next fourteen years the base would be closed seven times and reopened eight times. When World War II ended, "Roosey Roads" was in maintenance status, run by a Public Works officer supervising a unit of Seabees and a labor pool of Puerto Ricans.

But two years later, in the spring of 1947, the base was redesignated as a Naval Operating Base and used as a training installation and fuel depot for the Atlantic Fleet. In 1957 it again became a naval station, but with an important change in mission dictated by its crucial location and the rapid changes in naval weaponry. Henceforth Roosevelt Roads would be the center for the Atlantic Fleet's guided missile operations.

Major expansion of the station's facilities ensued. Between 1945 and 1957 the Navy completed the dredging of the harbor. Fort Bundy, built in 1940 as headquarters for coast artillery in Puerto Rico and abandoned ten years later when the 504th Artillery Battalion pulled out for the Panama Canal Zone, was taken over and transformed into the station's administration, personnel, comptroller, and security divisions. New buildings for assembling, maintaining, and testing missiles, as well as a liquid oxygen plant, an aviation electronics warehouse, jet fuel storage tanks, and a high explosives magazine, were constructed. A missile launching pad appeared, and the airfield runways were strengthened and extended. An ambitious effort to relieve the housing shortage got under way with construction of enlisted men's barracks, bachelor officers' quarters, new mess hall, and houses.

In the fall of 1958 Guided Missile Unit 51 arrived to supply Regulus I missile services to the Atlantic Fleet submarine units as well as to conduct training exercises for new submarine personnel in the firing of the Regulus I. A year later, this program was supplanted by Guided Missile Service Squadron Two. Under the direction of the Naval Air Force, U.S. Atlantic Fleet, the new operation encompassed the providing of services for all types of missiles.

Annually, Roosevelt Roads serves as the coordinating center for four exercises: Operation Springboard, the Navy's Caribbean wintertime maneuver, during which all weapons systems of the Atlantic Fleet Weapons Range are utilized; Operation Rimex, a multi-ship exercise to train and test participating units in weapons systems; Operation Stormfury, an exercise in monitoring tropical storms; and Operation Firex, largely a Marine Corps exercise.

Springboard, held from January to March, customarily involves 2,000 ships and aircraft and the firing of more than fifty guided missiles. Large numbers of transient aircraft and passengers and amounts of cargo are handled. For example, in 1974 the air terminal processed 30,588 passengers and 3,774 tons of freight. In 1975, in addition to hosting thirty-three deployed air squadrons (285 aircraft and 3,415 men), the station handled 7,219 aircraft from Cessna 150s to C-5A Air Force *Galaxys*, and during the peak period of the Springboard exercise conducted 12,534 flight operations while the Weapons Department serviced 28 ships, 10 aircraft squadrons, and handled 2,971,633 tons of ammunition. New records were set in 1982, when the station handled 57,200 takeoffs and landings, served 600 transient aircraft, and processed 12,000 transient passengers.

In the 1960s and 1970s the controversies with Cuba and Panama drew more attention to Guantanamo Bay (q.v.) and the Canal Zone Bases (*see* Panama Canal Zone, Post-World War II Defense Arrangements), though Roosevelt Roads played an important role in the 1965 Dominican intervention. Naval facilities on Puerto Rico made headlines when incidents involving nationalist groups on the island generated public interest, as in the controversy over the Navy's shelling of Vieques. But the uncertain status of Guantánamo and the prospective loss of military installations in Panama by the year 2000 meant that the Puerto Rican installations, especially Roosevelt Roads, had become more important than ever in protecting the sea lanes between the Venezuelan oil fields and the refineries of the Gulf Coast as well as the Atlantic sea routes north of Puerto Rico sailed by the oil tankers from Saudi Arabia too large for the Suez. When Puerto Rican activists made the Navy's shelling of Vieques a cause célèbre in 1979 and 1980, the Navy forcefully argued that Vieques and Roosevelt Roads were essential to maintaining an edge over the Soviet fleet. As Vice Adm. G.E.R. Kinnear II explained to the House of Representatives' Armed Services Committee in 1980:

> The overall training requirement is for a fully instrumented range for torpedo exercises, a live surface-to-air missile firing, an air-to-air missile firing against drone targets, electronic warfare simulation, aerial mining range, minesweeping areas, mobile land targets for strafing, targets for aerial bombing, shore targets for naval gunfire bombardment, and an amphibious landing area where close air support, naval gunfire support, and organic artillery can be exercised simultaneously. With this combination of requirements, one quickly comes to the realization that there is no other place that qualifies anywhere in the Atlantic Fleet.....
>
> The essential element that provides the U.S. Navy its advantage over the Soviets is our ability to deploy high performance aircraft; that is carrier aviation. They have us outnumbered in submarines and surface ships. Only in the area of high performance aircraft at sea do we have the edge....The Roosevelt Roads total training complex, of which Vieques is an integral part, is absolutely essential in enabling us to maintain that margin.

Roosevelt Roads Naval Station's tenant commands are: Commander Naval Forces Caribbean; U.S. South Atlantic Force; Fleet Analysis Center; Fleet Composite Squadron Eight; Naval Regional Dental Center; U.S. Naval Hospital; Mobile Construction Battalion Moscrip; Marine Barracks; and the Naval Special Warfare Group Two Detachment of the Caribbean.

''Roosey Roads'' has concentrated heavily upon improving relations between the servicemen at the station and the native Puerto Ricans. In 1974, for example, it hosted 88 groups totalling 5,502 individuals that took part in public relations programs. In 1975 in addition it started a disadvantaged youth program. To the Youth Action Center provided have come annually approximately one hundred teenagers recommended by the island government. The program, federally funded, runs for eight weeks. Station personnel also help out when disaster strikes, as when Hurricane David, the worst since 1928, hit Puerto Rico in 1979, by providing food, clothing, bedding, and fresh water to refugees. On 3 September 1979, after Hurricane Frederick hit the islands of Dominica and Martinique and the Dominican Republic, the station between 31 August and 25 October flew out relief supplies. Unfortunately, extremists groups demanding that the United States leave Puerto Rico have occasionally shown their hand. On 3 December 1979, for example, a bus carrying military personnel from Sabana Seca was ambushed. Two persons were killed and ten wounded. Moreover, on 9 December two Marines from the station's Marine Barracks were shot at during a routine security patrol. No one was injured, and no link was established with the Sabana Seca incident.

BIBLIOGRAPHY

A. U.S. Navy, Bureau of Yards and Docks, *Building the Navy's Bases in World War II*, 2 vols. (Washington: GPO, 1947); ''Command Historical Reports, U.S. Naval Station, Roosevelt Roads,'' 1959-1983 (Washington: Naval Historical Center, Operational Archives Branch); U.S. Congress, House of Representatives, Committee on Armed Services, 96th Cong., 2d Sess., *Naval Training Activities on the Island of Vieques, Puerto Rico: Hearings* (Washington: GPO, 1980), and *Report on the Inspection of U.S. Military Bases in Puerto Rico, Cuba, and the Panama Canal Zone* (Washington: GPO, 1980).

B. *El Navegante* (Roosevelt Roads, P.R.), 1942-

LESTER D. LANGLEY

ROSNEATH, SCOTLAND, U.S. NAVAL OPERATING BASE.
See United Kingdom, U.S. World War II Naval Bases.

ROTA, SPAIN, U.S. NAVAL BASE, 1955– Rota is a town of about 10,500 inhabitants located twenty miles to the north and across from the port of Cadiz at 36°37′N., 6°22′W., sixty air miles northwest of Gibraltar. It is on a projecting part of the coast forming the northern entrance point of Cadiz Bay, Province of Cadiz, in an ancient vineyard region in southwestern Spain.

Because of its form of government and close Axis ties during the first two years of World War II, Spain had been ostracized by the rest of the international community. In 1950, however, the United Nations approved the resumption of diplomatic relations with it, and in November of that year the United States granted it $62.5 million in economic aid. Adm. Forrest Sherman saw the value of strengthening U.S.-Spanish ties when in 1948 he served as Commander, Sixth Fleet, in the Mediterranean. In 1949 he returned to Washington as Chief of Naval Operations, and in 1950 he and Adm. Robert B. Carney, Commander of NATO forces in Northern Europe and the Mediterranean, pressed upon President Harry S. Truman the need for American bases in Spain, as did Secretary of

Defense George Marshall. In December 1950 Truman sent an ambassador to Madrid; early in 1951 he told Sherman, "I don't like Francisco Franco and I never will, but I won't let my personal feelings override the convictions of you military men."

In July 1951 Sherman and ambassador Stanton Griffis spoke with Franco about a bases agreement. An accord in principle was promptly reached and three American missions soon visited Spain, one to determine its economic status and financial needs, a military survey group, and a joint congressional study mission. Although the last highly recommended building bases in Spain, agreement was held up until 26 September 1953 because of the change of administrations in Washington and because of Spain's natural desire to get all it could from the United States in return for the base rights.

The Pact of Madrid, signed on 26 September 1953, was an executive agreement, and hence did not need senatorial approval. It included a Defense Agreement, an Economic Aid Agreement, and a Mutual Defense Assistance Agreement. Under the terms of the first, the United States was authorized to develop, build, and use jointly with Spain "such areas and facilities. . . as may be agreed upon." The bases, however, would remain under the "sovereignty" and "flag and command of Spain," thus limiting the freedom of American action therein. A Spanish captain would be in command; an American captain would command American activities. The agreement would last for ten years and would be extended automatically for two successive periods of five years each unless a specified termination procedure was followed. The United States thus obtained the right to build and operate air and naval bases in Spain. The first ground was broken in April 1955; naval activities began in January 1957, with the Naval Air Station following on 1 October. Rota had the first Navy Chapel and the first and only Navy Calibration Laboratory established in Europe. Moreover, in August 1975 the Military Sea Transport Service office was relocated from Naples, Italy (q.v.), to Rota.

To avoid wasteful building such as that in Morocco in 1951-1952, base construction policies called for a normal rather than crash program. Whenever possible, Spanish contractors would work under the prime U.S. contractor, Brown-Raymond-Walsh. The United States would spend $10 million for building, using equipment, materials, and supplies valued at up to $40 million from the air base construction program in Morocco. Maximum use would be made of the Spanish construction industry and labor force, the latter eventually numbering 6,000 men. Even some British, French, and West German engineering firms were involved in order to save the costs of transporting materials from the United States.

The small force of American naval aviation personnel assigned to Commander U.S. Naval Activities, Spain, supported contractors and the officer in charge of construction of the military bases being built. The R4D-8 that carried naval personnel and civilian engineers and cargoes (varying from concrete specimens to turkeys) was affectionately termed "the Toonerville Trolley." The plane and its crew provided the nucleus of the aviation facilities when the station at Rota was commissioned. By the spring of 1957 the original 8,000-foot runway had been extended to 12,000 feet and enjoyed such appurtenances as fixed field lighting, navigation aids, control tower, and Ground Control [Radar] Approach (GCA) for instrument landings. Although Naval Station Rota was commissioned in November 1957, it was not until September 1958 that the first squadron, VP-5, arrived, thus making unnecessary the use of supporting aircraft from Port Lyautey (*see* North Africa, U.S. Naval Bases). By July 1961 two major squadrons were homeported at Rota—but it also hosted as many as six Reserve squadrons that flew in from South Weymouth, Mass., Jacksonville, Fla., Minneapolis, Minn., Atlanta, Ga., and New York, N.Y., for their two-week active duty training periods. The major missions of the permanent squadrons were to operate on a nonscheduled basis in response to requests from Commander Fleet Air, Mediterranean, bringing personnel, mail, and cargo to and from the United States and the ships of the Sixth Fleet. When called upon, the squadrons also responded by delivering blankets, food, and medical supplies when tragedy struck—as during the great flood in India in 1955, the earthquake in Turkey in 1956, the flood in Lebanon in 1956, and the 1957 earthquake at Agadir, Morocco.

The strategic air bases built at Zaragoza (a U.S. SAC command), Torrejon (near Madrid), and Morón (near Seville) by the U.S. Navy as an Air Force agent need not detain us. For our purpose interest centers on Rota, which has been used to operate fleet reconnaissance aircraft, to support fleet communications, to act on occasion as a base for carrier aircraft and replacement units, and, beginning late in 1960, to serve nuclear-powered submarines. Major construction included dredging and building breakwaters and piers capable of servicing any Sixth Fleet ship, and the beginning of a petroleum pipeline 485 miles long that would run through Morón and Torrejon to Zaragoza and supply all the Air Force bases. Subsidiary naval centers included an oil storage depot and supply center in Franco's native town of El Ferrol, in northwestern Spain, and an ammunition storage depot at Cartagena, on the Mediterranean coast, both eventually disestablished. Because of rising labor and material costs, the $225 million provided for the Air Force and the $113 million for the Navy grew to $420 million by 1960. The value of the plant as of 31 December 1966 was $91.262 million; on 31 December 1977, $350 million. The population of the naval station numbered 4,130 in 1961 and 8,234 in 1966, but, following budget reductions, fell to 5,552 in 1978 and to only 3,341 in 1979, when the squadron of nuclear-powered submarines left.

The entrance to the naval base is just off the center of the city of Rota, which in Spanish means "course," "strong" or "fortress," yet the city is a combination of old and new, with sixteenth- and seventeenth-century Gothic and baroque churches mingling with the hotels of a major seaside resort town sporting beaches of golden sand. The naval station itself, which covers 6,096 acres, is quite complete, including as it does a personal services center; hospital and dental, fire, police, chaplain, recreational, educational, commissary, and exchange services; and housing and educational complexes in an area roughly twelve by sixteen blocks in extent. Security is provided by a detachment of U.S. Marines 100 strong. To the north is the airfield used by three naval aircraft squadrons and by Fleet Tactical Support Squadron 24, which delivers personnel, cargo, and mail to U.S. naval forces in the European and Mediterranean areas. Since 1959, in an isolated 4-acre compound, Rota has operated three generating units each capable of producing eight gallons of liquid oxygen or five gallons of liquid nitrogen per hour. With a storage capacity of 3,500 gallons for oxygen and 500 gallons for nitrogen, it is the most important facility of its kind in the Mediterranean area. Since 1963, the naval station has also hosted the Navy Overseas Air Cargo Terminal, one of the Navy's five NOACTs, with a monthly record of cargo moved set at 4,654,525 pounds. A new record for ships served, 75 during a thirty-one day period, was established in May 1969, with 569 ships serviced during that year. In 1970 air traffic included 274 aircraft, which carried 6,628 passengers, 91.6 tons of mail, and 1232.4 tons of cargo per month; and 574 ships were serviced (394 U.S. naval combatants, 70 Spanish, and 110 merchantmen). In 1971 a Publications and Printing Service Branch Office was added. In 1971 also, Mobile Construction Unit 4 (Seabees) returned after a five-year absence and used Rota as a base camp for battalions scattered throughout Europe. While a new high of 674 ships serviced was established, Rota also provided assistance to the Air Force's Apollo Recovery Team based in England.

Ships and submarines are serviced at three piers to the south of Rota; communications are taken care of by radio, communications, and courier stations. In addition Rota contains such tenant facilities as a Naval Oceanography Command Center, a Weapons Department, a Naval Security Group, a Salvage Disposal Group, the aforementioned small Marine Detachment and Mobile Construction Unit, and Europe's only U.S. Fleet Weather Central. Growing pains included poorly designed boilers for steam generators, insufficient electrical power and water (annual rainfall is only 9.1 inches), cliff erosion, and, in some areas, shortages of office space and housing for dependents, telephone systems considered substandard in American eyes, and difficulties in replacing skilled American supervisory personnel with qualified Spaniards.

Because the proud Spaniards dislike having foreigners on their soil, American commanders have followed a "low profile policy" including a requirement that only civilian clothes—and these to be with coat and tie—be used by men leaving the base. As on-base housing facilities increased, a bit of America grew on Spanish soil, American relations with the outside nevertheless being formal but friendly.

By 1958, just when construction of the bases in Spain was completed, the need for them began to evaporate. Spain disliked the idea of having air bases near some of its largest cities, which might become targets for Soviet missiles. In the United States, meanwhile, emphasis shifted from bombers to missiles, including those in Polaris submarines, as retaliatory weapons. The value of the air bases, from which an average of 32,000 sorties were made annually, consequently declined in subsequent years, as did the military aid granted Spain, which dropped from the $350 million for the first four years of the bases agreement to $32 million in 1960. The United States stopped its economic aid to Spain in 1963.

When the agreements came up for renewal in 1963, Spain asked for what the United States considered unreasonable financial terms. The United States preferred the existing *qui pro quo* program to Spain's desire for closer Spanish-American relations. Rather than the "alliance" Spain wanted, the renewed defense agreement called for granting Spain $100 million but for inactivating the Air Force base at Zaragoza while expanding the size and mission of Rota by merging the Naval Air Station and Naval Station and having it become the operational base for nine Polaris submarines and for many of the activities transferred there from Morocco after the United States closed its Moroccan bases in 1963. On 26 February 1964 the USS *Proteus* (AS-19) homeported in Rota as tender for eight nuclear submarines. The Air Force was hurt when one of its B-52s collided with a refueling plane and released four unarmed hydrogen bombs near the small farming village of Palomares. Although three of the bombs were recovered within twenty-four hours, the fourth was not recovered from the ocean until eighty days later. At Spanish request, the United States agreed to bar aircraft carrying nuclear weapons from overflying Spain.

Negotiations undertaken in 1968 to renew the bases agreement ran into congressional desire to reduce foreign commitments—the Vietnam War was nearing its peak—and opposition to exorbitant Spanish financial demands for $1.5 billion, and for American assistance in trying to get Britain to restore Gibraltar to Spain. Not until 20 June 1969 was an accord reached on a two-year extension of the agreements, for which the United States would give $50 million in arms aid, with both the time and money involved hinting at liquidation of the agreement in the near future, a prospect very pleasing to J. William Fulbright, Chairman of the Senate Foreign Relations Committee, who thought that the national interest did not require the bases. In April 1969 President Richard Nixon approved placing the air base at Morón on inactive status and reducing American troop strength in Spain from 15,000 to 10,000 by January 1970. In turn, Spain's purchase of thirty French Mirage 3-E jets showed that it was lessening its dependence upon the United States for military supplies. However, the deterioration of the U.S. strategic position in North Africa since the June 1967 Arab-Israeli War and its expulsion from Wheelus Air Force Base in Libya in March 1970 revived the need for the Spanish bases, and on 26 September 1970 a five-year extension for their use was signed that transferred Spanish workers from the employ of the U.S. Navy to that of the Spanish Navy. More important, on 1 July 1971 the nuclear capability of Naval Station Rota was reduced from that of an Operational Overseas Storage Site to that of a Modified Advanced Underseas Warfare Shop, meaning that the latter could no longer be associated with the Polaris program, that it had to phase out the Mk-101 depth bomb and the Mk-44 torpedo, and in addition that it had to reduce the personnel allowed in these programs. While about 23,000 tons of obsolescent ammunition were returned to the United States, Rota was designated a Surface Missile System Support Activity for emergency stowage of Terrier, Tartar, and Talos missiles. Extension and resurfacing of runways meanwhile permitted their use by C-5A *Galaxy* aircraft and the setting of a new record of service for 47,461 aircraft, including squadrons from several carriers and Naval Air Reserve Training Units from the United States.

During the Arab-Israeli War of 1973, Rota and the Air Force bases played an unintended role: with only 70 percent of its authorized enlisted strength, Rota in 1973 increased its cargo tonnage-handling by 47 percent. When all of Washington's allies except Portugal refused to permit the United States to refuel its planes supplying Israel, U.S. tanker planes from Torreon refueled U.S. planes over the Mediterranean despite Spanish protests, which raised the question in the minds of many Americans whether the bases would be available to further American interests in the future. In any event, VR-24 Detachment, Rota, Comdr. E.V. Thomas, provided nearly all of the airborne support for minesweeping of the Suez Canal in 1975 in operations *Nimbus Star, Nimbus Moon,* and *Nimrod Spar*. Although temperatures at the runway in Ismailia, Egypt, sometimes reach 130°F and the runways were less than 4,000 feet long, VR-24's *Hercules* made timely flights to the area in support of this critical mission.

With the death of Franco in November 1975 portending increased democratization in Spain and Spain's moving closer to NATO, much of the opposition in the United States was quieted. By a vote of 84 to 11 on 21 June 1976, the Senate approved a friendship treaty with Spain that renewed the bases agreement for another five years at a cost to the United States of $1.2 billion. The United States could continue to use the air bases at Morón, Torrejon, and Zaragoza and the naval base at Rota. Soon thereafter, however, the air bases were put in standby status or used as training stations, and operations at Rota promised to diminish because all nuclear-powered submarines were to be barred from it on 1 July 1979. When Submarine Squadron Sixteen left in June, more than 3,550 military personnel and 3,572 military dependents left with it, reducing the population of the base by almost a third and causing reductions in force and the consolidation of many personnel services. Yet, in 1979 Rota berthed almost 100,000 transient personnel, controlled 62,043 aircraft operations, moved 12,584 tons of air cargo, increased the number of American and Spanish naval ships as well as merchant ships serviced to a total of 801—levels matched in 1980. In 1980 Rota was designated as a Contingency Landing Site for NASA's space shuttle and celebrated its eleventh year of accident-free flight operations. Operating costs that year were almost $39 million, part of which went to defray charges for the transshipment of foods and supplies for the increased number of ships in the Middle East Force.

Military aid to Spain has been quite negligible—$3.8 million for fiscal year 1980, $3.6 million for 1981—and the United States will not sell Spain nuclear fuels unless it agrees to stated safeguards against using them to build weapons.

For 1982, however, aid under the Ronald Reagan administration was increased to $150 million.

By the summer of 1981 the Aircraft Intermediate Maintenance Department (AIMD) at Rota, which followed the slogan ''If it comes off an aircraft, we can fix it,'' had 276 personnel in nine divisions scattered through buildings that stretched more than a mile from the jet test cell to the AIMD hangar. They maintained four naval station aircraft, provided support for three tenant squadrons based at the station, and deployed units aboard ships in the Mediterranean. Naval Air Reserve Squadrons used Rota as a base during active duty for training. At the same time, Rota personnel were preparing equipment and space to support a new arrival, the P-3C *Orion*.

On 10 December 1981 NATO took a historic step and formally invited Spain to become its sixteenth member, an act clearly intended to fill a strategic gap on the southwestern flank of the alliance in Europe and to strengthen democracy in post-Franco Spain. In May 1982, when Spain recorded its accession to NATO with the U.S. Department of State, it was admitted to membership. The four U.S. bases in Spain therefore are under NATO rather than American control. In addition, the newly elected socialist president has announced that he will submit the issue of foreign bases on Spanish soil to close scrutiny and possibly a popular referendum. However, on 23 February 1983 it was announced that agreement had been reached on a five-year defense treaty that would allow U.S. forces to use one naval base and three air bases in Spain but with increased military aid for Spain and stricter Spanish control over American use of the bases. When approved, the treaty will provide for U.S. loans worth $400 million beginning October 1983 to modernize the Spanish armed forces; a $12 million grant in cooperation aid; and $3 million for military training of Spanish personnel in the United States.

BIBLIOGRAPHY

Capt. John D. Eaton, USN, ''United States-Spanish Military Relationship, 1968-1973'' (Newport, R.I.: U.S. Naval War College, Research Paper, 20 Oct. 1976); *Statement of Living and Working Conditions at Naval Base, Rota (Cadiz), Spain* (Rota, Spain: Commander Naval Activities, Spain/Commanding Officer U.S. Naval Station, Rota, Spain, rev. 18 Apr. 1969, courtesy Public Affairs Officer, Rota, Spain); Stanley B. Weeks, 'The Development and Implications of the United States Alliance with Spain since 1953'' (Annapolis, Md.: U.S. Naval Academy, Trident Scholar Project Report, 1970); U.S. Congress, Senate, Committee on Foreign Relations, *United States Security Agreements and Commitments Abroad, Hearings before the Subcommittee on United States Security Agreements and Commitments Abroad*, 91st Cong., 2d. Sess., 2 vols. (Washington: GPO, 1971); Command History of the Joint Spanish-U.S. Naval Base, Rota, Spain (Commanding Officer U.S. Naval Station, Rota, Spain, to Chief of Naval Operations, for the years 1957 and 1967 and 1967-1980, courtesy Public Affairs Officer, U.S. Naval Station Rota).

B. U.S. Department of State, *Department of State Bulletin*, 1950- ; Claude G. Bowers, *My Mission to Spain* (New York: Simon and Schuster, 1954); Arthur P. Whitaker, *Spain and the Defense of the West* (New York: Harper and Bros., 1961); Paul Hoffman, ''Rota

Shipshape as a U.S. Navy Base,'' *New York Times*, 28 Feb. 1963; ''Rota and Its Aviation Activities,'' *Naval Aviation News*, Nov. 1964, pp. 24-25; ''American Bases in Spain,'' *New York Times*, 12 Mar. 1969; ''The Spanish Bases,'' *Washington Post*, 17 Mar., 13 Apr. 1969; Tad Szulc, ''Accord Reported on Bases in Spain,'' *New York Times*, 15 Apr. 1970; ''U.S. and Madrid Resuming Talks,'' *New York Times*, 12 Apr. 1970; ''U.S., Spain Begin Talks on Bases Agreement,'' *Washington Post*, 14 Apr. 1970; R.A. Komorowski, ''Spain and the Defense of NATO,'' U.S. Naval Institute *Naval Review*, May 1976 pp. 190-203; Hal P. Klepak, *Spain: NATO or Neutrality* (Kingston, Ont.: Queen's University Centre for International Relations, 1980); F.R. Stevens, Jr., ''Spain and NATO: Problems and Prospects,'' *Air University Review* 31 (Mar.-Apr. 1980):2-14; ''The Fix Is in at AIMD Rota,'' *Naval Aviation News*, Sept. 1981, p. 54; Miguel Garcia De Lomas, Capitan de Fregata, Spanish Navy, ''Spain, NATO, and Gibraltar,'' *Air University Review* 32 (May-June 1981):88-89; Angel Vinas, *Los pactos secretos de Franco con Estados Unidos: Bases, ayuda, economica, recortes de soberania* (Colection 80) (Barcelona, Spain: Grijalbo, 1981); ''Spain Becomes 16th Member of NATO,'' *NATO Review* 30, No. 3 (1982).

RUSSELL ISLANDS, SOLOMON ISLANDS, U.S. NAVAL ADVANCE BASE, 1943-1946 Located about thirty miles northwest of Guadalcanal, the Russell Islands (9°6′S., 159°11′E.) comprise two main islands, Pavuvu and Banika, separated by narrow Sunlight Channel. They were part of the British Solomon Islands Protectorate. Pavuvu is rugged and densely wooded, while Banika is favored with level land on its east coast. Adm. William F. Halsey, Commander, South Pacific Area, desired occupation of the Russells as the next batch of islands north up the chain of the Solomons toward the Japanese base of Rabaul on New Britain. He intended to use them as a motor torpedo boat base, air base, and landing craft staging point for further operations in the Solomons. The invasion of the Russells (Operation Cleanslate) was approved on 23 January 1943 and mounted less than a month later. Troops made unopposed landings on 21 February. First priority for the Seabees was construction of two fighter fields with ancillary support facilities on Banika. The fields were ready by April 1943 to help support attacks on Munda airfield on New Georgia. The same day as the landings, PT service personnel set up a primitive base in Sunlight Channel and inaugurated anti-barge patrols toward New Georgia.

The immediate strategic use for the Russells came to an end in the summer of 1943 with the capture of New Georgia in the central Solomons. However, Banika became the location of important supply and light craft repair installations. That summer, construction troops created a number of small-craft landing areas on Banika, then erected the buildings for a large naval supply depot. Supplies were unloaded there, sorted, and repacked for shipment north to other advance bases in the Solomons. Operating in January 1944 as a part of this huge warehouse complex was an advance base construction depot to service the naval construction battalions operating in the Solomons. In connection with the small-craft base, by late 1943 Pontoon Assembly Detachment 2 was functioning on Banika. On

Pavuvu, the Marine Corps developed a staging camp and a large depot for the First Marine Division. The division rested there during the spring and summer of 1944 after its grueling campaign on New Britain, and returned there after the bloody invasion (September 1944) of Peleliu.

As with the other naval bases in the lower Solomons, the Russells last came into prominence in early 1945 with preparations for the assault on Okinawa. The First Marine Division was part of Task Force 53, Northern Attack Force for the Okinawa landings. Getting them ready to go and sending them off was the final effort of the Russell Islands naval advance base. Thereafter, there was a massive roll-up of facilities in the Solomons. The base at the Russells was disestablished the same day as its companions at Guadalcanal (q.v.) and Tulagi (q.v.) 12 June 1946.

BIBLIOGRAPHY

A. Russell Islands Naval Base, ''First Narrative of the Russell Islands Naval Command, Shore Establishment, 1945'' (Washington: Naval Historical Center, Operational Archives Branch); Service Squadron, South Pacific, ''History of Commander, Service Squadron, South Pacific, 7 December 1941-15 August 1945'' (Washington: Naval Historical Center, Operational Archives Branch); Fourth Base Depot, USMC, Russell Islands, ''History of Base Depot Russell Islands,'' Administrative History, Appendix, ''South Pacific Administration, History 74'' (Washington: Naval Historical Center, Operational Archives Branch).

B. Samuel E. Morison, *Breaking the Bismarcks Barrier 22 July 1942-1 May 1944* (Boston: Little, Brown, 1950); Robert Sherrod, *History of Marine Corps Aviation in World War II* (Washington: Combat Forces Press, 1952); Capt. Robert J. Bulkley, *At Close Quarters: PT Boats in the United States Navy* (Washington: Department of the Navy, History Division, 1962).

JOHN B. LUNDSTROM

S

SA DEC, REPUBLIC of VIETNAM, U.S. NAVAL SUPPORT ACTIVITY DETACHMENT, 1966–1971 Located on the south bank of the Mekong River in the center of the Republic of Vietnam's Mekong Delta, Sa Dec was the site of a forward combat base during the conflict in Southeast Asia. A ten-boat river patrol section of River Division 52 first deployed there during the summer of 1966 as part of the Game Warden operation, which sought to interdict enemy logistic traffic on the larger rivers.

Naval leaders chose Sa Dec as a staging area because the city lay astride the key waterway of the area and was accessible to logistic support vessels steaming upriver from the South China Sea. In addition, a Vietnamese Army compound there contained adequate facilities, including a boat yard and small marine railway, for the intermediate-level repair of river patrol craft.

A detachment of Naval Support Activity, Saigon (q.v.), provided the combat unit with basic logistic support and oversaw base development, including the installation of a pontoon pier, fuel storage bladder, and boat ramp. The naval facility at Sa Dec was turned over to the Vietnamese Navy as part of the Vietnamization program in April 1971.

BIBLIOGRAPHY

A. Commander Naval Forces, Vietnam, "The Naval War in Vietnam," May 1970 (Washington: Naval Historical Center, Operational Archives Branch); Service Force, U.S. Pacific Fleet, "Command Histories, 1967-1972" (Washington: Naval Historical Center, Operational Archives Branch).

B. Herbert T. King, "Naval Logistic Support, Qui Nhon to Phu Quoc," U.S. Naval Institute *Naval Review* 95 (May 1969):84-111; Edwin B. Hooper, *Mobility, Support, Endurance: A Story of Naval Operational Logistics in the Vietnam War, 1965-1968* (Washington: GPO, 1972).

EDWARD J. MAROLDA

SAFI, FRENCH MOROCCO.
See North Africa, U.S. Naval Bases.

SA HUYNH, REPUBLIC OF VIETNAM, U.S. NAVAL SUPPORT ACTIVITY DETACHMENT, 1967-1970 Sa Huynh, 100 miles south of Danang, marked the location of a remote naval logistic base during the Vietnam Conflict. The site, on an island at the southern end of the I Corps Tactical Zone, was chosen in 1967 as the least undesirable location from which to support Army operations in the Duc Pho region. Still, its drawbacks were significant; a channel through the surrounding lagoon required constant dredging to remain open; at the end of that year, an over-the-beach supply effort with civilian-manned tank landing ships (LSTs), an amphibious assault fuel line, and a pontoon causeway proved inadequate in the face of the seasonal monsoon that swept in off the South China Sea.

As a result, in August 1968 naval leaders established the Naval Support Activity, Danang, Detachment Sa Huynh, to put the logistic operation on a firmer footing. Thereafter, utility landing craft (LCU), ramps, portable fuel storage bladders, and various base facilities were constructed on the island. By September 1969 the detachment handled over 3,000 measurement tons of cargo monthly for Army troops fighting inland. As part of the general phase-out of the U.S. presence in South Vietnam, the Sa Huynh facility was closed in February 1970.

BIBLIOGRAPHY

A. Service Force, U.S. Pacific Fleet, "Command Histories, 1967-1972" (Washington: Naval Historical Center, Operational Archives Branch).

B. Frank C. Collins, Jr., "Maritime Support of the Campaign in I Corps," U.S. Naval Institute *Naval Review* 97 (May 1971):156-79; Edwin C. Hooper, *Mobility, Support, Endurance: A Story of Naval Operational Logistics in the Vietnam War, 1965-1968* (Washington: GPO, 1972).

EDWARD J. MAROLDA

SAIDOR, NEW GUINEA, U.S. NAVAL ADVANCE BASE, 1944 On 2 January 1944 troops from the Southwest Pacific Area landed at Saidor (5°35′S., 146°35′E.) on the north New Guinea coast about 115 miles west of Finchhafen. Their objective was to bypass strong Japanese forces at Sio, seize a base on the coast, and use the airfield there to help neutralize Sio and another big Japanese concentration at Wewak, to the west of Saidor. The invasion proceeded without trouble, and soon the airfield was operating. Other than supplying the forces ashore, main naval activity by the Seventh Fleet at Saidor was by PT boats. On 4 March 1944 Motor Torpedo Boat Squadron 24 set up a small operating base at Nom Plantation near Saidor. Barge hunting was particularly fruitful westward toward Hansa Bay and Wewak. PT patrols from Saidor finally ceased on 25 June 1944, and the PTs advanced to Mios Woendi off Biak (q.v.).

BIBLIOGRAPHY

A. Motor Torpedo Boat Squadrons, Philippine Sea Frontier, "Command History of MTB Squadrons, Philippine Sea Frontier, Formerly MTB Squadrons, 7th Fleet," 5 vols., Type Commands, 1945 (Washington: Naval Historical Center, Operational Archives

Branch); U.S. Navy, "7th Amphibious Force Command History 10 January 1943-23 December 1945" (Washington: Naval Historical Center, Operational Archives Branch); U.S. Navy, "U.S. Naval Bases in the South and Southwest Pacific (and Central Pacific Forward) in World War II," 1 November 1954 (Washington: Naval Historical Center, Operational Archives Branch).

B. Samuel E. Morison, *Breaking the Bismarcks Barrier 22 July 1942-1 May 1944* (Boston: Little, Brown, 1950); Capt. Robert J. Bulkley, *At Close Quarters: PT Boats in the United States Navy* (Washington: Navy Department, Naval History Division, 1962); Vice Adm. Daniel E. Barbey, *MacArthur's Amphibious Navy* (Annapolis, Md.: U.S. Naval Institute, 1969).

JOHN B. LUNDSTROM

SAIGON, REPUBLIC OF VIETNAM, U.S. NAVY HEADQUARTERS SUPPORT ACTIVITY, SAIGON, AND NAVAL SUPPORT ACTIVITY, 1950-1973 The U.S. Navy was long associated with Saigon, the capital and largest city in South Vietnam. In August 1950 eight officers and men arrived there to staff the Navy Section of the newly created Military Assistance Advisory Group (MAAG), Indochina, the function of which was to administer American military aid to the French. Between 1950 and 1954, hundreds of ships and craft, including the aircraft carrier *Belleau Wood* (CVL-24), amphibious ships and craft, armored river boats, yard craft, barges, and floating cranes were provided the French Expeditionary Force in its ultimately unsuccessful fight against Ho Chi Minh's Viet Minh forces.

The naval presence in Saigon surged during late 1954 and early 1955 when, under the provisions of the Geneva Agreement, Vietnamese living in areas to be controlled by the predominantly communist Viet Minh chose evacuation by sea to the noncommunist South. The U.S. Navy transported, in seventy-four of its ships and thirty-nine belonging to the Military Sea Transportation Service, over 310,000 passengers, 69,000 tons of cargo, and 8,000 vehicles, mostly to Saigon.

Even as the French withdrew from Indochina, the Navy Section of the MAAG worked to develop a viable naval force for the new Republic of Vietnam. Between 1955 and 1961 the American advisors made considerable quantitative progress, although qualitative improvement came slower. By the end of 1961, the 63-man naval advisory contingent had helped to create a Vietnamese Navy of 4,500 men and 119 ships, landing craft, and boats as well as an autonomous paramilitary junk force for coastal patrol. In addition, the advisors provided technological assistance at the Saigon Naval Shipyard, the largest facility of its kind in Southeast Asia.

Following the November 1961 visit to South Vietnam of a team headed by Gen. Maxwell Taylor, President John F. Kennedy's chief military advisor, the American role in the increasingly critical counterinsurgency struggle changed from advice to combat support. The resulting growth in the number of U.S.

support units deployed to South Vietnam called for a corresponding buildup of logistic resources. Because earlier, in a worldwide division of labor, the Navy had been assigned logistic responsibility for American forces in Southeast Asia, the service was directed to assume the task of supporting the primarily Army and Air Force commands in-country.

Established in July 1962, the Navy's Headquarters Support Activity, Saigon (HSAS), provided the U.S. military services in the capital region with supply, fiscal, public works, medical and dental, transportation, commissary and exchange, special services, security, and other support. The commanding officer of HSAS directed the activity's operations from the Cofat building on Hung Vuong Street, but subordinate offices, warehouses, and personnel quarters were spread all over the city. From this decentralized complex, HSAS personnel carried out such activities as managing bachelor officer and enlisted quarters and messes, rest and recreation flights to Asian cities, USO shows, and the Armed Forces Radio Service. In addition, the command ran the seventy-two-bed Saigon Station Hospital on Tran Hung Dao Street and a dental clinic. Also, naval chaplains ministered to the spiritual needs of American servicemen. In addition, HSAS transported mail and commissary and exchange items to other U.S. bases in-country, particularly along the coast.

Although in the minority, other naval units formed part of the growing Saigon military community. A subordinate of the Navy's Bureau of Yards and Docks, the Officer in Charge of Construction, established his office in the capital's Tu Do Street. He and his staff oversaw the burgeoning construction of airfields, warehouses, and other facilities by civilian contractors. To control the Seabee teams that were already in South Vietnam building Army Special Forces camps and accomplishing civic action tasks, the Navy established the headquarters of Commander Naval Construction Battalions, U.S. Pacific Fleet Detachment, Republic of Vietnam. Another unit, a detachment from the Seventh Fleet, flew aerial reconnaissance missions over South Vietnam from the nearby Tan Son Nhut Airfield during 1962 and 1963.

After the assassination of President Ngo Dinh Diem and the fall of his government in December 1963, the conflict entered a new, more critical phase wherein additional American forces were required to stem the rising communist tide. Hoping to better control the war and the military assistance effort, in May 1964 American leaders disestablished the MAAG and incorporated its personnel and resources into Military Assistance Command Vietnam (MACV). The old Navy Section of the MAAG became the Naval Advisory Group, and by the end of the year there were 235 naval personnel in the 4,900-man military assistance command. This increase reflected the growth of the Vietnamese Navy, by then manned by over 8,100 men, and the junk force.

At the same time, the number of American servicemen in South Vietnam approached 23,000, which severely taxed the personnel and material resources of the 600-man HSAS, originally intended only to support Saigon headquarters. The Port Terminal Division handled 30,000 to 40,000 measurement tons of cargo each month during 1964. HSAS supplied over 100 local and field exchanges and maintained 186,000 square feet of warehouse space, 200,000 cubic feet of cold storage space, and 127,000 square feet of open storage. And the activity continued to provide security, messing and quartering, medical and dental, administrative, and personnel services.

Recognizing in late 1964 that a major buildup of U.S. and allied forces was likely to occur soon, Pacific military leaders gradually transferred HSAS responsibilities to deploying Army logistic commands. Nonetheless, the Navy's support activity in Saigon accomplished much during 1965; in one month, the port unit handled 330,000 measurement tons of military supplies offloaded from ninety-six ships; another 40,000 measurement tons were transported to outlying ports; the activity acquired 2,730,000 cubic feet of warehouse space; fifty-four bachelor officer and enlisted quarters and four hotels for transient personnel were managed; a main library in Saigon dispatched over 60,000 books and magazines to in-country bases; the real estate division was managing 318 construction contracts at the end of the year; and 109 medical personnel at the Saigon Station Hospital treated thousands of patients, many of whom were battle casualties. Finally, in May 1966, with its resources turned over to the Army, HSAS was disestablished.

The deployment to South Vietnam of large combat forces during the years from 1965 to 1968 caused the naval establishment in Saigon to balloon. Early in 1965 the headquarters and operations center of Commander Coastal Surveillance Force was established at the advisory group facility to direct the Navy's country-wide Market Time anti-infiltration effort. Squadrons of SP-2 *Neptune* patrol planes, the aerial component of the coastal force, flew from Tan Son Nhut Airfield. Helicopter Combat Support Squadron 1 detachments also operated from the air facility. Operations to prevent the Viet Cong from mining the vulnerable river approaches to the inland port began when a unit composed of converted landing craft was based at the Saigon Naval Shipyard. Before being relocated to Can Tho (*see* Can Tho-Bin Thuy, Republic of Vietnam, U.S. Naval Support Activity) in the Mekong Delta, the headquarters of the River Patrol Force, which directed the effort to interdict communist logistic movement on the rivers, also was set up in Saigon.

By early 1966 the size and diverse nature of the Navy's headquarters, advisory, coastal surveillance, helicopter and fixed-wing aircraft, logistic support, river patrol, mine warfare, and harbor defense units made central control an essential requirement. Accordingly, on 1 April Commander Naval Forces, Vietnam (COMNAVFORV), with headquarters in Saigon, became the senior naval officer in-country and subordinate only to the MACV commander. In addition to directing the major combat and support commands, COMNAVFORV assumed responsibility for coordination with the Saigon-based Military Sea Transportation Service office, with the Officer in Charge of Construction, and with Commander Coast Guard Activities, Vietnam.

Although HSAS was replaced by the Army's own logistic commands for general support, naval units in the southern part of the Republic of Vietnam continued to need Navy-peculiar support. As a result, on the same day that HSAS passed into history, 17 May 1966, the Naval Support Activity (NSA), Saigon, began providing service to shore-based naval forces in all but the I Corps Tactical Zone. From scattered locations in the downtown area, NSA's operations, supply, repair, public works, and administrative departments handled such functions as transportation; ammunition, communications, ordnance, and registered publications supply; repair and maintenance; repair parts stowage and issue; base construction and support; special services; quartering and messing; and payroll.

To improve the logistic flow to the naval units in the field, which operated over 400 river patrol boats (PBR), fast patrol craft (PCF), landing craft, and various other vessels, NSA Saigon established subordinate detachments at An Thoi (q.v.), Cam Ranh Bay (q.v.), Cat Lo (q.v.), Nha Be (q.v.), Qui Nhon (q.v.), Can Tho-Bin Thuy, Dong Tam (q.v.), Sa Dec (q.v.), Vinh Long (q.v.), Vung Tau (q.v.), and Ben Luc (q.v.). These sites were chosen because of their proximity to the waterways on which the combat units operated and their accessibility to support ships and craft. In addition, an important criterion for site selection of a number of the bases was the existence of Vietnamese Navy or Army installations that could provide base facilities and defenses for the American naval tenants.

The NSA had assigned or operationally controlled many vessels, including the repair and maintenance ships *Tutuila* (ARG-4), *Markab* (AR-23), and *Krishna* (ARL-38), tank landing ships (LSTs), and a great variety of barges for berthing and messing, fuel and water supply, and repair. In addition, the activity's air transportation service, nicknamed ''Air Cofat'' for the compound in which the main headquarters was housed, operated C-47, TC-45J, HU-16, and H-46 aircraft from Tan Son Nhut Airfield.

As the war progressed, NSA Saigon took on additional responsibilities, such as support for the joint Army-Navy Mobile Riverine Force, the naval element of which consisted of heavily armed and armored landing craft used as monitors, troops transports, and command-control vessels. The Saigon activity also was charged with construction and supply of the radar facilities on Con Son and Hon Khoai, islands off the southern coast of the Mekong Delta.

At the same time, the development of facilities and refinement of logistic operations enabled NSA Saigon to accommodate new tasks. In that regard, in 1967 the Saigon support establishment relieved the Naval Supply Depot at Subic Bay (q.v.) in the Philippines of responsibility for stocking and issuing boat repair parts. A new naval supply facility at the outlying complex at Newport also eased the supply load. And subsequently some major vessel repairs were accomplished at the naval shipyard.

As the Navy began withdrawing from the Republic of Vietnam, from 1969 to 1973, the vast headquarters and support establishment in Saigon was gradually turned over to the Vietnamese Navy. In keeping with the Vietnamization program, the indigenous naval service was prepared by its American counterpart to assume the myriad and complex operational and logistic functions. On 30 April 1972 the headquarters of Commander Naval Construction Battalions, U.S. Pacific Fleet Detachment, Republic of Vietnam, was closed down and the staff transported to the United States. That June, Naval Support Activity, Saigon, turned over its resources to the Vietnamese and was disestablished. Shortly afterward, the Naval Supply Facility, Newport, carried out a similar transfer. As provided for in the Paris Agreement establishing the ceasefire in Southeast Asia, the Naval Advisory Group, Vietnam, and Naval Forces, Vietnam, commands were disestablished on 29 March 1973, ending the advisory and combat phase of the Navy's long sojourn in the Republic of Vietnam.

The only personnel remaining in South Vietnam after March 1973 were those officers and men assigned to the naval section of the Defense Attaché Office, which was subordinate to the U.S. Embassy in Saigon. For the next two years, the naval office administered the ever dwindling military assistance that was provided to the struggling South Vietnamese nation. This aid notwithstanding, the Republic of Vietnam was finally overrun by the communist enemy in the spring of 1975. By the end of April, all naval personnel were withdrawn from the doomed capital that had accommodated the U.S. Navy for twenty-five years.

BIBLIOGRAPHY

A. Commander Naval Forces, Vietnam, ''Monthly Historical Reports, 1965-1971,'' (Washington: Naval Historical Center, Operational Archives Branch); Service Force, U.S. Pacific Fleet, ''Command Histories, 1967-1972'' (Washington: Naval Historical Center, Operational Archives Branch).

B. Herbert T. King, ''Naval Logistic Support, Qui Nhon to Phu Quoc,'' U.S. Naval Institute, *Naval Review* 95 (May 1969):84-111; W.C. Wells, ''The Riverine Force in Action, 1966-1967,'' U.S. Naval Institute *Naval Review* 95 (May 1969):46-83; Charles J. Merdinger, ''Civil Engineers, Seabees, and Bases in Vietnam,'' U.S. Naval Institute *Naval Review* 96 (May 1970):254-75; S.A. Swarztrauber, ''River Patrol Relearned,'' U.S. Naval Institute *Naval Review* 96 (May 1970):120-57; Richard L. Schreadley, ''The Naval War in Vietnam, 1950-1970,'' U.S. Naval Institute *Naval Review* 97 (May 1971):180-211; Edwin B. Hooper, *Mobility, Support, Endurance: A Story of Naval Operational Logistics in the Vietnam War, 1965-1968* (Washington: GPO, 1972); Richard Tregaskis, *Southeast Asia: Building the Bases: The History of Construction in Southeast Asia* (Washington: GPO, 1975); Edwin B. Hooper, Dean C. Allard, and Oscar P. Fitzgerald, *The Setting of the Stage to 1959,* Vol. 1 of *The United States Navy and the Vietnam Conflict* (Washington: GPO, 1976).

EDWARD J. MAROLDA

ST. INGLEVERT, FRANCE.

See World War I U.S. Northern Bombing Group Bases in England and France.

ST. LUCIA, BRITISH WEST INDIES, U.S. NAVAL AIR STATION.

See Caribbean, The, U.S. Naval Bases.

ST. MAWES, ENGLAND.
See United Kingdom, U.S. World War II Naval Bases.

ST. NAZAIRE, FRANCE, U.S. DISEMBARKATION AND EMBARKATION PORT.
See World War I U.S. Naval Bases in Europe.

ST. THOMAS, VIRGIN ISLANDS, U.S. NAVAL BASES, 1917–1948 The main islands of the Virgin Islands are St. Thomas, St. John, and St. Croix (or Santa Cruz). St. Thomas, at 18°20′N., 64°55′W., forty miles east of Puerto Rico, is the seat of government, with the governor also being the commandant of the U.S. Naval Station originally established there. It is fourteen miles long, no more than four miles wide, and covers an approximate area of thirty-two square miles. Most of the island rises directly out of the sea in high rocky cliffs, with the major portion of the surrounding water either shallow or made useless for ships by barrier reefs. On the south side of the island, however, three bays are so situated that peninsulas and small islands form natural breakwaters.

In the 1850s, during the diplomatic bickering with Britain over an isthmian canal, with Spain over the purchase of Cuba, and over British expansion in Central America, the exploits of filibusterers William Walker and Narciso Lopez and the need to search American merchantmen suspected of being slavers caused the U.S. Navy Department to establish a supply depot at St. Thomas to support its ships operating in the Caribbean Sea.

Soon after the United States purchased the Danish West Indies from Denmark in 1917—to deny them to Germany and to provide protection for the Panama Canal—Rear Adm. James H. Oliver, USN, was appointed as the first governor of the Virgin Islands, as they were renamed. In addition to reorganizing life along American lines—85 percent of the 32,000 inhabitants were blacks and the rest mostly Danes or Germans—he was authorized to establish a station, a submarine base, a radio station, and a refrigerator plant. Since the islands were undisturbed by World War I, the Navy for many years did little beyond administering the islands and seeking to improve their public works, educational system, and other services, except for building a second radio station at St. Croix during the 1920s. The submarine base was discontinued after World War I ended. A Marine Corps Air Station to service thirty-six landplanes and emergency services for six seaplanes in the vicinity of Roosevelt Roads (q.v.) was commissioned on 1 September 1935, when it had 86 officers and 524 men on board.

In keeping with the Hepburn Board report approved by Congress in May 1939, Bourne Field, the small airfield at the head of Lindbergh Bay completed in 1935 at St. Thomas and occupied by the Marine Corps, was expanded to support a Marine squadron of eighteen planes on a permanent basis, and the adjacent waterfront was to be developed to serve a patrol-plane squadron in a tender-based status. A contract for the work was let on 8 July 1939. To plan further development of the naval shore establishment was the task of the Rear Adm.

John W. Greenslade Board appointed on 11 September 1940. Construction work was largely completed by the early months of 1943 as part of the fixed-fee contract for work done at San Juan, Puerto Rico (q.v.). Construction included greatly extending the runways (the NNW/SSE one was 2,900 feet long, the ENE/WSW one was 2,600 feet long) and providing additional hangars, quarters, public works, a new sixty-bed dispensary and hospital, and a concrete ramp, hangar, and utility shop to serve seaplane operations in Lindbergh Bay. In midsummer 1941 still further additions were made to the air station, and a completely new facility—a submarine base—was built on Gregerie Channel adjacent to the air station. To house the 40 officers and 700 enlisted men at the air station and the 42 officers and 900 men at the submarine base, additional quarters and public works were built, with potable water obtained by collecting rainfall. In October 1941, moreover, a section base and net and boom depot were constructed on the waterfront adjacent to the submarine base, which now had five finger piers and a new radio station to replace the one built in World War I. On 26 June 1943 the civilian construction contract was terminated and CBMU 507, with a complement of 4 officers and 256 enlisted men, carried to completion the buildings and installations left unfinished by the contractor.

As of August 1944, at a cost of $5 million, the principal military facilities at St. Thomas included the naval station, submarine base, radio station, net depot and target repair base, dispensary, section base and inshore patrol, and emergency fuel facility, the dry dock capable of supporting patrol craft having been disestablished. The Marines had an air facility near the Coast Guard Section Office at Charlotte Amalie with a capacity of seventy-two fighters and thirty-six patrol landplanes, twenty observation and ten patrol seaplanes at Lindbergh Bay, and a leased emergency field on Anguila Island. The Army had its own field. On 30 August 1946 the Chief of Naval Operations placed the naval facility in caretaker status but on 11 October modified his directive to permit the operation of a single plane there and to let Pan American Airways continue to use the field and facilities. The end came on 16 February 1948, when the Secretary of the Navy decommissioned the station and transferred all naval property to the Interior Department, which assumed responsibility for the administration of the Virgin Islands.

BIBLIOGRAPHY

A. "History of the United States Naval Facility on St. Thomas, Virgin Islands," 26 February 1942 (Washington: Naval Historical Center, Operational Archives Branch); U.S. Navy, Bureau of Yards and Docks, *Building the Navy's Bases in World War II*, 2 vols. (Washington: GPO, 1947), I:9-12; James B. Agnew, "Gold Braid and Sugarmills," October 1979 (Washington: Naval Historical Center, Operational Archives Branch); "St. Thomas, V.I." Shore Establishment Summary Cards (Washington D.C. Navy Yard, Naval Aviation History Office).

B. Luther Harris Evans, *The Virgin Islands: From Naval Base to New Deal* (Ann Arbor, Mich.: J.W. Edwards, 1945).

ST. TROJAN, FRANCE.
See World War I U.S. Naval Air Stations in Europe.

SAIPAN, MARIANA ISLANDS, U.S. NAVAL OPERATING BASE AND NAVAL AIR BASES, 1944–1949 Saipan is the second largest of the fifteen Marianas, lying to the north of Guam, Rota, and Tinian. An American, Captain Brown of the ship *Derby* from Salem, attempted to colonize the island in the nineteenth century only to be frustrated by the Spanish governor of the Marianas. As did the other Marianas except Guam, Saipan passed from Spain to Germany in 1899 and to Japan during World War I. Between the world wars the Japanese South Sea Development Company pressed the planting and refining of sugar on the island. On the eve of World War II the population of more than 20,000 was overwhelmingly Japanese, only 2,500 being native Chamoros.

Saipan is thirteen and one-half miles long by two and one-half to five miles wide. Its most prominent physical feature is Mt. Tapotchau, which rises 1,500 feet in the center of the island. Garapan, the administrative center of the Marianas, had a population of about 10,000 in the early 1940s; it lies on the island's west coast, to the south of the one good anchorage at Tanapag Harbor. For the Americans the most significant Japanese installation was the 4,500-foot runway at Isloto Field that the Japanese had constructed in southern Saipan.

In the spring of 1944, as the Navy completed its movement into the Marshalls, the Joint Chiefs of Staff ordered Adm. Chester W. Nimitz to occupy Saipan, Tinian, and Guam "starting 15 June. . . with the object of controlling the eastern approaches to the Philippines and Formosa, and establishing fleet and air bases." More specifically, Saipan and Tinian (q.v.) would provide the two air bases from which the Air Force could despatch the great B-29 bombers against Japan; Guam (q.v.) would be developed as the navy's most important fleet base in the Western Pacific to support operations against the Philippines, Formosa, and Japan; and submarines operating from Guam and Saipan would effectively interdict the flow of vital supplies from Southeast Asia to Japan proper. Between 15 June and 9 July, in Operation Forager, the Second and Fourth Marine Divisions, joined by the Twenty-seventh Army Division, secured Saipan against bitter enemy opposition.

Three days after the first Marine landings on Saipan, the base components of Gropac Eight moved ashore to control landings of supplies, to direct shipping, and to clear Tanapag Harbor of obstacles. On 25 July 1944 the first Navy ship tied up to a reconditioned dock in Tanapag, and on 1 September the Saipan Naval Operating Base was formally commissioned. Eventually as many as 400 ships anchored in Tanapag Harbor, where they were supported by Service Squadron Ten, the largest floating naval base in the world. In May 1945 alone, 475 ships called at Saipan, and shipping at the island came to rival that of New York and San Francisco. The base's administrative center was established on Mutcho Point, embracing Tanapag's southern shore. Among the base's more important shore facilities were a huge tank farm that was only half completed by VJ-Day;

a supply depot of sixty-four steel arch-rib warehouses, eleven refrigerator sheds, and numerous Quonsets; and an ammunition depot equipped with 112 steel magazines, 4 torpedo magazines, and shops. The 400-bed Naval Hospital cared for casualties from the Okinawa and Iwo Jima campaigns, supplementing the 5,600 beds in army hospitals and dispensaries.

Saipan also became a major center for Army and Navy air power during the last year of the Pacific War. Seabees reconstructed and expanded the former Japanese seaplane base at Tanapag Harbor. Iseley (the former Isloto) and Kobler Fields were developed to handle Air Force B-29s, the Kobler housed a naval refresher trainer center. The smaller Marpi Base in the north and the Kagman Base in the east cared for two carrier air groups, and Tanapag and Kobler were air transport centers.

The naval and air facilities on Saipan rivalled those on Guam by VJ-Day. For a period thereafter the island remained busy serving the fleet and as a staging point for demobilization of naval personnel. Inevitably, however, Saipan's facilities declined as the Navy's funds were devoted to maintaining Guam as the preeminent American naval position in the Western Pacific. A naval survey board in 1948 decided that the Naval Operating Base on Saipan should be disestablished. The base was formally rolled up on 30 June 1949.

BIBLIOGRAPHY

A. J.G. Ware, "History of U.S. Naval Base No. 3245 (Saipan), 15 October 1945" (Washington: Naval Historical Center, Operational Archives Branch, World War II Command File); U.S. Navy, Bureau of Yards and Docks, *Building the Navy's Bases in World War II*, 2 vols. (Washington: GPO, 1947), II:340-43.

B. Samuel E. Morison, *New Guinea and the Marianas, March 1944-August 1944* (Boston: Little, Brown, 1953), pp. 1-14, 149-54.

WILLIAM R. BRAISTED

SALCOMBE, ENGLAND.

See United Kingdom, U.S. World War II Naval Bases.

SALERNO, ITALY, U.S. NAVAL OPERATING BASE, 1943–1945 A decision was reached at the Trident Conference at Washington in May 1943 to expand the Sicilian operation into an invasion of mainland Italy. The original objectives of this move, which stemmed from the insistence of Prime Minister Winston Churchill, were to knock Italy out of the war and to tie up as many German divisions as possible in order to weaken their forces on the Western Front. The speedy success in Sicily and the fall of Mussolini on 25 July led to the selection of the Salerno Bay area as the landing zone for the Fifth Army. The plan called for the port of Salerno to be taken on D-Day and opened immediately to serve as the main port of entry until Naples could be taken (scheduled for D-plus-12) and opened. These ports were essential to the supply of the Fifth Army as well as the Eighth Army once it linked up.

On D-Day, 9 September 1943, Salerno was occupied by the Commandos, but the Germans maintained their position on the high ground dominating Salerno. On the tenth the Advanced Port Party landed and began to put the port into operable condition. Special harbor salvage groups had been set up to clear both Salerno and Naples (q.v.) as soon as they were occupied. A channel was quickly swept to permit the entrance of assault ships. On the eleventh the Naval Officer In Charge signaled that the port was open to shipping, with berths available for three coasters and three LSTs and a beach suitable for landing twelve LSTs. By late on the thirteenth more than 1,850 tons of cargo had been discharged through the port. The next morning, however, an LST entering the port was forced to beat a hasty retreat due to German shelling, and on the fifteenth the Port Party had to be withdrawn and the port closed. The port remained closed until 25 September, when the enemy was finally dislodged from the high ground. That day the Port Party relanded and reopened the port, with two coasters, a tug, and a boom vessel entering. The following day, the landing beaches were closed down because Salerno now offered an adequate port facility. All beach parties and repair groups were shifted to Salerno. The port was fully exploited, with ever-increasing tonnage being cleared through. Even with Naples opened, Salerno continued to serve as an entry port. By 1 November both ports had handled a total of 164 ships and 164 LSTs, 35,492 personnel, and 5,089 vehicles.

In February 1944 it was decided to set up an Advanced Amphibious Training Base at Salerno to train personnel for the landing planned in southern France rather than return the men and equipment to North Africa for training. Personnel and material for the new base were obtained from the training base at Arzew, Algeria (*see* North Africa, U.S. Naval Bases). The base continued in operation until October 1944. NOB Salerno was shut down in January 1945.

BIBLIOGRAPHY

A. United States Naval Administrative Histories of World War II. Commander U.S. Naval Forces, Northwest African Waters, "Naval Forces, Northwest African Waters and the Eighth Fleet," 5 vols. (Washington: Naval Historical Center, Operational Archives Branch, 1945).

B. Samuel E. Morison, *Sicily, Salerno, and Anzio* (Boston: Little, Brown, 1954).

FRANCIS X. HOLBROOK

SALINAS, ECUADOR, U.S. NAVAL AIR FACILITY.
See Hispanic South America, U.S. Naval Bases.

SAMAR, PHILIPPINE ISLANDS, U.S. NAVAL AIR CENTER AND NAVAL OPERATING BASE, 1944–1947 Within two months of the American landings at Leyte Gulf, the 12th, 61st, 93rd, and 105th Naval Construction Battalions (Seabees), the 5th and 33rd Special Seabees and 1024th Special Seabee Detachment, and the 821st Army Engineer Battalion began constructing a 7,000-foot runway at Guiuan, at the southernmost tip of Samar, for bomber and fighter use. Added were facilities for servicing aircraft; the housing and messing of assigned personnel and itinerant aircraft crews; supervisory communications personnel; field operations and local control of air traffic; ammunition and petroleum, lubricants, and oil dumps; aviation repair and overhaul; an aviation supply depot; and whatever ACORN (advanced air base construction teams) might be assigned. Although used mostly by bombers of the 5th and 15th Army Air Forces, the Naval Air Center, commissioned on 23 December 1944, was also used by naval transports, bombers, fighters, and aircraft of the Naval Air Transport Service. To support seaplanes came the seaplane tender *Currituck* (AV-7) on 6 November. These seaplanes, along with *Ventura* landplanes from the air strip at Tacloban, at the head of Leyte Gulf on the island of Leyte (q.v.), flew reconnaissance over the inland seas of the Philippine Islands. Joining them were aircraft from a naval air facility established at Mios Woendi, near Biak (q.v.).

Also included in the naval operating base were a naval station; pontoon assembly unit; antiaircraft training center and naval supply depot Calicoan; advance base construction depot and construction equipment parts depot; net depot; automotive equipment repair and overhaul unit; fleet hospital; motor torpedo boat base; receiving station Tubabao Islands; boat repair unit Inaloulan; amphibious boat pool; and naval ammunition depot.

By early November 1945, when a board inquired into what installations should be retained, the antiaircraft training center was training only local forces, and the following had been disestablished: the naval supply depot, advanced base construction depot, and automotive and construction equipment parts depot; pontoon assembly unit; automotive equipment repair and overhaul unit; boat repair unit; and naval ammunition depot. Pontoon assembly depot No. 14 was disestablished on 15 November 1945; the net depot was transferred to the buoy depot at Manicani Islands; the fleet hospital was transferred to Tubabao Island; the torpedo boat base had been reduced to caretaker status and would be disposed of as the Chief of Naval Operations directed; and the receiving station would be disestablished when the progress of demobilization permitted. The air center and a few other installations remained fully operational until 15 July 1947, when they were inactivated. Disestablishment occurred on 12 August 1947.

BIBLIOGRAPHY

A. "Monograph Histories of United States Overseas Bases. Vol. II. Pacific Area" (Washington: Naval Historical Center, Operational Archives Branch); "Report of the Board Appointed to Inquire into and Submit Recommendations on Postwar Developments Philippine Islands" (Washington: Naval Historical Center, Operational Archives Branch); Summary Cards (Washington, D.C., Navy Yard: Naval Aviation History Office).

SANGATTE, FRANCE. *See* World War I U.S. Northern Bombing Group Bases in England and France.

SANGLEY POINT, LUZON, REPUBLIC OF THE PHILIPPINES, U.S. NAVAL STATION, 1945–1971 In 1876 the Spaniards, who had captured Manila in 1570, established a naval hospital on Sangley Point, eight miles southwest of Manila on a peninsula jutting into Manila Bay. After Commo.

George Dewey defeated the Spanish fleet anchored off Cavite, just to the southwest, on 1 May 1898, the site was used by Americans as a rest camp and burial ground, and in 1899 U.S. Naval Hospital Canacao (q.v.) was built there. Between 1914 and 1941 the hospital was extended. In 1915 the U.S. Navy built Radio Sangley, and in 1921 all the industrial facilities located at Olongapo, Subic Bay (q.v.), were transferred to Sangley, then known as the Cavite (q.v.) U.S. Navy Yard and the main ship repair facility for the Asiatic Fleet. Although the Bureau of Aeronautics in late 1940 authorized the construction of a seaplane ramp and other aviation facilities, the projects were incomplete when war with Japan began on 7 December 1941.

Japanese forces occupied Cavite in January 1942, rehabilitated and extended its facilities, and used them to build and repair small craft useful for coastal patrol. Beginning in September 1944, American carrier planes began bombing Cavite, which was liberated by the U.S. Army in early February 1945. Soon thereafter Adm. Frank D. Wagner established the offices of Air Wing Ten at Sangley and began rehabilitating it, meanwhile using two undamaged wards and the galley of the Canacao hospital for administrative purposes.

The naval air base established by the U.S. Navy at Sangley Point on 23 March 1945 used a site covering 341 acres at an elevation of only 6.43 feet. Although the base was redesignated a naval air station on 27 February 1947, its mission of supporting fleet aircraft remained unchanged. The station was inactivated as an independent entity on 30 June 1949 and on the next day became part of the Sangley Point Naval Station, the latter a component of the Naval Operating Base disestablished on 1 June 1949 and redesignated Naval Station Philippines. It was the site of Headquarters, Commander Philippine Command; Commander Naval Philippines Movement Report Office; SubArea Petroleum Office; Headquarters, Commander Seventh Fleet; Fleet Weather Central; Naval Communication Facilities for receiving (San Miguel) and transmitting (Bababantay and Moron); a naval post office; and a Marine Barracks. Its mission now was: "to provide facilities to support regular operations of fleet reconnaissance, antisubmarine, transport, and utility aircraft; provide minimum special support for Commander Naval Forces Philippines; provide primary search and rescue facilities for area of responsibility assigned by Commander Pacific Fleet."

Its tasks were numerous: to perform aircraft maintenance and provide operational training facilities and services as required; maintain and operate an aircraft engine pool; provide special air logistics support and administrative aircraft and services as required; provide air surveillance radar services; serve as an all-weather station (meaning that it had Ground Control Approach); maintain and operate an air terminal; maintain and operate the U.S. Embassy Landing and U.S. Fleet Landing in Manila; operate a brig; maintain and operate seaplane facilities; operate a motion picture exchange; provide medical and dental services; and provide boat, ammunition, and transportation for ship's company and tenants. The various departments that performed these tasks included administration, supply, security, industrial relations, medical, dental, air operations, aircraft maintenance, public works, surface operations, and Navy exchange.

The Sangley runway, dedicated on 1 February 1951, was extended twice until it reached 8,000 feet by April 1953. Station personnel that year included 241 officers, 2,258 men, and 1,068 civilians. In addition, seaplane ramps were provided. Sangley was designated a permanent station in 1955.

Comdr. Donald W. Darby, USNR, commanded ACORN 45, which had refurbished Sangley's airstrip. From 20 April to 26 September 1945 he then served as Sangley's first commanding officer. Like his successors, he faced a difficult task in trying to reduce venereal disease among ship's company and transients. While a rest and recreation center was available in Manila, personnel flown to there from Vietnam for five days frequently became infected. Because about 5,000 men obtained liberty daily and there was almost that number of bar girls in the city of Olongapo, the latter was the only place in the Philippines put off limits.

A second challenge to commanders at Naval Station Sangley Point stemmed from the fact that, as one account has put it, "Manila is a city with an Oriental soul, Spanish ways, and American slang." Natives working at or living near Sangley can be placed under the same umbrella. Therefore a tremendous amount of effort went into Project Handclasp and the Philippine American Community Action Program. News about the station was spread through the weekly newspaper, the *Canacao Clipper*. Various weeks were devoted to Cub, Boy, and Explorer Scouts and to Girl Scouts. Sometimes as many as 80 professors and 200 students visited the station, and as many as 460 American and Filipino VIPs visited in only one year.

In 1954, personnel included 143 officers, 2,174 men, and 1,484 civilians. Other facilities included ship's service, ship's store, commissary, brig, chapel, bakery, and laundry. As yet, there was only a ten-bed dispensary, and the nearest hospital was at Guam (q.v.), 1,343 miles away. The air operations department controlled the functions of an operations department, communications department, Fleet Air Squadron 119, VR-23 Detachment, (transportation by Fleet Logistic Wing Pacific), and VW-1 Detachment A (weather).

By 1956 there were four squadron offices covering 13,628 square feet; aviation storage space covering 30,617 square feet; gasoline storage for 420,000 gallons; a landplane parking area covering 550,000 square feet; and an 8,000-by-150-foot concrete runway capable of handling planes with a 55,000-pound wheel load and weight of up to 60 tons. In addition there were two seaplane ramps, one 50 feet by 179 feet, the other 50 feet by 168 feet, and 240,000 square feet of parking space. Five seaplane channels were available, each 1,000 feet wide, 12,000 feet long, and 20 feet deep. Served were carrier aircraft support units, Naval Air Transportation Service, and training squadrons. There was a bombing range, capacity to handle one carrier, four patrol squadrons, one reconnaissance squadron, three utility squadrons, and nine seaplanes.

The year 1967 saw the deployment home of the last seaplane patrol squadron, with Commander Fleet Air Wing, however, rotating various landplane squadrons to Sangley. Aircraft operations in 1967 numbered 1,620, when ship's company included 61 officers, 600 men, and 1,680 civilians; but operations, construction, and activities would escalate because of increased U.S. participation in the Vietnam War. Construction alone amounted to $2,748,000, and special attention was given to providing inhouse activities in an alien land. There were councils and committees tasked with providing from a recreation fund such activities as theater, swimming pools, bowling alleys, a recreation hall, various hobby shops, water skiing, golf, picnic areas, organized parties and hiking trips, skeet shooting, and even a station hotel. In close cooperation with the USO there, five-day trips were organized for men from Vietnam on rest and recreation leave.

The facilities at Sangley Point would not have been able to answer all the demands for air support engendered by the Vietnam War, but it played its part while the larger and newer naval air station at nearby Cubi Point (q.v.) assumed a much more important role.

In April 1968 Ground Control Approach made Sangley an all-weather station. On 12 June Gen. William G. Westmoreland addressed station personnel on the Navy's role in Vietnam, and a number of Sangley sailors volunteered for duty there. Military and civilian personnel increased by a third in 1968, while aircraft operations more than doubled. In addition, Sangley was tasked with flying reconnaissance patrol in the Market Time Operation and was made responsible for providing all the supplies and assuming financial responsibility for U.S. Naval Air Facility Cam Ranh Bay (q.v.). In the period from March 1967 to the end of 1968 this involved airlifting 2,689,903 pounds of cargo to Cam Ranh Bay and in addition supporting VO-67 at Nakhon Phanom, Thailand. Moreover, late in 1966 Sangley agreed to assume responsibility for placing contracts for the repair and overhaul of U.S. Army vessels in the Philippines, Singapore, and Taiwan. In January 1965 the supply inventory at Sangley had included 23,728 line items with a value of $6,626,943; at the end of 1968 the totals were 60,772 and $23,537,775, with 4,743,312 pounds of cargo flown out during the period.

With no increase in station personnel, in 1969 Sangley assumed for five months all responsibility for shuttling mail, cargo, and passengers when C-2s at Cubi Point were grounded; continued to support Cam Ranh Bay with C-54 *Skymasters*; and supported the visit by President Richard Nixon in July and of Vice President Spiro Agnew in December. With funding cut back, however, all P-2 *Orion* aircraft left Sangley for NAS Alamitos, Calif., and reductions were made especially in Sangley's surface ship operations. On 10 December 1969 came word that Sangley would be turned over to the Republic of the Philippines in seven to nine months. One by one Sangley closed down its operations; on 1 July 1971 it was placed in inactive status and declared excess. On that date a Sangley Point Closure Detail of seven officers and ninety-five men was activated and in sixty days had readied Sangley for complete evacuation. On 20 August Filipino Marines took over perimeter security, and the transfer began of 350 items of automotive and construction equipment, 400 industrial buildings, and government quarters stripped of furnishings, while 2,500 tons of gear were shipped by sea and land to various other U.S. military bases. At 1000 hours on 31 August disestablishment ceremonies were held that transferred Sangley to the Republic of the Philippines.

BIBLIOGRAPHY

A. "Command History, U.S. Naval Station, Sangley Point. Luzon, Republic of the Philippines," 1966-1971, including files of the *Canacao Clipper* (Washington: Naval Historical Center, Operational Archives Branch); "Monograph Histories of U.S. Naval Overseas Bases, Vol. II. Pacific Area" (Washington: Naval Historical Center, Operational Archives Branch); "Naval Air Stations," 2 vols, n.d., Washington, D.C., Navy Yard, Naval Aviation History Office); Summary Cards (Washington, D.C., Navy Yard; Naval Aviation History Office).

SAN JUAN, PUERTO RICO, U.S. NAVAL STATION, 1898–1950 San Juan is located on the northern shore of the island of Puerto Rico toward its eastern end at 3°50′N., 66°10′W. The U.S. naval station built there lies mostly on the 340-acre Isla Grande, in San Juan harbor.

From 18 October 1898, when the American flag rose over the captured Spanish city, the U.S. Navy took over the former Spanish installations there and added a few. The Spaniards had a small navy yard on the bay abreast old San Juan that the U.S. Navy administered until the property passed to the Department of Commerce and Labor in 1912 and to the Coast Guard in 1939. In 1904 the Navy built a hospital for the station at Puerta de Fiera, and in 1905 a signal shore station at San Juan itself. The Navy also operated a radio station on 9 acres at Loiza, fifteen miles southeast of San Juan, acquired in June 1920 from Lt. Comdr. Virgil Baker, USN (Ret.), in return for a lease of 10.2 acres for a tract on San Geronimo naval reservation. In addition a 37.2-acre tract lying at 18°27′54″N., 66°5′11″W., was transferred at Loiza from the War Department to the Navy in March 1921. In 1927, except for 5 acres used as a site for a radio station, the property reverted to the War Department.

The U.S. Navy conducted various exercises in the Caribbean during the 1930s, their tempo increasing as the threat of war arose in Europe and rumors abounded about Japanese submarines operating off Puerto Rican harbors. More important, during 1939 Capt. Richmond Kelly Turner, of the cruiser *Astoria*, saw tested some new amphibious craft at Culebra Island. Capt. Raymond A. Spruance, who commanded the battleship *Mississippi* during the 1939 exercises, was promoted to flag rank and in late February 1940 began a "seasoning" process for a large command afloat as Commandant of the new Tenth Naval District, which included the entire Caribbean Sea and such American possessions in the West Indies as Guantánamo Bay, Cuba (q.v.), Puerto Rico, and the Virgin Islands (*see* St. Thomas, Virgin Islands, U.S. Naval Bases).

Knowing that the weather at San Juan made flying possible all year round, soon after the outbreak of the European war in 1939 Washington directed that the 340 acres of swamp and mud flat lying in San Juan harbor be transformed into a naval air station. Although Spruance provided all possible support to the extremely capable resident engineer, Harold W. Johnson, the latter had little initial success. As he described the swamp, it was "a quivering lake of mud 20 to 30 feet deep." He had thousands of piles driven and tons of solid fill dumped into it, but Isla Grande remained a pile of muck. When Johnson complained to Washington, he was told, "You were sent to San Juan to build an airfield and not to select a site." Spruance opposed the building of a naval base at San Juan because the restricted harbor was vulnerable to surprise attack. Although the Navy Department agreed with him, it directed him to press on with construction. When Washington wished to build a major fleet base at Portage Bay, on the south coast of Trinidad, Spruance objected on the grounds that it was foreign territory not subject to American control and that its government was unfriendly and uncooperative. Lastly, it was not strategically well located within the West Indies, and he recommended developing instead a site at the eastern end of Puerto Rico later known as Roosevelt Roads (q.v.), to which Washington agreed. Meanwhile, construction proceeded at San Juan under the direction of poorly trained men, while others better qualified worked elsewhere.

One of the French naval units left homeless when France fell in the summer of 1940 was that of Adm. Georges Robert. Rather than have his ships destroyed by the British, as French ships had been at Mers-el-Kebir, Robert agreed to neutralize his ships, and Spruance provided a permanent defensive destroyer patrol for them. When Spruance left with new orders in the summer of 1941 to command a four-cruiser division, he was succeeded by Rear Adm. John Hoover.

The officer who supervised the original construction work at San Juan was Lt. Comdr. Edward A. Cruise, who came on board on 7 August 1939. With Patrol Squadron 51 directed to use the base in September, on 14 September 1949 a revocable permit was agreed upon between the Navy and Pan American Airways whereby the latter's air strip and small hangar were taken over by the Navy. Cruise placed the station in commission on 1 May 1940 and served as its commander until 12 August 1940, when he was succeeded by Captain V. C. Griffin. In mid-January 1951 Patrol Squadrons 52 and 53 joined 51; in May 1951 the naval air station was designated a major supply point for NAS Antigua (q.v.) NAS Vieques Sound, and the USMC Air Station at St. Thomas (q.v.). Defense was provided by the 66th CAC (AA) U.S. Army; security by the Marine Barracks established on 1 January 1941. The main mission of the station was to provide aerial surveillance in an area about 600 miles north of Puerto Rico and east of Antigua in a 660-mile circle centering on San Juan.

Through a herculean dredging operation, topsoil covering was provided for some 70 percent of Isla Grande, and the Pan American strip was widened and lengthened to accommodate heavy military aircraft. The final cost of the station was $26,681,332.73 exclusive of providing the fresh water system, which cost $256,405.06.

Despite the large expenditures at San Juan, as late as the summer of 1941, when shipyards in the United States were operated round the clock to build the ships for a two-ocean navy, the Navy had no dry docks in the Caribbean except in the Canal Zone, and had inadequate sources of fuels, repairs, and supplies at Guantánamo Bay. The Navy took over a dock built by the Insular Government and transformed it into a dry dock supported by shops, warehouses, and other industrial facilities, all constructed and operated with heavy use of Puerto Rican men, heretofore employed largely in agriculture, and Puerto Rican women in clerical tasks. The sociological impact was considerable.

Despite U-boat attacks on supply ships bound for Puerto Rico, by mid-1943 the Navy was able to complete its work at San Juan and turn its attention to Roosevelt Roads, planned as the major fleet operations installation in the Caribbean. By mid-1943, however, it became apparent that the Caribbean area was diminishing in importance with respect to the war effort, and after that date the station served mainly as an aircraft overhaul facility and one that provided emergency services to Fleet aircraft and destroyers. Station complement began a steady decline after VE-Day, 8 May 1945, even though no change was made in its personnel allowance of 1,183 enlisted men. Men were discharged as quickly as possible, and by November the station had voluntarily cut its roster by about 350 men. Those remaining continued with their regular duties, such as dusting swamps for the control of anopheles mosquitos, servicing utility aircraft for the station and the Commander of the Tenth Naval District, engaging in air-sea rescue, providing training in instrument flying and aerial photography, and towing targets for aircraft firing practice. Another large undertaking was the salvaging of fifty-one excess TBM-3s. These were stripped and the parts sold for more than $2 million. The handwriting was on the wall, however. On 19 August 1949 the dry dock and repair facility was disestablished, as was the Office of the Commandant of Naval Air Bases, Tenth Naval District. The Branch Hydrographic Office was also closed, and the station itself was disestablished on 9 February 1950.

BIBLIOGRAPHY

A. U.S. Navy, Bureau of Yards and Docks, *Federal Owned Real Estate under the Control of the Navy Department* (Washington: GPO, 1937); U.S. Navy, Bureau of Yards and Docks, *Building the Navy's Bases in World War II*, 2 vols. (Washington: GPO, 1947); Commandant Tenth Naval District, ''Administrative Narrative, San Juan, Puerto Rico,'' and ''Naval Activities Disestablished since July 1949,'' in ''Monograph Histories of U.S. Naval Overseas Bases'' (Washington: Naval Historical Center, Operational Archives Branch); ''War History,'' Naval Air Station, San Juan, Puerto Rico, 30 November 1944-1 November 1945,'' and supplements (Washington: Naval Historical Center, Operational Archives Branch).

B. Thomas B. Buell, *The Quiet Warrior: A Biography of Admiral Raymond A. Spruance* (Boston: Little, Brown, 1974).

LESTER D. LANGLEY

SAN JULIAN, CUBA, U.S. NAVAL AIR FACILITY, 1942–1945 San Julian is located at 22°5′N., 84°9′W., ten miles east of La Fe and 120 miles west-south-west of Havana. The primary mission of the naval air facility the United States built there by arrangement with the government of Cuba was to support aircraft patrols in the Yucatan Channel, the narrow waters separating Cuba and the Mexican province of Yucatan and connecting the Gulf of Mexico and the Caribbean Sea. Its secondary mission was to base a blimp that would engage in night patrol of the channel.

Operations actually started from a Pan American Airways airfield while the U.S. Army built the facilities at San Julian and turned them over to the Navy on 1 November 1942. Included were two 7,000-by-150-foot runways, two taxiways, eight hardstands, storage for 100,000 gallons of gasoline, and housing for 160 officers and 900 men. Adjacent to the PAA field was a stick mast for blimps. Operations began with scouting squadron VS2D-7, later VS-40, in July 1943, when four PV-1 *Venturas* came on board, and LTA operations began on 18 September 1944. As of 17 September 1943 there was an Air Control Center under Comdr. F. G. Raysbrook as the Air Group Commander, with Raysbrook in command of both Army and Navy base units and Lt. Comdr. Carleton S. Richardson in command of the air facility. No formal commissioning exercises were held, but as of 1 December 1943 there were eight officers and seventy-seven men on board, numbers that increased to fifteen officers and 140 men on 1 February 1944, while the various squadrons had sixty-two officers and ninety men and the blimp detachment had an additional officer and fourteen men.

With the worst of the U-boat menace evaporated by late 1943, the LTA facility was closed and cancelled. However, the LTA mast was left intact. The rest of the facilities were reduced to functional status by 9 July 1945.

BIBLIOGRAPHY

A. "San Julian, Cuba, U. S. Naval Air Facility" (Washington, D.C., Navy Yard: Naval Aviation History Office).

SANSAPOR, DUTCH NEW GUINEA, U.S. NAVAL ADVANCE BASE, 1944–1945 Cape Sansapor, Dutch New Guinea (3°S., 133° E.), is located on the northwest coast of the Vogelkop Peninsula. On 30 July 1944 troops from the Southwest Pacific Area landed at Sansapor to complete the conquest of western New Guinea, the last of Gen. Douglas MacArthur's leap-frogging amphibious operations along the north coast of New Guinea. On Amsterdam Island just northeast of Cape Sansapor, the Seventh Fleet set up Motor Torpedo Boat Advance Base 3 to service the PTs of Squadron 24 in patrols against Japanese barge traffic along the Dutch New Guinea coast. PT operations began in early August and lasted until 28 September 1944, when the boats were withdrawn to Biak (q.v.). Sansapor was also the site of several important Army installations that helped stage the landings in Lingayen Gulf, Luzon, in January 1945. To facilitate transport, the Seventh Fleet operated a port director's office at Sansapor until 9 April 1945.

BIBLIOGRAPHY

A. Motor Torpedo Boat Squadrons, Philippine Sea Frontier, ''Command History of MTB Squadrons, Philippine Sea Frontier, Formerly MTB Squadrons, 7th Fleet,'' 5 vols., Type Commands, 1945 (Washington: Naval Historical Center, Operational Archives Branch); U.S. Navy, ''7th Amphibious Force Command History, 10 January 1943-23 December 1945'' (Washington: Naval Historical Center, Operational Archives Branch); U.S. Navy, ''U.S. Naval Bases in the South and Southwest Pacific (and Central Pacific Forward) in World War II,'' prepared by Op441H, 1 November 1954 (Washington: Naval Historical Center, Operational Archives Branch).

B. Samuel E. Morison, *New Guinea and the Marianas March 1944-August 1944* (Boston: Little, Brown, 1953); Capt. Robert J. Bulkley, *At Close Quarters: PT Boats in the United States Navy* (Washington: Navy Department, Naval History Division, 1962); Vice Adm. Daniel E. Barbey, *MacArthur's Amphibious Navy* (Annapolis, Md.: U.S. Naval Institute, 1969).

JOHN B. LUNDSTROM

SANTA FE, ISLE OF PINES, CUBA, U.S. NAVAL AIR FACILITY, 1943–1944 In 1940 agreement was reached between the Navy Department and the government of Cuba for the use of various Cuban sites for defense purposes. One of these was on the Isle of Pines, south of Cuba at roughly 22°N., 83°W. The site was to provide emergency operations for lighter than air craft using a one stick mast and observation-type landplanes, and housing for eighty officers and men in a local hotel.

By 21 February 1943 the facility was 25 percent completed, and some operations began to reconnoiter the Yucatan Channel, which separates Cuba from the Yucatan Peninsula. When the U-boat threat diminished in these waters late in 1943, the Navy Department decided to disestablish the facility. This was done on 2 September 1944, when it was transferred to NAF San Julian, Cuba (q.v.).

BIBLIOGRAPHY

A. ''Naval Air Facility, Santa Fe, Isle of Pines,'' Summary Cards (Washington, D.C., Navy Yard: Naval Aviation History Office).

SASEBO, JAPAN, U.S. NAVAL FLEET ACTIVITIES, 1945– U.S. Fleet Activities Sasebo is located at 33°12′N., 129°43′E., fifty-five miles from Nagasaki on the island of Kyushu. Its primary mission is to maintain base facilities and provide logistic support, especially through maintenance, storage, and issuance of weapons, to units of the Seventh Fleet.

Sasebo has enjoyed an extremely varied history as a naval facility under Japanese and American control. Its fine harbor and strategic position close to the Tsushima Strait made it a natural location for an Imperial Japanese Naval Station. As Japan's territorial empire expanded over Taiwan and Korea and her economic interests spread over coastal China, the base grew in functions and importance. By 1921 Sasebo homeported six submarines and possessed a dry dock capable of accommodating ships as large as small cruisers. By 1933 the base was the Imperial Navy's third largest, serving major fleet surface units, submarines, and one and a half air corps. Ship construction and repair facilities were expanded, creating an employment boom that helped double the surrounding city's population within twenty years. However, a single American incendiary bomb attack on 29 June 1945, followed by a devastating typhoon three months later, virtually razed the city and base facilities.

Marines of the Fifth Amphibious Corps, operating as part of the U.S. Sixth Army commanded by Gen. Walter Krueger, arrived to take over the Sasebo Naval Station on 22 September 1945. As they entered the harbor, they saw two beached hulks of Imperial Japanese Navy carriers; the sight prompted feelings of revenge for losses suffered during the long island-hopping campaign toward Japan. These first American occupiers were depressed by Sasebo; one officer ranked it first on his list of places he never wanted to visit again. Base and city were indeed forlorn and desolate. Almost immediately, however, relations between American forces and Japanese citizens shifted from mutual hostility to shared friendly pride. From their headquarters in the former Imperial Japanese Navy Officers Club, American officers directed the cleanup of the devastated base. In so doing they gave employment to workers who had formerly served the Imperial Navy, thus setting the stage for Sasebo's reemergence as a naval base.

For the next five years Sasebo remained a backwater, despite formal establishment of a U.S. Navy Fleet Activities command. Then the outbreak of war in Korea breathed new life into the place. During the first ninety days of conflict, Sasebo refueled and replenished ships that provided first air and naval gunfire support, then American ground forces, for the defense of the Republic of Korea. In mid-September 1950 Sasebo witnessed a historic event: Gen. Douglas MacArthur embarked on the USS *Mount McKinley* for his journey to the dramatic landings at Inchon. During the next three years the base hummed with activity. It fueled and provisioned ships bound for Korean waters and for the Taiwan Strait. It provided rest and recreation for those who survived the bitter battles on the Korean peninsula. Sasebo also served as the site of important conferences that brought together Commander Seventh Fleet, Commander in Chief Pacific Fleet, and Chief of Naval Operations. By 1952, when peace and security treaties with Japan were ratified and an administrative agreement regulating base usage was concluded, Sasebo had long since established its permanent value to the U.S. Navy.

When a year later the Korean conflict came to an end, the base once again slipped into obscurity. Junior officers serving ashore elsewhere in Japan joked that fouling up in their duties would guarantee assignment as laundry officer at Sasebo. Nonetheless, the base quietly served the fleet for fifteen years, when the visit of the nuclear-powered carrier *Enterprise* catapulted it into the headlines. Thousands of militant students opposed to the Vietnam War and to the American naval presence in Japan demonstrated in Tokyo. Eight hundred tried to invade the Sasebo base, and in the two days of rioting that followed nearly 200 persons were injured. While the ship's crew had enjoyed liberty in Sasebo and she left without further incident, the *Enterprise* visit transformed the naval relationship between the United States and Japan. Locally, the Sasebo Municipal Assembly, after receiving reports that nuclear wastes had been dumped in nearby waters, passed a resolution opposing the visit of nuclear-powered ships of any sort. Subsequent investigation confirmed that the material could not have come from an American nuclear-powered submarine. But Prime Minister Sato Eisaku declared that his government must, under the terms of the revised U.S.-Japan Security Treaty, be consulted prior to the visit of American nuclear-armed vessels. The incident at Sasebo thus laid the foundation for his proclamation of the three non-nuclear principles that have guided Japan's defense policy ever since.

As it did after the Korean War, Sasebo disappeared from public view after the Vietnam conflict. Nuclear-powered American submarines slipped in and out of the harbor without repetition of the tumultuous events of 1968. Indeed, in the twilight of the Vietnam War era, Sasebo's obscurity made it attractive to Japanese and American diplomats planning consolidation of American bases in Japan. In December 1970 a scheme for reduction and relocation of the American military and naval presence in Japan was made public. Seventh Fleet headquarters, and with it major ship repair and housing facilities, would be shifted from highly visible Yokosuka (q.v.), near Tokyo, to distant Sasebo. After talks between Chief of Naval Operations Adm. Thomas Moorer and Prime Minister Sato, however, the scheme was turned upside down. Sasebo's size and functions were greatly reduced. Its three tenant commands were combined into one—Fleet Activities. Skyrocketing civilian labor costs, which increased 64 percent in one two-year period, dictated drastic cuts in the number of civilian and naval personnel employed on the base. Following movement of Sasebo's major home-ported ship, the USS *White Plains* (AFS-4), to Yokosuka in 1975, U.S. Navy port visits dropped by 25 percent. It seemed as if the base might all but disappear.

Yet eight years later Sasebo still serves the fleet. Time has healed the wounds of the Vietnam War era. In 1976 throngs of Japanese visitors trooped through the base in celebration of the United States' Bicentennial. As is the case elsewhere, Japanese Maritime Self-Defense Forces as well as the U.S. Navy use base facilities. Port visits, made more infrequent by changed Seventh Fleet deployment patterns, have passed without incident. Indeed, the August 1983 visit of the USS *New Jersey*, refurbished and rearmed with batteries capable of launching nuclear missiles, promises to usher in a new era of Japanese-American naval relations. If it proceeds without demonstration and difficulties, then those ties can be said to have adapted to the new technology of naval warfare. If not, then still more changes in the history of the U.S. Navy's use of Sasebo seem certain.

BIBLIOGRAPHY

A. *Sasebo shi: seiji gyōsei Kan* (A History of Sasebo City: Politics and Administration) (Sasebo, 1957); "Command Reports, Fleet Activities Sasebo, 1975-1982" (Washington:

Naval Historical Center, Operational Archives Branch); Sherwood F. Moran Papers (Washington: History and Museums Division, Headquarters, USMC).

ROGER DINGMAN

SHANGHAI, CHINA.
See Far Eastern U.S. Naval Bases to 1898.

SIGONELLA, CATANIA, SICILY, U.S. NAVAL AIR STATION, 1959–
Approximately ten miles southwest of Catania, Sicily, NAS Sigonella is strategically located in a sparsely settled area virtually in the center of the Mediterranean Sea; it enjoys a climate similar to that of the U.S. Gulf Coast but without the high humidity. Commissioned as a Naval Air Facility in 1959, Capt. W. J. Frazier, USN, commanding, it is located at the site of a former Italian naval air base and was developed jointly by the United States and NATO to relieve overcrowding at Malta's Hal Far Naval Air Facility. Its host is the Italian Air Force Forty-first Wing Command, but it reports to the Commander in Chief U.S. Naval Air Europe, in London, via Commander Fleet Air Mediterranean. It is one of the fastest growing naval bases in Europe, with a tripling in size between 1970 and 1980 and further growth expected. Its mission is to maintain and operate facilities and provide services and material to support operations of aviation activities and units of operating forces of the U.S. Navy and other activities and units as designated by the Chief of Naval Operations. Primary tasks are to provide ordnance replenishment and aircraft maintenance, and forward supplies and mail to the Sixth Fleet. In addition it has a liquid oxygen plant, operates a patrol squadron, and engages in search and rescue.

There are two main parts of NAS Sigonella: the American Village (NAS 1), and the airfield, eight miles away (NAS II). Free bus transportation between the two is provided on a half-hour schedule. The two runways, each 8,000 feet long, are at NAS II. Among twenty tenants are VR-24, Marine Guard Barracks, Construction Battalion Detachment, Naval Communications Detachment, Naval Oceanographic Command Detachment, Medical and Dental Branch hospitals, Armed Forces Radio and Television Service, and Mobile Mine Assembly Group.

A sponsor meets new arrivals and old hands at "indoctrination week," explaining local customs and emphasizing the danger from Italian automobile driving habits. With the accident rate of NAS Sigonella personnel running at forty per month, great care in driving is urged and the use of cars larger than compacts is discouraged. Moreover, offbase disputes, as with a landlord, must be settled in accordance with Italian law rather than American military law. Government quarters are limited, and there is no Navy Lodge.

The station lies in the shadow of Mount Etna, Europe's most active volcano, in a fertile area principally producing citrus fruits, olives, wine, sheep, and cattle. An industrial metropolis of 700,000 inhabitants, Catania provides shopping, sports, and cultural activities utilized by personnel and dependents assigned to units at Sigonella. On base there are a Navy Exchange; Commissary Store;

elementary, junior, and senior high schools; a chapel; banking, legal, and security services; and recreational facilities. As of October 1982 there was a military population of 2,000 at NAS Sigonella, and about the same number of dependents. The present commanding officer, Capt. Lynn H. Grafel, assumed charge in June 1982.

BIBLIOGRAPHY

A. "Living Overseas: Sigonella," *Navy Times*, 4 Oct. 1982, p.54; Ens. Betty R. Jenkins, USNR, Assistant Public Affairs Officer, NAS Sigonella, to the writer, 19 Oct. 1982.

B. "Welcome Sign Is for Real at Sigonella," *Naval Aviation News*, May 1963, p. 23; "Sigonella Unit Manufactures LOX," *Naval Aviation News*, Apr. 1965, p. 37; "Under Secnav Flies with VP-44," *Naval Aviation News*, Apr. 1970, p. 25; "Sigonella," *Naval Aviation News*, May 1976, p. 30; PHD A.A. Clemons, "VP Sigonella Style," *Naval Aviation News*, Sept. 1976, pp. 38-39; "Sigonella," *Naval Aviation News*, May 1978, p. 24; Lt. J. A. Kendrick, USN, *Welcome Aboard U.S. Naval Air Facility Sigonella, Sicily: "The Biggest Little Air Base in the World* (Sigonella NAS: Public Affairs Office, 1980); "Naval Air Station, Sigonella" (n.p., n.d. mimeographed handout).

SINGAPORE, MALAYA

See Far Eastern U.S. Naval Bases to 1898.

SIPLE STATION, ANTARCTICA, U.S. NAVAL BASE.

See Antarctica, U.S. Naval and Air Bases.

SONG ONG DOC, REPUBLIC OF VIETNAM, U.S. NAVAL RIVERINE OPERATIONAL BASE, 1970 Located on the western coast of South Vietnam's Mekong Delta region, Song Ong Doc served for a short time during the Southeast Asian Conflict as an operational base for U.S. and Vietnamese river forces. During 1970 allied naval units patrolled the area's numerous waterways as part of the Sea Lords strategy to interdict Viet Cong supply lines and troop movements. As part of the Vietnamization program, the Song Ong Doc facility was completely turned over to the Vietnamese.

BIBLIOGRAPHY

A. Commander Naval Forces, Vietnam, "The Naval War in Vietnam," May 1970 (Washington: Naval Historical Center, Operational Archives Branch).

EDWARD J. MAROLDA

SOUTHAMPTON, ENGLAND.

See United Kingdom, U.S. World War II Naval Bases.

SOUTH SEYMOUR, GALAPAGOS ISLANDS, ECUADOR, U.S. NAVAL AIR FACILITY.

See Hispanic South America, U.S. Naval Bases.

SPEZIA, ITALY, U.S. NAVAL BASE.
See Mediterranean, The, U.S. Naval Bases, 1800-1917.

SPICKER, FRANCE.
See World War I U.S. Northern Bombing Group Bases in England and France.

SUBIC BAY, LUZON, PHILIPPINE ISLANDS, U.S. NAVAL FACILITIES, 1898– Subic Bay lies to the west of the Bataan Peninsula facing the South China Sea. The city of Olongapo, at the head of the bay, lies at 15°N., 121°E. After the United States acquired the Philippine Islands by the Treaty of Paris, signed in December 1898, the Navy set aside an area along both sides of the head of the bay as a naval reservation, in 1904 establishing at Olongapo a coaling station and in 1905 a naval station. In 1909, however, the Joint Board of the Army and Navy advised against any extensive outlays for insular fortifications in the Philippines and suggested that the facilities at Olongapo be limited to a floating dock towed from the United States and small repair shops. The 1922 Five Power Naval Treaty of the Washington Conference prohibited the increase in fortifications in American territories west of Hawaii. It was thus assumed that in the event of war in the Western Pacific the Philippines and Guam would fall at once to the Japanese and that bases for the support of our forces would have to be rewon against enemy opposition. Saying that the defense of the Philippines involved matters of national policy that took precedence over the military problem involved, the Rear Adm. Arthur J. Hepburn Board on the Shore Establishment recommended late in 1938 that existing facilities only be maintained. At the time of the Japanese bombing of Pearl Harbor, therefore, Subic Bay had only some floating dry docks, a rifle range, and Marine barracks, all of which were quickly captured by the Japanese in mid-December 1941.

On 30 January 1945 the Eighth Army secured Subic Bay and, following the occupation of Grande Island, the Seventh Fleet entered it and established an amphibious training center, fleet training command, advance base construction depot, automotive and construction equipment parts depot, recreation facilities (Mataan River area), petroleum products storage, naval supply depot, small-boat repair unit (Half Moon Bay), degaussing unit, Naval Station Olongapo, and submarine base. A board appointed to inquire into and submit recommendations on postwar developments in the Philippines recommended the disestablishment of all facilities except the receiving station, which would serve until demobilization was completed; the transfer of the construction and automotive depots to the naval supply depot; permanent construction for fuel storage, the retention and expansion of recreation facilities; and the building of a new naval station and submarine base.

By 1953, while most aerial activity occurred at NAS Sangley Point (q.v.), other naval activities were concentrated at Naval Station Subic Bay and U.S. Naval Reservation Olongapo, an element of the naval station that included the city of Olongapo and its population of about 15,000. Around the city was a huge tract of forest land containing tropical trees of great value as lumber, some of which had been damaged by gunfire when the U.S. Army captured it in February 1945. The current Naval Station Subic Bay is built on the same site as the naval station of 1905 and provides the main source of livelihood among the local inhabitants. As of 30 June 1952 the Navy had 2,800 military personnel there and hired 401 in civil service billets, with almost all of the latter being Filipinos. By September 1953 military personnel had increased to 1,764 and civilians to 5,306.

A prime task of the commander at Subic is community relations. In order to keep relations with natives good, he has when necessary delivered plane loads of relief goods to the victims of fires, earthquakes, and typhoons. He works primarily through the Philippine charity groups in Manila organized in the Filipino-American Benefit Committee. In addition he provides aerial medical evacuation. He has turned over such equipment as Swift boats and various aircraft to President Ferdinand E. Marcos of the Philippines and has opened U.S. Naval Hospital, Subic Bay, to natives hurt in natural disasters. He also does all he can to reduce the high incidence of venereal disease apparently endemic on the beach.

By 1966, like other naval facilities in the area, Subic Bay felt the pressure of the Vietnam War. A main service provided by Subic was to handle 2,036,546 men who left their ships and aircraft on liberty, or a daily quota of 5,579 in 1966 alone. To keep up with the demands of Vietnam, in that year 2,000 laborers worked for thirteen contractors to carry out $30,777,694 in construction work. Included were increased petroleum storage facilities, an offshore fuel terminal, electric power system, extension of a ship pier, and of an ammunition pier, augmented magazines and hardstand, more warehouses for the Naval Supply Depot, additional hangars and an aircraft paint shop, and a special landing forces camp provided with quarters for both officers and men. From Subic a 100km pipeline furnishes fuel to Clark Air Force Base.

Although the United States does not own the real estate it occupies at Subic Bay, it occupies it under the provisions of the Bases Agreement of 1947, as amended in 1965. Then, in 1966, President Marcos and President Lyndon Johnson agreed to set the date for evacuation at the end of twenty-five years, in 1991. In turn, Marcos said he would do what he could about the "squatter problem," that is, try to keep various families numbering 1,708 persons from living on the base without legal right. They cut timber, planted crops, burned brush, and endangered the base watershed and security—all because of the lack of a security fence around the base.

A major problem at Subic, in addition to the venereal disease rate, which affects 4 percent of the men going on liberty, is that of family housing. About half of the men and their dependents in 1966 were living on the base, the others outside. The waiting period for onbase housing for officers was from eight to ten months; for enlisted men, fourteen to eighteen months. Moreover, offbase housing was poor and expensive, running from $80 to $150 a month, unfurnished. Making matters worse, the American personnel at Subic are not eligible for full commissary and exchange privileges under the Bases Agreement. Because of the shortage of legitimate hotels in Olongapo, those sent to serve at Subic are encouraged to take unaccompanied tours.

On 4 February 1967, HMS *Victorious* visited Subic, followed by HMS *Hobart* on 5 April. On 17 April Rear Adm. Edwin Hooper, Commander Service Force Pacific, visited on an inspection tour. On 1 July Subic Base came under his operational control because of its part in resupplying Americans fighting in Vietnam. On 31 July the USS *Forrestal* arrived after having suffered a tragic fire at sea, with correspondents from around the world coming to Subic to obtain stories about it. Meanwhile the increase in traffic because of Vietnam can be measured by noting that Subic Bay was visited by 216 ships each month during 1967, with the fleet population numbering 4,224,503. Of these, 2,135,060 were granted liberty in Olongapo. Another measure was the increase to 15,350 of Filipino civilians hired at a time when there were only 478 American civilians on the base. These helped serve the 2,586 ships that required logistic support; manned tugs that made 9,196 ship moves in the harbor; and worked on three yard oilers (YOs) that pumped 162,322,487 gallons of fuel into ships and on $20.2 million of new construction. American servicemen reported 1,800 incidents of Filipino watch and wallet snatching, theft, and other crimes in 1967. According to the *Subic Bay News*, during that year more than 389,630 tons of aid were transferred to Filipinos through Project Handclasp, the venereal disease rate remained steady, and the lack of adequate housing continued to be the most insoluble problem at the base.

On 12 June 1968, on his way home to become the Chief of Staff of the Army, Gen. William Westmoreland visited Subic and thanked its personnel for their support while he was the commander of the U.S. Military Assistance Command in Vietnam. He spoke of what he knew, for during the first six months of 1968 Subic had resupplied allied ships in Vietnam that had fired 600,000 rounds of naval ordnance at the enemy. A total of 5,077 underway replenishments (UNREPs) had been performed by supporting ships out of Subic. These included 1,553 UNREPs at night. In June also, 890 UNREPs had been performed in addition by ships of Service Force Pacific. A gala day was 22 September, when the battleship *New Jersey* paid a call for the first time since she had been recommissioned to engage in the Vietnam conflict. In October Subic made a new record when it had forty-seven ships in port. Personnel at Subic now included 16,000 Filipinos and 600 American civil servants, with about 5,000 U.S. military personnel. Of the last, 500 families lived on base and 2,800 in Olongapo.

The Vietnam War kept Subic amply busy during 1968, with a daily average of twenty-seven ships in port and a population of 3,418,752. Of these, 2,074,668, or 5,410 a day, went on liberty. For ships undergoing training, Subic provided drones, towed air sleeves, and provided missile ranges and rockets. It had twenty-one offshore areas and six onshore ranges including four beaches that were available for amphibious assault exercises. An unfortunate fire on 7 June burned the naval supply depot warehouse with the loss of 18,000 line items worth more than $10 million—cause undetermined. The year 1968 put a great strain on Subic because it had to process the logistic requirements of 2,743 ships, or an average of 228 ships a month, an increase of 6 percent over 1967. Fuel pumped totaled 179,837,840 gallons; water, 53,312,250 gallons. Although thirty major construction projects worth $20 million were under way, including 100 new units of family housing costing $1.5 million, housing still remained Subic's major problem.

If the visit by Adm. Arthur W. Radford, who had been responsible for the building of the nearby Cubi Point Naval Air Station (q.v.), was a happy occasion on 26 March, sad news came on 3 June of the collison at sea between the carrier HMAS *Melbourne* and USS *Frank E. Evans* (DD-754), which occurred about 240 miles southwest of Manila in the South China Sea and cut the *Evans* in half. On the sixth, the USS *Kearsarge* brought to Subic 196 of the 199 survivors; on the ninth a Joint Australian/U.S. Board of Inquiry convened in the library of George Dewey High School; also on the ninth, the stern section of the *Evans* arrived under tow by a tug. It was stripped and towed to sea to serve as a gunnery target. Happier notes were the completion of a 600-foot extension to the Alfa wharf and of two new warehouses for the Naval Supply Depot. At year's end there were 5,700 American military officers and enlisted personnel at Subic.

The year 1969 caused Subic to feel the reverse flow from Vietnam. With two ships in port on any day, it was visited by fleet personnel numbering 3,428,470, with 2,074,106 of these, or about 5,700 daily, granted liberty. Services were nevertheless provided, as in training in air-to-air, surface-to-surface, and surface-to-air missiles; aircraft mining; surface gunnery; aircraft intercept control; naval gunfire support; close air support; amphibious landings; jungle training; ASW; and electronic warfare. Although operating tempo slowed somewhat, ninety-one construction projects costing more than $48 million were under way. Despite all that could be done including the use of a team of medical personnel numbering 196 over a three-year period, venereal disease remained endemic, and housing was still the number one problem.

Subic was most directly involved with the logistic support of ships that operated off Vietnam from 1967 to 1970. Since that date, operations have been normal, its main mission still being to provide logistic support and training for Seventh Fleet ships. It has remained a favorite target for visiting VIPs from CINCPACLFT Commander in Chief Pacific Fleet to the Secretary of the Navy, despite the slowing down of its operations and reductions in personnel. In 1974, for example, its allowance was of 33 officers, 492 enlisted men, and 428 civilians and 3,037 nonappropriated civilians. During that year it had 1,316 ships in port; it processed 697 logistic requests for naval ships and 688 for merchant ships; its tugs made 6,097 ship moves and its pilots 2,678 moves; and it pumped 43 million gallons of fuel and 4.4 million gallons of water. Its post office handled 6 million pounds of mail. Among other training courses, it taught fire fighting and police work to both Americans and foreigners.

The U.S. Naval Station, Subic Bay, remains home for Headquarters, Commander Navy Philippines/Commander Naval Base; Commander in Chief Pacific Representative Philippines. It has a hospital, public works center, naval supply depot, ship repair facility, commissary store, berthing and messing for ship's company and transients, terminal post office, mobile technical unit, motion picture exchange, disaster control and services, dependents' schools, various clubs, huge recreation facilities, religious services, PX, health care, boats, weapons, ordnance, and electronics and utilities, and its people-to-people program including the hire of Filipino youths during the summer season. Its Counseling and Assistance Center/Alcohol Rehabilitation Drydock keeps busy; its brig, quite full; its educational programs, burgeoning. It has numerous transients—14,000 of these in 1977 alone. However, starting in late 1973, it lost a number of employees to the Middle East OPEC countries. Indeed, in 1977 800 highly skilled or supervisory employees left Subic for better pay in the Middle East. Subic nevertheless has kept busy. In 1977 its 7,340 military personnel and 573 civilians served 30,000 visiting Seventh Fleet personnel, 521 Seventh Fleet ships, 112 U.S. Naval Service ships, 43 foreign ships, and 157 merchant ships. In 1978 it serviced 738 ships; in 1979, 840; in 1981, 562; with many of these now coming from the Indian as well as the Pacific Ocean.

BIBLIOGRAPHY

A. "Command History, U.S. Naval Station, Subic Bay, Republic of the Philippines" (Washington: Naval Historical Center, Operational Archives Branch); "Monograph Histories of U.S. Naval Overseas Bases. Vol. II. Pacific Area" (Washington: Naval Historical Center, Operational Archives Branch); "Report of Board Appointed to Inquire into and Submit Recommendations on Postwar Developments Philippine Islands" (Washington: Naval Historical Center, Operational Archives Branch); U.S. Navy Department, "Report on Need of Additional Naval Bases to Defend the Coasts of the United States, Its Territories, and Possessions [The Hepburn Board Report]" (Washington: U.S. Congress, House of Representatives, 76th Cong., 1st Sess., Doc. No. 65).

SUMMIT, PANAMA CANAL ZONE, RADIO STATION.
See Panama Canal Zone, Naval Operating Base/Naval Station, and Balboa, Panama Canal Zone, U.S. Naval Radio Stations.

SURABAYA, JAVA, U.S. NAVAL ADVANCE BASE, 1942 In December 1941, the Asiatic Fleet, withdrawing south from the Philippines in the face of overwhelming Japanese attacks, was ordered to head for a new Allied operating base at Surabaya (7°S., 112°30′E.) in the Netherlands East Indies. A large city and important port on Java's northeast coast, Surabaya in early January 1942 became a main base for the Asiatic Fleet's cruiser-destroyer Striking Force (Task Force 5) and submarines (Task Force 3). Available at Surabaya were fuel and some supplies, but only limited ship repair facilities. The fleet depended heavily upon its tenders and auxiliaries based at Darwin (q.v.), 1,200 miles to the southeast.

On 15 January 1942 the Asiatic Fleet came under the control of the Allied

American, British, Dutch, and Australian (ABDA) Command in a vain effort to prevent Japanese offensives in Malaya and the East Indies. After 3 February Surabaya was attacked almost daily by Japanese aircraft. Nevertheless, it remained the main ABDA naval base, although threatened by Japanese air and sea power. American base personnel began leaving on 19 February for Tjilatjap (q.v.) on Java's south coast. The ABDA Combined Striking Force sortied from Surabaya on 27 February 1942 to do battle with the Japanese in the Java Sea and, after the defeat, American destroyers sheltered there briefly before heading south. The last American naval units left Surabaya on 1 March 1942.

BIBLIOGRAPHY

B. U.S. Navy, Office of Naval Intelligence, *Combat Narrative. The Java Sea Campaign* (Washington: GPO, 1943); Samuel E. Morison, *The Rising Sun in the Pacific 1931-April 1942* (Boston: Little, Brown, 1948).

JOHN B. LUNDSTROM

SUVA, FIJI ISLANDS.
See Nandi-Suva, Fiji Islands, U.S. Naval Advance Base.

SYDNEY, AUSTRALIA, U.S. NAVAL ADVANCE BASE, 1942–1945 The capital of New South Wales, Sydney is Australia's largest city and port. On 1 February 1942 a U.S. naval base at 33°50′S., 151°10′E. was established there in connection with the main Royal Australian Naval Base and extensive commercial harbor facilities. The base came under the jurisdiction of Commander, Naval Forces, Southwest Pacific, which in March 1943 became the Seventh Fleet. Beginning in May 1942, the destroyer tender *Dobbin* operated in Sydney harbor to help repair naval vessels. In late 1942 and early 1943, battle-damaged cruisers and destroyers began arriving at Sydney for repairs at the Royal Australian Navy's dockyard and the large graving dock at Wooloomooloo, as well as at commercial facilities. Sydney also was an important place for normal overhauls as well as for all classes of naval warships. By early 1943 it had become an assembly point for the many small- and medium-sized landing craft (LSTs, LCIs, and LCMs) heading out to the Southwest Pacific Area. There they were repaired and made ready before heading north to other amphibious installations.

With the help of Australian labor, Seabees in the summer of 1943 increased U.S. naval facilities at Sydney by the construction of a naval supply depot, ammunition depot, and base hospital. Sydney functioned as a rear area supply base in addition to its important ship-repair role. However, with the increasing complexity of forward bases in New Guinea and the Admiralty Islands, its supply installations were dismantled in the summer of 1944 for shipment elsewhere. Only the ammunition depot remained to service ships under repair. Meanwhile, Sydney had become the main base for the British Pacific Fleet. U.S. facilities at Sydney were disestablished on 5 December 1945.

BIBLIOGRAPHY
A. U.S. Navy, Bureau of Yards and Docks, *Building the Navy's Bases in World War II,* 2 vols. (Washington: GPO, 1947); U.S. Navy, "U.S. Naval Bases in the South and Southwest Pacific (and Central Pacific Forward) in World War II," 1 November 1954 (Washington: Naval Historical Center, Operational Archives Branch).
B. Rear Adm. Worrall Reed Carter, *Beans, Bullets, and Black Oil* (Washington: GPO, 1953).

JOHN B. LUNDSTROM

SYDNEY, CAPE BRETON ISLAND.
See World War I U.S. Naval Air Stations in Canada.

T

TABOGA ISLAND, PANAMA CANAL ZONE, U.S. NAVAL STATION, 1942–1945 In March 1942 the strategically located Taboga Island at the Pacific terminus of the Panama Canal was made to serve as an advanced major overhaul and training center for motor torpedo boats (MTBs). Concluded on 18 May 1942 were diplomatic negotiations with the Republic of Panama that enabled the U.S. Navy to use thirty-six acres thereon for the duration of the war plus one year.

Taboga Island was used primarily to service MTBs and as an operational training center for PT squadrons en route to combat zones. Construction there beginning 6 July 1942 included a timber pier, two small marine railways, overhaul shops, power plant, light and power systems, refrigeration building, water storage and supply, and a radio building. Later construction included a storehouse, mess hall, barracks, quarters, fuel oil and gasoline storage tanks, a torpedo workshop, munitions storage, and various other facilities. Although work was slowed because of the need to deliver all materials by barge from Balboa (q.v.) and because the lava soil was hard to dig, 90 percent of the work was completed by the end of the year. Additional construction was undertaken by Seabees from Detachment 1012, who in 1943 took over construction and repair and in September assembled two pontoon dry docks and built a recreation camp. During the two remaining years of the war approximately 340 MTBs with their personnel of 1,000 officers and 4,000 men performed complicated training maneuvers by day and by night from the base. Subsequently nineteen squadrons of these MTBs participated in engagements throughout the rest of the war from Guadalcanal to the Aleutians. While at Taboga Island they were supported by eleven barracks buildings, a large mess hall, administration and recreation buildings, a hospital, machine shops, an engine storage building, a radio building, two power plants, and a long finger pier.

By agreement, beginning in August 1945 and ending in December, all fixed installations were turned over to the Republic of Panama.

BIBLIOGRAPHY
A. U.S. Navy, Bureau of Yards and Docks, *Building the Navy's Bases in World War II*, 2 vols. (Washington: GPO, 1947), II:17, 36, 40; "U.S. Naval Administration in World War II. Commander 15th Naval District and Commander Panama Sea Frontier," 2 vols., microfilm (Washington: U.S. Navy Department Library).

TALARA, PERU, JOINT U.S. ARMY/U.S. NAVY AIR BASE.
See Hispanic South America, U.S. Naval Bases.

TAN AN, REPUBLIC of VIETNAM, U.S. NAVAL ADVANCED TACTICAL SUPPORT BASE, 1968–1969 The Navy established an advanced tactical support base at this site on South Vietnam's Vam Co Tay River for a short time during the conflict in Southeast Asia. Initially, naval leaders planned to support anti-infiltration river patrols on the river northwest of Saigon from a repair, berthing, and messing barge stationed at Tan An. However, when the vessel was deployed to another location downriver, the shore facilities proved inadequate to support the river patrol boat (PBR) unit based there. As a result, in March 1969 the naval force reestablished its base of operations on board Mobile Support Base II, which consisted of connected pontoons moored in the river.

BIBLIOGRAPHY
A. Commander Naval Forces, Vietnam, "The Naval War in Vietnam," May 1970 (Washington: Naval Historical Center, Operational Archives Branch).

EDWARD J. MAROLDA

TAN CHAU, REPUBLIC of VIETNAM, U.S. NAVAL RIVER PATROL BASE, 1969–1970 Tan Chau was the site of a naval operating base during the Vietnam War. Located on the Mekong River on the South Vietnamese-Cambodian border, Tan Chau provided U.S. river patrol boat (PBR) units with a relatively secure haven from which to patrol the waterways of the region. The facility served as a key staging base during the Sea Lords anti-infiltration campaign of 1969-1970. The Tan Chau installation was turned over to the Vietnamese Navy in December 1970.

BIBLIOGRAPHY
A. Service Force, U.S. Pacific Fleet, "Command Histories, 1967-1972" (Washington: Naval Historical Center, Operational Archives Branch).
B. S. A. Swarztrauber, "River Patrol Relearned," U.S. Naval Institute *Naval Review* 96 (May 1970):120-57; Edwin B. Hooper, *Mobility, Support, Endurance: A Story of Naval Operational Logistics in the Vietnam War, 1965-1968 (Washington: GPO, 1972).*

EDWARD J. MAROLDA

TAN MY, REPUBLIC OF VIETNAM.
See Hue-Tan My-Phu Bai, Republic of Vietnam, U.S. Naval Support Activity.

TARAWA ATOLL, GILBERT ISLANDS, U.S. AIR BASES, 1943–1945 Tarawa is an atoll in the Gilbert Islands that lies about equidistant between Apamama to the south and Makin to the north. Triangular in shape, Tarawa measures about twenty-two miles in length and fifteen miles in width. At its southwest corner lies Betio, a gun-shaped island about two and one-half miles long by one-half mile wide that is surrounded by a dangerous reef. Once they captured the atoll from the British early in World War II, the Japanese were positioned to strike at Allied communications between Hawaii and Australia or to attack the flank of American expeditions moving westward into the Marshalls. When American air reconnaissance reported in 1943 that the Japanese had constructed a landing strip on Betio, therefore, the Joint Chiefs of Staff decided to capture the Gilberts by occupying Tarawa, Apamama, and Makin. Dubbed ''Galvanic,'' the American operation had three main objectives: to win sites for air bases from which to launch attacks on the Marshalls and to neutralize the enemy in other neighboring islands; to remove the Japanese threat to Allied communications between Hawaii an the Southwest Pacific, and to divert the Japanese from the Indian Ocean. The attacks on Tarawa and Apamama were undertaken by the Navy and the Marines; that on Makin by the Army. Heavily fortified Betio Island was captured by the Second Marine Division of the Fifth Amphibious Force in a bloody assault that lasted from 21 to 23 November 1943, and the remaining islets of Tarawa were occupied two days later.

The Seventy-fourth and Ninety-eighth Construction Battalions arrived in the atoll's lagoon the day after Betio was secured, and the Ninety-eighth Seabees began forthwith to clear up the dreadful mess. Fighter planes operated almost immediately from the former Japanese airfield, renamed Hawkins Field after a fallen Marine officer, and bombers employed the field as a staging point for operations against the Marshalls from mid-December. Because the original field proved too weak to support the weight of loaded bombers, the runway was resurfaced and extended from 4,000 to 6,000 feet in length—in just eighteen days. A second, entirely new 6,000-foot strip, named Mullinix Field after the admiral lost in the sinking of the *Liscombe Bay*, was completed on Buoto Island on the eastern side of the atoll, which also served as a base for bombers attacking the Marshalls and as a fueling station for flights between Hawaii and the Southwest Pacific. Other facilities completed by the Seabees included a tank farm, gasoline station, medical station, quarters, and water system.

By late December 1943 personnel on Tarawa had increased to 11,567 Marines and Navy armed with fifty-seven antiaircraft guns. As the war progressed westward, however, activity declined on Tarawa, and personnel dropped to 5,797 by April 1944. Mullinix Field was decommissioned on 9 December 1944. Hawkins Field was transferred to the Army on 1 June 1945 for use by the Air Transport Command.

BIBLIOGRAPHY

A. Commander in Chief, Pacific Fleet, ''Administrative History of the Marshalls-Gilberts Area,'' 6 vols., (Washington: Naval Historical Center, Operational Archives Branch 1946); U.S. Navy, Bureau of Yards and Docks, *Building the Navy's Bases in World War II*, 2 vols. (Washington: GPO, 1947), II:313-17.

B. Samuel E. Morison, *Aleutians, Gilberts, and Marshalls June 1942-April 1944* (Boston: Little, Brown, 1951), pp. 146-86, 211-12.

WILLIAM R. BRAISTED

TEIGNMOUTH, ENGLAND.
See United Kingdom, U.S. World War II Naval Bases.

TENES, ALGERIA.
See North Africa, U.S. Naval Bases.

THUAN AN, REPUBLIC OF VIETNAM, U.S. NAVAL INTERMEDIATE SUPPORT BASE, 1971 Situated on an island near Tan My in the Republic of Vietnam, the naval installation at Thuan An provided logistic support to American and Vietnamese naval forces during the Southeast Asian War.

When American forces withdrew from the Hue area in early 1971 as part of the lessening of U.S. involvement in the conflict, the logistic tasks of the Hue, Phu Bai, and Tan My bases (*see* Hue-Tan My-Phu Bai, Republic of Vietnam, Naval Support Activity) were concentrated at the newly constructed Thuan An intermediate support base. The Navy's Seabees prepared facilities for the provision of fuel, maintenance, administrative, financial, and other support of river and coastal patrol bases in the northern I Corps Tactical Zone. In September 1971 the Vietnamese Navy relieved American naval forces at Thuan An and the intermediate support base was disestablished.

BIBLIOGRAPHY

A. Commander Naval Forces, Vietnam, "Monthly Historical Reports, 1965-1971" (Washington: Naval Historical Center, Operational Archives Branch).

EDWARD J. MAROLDA

THURSDAY ISLAND, AUSTRALIA, U.S. NAVAL ADVANCE BASE, 1943–1944 In response to a perceived Japanese threat to south-central New Guinea, the Seventh Fleet (Sothwest Pacific Area) established a temporary motor torpedo boat operating base on Thursday Island (10°40′S., 142°15′E.) in Torres Strait. Thursday Island lies off Australia's Cape York and is in close proximity to the Royal Australian Air Force bases on Horn Island. On 16 April 1943 U.S. Army Engineers arrived on Thursday Island to begin constructing a fighter strip. Early in May PT boats from MTB Squadron 7 began patrols from Thursday Island to protect the route to Merauke, Dutch New Guinea (q.v.), across the straits to the northwest. They had to cope with primitive conditions at Thursday and very shallow water off the south New Guinea coast. The PTs remained at Thursday Island until July 1943, when they returned to Milne Bay, New Guinea (q.v.). Thursday continued as an airfield, and a small naval air center there operated until July 1944, when all naval activities ceased there.

BIBLIOGRAPHY
A. Motor Torpedo Boat Squadrons, Philippine Sea Frontier, "Command History of MTB Squadrons, Philippine Sea Frontier, Formerly MTB Squadrons, 7th Fleet," 5 vols., Type Commands, 1945 (Washington: Naval Historical Center, Operational Archives Branch); U.S. Navy, Bureau of Yards and Docks, *Building the Navy's Bases in World War II*, 2 vols. (Washington: GPO, 1947); U.S. Navy, "U.S. Naval Bases in the South and Southwest Pacific (and Central Pacific Forward) in World War II," 1 November 1954 (Washington: Naval Historical Center, Operational Archives Branch).
B. Capt. Robert J. Bulkley, *At Close Quarters: PT Boats in the United States Navy* (Washington: Navy Department, Naval History Division, 1962).

JOHN B. LUNDSTROM

THUYEN NHON, REPUBLIC OF VIETNAM, U.S. NAVAL ADVANCED TACTICAL SUPPORT BASE, 1969–1971 As part of the Giant Slingshot anti-infiltration operation during the Vietnam War, the Navy established an advanced tactical support base at Thuyen Nhon on the Vam Co Tay River. River patrol boat (PBR) units staged there while acting to cut the flow of communist men and supplies into South Vietnam from the nearby "Parrot's Beak" section of Cambodia.

During 1969 and 1970 Seabees, using materials brought in from Danang (q.v.), constructed an operations center, defensive bunkers, ammunition and fuel storage facilities, a helicopter pad, sleeping quarters, and a mess hall.

As part of the Vietnamization of the war, the Vietnamese Navy relieved U.S. naval forces at Thuyen Nhon in April 1971.

BIBLIOGRAPHY
A. Commander Naval Forces, Vietnam, "The Naval War in Vietnam," May 1970 (Washington: Naval Historical Center, Operational Archives Branch).

EDWARD J. MAROLDA

TINIAN, MARIANA ISLANDS, U.S. NAVAL BASE AND NAVAL AIR BASE, 1944–1947 Tinian, the third largest of the Mariana Islands, lies immediately south of Saipan across a three-mile strait. Measuring approximately twelve miles by six miles, it embraces a series of plateaus that the Japanese developed into sugar plantations during the thirty years of their occupation. Taking advantage of the flat terrain, the Japanese by 1944 had also finished or were constructing four airfields: two in the north, a 5,000-foot strip halfway up the west coast, and one in the island's mid-section. For a harbor, Tinian possessed only an unprotected indentation on the southwest coast, Sunharon Bay, at which was situated the town of Tinian.

Through the planning for Operation Forager in 1943-1944, it was assumed that Tinian would be captured along with Saipan. This was partly because Saipan could not be occupied alone without exposing it to menace from the Japanese across the strait in Tinian. More important, the Tinian flatlands and the airfields already under development were promising sites for the bases from which

American B-29 bombers would launch devastating raids against Japan. After a feint in the Sunharon Bay region, the Second and Fourth Marine Divisions made a successful surprise landing on the narrow beaches of northwest Tinian on 21 July 1944 and swept to occupy the entire island by 1 August. Moving ashore with the invading Marines were the elements of Gropac Six that would be commissioned as Naval Base, Tinian, in December.

Beginning on 27 July 1944 with the repair of the 4,700-foot runway on northern Ushi Point, the battalions of the Navy's Sixth Construction Brigade, joined by the Sixty-fourth Army Engineers, pressed ahead with the construction of two large air base complexes: West Field in the island's western mid-section, and North Field at the northern extremity. Completed first for the Navy on 15 November at West Field was a 6,000-foot runway with accessories that included 16,000 feet of taxiways, seventy hardstands, 345 Quonsets, thirty-three other buildings for repair and maintenance, seven magazines, and a 75-foot control tower. To this were later added at West Field two 8,500-foot runways with elaborate appurtenances for the Army Air Forces' B-29s. By its completion in May 1945 North Field comprised four 8,500-foot strips interlaced with eleven miles of taxiways and equipped with 265 hardstands, two service aprons, and maintenance buildings. To support the great weight of bombers, the runways were paved with eighteen inches of crushed coral topped by two inches of rolled asphalt. Building the air fields involved immense earthmoving and cutting operations: 4,789,400 cubic yards of coral fill were required at North Field, and 3,298,490 cubic yards at West Field. The first B-29 landed on Tinian in December 1944, and it was from Tinian that the *Enola Gay* with two other B-29s took off for Hiroshima to drop the atomic bomb on 6 August 1945.

Truly perplexing was the fabrication of a harbor at Tinian Town, where Sunharon Bay was no more than an open roadstead. Initially, the Seabees sought to meet the problem with temporary measures, such as the repair of two former Japanese piers and the construction of two marine railways, a pontoon pier, and a section base. After these expedients were wrecked by a typhoon in early October, the Seabees built more permanent bulk-heads, piers, and a protective breakwater. The breakwater was constructed on a coral reef with 120 circular steel sheet pilings thirty feet in diameter filled with coral. Two 80-by-500-foot cargo piers were constructed of sheet piling parallel to a cargo ship bulkhead of sheet piling and coral fill all linked by an 88-foot-wide causeway. Until the harbor's completion, cargo was moved to the beaches in lighters.

The Americans inherited a road system from the Japanese similar to the grid plan of Manhattan's streets. These roads were surfaced and broadened to link the port with the airfields and other utilities. Large storage areas were provided for the Army, the Navy, and the Sixth Construction Brigade. The ammunition dump of 254 coral-surfaced revetments linked by fourteen miles of roads was completed in February 1945, and a 20,000-bomb dump in 468 revetments was commissioned at West Field early the following summer. The 13,000 mines assembled by the Mine Assembly Plant, No. 4, Tinian, during the final months of the war exceeded the production of all other American mine depots combined and probably established a world record for mine assemblies.

Fuel storage was provided on Tinian in a 14,000-barrel fuel oil storage farm, a 20,000-barrel motor gasoline farm, and six aviation gasoline farms of 165,000 barrels total capacity located close to the main airfields. Fuel oil and motor gasoline tanks were sufficiently close to tanker moorings to permit filling from tanker pumps, but aviation gasoline was distributed through pipelines to eight dispersing stations close to North and West Fields.

With the end of World War II Tinian lost its naval significance, and the Tinian Naval Base and Naval Air Base were both disestablished on 1 June 1947.

BIBLIOGRAPHY

A. H. F. Ely, "Base History, Tinian, M.I., 11 October 1945" (Washington: Naval Historical Center, Operational Archives Branch, World War II Command File); U.S. Navy, Bureau of Yards and Docks, *Building the Navy's Bases in World War II*, 2 vols. (Washington: GPO, 1947), II:358-60.

B. Samuel E. Morison, *New Guinea and the Marianas*, (Boston: Little, Brown, 1953), pp. 149-54.

WILLIAM R. BRAISTED

TIVERTON, ENGLAND.
See United Kingdom, U.S. World War II Naval Bases.

TJILATJAP, NETHERLANDS EAST INDIES, U.S. NAVAL ADVANCE BASE, 1942 Located on the south coast of Java, Netherlands East Indies, Tjilatjap (7°S., 108°30′E.) became in January 1942 a base for auxiliaries of the Asiatic Fleet, fighting within the American, British, Dutch, Australian (ABDA) Command for the defense of the Malay Barrier against the Japanese. The auxiliaries had been operating out of bases on the northwest coast of Australia. On 10 February the submarine tenders *Holland* and *Otus* arrived at Tjilatjap, but they were not fated to operate there long. In late February the *Holland* retired to Australia and the *Otus* escorted the badly damaged cruiser *Marblehead*, given emergency repairs in commercial facilities at Tjilatjap, to safety in the Indian Ocean. Beginning 19 February, Asiatic Fleet administrative offices were transferred from Surabaya (q.v.) to Tjilatjap. However, the Japanese invasion of Java compelled the dissolution of the ABDA naval forces and on 1 March 1942 the evacuation of Tjilatjap.

BIBLIOGRAPHY

B. U.S. Office of Naval Intelligence, Combat Narrative, *The Java Sea Campaign* (Washington: GPO, 1943); Samuel E. Morison, *The Rising Sun in the Pacific, 1931-April 1942* (Boston: Little, Brown, 1948).

TONGAREVA, NORTHERN COOK ISLANDS, U.S. NAVAL AIR TRANSPORT SYSTEM BASE, c. 1943–1944 Tongareva (also known as

Penryhn) is an atoll located at 9°3′S., 157°58′W. in the Northern Cook Islands, administered by New Zealand. Located northeast of Samoa and northwest of Bora Bora, it offered a convenient stopping point for aircraft flying into the South Pacific. Probably in 1943, an airfield on Tongareva's Omoka Island was constructed for the Naval Air Transport System. Additional installations included a weather station and a radio range. The airfield functioned as a fueling stop for naval transport planes until May 1944, with the opening of shorter flying routes to the north.

BIBLIOGRAPHY

A. U.S. Navy, "U.S. Naval Bases in the South and Southwest Pacific (and Central Pacific Forward) in World War II," 1 November 1954 (Washington: Naval Historical Center, Operational Archives Branch).

JOHN B. LUNDSTROM

TONGATABU ISLAND, U.S. NAVAL STATION, 1942–1945 [BLEACHER] Tongatabu (preferred spelling is Tongatapu), at 21°7′S., 175°10′W., is the main island of Tonga, in 1942 a British protectorate ruled by the Tongan Queen Salote Tupou. Roughly eighteen by nine miles in size, Tongatabu features a low, even terrain. The principal settlement and port is Nukualofa, a protected anchorage on the north coast. Tongatabu is about 400 miles southwest of Fiji and nearly 500 miles southwest of Samoa.

On 22 February 1942 Adm. Ernest J. King, Commander in Chief, U.S. Fleet, ordered development of Tongatabu as an advanced naval operating base capable of handling one carrier task force's demands for fuel, supplies, and minor repairs. He chose Tongatabu in preference to Fiji and Samoa (q.v.), both of which he considered too exposed to Japanese attack. Admiral King intended at that time that Tongatabu would ultimately serve as the main South Pacific base for transshipment of materiel for future South Pacific advanced bases. That ambitious role for Tongatabu never came to pass. On 12 March the Joint Chiefs of Staff issued the basic plan for Tongatabu, calling for a naval operating base, fuel depot, and air base. They allocated Army garrison troops and naval construction forces to sail in April from the United States.

Before the Tongatabu base forces even arrived, the island served as a welcome haven for Pacific Fleet warships. On 31 March King directed Rear Adm. Frank Jack Fletcher's Task Force 17, including the carrier *Yorktown*, to replenish from stores and repair ships ordered to Tongatabu. After more than two months of continuous steaming, Task Force 17 sheltered there from 20 to 27 April and returned there on 15 May to lick its wounds after the Battle of the Coral Sea (4-8 May 1942). Meanwhile, on 9 May, the Tongatabu base convoy had arrived and began constructing base facilities: a naval camp, a tank farm, a seaplane ramp, and an Army Air Forces airfield. Initial construction lasted about nine months.

In the summer of 1942 Tongatabu served as a fuel staging point and rendezvous for chartered tankers stockpiling fuel during the early portion of the Solomons offensive. In September the carrier *Saratoga* availed herself of Tongatabu's submarine-protected anchorage to effect emergency repairs after being torpedoed on 30 August west of the Santa Cruz Islands. Likewise, the battleship *North Carolina*, torpedoed on 15 September northwest of Espiritu Santo, sheltered at Tongatabu for temporary repairs before heading north for Pearl Harbor. However, the successful development of such strategically located bases as Noumea (q.v.) and Espiritu Santo (q.v.) rendered further effort on remote Tongatabu unprofitable. By the fall of 1942, the naval station was reduced in function to that of a reserve fueling point and Naval Air Transport System service base. Seabees dismantled the oil tank farm and shipped it to Samoa. Some facilities remained open until late in the war, and Tongatabu served as a stopping point for barge fleets being towed out to the South Pacific. The naval station at Tongatabu was disestablished on 10 December 1945.

BIBLIOGRAPHY

A. Tongatabu Advance Naval Base, "History of Tongatabu," 1945 (Washington: Naval Historical Center, Operational Archives Branch); U.S. Navy, Bureau of Yards and Docks, *Building the Navy's Bases in World War II*, 2 vols. (Washington: GPO, 1947).

B. John B. Lundstrom, *The First South Pacific Campaign: Pacific Fleet Strategy December 1941-June 1942* (Annapolis, Md.: Naval Institute Press, 1976).

JOHN B. LUNDSTROM

TOROKINA, BOUGAINVILLE, SOLOMON ISLANDS, U.S. NAVAL ADVANCE BASE, 1943–1945 Cape Torokina (Empress Augusta Bay) is located on the west central coast of Bougainville, which is geographically part of the Solomon Islands. However, in 1942, at the time of Japanese occupation, Bougainville was administered by Australia in its Mandated Territory of New Guinea. Bougainville is 130 miles long and up to fifty miles wide, a wilderness of mountains and dense forests. On 1 November 1943 the I Marine Amphibious Corps landed at Torokina to establish an air base surrounded by a defense perimeter. Capture of the whole of Bougainville was not intended; it would be enough to merely neutralize its strong Japanese garrison. Airfields at Torokina would reinforce the massive air effort against the powerful Japanese fortress of Rabaul on New Britain. The first fighter field at Torokina was completed on 10 December 1943, and Piva Field for bombers was ready by 30 December.

Beginning on 3 November 1943, eight PT boats set up a temporary motor torpedo boat operating base at Purata Island in Torokina anchorage (6°22′S., 155°6′E.). The PTs hunted enemy coastal barge traffic, but, lacking targets, they discontinued combat patrols on 25 April 1944. Torokina remained an active PT center, but its main naval function involved its small-boat repair unit, completed in July 1944, which serviced small landing craft such as LCMs and LCVPs. Meanwhile, on 15 June 1944, Bougainville, along with other islands in the Northern Solomons, passed from jurisdiction of the South Pacific Area Force to that of the Southwest Pacific Area, specifically Seventh Fleet. Commo. Edward J. Moran, formerly Commander, MTB Squadrons, South Pacific Force, became Commander, Allied Naval Forces, Northern Solomons Area (Task Group 70.8), controlling naval forces and bases from New Georgia (q.v.) north to Emirau, New Ireland (q.v.). On 18 June 1944 he established his headquarters at Torokina for closer liaison with the commander of air forces in the Northern Solomons and the Army's XIV Corps handling operations on Bougainville.

With decreasing enemy operations in the Bougainville-Rabaul area, combat forces in the area could be sent northward to more active areas. Roll-up of naval facilities at Torokina began early in 1945, and the base was formally disestablished in March 1945, although Seabee maintenance forces operated there until June of that year.

BIBLIOGRAPHY

A. Motor Torpedo Boat Squadrons, Philippine Sea Frontier, "Command History of MTB Squadrons, Philippine Sea Frontier, Formerly MTB Squadrons, 7th Fleet," 5 vols., Type Commands, 1945 (Washington: Naval Historical Center, Operational Archives Branch); Service Squadron, South Pacific, "History of Commander, Service Squadron, South Pacific 7 December 1941-15 August 1945" (Washington: Naval Historical Center, Operational Archives Branch); U.S. Navy, Bureau of Yards and Docks, *Building the Navy's Bases in World War II*, 2 vols. (Washington: GPO, 1947); U.S. Navy, "U.S. Naval Bases in the South and Southwest Pacific (and Central Pacific Forward) in World War II, "1 November 1954 (Washington: Naval Historical Center, Operational Archives Branch).

B. Samuel E. Morison, *Breaking the Bismarcks Barrier 22 July 1942-1 May 1944* (Boston: Little, Brown, 1950); Robert Sherrod, *History of Marine Corps Aviation in World War II* (Washington: Combat Forces Press, 1952); Capt. Robert J. Bulkley, *At Close Quarters: PT Boats in the United States Navy* (Washington: Navy Department, Naval History Division, 1962).

JOHN B. LUNDSTROM

TOWNSVILLE, AUSTRALIA, U.S. NAVAL ADVANCE BASE, 1943–1944 A small port in Queensland on Australia's northeastern coast, Townsville (19°10′S., 147°30′E.) was in 1942 the site of a Royal Australian naval station, several airfields important for searches into the Coral Sea, and bomber fields supporting Port Moresby (q.v.) in Papua. Also situated nearby were a number of U.S. Army camps and troop staging areas.

In connection with amphibious activities, Townsville in the spring of 1943 developed into a U.S. naval advance base offering support for Seventh Fleet activities in northeastern Australia and eastern New Guinea. It also served as a staging and training area for the Seventh Amphibious Force. In June 1943 troops intended for the invasion of Kiriwina Island, off eastern New Guinea, assembled there. In August Seabees completed a naval magazine and constructed other minor base facilities. A small-boat repair unit helped service landing craft. In the spring of 1944 advance bases in New Guinea began usurping Townsville's functions, and the base was rolled up and disestablished in July 1944.

BIBLIOGRAPHY

A. U.S. Navy, "7th Amphibious Force, Command History 10 January 1943-23 December 1945" (Washington: Naval Historical Center, Operational Archives Branch); U.S. Navy, Bureau of Yards and Docks, *Building the Navy's Bases in World War II*. 2 vols. (Washington: GPO, 1947); U.S. Navy, "U.S. Naval Bases in the South and Southwest Pacific (and Central Pacific Forward) in World War II," 1 November 1954 (Washington: Naval Historical Center, Operational Archives Branch).

B. Vice Adm. Daniel E. Barbey, *MacArthur's Amphibious Navy* (Annapolis, Md.: U.S. Naval Institute, 1969).

JOHN B. LUNDSTROM

TRA CU, REPUBLIC of VIETNAM, U.S. NAVAL ADVANCED TACTICAL SUPPORT BASE, 1968–1971 Tra Cu, a small town on South Vietnam's Vam Co Dong River, was the location of a U.S. naval advanced tactical support base during the Southeast Asian Conflict. River forces operated from the base as part of the overall strategy to interdict the enemy's movement of troops and supplies into the Saigon area from Cambodia. The operation, named Giant Slingshot, entailed the forward basing of river patrol boat (PBR) units at key points on the Vam Co Dong and Vam Co Tay rivers for aggressive sector patrolling.

From December 1968 to the end of the following year, Seabees brought in from the I Corps Tactical Zone developed the base at Tra Cu. The naval constructionmen installed defensive works, ammunition bunkers, an operational command center, a helicopter pad, sleeping huts, and a mess hall. The site also boasted a 70,000-gallon fuel storage pontoon. Additional facilities were required when the PBR unit at nearby Hiep Hoa (q.v.) redeployed to Tra Cu because of the growing ground threat at the former base.

The base at Tra Cu was turned over to the Vietnamese Navy in April 1971 as U.S. forces withdrew from the combat area.

BIBLIOGRAPHY

A. Commander Naval Forces, Vietnam, "The Naval War in Vietnam," May 1970 (Washington: Naval Historical Center, Operational Archives Branch).

EDWARD J. MAROLDA

TREASURY ISLANDS, SOLOMON ISLANDS, U.S. NAVAL ADVANCE BASE, 1943–1945 Located only twenty-eight miles off the southwest coast of Bougainville, the Treasury Islands (British Solomon Islands Protectorate) were admirably situated to help neutralize strong Japanese forces in southern Bougainville and on Shortland. The Treasuries comprise two main islands; rugged, steep Mono (nine by five-and-one-half miles) and low, flat Stirling, only four miles long and less than one mile wide. Between the two is a narrow channel, the southern terminus of which forms Blanche Harbor. The Treasury Islands were secured by the Eighth New Zealand Infantry Brigade, which landed on 27 October 1943.

The day after the invasion, Motor Torpedo Boat Squadron 9 advanced to Stirling, and that evening (28 October) conducted its first patrols against barge traffic off Bougainville and Shortland. They also helped to support the invasion of Cape Torokina on Bougainville's west coast. Naval construction troops on Stirling set to work leveling the terrain for an airfield from which heavy and medium bombers could strike Rabaul on New Britain. Operational in late December, Stirling's airfield mounted its first strikes on Rabaul in mid-January 1944. Seabees also improved port facilities, so that by January 1944 large cargo ships were able to use Blanche Harbor. They also erected an important small-boat repair unit. In February 1944, MTB Base 9 arrived at Stirling and by April was functioning as a major overhaul and repair base for PTs in the Northern Solomons.

The Treasury Island naval base in 1944-1945 supported the containment campaign against Japanese troops on Bougainville and Choiseul. However, its small-boat repair and PT base assisted preparations for such far-flung operations as the invasions of the Western Carolines (September 1944) and Leyte (October 1944). Meanwhile, on 15 June 1944, the Treasury Islands, along with various naval forces in the Northern Solomons, passed from the jurisdiction of the South Pacific Area to that of the Southwest Pacific Area. The Treasury Islands came under control of Task Group 70.8, Allied Naval Forces, Northern Solomons Area. With the winding down of combat operations against Bougainville, the Treasury Islands PTs secured from combat patrols on 24 November 1944. Likewise, the air effort against Rabaul and Bougainville also ceased from Stirling field. Roll-up was complete by late 1944, and the base was disestablished in March 1945.

BIBLIOGRAPHY

A. Motor Torpedo Boat Squadrons, Philippine Sea Frontier, "Command History of MTB Squadrons, Philippine Sea Frontier, Formerly MTB Squadrons, 7th Fleet," 5 vols., Type Commands, 1945 (Washington: Naval Historical Center, Operational Archives Branch); Service Squadron, South Pacific, "History of Commander, Service Squadron, South Pacific 7 December 1941-15 August 1945" (Washington: Naval Historical Center, Operational Archives Branch); U.S. Navy, Bureau of Yards and Docks, *Building the Navy's Bases in World War II*, 2 vols. (Washington: GPO, 1947); U.S. Navy, "U.S. Naval Bases in the South and Southwest Pacific (and Central Pacific Forward) in World War II," 1 November 1954 (Washington: Naval Historical Center, Operational Archives Branch).

B. Samuel E. Morison, *Breaking the Bismarcks Barrier 22 July 1942-1 May 1944* (Boston: Little, Brown, 1950); Robert Sherrod, *History of Marine Corps Aviation in*

World War II (Washington: Combat Forces Press, 1952); Capt. Robert J. Bulkley, *At Close Quarters: PT Boats in the United States Navy* (Washington: Navy Department, Naval History Division, 1962).

JOHN B. LUNDSTROM

TREGUIER, FRANCE.
See World War I U.S. Naval Air Stations in Europe.

TRINIDAD, BRITISH WEST INDIES, U.S. NAVAL OPERATING BASE.
See Caribbean, The, U.S. Naval Bases.

TUFI, PAPUA, U.S. NAVAL ADVANCE BASE, 1942–1943 A small anchorage situated on the east side of Cape Nelson in New Guinea's Territory of Papua, Tufi (9°6′S., 149°16′E.) became the first forward operating base for PT boats on New Guinea. On 19 December 1942 PT boats from Motor Torpedo Boat Squadron 6 advanced from Milne Bay (q.v.) to Tufi, which is located southeast of Buna. From Tufi, the PTs patrolled past Buna toward Huon Gulf to disrupt Japanese coastal barge traffic and help prevent evacuation of Japanese troops from the Buna area. After April 1943 the PTs advanced to Morobe (q.v.), further west along the coast. Tufi was used for a time as an emergency fueling and staging point for coastal traffic bringing supplies to Seventh Fleet advance bases on the New Guinea coast.

BIBLIOGRAPHY

A. Motor Torpedo Boat Squadrons, Philippine Sea Frontier, "Command History of MTB Squadrons, Philippine Sea Frontier, Formerly MTB Squadrons, 7th Fleet," 5 vols., Type Commands, 1945 (Washington: Naval Historical Center, Operational Archives Branch); U.S. Navy, "7th Amphibious Force, Command History, 10 January 1943-23 December 1945" (Washington: Naval Historical Center, Operational Archives Branch); U.S. Navy, "U.S. Naval Bases in the South and Southwest Pacific (and Central Pacific Forward) in World War II," 1 November 1954 (Washington: Naval Historical Center, Operational Archives Branch).

B. Capt. Robert J. Bulkley, *At Close Quarters: PT Boats in the United States Navy* (Washington: Navy Department, Naval History Division, 1962); Vice Adm. Daniel E. Barbey, *MacArthur's Amphibious Navy* (Annapolis, Md.: U.S. Naval Institute, 1969).

JOHN B. LUNDSTROM

TULAGI, FLORIDA ISLAND, SOLOMON ISLANDS, U.S. NAVAL ADVANCE BASE, 1942–1946 The Tulagi Naval Advance Base (which included the southern shore of nearby Florida Island) grew into a massive support installation for fleet operations, a perfect complement to Guadalcanal (q.v.) some eighteen miles to the south, which acted as a troop staging and supply base. A small island only two-and-one-half miles long and less than a half-mile wide, Tulagi (9°6′S., 160°9′E.) in 1942 was the administrative center of the British

Solomon Islands Protectorate. With its associated islets of Gavutu, Tanambogo, and Macambo, Tulagi's harbor encompassed a bay six miles across, the finest in the Solomons. Less than a mile north of Tulagi is Florida (Nggela) Island, twenty-five miles long, and its southern coast localities, such as Halavo and Purvis Bay, east of Tulagi, would be incorporated in the Tulagi base.

On 3 May 1942 Tulagi, with its small Royal Australian Air Force seaplane base, was taken by the Japanese as part of their MO Operation, the attempted invasion of Port Moresby. In July Tulagi became one of the primary objectives of the Allied plan to reconquer the southern Solomons (Operation Watchtower). Between 7 and 9 August, elements of the First Marine Division (reinforced) captured Tulagi and the harbor area in the face of determined Japanese resistance. There were no immediate plans for the development of Tulagi as a base, and in August and September it was a spectator to the dramatic events taking place at Guadalcanal and in the waters to the north. Only in early October 1942 were steps taken to utilize Tulagi as a small naval base. Elements of the Sixth Naval Construction Battalion crossed over from Guadalcanal to build a small PT boat base at Sesaspi on Tulagi's north coast. On 12 October the first motor torpedo boats (from MTB Squadron 3) arrived at Sesaspi and began patrols into Iron-bottom Sound against Japanese ships operating off Guadalcanal. In the next few months more PTs were committed to Tulagi, and on 15 December 1942 head-quarters MTB Flotilla 1 was set up there. The small, nimble PT boats departed nightly from Tulagi to do battle with the "Tokyo Express."

With the wild succession of naval battles off Guadalcanal, Tulagi also became important as a place where badly damaged warships could take refuge for emer-gency repairs before heading south for better-equipped naval repair centers. In mid-November 1942, after the Naval Battle of Guadalcanal, the heavy cruiser *Portland* and the destroyer *Aaron Ward* limped into Tulagi, as did heavy cruisers *Pensacola, Minneapolis*, and *New Orleans* after their defeat off Tassafaronga. Tulagi's specialists did what they could to make the ships seaworthy while they hid under foliage and nets in Purvis Bay and other anchorages around the harbor.

By early 1943 a concerted effort had begun to convert Tulagi into a major naval base to service and repair most classes of warships, just as Guadalcanal developed into a main staging and supply center for the advance bases. For the PT boats, the Sesaspi base was expanded when in March 1943 PT Base 3 and part of PT Base 1 reached Tulagi. They set up additional PT repair facilities on Macambo Island and completed a camp across the bay at "Calvertville" on Florida Island. Boats from MTB Squadrons 1, 3, and 8 made their last active patrols from Tulagi on 6 July. Thereafter, Tulagi served as an important rear area base for PTs in the northern Solomons until April 1944, when facilities were dismantled and moved north to Green Island (q.v.). Along with the PT boats, an early naval activity at Tulagi was the seaplane base started in late 1942 at Halavo, a peninsula of Florida jutting into Tulagi harbor. Patrol planes began operating from there in June 1943, and the base was expanded, so that by late

1943 it provided most reconnaissance flights for the southern Solomons and security patrols for the very busy ship traffic in and out of Tulagi.

Tulagi's most vital task involved service and repair for ships and small craft. In the spring and summer of 1943 its harbor continued as a fleet anchorage for cruiser-destroyer task forces operating in the Slot. They rested at Tulagi by day before sorties northward to engage Japanese naval forces in the central Solomons. The big ships were serviced by numerous fleet repair, supply, and ammunition vessels, mainly at Purvis Bay. This continued well into 1945. In one month, for example (March 1944), Tulagi handled 261 ships for major and minor repairs, utilizing repair ships and a number of floating dry docks. The base likewise contained several installations to deal with the fleets of landing craft involved in the many amphibious operations in the South Pacific. Begun in April 1943 was a landing craft repair center at "Carter City," on Florida; next placed in operation was a similar facility on little Gavutu Island. "Turner City" on Florida was organized as an amphibious training command to help train landing craft crews. In September 1943 an advance submarine base was set up at Tulagi to refuel the submarines based in Brisbane (q.v.) making war patrols east of Bougainville. These boats were able to top off their tanks while headed in or out from their patrol areas. For fueling needs in general, in March 1944 Seabees completed on Florida's Phillips Peninsula an oil tank farm for 280,000 barrels of fuel oil and 50,000 barrels of diesel.

By the spring of 1944 construction at Tulagi was largely finished. Some roll-up of specific installations took place, but Tulagi's facilities remained crucial through the fall of 1944 as a ship repair and service base. In August 1944 the ship repair unit was reinforced with numerous repair ships and floating workshops in anticipation of Operation Stalemate II, the invasion of the Western Carolines. In September alone, the Tulagi base handled 383 ships, including 4 battleships, 1 carrier, 2 cruisers, and 9 destroyers. It proved invaluable in helping to keep ships combat-ready after months of continuous activity. In the fall of 1944 Tulagi likewise prepared ships for the invasion of the Philippines. By 1945, however, it had wound down to a minor repair and fueling base as effort shifted to Manus (q.v.) in the Admiralty Islands and to Leyte (q.v.), but the base still played a useful role in the preparations (February-March 1945) for the invasion of Okinawa. Thereafter final roll-up took place, and the base was disestablished (along with Guadalcanal) on 12 June 1946.

BIBLIOGRAPHY

A. Service Squadron, South Pacific, "History of Commander, Service Squadron, South Pacific 7 December 1941-15 August 1945," (Washington: Naval Historical Center, Operational Archives Branch); Tulagi Advance Naval Base, "History of Advance Naval Base, Tulagi, British Solomon Islands," Shore Establishment, 1 August 1945 (Washington: Naval Historical Center, Operational Archives Branch).

B. Samuel E. Morison, *Coral Sea, Midway, and Submarine Actions May 1942-August 1942* (Boston: Little, Brown, 1949); Samuel E. Morison, *The Struggle for Guadalcanal August 1942-February 1943* (Boston: Little, Brown, 1949); Samuel E. Morison, *Breaking the Bismarcks Barrier 22 July 1942-1 May 1944* (Boston: Little, Brown, 1950); Rear Adm. Worrall Reed Carter, *Beans, Bullets and Black Oil* (Washington: GPO, 1953); Capt. Robert J. Bulkley, *At Close Quarters: PT Boats in the United States Navy* (Washington: Navy Department, Naval History Division, 1962); Vice Adm. George C. Dyer, *The Amphibians Came to Conquer*. 2 vols. (Washington: GPO, 1972).

JOHN B. LUNDSTROM

TUNIS, TUNISIA.
See North Africa, U.S. Naval Bases.

TUTUILA, SAMOA, U.S. NAVAL STATION, 1900–1951 From 1900 to 1951 the U.S. Navy had a station on the island of Tutuila in American Samoa. Its commandant was a busy man, for he wore another hat: he was also governor of that island group. Pago Pago (pronounced Pong-o Pong-o), the capital, lies 2,263 miles south of Honolulu, 1,580 miles east of Auckland, New Zealand, and 4,160 miles southwest of San Francisco.

During the twentieth century the two political divisions of the Samoan Archipelago have usually been known as Western Samoa and American Samoa. (Western Samoa, now independent, changed its name to simply Samoa in 1977, but the older form is retained here to avoid confusion.) Of these two divisions, the former is by far the larger in both area and population. Its principal islands are Upolu and Savaii; its principal city is Apia, on Upolu. Tutuila, which measures about eighteen miles by six miles, is much the largest of the American group. Aunuu, one of the four other inhabited islands, is administratively part of Tutuila; the other three, lying well to the east, are known collectively as Manua. Pago Pago Harbor, Tutuila, on the south side of which the Naval Station stood, is the finest harbor in the South Sea Islands. It extends northward one-and-one-half miles into mountainous Tutuila and then westward for the same distance.

The Samoan people were Christianized early in the nineteenth century by missionaries sent out by various denominations. Their form of government was oligarchy. Each family group ("family" in the broadest sense) elected or appointed a representative called a matai; these matais met in a fono (council) and, along with certain higher chiefs, ran the government.

Lt. Charles Wilkes, USN, commander of a U.S. Exploring Expedition, made the first U.S. naval contact with the islands in 1838. He visited both Apia and Tutuila and was impressed by their possibilities as supply and repair depots for American whalers.

During the next thirty years the islands began to have, or to seem to have, commercial value. Both French and German firms appeared at Apia. As the transcontinental railroad connected the American coasts, and as rumors were heard of a possible isthmian canal, American, Australian, and New Zealand businessmen became interested in using Pago Pago as a coaling station between Honolulu and "down under." Comdr. Richard W. Meade, USN, persuaded the

Mauga, the principal chief on Tutuila, to accept a treaty (1872) giving the United States the exclusive right to build and maintain a naval station in Pago Pago Harbor in exchange for which Tutuila was to have the friendship and protection of the United States. However, the U.S. Senate, distrustful of "entangling alliances," rejected the treaty.

Eager to obtain protection, particularly against Germany, the Samoans in 1877 tried to obtain treaties both from Great Britain and from the United States. When the British would make no promises, the Samoan secretary of state negotiated a treaty with the Rutherford B. Hayes administration. The U.S. Senate ratified it on 13 February 1878 but refused an offer of annexation. The treaty affirmed the right of the United States to establish a naval station at Pago Pago, though that right was no longer exclusive, and stated that, in the event that Samoa should quarrel with a third nation, the United States would use its "good offices."

During the 1880s, while rival native claimants disputed the throne of Samoa, Britain and the United States, as well as the Samoans, feared German expansionism, as illustrated by the fact that German ships had fired upon Samoans and endangered American property. Germany made the conciliatory gesture of arranging a three-power conference at Berlin in 1889, but meanwhile potentially hostile warships—three American and one British, as against three Greman—gathered in Apia Harbor. On 15 March 1889 one of the most savage of recorded hurricanes struck there. Only HMS *Calliope* managed to fight her way out of the harbor and get to sea. Every other ship either sank or went aground. Two—one American, one German—were ultimately salvaged.

The storm, however, did some good: it relaxed international tensions and taught people to work together for the good of others. Thus when the Berlin Conference met in the following month, the atmosphere was far friendlier than it might otherwise have been. The conferees set up a new government built around a "king," who would be advised by two foreigners selected by the three powers. The plan lasted for about ten years, but it never worked. The government became increasingly chaotic. Several times armed intervention by one or more of the three powers occurred. Finally, early in 1899, matters came to a head, following the murders of an Englishman and an American and sporadic firing at sentries outside the two embassies. British and American warships thereupon shelled Apia and some native villages. A joint landing party was sent ashore to destroy some villages and drive the aggressors away. The result was a disastrous fight in which four Americans (including the senior U.S. naval officer present) and three Englishmen were killed. Rear Adm. Albert Kautz, USN, believed that the effectiveness of the resistance was due to German help.

Since the existing government was not working, Germany proposed that the islands be partitioned among the three powers. The United States agreed to accept Tutuila and the other islands east of the 171st meridian of west longitude. However, Germany offered Britain certain concessions, chiefly in the Tonga and Solomons archipelagoes, if Britain would renounce all claim to Samoa. Britain agreed, and a three-power agreement to that effect was signed on 14 November

1899. Thus Western (i.e., German) Samoa and American Samoa came into existence.

The treaty of 1878 had given the United States the right to maintain a coaling station on Tutuila. Accordingly, land was rented in Fagatoga village, on the south side of Pago Pago Harbor, for $10 a month. The coal lay piled up on the piers; when rain fell, the coal discolored the waters of the bay. The U.S. consul at Apia managed the station; that is, he hired a man to tend it.

About 1889 the Navy Department became serious about constructing a naval station in addition to the coaling station. After the disastrous hurricane at Apia, Rear Adm. Lewis A. Kimberly, USN, went to Tutuila to choose a site. He recommended a tract of land east of Fagatoga, on and near Goat Island, which is actually a peninsula. Buying up the necessary land took several years. Not until 1898 did the Navy make a contract with a San Francisco firm to construct such a station. As an American naval officer reported,

> work on the coaling station at the United States naval station was begun in 1898 and completed in 1902. The station consists of a coal shed with a capacity of about 4,200 tons, and a steel wharf with 30 feet of water alongside. Coal is supplied only to vessels of the United States Navy. The station also contains storehouses for naval stores of all kinds. There is no manufacturing plant, and no shop using power machinery; the expenses of maintenance of the station are kept down to a minimum. The complement of officers includes the commandant, captain of the yard, general storekeeper, medical officer, and chaplain. A lieutenant, a pay officer, a chief machinist, and a pay clerk have duties on the station ship as well as on the naval station. The power plant comprises the refrigerating and electric-lighting machinery. Fresh water is supplied from a reservoir in a valley behind the village of Fagatogo [*sic*], but the supply is not nearly enough during the dry season. For months at a time the water is turned on in the water mains only during meal hours.

This description of the station, written by Comdr. William M. Crose, the Commandant, in 1913, is probably accurate for most of the period preceding World War I.

In August 1899 Comdr. Benjamin F. Tilley, USN, took office as the first commandant of the naval station. When the three-power treaty created American Samoa, Secretary of the Navy John Davis Long issued this order: "The island of Tutuila, of the Samoan group, and all other islands of the group east of longitude 171° west of Greenwich, are hereby established into a naval station, to be known as the Naval Station, Tutuila, and to be under the command of a commandant." Assistant Secretary Charles H. Allen thereupon wrote to Tilley appointing him to the larger job and saying, "While your position as commandant will invest you with authority over the islands embraced in the limits of the station, you will at all times exercise care to conciliate and cultivate friendly relations with the natives. A simple, straightforward method of administration, such as to win and hold the confidence of the people, is expected of you." Thus, as the first commandant of "Naval Station, Tutuila," Tilley was also, for all practical purposes, the first governor of American Samoa, although the title was not formally adopted until 1905. He was a splendid choice.

It was important that the Samoans should accept American sovereignty. Somehow Tilley persuaded the chiefs of Tutuila Island to draw up and sign a deed of cession to the United States, dated 2 April 1900. The official flag-raising ceremony took place on 17 April. The chiefs of Manua were more difficult to persuade, but Tilley did obtain an informal agreement that placed Manua under the sovereignty and protection of the United States. The cession was formalized in 1904.

Tilley established the form of government that endured, with minor changes, for fifty-one years. Comdr. William M. Crose, governor from 1910 to 1913, describes it as follows:

> The seat of government is at the naval station in Pago Pago Bay. The governor. . . is also the commandant of the naval station and commands the station ship. The secretary of native affairs, an executive [and civilian] official, has cognizance of all native affairs and native officials, acting under the directions of the governor. The position of chief customs officer is held by the naval captain of the yard; he is also superintendent of roads and sheriff. The treasurer is a naval paymaster, who also acts as storekeeper of the naval station. The health officer is a naval medical officer, who is also in charge of a naval dispensary and sick quarters on the station.
>
> American Samoa is divided into three general administrative divisions, Eastern District of Tutuila, Western District of Tutuila, and Manua District, these corresponding to the Samoan divisions which have existed since early days. Each district is administered by a native district governor appointed by the governor. . . . [Crose goes down the hierarchy of rulers—county chief, village chief—and then:] The village councils are composed of the "matais" (heads of families) in each village, and each is presided over by the village chief. . . . The suffrage is restricted to the "matais," in accordance with the Samoan custom, whereby the family, not the individual, is the unit of society. . . .
>
> The organic law of American Samoa is [Tilley's] regulation No. 5 of 1900, "A declaration concerning the form of government for the United States naval station, Tutuila." This provides that the laws of the United States be in force unless expressly modified; that the Samoan customs, not in conflict with the law, shall be preserved; that the Samoans shall retain their village, county, and district councils who meet to recommend laws, and who are charged with the cleanliness of the villages, counties, and districts, the planting of lands, the making of roads, and matters of local interest.

One very important rule is omitted here: foreigners were not allowed to buy and "alienate" land; thus industrialization was essentially forbidden. In general, Tilley's laws pleased the Samoans; they were able to retain their way of life. The autocratic power of the naval governor was the only obvious source of future trouble. Tilley also formed a Samoan military organization known as the Fita Fita, or "guard." Its members ranked as Navy "landsmen." Tilley's successor established a Fita Fita band which, in later years, welcomed official visitors.

For the first fourteen years of the twentieth century, life in American Samoa was pleasant and calm. Then in August 1914 a small German warship and a 15,000-ton liner entered Pago Pago Bay from Apia and asked to be interned "for the duration." The request was granted, and none too soon from the German point of view, for on 29 August a New Zealand expeditionary force of 1,473, escorted by overwhelming British naval force (plus a French cruiser), landed at Apia and took possession. Thereupon "German" Samoa ceased to exist. (When the United States entered the war in 1917, the Navy seized the two interned German ships but was unable to make effective use of them.) Western Samoa remained under a friendly New Zealand rule, at first under occupation during World War I, then as a League of Nations mandate, and then, after World War II, as a United Nations trust territory. In 1962 it was given its independence.

Until about 1920 the naval commandant-governors had been consistently satisfactory to the Samoans, but the 1920 incumbent, Comdr. Warren J. Terhune, USN, was the least successful administrator ever given the job. Details of all the moves and countermoves are missing, but the fact that Terhune's executive officer, Lt. Comdr. Creed H. Boucher, USN, and then Boucher's successor, Comdr. Arthur C. Kail, USN, sided with the Samoan opposition rather than with their superior officer suggests that the government must have been chaotic. Boucher was court-martialed and dismissed from the Navy, Kail was transferred to other duty, and Terhune himself committed suicide rather than face a court of inquiry. Fortunately, Terhune's successor was able to restore relative peace and happiness although the opposition party, which came to be known as the Mau, continued to exist.

By the middle 1920s life in American Samoa was much as it had been before World War I. Capt. Henry F. Bryan, USN (Ret.), Governor from March 1925 to September 1927, described the naval station proper as follows:

The naval station is primarily a supply base. There is a coal shed with a capacity of about 4,500 tons and a new modern concrete wharf with 30 feet of water alongside. Coal is supplied only to vessels of the United States Navy, but in case of emergency merchantmen have been given a sufficient amount to carry them to the nearest port.

A naval dispensary is maintained for naval personnel.

The station is equipped with storehouses for naval stores of all kinds and has limited facilities for repair work. The power plant comprises refrigerating and electric lighting machinery.

There is an ample supply of the best water and vessels may obtain any amount at almost any time. The water is of excellent quality for both drinking and boiler use.

In November, 1922, the United States Shipping Board completed the erection on the naval station of two fuel-oil storage tanks of 55,000 barrels capacity each, and a pumping plant to handle the oil. This equipment has never been used; and the tanks are now filled with water.

A new hydro-electric power plant began to operate in August, 1926.

The station ship is a Navy tug, assigned to the station for general harbor and island duty; enlisted complement, 54.

The complement of naval officers attached to the naval station consists of the commandant, captain of the yard, aide to the commandant and engineer officer, supply officers, medical officers, a dental officer, a radio officer, civil engineer, and a chaplain, a total of 16.

The enlisted complement is 147, including 70 members of the native guard and band [i.e., the Fita Fita], and 6 native apprentice seamen (at present, 6 native seamen, second class, unattached) for duty in the medical department.

Note the presence of the radio officer. In World War II the station would be important as a communications base.

Although the cession of Tutuila had occurred in 1900 and that of Manua in 1904, Congress did not get around to accepting these cessions until 1929. It then appointed a commission to report on conditions in American Samoa. The commissioners investigated thoroughly and drew up a 137-page report recommending some changes. Congress failed to act on these recommendations.

Because of increasing international tensions that might lead to war, in 1940 the United States began to expand the naval station at Tutuila and in addition to establish "facilities to support land, sea, and air forces" on Upolu in Western Samoa and on Wallis Island 300 miles to the west.

The civilian construction workers found the Tutuila station little changed since Governor Bryan's 1927 report. According to the Bureau of Yards and Docks:

Before the war, the Navy installations in Samoa consisted of a refueling station and a communication center at Pago Pago Harbor. The station was a minor establishment until construction under contract was begun in 1940 as part of the national defense program. At that time the station comprised a 300-foot wharf, a radio station, housing facilities, office space for four desks, shops, and a garage (all poorly equipped), a small power plant, water-supply system, and several miles of narrow, crooked roads.

After Pearl Harbor that placid backwater changed drastically. The general calm of the islands was shattered in January 1942 when a Japanese submarine fired on Pago Pago Harbor, doing minor physical but considerable psychological damage. In any event,

marine forces arrived at Tutuila in January 1942, under a brigadier general [Henry L. Larsen] who was empowered by the President to assume military governorship and command of the defense forces. He took charge of all construction operations and concentrated attention on the airfield. . . . By virtue of concentration, a 2,500-by-250 foot section was ready for operation by April 6, 1942, and the runway was completed in late June. Construction of a fuel wharf, an additional power plant, a 100-foot extension of the old naval station wharf, and additions to the net facilities on Goat Island and the storehouse at the naval station were undertaken. In April 1942, facilities for the construction of the 300-bed Naval Mobile Hospital 3 [called "Mob 3"] arrived, and the naval personnel attached to the hospital started construction of the unit. (U.S. Navy, Bureau of Yards and Docks, *Building the Navy's Bases in World War II*, 2 vols. [Washington: Government Printing Office, 1947], II:210-12).

General Larsen and his successor, Maj. Gen. F. B. Price, USMC, were officially in command of the Samoan Defense Group, which included all of the Samoan Islands and also the Cook, Wallis, and Society groups. No doubt their presence on Tutuila was slightly irksome to the naval governor-commandant, but as a naval captain he was outranked by the generals. One commandant reported, ''Until December 7, 1941, the native political situation was a continuation of that of previous years. The Island Government, until that date, maintained the policy 'Samoa for the Samoans.' Since that date the policy has been and is, 'Samoa for the Defense of the Australian Life Line.' '' When Capt. Allen Hobbs, USN, relieved General Price and also the Navy commandant in March 1944, the situation in American Samoa became more normal.

In July 1942 the Seventh Construction Battalion arrived at Tutuila to relieve the civilian construction workers, who went aboard ship to go home. Thereupon the Seabees' orders were changed: they were to proceed to the New Hebrides. It looked as if most of the work on Tutuila would stop, but then a hundred of the already embarked civilians volunteered to stay while they were needed. The Eleventh Construction Battalion arrived in late August and relieved them.

World War II had a much greater impact on Samoa than World War I had had. After 23 January 1942, contingents of Marines arrived regularly, until, it was believed, the Marines outnumbered the Tutuilans. Part of the Guadalcanal attack of 7 August 1942 was staged from Pago Pago. On 27 August the first load of wounded Marines was brought to Mob 3 from the Solomons.

Meanwhile the work at Tutuila proceeded. According to the Bureau of Yards and Docks:

> The major project of the 11th Battalion at Tutuila was the construction of a destroyer repair base. . . . Quarters for officers and enlisted men, water-supply facilities, fourteen 50-by-200-foot frame warehouses, three 20-by-40 feet timber piers, and a 600-foot timber bulkhead were installed. . . . The Marine airfield, with two coral-surfaced runways—one 6,000 feet by 500 feet; the other 3,000 feet by 500 feet—was completed at Tafuna, together with industrial facilities, warehouses, a 6,000 kw power plant, a 50-bed dispensary, quarters, and mess halls. The Seabees also constructed Leone Airfield, a 6,000-by-400-foot bomber strip. . . and necessary supportive facilities.

The Seabees also completed Mobile Hospital 3 and built fuel storage tanks, a pump system, a fuel pier, and a net depot, and they developed the island water supply, power plants, and services. They constructed and maintained roads.

But the war moved on, and soon American Samoa lost its military importance. The station was cut down rapidly. By August 1944 the salvage of valuable materials was complete. By January 1945 there was only a token Navy garrison on Tutuila, and the base conducted virtually nothing but emergency seaplane operations, weather reporting, and communications.

When peace came, the economy of American Samoa was in trouble. The export of copra had hitherto been its chief resource, but the cutting of copra had ceased during the war because there had been no freighters available to export it. During the final six years of Navy administration (1945-1951) the copra trade revived somewhat, but even so the exports were not over 2,000 tons annually. As there were no other exports except handicrafts, something had to be developed. The final answer was the export of tuna. In 1948 Island Packers, Inc., leased Navy property for a fish cannery, but that project closed in 1950; there were too few fish. The solution came after the naval station had closed; in 1954 Japanese fisherman entered Samoan waters and, using a new technique, showed that tuna abounded there and could easily be caught. Thereupon the Van Camp Seafood Company of California leased the cannery.

Meanwhile Washington had decided to close the naval station and turn the government of the islands over to the Department of the Interior. Although American Samoa can hardly be regarded as a part of the interior United States, the decision made sense because that department was responsible for American Indian affairs and thus had some experience in governing people whose lifestyle differed from that of the average mainland American.

On 22 February 1951, therefore, the Honorable Phelps Phelps arrived at the naval station by ship and was met at the wharf by Capt. Thomas F. Darden, the last of the twenty-seven naval governors. The next day Phelps, representing the Navy Department until the actual transfer date of 1 July 1951, relieved Darden.

In the program printed for that occasion, the Fono (i.e., council) of American Samoa said:

> The Fono, in behalf of the people of American Samoa, wishes to place in the record of history the significance of the termination of 51 years of naval administration. Mutual respect, understanding, and cooperation has been the keynote of our long relationship. Our appreciation for the guidance and leadership of the Navy in helping American Samoa to move forward is deep-seated and everlasting. Turning its head to the past, Samoa is sorrowful to bid farewell to a good and loyal friend, the Navy.

And so, in June 1951, the Fita Fita was disbanded and the last sizable naval contingent sailed from Pago Pago Harbor.

Was the Fono's tribute justified? Apparently it was. A scholarly investigation of the topic came to these conclusions:

> The transfer [to the Department of the Interior] was largely the result of forces outside of the Samoan polity, although there were numerous Samoans who favored such a change. . . . Had the decision been left in their hands it is likely that the majority of Samoans would have opted to retain naval administration of their islands. . . .
>
> The Navy's policy of "Samoa for the Samoans" provides a sharp contrast with the treatment of the American Indians, who were subjected to formal Americanization and suffered the loss of much of their reservation land. Neither fate was shared by the American Samoans. . . .
>
> The policy of "Samoa for the Samoans" reflected the conservative nature of the naval administration. As a caretaker regime, the naval administration maintained the status quo. This the Samoans considered very much to their benefit, since it allowed them a rare privilege for any non-Western people in the twentieth century—to develop without breaking with their past.

BIBLIOGRAPHY

A. U.S. Navy Department, *Annual Report of the Secretary of Navy, 1900* (Washington: GPO, 1900); Comdr. William M. Crose, *American Samoa: A General Report by the Governor* (Washington: GPO, 1913); Capt. H. F. Bryan, USN (Ret.). *American Samoa:*

A General Report by the Governor (Washington: GPO, 1927); U.S. President, *The American Samoan Commission: Report* (Washington: GPO, 1931); Capt. Lawrence Wild, USN, ''Annual Report for the Fiscal Year Ending 30 June 1942, Government of American Samoa'' (Washington: Naval Historical Center, Operational Archives Branch); Samoan Defense Group, ''U.S. Naval History of the Samoan Defense Group,'' Administrative Historical Appendix, SoPac Administrative History 97 (Sept. 1945) (Washington: Naval Historical Center, Operational Archives Branch); Samoan Defense Group, ''U.S. Naval History of the Samoan Defense Group,'' Administrative Historical Appendix, SoPac, Administrative History 84, 1 Oct. 1945 (Washington: Naval Historical Center, Operational Archives Branch); U.S. Navy, Bureau of Yards and Docks, *Building the Navy's Bases in World War II,* 2 vols. (Washington: GPO, 1947); U.S. Navy, Hydrographic Office, *Sailing Directions for the Pacific Islands,* Vol. 3, *South Central Group,* rev. ed. Pub. No. 80. (Washington: GPO, 1976); Capt. Thomas F. Darden, USN (Ret.), *Historical Sketch of the Naval Administration of the Government of Samoa, April 17, 1900-July 1, 1951* (Washington: GPO, n.d.).

B. George H. Ryden, *The Foreign Policy of the United States in Relation to Samoa* (New Haven: Yale University Press, 1933); Capt. Robert P. Parsons, MC, USM, *Mob 3: A Naval Hospital in a South Sea Jungle* (Indianapolis: Bobbs-Merrill, 1945); David O. Woodbury, *Builders for Battle: How the Pacific Naval Air Bases Were Constructed* (New York: E. P. Dutton, 1946); Capt. J.A.C. Gray, MC, USN, *Amerika Samoa: A History of American Samoa and Its United States Naval Administration* (Annapolis, Md.: U.S. Naval Institute, 1960); Frederick Harris Olsen, ''The Navy and the White Man's Burden: Naval Administration of Samoa,'' Ph.D diss. Washington University, 1976.

EDWIN M. HALL

U

ULITHI ATOLL, CAROLINE ISLANDS, U.S. ADVANCED FLEET ANCHORAGE, 1944-1948 Ulithi is an atoll in the Western Carolines 93 miles northeast of Yap, 370 miles southwest of Guam, and 370 miles northeast of Peleliu. Its principal islands lie on the atoll's edge: Mogmog, Falalop, Asor, Potangeras, and Sorlen. The Joint Chiefs of Staff planned to occupy Ulithi along with Yap in early October 1944 as part of a movement against the Japanese in the Philippines. When Adm. William F. Halsey, then commanding the fast carrier force of Task Force 38, urged an earlier invasion of the Philippines, where he had found Japanese defenses a "hollow shell," however, the Joint Chiefs decided to abandon occupation of Yap and to seize Ulithi forthwith as a fleet anchorage and logistic support base. An expeditionary force under the direct command of Rear Adm. W.H.P. Blandy seized the atoll's five principal islands without opposition on 22 September 1944, and unloading from transports and cargo ships began after two days of minesweeping. The stated mission of the operation was to occupy Ulithi so that it could be developed as a fleet anchorage, seaplane base, and air base. All supplies of fuel, ammunition, and spare parts were to be stored afloat.

Perhaps the most important facility ashore was the former Japanese airfield on Falalop Island, which the Fifty-first Construction Battalion rebuilt to include a 3,500-foot runway, six taxiways, and hardstands. At the end of the runway the Seabees also built a seaplane ramp. New types of piers were devised by sinking gravel-filled pontoons. Mogmog Island served as a fleet recreation area with a 1,200-seat theater and accommodations for 8,000 enlisted men and 1,000 officers. Sorlen Island was developed to serve a standard landing craft unit. Other construction included housing, sewage and water distilling units, three strips for light planes operating between the atoll's islands, three theaters, a chapel, housing, and a headquarters building.

The Ulithi base operated at full capacity until VJ-Day. Except for an aerological station that continued until 1948, however, all facilities were rolled up by 27 December 1945.

BIBLIOGRAPHY
A. J. C. Webb, "Ulithi Base History, 5 December 1945" (Washington: Naval Historical Center, Operational Archives Branch, World War II Command File); U.S. Navy, Bureau of Yards and Docks, *Building the Navy's Bases in World War II*, 2 vols. (Washington: GPO, 1947), II:332-35.
B. Samuel E. Morison, *Victory in the Pacific, 1945* (Boston: Little, Brown, 1961), pp. 108-17, 156-59.

WILLIAM R. BRAISTED

UNITED KINGDOM, U.S. WORLD WAR II NAVAL BASES, 1941-1945 Allied planning for a cross-Channel landing in Normandy began in July 1942, when it was thought in Washington at least that a beachhead in France could be seized in the late summer of 1942 (Operation Sledgehammer) and a major invasion could be launched in 1943 (Operation Roundup). For Roundup there were to be established five amphibious training bases along the Devon and Cornwall coast that would double as stock points. As planned, each base would have buildings, water systems, refrigeration, fuel stations, electrical equipment, general supplies and equipment storage, waterfront structures including pontoon gear, transportation equipment, and construction equipment, the whole to come to 27,950 ship tons of 40 cubic feet. These bases would be built in addition to the advanced bases built at Londonderry, Ireland, and Rosneath, Scotland, and would be under the command of Commander Advanced Group Amphibious Forces, Atlantic. Involved would be 125 LSTs (316-feet), 150 LSMs (153 feet), 340 LCI(5s) (105 feet), 600 LCMs (50 feet), 336 LCP (R)s(36 feet), and 252 LCVs (36 feet), as well as 1,650 officers and 18,349 men. The first such base would be readied as soon as possible and the last by 15 February 1943.

Before turning to these bases, let us look at Londonderry and Rosneath.

Londonderry, Northern Ireland, U.S. Naval Operating Base 1941-1944

Londonderry is located four miles up the River Foyle at the base of Lough Foyle, Northern Ireland, at 55°10′N., 7°20′W. Like similar installations at Rosneath, Scotland, and at Loch Erne and Lough Foyle, Ireland, it was financed by American Lend-Lease. Construction work by Navy Seabees began in the summer of 1941, and after it was commissioned on 5 February 1942 the base served as a turnaround point for convoys on the North Atlantic run. Construction included 749 Quonset huts for housing and messing; 8 60-by-90-foot utility buildings; 25 20-by-50-foot steel magazines; 17 40-by-100-foot storage buildings; 153 7-by-25-foot air raid shelters; three 10,000-barrel diesel oil tanks and four 100,000-barrel fuel oil tanks; and a pipeline twenty-five miles long of 12-inch pipe for fuel oil and one thirty-three miles long for diesel. The work was accomplished by about 1,500 men of the Twenty-ninth Seabees and 4,800 local workers. After these men completed the original contract they finished the fuel depot and a repair pier and accomplished other minor work.

A purely defensive installation, NOB Londonderry was a vast establishment containing a radio station; naval station; destroyer base; base hospital No. 1 of 500 beds; medical supply storehouse No. 5; supply depot; fuel depot; convoy escort maintenance station; repair base; commercial dry dock; ammunition depot; degaussing facilities; a radio, radar, and underwater sound pool; an ASW training center; a torpedo depot; and a spare parts distribution center. While administrative headquarters were in downtown Londonderry, the various facilities were scattered throughout a four-mile area. An abandoned Admiralty shipyard served as the center of industrial facilities for ship repair. At Lisahally a deep-water unloading wharf, storehouses, and a tank farm were established. Tanker and fueling berths were available along an existing Admiralty pier. Living quarters were established in three different locations because emphasis was placed on dispersal as a defense against bombing attacks which, fortunately, never materialized.

With the entry of the United States into the war, plans changed and Londonderry was commissioned as a naval operating base at which extensions were made to the loading wharf at Lisahally and to the radio station, while the size of the hospital was reduced from 500 to 200 beds. As the various construction projects were completed, workers not retained for maintenance were transferred to other projects in Scotland. Indeed, the office of the officer in charge of construction was moved on 5 September 1942 to Helensburgh, Scotland, where the Dumbartonshire pipeline was the last major project to be constructed. The small local office left in Londonderry supervised a 1,000-man force that handled base maintenance and additional construction.

In an area covering 425 acres, 1,350 separate buildings had been constructed, many of them prefabricated structures such as the new Quonset huts.

With the successful completion of the North African landings by January 1943, most of the Twenty-ninth Seabees were transferred to Londonderry from Rosneath and carried on maintenance and improvement work until relieved by the Ninety-seventh Battalion in September. In mid-April 1943 the Ninety-seventh was transferred to the Scottish pipeline project, while the Seabees left behind maintained the base and operated the transportation department and the tank farm, the last of which was greatly enlarged in anticipation of the Normandy landings.

Too far from the English Channel, along which most of the amphibious training bases were located for the cross-Channel operation, NOB Londonderry was disestablished, except for the radio station, on 14 August 1944, and turned over to the British. The Seabees, meanwhile, had removed all critical material for shipment home except for building quarters for personnel remaining at the sole American activity in the area, the radio station. That station operated until 3 October 1947, when it was transferred to Commander in Chief of North Atlantic and Mediterranean (CINCNELM). In 1950 it became the U.S. Naval Communication Facility London under title of U.S. Naval Facility (T) (R), Londonderry.

Londonderry had served well as a refueling stop for convoy escorts on their return trip across the Atlantic and as a repair base for ships and machinery. Until the creation of the huge supply depot at Exeter, England, it was the main supply depot for American naval activities in the British Isles, and throughout the war it had the major U.S. naval radio station in the European theater.

Rosneath, Scotland, U.S. Naval Operating Base, 1941-1944

Rosneath is located west of Glasgow opposite Greenock on the Firth of Clyde at 56°10′N., 5°30′W. It was one of the four bases in the United Kingdom financed by Lend-Lease—the others being at Londonderry, Northern Ireland, and Lough Foyle and Loch Erne, Ireland. Construction by Seabees began in the summer of 1941. After it was completed and commissioned, on 5 February 1942, it began serving as a turnaround point for convoys on the North Atlantic run. The naval operating base turned over to the British was purely defensive in nature and specialized in servicing and repairing destroyers. For this purpose it was provided with machine tools equivalent to those carried in a destroyer tender; a supply depot that covered 160,000 square feet; a tank farm that stored 200,000 gallons of fuel oil, 30,000 barrels of diesel oil, and 30,000 barrels of aviation gasoline; a 600-bed hospital; an ammunition dump; and personnel facilities for approximately 5,000 men. The last used 994 Quonset huts for berthing and messing. Of the 45 40-by-100-foot storage buildings, seven were refrigerated. There were 10 60-by-90-foot repair buildings; 36 20-by-50-foot steel magazines; 233 7-by-25-foot air raid shelters; and a radio transmitting station not commissioned until 10 July 1944. After the 600 men of the Twenty-ninth Seabees finished the original contract they went on to complete the fuel depot, build a repair pier, and undertake other minor work. At the peak of use, there were 136 U.S. Navy officers and 5,027 men and 24 officers and 544 men of the Marine Corps at Rosneath.

U.S. Naval Advanced Amphibious Training Bases, 1942-1945

On 16 July 1942 Commander in Chief U.S. Fleet (COMINCH) established Advance Group, Amphibious Forces, Atlantic, and on 25 September detached it and assigned it to Commander, U.S. Naval Forces, Europe, as U.S. Amphibious Forces, Europe effective 1 October 1942. Because of its great distance from the assault area, Rosneath was used principally as a receiving base for personnel and ships arriving from the United States and destined for such major amphibious bases as those at Appledore, Fowey, Salcombe, and Teignmouth for training, and at Falmouth, Plymouth, and Dartmouth for both training and assault. On 29 July 1943 the U.S. Naval Advanced Amphibious Base, Appledore, Devon, was commissioned, Comdr. C. Camp, USNR, commanding. Housing, offices, and ship facilities for 768 ships and craft were made available by the British at Appledore, Falmouth, Fowey, Salcombe, Teignmouth, and Plymouth. Additional construction was performed by the Twenty-ninth, Eighty-first, Ninety-seventh and part of the Tenth Special Battalion of the Seabees reorganized on

24 September 1943 as the Thirteenth Naval Construction Battalion, with headquarters at Exeter until March 1944, when it moved to Heathfield, Devon.

With the date for Operation Overlord set for June 1944 by the Casablanca Conference held in January 1943, providing the necessary forces in the United Kingdom began immediately. The Chief of Naval Operations set a schedule for the arrival of landing craft in England for the rest of the year 1943, and on 15 July of that year Rear Adm. John Wilkes, USN, was appointed as Commander Landing Craft and Bases Europe (ComLanCrabEU) as well as Commander, Amphibious Forces, Europe. Upon arriving in London, Wilkes took over command of Rosneath and Appledore and of the supply depot at Exeter. On 7 September a sub-base was established at St. Mawes, Cornwall, and on 25 October that at Fowey, Wilkes meanwhile on 13 October having moved to Falmouth when the latter base was commissioned. The base at Plymouth was commissioned on 8 November 1943, and three sub-bases at Salcombe were commissioned on the twenty-fifth. With Dartmouth commissioned on 24 December, by the end of the year, in addition to the bases and sub-bases already mentioned, partly operational bases were in existence at Milford Haven, Penarth, Launceton, and Tiverton. Because British ship repair and servicing facilities were available, little new construction was necessary in the bases on the southern coast of England.

With the establishment of the headquarters of ComLanCrab in Plymouth on 3 January 1944, large training exercises began. On 4 February, since Adm. Alan G. Kirk had been billeted as Commander Task Force 112, Wilkes became Commander Landing Craft and Bases, Eleventh Amphibious Force. By the seventh, 983 landing craft had been gathered at eleven bases and sub-bases, with Force "O" under Vice Adm. John L. Hall destined for Omaha Beach and Force "U" under Rear Adm. Don P. Moon destined for Utah Beach. On 1 May 1944, 1,257 craft had been gathered and Admiral Wilkes established a staff organization for "far shore" activities including Mulberries and Gooseberries, captured ports, Commander Service Group Omaha Beach, Commander Service Group Utah Beach, and shuttle control. On 10 April, meanwhile, Deptford was designated as the main LST base, and the sub-base at Teignmouth was decommissioned. As the day of the assault by 1,638 craft approached, additional bases not directly contributing to the effort were closed in favor of those nearer to the Normandy coast. For example, St. Mawes and Appledore were decommissioned in May, but new bases were opened at Portland-Weymouth, Poole, and Southampton. It is difficult to believe, but of the 2,493 ships and craft involved in the assault, only 14 were not ready to operate.

With the invasion a success, beginning as early as June 1944 various bases were decommissioned as soon as possible. Poole, for example, was closed on 7 August. All medical supplies were sent to Exeter for retention or redistribution. An inventory of all real estate, property, and equipment obtained from the British was made and receipts were given therefor, and all surplus property was returned to the United States. Between D-Day (6 June) and 31 August, 950 officers and 11,432 men were returned home, and on 1 September Deptford was decommissioned. On 12 September a U.S. Naval Air Service was established to transport passengers, special freight, and personal and official mail from the United Kingdom and the United States and U.S. ports and bases on the Continent, with daily service provided to Cherbourg and to London and Paris three times a week. By the end of September 2,652 additional officers and men had been returned home and the number of ships and craft had dropped to 1,825. All in all, during two years of Construction Battalion activity in the United Kingdom, 250 officers and 11,000 men had built housing for 2,400 officers and 30,000 men, hospital space for 2,700 beds, and 842,000 square feet of industrial building space. The largest construction project had been at the naval supply depot at Exeter, the second largest the pontoon assembly program at Falmouth, Plymouth, and Dartmouth.

Although advanced naval bases or port officers remained at Antwerp, Brest, and Cherbourg as late as 10 September 1946, the bases at Dartmouth, Exeter, Falmouth, Fowey, and Inverness were disestablished between 23 October 1944 and 31 July 1945. Dates of the commissioning and decommissioning of the advanced amphibious bases in the United Kingdom were: Milford Haven, December 1943-16 October 1944; Deptford, 10 April 1944-1 September 1944; Plymouth, 8 November 1943-7 December 1945; Poole, May 1944-7 August 1945; St. Mawes, 7 September 1943-May 1944; Salcombe, 25 November 1943-15 June 1945; and Southampton, 11 May 1944-12 July 1945. Within five years of the invasion of Normandy visitors who examined the pre-invasion amphibious bases could find no trace of American use or facilities. All had been restored to its original condition.

Loch Erne, Northern Ireland, and Loch Ryan, Scotland, U.S. Naval Seaplane Bases, 1941-1942

Mention should be made of two additional bases built for the British at Loch Erne, Northern Ireland, and at Loch Ryan, Scotland, under the Lend-Lease program. These seaplane bases, capable of operating four squadrons of patrol planes, had only limited aircraft overhaul shops, yet they had hangars, seaplane ramps, a 200-bed hospital, ammunition dump, supply buildings, and housing and messing for 4,000 officers and men. They were built by George A. Fuller Co. and Merritt-Chapman and Scott Corporation, with the work done at Loch Erne coming to $7.5 million and that at Loch Ryan to $7.2 million. Both were turned over to the British in June 1942.

Dunkeswell, Devonshire, England, U.S. Naval Air Facility, 1943-1945

Dunkeswell, in the southwesternmost shire of England, was a former Royal Air Force station at which the U.S. Navy performed additional construction so that its aircraft, in cooperation with 19 Group Coastal Command, RAF, could patrol the Bay of Biscay and adjacent waters. The weather there was miserable, with precipitation on 200 days of the year and frequent fogs. The heating system in the crowded Nissen huts was poor, and the water supply so low that a bath was a treat until some Seabees improved the situation. In any event, Dunkeswell was home for Fairwing 7 Headquarters, Squadron Headquarters 7, VB-103, VB-105, VB-110, and the Ninety-seventh Construction Battalion Mobile Unit. Provided were underground storage for 144,000 gallons of aviation gasoline, 5,000 gallons of motor gasoline, and 7,000 gallons of lubricating oil, a small cold storage cubicle, and nine storage buildings.

After the Navy in late 1943 replaced four American *Liberator* squadrons that had flown ASW patrols, its personnel used the three rather small runways, of 4,200 by 50, 2,000 by 50, and 1,245 by 50 feet, that nevertheless could handle any four-engine aircraft then in the naval service. With ample parking area, the facility had a capacity of sixty PB4Ys.

When NAF Dunkeswell was commissioned, on 24 March 1944, American naval personnel there numbered 3,635, with the number growing to 498 officers and 3,706 men on 15 May 1944. The five hangars were able to accommodate the fifty-one PB4Ys stationed there, but there was only minor aircraft overhaul available and no engine overhaul whatever.

On 11 July 1945, FAW 7 was inactivated and departed aboard the *Albemarle* for Norfolk, Va., to be decommissioned, and on 31 July Capt. G. C. Miller, USN, handed the facility back to the British via Group Captain W. S. Caster and declared it decommissioned.

BIBLIOGRAPHY

A. Commander, Amphibious Bases, United Kingdom (Plymouth, Devon, 1 November 1944), ''A History of the United States Naval Bases in the United Kingdom'' (Washington: Naval Historical Center, Operational Archives Branch); U.S. Navy, Bureau of Yards and Docks, *Building the Navy's Bases in World War II,* 2 vols. (Washington: GPO, 1947), II:95–119; ''Loch Erne, Northern Ireland and Loch Ryan, Scotland,'' and ''Dunkeswell, Devonshire England,'' Shore Establishment Summary Cards (Washington, D.C. Navy Yard: Naval Aviation History office.)

V

VELLA LAVELLA, SOLOMON ISLANDS, U.S. NAVAL ADVANCE BASE, 1943-1944 A densely forested, rugged island in the Central Solomons (British Solomon Islands Protectorate), Vella Lavella lies north of New Georgia and is separated from it by Kolombangara and Gizo Islands. In the summer of 1943 South Pacific Area strategists decided to bypass strong Japanese troop concentrations on Kolombangara and invade weakly defended Vella Lavella to establish air and PT boat bases, thereby cutting off Kolombangara's garrison and threatening Choiseul and southern Bougainville.

Beginning 13 August 1943, U.S. Army troops landed on Vella Lavella's southern coast at Barakoma (7°55′S., 156°42′E.) and began a campaign that finally secured the island two months later. By 24 September Seabees had constructed an airfield near Barakoma. In October a strong force of Marine Vought F4U *Corsair* fighters advanced to Barakoma Field to contest control of the skies with Japanese *Zeros* operating from Kahili on Bougainville, only ninety miles to the north. Marine air operations greatly supported the landings on the Treasury Islands in October and at Cape Torokina on 1 November 1943.

The South Pacific Motor Torpedo Boat squadrons were equally eager to advance from Rendova (q.v.) to Vella Lavella. On 25 September seven PTs and an APC coastal transport set up a small base at Lambu Lambu Cove on the northeastern coast of Vella Lavella. From there they executed long patrols against Japanese barge traffic at Choiseul and southern Bougainville-Shortlands. Surprisingly, the patrols proved generally unproductive, and the PTs engaged in only three antibarge actions before they left Lambu Lambu on 17 December 1943 for the new base in the Treasury Islands (q.v.).

In connection with the planned landings on Bougainville, Vella Lavella was built into a minor naval support base. Near the small anchorage at Biloa, not far from Barakoma, Seabees constructed a small naval supply depot, hospital facilities, and a small-boat repair base to handle landing craft maintenance and overhaul. Until mid-1944 Vella Lavella performed its supporting role for the Bougainville-Choiseul containment, but as operations became less active installations on Vella Lavella were rolled up. On 15 June 1944 administrative control of forces in the Northern Solomons passed from the South Pacific Area to the Southwest Pacific Area. On the same day, operations ceased at Barakoma Field, and the island base was disestablished in September 1944.

BIBLIOGRAPHY

A. Motor Torpedo Boat Squadrons, Philippine Sea Frontier, ''Command History of MTB Squadrons, Philippine Sea Frontier, Formerly MTB Squadrons, 7th Fleet,'' 5 vols., Type Commands, 1945 (Washington: Naval Historical Center, Operational Archives Branch); Service Squadron, South Pacific, ''History of Commander, Service Squadron, South Pacific, ''History of Commander, Service Squadron, South Pacific 7 December 1941-15 August 1945'' (Washington: Naval Historical Center, Operational Archives Branch); U.S. Navy, Bureau of Yards and Docks, *Building the Navy's Bases in World War II,* 2 vols. (Washington: GPO, 1947); U.S. Navy, ''U.S. Naval Bases in the South and Southwest Pacific (and Central Pacific Forward) in World War II,'' prepared by Op441H, 1 November 1954 (Washington: Naval Historical Center, Operational Archives Branch).

B. Samuel E. Morison, *Breaking the Bismarcks Barrier 22 July 1942-1 May 1944* (Boston: Little, Brown, 1950); Robert Sherrod, *History of Marine Corps Aviation in World War II* (Washington: Combat Forces Press, 1952); Capt. Robert J. Bulkley, *At Close Quarters: PT Boats in the United States Navy* (Washington: Navy Department, Naval History Division, 1962).

JOHN B. LUNDSTROM

VERACRUZ, MEXICO, U.S. NAVAL BASE, 1846-1848, 1914 Veracruz, the chief port on the east coast of Mexico, lies at 19°11′N., 96°8′W. During the nineteenth century the open roadstead between the town and the massive fortification of San Juan de Ulloa, on Gallega Reef about a mile offshore, offered scant protection for large vessels. As a result, most large ships, including visiting warships, normally anchored at Anton Lizardo about twelve miles down the coast. After the construction of a breakwater late in the century, vessels could safely anchor off the city except during extremely poor weather.

During 1845 and early 1846, while the United States attempted to exert pressure on Mexico to negotiate the differences between the two nations, vessels of Commo. David Conner's Home Squadron swung at anchor at Anton Lizardo. After the outbreak of hostilities in May 1846 Conner converted the anchorage into a base for operations in the Gulf of Mexico. The Anton Lizardo base consisted of a lagoon protected by a chain of shoals, reefs, and low islands about nine miles long. The squadron established a coal depot on one of the islands and maintained a series of storeships elsewhere to dispense other provisions. During the height of the yellow fever seasons a hospital was also established on one of the other islands. A secondary anchorage behind the Isla de Sacrificios was only about four miles from Veracruz. From the Anton Lizardo anchorage Conner's squadron maintained a blockade of the Mexican coast and dispatched expeditions to seize smaller ports when the opportunity offered.

In March 1847 the transports carrying Maj. Gen. Winfield Scott's army arrived. On 9 March 1847 the vessels of Conner's squadron landed approximately 10,000 men south of Veracruz in America's first large-scale amphibious assault. They quickly laid siege to the port, which surrendered on 29 March. Veracruz served as the chief offloading point for materials and men destined for Scott's brilliant campaign against Mexico City and replaced Anton Lizardo as the Navy's main installation in Mexico. The naval forces withdrew from the port in June 1848.

American naval vessels did not return to Veracruz, except as visitors, for fifty-six years. On 21 April 1914 a landing party of sailors and Marines seized the port as part of an effort to bring about the overthrow of the government of President Victoriano Huerta. They remained ashore until 23 November, during which period a substantial portion of the Atlantic Fleet made the port its base.

BIBLIOGRAPHY

B. Jack Sweetman, *The Landing at Veracruz: 1914* (Annapolis, Md.: U.S. Naval Institute, 1968). K. Jack Bauer, *Surfboats and Horse Marines* (Annapolis, Md.: U.S. Naval Institute, 1969).

K. JACK BAUER

VICARAGE BARRACKS, PLYMOUTH, DEVON, ENGLAND, U.S. NAVAL AMPHIBIOUS BASE, 1943-1945. One of the numerous sub-bases established in England to prepare for the invasion of the Continent in Overlord-Neptune, on 8 November 1943 Capt. F.M.S. Quinby, USN, commissioned Vicarage Barracks on the site of a barracks previously used by a British Army garrison and extended by construction undertaken by American Seabees. Its mission was to feed, clothe, billet, and process transient personnel, particularly those who would participate in the cross-Channel expedition. With the end of the war it then served as an important demobilization site.

Plymouth was the nerve center of the American amphibious forces sent to England. Because of the need for speed, which precluded much construction, the British Admiralty provided many billets and authorized the U.S. Navy to take over some of its installations. Among these was the Royal Navy encampment at Saltash, on the banks of the River Tamur, which Americans would use to house the crews of landing craft repair units. A second camp turned over was that at the St. Budeau section of Plymouth. There the Admiralty requisitioned two properties for use as a U.S. naval dispensary and recreation hall. To the 44 British-type huts on the 3 acres Americans added 103 American-type huts and 11 miscellaneous structures. Men billeted there were employed on LCIs and AKAs, with LCTs, LSTs, and LCIs located at other points along the river or Plymouth harbor. As a Payroll Record Office, disbursing officers at Vicarage dispensed more than $1 million a month. During the assault, men at Vicarage put in many long hours of back-breaking labor to support the units that made the crossing and after V-E Day cared for the crews of twenty surrendered German vessels that were forwarded to the United States. With a normal base complement of 10 officers and 225 men, as many as 2,000 men a month were processed, with the peak month including 4,000 officers and men. After exchanging a bewildering number of foreign monies, Vicarage transferred men who had served eighteen months overseas to the United States for rest and recreation. To keep up morale, they showed movies five days a week, operated a recreation hall, had a Navy band provide music for dances two nights a week, and arranged for shows put on by USO troupes. They operated a wet canteen, barber shop, tailor shop, shoe repair facility, laundry, and ship's service, while fifteen men handled all-important mail. Other men handled frozen food for the base and for the Thirtieth Construction Battalion. Still others served as shore patrol. After Prime Minister Clement Atlee announced the cessation of hostilities against Japan, Vicarage Barracks was used as a demobilization point for those men who by length of service warranted being sent home. On 14 August 1945 the barracks were decommissioned and surplus personnel sent to the U.S. Naval Amphibious Supply Base at Exeter (*see* United Kingdom, U.S. World War II Naval Bases), while those who were to go home boarded the SS *Aquitania* for the United States.

BIBLIOGRAPHY
A. "History of U.S. Naval Amphibious Base, Vicarage Barracks, Plymouth, Devon, England" (Washington: Naval Historical Center, Operational Archives Branch).

VIEQUES ISLAND, PUERTO RICO, U.S. MARINE CORPS CAMP GARCIA, 1959-1978 Eight miles off the east coast of Puerto Rico lies the island of Vieques. From 1959 to 1978 the Marine Corps maintained a training base there for the Atlantic Fleet Marine Force. Forty-eight square miles in size, Vieques contained "a lot of wide open spaces," as a participant in an early exercise there recalled, making it an ideal location for amphibious warfare training.

In 1939 the Navy had purchased 27,000 of the island's 33,000 acres for $1.5 million, and during World War II it began utilizing the island as a target range and for amphibious exercises for the Marines. Then in 1947 it turned title of the land over to the Marine Corps in return for continued "use of parts of it for impact areas for naval gunfire training." During the ensuing decade the Marines held annual training exercises on the island but did not establish a permanent presence there until the late 1950s, when they assigned a small security detachment to it. On 20 January 1959 the Marine Corps officially activated Camp Garcia, named in honor of Pfc Fernando Luis Garcia, the first Puerto Rican to win the Congressional Medal of Honor. He earned it during the battle for Bunker Hill on 5 September 1952 in the Korean War by throwing himself on a grenade in order to save his comrades. The Navy also honored him by commissioning the USS *Garcia* (DE-1040) in 1963.

Initially, the only permanent structures at the camp were a few buildings from an old sugar mill. The security detachment occupied them, while the training forces that were sent to the island inhabited a massive tent city constructed nearby. In 1960 a Marine engineering company built a landing strip at the camp that subsequently served as the base's primary logistical lifeline. Twice a week air transports flew in supplies, replacements, and training units from the Naval Air Station at Roosevelt Roads (q.v.). On their return flights the planes ferried out materials and personnel departing the island. A Navy Landing Craft Utility (LCU) also provided transportation to and from Puerto Rico by weekly plying the waters between Vieques and Roosevelt Roads. In 1964 surplus Quonset huts from Camp Lejeune, N.C., replaced the tent city at Camp Garcia.

Throughout its existence Camp Garcia was a unique facility in that, instead of being operated by a host command to support the training of the Fleet Marine Force, it was manned directly by the units that utilized it. The Atlantic Fleet Marine Force rotated personnel from its units to the camp for five-month tours of duty. At the peak of Camp Garcia's operation, nearly 300 Marines manned it. It served as a training site not only for the Atlantic Fleet Marine Force but also for Marine Reserve units, the Puerto Rican National Guard, and for Marines from the nations of Brazil, Venezuela, and Great Britain.

In the 1970s the military control and use of the bulk of Vieques Island became a major dispute between the Navy and the government of the Commonweath of Puerto Rico. Local inhabitants of Vieques complained that the naval bombardment of the island and the Marines' amphibious exercises disrupted the local fishing industry and prevented the development of the island for tourism. A similar dispute involving the use of the smaller island of Culebra led the Navy to abandon it as a target range in 1975. In 1978 the Commonwealth of Puerto Rico filed suit against the Secretary of Defense and a number of Navy and Marine officers on the grounds that the Navy had "violated a number of environmental laws" in its use of Vieques. Governor Carlos Romero-Barcelo charged that "a community of American citizens is being denied the right to live and work in peace and tranquility, because the U.S. Navy obstinately and. . . illegally persists in pursuing a high-handed policy of brazen disregard for their well-being."

The courts ultimately ruled in the Navy's favor and issued injunctions against any local interference with training exercises being held on the island. Nevertheless, on 14 December 1978, while the case was still in litigation, the Marine Corps deactivated Camp Garcia. Since then the Navy has continued to shell the island, and amphibious exercises are still being held there, albeit without the convenience of an active installation to support them. Agitation and protest against the further military use of the island have likewise continued. In May 1982, for instance, an organization calling itself the Group for the Liberation of Vieques claimed responsibility for a shooting attack on four American sailors in San Juan, Puerto Rico, which left one dead and the other three seriously wounded.

BIBLIOGRAPHY

A. Carlos Romero-Barcelo, "Statehood for Puerto Rico: The Island of Vieques," *Vital Speeches of the Day*, 1 July 1979, pp. 564-68; U.S. Congress, Senate, Committee on Veterans Affairs, *Medal of Honor Recipients, 1863-1978*, 96th Cong., 1st Sess. 1979; Camp Garcia, Posts and Stations Files (Washington: U.S. Marine Corps Historical Center).

B. SSgt. Thurlow D. Ellis, "Vieques," *Leatherneck*, Dec. 1960, pp. 30-33; Maj. E. W. Burchart, "Camp Garcia, Vieques, Puerto Rico," *Leatherneck*, Sept. 1971, pp. 44-49; *Dictionary of American Naval Fighting Ships*, 8 vols. (Washington: GPO, 1959-1981).

ROGER T. ZEIMET

VILLEFRANCHE, FRANCE, U.S. NAVAL BASE.
See Mediterranean, The, U.S. Naval Bases, 1800-1917.

VINH LONG, REPUBLIC OF VIETNAM, U.S. NAVAL FACILITY, 1966-1971 This South Vietnamese city, in the eastern sector of the Mekong Delta, was the site of a U.S. naval facility during the conflict in Southeast Asia. Vinh Long was selected for a number of reasons: U.S. naval leaders intended to interdict communist waterborne movement with units patrolling the major rivers, in the Game Warden operation, and the city was located on the wide Co Chien River; it was accessible to U.S. logistic support vessels steaming in the South China Sea; and facilities at the Vietnamese River Assault Group base were ready to accommodate an American river force.

Beginning in August 1966, river patrol boat (PBR) units of the River Patrol Force deployed to Vinh Long, from which they operated against the Viet Cong supply network. The following year, the surface force was joined by a detachment of Helicopter Attack (Light) Squadron 3, the Seawolves.

Initially, base support was rudimentary. Spare parts and supplies were dispensed from small shacks, and boat repairs were performed using a boat ramp, an engine lifting rig, and a small crane. Quarters for the men were established in the city in two crowded villas six kilometers from the PBR base.

Conditions gradually improved as the Navy devoted resources to base development. Seabees installed a pier with Army-supplied pontoons and a portable fuel storage bladder. However, initial progress in the creation of support facilities suffered a setback when Viet Cong forces overran the base during the Tet Offensive of early 1968, destroying the tactical operations center, with its communications equipment, as well as the supply and spare parts buildings, and forcing the evacuation of personnel to the *Garrett County* (LST-786).

Naval leaders acted quickly to provide mobile support. YR-9, a converted large covered lighter, was based at Vinh Long to handle maintenance and repair tasks, and APL-46, a messing and berthing barge, dropped anchor off the river city in October 1968. At that time, the twenty-boat PBR force, a detachment of SEALs (naval special forces), and the Naval Support Activity, Saigon, Detachment Vinh Long, moved afloat. Following the relief in January 1969 of YR-9 and APL-46 by YRBM-20, a vessel that performed all the functions of the two former craft, the U.S. naval contingent was completely mobile. Consequently, on 1 February 1969, the Naval Support Activity, Saigon, Detachment Vinh

Long, was disestablished. However, the facility continued to serve as an intermediate support base until September 1971, when the Vietnamese Navy assumed control.

BIBLIOGRAPHY
A. Commander Naval Forces, Vietnam, "The Naval War in Vietnam," May 1970 (Washington: Naval Historical Center, Operational Archives Branch); Service Force, U.S. Pacific Fleet, "Command Histories, 1967-1972" (Washington: Naval Historical Center, Operational Archives Branch).
B. Herbert T. King, "Naval Logistic Support, Qui Nhon to Phu Quoc," U.S. Naval Institute *Naval Review* 95 (May 1969):84-111; S. A. Swarztrauber, "River Patrol Relearned," U.S. Naval Institute *Naval Review* 96 (May 1970):120-57; Edwin B. Hooper, *Mobility, Support, Endurance: A Story of Naval Operational Logistics in the Vietnam War, 1965-1968* (Washington: GPO, 1972).

EDWARD J. MAROLDA

VIRGIN ISLANDS.
See St. Thomas, Virgin Islands, U.S. Naval Bases.

VUNG TAU, REPUBLIC OF VIETNAM, U.S. NAVAL SUPPORT ACTIVITY DETACHMENT, 1965-1971 Situated on a peninsula jutting out from the Republic of Vietnam into the South China Sea, Vung Tau was a natural site for the U.S. naval facilities developed there during the Southeast Asian Conflict. In addition, the resort town overlooked the entrance to the serpentine river approach to Saigon, the nation's capital and main port.

The American naval presence at Vung Tau dated from 1954, when Naval Beach Group 1 helped French authorities to construct an emergency tent camp for thousands of refugees evacuated from North Vietnam in the "Passage to Freedom" sealift operation. Eleven years later, the Navy established a base there for surface and air units of the Coastal Surveillance Force, which patrolled the South Vietnamese littoral in search of infiltrating communist ships and craft. A coastal surveillance command center at Vung Tau coordinated the operations of fast patrol craft (PCF) and SP-2 *Neptune* aircraft patrol units.

The site also was an interim staging area for the Navy's forces deploying deeper into the Mekong Delta region south and west of Saigon. Beginning in January 1967, ships carrying the men and specialized landing craft soon to form the naval component of the joint Army-Navy Mobile Riverine Force, anchored off Vung Tau, where the units were made ready for operations inland. At the same time, the repair and maintenance ships *Tutuila* (ARG-4) and *Askari* (ARL-30), barracks ship APL-26, and repair, berthing, and messing barge YRBM-17 arrived to provide the force with mobile support. Although the Mobile Riverine Force shifted to Dong Tam (q.v.) in June, after training and material preparations were completed, Vung Tau continued to serve its logistic needs.

Vung Tau also provided an operating base for the Navy's helicopter and fixed-wing assault units. In May 1967 Helicopter Attack (Light) Squadron 3 established a headquarters at Vung Tau, initiating its combat operations in South Vietnam. While the command center later moved to Binh Thuy (*see* Can Tho-Binh Thuy, Republic of Vietnam, U.S. Naval Support Activity), deep in the Mekong Delta, detachments of the Seawolves squadron continued to use the air facilities at Vung Tau. And from April 1969 on, one-half of the fixed-wing Light Attack Squadron 4 flew from the nearby U.S. Army airfield.

Under the direction of Naval Support Activity, Saigon, Detachment Vung Tau, logistic support was provided the locally based air and coastal patrol units as well as the river units deployed forward. On a weekly basis, a tank landing ship (LST), usually stationed off Cape Vung Tau, delivered food, fuel, ammunition, and other supplies to the floating base of the Mobile Riverine Force operating near Dong Tam. An Army-Navy liaison team used a small pier and warehouse to process and transship incoming cargo to the LST. Also normally anchored in the roadstead was the *Tutuila*, and later the *Markab* (AR-23), which provided depot-level repair and maintenance support to myriad river and coastal combat vessels, including LSTs. In addition to these units, harbor defense and harbor clearance units were based at Vung Tau. Two heavy lift craft and other vessels of the latter command, belonging to Service Force, U.S. Pacific Fleet, were positioned offshore prepared to salvage vessels in distress from the many waterways of South Vietnam.

As the Navy's installations at nearby Cat Lo (q.v.) and in the Mekong Delta completed their development and took on greater logistic responsibilities, the facility diminished in importance. However, Vung Tau continued to serve as the maritime gateway to the southern regions of the Republic of Vietnam.

BIBLIOGRAPHY

A. Commander, Naval Forces, Vietnam, "The Naval War in Vietnam," May 1970 (Washington: Naval Historical Center, Operational Archives Branch); Commander Naval Forces, Vietnam, "Monthly Historical Reports, 1965-1971" (Washington: Naval Historical Center, Operational Archives Branch).

B. W. C. Wells, "The Riverine Force in Action, 1966-1967," U. S. Naval Institute *Naval Review* 95 (May 1969):46-83; S. A. Swarztrauber, "River Patrol Relearned," U.S. Naval Institute *Naval Review* 96 (May 1970):120-57; Richard L. Schreadley, "The Naval War in Vietnam, 1950-1970," U.S. Naval Institute *Naval Review* 97 (May 1971):180-211; Edwin B. Hooper, *Mobility, Support, Endurance: A Story of Naval Operational Logistics in the Vietnam War, 1965-1968* (Washington: GPO, 1972); Edwin B. Hooper, Dean C. Allard, and Oscar P. Fitzgerald, *The Setting of the Stage to 1959*, Vol. 1 of *The United States Navy and the Vietnam Conflict* (Washington: GPO, 1976).

EDWARD J. MAROLDA

W

WAKDE, DUTCH NEW GUINEA, U.S. NAVAL ADVANCE BASE, 1944–1945 Wakde (2°30′S., 138°E.) is a small island located close to the north Dutch New Guinea coast about 120 miles west of Hollandia. Capture and use of the Japanese airfield on Wakde was vital for the Southwest Pacific Area to gain air superiority over Biak to the west. On 17 May 1944 American troops landed first at Toem on the New Guinea coast about two miles from Wakde; the next day they assaulted the little island itself. Resistance was bitter, but Wakde field was operational by 21 May and supported Army heavy bombers as well as Navy PB4Y *Liberator* long-range patrol planes conducting reconnaissance flights deep into the enemy rear area. PT boats operated from Wakde for a time in June 1944 before advancing to Biak (q.v.). Naval installations at Wakde included a port director's office and communications center that remained open until 31 March 1945.

BIBLIOGRAPHY

A. Motor Torpedo Boat Squadrons, Philippine Sea Frontier, "Command History of MTB Squadrons, Philippine Sea Frontier, Formerly MTB Squadrons, 7th Fleet," 5 vols., Type Commands, 1945 (Washington: Naval Historical Center, Operational Archives Branch); U.S. Navy, "7th Amphibious Force, Command History 10 January 1943-23 December 1945" (Washington: Naval Historical Center, Operational Archives Branch); U.S. Navy, "U.S. Naval Bases in the South and Southwest Pacific (and Central Pacific Forward) in World War II," 1 November 1954 (Washington: Naval Historical Center, Operational Archives Branch).

B. Samuel E. Morison, *New Guinea and the Marianas March 1944-August 1944* (Boston: Little, Brown, 1953); Capt. Robert J. Bulkley, *At Close Quarters: PT Boats in the United States Navy* (Washington: Navy Department, Naval History Division, 1962); Vice Adm. Daniel E. Barbey, *MacArthur's Amphibious Navy* (Annapolis, Md.: U.S. Naval Institute, 1969).

JOHN B. LUNDSTROM

WAKE ISLAND, U.S. NAVAL AIR BASE, 1941–1947 Wake Island is actually a coral atoll composed of three small islands—Wake Island and smaller

Peale and Wilkes islands. Totaling only 2,600 acres and rising to a maximum elevation of only 24 feet, the islands form a V roughly four miles long and two and a half miles wide with Wake at the heart of the V. Wake is strategically located on the Navy's trans-Pacific route about 2,004 miles west of Hawaii and 1,334 miles northeast of Guam. On 4 July 1898 Maj. Gen. Francis V. Green and the second echelon of the Philippine Relief Expedition touched at the uninhabited atoll as they moved across the Pacific to reinforce Adm. George Dewey at Manila Bay (*see* Far Eastern U.S. Naval Bases to 1898), and Comdr. E. D. Taussig on the USS *Bennington* in 1899 claimed Wake for the United States for a trans-Pacific cable landing.

After 1899 Wake remained largely unnoticed until the mid-1930s, when the United States was moved by the increasing importance of air power to search for islands in the Pacific suitable for fueling stations for American naval and commercial aircraft. In 1934 President Franklin D. Roosevelt placed Wake under the jurisdiction of the Navy Department, and the following year the Navy granted to Pan American Airways the right to develop staging facilities there for its prospective trans-Pacific air service, the China Clipper. Since Pan Am agreed to make the facilities available to naval aircraft in an emergency, the Navy acquired support facilities for seaplanes that it could not itself construct in the western Pacific under the restriction of Article XIX of the 1922 Washington naval treaty.

Once the naval treaties expired on 31 December 1936, the Navy moved only slowly to build light naval facilities at Wake. In December 1938 the Hepburn Board on naval bases declared that Wake was second only to Midway Island as a point in the mid-Pacific that should be provided with fuel and shore facilities to support a twelve-plane patrol squadron. These facilities were to include stored fuel, a pier, and a channel and turning basin within the lagoon sufficiently deep to accommodate a large tender or tanker. Two years later (6 January 1941) the Greenslade Board confirmed that Wake should be built up as an outlying subsidiary base capable of supporting air and submarine forces charged with surveillance of the line of communications between Hawaii and the Philippines. Because Congress repeatedly struck Wake from the naval appropriations bills, construction of the base was only begun in January 1941 with the arrival of the first eighty workers of a private construction firm.

By the outbreak of the Pacific War in December 1941, an estimated 65 percent of the installations were completed by a civilian work force that had increased to 1,146. A channel had been cut from the open sea into the lagoon capable of accommodating a 1,000-foot barge; living accommodations were about 50 percent completed for the Marine defenders; and storage had been provided for 150,000 barrels of gasoline, 20,000 barrels of fuel oil, and 6,000 barrels of diesel oil. The hastily contrived defenses of Wake by December 1941 included 450 Marines, a dozen 3-inch antiaircraft guns, a half dozen old 5-inch guns, and a dozen F4F *Wildcat* fighting planes. Without reinforcement from Pearl Harbor, these defenders, supported by the untrained civilian workmen, defended

Wake against great odds until they were obliged to surrender on 23 December. The fate of the interned civilian workers led the Navy to begin the enlistment of Construction Battalions, the Seabees, composed of men in the construction trades who were given basic military training.

Wake was recovered by the Navy when Japan surrendered in August 1945, and it served as a Naval Air Facility until its transfer by the Navy to the Civil Aeronautics Authority in 1947.

BIBLIOGRAPHY

A. U.S. Navy, Bureau of Yards and Docks, *Building the Navy's Bases in World War II*, 2 vols. (Washington: GPO, 1947), II: 154-58; Record Group 80, General Records of the Navy Department, 1927-1940, A21-5 File (Washington: National Archives); "Wake Island" (Washington: Naval Historical Center, Operational Archives Branch, Base Maintenance File).

B. Francis X. Holbrook, "United States National Defense and Trans-Pacific Commercial Air Routes, 1933-1941," Ph.D. diss., Fordham University, 1969.

WILLIAM R. BRAISTED

WEDDELL SEA COASTAL STATION, ANTARCTICA, U.S. NAVAL BASE.

See Antarctica, U.S. Naval and Air Bases.

WELLINGTON, NEW ZEALAND, U.S. ADVANCE NAVAL BASE, 1942–1944 The capital of New Zealand, Wellington is situated on the lower tip of North Island at 41°17′S., 174°47′E. It was utilized by the South Pacific Area's Amphibious Force as a staging area and minor landing craft base. In June 1942 advance elements of the First Marine Division arrived there and assembled at a camp about thirty miles to the north. During the hasty preparations in July 1942 for Operation Watchtower (the invasion of Guadalcanal and Tulagi in the British Solomon Islands), Rear Adm. Richmond Kelly Turner, Commander, South Pacific Amphibious Force, assembled forces at Wellington to stage for the invasions scheduled for early August 1942. He intended to form an amphibious force boat pool at Wellington, but almost all other U.S. naval activities in New Zealand were conducted from Auckland (q.v.). Meanwhile, the First Marine Division departed Wellington in late July to execute landings in the Solomons.

In March 1943 the Second Marine Division assembled at Wellington for rest and recuperation after fighting in the Solomons. That July, secret preparations began for an offensive in the Central Pacific that would involve Admiral Turner's amphibious forces and the Second Marine Division. In connection with this buildup, the naval base at Wellington was formally commissioned on 23 August 1943. Unfortunately, the amphibious boat pool had never amounted to much, and Turner scavenged it to prepare for Operation Galvanic, the invasion of the Gilbert Islands. Wellington's last important naval role was as a staging and practice point for the Second Marine Division's preparations for assaulting Tarawa in the Gilberts. With the departure of the division on 1 November 1943,

Wellington's high point as an American naval base was over. Installations such as the base hospital and receiving barracks remained open until May 1944, when the base at Wellington was disestablished.

BIBLIOGRAPHY

A. U.S. Navy, "U.S. Naval Bases in the South and Southwest Pacific (and Central Pacific Forward) in World War II," 1 November 1954 (Washington: Naval Historical Center, Operational Archives Branch); South Pacific Area and Force, "History of New Zealand during World War II," Administrative History, Appendix 34 (16) (Washington: Naval Historical Center, Operational Archives Branch).

B. Vice Adm. George C. Dyer, *The Amphibians Came to Conquer*. 2 vols. (Washington: GPO, 1972).

JOHN B. LUNDSTROM

WEST BASE, LITTLE AMERICA, BAY OF WHALES, U.S. NAVAL BASE.
See Antarctica, U.S. Naval and Air Bases.

WEXFORD, IRELAND, SEAPLANE STATION.
See World War I U.S. Naval Air Stations in Europe.

WEYMOUTH, ENGLAND.
See United Kingdom, U.S. World War II Naval Bases.

WHIDDY ISLAND, IRELAND, SEAPLANE STATION.
See World War I U.S. Naval Air Stations in Europe.

WOODLARK ISLAND, PAPUA, U.S. NAVAL ADVANCE BASE, 1943–1944 Woodlark Island, at 9°5′S., 152°0′E., is one of the Trobriand Islands (part of the Territory of Papua) situated northeast of New Guinea's eastern extremity. The Allies occupied Woodlark, a rugged, irregularly shaped island about forty miles long, as the site of an air base for attacks against New Britain and Bougainville. Seabees, following the landings, first constructed the airfield for the Allied air forces, then during the fall of 1943 worked on a small naval base. Naval facilities on Woodlark engaged in the repair of small boats, such as landing craft and PTs, and helped to maintain the large numbers of such vessels operating along New Guinea's northeast coast. The Seabees completed construction by November 1943 and remained on maintenance duties until March 1944. Roll-up was completed by July 1944 when Seventh Fleet (Southwest Pacific Area) ceased using the facility.

BIBLIOGRAPHY

A. U.S. Navy, "7th Amphibious Force Command History, 10 January 1943-23 December 1945" (Washington: Naval Historical Center, Operational Archives Branch); U.S. Navy, Bureau of Yards and Docks, *Building the Navy's Bases in World War II*, 2 vols. (Washington: GPO, 1947); U.S. Navy, "U.S. Naval Bases in the South and Southwest

Pacific (and Central Pacific Forward) in World War II,'' 1 November 1954 (Washington: Naval Historical Center, Operational Archives Branch).

B. Samuel E. Morison, *Breaking the Bismarcks Barrier 22 July 1942-1 May 1944* (Boston: Little, Brown, 1950); Capt. Robert J. Bulkley, *At Close Quarters: PT Boats in the United States Navy* (Washington: Navy Department, Naval History Division, 1962); Vice Adm. Daniel E. Barbey, *MacArthur's Amphibious Navy* (Annapolis, Md.: U.S. Naval Institute, 1969).

JOHN B. LUNDSTROM

WORLD WAR I U.S. NAVAL AIR STATIONS IN CANADA: HALIFAX, NOVA SCOTIA; AND SYDNEY, CAPE BRETON ISLAND To extend the string of air patrol stations along the East Coast from the Canadian border to Key West, two extracontinental stations were established in Canada and one at Coco Solo, Panama Canal Zone (q.v.). The station at Halifax, Nova Scotia, was commissioned in August 1918, Lt. Richard E. Byrd, USN, commanding; that at Sydney, Cape Breton Island, on 31 July 1918, Lt. Robert Donahue, USCG, commanding. Operations were routine at both places. At the end of the war, all American equipment at the stations was turned over to Canada.

BIBLIOGRAPHY

A. "Log Book of the Naval Air Station, Halifax, N.S., Aug. 1, 1918-Jan. 7, 1919" (Washington: Naval Historical Center, Operational Archives Branch); Bureau of Aeronautics, "World War II Administrative History," 20 vols. (Washington: Bureau of Aeronautics, 8 November 1957), Vol. XI.

B. Archibald D. Turnball and Clifford L. Lord, *History of United States Naval Aviation* (New Haven: Yale University Press, 1949), pp. 126-27, 142-49; *United States Naval Aviation 1910-1960* (Prepared at the Direction of Deputy Chief of Naval Operations [Air] and Chief of the Bureau of Naval Weapons, Washington: 1960).

WORLD WAR I U.S. NAVAL AIR STATIONS IN EUROPE On 20 April 1917, three weeks after the United States entered World War I, Secretary of the Navy Josephus Daniels asked Rear Adm. William S. Sims, representing the Navy Department in London, what the Allies were doing with respect to naval aviation. After consulting the British and French, on 3 July Sims replied that the British needed at least 100 kite balloon units and complete squadrons of seaplanes. Meanwhile, among the first seven U.S. naval aviators to get "over there" was the extremely energetic Lt. Kenneth Whiting, Naval Aviator No. 16. Although sent primarily to bolster Allied morale, he quickly saw the need of coastal air patrol stations and greatly stretched his orders by making commitments whereby American naval aviation personnel would be trained in France and then serve there. Specifically, he endorsed American use of a school at Moutchic, a bombing base at Dunkirk, and seaplane stations at the mouths of the Loire and Gironde rivers. Fortunately, now Vice Adm. William S. Sims, Commander, U.S. Naval Forces Operating in European Waters, supported the arrangements Whiting had made. Seeing the need for aircraft to protect ships at the entrances to Allied harbors and near their shores in general, he extended the work to Great Britain and Ireland as well. Plans for France called for an assembly and repair base at Pauillac, two kite balloon stations, three dirigible stations, and nine seaplane stations. When the bombing base at Dunkirk proved unsuitable, it was replaced by the Northern Bombing Group (*see* World War I U.S. Northern Bombing Group Bases in England and France).

Although Capt. Hutch I. Cone was not an aviator, he was an excellent administrator. He had served as the Engineer in Chief of the Navy; when Sims on 21 August 1917 called for him to serve him in the field of aviation, he was the Marine Superintendent of the Panama Canal. He arrived in England on 27 September 1917, offered to cooperate with the Royal Navy Air Service on the building and operating of air stations in England and Ireland, and established his office first in Paris, late in the summer of 1917, and then in London on 1 July 1918. On 24 October 1917 he relieved Whiting as Commander Naval Aviation Forces, Foreign Service, and directed that Aviation Intelligence officers be specially trained. Early in October he began a tour of possible station sites in England, Ireland, and France. One limitation he had to live with was the order from the Chief of Naval Operations, Adm. William S. Benson, that no seaplane carrier would be provided him. In July 1918 Cone moved his office from Paris to London, and in September 1918 Sims made him his aide for naval aviation. For about a year Cone served as an air station builder, while Capt. Thomas T. Craven handled operational matters. When Cone was wounded while in the *Leinster*, he was succeeded by Lt. Comdr. W. A. Edwards.

The Navy's Bureau of Yards and Docks began in November 1917 to provide materials for building and for public works at the sites Cone had selected. Except where existing buildings were available for stated purposes, new construction "from plan to paint" was provided for each station. Construction included hangars, slipways, aprons, barracks, storehouses, mess halls, galleys, garages and repair shops, recreation and YMCA halls, power houses, administration buildings, roads, water tanks, gasoline tanks, piers, telephone systems, and water lines.

During the first year the United States was at war, naval air stations were established in Ireland, England, France, and Italy.

Ireland

Bantry Bay, located at the center of southern Ireland, was the easternmost of all the U.S. naval seaplane stations. Its planes met convoys as they approached the British Isles.

Berehaven is located halfway up the north shore of Bantry Bay. There the British had built a kite balloon station that would be transferred to the United States and use kite balloons on patrol in cooperation with American destroyers. The base was located well down Bantry Bay from Whiddy Island and was built on a golf course three miles from the town of Castletownbere, behind Bere Island and near the mouth of Bantry Bay. It was turned over by the Royal Air Force on 26 April 1918, Ens. Carl E. Shumway commanding. Although on 29 July 1918 many men and much material were transferred to Brest, the station operated to the end of the war. Like the other Irish stations, Berehaven was closed down between 29 January and 15 February 1919, with all equipment returned to the United States.

Castletownbere, a few miles west of Berehaven, also served as a kite balloon station. It was commissioned on 29 April 1918, Ens. Carl E. Shumway commanding.

Lough Foyle, in northern Ireland, is located at the base of this fjord about nine miles north of Londonderry. The seaplane station established there provided patrols over the North Channel entrance to the Irish Sea. It was commissioned on 1 July 1918, Comdr. H. D. Cooke commanding until relieved by Lt. Carl T. Hull. Patrols began on 3 September and continued until the Armistice. It was closed down between 29 January and 15 February 1919, with all salvageable material sent to Dublin for shipment home. It was closed on 22 February 1919.

Lough Swilly (Buncarana), about fifteen miles west of Lough Foyle, was a kite balloon station and served both American and British destroyers in northern waters.

Queenstown, located about a third of the way eastward along the southern Irish coast and a dozen miles from Cork and on the edge of Cobh, was both a repair base and seaplane base. The seaplane base was commissioned on 22 January 1918, Lt. Comdr. P. J. Peyton commanding.

Wexford, a naval seaplane station, was located at a site formerly used by the British at Ferrybank, on sheltered Wexford Harbor at the southeasternmost point of Ireland. The mission of the station, to patrol over St. George's Channel, did not change when about 200 Americans began operations on 18 October 1918. The station was closed down between 29 January and 15 February 1919, with all salvageable materials sent to Dublin for shipment home.

Whiddy Island, located toward the northern end of Bantry Bay, was the site of a seaplane station commissioned on 4 July 1918. Its mission was to provide escort for convoys approaching the British Isles. Although about 200 Americans worked to build the base and it was declared operational on 25 September 1918, it operated for only seven weeks under wartime conditions. It was closed down between 29 January and 15 February 1919. Salvageable materials were sent to Dublin for shipment home to the United States.

BIBLIOGRAPHY

U.S. Navy, Bureau of Yards and Docks, *Activities of the Bureau of Yards and Docks, Navy Department: World War 1917-1918* (Washington: GPO, 1921), pp. 395-416. Bureau of Aeronautics, "World War II Administrative History," 20 vols. (Washington: Bureau of Aeronautics, 8 November 1957), Vol. II.

B. Archibald D. Turnbull and Clifford L. Lord, *History of United States Naval Aviation* (New Haven: Yale University Press, 1949); *United States Naval Aviation 1910-1960* Prepared at the Direction of Deputy Chief of Naval Operations [Air] and Chief of the Bureau of Naval Weapons (Washington: 1960).

England

Eastleigh, about five miles north of Portsmouth on England's southern coast, was used as the assembly and repair base of the Northern Bombing Group, whose mission was to bomb U-boat bases in the Dunkirk-Zeebrugge area. It superseded Dunkirk because of fear that the latter might be taken by the Germans if they drove down the Channel coast of France. The construction required there may be estimated from the fact that an English reception park for aircraft that had accommodations for only 100 men had to be enlarged to accommodate 5,000 Americans. In some stations, such as the one in the city of Dunkirk and the great British naval aviation station at Felixstowe, bombproof shelters had to be built because the Germans subjected them to nightly bombing. At Eastleigh the quarters built for the 20,962 American officers and men there, if joined end to end, would have extended for twelve miles.

Killingholme, Lincolnshire, on the North Sea a bit inshore from the estuary of the Humber, was largely unknown to Americans before the outbreak of the Great War. In June 1916, however, about two dozen members of the Royal Air Force were stationed there to protect large oil fuel tanks from air raids conducted by German zeppelins. Under Wing Comdr. (later Air Chief Marshal) Sir Arthur Longmore, the site was developed into a land- and seaplane station, and by 1917 it had become one of the leading air stations in Britain. With about 900 officers and men on board, it served particularly as a training station for seaplane pilots and as a construction base, and serviced about 100 aircraft.

Following the decision to make Killingholme an all-American air station, American men began to arrive in March 1918, and Lt. Kenneth Whiting relieved Wing. Comdr. F. W. Bowhill, RNAS. The primary task of the Americans was to provide escort of convoy, conduct submarine search and long-distance reconnaissance, and give early warning of the approach of hostile aircraft or surface ships. Flights were conducted as far as 225 miles at sea. There were 67 American officers and 902 men cooperating with the British at Killingholme during the summer of 1918.

A major project devised by Whiting was to bomb the German naval bases. For this purpose he returned to the United States to pick up twenty-three H-16 flying boats, eight lighters, and 7 officers and 150 men. The U.S. Chief of Naval Operations, Adm. William S. Benson, first approved, then vetoed the use of aircraft carriers in the North Sea. Whiting thereupon proposed to use seaplanes on lighters towed by destroyers to bomb German coastal works along the Heligoland Bight. Unfortunately, a test of the lighters was witnessed by a zeppelin and the plan had to be scrapped. Whiting thereafter used all the British Short seaplanes at the RNAF station at Killingholme and the American aircraft he had ready for use after 1 July to conduct ASW patrols, escort ships, and keep German minesweepers away from Allied minefields. The station was commissioned under the American flag on 20 July 1918. The fifty seaplanes supported by 2,000 men at Killingholme patrolled for 10,000 miles and were credited with destroying one U-boat and damaging several others. It was the most successful of all U.S. air stations in Europe. While it bombed enemy submarines—one sunk and several "probables"—it also warded off zeppelin attacks on England. Whiting performed so well that he was awarded the Navy Cross. NAS Killingholme was disestablished shortly after the Armistice, its facilities reverting to the British.

BIBLIOGRAPHY

A. "Aviation, U.S. Navy, General, I," ZO File, Box 10 (Washington: Naval Historical Center, Operational Archives Branch); "Command History, U.S. Naval Air Station, Killingholme, England, 1918" (Washington: Naval Historical Center, Operational Archives Branch); "History of United States Naval Air Station, Killingholme, England, July 20-11 November 1918" (Washington: Naval Historical Center, Operational Archives Branch); Bureau of Aeronautics, "World War II Administrative History," 20 vols. (Washington: Bureau of Aeronautics, 8 November 1957), Vol. XI.

B. Sir Walter Raleigh and Henry Albert Jones, *The War in the Air: Being the Story of the Part Played in the Great War by the Royal Air Force*, 6 vols. (Oxford: Clarendon Press, 1922-1937), IV:19, V:440; Air Chief Marshal Sir Arthur Longmore, *From Sea to Sky, 1910-1915* (London: Geoffrey Bles, 1946); Archibald D. Turnbull and Clifford L. Lord, *History of United States Naval Aviation* (New Haven: Yale University Press, 1949); *United States Naval Aviation 1910-1960* (Prepared at the Direction of Deputy Chief of Naval Operations [Air] and Chief of the Bureau of Naval Weapons, Washington: 1960).

France

Following its examination of the French coasts during the summer of 1917, the U.S. Navy's Bureau of Yards and Docks began in November to provide materials for building and for public works at the naval air stations sites Cone had selected as well as materials for aircraft and hangars. The appraised value of all these installations was $11,216,758.

In 1914 Lt. Comdr. J. C. Porte, RN, and Glenn Curtiss had developed the flying boat *America* with which to attempt the first trans-Atlantic flight. When war erupted, Porte returned to England, had his government buy the *America*, and improved her hull design. Designated the *Felixstowe*, subsequent models were produced with successive modifications from Curtiss designs as the F-2, F-3, and F-5. These became the primary British ASW aircraft and were the aircraft used mostly by American pilots when they first arrived in England. Incidentally, the F-5, with different engines and hull modifications, was designated the F5-L by the U.S. Navy and saw service as the standard seaplane until 1929.

The first American float planes and flying boats, adapted from private designs, included the HS-1, HS-2, and H-16. Until these arrived overseas American pilots flew *Felixstowes*. France, meanwhile, provided such flying boats as the Donnet-Denhaut, Tellier, and Levy Le Pen. By the end of the war about 300 HS-1s, HS-2Ls, H-16s, and R-9s were operating, to which some F-5Ls were added toward the end of hostilities, as were various blimps of the B and C types. The first lighter-than-air pilots were sent to RNAS Cranwell, England, in August

1917, and received further training. It was determined in November, however, that they would be sent to French bases for familiarization with the French airships they would fly on patrol.

Because the British used ports and railroads in northern France while the French used ports and railroads somewhat to the south, the American Expeditionary Force used ports and railroads still farther south. For their protection, and that of shipping, the various U.S. naval air stations were built.

Arcachon is located on a site of sand dunes on the Bassin d'Arcachon on the eastern side of Cape Ferret, about three miles from the southern end of the point of the Cape, about thirty-five miles southwest of Bordeaux. Construction work by a French contractor began there in November 1917. The southernmost of the seaplane stations in France, it was commissioned as a U.S. Naval Air Station on 8 June 1918, Ens. J. N. Brown commanding until relieved by Lt. Zeno W. Wicks on 15 June 1918. The first planes arrived in mid-August and the first patrol was executed on 4 October over the waters of the Bay of Biscay south of the Garonne River. Following the end of the war it was transferred to the French Army.

Brest, the site of the large French naval and air station at the western tip of the Breton peninsula, was provided with an H-16 seaplane and kite balloon station on land fronting the inner harbor at the extreme western end of the French navy yard. Work proceeded more quickly after hangar lumber, tools, and portable barracks were delivered from the United States in April 1918. The crates in which aircraft were shipped were also used to build the hangars in which the same aircraft, delivered as deck loads on troop transports and too bulky to forward by rail, were assembled. After the Armistice the station was transferred to the French Navy.

At Belle Isle, 100 miles southeast of Brest and well located to guard the mouth of the Loire River, Cone decided that a submarine tender sufficed.

Fromentine is located below the Loire estuary. The site chosen for a U.S. Naval Air Station was a bleak, windswept waste of sand at the southern end of the island of Noirmoutier, thirty-five miles from the nearest town. However, the sheltered water between the island and the mainland made it ideal for a seaplane station. It was built between 23 February and 26 October by Americans using American materials. The commanding officers were, successively, Gunner (R) R. J. McGee, Lt. Comdr. W. G. Child, and Lt. Comdr. W. Capehart. It began the first of its 200 convoy escort trips on 17 August. Because the French opposed the sale of materials from the American bases for fear they would glut the market, the wooden structures were razed and the lumber and other materials were given to the American Army or to Herbert Hoover for Belgian relief.

Guipavas, the site of a dirigible station, was near the town of the same name about seven miles from Brest. Construction began on 10 March 1918, but the station was declared fit for operations only after 24 November by the commanding officer, Lt. Comdr. A. Landsdowne. Construction was of lumber trucked from

Brest. Men had to be trained to do "high" work, and some life was lost in getting the various hangar trusses in place.

While the French Navy took over the hangar after the Armistice was signed, the camp buildings and surplus lumber were transferred to the American Army for use near Brest.

Gujan lay on the flat, sandy shores of the Bassin d'Arcachon, west of Bordeaux. The mission of the base was to patrol south of the Gironde over the Bay of Biscay and also to escort vessels sailing between Bayonne and the mouth of the Gironde. However, because of the lack of men and materials, progress was never made beyond the construction stage. Following the Armistice the materials were given to the American Army and to Herbert Hoover for Belgian relief.

Ile Tudy lies directly south of Brest and not far from it on the other side of the Breton peninsula. Americans extended work already undertaken there by the French. They built barracks, a recreation hall, and a dispensary in addition to concrete aprons and launching ways, the latter replacing the French track lying on mud flats. The site was on a low, flat sand spit to the south of which was the Bay of Biscay. To the north was a shallow basin that connected with the sea through an inlet at the western end of the spit.

Operations began at Ile Tudy on 28 February 1918, before the station was commissioned, the latter event occurring on 14 March, Lt. Charles E. Sugden, USCG, commanding. Because of its location, flyers out of Ile Tudy saw more ASW action than the other overseas stations. In addition to covering two daily coastal convoys, its aircraft flew in twenty-five-square-mile areas and reported their position every half hour by radio and pigeons. One of the planes, piloted by Ens. Edwin S. Pout and Quartermaster second class F. H. Tittle, while on convoy patrol near Point Penarch, dropped bombs on a pestiferous U-boat nicknamed "Penmarch Pete" that loitered in the Ras de Sein, a narrow channel through which ships sailing north or south had to pass and for which Ile Tudy had particular responsibility. They were given the assessment of having "probably damaged the U-boat." After the Armistice all usable material was turned over to the U.S. Army to expand its embarkation camp near Brest.

L'Aber Vrach, one of the eight seaplane stations the United States built in France, was situated on a rocky island named Ile d'Ehre near L'Aber Vrach. The site covered 16 acres about twenty miles north of Brest at the entrance to the English Channel. It was the seventh station to go into construction and the sixth to go into operation. Its mission was to support air patrols over the shipping lanes in the Southwestern Approaches to the English Channel.

A nonaviator, Lt. Comdr. Carlton A. McKelvey, USN, was successively officer in charge of construction, commanding officer, executive officer, and radio officer at L'Aber Vrach. According to his memoirs of the station, with their modern machines the Seabees of World War II could have built it in a quarter of the time it took men with hand labor in 1918. In any event, McKelvey, transferred overseas in December 1917, was interviewed by the Commander at Headquarters, U.S. Naval Aviation Forces, Foreign Service, in Paris in January

1918 and ordered to report to the Commandant of French Air Patrols and also to the Commanding Office of the U.S. Naval Air Station at Brest. He arrived at L'Aber Vrach on 24 January 1918 in company with Lt. C. P. Coarad, Assistant Civil Engineer, USN, who had plans and specifications for building a naval air station. On the next day they inspected Ile d'Ehre, where the station was to be built. Ile d'Ehre was half a mile from the village of L'Aber Vrach in a small bay. The uninhabited island was formed mostly of rock, with little soil, and was 1,500 yards long and 500 yards wide at its widest part. Headquarters for the increasing number of Americans sent there was the Hotel Belle-vue, which in the summertime served mostly men engaged in lobster fishing, the most important business in the area. There was a narrow-gauge railroad connecting with Brest, which was the main provider of supplies, and also a good service road to that main port.

Fortunately, among the men who began to arrive late in January were some who were riggers or qualified to handle explosives, for the seaplane ramp and airfield had to be blasted from rock. Other problems encountered were a tidal range of 26 feet and, initially, the lack of a causeway between the Ile d'Ehre and L'Aber Vrach. All work in constructing the level ground for hangars and other buildings, parking areas for aircraft, and the seaplane ramp and boat pier had to be done by hand, with concrete being hand-mixed and poured out of wheelbarrows. Because potable water was scarce, it was brought from L'Aber Vrach in fifty-gallon drums. A ginpole was used for hoisting, and barracks were made from prefabricated parts. Some help came from French drivers using horse-drawn two-wheeled carts, and more from trucks after a causeway was built connecting Ile d'Ehre and L'Aber Vrach.

Although the station was as yet incomplete, aircraft arrived on 18 July 1918. These were pusher-type HS-1 flying boats with a Liberty V-12 motor. By the time the station was considered complete, on 11 October, there were six HS-1s on board that regularly engaged in patrols over the English Channel. Except for the constant profferring of veal by the French, the food sent from Brest was excellent.

With the Armistice all operations ceased and steps were taken to dismantle the station. The last to leave L'Aber Vrach was McKelvey, whose departure at 1600 hours on 22 January 1919 marked the disestablishment of the station. When the French said that they did not want the station, it was torn down and all salvaged building material was turned over to the Army for camp construction near Brest.

La Pallice is on the shore of the Bay of Biscay just a few miles west of La Rochelle. To the west is Ile de Re; to the south, Ile d'Oleron. It was still under construction at the time of the Armistice, however, and saw no wartime operations. It was transferred to the U.S. Army following the Armistice.

La Trinite is a little fishing village in the Rochefort-sur-mer area six miles from the nearest railroad station. The naval air station to be built there was to provide kite balloons to patrol for vessels sailing between the Bay of Quiberon and La Pallice. Construction began in mid-March 1918 and was completed in September. Although one balloon was received on 18 October and another on 8 November, no operations had occurred before the signing of the Armistice on 11 November. After that the United States simply abandoned the base.

Le Croisic is located just below the Breton peninsula about eighteen miles from St. Nazaire. The U.S. naval aviation station was situated on two small islands that had been used by fishermen to dry their nets. The rise and fall of the tide is so great that it necessitated the use of a derrick to handle seaplanes. Its supreme task was to provide aerial escort for troop convoys coming into the Loire River. The station was in operation on 26 July 1917; the first seaplane, a French Tellier, was received on 6 October; and the first patrol flight occurred on 18 November.

The work at Le Croisic was pushed by Lt. John L. Callan, USNR, one of Glenn Curtiss's early civilian pilots who had flown with Theodore G. Ellyson and John Towers. The base was built largely by German prisoners, whom Lt. Kenneth Whiting called "the best workmen in Europe." The first patrol station to go into operation, it was commissioned on 27 November 1917, Lt. William M. Corry commanding.

On 15 November 1918 Vice Adm. William S. Sims, Commander, U.S. Forces Operating in European Waters, directed the regional headquarters of naval aviation to return 50 percent of the personnel at their stations and prepare for full mobilization. They were to dispose of all material at hand and package salvageable material for shipment home. Le Croisic was closed shortly thereafter.

Moutchic-Lacanau lies four miles from the Atlantic Ocean on the north shore of Lake Lacanau, thirty-two miles west and slightly north of Bordeaux and enjoys an excellent climate.

Soon after the United States entered World War I, Lt. Kenneth Whiting went to France and arranged for American naval aviation personnel to be trained at French military schools.

Aeronautic Detachment 1 of the U.S. Navy left Pensacola Naval Air Station in two sections, which crossed in the USS *Jupiter* and the USS *Neptune*, one landing at Pauillac, the other in St. Nazaire. Immediately upon his arrival Whiting headed for Paris, leaving Lt. (jg) V. C. Griffin, USN, in charge of the St. Nazaire party and Lt. G. C. Dichman, USN, in charge of the other. As arranged, American quartermasters would be instructed in the French Army Flying School at Tours and then sent to learn smooth-water flying in seaplanes at the French School of Naval Aviation at Hourtin. Their final stop would be at the French Naval School for Pilots and Observers at St. Raphael, on the Mediterranean, before heading for Moutchic and establishing the mother station of U.S. naval aviation in France.

The history of the station at Moutchic began on 17 July when Lt. John L. Callan, USNRF, with three men, selected a site four miles from the ocean at Lake Lacanau. The site was half a mile from a railroad station and surrounded by pine forests containing few inhabitants and only one poor road. It was built "from pine needles up" by a French contractor. The men trained in the French schools arrived between 31 August and 11 September, with the latter date considered the real beginning of the station.

While five flying boats were being assembled, construction work was entrusted to Georges Hauret, a French civilian contractor who had also built the U.S. naval air stations at Arachon and St. Trojan. Because of the scarcity of labor, the station was still incomplete after fifteen months. Meanwhile the men lived and ate in tents and later in huts rudely constructed from the wooden crates their aircraft came in and during the winter months suffered from a damp and penetrating cold because the only heat they had was from the sticks and pine cones they could gather in the forest. In any event, on 27 September 1917 Ens. Robert A. Lovett (later Secretary of War for Air and Secretary of Defense), already trained in the United States, made the first flight in a flying boat, a six-minute solo flight using sandbags as ballast. He flew again on 16, 18, and 22 October, the last two days before flight instruction began at the station, such instruction being its main mission. Involved were a ground school, solo flights for pilots, and flights of pilots with observers as passengers. There being no gunnery range, learning proceeded by the dropping of dummy bombs. By 17 October Moutchic was providing trained men for such stations as those at Le Croisic and Loire-Inferieur. When trained ensigns began to arrive from the United States, Americans took over training functions from British and French officers, but enlisted men were sent to Casaux for training. It must be added that until about 1 July 1918 French planes were used exclusively because the DDs and Telliers were much better than the F.B.A.s, which were gradually discarded. Also, a constant exchange of ideas was maintained with the French; several instructors were sent to England as well, particularly to learn about gunnery.

By 1 July 1918 Moutchic had administration, instruction, and engineering buildings, an armory, five hangars, bunkhouses, mess halls, a sick bay, head, and washhouse but as yet no officers' quarters, so the officers lived in Lacanau-Ocean, four miles away, and were transported in trucks to and from the station. There was an athletic program, theatricals, and a band, and half the crew was granted weekend liberty in Bordeaux. American pride soared when American planes equipped with Liberty motors began to arrive, among them two Curtiss HS-1 flying boats. Yet of the fifteen planes on board for instruction, the rest were French.

When the Northern Bombing Project got under way—in which naval personnel would use land machines to bomb the Belgian ports invested by the Germans—a number of pilots, observers, and enlisted men were at once sent to the U.S. Bombing School at Clermont-Ferrand and to the French Army Bombing School at Avord for special courses in bombing. Pilots and observers trained in bombing and gunnery were also sent to the American naval air station established at Porto Corsini, Italy, which was occupied on 24 July 1918. On 14 August, when Lt. Comdr. R. W. Cabaniss assumed command from Lt. W. Wicks, Moutchic had sent out 104 commissioned officers and 103 enlisted students.

The end of hostilities on 11 November found Moutchic thoroughly organized and equipped, with 33 permanent officers, 35 officers under instruction, and 493 enlisted men. There were twenty-four planes on the station, eleven of which were HS-1s, and construction was practically complete. When 200 men were demobilized to the United States on 24 November, for all practical purposes the station had fulfilled its role.

Paimboeuf, about ten miles upstream from the mouth of the Loire River on its eastern bank and about twenty-five miles west of Nantes, had already been used as an air center and, like Treguier, was ready for American use when Lt. Comdr. L. H. Maxfield arrived on 4 January 1918. The dirigible station, commissioned on 1 March 1918, had 308 Americans on board by 6 June. By the end of the war it had three dirigibles, which had flown 48,630 miles. At decommissioning time, shortly after the Armistice, there were 30 American officers and 477 men on board. It was then transferred to the French Navy.

Pauillac is located on the Gironde River about halfway between Bordeaux and the Bay of Biscay and was centrally located with respect to the American air stations built in France. On 5 June 1917, it had received part of the first Aeronautical Detachment from Pensacola, Fla., from the USS *Jupiter*, and the second part from the USS *Neptune*, its 7 officers and 122 men commanded by Lt. Kenneth Whiting. After Whiting was called to Paris and then to Killingholme, England, its command fell first to Ens. R. F. Nourse and in February 1918 to Lt. Henry B. Cecil.

The most important aircraft assembly and repair base in France, Pauillac was commissioned on 1 December 1917. It soon became a factory town, with sawmills, sail lofts, machine shops, warehouses, hospitals, barracks, and garages in addition to several long docks that handled both merchantmen and the so-called Suicide Fleet, the small group of converted yachts that escorted French-bound convoys. It also had excellent railroad connections and a pigeon loft whose 78 birds delivered 698 messages a month and 219 messages about emergencies. Eventually command fell to Capt. Frank Taylor Evans, son of "Fighting Bob" Evans. From Pauillac men were sent to the twenty-eight naval bases the U.S. Navy established in Europe, all but three (Eastleigh, England, Moutchic, and Pauillac itself) being operating bases, i.e., used for combat activities. Unfortunately, although it distributed materials worth $1 million a month, motors and planes destined for Pauillac did not begin to arrive from the United States until April 1918. Moreover, some were badly damaged, while others, along with spare parts, were sent to different destinations. Meanwhile Americans used British or French planes. It was closed down after the Armistice.

Rochefort is located on the shore of the Bay of Biscay midway between the Spanish border and Brest. It had been used as a naval station since the days of Colbert. American plans called for building a dirigible station there, but the great German push on the French front beginning in March 1918 caused it to be returned to the French for use as a storage facility for dirigible materials.

St. Trojan, near the mouth of the Gironde River, was a site covered with pine forests and sand dunes on the Straits of Maumusson, which separate the southern end of the Ile D'Oleron from the mainland. Strategically located to cover ships at the mouth of the river, the twenty buildings erected there were completed by 16 June 1918 by a French contractor at a cost of 1.2 million livre, or $250,000. The station was commissioned under the American flag on 14 July, Lt. V. C. Griffin commanding. The first two French seaplanes arrived on 29 June, and regular ship escort flights were undertaken beginning 19 July. Because of the lack of American aircraft, use was made there of French Levy Le Pens. After the Armistice it was transferred to the French Army.

Treguier lies twelve miles from the sea on the Breton shore of the English Channel. Unlike the stations at Brest, L'Aber Vrach, and Guipavas, which Americans built or completed, the seaplane station at Treguier had been operated by the French since 1917. It was turned over to Americans on 15 August 1918, Lt. A. M. Baldwin commanding, and serviced seaplanes that patrolled the English Channel. After the Armistice the French kept the station, except for the barracks the Americans had erected, which were transferred to the U.S. Army at Brest.

BIBLIOGRAPHY

A. U.S. Navy, Bureau of Yards and Docks, *Activities of the Bureau of Yards and Docks, Navy Department: World War 1917-1918* (Washington: GPO, 1921); Bureau of Aeronautics, "World War II Administrative History," 20 vols. (Washington: Bureau of Aeronautics, 8 November 1957), Vol. XI; "A History of the United States Naval Air Station Moutchic-Lacanau, France" (Washington: Naval Historical Center, Operational Archives Branch); Carlton A. McKelvey, Lt. Comdr, USN (Ret.) "Construction of United States Naval Air Station, L'Aber Vrach, France" (Washington: Naval Historical Center, Operational Archives Branch).

B. John Langdon Leighton, *Simsadus London: The American Navy in Europe* (New York: Henry Holt, 1920), pp. 85-86; Josephus Daniels, *The Wilson Era: Years of War and After, 1917-1923* (Chapel Hill: University of North Carolina Press, 1946), pp. 115-16; Archibald D. Turnbull and Clifford L. Lord, *History of United States Naval Aviation* (New Haven: Yale University Press, 1949), pp. 126-27, 142-49; *United States Naval Aviation 1910-1970*. Prepared at the Direction of the Deputy Chief of Naval Operations (Air), and Chief of the Naval Air Systems Command (Washington: GPO, 1971).

Italy

In November 1917 Italy asked the United States to furnish aircraft and personnel for two naval air bases to be established on her eastern, or Adriatic, coast. Somewhere along the line a misunderstanding occurred, the result being that instead of obtaining trained men from the United States Italy was offered Americans to train. In December Capt. Hutch I. Cone sent Lt. John Lansing Callan to make the necessary arrangements with the commander of Italian naval aviation, Capitano de Vascello L. De Filippi. By February 1918 Callan had men in training and in August Americans began to operate Italian aircraft from two of the bases that were under construction.

Lake Bolsena, a seaplane station sixty miles northeast of Rome, had various buildings, seven runways, and hangars. Its primary mission after training was to bomb the Austrian works at Pola, on the Dalmatian shore of the Adriatic. American aviators arrived there on 19 February 1918, Ens. W. B. Atwater commanding, with commissioning ceremonies taking place two days later. Seventy-three Americans finished the course in handling Italian Macchi flying boats and were sent to various Italian stations or to Moutchic, France. In orders dated 8 November 1918 sent by Vice Admiral Sims to regional headquarters of naval aviation, no more students were to be posted to Lake Bolsena. New orders dated the fifteenth directed the return of 50 percent of the personnel and preparations for full demobilization, including the disposition of all materials and the packaging of all useful materials for shipment home. The facility was decommissioned by 15 January 1919.

Pescara, located on the Adriatic coast at 42°N., 14°E., had excellent railroad communications, food and water, and hangars and slips that supported three squadrons of nine patrol planes each. As arranged with the Italians, the United States assumed command of the largest air station it opened in Europe in March 1918; the United States would pay its men and provide their subsistence while Italy furnished the aircraft. On 8 November 1918 Vice Admiral Sims directed regional headquarters of naval aviation to return 50 percent of personnel at all speed and to prepare for full demobilization. New orders of the fifteenth called for the disposition of all material at hand and the packaging of useful materials for shipment home. Pescara was decommissioned by 15 January 1919.

Porto Corsini is located about ten miles northeast of Ravenna and seventy miles southwest of Venice. It received its first American detachment on 24 July 1917 from Pauillac, France, Lt. Willis B. Haviland, USNRF, commanding. The Austrians commemorated the occasion with a bombing raid, which fortunately did no damage to the 331 men Haviland had brought with him or to the 250 tons of supplies that had come in a special train.

By agreement, the United States would supply everything but food and clothing for the personnel at Porto Corsini, which started with three aircraft and finally built up to twenty-one. The Americans flew Macchis, either single-seater flying boats or two-seater M-8s. The major target for the Americans was the Austrian naval and air base at Pola, only sixty-four miles away across the Adriatic, where Austrian battleships and cruisers and German and Austrian U-boats were serviced. The base and city were defended by eighteen forts and batteries containing no less than 114 antiaircraft guns.

Although strategically located, Porto Corsini had one tremendous disadvantage in that all landings had to be made on a canal about 100 feet wide, with problems exacerbated when the wind blew across the canal. The greatest undertaking of the Americans at Porto Corsini, aside from one successful bombing raid on Pola on 22 October 1918, was to drop propaganda leaflets over Austrian installations. However, a heroic rescue was also accomplished. When Lt. (jg) William C. Ludlow, Jr., USNRF, was forced to ditch by three Austrian aircraft when near Pola, Ens. Charles Hazeltine Hammann, also USNRF, took his damaged craft down. After sinking his *Macchi*, Ludlow held onto the struts under the engine of Hammann's single-seater plane and suffered a bad gash in the head when the plane, damaged in the bow, flipped over in the canal at the base. Ludlow received a Navy Cross and Hammann the first Medal of Honor awarded a naval aviator.

At the end of the war Porto Corsini had 45 American officers and 360 men on board, yet it never reached full operational status. Desiring to clear out of American bases in Europe as soon as possible as the Armistice approached, Vice Admiral Sims on 8 November directed that Porto Corsini be kept in full commission until demobilization orders were issued by him. Such orders were issued on 15 November to the regional headquarters of naval aviation. They called for the return home of 50 percent of personnel with full speed while preparing for demobilization, including the disposition of all material at hand and the packaging of all useful material for shipment home. Porto Corsini was demobilized on 31 December 1918.

See also World War I U.S. Northern Bombing Group Bases in England and France.

BIBLIOGRAPHY

A. U.S. Navy, Bureau of Yards and Docks, *Activities of the Bureau of Yards and Docks, Navy Department: World War 1917-1919* (Washington: GPO, 1921), pp. 395-416; Bureau of Aeronautics, "World War II Administrative History, Bureau of Aeronautics," 20 vols. (Washington: Bureau of Aeronautics, 8 November, 1957). Vol. XI.

B. Archibald D. Turnbull and Clifford L. Lord, *History of United States Naval Aviation* (New Haven: Yale University Press, 1949); *United States Naval Aviation 1910-1960*. Prepared at the direction of the Deputy Chief of Naval Operations (Air) and Chief of the Bureau of Naval Weapons (Washington: GPO, 1960).

WORLD WAR I U.S. NAVAL BASES IN EUROPE Shortly after the United States entered World War I, the ports on the west coast of France were inspected by a joint Franco-American commission and then by a joint U.S. Army-Navy commission. In consequence, base sites were selected at Bassens, Bordeaux, Brest, and St. Nazaire. Additional bases were created in the Azores Islands and at Corfu, Greece, for antisubmarine warfare, and mine forces bases were established at Inverness and Invergordon, Scotland. These bases are discussed below in alphabetical order of the country in which they were established.

France

Bassens, 1918-1919

Bassens, six miles below Bordeaux and about fifty-six miles up the Gironde River—actually it is on the east bank of the Garonne River—provided wharfage for ships too large to ascend to Bordeaux. The facilities there were originally commanded by Comdr. John B. Patton, USN, a naval constructor recalled to active duty from retirement and serving as naval port officer for Pauillac and Bordeaux as well, all with the purpose of berthing ships carrying American cargoes and troops for the French front. When Patton was shifted to command at Pauillac and to develop it as a naval aviation station, command of Bassens fell to a U.S. Naval Dock Officer who would act as liaison between the captains and masters of American ships and the French captain of the port of Bordeaux in matters connected with mooring and navigation. There between August 1917 and April 1918 the Army Corps of Engineers built a pile dock containing ten berths, the largest construction of this type undertaken by the Army in France.

The engineers used 6 million feet of lumber, 25,000 cubic yards of concrete, and rails for fifty miles of railroad track to provide the whole series of wharves with three parallel lines of track along their entire length. Almost all the material was brought from the United States, as were all the cranes, locomotives and freight cars. They also built motor parks, rest camps, a huge refrigerator plant, and railway yards, and in addition sunk artesian wells. By the end of 1918 a force of well over 6,000 Negro stevedores was employed in the unloading of ships. In consequence New (or American) Bassens became the most efficient port in France.

To move troops and supplies forward was the task undertaken by representatives of the Army Transport Service, who left the handling of ships to a Marine Superintendent, Lt. Comdr. Henry W. Barstow, a former ship captain of the Clyde-Mallory Line. Although the discharge of ships was assigned to the service they served, in order to speed turnaround time naval personnel helped unload Army ships while armed guard crews served as sentries at the gangways and at the holds from which the cargo was taken. A naval ferry took naval personnel to and from liberty in Bordeaux, the largest city in the region. The port officer at Bassens also provided ships making passage for home with their sailing orders and insured that the ships carried no stowaways; handed in a muster list of all persons carried on board and left behind; and provided it with ballast, usually iron pyrites. Once a ship left the dock, it again came under naval authority while on its way to the convoy station at Le Verdon and while in convoy. All ships making for Bassens or Bordeaux checked in with Vincent Astor, the port officer at Royon, down the right bank of the Gironde across from Bordeaux, and again when they proceeded to sea.

The homeward movement of troops began at the end of November 1918 and continued for over seven months. As late as March 1919, the port officer at Bassens still cooperated with similar port officers at Bordeaux, Le Verdon, and Pauillac in returning Army cargo that could not be disposed of abroad, including $7 million worth of surplus food and supplies for the American Relief Administration. Soon thereafter the port officer of Bordeaux relocated at Bassens near the office of the Army Transport Service and cooperated in loading the transports there. Both offices were closed on 30 September 1919.

BIBLIOGRAPHY

A. Henry P. Beers, *U.S. Naval Port Officers in the Bordeaux Region, 1917-1919* (Washington: Navy Department, Sept. 1943).

B. Elliott Roosevelt, ed., *F.D.R.: His Personal Letters 1905-1928* (New York: Duell, Sloan and Pearce, 1948).

Bordeaux, 1917-1919

U.S. Navy officers who inspected Bordeaux, located sixty miles from the sea up the Gironde River, collected data on the railroad lines connecting with the Bay of Biscay. While Bordeaux could not accommodate the largest ocean liners of the day, it possessed shipbuilding, repair, and supply organizations, was well protected from the weather and from attack by German naval forces, and had been developed by the French into a revictualing base. In the Spring of 1917, however, it could berth only two ships at a time, and even as late as November 1917 it could handle only 26,000 tons of freight per day. Despite the extension of quays and facilities there and also at downriver areas at Bassens, Pauillac, and Blaye, even more had to be done to service the American troops that would arrive. This fact was well realized by Rear Adm. Albert Gleaves, Commander Cruiser and Transport Force, and by the Navy Department in Washington. On 8 May 1918 Secretary of the Navy Josephus Daniels informed Vice Adm. William S. Sims, Commander, U.S. Naval Forces Operating in European Waters, that France had requested the establishment of temporary bases at Bordeaux and Brest. Sims approved, providing that the destroyer bases he was using did not suffer. At the end of June, the Bureau of Navigation detailed Comdr. John B. Patton, recalled from retirement for the duty, to proceed to Bordeaux and command the naval base to be established there. In July Patton spoke with Sims and Capt. Richard H. Jackson, the U.S. Navy Representative in Paris, and also with Capt. William B. Fletcher, commanding U.S. Naval Forces in France. Lacking concrete instructions from Washington, Patton began to develop Pauillac as a coaling and supply station for naval patrol and escort vessels operating along the Biscay coast. While he was so doing, Sims asked the Chief of Naval Operations, Adm. William S. Benson, for needed funds. Benson replied that he opposed the establishment of shore bases except for aviation purposes and was sending two repair ships for the use of the small craft operating on the French coast. Although Sims retorted that a base at Pauillac was needed in addition to the repair ships, Benson's order meant that Pauillac would be used merely as a coaling station and would not engage in repair work.

Meanwhile Patton organized a staff for the American naval base at Bordeaux. With a chief yeoman and three yeomen, he acted as naval, or port officer, taking charge of ship movements, personnel records, and communications. Paymaster F. D. Colby acted as the accounting, supply, and disbursing officer and also handled contracts. To direct construction was the task assumed by Lt. Louis L. Bernier, a native of France who had lived in the United States and was enrolled in the Naval Reserve Force. Including a small medical department, by the end of 1917 there were only twenty-four enlisted men at Bordeaux.

On 24 September 1917 Sims designated Patton as naval port officer at Bordeaux, Pauillac, and Bassens, with Comdr. Frank P. Baldwin to assume duty as naval port officer at St. Nazaire. As yet, American ship arrivals were few, with only 9,800 tons of general cargo, 28,300 tons of coal, and 6,600 tons of lumber delivered there by the end of the year. Meanwhile Sims obtained the services of Capt. Hutch I. Cone as Commander, U.S. Naval Aviation Forces, Foreign Service. Sims agreed with Cone that Pauillac rather than Bordeaux should serve as a naval aviation center that would assemble and repair aircraft and contain general storehouses and barracks from which enlisted aviation personnel would be distributed throughout France.

On 4 January 1918 Sims replaced Captain Fletcher with Rear Adm. Henry B. Wilson as "Senior U.S. Naval Officer in France" and divided the west coast of France into three districts whose headquarters were at Brest, St. Nazaire, and Bordeaux. A fourth district, at Cherbourg, was added in April 1918. This decentralized system lasted for the rest of the war and served very well.

Dissatisfied with Patton's serving as a naval port officer when he had been directed to establish a repair base, Wilson shifted him to command the aviation center at Pauillac and had Lieutenant Bernier serve as port officer at Bordeaux. Bernier was relieved on 28 May 1918 by Comdr. Ralph P. Craft. With a staff of eleven officers, Bernier handled the greatly increased amount of shipping that arrived in the Gironde, including colliers from Wales and ships carrying the material needed to build the U.S. Naval Radio Station at Croix d'Hins (q.v.). Now Bordeaux could berth fifteen ships a day and handle more than 236,000 tons of freight per day. The direction of troop distribution was vested in Army Base Sections of the Army Transport Service. These were located at St. Nazaire, Bordeaux, Le Havre, Brest, Marseilles, and La Pallice. Although the despatch of troopships to Bordeaux meant dividing their convoys somewhere in the eastern Atlantic Ocean and straining the Navy's ability to provide escort vessels, Washington insisted on the division in order to speed up turnaround time. Driblets of troops—5,549 in March, 6,161 in April—increased to 11,000 in both May and June, with the American ships paying pilotage, ballast, and towage fees but not sanitary and quay duties. Under the watchful eyes of the naval port officer, repairs beyond the capacity of ship's force and of the repair ship *Panther* were made in the French shipyards and dry dock at Bordeaux.

By the second half of 1918, American ship convoys of from twenty-two to thirty-six ships arrived at Bordeaux, with a total of 437 ships entering by October. These going over (HB) convoys remained under British Admiralty control until September, when the U.S. Navy took over. Air and surface escort for them was provided by Admiral Wilson at Brest, to which Sims sent some destroyers toward the end of the war. Ships returning home, the returning home (OV) convoys, were under American control. While on an inspection trip to American naval bases in Europe, Assistant Secretary of the Navy Franklin D. Roosevelt wrote on August 14, 1918:

> Met General Connor after breakfast and crossed the river to the docks, which have been taken over by the army. The length of the docks is being doubled and when the work is completed ten ships can unload at the same time. Temporary storehouses and additional trackage facilities have been put in along the docks, but it is not intended that any army supplies should remain here more than over night. After the enormous storage

base, about 6 miles away, is completed and filled, and after railroad equipment becomes sufficient, it is the intention to move all the incoming cargoes direct on to the flat cars and thence by rail up to the supply bases back of the front. Thus the big supply base outside of Bordeaux will become a huge reserve to be used only in case of emergency, as, for instance, in case heavy German ships should get out of the North Sea and temporarily stop the flow across the trans-Atlantic lane. By shipping the cargoes in normal times direct from the ship to the front one process of handling will be avoided.

The bulk of the unloading is being handled by negro troops, and General Connor told me that he is now getting out an average of about 700 tons per ship per day. This is a splendid achievement, even when compared with commercial practice, but Connor is not satisfied and hopes eventually to get out over 800 tons per ship per day. It should be borne in mind that according to the plans Bordeaux and St. Nazaire are to handle the greater part of the army stores. Some will come in through smaller ports, and the principal troop debarkation port will continue to be Brest.

Although the Armistice was signed on 11 November 1918, the U.S. Naval Port Office remained at Bordeaux for almost a year longer in order to help return soldiers home, handle storeships bringing supplies for troops still in France, and aid Shipping Board ships that arrived with commercial cargoes as well as ships carrying relief food and supplies sent over by the Food Administration and the American Relief Administration. By March 1919 naval personnel at Bordeaux numbered only five officers and twenty-five men. On 30 September 1919 the Naval Port Office was closed.

BIBLIOGRAPHY

A. Henry P. Beers, *U.S. Naval Port Officers in the Bordeaux Region, 1917-1919* (Washington: Navy Department, Sept. 1943); Records of the Office of Naval Records and Library: Files KO, U.S. Naval Forces in France, Demobilization: P. Bordeaux; PO, Bordeaux (Washington: National Archives).

B. Rear Adm. Albert Gleaves, *A History of the Transport Service: Adventures and Experiences of United States Transports and Cruisers in World War I* (New York: George A. Doran, 1921); Herbert A. Gibbons, *Ports of France* (New York: Century Co., 1926); Elliott Roosevelt, ed., *F.D.R.: His Personal Letters 1905-1928* (New York: Duell, Sloan and Pearce, 1948), pp. 437-38.

Brest, 1918-1919

Like St. Nazaire, Lorient, and several other French ports, Brest occasionally served American warship captains before the War of the American Revolution. As the cruise of Lambert Wickes shows, the French, who hated Britain and desired vengeance on "the mistress of the seas," even while neutral before February 1778 permitted him to repair his ship, alter its appearance, and take on water, stores, and crewman as well.

During World War I, Brest was to the American Expeditionary Force (AEF) what Queenstown, Ireland, was to the American destroyers that hunted submarines and escorted convoys to and from the southern ports of Great Britain. The French Fleet saw no great naval battles during World War I. Rather, it engaged in the mundane duties of transporting the colonial Army from Algeria to France, escorted convoys, helped Italy and Britain guard against an Austrian naval menace that never really materialized, and aided the British at the Dardanelles campaign far from home and from any direct threat to French survival. In addition, the handing over of the Navy's shipyards to the Army for the manufacture of arms for the Western Front meant that ship maintenance was delayed and little was done to improve the ports, whose channels were not of sufficient depth to admit the largest ships and were poorly supplied with berths and facilities. Except for sending out some small craft on antisubmarine patrol, naval activity was quite passive at Brest until eight converted American yachts arrived at the end of June 1917. To these were added two squadrons of converted yachts in August and September and a destroyer squadron in October. Part of the command of Vice Adm. William S. Sims, Commander, U.S. Naval Forces Operating in European Waters, their first immediate commander was Capt. William B. Fletcher, USN, Commander, U.S. Patrol Squadrons Operating in European Waters. Fletcher immediately had to provide facilities lacking at Brest for his ships and as the major debarkation and embarkation port for the American Expeditionary Force. As directed from Washington when the great crisis of U-boat warfare began to wane during the late summer of 1917, Sims sent some destroyers from Queenstown to Brest and also designated Lorient, St. Nazaire, Rochefort, and Bordeaux as bases, these southern French ports being selected because the British and French were using the ports in northern France. In October 1917 Sims ordered Rear Adm. Henry Wilson, commanding at Gibraltar (q.v.), to shift his flag to Brest and appointed him Commander, U.S. Naval Forces in France, responsible for both operations and administration to him in an area including Brest and extending from Brehat to Penmarch, including Ushant. Although Admiral Wilson preferred to remain afloat, at the insistence of the French he moved ashore, a wise move because he could get quicker and more complete information there. His offices were at first in a small building along the Penfield River, which flows through the city, then at the Credit Lyonnaise, one of the most modern buildings in Brest.

Both coastal and deep-sea convoys were escorted from Brest. After January 1918 the base grew rapidly, with new spaces for quarters, offices, coal, oil, water, repairs, salvage, mail, aviation, intelligence, communications, engineering, ordnance, administration, a beachmaster, shore patrol, one of the four naval hospitals built in Europe, and supplies and disbursements.

There was also a Naval Band and Orchestra that gave daily concerts, played twice a week in the public square, and provided music for entertainments and dances and at the hospital. A combined vaudeville and minstrel show entertained many, and generous services were provided by the YMCA and the Knights of Columbus. The large Carola castle near the waterfront, including six buildings, was practically rebuilt and used as a naval barracks. The Port Director, who had only four or five assistants, supervised all American ships in Brest and in addition cooperated with the U.S. Army and French harbor personnel as well. It was he who supervised the berthing of incoming troop and cargo transports and provided them with fuel and water. He was also responsible for offloading the U.S. Naval Railway Batteries sent to France and the materials used to build the Lafayette Naval Radio Station at Croix d'Hins (q.v.). Some construction was undertaken by the U.S. Navy itself, the rest by contract with the French Navy.

Repairs were undertaken in the French navy yard located some distance up the Penfield River, with great improvement in the speed and quality of work after the arrival of two destroyer tenders. The latter also did some repair work for the French Navy. With the increased number of American ships arriving, however, during the spring of 1918 men and materials were sent from the United States to build a repair base ashore. By the time of the Armistice 540 men were at work in the various repair shops. Salvage work was accomplished by the USS *Favorite*, which reached Brest on 5 August 1918, the USS *Utowana*, and a lighter fitted with pumps and diving gear.

In his report on a visit to Brest dated 5 August 1918, Capt. Harry E. Yarnell, of Sims's Planning Section in London, found that 10,000 troops could be handled daily, that 40,000 had been landed in a twelve-hour period, and that 150,000 could be quartered in the immediate vicinity. As for Army-Navy relations, they were "most cordial, and complete cooperation exists." Brest was congested and its sanitary conditions were poor, but an increase in the water supply would improve the situation. Destroyers based there were "worked to the limit," and while twelve additional ones could be accommodated, Brest could support only sixty of them. For the AEF, Naval Operating Transport Service ships delivered 3,102,462 tons of supplies and, from Cardiff, Wales, to Brest, 96,000 tons of coal. Late in 1918 U.S. naval ships at Brest included one gunboat, sixteen yachts, three tenders, thirty-eight destroyers, nine tugs, four steam barges, four barges, nine minesweepers, and four submarine chaser units each comprised of three boats.

Until the Armistice, ships based at Brest escorted 91 percent of all convoys in and out of France; at the Armistice, there were seventy-eight vessels and 12,000 men there, and 1,600,000 American troops had passed through it on their way to the front.

At the time of the Armistice there were 88 U.S. Navy officers and 837 men on board at Brest. Then the Port Director inventoried his materials and supplies and decided which of them to dispose to Allied governments, transfer to the U.S. Army, place on public sale, or return to the United States. Land taken over was released back to the French Department of the Seine. Within just two months, a 72 percent reduction in operations had occurred, and sales recouped about half the cost of construction work at the base.

Part of the naval base was a kite balloon facility established on 4 July 1918 and a seaplane facility established on 29 October 1918. The aerial facility was commissioned on 7 October 1917 but not as an air station. The seaplanes proved useful in patrol work and escort of convoy, but with the end of the war all the aerial facilities were transferred on 15 February 1919 to the French Navy.

BIBLIOGRAPHY
A. "A Brief History of the U.S. Naval Forces in France, from 11 November 1918 to 1 October 1919" (Washington: Naval Historical Center, Operational Archives Branch); Admiral Henry B. Wilson, USN, *An Account of the Operations of the American Navy in France during the War with Germany* (USS *Pennsylvania*, July 1, 1919); U.S. Navy Department, Office of Naval Intelligence, Historical Section, *The American Naval Planning Section in London*, Pub. No. 7 (Washington: GPO, 1923); Lewis P. Clephane, *History of the Naval Overseas Transportation Service in World War I* (Washington: Naval History Division, 1969); "Brest," in *Naval Air Stations*, 3 vols. (Washington, D.C., Navy Yard: Naval Aviation History Office, n.d.).

B. Joseph Husband, *On the Coast of France: The Story of the United States Naval Forces in French Waters* (Chicago: A. C. McClurg & Co., 1919); Rear Adm. William Sowden Sims, USN, *The Victory at Sea* (Garden City, N.Y.: Doubleday, Page, 1920); Albert Gleaves, *A History of the Transport Service: Adventures and Experiences of United States Transports and Cruisers in World War I* (New York: George Doran, 1921); William Bell Clark, *Lambert Wickes: Sea Raider and Diplomat* (New Haven: Yale University Press, 1932); Josephus Daniels, *The Wilson Era: Years of War, 1917-1923* (Chapel Hill: University of North Carolina Press, 1946).

Lorient, 1917-1918

Among the various sites for U.S. naval facilities along the coast of France south of Brest was Lorient, designed to serve as a fuel oil depot for slower and smaller ships escorting cargo and troop transports entering the Gironde River. Lorient lies about halfway along the southern coast of the Breton peninsula, north of Belle Isle and west of Quiberon peninsula. Between 13 December 1917 and 2 February 1918 a division of minesweepers, Squadron Four Patrol Force, arrived there. This was comprised of a converted yacht as flagship and ten converted menhaden fishing craft armed with two 3-inch guns each, Capt. Thomas P. Magruder, USN, commanding. These left Provincetown, Mass., on August 1917 and proceeded to France via the Azores and Brest, making the voyage in a record seventeen days. They were accompanied by a supply ship and various submarine chasers. Magruder was eventually given office space in the Inscription Maritime Building at the French Arsenal.

The mission of Squadron Four Patrol Force was the important one of keeping clear of mines the approaches to St. Nazaire, to which an increasing number of American cargo and troop transports were sent. They were also to sweep for mines in a district extending from Penmarch to Fromentine with sweeping gear provided by the French. They also engaged in rescue and salvage work, and occasionally, as during the height of the U-boat campaign, escorted convoys proceeding southward from Brest. Hospitalization for the Americans was provided by a French hospital at La Perrier, a suburb of Lorient.

As more and more American ships arrived from the United States, Vice Adm. Henry B. Wilson, commanding American naval forces in France from headquarters in Brest, determined that the United States should send the necessary buildings, tools, equipment, supplies, and personnel to establish repair shops at

Brest, Lorient, and Pauillac. The movement of materials, begun on 1 June 1918, reached Lorient between 15 September and 5 December 1918. With the signing of the Armistice on 11 November, however, a small quantity of material remaining undelivered was cancelled by cable. Administration and supplies for Squadron Four Patrol Force were taken care of by Base 19, located at the French Arsenal, and the 260 enlisted men were quartered in a converted hotel located near the Place Alsace Lorraine.

Minesweeping undertaken by Magruder's boats was steady, continuous, persevering, and unspectacular for about a year in the area between Belle Isle and St. Nazaire. They were sometimes joined by French minesweeping squadrons and followed a schedule of eight days out and three days in port for taking on coal, water, and provisions.

At the time of the Armistice Lorient verged upon assuming direction over all naval units and air operations in the District of Lorient, which included the supervision of the Naval Port Officers at St. Nazaire, Nantes, and Quiberon, five U.S. naval air stations, and a total of 196 officers and 2,529 men. Large oil tanks were being built for the use of oil-burning destroyers and patrol boats. With the Armistice construction work ended, but Magruder's boats continued sweeping out to the 100-meter curve to make sure no German mines were left.

It being thought that many American transports would be sent to Lorient, plans were made for extensive repair facilities there. When the ships did not materialize, the repair shop was redesigned to take care of the minesweepers there only. The shop was located in an empty 40-by-60-foot building provided by the French, who also offered a 40-by-100-foot plot of ground for new construction by Americans. Storage space was available in an old storehouse provided by the French. With the Armistice, most of the tools and the shop buildings intended for Lorient were delivered to Brest instead.

For communications, naval operators were installed at the telephone and telegraph offices at the French Prefecture at Lorient. With the U.S. Army's Signal Corps agreeable, plans were made to construct a separate naval telephone line connecting the District Commander's Office at Lorient with the naval air stations at La Trinite, Le Croisic, Fromentine, and Paimboeuf. Busy with the Army's needs, the Signal Corps did not complete the lines until August 1918, when connections were also made with Admiral Wilson's office in Brest and with the Port Officer at St. Nazaire. A simplex line leased from the French also connected Brest-Lorient-St. Nazaire. Radio communications for Lorient were available at the French radio station at Penmane.

Base 19 supported Squadron Four Patrol Force well as it kept the sealanes south of Brest clear of mines, engaged in salvage and rescue work, and occasionally engaged in escort of convoy.

BIBLIOGRAPHY

A. Adm. Henry B. Wilson, USN, *An Account of The Operations of the American Navy in France during the War with Germany* (USS *Pennsylvania*, July 1, 1919, n.p.).

St. Nazaire, U.S. Disembarkation and Embarkation Port, 1917-1919

One of the principal French ports selected for the disembarkation and then embarkation of American troops was St. Nazaire, located twenty-five miles inland from the mouth of the Loire River. Because the French and the British used ports and land communications farther north and because routes to and through the Mediterranean meant meeting U-boats, the Americans used French ports south of Brest along the Bay of Biscay including Bassens, Bordeaux, and Pauillac on the Gironde River. St. Nazaire was especially important because it lay south of the major U-boat operating areas and had the only cranes in France able to handle the 1,761 railroad locomotives and 26,994 freight cars sent over by the United States as well as five units of the mobile railmounted 14″/50 naval guns that were used to bombard the German front. However, the United States had to create facilities for disembarkation so that men and supplies could reach the front. Needed were an organization, port facilities, depots, and lines of transportation.

In the purely artificial harbor at St. Nazaire there were in 1917 two docks located in a series of lock basins separated from the estuary by a narrow strip of land, but even ships with less than a 30-foot draft could enter and sortie only at high tide. The U.S. Naval Port Office overlooked the locks. Other impediments were the 13-foot rise and fall of the tide and the swift current, which meant that ships must be wharfed because cargo and troops could not be moved by lighters, and the presence of a number of Greek ships, interned by the Allies because Greece would not join them in the war against Germany, which took up usable space. Yet of the six ports of disembarkation for the American Expeditionary Force St. Nazaire ranked second. Brest was first with 791,000 troops, St. Nazaire second with 198,000, Bordeaux third with 50,000, and the others barely in the running: Le Havre, 13,000; La Pallice, 4,000; and Marseilles, 1,000.

The problem of offloading men and cargoes was compounded because the French had done nothing to prepare the port to receive great numbers of men and mountains of supplies, and there was a great shortage of labor. When the 500 Negro stevedores sent to discharge ships proved unequal to the task, Marines on board troopships unloaded their own ships. American sailors jumped in, as did some French stevedores as well as some German POWs. Many of the supplies, food, and clothing for the U.S. naval air stations at nearby Fromentine, Paimboeuf, and La Trinite came from St. Nazaire.

Both American and French warships escorted the American troop and cargo ships through the U-boat danger zones, following minesweepers, and the French in addition provided a dirigible and several aircraft. By 1 January 1918 American personnel in the Port Office had increased from three to thirty-three. Among the departments into which the office was divided were those for supplies, medicine, engineering, radio, post office, and convoy routing.

While cargo was transferred to trains for delivery to the fighting front, an almost continuous stream of soldiers marched off over the cobblestones of the narrow, winding streets to a camp built by German POWs a few miles behind the town. A repair base was established by 1 December 1917, and the seventy-five bed dispensary proved to be invaluable, particularly during the influenza epidemic in the early fall of 1918. Traffic was especially heavy from August to November 1918, when 172 ships entered port and discharged 604,598 tons of cargo and handled 47,961 passengers.

Protecting the approaches to St. Nazaire from Penmarch to the Loire were six American yachts based at Rochefort, Capt. N. A. McCully, USN, and a mine-sweeper division (ten boats), Capt. Thomas P. Magruder, USN, at Lorient, with the latter connected by telephone with the Port Office at St. Nazaire. To permit the cooperation of air forces, the port officer was connected to the American naval air stations at Fromentine and Le Croisic, telegraph circuits linked St. Nazaire with Lorient and Brest, and an American-manned radio station at Chemoulin enabled St. Nazaire to handle all communications for American ships.

The American facilities at the port were disestablished on 10 October 1919.

BIBLIOGRAPHY

A. "A Brief History of the United States Naval Forces in France from 11 November 1918 to 1 October 1919," in *Wars, World War I*, ZO File, Box 2 (Washington: Naval Historical Center, Operational Archives Branch); Vice Adm. Henry B. Wilson, USN, *An Account of the Operations of the American Navy in France during the War with Germany* (USS *Pennsylvania*, July 1, 1919 n.p.); Lewis P. Clephane, *History of the Naval Overseas Transport Service in World War I* (Washington: Naval History Division, 1969).

B. Benedict Crowell and Robert Forrest Wilson, *The Road to France: The Transportation of Troops and Military Supplies,* 2 vols. (New Haven: Yale University Press, 1921), I:238, II:478-79; Vice Adm. Albert Gleaves, USN, *A History of the Transport Service: Adventures and Experiences of United States Transports and Cruisers in the World War* (New York: George H. Doran Co., 1921); Thomas G. Frothingham, *The Naval History of the World War: The United States Navy in the World War, 1917-1918*, 3 vols. (Cambridge, Mass.: Riverside Press, 1924-1926); Thomas G. Frothingham, *The American Reinforcement in the World War* (Garden City, N.Y.: Doubleday, Page, 1927); *The [London] Times History of the War*, 22 vols. (London: *The Times*, 1914-1921, XX:40-47).

Great Britain

Cardiff, Wales, 1918

In January 1918 Vice Adm. William S. Sims, Commander, U.S. Naval Forces Operating in European Waters, ordered the executive officer of the USS *Leviathan*, Comdr. H. M. Jeffers, USN, to Cardiff, Wales, to organize a naval base from which coal could be transported to France. Sims took the step because of the need to provide coal for the ships that transported Gen. John J. Pershing's American Expeditionary Force (AEF). Manned by men of the Naval Reserve Force, an increasing number of ships engaged in what was known as the Army coal trade, taking coal from Cardiff to Le Havre, Cherbourg, Brest, and French Bay of Biscay ports. Base 29, Cardiff, was officially established on 24 September 1918. Although Jeffers had been promoted to captain, the work of the base had so expanded that it was necessary to place an admiral in command. Rear Adm. Philip Andrews, USN, was selected for the billet.

From Cardiff, fifty-three colliers in the Naval Overseas Transportation Service delivered 96,000 tons of coal for the AEF. Ships loaded either at Cardiff or Barry, with projected establishments at Penarth, Newport, and Swansea going into operation in October and November. At the Armistice, 1,758 American officers and 4,101 men worked at Cardiff alone and there were one tender, one refrigerator ship, and fifty-five colliers there. Base 29 was shut down after the AEF had been returned home.

BIBLIOGRAPHY

A. Lewis P. Clephane, *History of the Naval Overseas Transport Service in World War I* (Washington: Naval History Division, 1969), pp. xix, 211, 261-63.

B. John Langdon Leighton, *Simsadus London: The American Navy in Europe* (New York: Henry Holt, 1920), pp. 88-89.

Bantry Bay, Ireland, 1918

To counter the German High Sea Fleet or German cruiser raiders that got by the British Grand Fleet, Vice Adm. William S. Sims, Commander, U.S. Naval Forces Operating in European Waters, obtained permission from Washington in November 1917 to have a squadron of coal-burning battleships operate with the Grand Fleet and in August 1918 to station three additional battleships, Rear Adm. Thomas S. Rodgers, at Bantry Bay, Ireland, the southernmost point of Ireland. Out of Berehaven, on the north coast of the bay, also operated seven American L-class submarines, their duty to prevent U-boats from operating in the Western Approaches. (To distinguish themselves from British L-boats, the Americans used the designation AL.) Their immediate needs were taken care of after 28 January 1918 by the submarine tender *Bushnell* (AS-2). In July 1918, the destroyer tender *Dixie* (AD-1), based at Queenstown, relocated at Bantry Bay and furnished supplies and made minor repairs to ships there until she returned to Queenstown in September.

BIBLIOGRAPHY

A. U.S. Navy Department, Office of Naval Records and Library, Historical Section, *History of the Bureau of Engineering Navy Department during the World War*, Pub. No. 5 (Washington: GPO, 1922), p. 126; *Bushnell, Dixie*, and *L-Boats*, in *Dictionary of American Naval Fighting Ships*, 8 vols. (Washington: GPO, 1959-1981), I:181, II:282, IV:1-4.

B. Carroll Storrs Alden, ''American Submarine Operations in the War,'' U.S. Naval Institute *Proceedings* 46 (July 1920): 1013-48; John Langdon Leighton, *Simsadus London: The American Navy in Europe* (New York: Henry Holt, 1929), pp. 59-65; Rear Adm. William Sowden Sims, USN, and Burton J. Hendrick, *The Victory at Sea* (Garden City, N.Y.: Doubleday, Page, 1920), pp. 279-80.

Queenstown, Ireland, U.S. Naval Base, 1917-1919

Allied ships heading for or leaving the southern and western ports of Great Britain during World War I were given as much escort protection as possible in the Southwest Approaches. To base its escorts, the U.S. Navy chose Queenstown, Ireland, a halfway point between the western ports of England and a convoy rendezvous point between 200 and 300 miles to the west. Among others, Vice Adm. Sir Lewis Bayly, commanding the British naval station at Queenstown, met the first six American destroyers, which arrived on 4 May 1917, Comdr. Joseph Taussig commanding, and all subsequent arrivals as well. To cement good relations and obtain unity of command, Vice Adm. William Sowden Sims, Commander, U.S. Naval Forces Operating in European Waters, whose headquarters were in London, put his ships under Bayly's operational command. Administrative command, however, remained with Sims and was exercised by his chief of staff at Queenstown, Capt. J.R.P. Pringle. Although Bayly offered the Americans all the support facilities in his command, Sims deemed them so poor and overworked that he determined to repair and supply his eventually thirty-six destroyers and thirty-six submarine chasers from floating facilities. These took the form of the destroyer tenders *Melville* (flagship) and *Dixie*, but he acquired warehouses and barracks, as well as hospital, recreation, and some repair facilities on the beach. The tenders did three-fourths of the repair work needed except major repairs and those that required docking.

American ships returning from a normal four days at sea to Queenstown would radio the *Melville* about needed repairs. Soon after they tied up alongside, working parties from the tenders would undertake the repairs. Two days later, the destroyers would shove off again. The system was so efficient that the destroyers spent 66 percent of their time at sea and escorted 39 percent of all the traffic passing in and out by way of the southern coast of Ireland.

Because of their attitude toward the war, cocky independence, lower pay, and jealousy of their women, Irishmen soon clashed with American sailors. To prevent further trouble, Sims and his associates established a Men's Club in which dances or amateur theatrical productions were held or movies shown to crews in port, who were denied liberty in the town of Cork, twelve miles distant. The officers were entertained in Admiral Bayly's quarters, Admiralty House. By the end of the war, nearly 8,000 Americans were at Queenstown, itself containing only 6,000 or 7,000 people.

American destroyers were larger and hence had more range than British destroyers, yet under the direction of British Capt. E.R.G.R. Evans, later Evans of the *Broke*, they lowered their mast heights to foil German range-finding, improved their camouflage, and modified their doctrine in keeping with British experience at sea. Throughout America's participation in the war, Queenstown was the largest American base for convoy escorts and, beginning in late 1917, for troop transport escorts as well. By early 1919 all American ships had left except the *Melville*, which stayed on to wrap up loose ends until 4 January 1919, when she too returned home.

BIBLIOGRAPHY

A. U.S. Navy Department, Office of Naval Intelligence, Historical Section, *The American Naval Planning Section in London*, Pub. No. 7 (Washington: GPO, 1923); "*Dixie*" "*Fanning,*" and "*Melville,*" in *Dictionary of American Naval Fighting Ships,* 8 vols. (Washington: GPO, 1959-1981): II:338, II, 181-82; IV:314-15.

B. John Langdon Leighton, *Simsadus London: The American Navy in Europe* (New York: Henry Holt, 1920); Rear Adm. William Sowden Sims, USN, and Burton J. Hendrick, *The Victory at Sea* (Garden City, N.Y.: Doubleday, Page, 1920): Joseph K. Taussig, "Destroyer Experiences during the Great War," U.S. Naval Institute *Proceedings* 48 (Dec. 1922):215-40, and 49 (Jan.-Mar. 1923):221-48, 383-408.

Invergordon and Inverness, Scotland, U.S. Naval Mine Force Bases, 1918-1919

By late 1916 various Englishmen and Americans saw the need for a large mine barrage across the top of the North Sea to destroy U-boats that tried to sortie via that sea to the Atlantic. Problems encountered included the length of time it would take to lay the field, inefficient mines, an average depth of water of 600 feet, tempestuous weather, and the need to patrol it when ASW vessels were extremely difficult to come by. In the summer of 1917, however, an electrical engineer from Salem, Mass., asked Comdr. Simon P. Fullinwider, in charge of the mining section of the U.S. Bureau of Ordnance, to evaluate a submarine gun. Fullinwider disliked the gun but saw that its electrical firing device might prove useful in firing mines. American and British officers brought the device to perfection and created the antenna mine. Rather than having merely contact "horns," the new mine would be exploded when a hull set up an electrical current in a long copper wire suspended by a float a few feet below the surface of the water. In consequence, only about 100,000 of these would be needed instead of 400,000 of the older contact type. This, in turn, meant fewer minelaying ships, crews, officers, bases, supplies, and costs—which turned out to be $400 million—and on 2 November the American and British governments formally approved the "Northern Barrage" project.

Command of the minelaying squadron of the Atlantic Fleet lay with Capt. Reginald R. Belknap. Before he could lay mines, however, he had to create bases both in the United States and in Scotland. Loaded in the Norfolk area, the mines began leaving for Scotland in February 1918. In Scotland, use was made of Fort William and Kyle of Loch Alsh, on the western coast, whence the mines were transported to bases in the ports of Inverness, Base 18, and Invergordon, Base 17, thirty miles apart on Moray Firth, the former served by the Highland Railway, the latter by the Caledonian Canal. Because of transportation difficulties, two bases were used instead of one.

By May 1918, when the American Mine Force arrived, Capt. Orin G. Murfin, USN, had designed and built bases capable of handling more than 2,000 men and as many as 20,000 mines at one time, with largely reserve personnel fitting the firing devices into as many as 1,200 mines a day. At Dalmore, three miles from Invergordon, and at Glen Albyn, Muirtown, two idle distilleries—clean, dry, and well-ventilated—provided excellent living accommodations for the 20 officers and 1,000 men at each base and for the 3 officers and 60 men at each mine unloading point. In addition, Murfin erected a YMCA hut and transformed a small hotel into a sickbay. A 1,000-bed U.S. Naval Base Hospital was established at Strathpeffer, twenty miles from either base, under Capt. E. S. Bogert, MC (Medical Corps). Supplies and repairs for the minelayers were provided by the Royal Dockyard and depot at Invergordon and by the depot at Inverness until the repair ship *Black Hawk* arrived in June. Capt. Dudley W. Knox, of Vice Adm. William S. Sims's Planning Section in London, who reported on a visit to the bases on 24 May 1918, said that "the two bases at Inverness and Invergordon are complete and ready for operations, except for some mine equipment. They appear to be well-organized, going concerns, with a fine spirit, and may be expected to be very efficient in operation."

Minelayers escorted by patrol craft and units of the British Grand Fleet, including the American battleship squadron assigned to it, dropped the mines off from the Orkney Islands to the coast of Norway, Americans to about fifty nautical miles from Norway, Britons the rest of the way. To supervise an operation of such magnitude was the task of the Commander, Mine Force, Atlantic Fleet, Rear Adm. Joseph Strauss, a former Chief of the Bureau of Ordnance, who arrived in Scotland in March 1918, and Rear Adm. Clinton-Baker, RN. By the time of the Armistice, the Americans had laid 56,571 mines, the British, 13,546.

Three weeks after the Armistice, on 2 December 1918, the Mine Force started departing Invergordon for the Azores and Bermuda en route to Hampton Roads. The base there and the one at Inverness were rolled up, and the minesweepers began their dangerous work.

BIBLIOGRAPHY

A. U.S. Navy Department, Office of Naval Intelligence, Historical Section, *The American Naval Planning Section in London*, Pub. No. 7 (Washington: GPO, 1923), pp. 1-6, 12-13, 52-53, 139-53, 146-49, 162-70.

B. Reginald R. Belknap, "The North Sea Mine Barrage," *National Geographic Magazine* 35 (Feb. 1919):85-110; Reginald R. Belknap, *The Yankee Mining Squadron: Or Laying the North Sea Mine Barrage* (Annapolis, Md.: U.S. Naval Institute, 1920); Rear Adm. William Sowden Sims, USN, and Burton J. Hendrick, *The Victory at Sea* (Garden City, N.Y.: Doubleday, Page, 1920), pp. 285-309.

Greece

Corfu, 1918

During World War I, to base a number of submarine chasers near Otranto Strait, through which German and Austrian U-boats might sortie from the Adriatic to the Mediterranean Sea, Vice Adm. William S. Sims, Commander, U.S. Naval Forces Operating in European Waters, ordered an installation built on the island of Corfu. The site, never before used as a naval base, had to be converted into a useful utility in a barren and uncivilized cove. The work was accomplished in June 1918 by the 1,000 officers and men of the destroyer tender *Leonidas* (AD-7) and thirty-nine submarine chasers, Capt. Charles P. "Juggy" Nelson commanding, in record time, with the cooperation of both French and English naval officers. Up went shacks for staff offices, barracks, and a hospital. By the end of June the job at Base 25 was done and the forces were ready for operations. Usually three units, of three boats each, went hunting. They kept U-boats down and may have sunk one, and eleven of them took part in the antisubmarine operations connected with the bombardment of Durazzo, on the eastern coast of the Adriatic, on 2 October 1918. On 20 November 1918, soon after the signing of the Armistice, the *Leonidas* left for home and the base was closed.

BIBLIOGRAPHY

A. "*Leonidas*," in *Dictionary of American Naval Fighting Ships*, 8 vols. (Washington: GPO, 1959-1981), IV:90-91.

B. John Langdon Leighton, *Simsadus London: The American Navy in Europe* (New York: Henry Holt, 1920); pp. 78-82; William W. Nutting, *The Cinderellas of the Fleet* (Jersey City, N.J.: The Standard Motor Construction Co., 1920); Rear Adm. William Sowden Sims, USN, and Burton J. Hendrick, *The Victory at Sea* (Garden City, N.Y.: Doubleday, Page, 1920), pp. 228-39; Vice Adm. Cecil Vivian Usborne, "Anti-Submarine Campaign in the Mediterranean Subsequent to 1916," *Royal United Service Institution Journal* 69 (Aug. 1924):444-64; Vice Adm. Cecil Vivian Usborne, *Smoke on the Horizon: Mediterranean Fighting 1914-1918* (London: Hodder & Stoughton, 1933); Vice Adm. Cecil Vivian Usborne, *Blast and Counterblast: A Naval Impression of the War* (London: J. Murray, 1935).

Portugal

Azores Islands, 1917-1919

American whalers from such Massachusetts towns as Nantucket and New Bedford stopped at Horta, Fayal, for water and fresh fruit as early as 1790, when the United States sent a consul to Fayal to provide for the relief and protection of American seamen. During the War of 1812, the *General Armstrong*, Samuel C. Reed commanding, was surprised while at anchor by three British ships; he scuttled her rather than have her seized. Subsequent American trade and involvement with the nine Azores Islands 800 miles west of Portugal were quite limited until the United States entered World War I.

On 4 July 1917 a German U-boat used its guns to bombard the town of Ponta Delgada, Azores Islands, which lies 800 miles west of Lisbon, Portugal, at 37°44′N., 25°39′W. To extend convoy protection and prevent U-boats from using the islands as refueling sites, the U.S. Navy Department on 16 August 1917 decided that a naval base was needed in the Azores and assigned Rear Adm. Herbert Dunn to command the five submarines, two yachts, one tender, one oiler, two minesweepers, one tug, and several submarine chasers sent there. In addition, the First Marine Aeronautic Company was dispatched from the

United States and on 21 January 1918 arrived at Naval Base 13, Azores Islands, Capt. Frank T. Evans commanding. It was the first completely trained and equipped patrol aviation unit to be sent overseas. The Marines used a mixed bag of obsolete and short-range aircraft including ten R-6 scouts, two N-9 trainers and six later models that still had limited endurance, and HS-2L flying boats, none with radios. No report mentions the sighting of a U-boat by an American ship or aircraft, and the base was disestablished on 1 September 1919.

See also World War I U.S. Naval Air Stations in Europe.

BIBLIOGRAPHY

A. Bureau of Aeronautics, "World War II Administrative History," 20 vols. (Washington: Bureau of Aeronautics, 8 November 1957), Vol. XI.

B. Frances M. Rogers, *Atlantic Islands of the Azores and Madeiras* (North Quincy, Mass.: The Christopher Publishing House, 1979).

WORLD WAR I U.S. NORTHERN BOMBING GROUP BASES IN ENGLAND AND FRANCE. Various American plans for bombing the German-occupied bases at Ostend, Zeebrugge, and Bruges were suggested, among them the use of seaplane carriers or of lighters bearing seaplanes and towed by destroyers. These ideas were vetoed by the Chief of Operations, William S. Benson. Moreover, when bombing from Dunkirk proved ineffective—the site was often under German aerial attack—it was decided to use landplanes rather than seaplanes. With the U.S. Army agreeable, the Navy would bomb the submarine pens in Belgium by day, and Marine Corps pilots would bomb them by night.

Dunkirk was across the English Channel from Dover, just north of Calais and only a few miles from the Franco-Belgian border. The German U-boat, destroyer, and minelayer bases in the Ostend-Zeebrugge-Bruges area lay only about thirty miles to the northeast.

The French had established a seaplane base on the eastern side of Dunkirk Harbor, to which a British naval air station adjoined, Capt. C. L. Lambe, commanding. When Lt. Kenneth Whiting, USN, visited Dunkirk on 18 June 1917 he found there "miles of hangars and thousands of machines." Construction work by the French had begun on 20 July; by 25 September barracks and other facilities had been completed. The first plane arrived in October. Although the station was commissioned on 1 January 1918, there were no pilots there, and the Germans bombed the site by night. When the British suggested that the United States take over the station, Capt. Hutch I. Cone, in charge of American aviation in Europe, agreed but recommended that airfields be dispersed in order to avoid German bombing. Moreover, he saw the need of landplanes to fight off German bombers so that seaplanes could bomb the German naval works in Belgium. On 24 January 1918 Capt. A. A. Cunningham, USMC, suggested that his Corps provide the fighters to protect the seaplanes. In consequence, some 30 seaplanes were protected by 64—later 200—landplanes.

On 10 March 1918 the Navy Department in Washington ordered Vice Adm. William S. Sims, Commander, U.S. Naval Forces Operating in European Waters, to prepare stations for four land fighter squadrons and have them ready by 1 June. However, it was found that landplanes and seaplanes were "incompatible" and that landplanes should be used for bombing purposes. Asked if it had any objection to the use of naval planes for bombing naval targets, the U.S. Army said that it did not. In consequence, the Navy took over and recommended the use of bombers capable of self-defense.

To bomb the German naval works in Belgium the Navy on 30 April 1918 organized what became known as the Northern Bombing Group. It was to consist of six day and six night squadrons. The Marines would operate the day squadrons and be supported by a northern repair base at St. Inglevert. Fields requisitioned from the French for night bombing were at Campagne, Sangatte, La Frene, Oye (Calais), and Spicker. The first four fields would have two squadrons of ten Italian Caproni bombers each, while Oye would have four squadrons (eighteen DH-4s for each), and Spicker two squadrons (eighteen DH-4s each). Because of the U.S. Army's need for aircraft, on 31 May the Navy Department reduced the Naval Bombing Group to four day and four night squadrons and on 20 July directed that they use a repair base on the western side of the English Channel at Eastleigh, four miles from Southampton.

Eastleigh had been used by the Royal Air Force as an aircraft reception park. It had enormous storehouses and hangars but quarters for only 100 men when 5,000 Americans were expected. In any event, under Lt. Comdr. F. N. Bolles, USN, as Officer in Charge, a capacity was developed to assemble five planes and overhaul and repair three aircraft and engines per day. The base was fully operational by the time of the Armistice.

Changes in plans dated 31 May caused Night Squadrons 1 and 2 to use St. Inglevert and 3 and 4 to use Campagne, while Sangatte was used as a dummy field. Day Squadrons 7 and 8 would operate from Oye; 9 and 10 from La Frene, with a dummy field at Alembon; and Spicker Field was eliminated. Headquarters for the Northern Bombing Group, which lacked an airfield, was at Antigues, a few miles south of Ardres.

St. Inglevert was located on high ground about six miles southwest of Calais. A British Handley-Page night bombing station was adjacent to it. While officers were quartered in an old chateau, the enlisted lived in standard Navy-type housing.

La Frene, near Ardres, served Marines who used DH-4s and DH-9s for day bombing.

Oye, near Gravelines, was headquarters for Captain Cunningham. It was being developed, yet at the end of the war it had hangars but no planes.

Campagne, 4 and a half miles south of Calais, was used for night bombing.

Guines, seven miles south of Calais, was used as an advanced repair base and contained 360 officers and men.

Commanding the Northern Bombing Group was Capt. D. C. Hanrahan, USN, who served under the command of the British vice admiral commanding at Dover.

The operations of the Northern Bombing Group were hampered not only by the lack of planes but by the especially poor quality of the Italian Caproni. The first was flown from Furino, Italy, by American personnel on 11 August 1918. While they were used for a raid against Ostend on 15 August, that they survived was a miracle because of their extraordinarily unreliable Fiat engines. With Handley-Pages very difficult to obtain, American pilots helped the RAF in their raids.

Active operations by the American squadrons did not begin until 13 October 1918. Their major objective was the German submarine pens in Belgium. When the Germans abandoned these under Allied military pressure, the Northern Bombing Group hit railroads, canal locks, supply and ammunition depots, and aerodromes. By 27 October the Northern Bombing Group was preparing to move to Belgium. Before the Armistice, one squadron had advanced to Knessalare and two night squadrons to Mari Alta, and the seaplane station at Dunkirk was being transferred to the mole at Zeebrugge. Following the Armistice the American squadrons returned to British bases before being decommissioned. Eastleigh was not closed down until 27 May 1919, and many of the materials there, at Dunkirk, which was closed down on 1 January 1919, and at the other French fields were given to Herbert Hoover for Belgian relief.

BIBLIOGRAPHY

A. "Summary of Activities of U.S. Naval Forces Operating in European Waters," 23 December 1918 (Washington: Naval Historical Center, Operational Archives Branch); U.S. Navy, Bureau of Yards and Docks, *Activities of the Bureau of Yards and Docks, Navy Department, in the World War 1917-1918* (Washington: GPO, 1921), pp. 395-416; Bureau of Aeronautics, "World War II Administrative History," 20 vols. (Washington: Bureau of Aeronautics, 8 November 1957), Vol. XI:171-185.

B. Archibald D. Turnbull and Clifford L. Lord, *History of United States Naval Aviation* (New Haven: Yale University Press, 1949); *United States Naval Aviation 1910-1960*. Prepared at the direction of the Deputy Chief of Naval Operations (Air) and Chief of the Bureau of Naval Weapons (Washington: GPO, 1960).

Y

YOKOSUKA, JAPAN, U.S. NAVAL BASE, 1945– Yokosuka Naval Base is located at 35°17′N., 139°40′E., approximately forty miles southwest of the Japanese capital, Tokyo. It is the principal U.S. Navy base in the Western Pacific, with more than twenty tenant commands. As the homeport of the Seventh Fleet, the base provides administrative, logistic, communications, medical, and ship repair support for the ships and men of that fleet.

Long before the first American forces occupied Yokosuka Naval Base on 30 August 1945, it had become the premier naval station of the Imperial Japanese Navy. Ironically, the idea for its establishment was born just eight-five years earlier in the United States. Oguri Kozukenosuke, a member of the Japanese mission sent to Washington in 1860 to exchange ratifications of a new treaty of friendship and commerce, was strongly impressed by what he saw in American Atlantic ports. Returning home convinced that Japan must have a modern navy, he became finance minister and pressed the shogun's government to build a shipyard on Tokyo Bay. Five years later, in 1865, contracts were signed with French engineers to build an iron and steel foundry and dry dock at Yokosuka.

That agreement set the pattern for Yokosuka's growth over the next half century. Progress was uneven, and Japanese naval officials repeatedly turned to foreign experts for technical assistance in building both the base and the fleet it would serve. It took four years to complete the first dry dock, and four more passed before the hybrid steam- and sail-powered *Seiki* was completed. In 1878 workers began building a third dry dock. But Imperial Japanese Navy leaders were not satisfied with the progress being made. In 1883 they brought two English ship architects to the base to provide appropriate advice; the fruits of their labors slid down the ways in 1890, when the *Yaeyama*, Japan's first all-steel warship (powered by British engines), was launched. By that time, German ordnance experts had also been summoned to improve weapons manufacture and storage on the base.

For the first two decades of its existence, Yokosuka was administratively subordinate to Tokai District Headquarters in Yokohama. In 1886, however, it became headquarters of the first naval district. That change ushered in diversification of its functions. A branch of the naval academy, a torpedo testing facility, and a naval hospital were established. In 1889 the Imperial Marines arrived, and a naval weapons testing station was added four years later. The surge of popular support for naval expansion that accompanied the Sino-Japanese (1894-1895) and Russo-Japanese (1904-1905) wars provided funds for more growth and innovation. Yokosuka's workers built many of the ships of the so-called six-six fleet, the nucleus of which was six battleships and six cruisers, approved after Japan's war with China. By 1905 they were assembling the Imperial Navy's first submarine—an American designed boat. In 1912 Yokosuka became a seaplane base, and four years later a permanent naval air group was established there. Eager to profit from the European powers' experience in World War I, Japanese navy officials in 1921 brought British instructors to Yokosuka to train pilots for landbased aircraft.

The launching of the *Hosho*, the world's first true aircraft carrier, in 1922 marked the end of Yokosuka's dependence on foreign expertise. Over the next two decades the base grew into a center for independent innovation as well as unprecedented naval construction. Within the base, a sixth dry dock, designed to accommodate vessels of 80,000 tons' displacement (a volume greater than that of any ship in existence) was completed. Laboring behind a high wall that shielded their endeavors from the eyes of ordinary citizens and foreign spies, Yokosuka's huge work force in 1937 laid down the carrier *Shokaku*, the first to be equipped with sonar. They also built the *Shinano*, intended to be the world's largest battleship, then redesigned it as a carrier. That behemoth was sunk by an American submarine only nineteen days after they finished their work. Innovators within the Technical Area Arsenal produced the so-called baka-bomb, a jet-propelled suicide aircraft used with devastating effect during the last days of the Pacific War. By the time it was drawing to a close, Yokosuka's engineers were experimenting with turbo-jet and ram-rocket forms of propulsion and had begun testing a twin turbo-jet aircraft intended for kamikaze use.

Technical growth demanded physical expansion. By 1941 Yokosuka had acquired a submarine base. Satellite housing and weapons storage facilities were built on the far side of the Miura peninsula, and Yokosuka had administrative control over naval aviation stations across Tokyo Bay in Ibaraki and Chiba prefectures. The work force at the Oppama Naval Air Station alone mushroomed to some 18,000. By 1944 7,000 more workers had completed an extensive network of caves, designed to provide protection from air attack for Yokosuka's many commands. A year later American planes bombed the base three times. But despite the damage done, it remained the most modern center for naval construction and innovation in all Asia.

When elements of the Sixth Marine Division came ashore at Yokosuka in August 1945, neither they nor their masters in Washington had any intention of making it an American naval base. The occupiers' immediate mission was to destroy facilities like Yokosuka from which Japan might again wage war. Naval planners in Washington saw no particular need for a base in Japan. Their thoughts focused instead on retaining control of the mid- and western Pacific islands that had been seized along the road to Tokyo. Deterrence from a distance, together with disarmament, would keep the foe just defeated in check.

Five years later, on the eve of war in Korea, American policy had completely reversed itself. Now admirals and diplomats agreed that the United States must be assured control or, at the very least, use of the Yokosuka base. That shift came about for several reasons. First, in April 1946 Yokosuka gained an energetic and shrewd naval advocate in the person of its third American commander, Capt. Benton W. Decker. He very quickly recognized the base's potential utility to the fleet: it provided modern facilities and cheap labor in an area likely to be of continuing concern to the Navy. Moreover, Decker and his able wife sensed that Yokosuka had political and diplomatic as well as naval value. Rebuilt, democratized, and even Christianized, it could become a cornerstone for the restoration of Japanese-American friendship. Thus Decker seized every opportunity to tout Yokosuka's value, briefing high-ranking visitors such as Chief of Naval Operations Louis Denfeld and entertaining journalists who educated their readers on the base's importance.

Second, Washington's strategic perspectives changed as the Cold War confrontation with the Soviet Union developed. By mid-1947 American policy planners recognized that the United States must not simply dominate Japan but rather deny it to Russian control. At first diplomats and even some naval officers thought that objective could be accomplished by building air and naval bases on Okinawa (q.v.). Sober second thoughts about that island's typhoons and the difficulties of getting Congress to fund base construction made that idea less attractive. More important, evolving strategic plans for global war gave Japan new importance. With bases on the Chinese mainland lost during the revolution there, planners now envisaged making air and naval attacks on the Soviet Union in East Asia as well as in Europe and the Middle East. Secure and developed bases for the fleet in Japan thus became essential to the U.S. Navy.

Finally, Yokosuka appealed to both American and Japanese political leaders' sense of economy. As Captain Decker pointed out, Washington paid only slightly more than half of the base's operating costs. Holding on to an asset of that sort amid all the criticism of his "loss" of China to communism made good sense to President Harry S. Truman. It also set in motion negotiations for peace with Japan that would assure Yokosuka's retention. In those talks, Japanese Prime Minister Yoshida Shigeru and his advisors came to recognize the importance of the American naval presence at Yokosuka for their nation. Japanese naval officers saw the base as a way of assuring access to American assistance in rearmament. The prime minister, by contrast, accepted a prolonged U.S. Navy presence at Yokosuka as a means of resisting Washington's pressures for quick, expensive, and potentially politically dangerous rearmament. For him, the cost of bases like Yokosuka was far lower than the risks of rearmament.

The peace and security treaties which would assure continued American presence at Yokosuka were not signed until September 1951. By that time, however, the base had proven in fact the value that Captain Decker had proclaimed in prospect. The outbreak of war in Korea in June 1950 transformed Yokosuka into a major forward operating base for the fleet. The Seventh Fleet doubled its carriers within six months, tripled them within a year, and by January 1952 reached the semipermanent level of four. This growth demanded that Yokosuka expand rapidly to meet the needs of hordes of visitors en route to or from the war in Korea. So it did. During the first sixty days of the war, Ship Repair Facility workers reactivated nine of twenty-seven Lend-Lease frigates returned by the Soviet Union. Over the longer term, the base would provide 85 percent of the repair, maintenance, and resupply of ships that fought in the war. Yokosuka also became an important naval personnel processing center. This required establishment of a receiving station, augmentation of berthing space for officers and men, and reclamation of lands previously turned back to the Japanese government or private use. Growth also demanded administrative streamlining of tenant command activities and of the command structure. In December 1952, following conclusion of an administrative agreement with Japan on the operation of American bases, Commander Naval Forces Far East (later, Japan) shifted his headquarters from Tokyo to Yokosuka.

The Korean War emergency ended in 1953 with the conclusion of a truce. Yet, during the decade between that agreement and the 1964 Tonkin Gulf incident in Vietnam, Yokosuka experienced changes that enhanced its importance to the U.S. Navy. The return of peace did not bring reversion to prewar levels and patterns of base operations. Continued tension on the Korean peninsula, the omnipresent threat of conflict in the Taiwan Strait, and war and crisis in Southeast Asia produced a fundamental shift in carrier deployment patterns. In every year save one of the post-Korean War decade, more carriers were assigned to the Pacific than to the Atlantic and Mediterranean combined. Yokosuka had to service ships from four carrier task groups that patrolled East Asian waters from Japan south to Singapore. Their presence demanded retaining command personnel strengths and streamlining of base operations. In addition, new conglomerate commands, such as Naval Communications Station Japan, were brought together from units once scattered throughout the Japanese islands.

During the post-Korea decade, the framework that would assure continued American use of the Japanese-built base was also strengthened. Yokosuka became the vital link between the U.S. Navy and the growing Japanese Maritime Self-Defense Force (JMSDF). In 1958 the two navies signed the first joint use agreement for American naval base facilities in Japan. While more senior officers cooperated with the JMSDF Staff College, junior officers helped cadets at the newly established Defense College to improve their English. At the highest levels of government, the United States-Japan Security Treaty was revised in 1960, establishing a binational security committee to deal with base problems. Locally, skillful management of civil-naval relations helped strengthen awareness of the base's importance for Japanese and Americans alike. A film entitled *Pigs and*

Battleships lamenting the social impact of the American presence in Yokosuka was released in 1961. But by that time the base had become a vital force in the city's economic life. Civilian employment, which had doubled during the Korean War, remained high; the Ship Repair Facility alone employed almost 1 percent of Yokosuka's population. Give and take marked both labor and property negotiations. Thus the Japanese reversed an initial American decision to release hundreds of base workers, and the base commander cheerfully returned excess property, including the Tadodai residence occupied by his predecessors since 1913.

In 1964 the Yokosuka City Assembly passed a resolution calling for return of the Oppama naval air facility to Japanese use. That action symbolized in many ways the impact of the Vietnam War on the Yokosuka base. The war in Southeast Asia did not dramatically alter the pattern or intensity of base usage to the degree that the Korean War had. To be sure, more ships had to be replenished as the number of Seventh Fleet carriers rose from four to seven before leveling off again. The Ship Repair Facility workload climbed once again, reaching over 800 vessels in 1967. The base hospital provided advanced surgical techniques and much-needed rest to those wounded in Vietnam. But this time Yokosuka was much more a rear support than a forward combat action-oriented base.

Nonetheless, the Vietnam era witnessed fundamental shifts in the terms of the U.S. Navy's usage of Yokosuka. At first glance, these might seem to have been politically caused, arising from Japan's chariness of the conflict in Southeast Asia and her fear of being drawn into it. In fact, political protests at Yokosuka during the decade between the 1965 attack on Pleiku and the 1975 fall of Saigon occurred only twice. The first, in February 1968, brought 2,000 students and workers to oppose the arrival of the nuclear submarine *Queenfish*; the second was prompted by the arrival of the USS *Midway* five and a half years later. What lay behind these events was not the war thousands of miles away but rather popular concern lest the Japanese government compromise or abandon the so-called three nonnuclear principles. The public rejected the manufacture, import, or transit of nuclear weapons; and thousands demonstrated at Sasebo (q.v.) when the nuclear-powered carrier *Enterprise* arrived. But these feelings had little impact on base operations at Yokosuka. More and more nuclear-powered ships visited the port, their numbers peaking in 1971-1973 before stabilizing at a level four times greater than that of the pre-Vietnam War era.

The taproots of change at Yokosuka were fundamentally economic. On the one hand, Japan's rapid economic growth fostered a climate of entrepreneurship that produced new employment opportunities and pushed land values sky high. These trends intensified local pressures for reduction of the base's area. On the other hand, skyrocketing costs of American defense worldwide prompted reconsideration in Washington of base policy around the globe. By late 1968 the United States announced its intention to reduce base facilities in Japan by one-third. The new Republican Secretary of Defense, Melvin Laird, insisted early in 1969 that $3 billion be cut from the defense budget. His demand coincided with the logic of the Nixon Doctrine, proclaimed almost simultaneously, which asked allies like Japan to provide more for their own defense. The result was negotiations with Tokyo, which by December 1970 produced agreement to shift most of Yokosuka's functions to Sasebo. Commander Seventh Fleet, his ships and men, dependents and ancillary tenant commands would all move to that distant Kyushu port, far from the Japanese public's eye. The Ship Repair Facility, gem of the base, would revert to Japanese control, and thousands of base employees would lose their jobs.

This drastic change proved simply too much for Japanese and Americans alike. Labor union leaders protested the planned dismissals, and the Navy, in the person of then Commander in Chief of the Pacific (CINCPAC) John S. "Jocko" McCain, had never been happy with the scheme. In January 1971, Adm. Thomas Moorer, Chairman of the Joint Chiefs of Staff, came to Tokyo for talks with Japanese Prime Minister Sato Eisaku. The admiral shrewdly pointed out that reduced U.S. Navy presence in the Japanese home islands might have to be compensated for by an expansion of base operations in Okinawa—something which Sato desperately wanted to avoid. By March 1971 the Japanese Government reluctantly announced postponement of the changes originally set for June. This marked the beginning of a retreat from, and indeed reversal of, the December 1970 decisions. By the end of 1971, the Pentagon, too, had changed its mind. Now Washington hoped to make Yokosuka one of the four major overseas naval bases at which carrier task forces would be homeported. By stationing a ship there for three years rather than six months and moving dependents along with the crew, Pentagon planners hoped to cut costs and boost morale.

It was October 1973 before the *Midway*, the embodiment of this new deployment scheme, arrived amid protests at Yokosuka. But the noise and media coverage mattered little. Negotiations had already yielded agreement on three basic points. First, housing and other ancillary facilities physically separate from the main base at Yokosuka would gradually be returned. Second, there would be greater joint use of facilities, in particular the drydocks, on the base. This satisfied Japanese desires for commercial and Maritime Self Defense Forces use. It also corresponded with the changing needs of the Seventh Fleet. During the latter half of the 1970's, the number of ships served by Fleet Activities declined and American use of the drydocks fell from nearly 50 to less than 40 percent of capacity. Third, more Americans would have to make more intense use of less space. By 1976 more than 80 percent of U.S. Navy personnel in Japan were assigned to commands in Yokohama or Yokosuka and the first of six new high rise apartments designed to accommodate them and their dependents was nearing completion on the base.

These changes demonstrated the resiliency of the American-Japanese naval relationship as it had evolved at Yokosuka. Occupation by the victor of the vanquished's finest naval facility had metamorphosed into mutually beneficial joint use of the base. Yokosuka served the fleet and contributed to the economic well-being of the surrounding city's people. Indeed, it became a bridge that reduced the distance across the pacific. More U.S. Navy men visited Yokosuka than perhaps any other foreign port during its nearly forty years under American control; and as former base commander Rear Adm. Kemp Tolley recently pointed out, every U.S. Navy officer is likely to visit the base sometime during his career. The hundreds of thousands of Americans who visited Yokosuka brought with them tokens of their culture, ranging in complexity from popular music to management systems to religious and political values, that in subtle ways changed the life of the Japanese people. They carried home not only spouses and souvenirs but also awareness of and openness to a culture and way of life radically different from their own. In so doing, Yokosuka's naval ambassadors helped solidify the political and economic as well as naval basis for American-Japanese friendship.

What, then, does the future hold for the U.S. Navy Base at Yokosuka? The foundations for its use well into the next century have been laid during the past forty years. But at the same time forces just beyond the horizon threaten to change, if not terminate, the Navy's use of the base. Some of those forces are political. As Washington presses Tokyo to assume more of the burden of Japan's naval defense, Japanese political leaders are likely to foster nationalism that will eventually demand greater control over more, if not all, of the base. The time might well come when Seventh Fleet ships will be serviced by Japanese rather than American-controlled port facilities. Other forces for change are strategic. Crises elsewhere have already drawn the Seventh Fleet down to its lowest level in thirty years; and in 1983 a scheduled port visit by the refurbished USS *New Jersey* was cancelled so that she might proceed to troubled Central American waters. Naval thinkers have also begun to reconsider Pacific strategy. Given the decreasing likelihood that the United States will once again have to project the kind of amphibious power onto the East Asian mainland that it has during the past thirty years, submarines less in need of substantial shore support than carrier task forces might better serve American naval needs in the Western Pacific.

Changing economic and political forces might also alter radically the American naval presence at Yokosuka. The cost advantages that Captain Decker pointed out more than three decades ago have long since vanished. In 1982 operating Commander Fleet Activities Yokosuka alone cost four times what it had a decade earlier. Ship repair work of comparable quality can now be obtained at less cost in other Asian ports. Budgeteers in Washington might well find it expedient to reduce still further American operations on the base. Finally, U.S. civilian and naval leaders might, through indifference, ignorance, or insensitivity, threaten the delicate network of Japanese-American cooperation that makes use of Yokosuka possible. The absence of overt controversy over the base has hidden its importance from congressional eyes. In 1983 the Navy and State departments planned a port visit by the *New Jersey* for August, when sensitivity to nuclear matters peaks annually in Japan. Mass demonstrations were being organized, only to be averted by a sudden change in the ship's deployment. As the United

States and Japan become competitors as well as allies, it seems all the more important that naval leaders on both sides of the Pacific work to ensure continued, mutually beneficial use of the Yokosuka Naval Base.

See also Far Eastern U.S. Naval Bases to 1898.

BIBLIOGRAPHY

A. "Carriers with the Seventh Fleet 1950-1964 Study" (Washington: Naval Historical Center: Operational Archives Branch); Commander Fleet Activities Yokosuka, "Command Histories," 1975-1980 (Washington: Naval Historical Center, Operational Archives Branch); Commander Fleet Activities Yokosuka to the writer, 3 Sept. 1982; Radio Japan broadcasts, 18, 22 July 1983.

B. C. Ray Stokes and Tad Darling "Yokosuka Naval Air Base and Japanese Naval Aviation," U.S. Naval Institute *Proceedings* 74 (Mar. 1948):339-42; Desmond P. Wilson, Jr., *Evolution of the Attack Aircraft Carrier: A Case Study in Technology and Strategy* (Cambridge, Mass.: MIT Institute of Naval Studies, 1965); Yokosuka Hyakunen shi hēnsan iinkai, ed., *Yokosuka Hyakunen shi [A Centennial History of Yokosuka]* (Yokosuka: Yokosuka City Office, 1965); Elmo R. Zumwalt, Jr., *On Watch* (New York: Quandrangle Books, 1976); Roger Dingman, "Strategic Planning and the Policy Process: American Plans for War in East Asia, 1945-1950," *U.S. Naval War College Review* 32 (Nov.-Dec. 1979):4-21; *New York Times*, 22 Jan., 18 Feb., 15 May, 24 Dec. 1968, 17 Jan., 9 Feb., 16 Dec. 1971, 1 Oct. 1973; Roger Dingman, "The U.S. Navy and the Cold War: The Japan Case," in Craig L. Sumonds, ed., *New Aspects of Naval History* (Annapolis, Md.: Naval Institute Press, 1981), pp. 291-312: Takei Hideo, *Kanagawa ken no Beigun Kichi* [American Bases in Kanagawa Prefecture] (Yokohama: Kanagawa ken shogai bu, 1982).

ROGER DINGMAN

Z

ZAMBOANGA FIELD, MINDANAO, PHILIPPINE ISLANDS, U.S. FLEET AIR BASE, 1945 Zamboanga is located at the extreme southwestern tip of the island of Mindanao, the largest southern island of the Philippines. There, on 15 May 1945, the U.S. Navy established a naval air facility and fleet air base to serve the Naval Air Transport Service and aircraft engaged in reconnaissance; a section base; PT Base No. 17; and a port director's office. The war ended on 2 September 1945, and the facilities were disestablished on 26 December 1945.

BIBLIOGRAPHY

A. ''Monograph Histories of U.S. Naval Overseas Bases. Vol. II. Pacific Area'' (Washington: Naval Historical Center, Operational Archives Branch); Summary Cards (Washington, D.C., Navy Yard: Naval Aviation History Office.

APPENDIXES

APPENDIX A

Subject Listing of Bases

ADVANCE AMPHIBIOUS TRAINING BASES

North Africa, U.S. Naval Advance Section and Advance Amphibious Training Bases
United Kingdom, U.S. Naval Advanced Training Bases

ADVANCED FLEET ANCHORAGES

Eniwetok Atoll, Marshall Islands
Long Xuyen, Republic of Vietnam
Majuro, Marshall Islands
Ulithi Lagoon, Caroline Islands

ADVANCE SUBMARINE BASE

Albany, Australia

HEADQUARTERS, COMMANDER NAVAL FORCES NORTHWEST AFRICAN WATERS, AND HEADQUARTERS, ALLIED FORCES SOUTH (NATO)

Naples, Italy

MARINE CORPS AIR FACILITIES

Charlotte Amalie, Virgin Islands
Lindbergh Bay, Virgin Islands

MINE FORCES AND BASES

Invergordon, Scotland
Inverness, Scotland

NAVAL ACTIVITIES

Ie Shima, Okinawa, Ryukyu Islands
Inchon, Korea
Pusan, Korea
Sasebo, Japan

NAVAL ADVANCE BASES

Aitape, New Guinea
Balikpapan, Dutch Borneo

Biak, Dutch New Guinea
Brunei Bay, British North Borneo
Buna, New Guinea
Cairns, Australia
Chorrera, Republic of Panama
Darwin, Australia
Emirau, New Ireland, New Guinea
Finchhafen, New Guinea
Freetown, Sierra Leone
Fremantle-Perth, Australia
Funafuti, Ellice Islands
Go Dau Ha, Republic of Vietnam
Green Island, Solomon Islands
Guadalcanal, Solomon Islands
Hollandia, Dutch New Guinea
Kiriwina Island, New Guinea
Mackay, Australia
Madang-Alexishafen, Dutch New Guinea
Merauke, Dutch New Guinea
Milne Bay, Dutch New Guinea
Nanomea, Ellice Islands
New Georgia, Solomon Islands
Palm Island, Australia
Port Moresby, New Guinea
Port Stephens, New South Wales, Australia
Recife, Brazil
Russell Islands, Solomon Islands
Saidor, New Guinea
Sansapor, Dutch New Guinea
Surabaya, Java
Sydney, Australia
Thursday Island, Australia
Tjilatjap, Netherlands East Indies
Torokina, Bougainville, Solomon Islands
Townsville, Australia
Treasury Islands, Solomon Islands
Tufi, Papua
Tulagi, Florida Island, Solomon Islands
Vella Lavella, Solomon Islands
Wakde, Dutch New Guinea
Wellington, New Zealand
Woodlark Island, Papua

NAVAL ADVANCED AIR BASE

Nukufetau, Ellice Islands

NAVAL ADVANCED TACTICAL SUPPORT BASES

Ben Keo, Republic of Vietnam
Hiep Hoa, Republic of Vietnam

Moc Hoa, Republic of Vietnam
Phu Cuong, Republic of Vietnam
Phuoc Xuyen, Republic of Vietnam
Tan An, Republic of Vietnam
Thuyen Nhon, Republic of Vietnam
Tra Cu, Republic of Vietnam

NAVAL AIR BASES

Amapa, Brazil
Antarctica
Camocin, Brazil
Eniwetok Atoll, Marshall Islands
Iwo Jima
Jamaica, British West Indies
Kwajelein, Marshall Islands
Pauillac, France
Saipan, Mariana Islands
Wake Island

NAVAL AIR FACILITIES

Atsugi, Japan
Bahia, Brazil
Barranquilla, Colombia
Belem, Brazil
Caravellas, Brazil
Dunkeswell, England
Essequibo, British Guiana
Fonseca, Nicaragua
Fortaleza, Brazil
French Frigate Shoals
Galeao, Brazil
Georgetown, British Guiana
Igarape Assu, Brazil
La Fe, Cuba
Lajes, Azores Islands, Portugal
Maceio, Brazil
Majuro, Marshall Islands
Mildenhall, Suffolk, England
Misawa, Japan
Natal, Brazil
Salinas, Ecuador
San Julian, Cuba
Santa Fe, Isle of Pines, Cuba
South Seymour, Galapagos Islands, Ecuador

NAVAL AIR STATIONS

Almirante, Panama
Antarctica

Antigua, British West Indies
Apamama Atoll
Arcachon, France
Argentia, Newfoundland
Berehaven, Ireland
Bermuda
Coco Solo, Panama Canal Zone
Fromentine, France
Georgetown, British Guiana
Guipavas, France
Gujan, France
Ile Tudy, France
Killingholme, England
L'Aber Vrach, France
La Pallice, France (LTA)
La Trinite, France (LTA)
Le Croisic, France
Lough Foyle, Ireland
Mandinga, Republic of Panama (LTA)
Midway Islands
Moutchic-Lacanau, France
Paimboeuf, France
Palmyra Island
Port Lyautey, French Morocco
Porto Corsini, Italy
Queenstown, Ireland
Rochefort, France
St. Lucia, British West Indies
St. Trojan, France
Sigonella, Catania, Sicily
Tarawa Atoll, Gilbert Islands
Tinian, Mariana Islands
Wexford, Ireland
Whiddy Island, Ireland
World War I, U.S. Northern Bombing Group Bases in England and France
World War I Overseas Naval Air Stations

NAVAL AIR TRANSPORTATION SERVICE BASES

Aitutaki, South Cook Islands
Tongareva, Northern Cook Islands

NAVAL AMPHIBIOUS BASE

Vicarage Barracks, Plymouth, Devon, England

NAVAL AUXILIARY AIR FACILITIES

Almirante, Panama
Atsugi, Japan
Corinto, Nicaragua

Lajes, Azores Islands, Portugal
Puerto Castillo, Honduras

NAVAL AUXILIARY AIR STATION

Almirante, Panama

NAVAL BASES

Algiers, Algeria
Azores Islands, Portugal
Bantry Bay, Ireland
Bassens, France
Bermuda
Bordeaux, France
Brest, France
Cam Ranh Bay, Republic of Vietnam
Cardiff, Wales
Casablanca, French Morocco
Chefoo, Korea
Constantinople, Turkey
Corfu, Greece
Diego Garcia Island, Indian Ocean
Gibraltar
Greenland. *See* Naval Facilities
Guantánamo Bay, Cuba
Hong Kong, China
Lisbon, Portugal
Lorient, France
Macao, China
Madisonville, Massachusetts Bay, Marquesas Islands
Majuro, Marshall Islands
Malta
Manila, Philippine Islands
Nagasaki, Japan
Naha, Okinawa
North Africa
Oran, Algeria
Paramaribo, Surinam, Dutch Guiana
Pisa, Italy
Port Hamilton, Korea
Port Lloyd, Bonin Islands
Port Mahon, Minorca, Spain
Puerto Castillo, Honduras
Queenstown, Ireland
Recife, Brazil
Roosevelt Roads, Puerto Rico
Rota, Spain
St. Thomas, Virgin Islands
Shanghai, China

Singapore, Malaya
Spezia, Italy
Tinian, Mariana Islands
Veracruz, Mexico
Villefranche, France
United Kingdom, World War II
Yokosuka, Japan

NAVAL COMBAT AND LOGISTIC BASE

Cat Lo, Republic of Vietnam

NAVAL COMBAT BASE

Chau Doc, Republic of Vietnam

NAVAL FACILITIES

Bluie East 1, Torgilsbu, Greenland
Bluie East 2, Ikateq, Greenland
Bluie East 3, Gurreholm, Greenland
Bluie East 4, Ella Island, Greenland
Bluie East 5, Eskimonaes, Greenland
Bluie West 1, Narssarssuaq, Greenland
Bluie West 2, Kipisaka, Greenland
Bluie West 3, Simiutak, Island, Greenland
Bluie West 4, Faeringhavn, Greenland
Bluie West 5, Godhavn, Greenland
Bluie West 6, Thule, Greenland
Bluie West 7, Gronnedal, Greenland
Bluie West 8, Sondre Stromfjord, Greenland
Vinh Long, Republic of Vietnam

NAVAL FLEET ACTIVITY

Sasebo, Japan

NAVAL HOSPITAL/NAVAL REGIONAL MEDICAL CENTER

Canacao, Manila, Philippine Islands

NAVAL INTERMEDIATE SUPPORT BASES

Cat Lai, Republic of Vietnam
Long Phu, Republic of Vietnam
Rach Soi, Republic of Vietnam
Thuon An, Republic of Vietnam

NAVAL LOGISTIC INSTALLATION

Cho Moi, Republic of Vietnam

NAVAL MOBILE FACILITY

Nam Can, Republic of Vietnam

NAVAL OPERATING BASES

Auckland, New Zealand
Balboa, Panama Canal Zone
Bermuda
Brisbane, Australia
Casablanca, French Morocco
Curacao/Aruba, Netherlands West Indies
Efate, New Hebrides
Eniwetok Atoll, Marshall Islands
Espiritu Santo, New Hebrides Islands
Guam, Mariana Islands
Kwajalein, Marshall Islands
Londonderry, Ireland
Manus, Admiralty Islands
Noumea, New Caledonia
Okinawa, Ryukyu Islands
Oran, Algeria
Palermo, Sicily
Rosneath, Scotland
Saipan, Mariana Islands
Salerno, Italy
Trinidad, British West Indies

NAVAL OPERATING FACILITIES

Bahia, Brazil
Florianopolis, Brazil

NAVAL OPERATING STATION

Nha Trang, Republic of Vietnam

NAVAL RADIO AND COMMUNICATIONS FACILITIES

Balboa, Panama Canal Zone
Colon, Panama Canal Zone
Croix D'Hins, France, Lafayette Radio Station

NAVAL RIVERINE OPERATIONAL BASE

Song Ong Doc, Republic of Vietnam

NAVAL RIVER PATROL BASE

Tan Chau, Republic of Vietnam

NAVAL SECTION BASES

Dakar, French Morocco
Exmouth Gulf, Australia
Fedala, French Morocco
Safi, French Morocco
St. Thomas, Virgin Islands

NAVAL SECURITY GROUP

Edzell, Scotland

NAVAL STATIONS

Azores
Balboa, Panama Canal Zone
Bora Bora, Society Islands
Guam, Mariana Islands
Keflavik, Iceland
Sangley Point, Luzon, Philippine Islands
San Juan, Puerto Rico
Taboga Island, Panama Canal Zone
Tongatabu Island
Tutuila, Samoa

NAVAL SUPPORT ACTIVITIES

An Thoi, Republic of Vietnam
Can Tho-Bin Thuy, Republic of Vietnam
Chu Lai, Republic of Vietnam
Cua Viet, Republic of Vietnam
Danang, Republic of Vietnam
Dong Ha, Republic of Vietnam
Dong Tam, Republic of Vietnam
Hue-Tan Phu Bai, Republic of Vietnam
My Tho, Republic of Vietnam
Nha Be, Republic of Vietnam
Qui Nhon, Republic of Vietnam
Sa Dec, Republic of Vietnam
Sa Huynh, Republic of Vietnam
Saigon, Republic of Vietnam
Vung Tau, Republic of Vietnam

NAVAL SUPPORT BASE

Ben Luc, Republic of Vietnam

NAVAL SUPPORT OFFICE

La Maddalena, Sardinia

NAVAL UNDERWATER SYSTEMS CENTER

Tudor Hill Laboratory, Bermuda

NORTHERN BOMBING GROUP BASES

See World War I, Overseas Naval Air Stations

PATROL BOAT BASE

Hoi An, Republic of Vietnam

POST-WORLD WAR II DEFENSE ARRANGEMENTS WITH THE REPUBLIC OF PANAMA

RIVER FORCES OPERATING BASES

Kien An, Republic of Vietnam
Long Binh, Republic of Vietnam

RIVER PATROL BOAT STAGING AREA

Ha Tien, Republic of Vietnam

SUBMARINE BASE

Coco Solo, Panama Canal Zone

TENANT PORT

Monrovia, Liberia

APPENDIX B

Overseas U.S. Naval Bases by Geographic Area

AFRICA

Algiers, Algeria, Naval Base
Arzew, Algeria, Naval Advance Amphibious Training Base
Beni-Saf, Algeria, Naval Advance Amphibious Training Base
Bizerte, Tunisia, Naval Advance Amphibious Training Base
Casablanca, French Morocco, Naval Operating Base
Cherchel, Algeria, Naval Advance Amphibious Training Base
Dakar, French Morocco, Naval Section Base
Dellys, Algeria, Naval Advance Amphibious Training Base
Fedala, French Morocco, Naval Section Base
Ferryville, Tunisia, Advance Amphibious Training Base
Freetown, Sierra Leone, Naval Advance Base
La Goulette, Tunisia, Naval Advance Amphibious Training Base
Mers-El-Kebir, Algeria, Naval Advance Amphibious Training Base
Monrovia, Liberia, Naval Tenant Port
Mostaganem, Algeria, Naval Advance Amphibious Training Base
Nemours, Algeria, Naval Advance Amphibious Training Base
Oran, Algeria, Naval Operating Base
Port Lyautey, French Morocco, Naval Air Station
Safi, French Morocco, Naval Section Base
Tenes, Algeria, Naval Advance Amphibious Training Base
Tunis, Tunisia, Naval Advance Amphibious Training Base

ANTARCTICA

Amundsen Station
Byrd Station
Cape Crozier Station
Cape Hallett Coastal Station, Ross Sea
Christchurch, New Zealand, Antarctic Supply Base and U.S. Naval Technical Communications Group
Knox Coastal Station
Lake Bonney
Little America

McMurdo Sound
Palmer Station
Plateau Station
South Pole Station
Siple Station
Weddell Sea Coastal Station
West Base, Little America

ARCTIC

Greenland

ATLANTIC OCEAN

Azores Islands
Bermuda
Keflavik, Iceland

CANADA

Argentia, Newfoundland
Halifax, Nova Scotia
Sydney, Cape Breton Island

CARIBBEAN

Antigua, British West Indies
Charlotte Amalie, Virgin Islands
Curacao/Aruba, Netherlands West Indies
Guantánamo Bay, Cuba
Jamaica, British West Indies
La Fe, Cuba
Lindbergh Bay, Virgin Islands
Roosevelt Roads, Puerto Rico
St. Lucia, British West Indies
San Juan, Puerto Rico
San Julian, Cuba
Santa Fe, Isle of Pines, Cuba
Trinidad, British West Indies
Vieques Island, Puerto Rico, U.S. Marine Corps Camp Garcia

CENTRAL AMERICA

Almirante, Panama
Balboa, Panama Canal Zone
Chorrera, Republic of Panama
Coco Solo, Panama Canal Zone
Corinto, Nicaragua
Farfan, Panama Canal Zone
Fonseca, Nicaragua
Gatun, Panama Canal Zone
Mandinga, Republic of Panama
Puerto Castillo, Honduras

Summit, Panama Canal Zone
Taboga Island, Panama Canal Zone

EUROPE

Antigues, France
Appledore, England
Arcachon, France
Bantry Bay, Ireland
Bassens, France
Berehaven, Ireland
Bordeaux, France
Bremerhaven, Germany
Brest, France
Calais (Oye), France
Campagne, France
Cardiff, Wales
Castletownbere, Ireland
Cherbourg, France
Constantinople, Turkey
Croix D'Hins, France
Deptford, England
Dunkeswell, England
Dunkirk, France
Eastleigh, England
Edzell, Scotland
Exeter, England
Falmouth, England
Fowey, England
Fromentine, France
Guines, France
Gujan, France
Holy Loch, Scotland
Ile Tudy, France
Invergordon, Scotland
Inverness, Scotland
Killingholme, England
L'Aber Vrach, France
La Frene, France
Lake Bolsena, Italy
Lake Pallice, France
Le Croisic, France
Lisbon, Portugal
Loch Erne, Ireland
Loch Ryan, Scotland
Londonderry, Ireland
Lorient, France
Moutchic-Lacanau, France
Naples, Italy

Oye (Calais), France
Paimboeuf, France
Palermo, Sicily
Pauillac, France
Pescara, Italy
Pisa, Italy
Poole, England
Portland-Weymouth, England
Porto Corsini, Italy
Queenstown, Ireland
Rochefort, France
Rosneath, Scotland
Rota, Spain
St. Mawes, England
St. Nazaire, France
St. Trojan, France
Salcombe, England
Salerno, Italy
Sangatte, France
Sigonella, Sicily
Southampton, England
Spezia, Italy
Teignmouth, England
Treguier, France
Vicarage Barracks, Plymouth, England
Villefranche, France
Wexford, Ireland
Whiddy Island, Ireland

FAR EAST

Atsugi, Japan
Chefoo, Korea
Hong Kong, China
Inchon, Korea
Iuakuni, Japan
Macao, China
Manila, Philippines
Misawa, Japan
Nagasaki, Japan
Okinawa, Ryukyu Islands
Port Hamilton, Korea
Port Lloyd, Bonin Islands
Pusan, Korea
Sasebo, Japan
Shanghai, China
Singapore, Malaya
Yokosuka, Japan

INDIAN OCEAN

Diego Garcia Island

LATIN AMERICA

Amapa, Brazil
Bahia, Brazil
Barranquilla, Colombia
Belem, Brazil
Callao, Peru
Camocim, Brazil
Caravellas, Brazil
Essequibo, British Guiana
Florianopolis, Brazil
Fortaleza, Brazil
Galeao, Brazil
Igarape Assu, Brazil
Maceio, Brazil
Natal, Brazil
Paramaribo, Surinam, Dutch Guiana
Recife, Brazil
Salinas, Ecuador
South Seymour, Galapagos Islands, Ecuador
Talara, Peru
Veracruz, Mexico

MEDITERRANEAN SEA

Corfu, Greece
Gibraltar
La Maddalena, Sardinia
Malta
Pisa, Italy
Spezia, Italy
Villefranche, France

PACIFIC OCEAN

Aitape, New Guinea
Aitutaki, South Cook Islands
Albany, Australia
Auckland, New Zealand
Biak, Dutch New Guinea
Bora Bora, Society Islands
Brisbane, Australia
Brunei Bay, British North Borneo
Buna, New Guinea
Cairns, Australia
Canton Island
Christchurch, New Zealand
Darwin, Australia

Efate, New Hebrides Islands
Emirau, New Ireland, New Guinea
Eniwetok Atoll, Marshall Islands
Espiritu Santo, New Hebrides Islands
Exmouth Gulf, Australia
Fremantle-Perth, Australia
French Frigate Shoals
Funafuti, Ellice Islands
Guadalcanal, Solomon Islands
Guam, Mariana Islands
Hollandia, Dutch New Guinea
Ie Shima, Ryukyu Islands
Iwo Jima, Volcano Island
Johnston Island
Kwajalein, Marshall Islands
Mackay, Australia
Madang-Alexishafen, Dutch New Guinea
Madisonville, Massachusetts Bay, Marquesas Islands
Majuro, Marshall Islands
Manus, Admiralty Islands
Merauke, Dutch New Guinea
Milne Bay, New Guinea
Morobe, New Guinea
Morotai, Netherlands East Indies
Nanomea, Ellice Islands
New Georgia, Solomon Islands
Noumea, New Caledonia
Nukufetua, Ellice Islands
Okinawa, Ryukyu Islands
Palm Island, Australia
Palmyra Island
Peleliu, Palau Islands
Port Moresby, New Guinea
Port Stephens, Australia
Russell Islands, Solomon Islands
Saidor, New Guinea
Saipan, Mariana Islands
Sansapor, Dutch New Guinea
Surabaya, Java
Sydney, Australia
Tarawa Atoll, Gilbert Islands
Thursday Island, Australia
Tinian, Mariana Islands
Tjilatjap, Netherlands East Indies
Tongareva, Northern Cook Islands
Tongatabu Island
Townsville, Australia
Treasury Islands, Solomon Islands

Tulagi, Florida Island, Solomon Islands
Tutuila, Samoa
Ulithi Atoll, Caroline Islands
Vella Lavella, Solomon Islands
Wakde, Dutch New Guinea
Wake Island
Woodlark Island, Papua

SOUTHEAST ASIA

An Thoi, Republic of Vietnam
Ben Keo, Republic of Vietnam
Ben Luc, Republic of Vietnam
Cam Ranh Bay, Republic of Vietnam
Canacao, or Bilibid Prison, Manila, Philippine Islands
Can Tho-Bin Thuy, Republic of Vietnam
Cat Lai, Republic of Vietnam
Cat Lo, Republic of Vietnam
Cavite, Luzon, Philippine Islands
Chau Doc, Republic of Vietnam
Cho Moi, Republic of Vietnam
Chu Lai, Republic of Vietnam
Cua Viet, Republic of Vietnam
Cubi Point, Luzon, Republic of the Philippines
Danang, Republic of Vietnam
Dong Ha, Republic of Vietnam
Dong Tam, Republic of Vietnam
Go Dau Ha, Republic of Vietnam
Ha Tien, Republic of Vietnam
Hiep Hoa, Republic of Vietnam
Hoi An, Republic of Vietnam
Hue-Tan My-Phu Bai, Republic of Vietnam
Kien An, Republic of Vietnam
Leyte, Republic of the Philippines
Lingayen, Luzon, Republic of the Philippines
Long Binh, Republic of Vietnam
Long Phu, Republic of Vietnam
Long Xuyen, Republic of Vietnam
Moc Hoa, Republic of Vietnam
My Tho, Republic of Vietnam
Nam Can, Republic of Vietnam
Nha Be, Republic of Vietnam
Nha Trang, Republic of Vietnam
Phu Cuong, Republic of Vietnam
Phuoc Xuyen, Republic of Vietnam
Qui Nhon, Republic of Vietnam
Rach Soi, Republic of Vietnam
Sa Dec, Republic of Vietnam
Sa Huynh, Republic of Vietnam

Saigon, Republic of Vietnam
Song Ong Doc, Republic of Vietnam
Subic Bay, Luzon, Republic of the Philippines
Tan An, Republic of Vietnam
Tan Chau, Republic of Vietnam
Thuan An, Republic of Vietnam
Thuyen Nhon, Republic of Vietnam
Tra Cu, Republic of Vietnam
Vinh Long, Republic of Vietnam
Vung Tau, Republic of Vietnam
Zamboanga Field, Mindinao, Philippine Islands

APPENDIX C

Time Line

This time line is offered to show the times and places the U.S. Navy chose to establish its continental and overseas naval and Marine Corps bases. It clearly shows how the demands for support during wars and the requirements of U.S. foreign policies in times of peace have dictated the employment of the various geographical locations.

1767

Norfolk, Va., Naval Shipyard

1775

Whitehall, N.Y., Naval Base

1776

Far Eastern U.S. Naval Bases: Hong Kong, Macao, Shanghai, and Singapore, China; Manila, Philippine Islands; Naha, Okinawa; Port Lloyd, Bonin Islands; Chefoo and Port Hamilton, Korea; Nagasaki, Yokohama, and Yokosuka, Japan

1800

Lisbon, Portugal, U.S. Naval Tenant Base

1800

Mediterranean, U.S. Naval Bases: Gibraltar, Malta, Pisa, Port Mahon, Spezia, Villefranche

1800

Boston, Mass., Navy Yard

1800

New York, N.Y., Navy Yard

1800

Portsmouth, N.H., Navy Yard

1801

Gibraltar, U.S. Naval Tenant Base;
Philadelphia, Pa., Navy Yard

1803

New Orleans, La., Naval Station

1812

Black Rock, N.Y., Ship Base and Storage Depot
Presque Isle (Erie), Pa., Shipyard and Base
Sackett's Harbor, N.Y., Shipyard and Base

1813

Madisonville, Massachusetts Bay, Marquesas Islands, U.S. Naval Base

1822

Key West, Fla., Naval Station and Naval Base

1825

Pensacola, Fla., Navy Yard

1830

District of Columbia, Naval Observatory

1836

Chelsea, Mass., Naval Hospital

1846

Monterey, Calif., Naval Port
San Pedro, Calif., Naval Operating Base
Veracruz, Mexico, U.S. Naval Base

1849

New Orleans, La., Naval Support Activity

1861

Newport, R.I., Naval Academy
Parris Island, S.C., Naval Station and Marine Corps Recruit Depot

1862

Mound City, Ill., Shipbuilding and Repair Base
New London, Conn., Naval Base, later Submarine Base

1864

Newport, R.I., Naval Hospital

1869

Goat Island, Newport, R.I., Naval Torpedo Station and Successor Commands

1883

Coasters Harbor Island, Newport, R.I., Naval Training Station and Its Successor Commands and Major Components

1884

Coasters Harbor Island, Newport, R.I., U.S. Naval War College

1885

Widow Island, Me., Naval Hospital and Sanitarium

1891

Puget Sound, Wash., Naval Shipyard

1896

San Francisco Bay, Yerba Buena Island, Naval Training Station

1898

Cavite, Luzon, Philippine Islands, U.S. Naval Base
Guam, Mariana Islands, U.S. Naval Station and Naval Operating Base
Guantánamo Bay, Cuba, U.S. Naval Base
San Juan, Puerto Rico, U.S. Naval Station
Subic Bay, Luzon, Philippine Islands, U.S. Naval Facilities

1900

Tutuila, Samoa, U.S. Naval Station

1901

Charleston, S.C., Naval Base

1902

East Lamoine, Me., Coaling Station

1903

Lake Bluff, Ill. Great Lakes Naval Training Station

1904

Tiburon, Calif., Naval Net Depot

1905

Panama Canal Zone, U.S. Naval Radio Stations

1909

Hingham, Mass., Naval Ammunition Depot

1911

Annapolis, Md., Naval Aviation Camp

1914

Keyport, Wash., Naval Torpedo Station
Pensacola, Fla., Naval Air Station, 1914
San Diego, Calif., Marine Corps Recruit Depot
Veracruz, Mexico, U.S. Naval Base

1917

Akron, Ohio, Lighter-Than-Air Station
Antigues, France, World War I U.S. Northern Bombing Group Base
Arcachon, France, U.S. Naval Air Station
Azores Islands, Portugal, U.S. Naval Base
Balboa, Panama Canal Zone, U.S. Naval Station
Bantry Bay, Ireland, U.S. Naval Air Station and Naval Base
Bassens, France, U.S. Naval Base
Bay Shore, Long Island, Naval Air Patrol Station
Berehaven, Ireland, U.S. Naval Air Station
Bordeaux, France, U.S. Naval Base
Brest, France, U.S. Naval Base and Naval Air Station
Brunswick, Ga., Naval Air Patrol Station
Calais (Oye), France, World War I U.S. Northern Bombing Group Base
Champagne, France, World War I U.S. Northern Bombing Group Base
Cape May, N.J., Naval Air Patrol Station
Cardiff, Wales, Great Britain, U.S. Naval Base
Chatham, Mass., Naval Air Patrol Station
Croix D'Hins, France, Lafayette Radio Station
Curtiss Exhibition School, Newport News, Va., Naval Air Patrol Station
District of Columbia, Anacostia Naval Air Station
Dunkirk, France, World War I U.S. Northern Bombing Group Base
East Greenwich, R.I., Naval Air Patrol Station
Eastleigh, England, U.S. Naval Air Station
Ediz Hook, Ore., Naval Air Patrol Station
Fromentine, France, U.S. Naval Air Station
Galveston, Tex., Naval Air Patrol Station
Gibraltar, U.S. Naval Tenant Base
Guines, France, World War I U.S. Northern Bombing Group Base
Guipavas, France, U.S. Naval Air Station
Gujan, France, U.S. Naval Air Station
Halifax, Nova Scotia, U.S. Naval Air Station
Il Tudy, France, U.S. Naval Air Station
Imperial Beach, Calif., Ream Field, Naval Air Station
Invergordon, Scotland, U.S. Naval Mine Force Base
Inverness, Scotland, U.S. Naval Mine Force Base
Key West, Fla., Naval Air Patrol Station
Killingholme, England, U.S. Naval Air Station
L'Aber Vrach, France, U.S. Naval Air Station
La Frene, France, World War I U.S. Northern Bombing Group Base
Lake Bolsena, Italy, U.S. Naval Air Station
La Pallice, France, U.S. Naval Air Station
La Trinite, France, U.S. Naval Air Station
Le Croisic, France, U.S. Naval Air Station
Lorient, France, U.S. Naval Base
Lough Foyle, Ireland, U.S. Naval Air Station
Lough Swilly, Ireland, U.S. Naval Air Station

Marginal Parkway, Brooklyn, N.Y., Naval Air Patrol Station
Mastic, Long Island, N.Y., Naval Air Patrol Station
Miami, Fla., Naval Air Patrol Station
Moutchic-Lacanau, France, U.S. Naval Air Station
Norfolk, Va., Naval Air Station
Norfolk, Va., Naval Operating Base
Otter Cliffs, Mount Desert Island, Me. Radio Station
Paimboeuf, France, U.S. Naval Air Station
Parris Island, S.C., Naval Air Patrol Station
Paulliac, France, U.S. Naval Air Station
Pensacola, Fla., Naval Air Patrol Station
Pescara, Italy, U.S. Naval Air Station
Porto Corsini, Italy, U.S. Naval Air Station
Quantico, Va., Marine Corps Kite Balloon Station and Base
Queenstown, Ireland, U.S. Naval Air Station and Naval Base
Rockaway Beach, Long Island, N.Y., Naval Air Patrol Station
St. Nazaire, France, U.S. Disembarkation and Embarkation Port
St. Thomas, Virgin Islands, U.S. Naval Base
St. Trojan, France, U.S. Naval Air Station
San Diego, Calif., Naval Air Patrol Station
Sangatte, France, World War I U.S. Northern Bombing Group Base
Savannah, Ga., Naval Air Patrol Station
Spicker, France, World War I U.S. Northern Bombing Group Base
Squantum, Mass., Naval Air Patrol Station, later Naval Air Station
Sydney, Cape Breton Island, U.S. Naval Air Station
Tongue Point, Ore., Naval Air Patrol Station
Treguier, France, U.S. Naval Air Station
Wexford, Ireland, U.S. Naval Air Station
Whiddy Island, Ireland, U.S. Naval Air Station
Yorktown, Va., Naval Air Patrol Station, Naval Coal, Oil, and Mine Depot, later Naval Weapons Station

1918

Berehaven, Ireland, World War I U.S. Naval Air Station
Bermuda, Naval Base #24, White's Island, Hamilton Harbor
Cape May, N.J., Naval Air Station
Cardiff, Wales, U.S. Naval Base
Charleston, W. Va., Armor and Projectile Plants
Corfu, Greece, U.S. Naval Base
Dahlgren, Va., Naval Surface Weapons Center
District of Columbia, Anacostia Naval Air Station
Miami, Fla., Naval Air Station

1919

Alexandria, Va., Naval Torpedo Factory
Constantinople, Turkey, U.S. Naval Base

1921

Lakehurst, N.J., Naval Air Station

1922

Sand Point, Seattle, Wash., Naval Air Station

1923

Point Barrow, Alaska, Petroleum Reserve

1925

Annapolis, Md., Naval Air Facility
Grosse Ile, Mich., Naval Air Station

1928

Livermore, Calif., Naval Air Station
Los Alamitos, Calif., Naval Air Station
Minneapolis/Twin Cities, Minn., Naval Air Station
New York, N.Y., Floyd Bennett Field, Naval Air Station

1929

Antarctica, U.S. Naval and Air Bases

1930

St. Louis, Mo., Naval Air Station

1931

Moffett Field, Calif., Naval Air Station

1935

Los Angeles, Long Beach, Calif., Naval Bases
Winter Harbor, Me., Radio Station

1937

San Francisco Bay, Calif., Treasure Island

1938

Alameda, Calif., Naval Air Station
Balboa, Panama Canal Zone, U.S. Naval Operating Base, Naval Station
San Pedro, Calif., Terminal Island, Naval Air Station

1939

Banana River, Fla., Naval Air Station

1940

Antigua, British West Indies, U.S. Naval Air Facility
Astoria, Ore., Naval Air Station
Carderock, Md., David W. Taylor Naval Ship Research and Development Center

Casco Bay, Me., Destroyer Base
Curacao and Aruba, Netherlands East Indies, U.S. Naval Operating Base
Dallas, Texas, Naval Air Station
Georgetown, British Guiana, U.S. Naval Air Station, and Naval Air Facility
Jamaica, British West Indies, U.S. Naval Air Station
Jacksonville, Fla., Naval Air Station
Kaneohe, Oahu, Hawaii, Naval Air Station
Oakland, Calif., Naval Supply Center
Oceana, Va., Naval Auxiliary Air Station, Naval Air Station, and Master Jet Base
St. Lucia, British West Indies, U.S. Naval Air Station
Sitka, Alaska, Naval Air Station, later Section Base and Naval Operating Base

1941

Port Althorp, Alaska, Naval Auxiliary Air Facility
Port Armstrong, Alaska, Naval Auxiliary Air Facility
Quonset Point, R.I., Naval Air Station
Willow Grove, Pa., Naval Air Station

1942

Adak, Alaska, Naval Operating Base
Afognak, Alaska, Naval Auxiliary Air Facility
Agadir, French Morocco, U.S. Naval Advance Base
Almirante, Panama Canal Zone, U.S. Naval Auxiliary Air Station
Appledore, England, U.S. Naval Advance Amphibious Training Base
Annette, Alaska, Naval Auxiliary Air Facility
Arzew, Algeria, U.S. Naval Advance Amphibious Training Base
Atka, Alaska, Naval Air Facility
Atlantic City, N.J., Naval Air Station
Attu, Alaska, Naval Air Station
Auckland, New Zealand, U.S. Naval Operating Base
Bainbridge, Md., Naval Training Station
Barbers Point, Oahu, Hawaii, Naval Air Station
Beaufort, S.C., U.S. Marine Corps Air Station
Beni-Saf, Algeria, U.S. Naval Section Base
Bora Bora, Society Islands, U.S. Naval Station
Brisbane, Australia, U.S. Naval Operating Base
Bunker Hill, Ind., Naval Air Station
Cairns, Australia, U.S. Naval Advance Base
Callao, Peru, U.S. Naval Supply Base
Cape May, N.J., Naval Air Station
Casablanca, French Morocco, U.S. Naval Operating Base
Charlestown, R.I., Naval Auxiliary Air Station
Cherchel, Algeria, U.S. Naval Advance Amphibious Training Base
Clinton, Okla., Naval Air Station
Cold Bay, Alaska, Naval Air Facility
Columbus, Ohio, Naval Air Facility
Concord, Calif., Naval Weapons Station
Corinto, Nicaragua, U.S. Naval Auxiliary Air Facility

Dakar, French Morocco, U.S. Naval Section Base
Dartmouth, England, U.S. Naval Advance Amphibious Training Base
Darwin, Australia, U.S. Naval Advance Base
Davisville, R.I., Advanced Base Depot and Naval Construction Battalion Center
Daytona Beach, Fla., Naval Air Station
Dellys, Algeria, U.S. Naval Advance Amphibious Training Base
Deptford, England, U.S. Naval Advance Amphibious Training Base
Dunkeswell, Devon, England, U.S. Naval Air Facility
Eagle Mountain Lake, Fort Worth, Tex., Marine Corps Air Station and Naval Air Station
Edenton, N.C., Marine Corps Air Station
Efate, New Hebrides Islands, U.S. Naval Operating Base
El Toro (Santa Ana), Calif., Marine Corps Air Station
Espiritu Santo, New Hebrides Islands, U.S. Naval Operating Base
Exeter, England, U.S. Naval Supply Base
Falmouth, England, U.S. Naval Advance Amphibious Training Base
Farragut, Idaho, Naval Training Station
Fedala, French Morocco, U.S. Naval Section Base
Ferryville, Tunisia, U.S. Naval Advance Amphibious Training Base
Fowey, England, U.S. Naval Advance Amphibious Training Base
Fort Lauderdale, Fla., Naval Air Station
Freetown, Sierra Leone, U.S. Advance Base
Fremantle-Perth, Australia, U.S. Naval Advance Base
Funafuti, Ellice Islands, U.S. Naval Advance Base
Glenview, Ill., Naval Air Station
Guadalcanal, Solomon Islands, U.S. Naval Advance Base
Harvey Point, N.C., Naval Auxiliary Air Station
Hitchcock, Tex., Naval Air Station, LTA
Hutchinson, Kans., Naval Air Station
La Goulette (Tunis), Tunisia, U.S. Naval Advance Amphibious Training Base
Lake City, Fla., Naval Air Station
Launceton, England, U.S. Naval Advance Amphibious Training Base
Loch Erne, Ireland, U.S. Naval Seaplane Base
Loch Ryan, Scotland, U.S. Naval Seaplane Base
Londonderry, Ireland, U.S. Naval Operating Base
Melbourne, Fla., Naval Air Station
Memphis, Tenn., Naval Air Station. *See* Millington, Tenn., Naval Air Station Memphis.
Mers-El-Kebir, Algeria, U.S. Naval Advance Amphibious Training Base
Milford-Haven, England, U.S. Naval Advance Training Base
Millington, Tenn., Naval Air Station Memphis
Milne Bay, New Guinea, U.S. Naval Advance Base
Mojave, Calif., Marine Corps Air Station
Mostaganem, Algeria, U.S. Naval Advance Amphibious Training Base
Nandi-Suva, Fiji Islands, U.S. Naval Advance Base
Nemours, Algeria, U.S. Naval Advance Amphibious Training Base
Noumea, New Caledonia, U.S. Naval Operating Base
Oakland, Calif., Naval Regional Medical Center
Olathe, Kans., Naval Air Station
Oran, Algeria, U.S. Naval Operating Base

Otter Point, Alaska, Naval Air Facility
Ottumwa, Ia., Naval Air Station
Paramaribo, Surinam, Dutch Guiana, U.S. Naval Base
Pasco, Wash., Naval Air Station
Penarth, Wales, U.S. Naval Advance Amphibious Training Base
Plymouth, England, U.S. Naval Advance Amphibious Training Base
Port Hueneme, Calif., Naval Construction Battalion Center
Port Lyautey, French Morocco, U.S. Naval Air Station
Portland-Weymouth, England, U.S. Naval Advance Amphibious Training Base
Richmond, Fla., Naval Air Station, LTA
Roseneath, Scotland, U.S. Naval Operating Base
Safi, French Morocco, U.S. Naval Section Base
St. Mawes, England, U.S. Naval Advance Amphibious Training Base
St. Simons Island, Ga., Naval Air Station
Salcombe, England, U.S. Naval Advance Amphibious Training Base
Salinas, Ecuador, U.S. Naval Air Facility
Sampson, N.Y., Naval Training Center
San Diego, Calif., Marine Corps Base Camp Joseph H. Pendleton
Sanford, Fla., Naval Air Station
San Julian, Cuba, U.S. Naval Air Facility
Santa Ana, Calif., Naval Air Station, LTA
Santa Barbara (Goleta), Marine Corps Air Station
Shawnee, Okla., Naval Air Station
Solomons Island, Md., Naval Amphibious Training Base
Southampton, England, U.S. Naval Advance Amphibious Training Base
South Weymouth, Mass., Naval Air Station LTA
Surabaya, Java, U.S. Naval Advance Base
Sydney, Australia, U.S. Naval Advance Base
Taboga Island, Panama Canal Zone, U.S. Naval Station
Teignmouth, England, U.S. Naval Advance Amphibious Training Base
Tenes, Algeria, U.S. Naval Advance Amphibious Training Base
Tillamook, Ore., Naval Air Station, LTA
Tiverton, England, U.S. Naval Advance Amphibious Training Base
Tjilatjap, Netherlands East Indies, U.S. Naval Advance Base
Tongatabu, Tonga Island, U.S. Naval Station
Tufi, Papua, U.S. Naval Advance Base
Tulagi, Florida Island, Solomon Islands, U.S. Naval Advance Base
Vero Beach, Fla., Naval Air Station
Weeksville, Elizabeth City, N.C., Naval Air Station (LTA)
Wellington, New Zealand, U.S. Naval Advance Base
Westmorland, Calif., Salton Sea Naval Air Base
Whidbey Island, Oak Harbor, Wash., Naval Air Station
Yakutat, Alaska, Naval Air Facility

1943

Aitutaki, South Cook Islands, U.S. Naval Air Transport System Base
Akutan, Alaska, Naval Fueling Depot
Amchitka, Alaska, Naval Air Facility

Apamama (Abemama) Atoll, U.S. Naval Air Base
Azores Islands, Portugal, U.S. Naval Base
Barranquilla, Columbia, U.S. Naval Air Facility
Barstow, Calif., Marine Corps Logistics Base
Beeville, Tex., Chase Field, Naval Air Station
Brunswick, Me., Naval Air Station
Buna, New Guinea, U.S. Naval Advance Base
Chincoteague Island, Va., Naval Air Facility and Naval Aviation Ordnance Test Station
Chorrera, Republic of Panama, U.S. Naval Advance Base
Crows Landing, Calif., Naval Auxiliary Air Station
Dunkeswell, Devonshire, England, U.S. Naval Air Facility
El Centro, Calif., Marine Corps Air Station
Exmouth Gulf, Australia, U.S. Naval Section Base
Fallon, Nev., Naval Air Station
Finchhafen, New Guinea, U.S. Naval Advance Base
Franklin, Va., Naval Auxiliary Air Station
French Frigate Shoals, U.S. Naval Air Facility
Houma, La., Naval Air Station (LTA)
Inyokern/China Lake, Calif., Naval Air Facility
Kiriwina Island, New Guinea, U.S. Naval Advance Base
Kiska, Alaska, Naval Auxiliary Air Facility
La Fe, Cuba, U.S. Naval Air Facility
Livermore, Calif., Camp Parks Seabee Activity
Mackay, Australia, U.S. Naval Advance Base
Mandinga, Republic of Panama, U.S. Naval Station (LTA)
Merauke, Dutch New Guinea, U.S. Naval Advance Base
Monrovia, Liberia, U.S. Naval Tenant Port
Morobe, New Guinea, U.S. Naval Advance Base
Nanomea, Ellice Islands, U.S. Naval Advance Base
New Georgia, Solomon Islands, U.S. Naval Advance Base
Nukufetau, Ellice Islands, U.S. Naval Advance Base
Palermo, Sicily, U.S. Naval Operating Base
Palm Island, Australia, U.S. Naval Advance Air Base
Port Moresby, New Guinea, U.S. Naval Advance Base
Port Stephens, New South Wales, Australia, U.S. Naval Advance Base
Russell Islands, Solomon Islands, U.S. Naval Advance Base
Salerno, Italy, U.S. Naval Operating Base
Sand Bay, Alaska, Fueling and Net Station
Sand Point, Alaska, Naval Auxiliary Air Facility
Santa Fe, Isle of Pines, Cuba, U.S. Naval Air Facility
Scotia, N.Y., Naval Supply Depot
Seward, Alaska, Naval Auxiliary Air Facility
Shemya, Alaska, Naval Auxiliary Air Facility
Tanaga, Alaska, Naval Auxiliary Air Facility
Tarawa Atoll, Gilbert Islands, U.S. Air Bases at Hawkins Field, Betio Island, and Mullinix Field, Buoto Island
Thursday Island, Australia, U.S. Naval Advance Base
Tongareva, Northern Cook Islands, U.S. Naval Air Transport System Base

Torokina, Bougainville, Solomon Islands, U.S. Naval Advance Base
Townsville, Australia, U.S. Naval Advance Base
Treasury Island, Solomon Islands, U.S. Naval Advance Base
Vella Lavella, Solomon Islands, U.S. Naval Advance Base
Vicarage Barracks, Plymouth, Devon, England, U.S. Naval Amphibious Base
Woodlark Island, Papua, U.S. Naval Advance Base

1944

Aitape, New Guinea, U.S. Naval Advance Base
Bangor, Wash., Naval Magazine and Trident Submarine Base
Biak, Dutch New Guinea, U.S. Naval Advance Base
Cherbourg, France, U.S. Naval Advance Base
Emirau, New Ireland, New Guinea, U.S. Naval Advance Base
Eniwetok Atoll, U.S. Advanced Fleet Anchorage, Naval Air Base, and Naval Operating Base
Green Cove Springs, Fla., Naval Auxiliary Air Station
Green Island, Solomon Islands, U.S. Naval Advance Base
Hollandia, Dutch New Guinea, U.S. Naval Advance Base
Klamath Falls, Ore., Naval Air Station
Kwajalein, Marshall Islands, U.S. Naval Air Base, Naval Operating Base, and Headquarters Commander Marshalls-Gilbert Area
La Maddalena, Sardinia, U.S. Naval Support Office
Leyte, Republic of the Philippines, U.S. Naval Shore Facilities
Litchfield Park, Ariz., Naval Air Facility
Madang-Alexishafen, Dutch New Guinea, U.S. Naval Advance Base
Majuro, Marshall Islands, U.S. Fleet Anchorage, Naval Base, and Naval Air Facility
Manus, Admiralty Islands, U.S. Naval Operating Base
Morotai, Netherlands East Indies, U.S. Naval Advance Base
Naples, Italy, Headquarters, Commander Naval Forces North African Waters
Palmyra Island, U.S. Naval Air Station
Peleliu, Palau Islands, U.S. Naval Base
Saidor, New Guinea, U.S. Naval Advance Base
Saipan, Mariana Islands, U.S. Naval Operating Base and Naval Air Bases
Samar, Philippine Islands, U.S. Naval Operating Base
Sansapor, Dutch New Guinea, U.S. Naval Advance Base
Tinian, Mariana Islands, U.S. Naval Base and Naval Air Base
Ulithi Atoll, Caroline Islands, U.S. Advanced Fleet Anchorage
Wakde, Dutch New Guinea, U.S. Naval Advance Base
Warminster, Pa., Naval Air Development Center

1945

Balikpapan, Dutch Borneo, U.S. Naval Advance Base
Bar Harbor, Me., Naval Auxiliary Air Facility
Bremerhaven, Germany, U.S. Naval Advance Base
Brunei Bay, British North Borneo, U.S. Naval Advance Base
Iwo Jima, U.S. Advanced Air Base
Lingayen, Luzon, Republic of the Philippines, U.S. Naval Facilities
Mactan Island, Cebu Island, Republic of the Philippines, U.S. Naval Air Base

Mindoro Island, Republic of the Philippines, U.S. Naval Facilities
Okinawa, Ryukyu Islands, Japan, U.S. Naval Air Bases and Operating Base
Panama Canal Zone, Post–World War II Defense Arrangements
Sangley Point, Luzon, Republic of the Philippines, U.S. Naval Station
Sasebo, Japan, U.S. Naval Fleet Activities
Yokosuka, Japan, U.S. Naval Base
Zamboanga Field, Mindanao, Philippine Islands, U.S. Fleet Air Base

1946

Denver, Colo., Buckley Field Naval Air Station
Point Mugu, Calif., Naval Missile Center

1948

Birmingham, Ala., Naval Air Station
Lincoln, Neb., Naval Air Station
Niagara Falls, N.Y., Naval Air Reserve Training Unit

1949

Albuquerque, N.M., Kirtland Air Force Base, Naval Weapons Evaluation Facility
El Centro, Calif., Naval Air Facility

1950

Atsugi, Japan, U.S. Naval Air Facility
Inchon, Korea, U.S. Naval Fleet Activities
Pusan, Korea, U.S. Naval Fleet Activities
Saigon, Republic of Vietnam, U.S. Navy Headquarters Support Activity

1951

Bridgeport, Calif., Marine Corps Mountain Warfare Training Center
Cubi Point, Luzon, Republic of the Philippines, U.S. Naval Air Station
Monterey, Calif., Naval Postgraduate School
Naples, Italy, Headquarters, Allied Forces South (NATO)
Sanford, Fla., Naval Air Station

1952

Kaneohe, Oahu, Hawaii, Marine Corps Air Station
Twentynine Palms, Calif., Marine Corps Air Ground Combat Center

1953

Rota, Spain, U.S. Naval Base
San Francisco Bay, Mare Island Naval Shipyard, Vallejo
Stockton, Calif., Naval Supply Depot Oakland Annex

1956

Cutler, Me., Naval Communications Unit
Oahu, Hawaii, Marine Corps Camp H. M. Smith

1957

Lajes, Azores Islands, Portugal, U.S. Naval Air Facility
Okinawa, Japan, U.S. Marine Corps Camp Smedley D. Butler

1959

Sigonella, Catania, Sicily, U.S. Naval Air Station
Vieques Island, Puerto Rico, U.S. Marine Corps Camp Garcia
Yuma, Ariz., Marine Corps Air Station

1960

Iberia, La., Naval Air Station
Stockton, Calif., Naval Communications Station
Tudor Hill Laboratory (Office of Naval Research, later Naval Underwater Systems Center), Bermuda

1961

District of Columbia, Andrews Air Force Base, Naval Air Facility
Holy Loch, Scotland, U.S. Fleet Ballistic Submarine Base
Lemoore, Calif., Naval Air Station

1964

Chu Lai, Republic of Vietnam, U.S. Naval Support Activity
Danag, Republic of Vietnam, U.S. Naval Support Activity
Mildenhall, Suffolk, England, U.S. Naval Air Facility

1965

An Thoi, Republic of Vietnam, U.S. Naval Support Activity
Cam Ranh Bay, Republic of Vietnam, U.S. Naval Base
Cat Lai, Republic of Vietnam, U.S. Naval Intermediate Support Base
Cat Lo, Republic of Vietnam, U.S. Naval Combat and Logistic Base
Hue-Tan My-Phu Bai, Republic of Vietnam, U.S. Naval Support Activity
Nha Trang, Republic of Vietnam, U.S. Naval Operating Station
Qui Nhon, Republic of Vietnam, U.S. Naval Support Activity
Vung Tau, Republic of Vietnam, U.S. Naval Support Activity Detachment

1966

Can Tho-Binh Thuy, Republic of Vietnam, U.S. Naval Support Activity
Cua Viet, Republic of Vietnam, U.S. Naval Support Activity
Dong Tam, Republic of Vietnam, U.S. Naval Support Activity
Long Xuyen, Republic of Vietnam, U.S. Naval Advanced Support Base
My Tho, Republic of Vietnam, U.S. Naval Support Activity
Nha Be, Republic of Vietnam, U.S. Naval Support Activity
Trenton, N.J., Naval Air Propulsion Center
Vinh Long, Republic of Vietnam, U.S. Naval Facility

1967

Albany, Ga., Naval Air Station
Dong Ha, Republic of Vietnam, U.S. Naval Support Activity
Sa Huynh, Republic of Vietnam, U.S. Naval Support Activity Detachment

1968

Ben Luc, Republic of Vietnam, U.S. Naval Support Base
Ha Tien, Republic of Vietnam, U.S. River Patrol Boat Staging Area
Moc Hoa, Republic of Vietnam, U.S. Naval Advanced Tactical Support Base
Tan An, Republic of Vietnam, U.S. Naval Advanced Tactical Support Base
Tra Cu, Republic of Vietnam, U.S. Naval Advanced Tactical Support Base

1969

Ben Keo, Republic of Vietnam, U.S. Naval Advanced Tactical Support Base
Chau Doc, Republic of Vietnam, U.S. Naval Combat Base
Cho Moi, Republic of Vietnam, U.S. Naval Logistic Installation
Detroit, Mich., Naval Air Facility
Go Dau Ha, Republic of Vietnam, U.S. Naval Advanced Base
Hiep Hoa, Republic of Vietnam, U.S. Naval Advanced Tactical Support Base
Hoi An, Republic of Vietnam, U.S. Patrol Boat Base
Iwakuni, Japan, U.S. Marine Corps Air Station
Long Binh, Republic of Vietnam, U.S. River Forces Operating Base
Long Phu, Republic of Vietnam, U.S. Intermediate Support Base
Nam Can, Republic of Vietnam, U.S. Naval Mobile Facility
Phu Cuong, Republic of Vietnam, U.S. Naval Advanced Tactical Support Base
Phuoc Xuyen, Republic of Vietnam, U.S. Naval Advanced Tactical Support Base
Rach Soi, Republic of Vietnam, U.S. Naval Intermediate Support Base
Tan Chau, Republic of Vietnam, U.S. Naval River Patrol Base
Thuyen Nhon, Republic of Vietnam, U.S. Naval Advanced Tactical Support Base
Tustin, Calif., Marine Corps Air Station (Helicopter)

1970

Son Ong Doc, Republic of Vietnam, U.S. Naval Riverine Operational Base

1971

Thuan An, Republic of Vietnam, U.S. Naval Intermediate Support Base

1973

Diego Garcia Island, Indian Ocean, U.S. Naval Base

1974

San Francisco Bay, Calif., Navy Public Works Center

1975

Misawa, Japan, U.S. Naval Air Facility

1977

Lakehurst, N.J., Naval Air Engineering Center

1978

Indianapolis, Ind., Naval Avionics Center
Kings Bay, Ga., Fleet Ballistic Submarine Base

1979

Keyport, Wash., Naval Undersea Warfare Engineering Station

Index

About the Contributors

K. JACK BAUER obtained his Ph.D. at Indiana University. A former member of the historical staffs of the Marine Corps and Navy, he is Professor of History at Rensselaer Polytechnic Institute. He has lectured at the Naval War College and served as a visiting professor of military history at the U.S. Army Command and General Staff College. Dr. Bauer is the author or editor of numerous books and articles, including *Surfboats and Horse Marines* (1969); *Ships of the Navy; Combat Vessels* (1970); *The Mexican War 1846–1848* (1974); and *The New American State Papers: Naval Affairs* (1981). He is also a contributing editor of *American Secretaries of the Navy* (1980) and *Ports of the West* (1982).

JAMES H. BELOTE obtained his Ph.D. at the University of California, Berkeley. He has since served as Professor of History at Principia College, Elsah, Ill. With his brother William he has published *Corregidor* (1968), *Typhoon of Steel* (1970), and *Titans of the Seas* (1975).

WILLIAM R. BRAISTED obtained his Ph.D. at the University of Chicago and progressed from Instructor to Professor of History at the University of Texas, Austin. In addition to publishing numerous articles in historical and military journals, he is the world's foremost authority on the U.S. Navy in the Pacific, with two books published and a third forthcoming.

WILLIAM L. CALDERHEAD obtained his doctorate at the University of Pennsylvania. Since then he has served as Professor of History at the U.S. Naval Academy. He has published numerous articles on military history in various scholarly journals.

PAOLO E. COLETTA obtained his Ph.D. at the University of Missouri, Columbia, where he taught history prior to serving for three years in the Navy in World War II. He taught from 1946 until his retirement in 1983 at the U.S. Naval Academy. In addition to publishing more than fifty articles in historical and military magazines, he has produced a three-volume biography of W. J. Bryan, a study of the presidency of William Howard Taft; two editions of a naval history text; a bibliography of American naval history; and biographies of three naval officers. With Robert G. Albion and K. Jack Bauer, he was a contributing editor of *American Secretaries of the Navy.*

ROGER DINGMAN obtained his Ph.D. degree at Harvard University. Since then he has taught at Harvard, at the U.S. Naval War College, and at the University of Southern California. His published works include *Power in the Pacific*, *Kindai Nihon no taigai taido* (Japan and the Outside World) (1982), and numerous articles on American-East Asian relations and twentieth-century naval history. He is currently completing a study of American strategy, politics, and diplomacy in the Korean War.

EDWIN M. HALL obtained his doctorate at Pennsylvania State University. He taught from 1942 until his retirement at the U.S. Naval Academy. He has contributed to E. B. Potter, ed., *Seapower*, and Paolo E. Coletta, Robert G. Albion, and K. Jack Bauer, eds., *American Secretaries of the Navy* (1980).

FRANCIS X. HOLBROOK obtained his doctorate at Fordham University and has taught at Fordham Preparatory School, Bronx, N.Y., and served as a Lecturer at Mercy College, Dobbs Ferry, N.Y. He has published widely in professional journals on American naval and diplomatic history.

ROBERT E. JOHNSON obtained a doctorate from the Claremont Graduate School in 1956. Since then he has been a member of the history faculty at the University of Alabama. His major books are *Thence Round Cape Horn* (1963), *Rear Admiral John Rodgers, 1812–1882* (1967), and *Far China Station* (1979).

LESTER D. LANGLEY obtained his doctorate at the University of Kansas in 1965. Since 1981 he has served as a Professor at the University of Georgia. His major publications include *The Cuban Policy of the United States* (1968); *Struggle for the American Mediterranean* (1976); *The Caribbean in the Twentieth Century* (1980, 1982); and *The Banana Wars: An Inner History of American Empire* (1983).

JOHN B. LUNDSTROM obtained his M.A. at the University of Wisconsin-Milwaukee. From 1974 on he has served as an Assistant Curator of History at the Milwaukee Public Museum. He has published *The First South Pacific Campaign: Pacific Fleet Strategy December 1941–June 1942* (1976), and *The First Team: U.S. Naval Carrier Fighters, Friends, and Foes from Pearl Harbor through Midway* (1978).

WILLIAM MCQUADE obtained a B.A. degree from Pennsylvania State University and Master of Library Science from the University of Pittsburgh. He has had experience as a cataloger and reference librarian at West Virginia University Library and at the U.S. Naval Academy's Nimitz Library.

EDWARD J. MAROLDA is currently a doctoral student at George Washington University, from which he earned an M.A. in history in 1971. Since then he has served as an historian on the staff of the U.S. Naval Historical Center, Washington. He has published several articles in military journals, co-authored volume 2 in a series, *The United States Navy and the Vietnam Conflict*, and has been a co-compiler of *Guide to United States*

Naval Administrative Histories of World War II (1976) and *A Select Bibliography of the United States Navy and the Southeast Asian Conflict, 1950–1975* (1982).

BRADLEY REYNOLDS obtained his Ph.D. from the University of Southern California and has since served as a Professor of History at College of the Canyons, Valencia, Calif. He has published several articles on Guantánamo Bay, Cuba, and is currently working on a book dealing with the U.S. Navy's role there.

Captain PAUL B. RYAN, USN (Ret.) obtained an A.M. from Stanford University and an M.A. in history at San Jose State University following service in submarines and three command tours afloat, ending in the billet of Deputy Director of Naval History at the Navy Department. He has published *First Line of Defense: The U.S. Navy Since 1945* (1981) and *The Panama Canal Controversy* (1977); co-authored with Thomas A. Bailey *The Lusitania Disaster* (1978); and *Hitler vs. Roosevelt: The Undeclared War in the Atlantic* (1979); and in addition to publishing numerous articles in professional journals and the national press has contributed to Paolo E. Coletta, Robert G. Albion, and K. Jack Bauer, eds. *Secretaries of the American Navy* (1980).

WILLIAM N. STILL obtained his doctorate at the University of Alabama. Since 1968 he has served as Professor at East Carolina University. In addition to publishing numerous articles and being involved in the *Monitor* project, he has published *American Sea Power in the Old World: The United States Navy in European and Near Eastern Waters, 1865–1917* (1983), *Iron Afloat: The Story of the Confederate Armorclads* (1971), and *Confederate Shipbuilding* (1969).

DAVID L. WOODS obtained a Ph.D. from Ohio State University. Following work in academia, with the U.S. Navy, and in the aerospace/electronics industry, he joined the Department of the Navy as a civilian in 1965 and among other billets served as speech writer and historian. He is the author of two books on naval signalling and communications and is a captain in the U.S. Naval Reserve with a specialty in public affairs.

ROGER T. ZEIMET obtained his doctorate at Marquette University. Since then he has taught at Marquette, the University of Sisconsin-Milwaukee, Milwaukee Area Technical College, and Concordia College-Milwaukee. In 1981 he was brought aboard the History Department at the U.S. Naval Academy in the grade of lieutenant commander. He has the prospect of publishing a life of Gen. Philip Sheridan and is contributing an essay on Gen. Ben Fuller, USMC, for an anthology on the Commandants of the U.S. Marine Corps.